HAROLD NICOLSON

In memoriam Michael Bristow-Smith

HAROLD NICOLSON

Half-an-Eye on History

Laurence Bristow-Smith

The Letterworth Press

Published in Switzerland by the Letterworth Press
http://www.TheLetterworthPress.org

© Laurence Bristow-Smith 2014

Frontispiece photograph of Harold Nicolson in 1935
by Howard Coster, © National Portrait Gallery, London

ISBN 978-2-9700654-5-6

1 3 5 7 9 8 6 4 2

Contents

	Acknowledgements	ix
	Preface	xiii
1	Nicolsons	1
2	Hamiltons	11
3	Childhood	17
4	School	28
5	Weimar	38
6	Oxford	42
7	Preparation	58
8	Office	66
9	Courtship	73
10	Vita	78
11	Constantinople	85
12	Marriage	97
13	War	103
14	Revelation	117
15	Violet	124
16	Peace	134
17	Crisis	154
18	Author	167
19	Balance	182
20	Tennyson	188
21	Curzon	193
22	Lausanne	200
23	Bloomsbury	211
24	Byron	216
25	Affair	223
26	Policy	237
27	Change	244
28	Journey	253
29	Legation	260
30	Visit	269
31	Chargé	277

32	Return	289
33	Berlin	298
34	Fathers	305
35	Decision	321
36	Reasons	333
37	Journalist	336
38	Sissinghurst	344
39	Mosley	350
40	Recovery	359
41	Morrow	368
42	Election	380
43	Drama	386
44	Fifty	393
45	Munich	399
46	Outbreak	412
47	Role	421
48	Minister	428
49	Might-Have-Been	435
50	Survival	448
51	Post-War	454
52	Labour	469
53	Proposition	478
54	Biographer	485
55	Meanwhile	492
56	Reward	504
57	Health	511
58	Cruising	520
59	Endings	532
60	Epilogue	543
	Notes	547
	Bibliography	573
	Index	579

Acknowledgements

I am extremely grateful to Juliet Nicolson for allowing me to make full use of Harold Nicolson's books, letters and diaries. Extracts from the following works are reproduced with permission of Curtis Brown Group Ltd on behalf of the Estate of Harold Nicolson:
  Sweet Waters (© Harold Nicolson 1921)
  Verlaine (© Harold Nicolson 1921)
  Tennyson (© Harold Nicolson 1923)
  Byron: the Last Journey (© Harold Nicolson 1924)
  Some People (© Harold Nicolson 1926)
  Swinburne (© Harold Nicolson 1928)
  Lord Carnock (© Harold Nicolson 193 0)
  Curzon: the Last Phase (© Harold Nicolson 1934)
  Dwight Morrow (© Harold Nicolson 1935)
  Politics in the Train (© Harold Nicolson 1936)
  Small Talk (© Harold Nicolson 1937)
  Helen's Tower (© Harold Nicolson 1937)
  The Desire to Please (© Harold Nicolson 1943)
  Peacemaking (© Harold Nicolson 1944 edition)
  Friday Mornings 1941–1944 (© Harold Nicolson 1944)
  Comments 1944–1948 (© Harold Nicolson 1948)
  The Congress of Vienna (© Harold Nicolson 1948)
  King George V: His Life and Reign (© Harold Nicolson 1952)
  Good Behaviour (© Harold Nicolson 1955)
  Sainte-Beuve (© Harold Nicolson 1957)
  Journey to Java (© Harold Nicolson 1957)
  Harold Nicolson: Diaries and Letters 1930–1939 (© Harold Nicolson 1966)
  Harold Nicolson: Diaries and Letters 1939–1945 (© Harold Nicolson 1967)
  Harold Nicolson: Diaries and Letters 1945–1962 (© Harold Nicolson 1968)

Juliet Nicolson also kindly allowed me to make use of Vita Sackville-West's books and letters. Extracts from the following works are reproduced with permission from Curtis Brown Group Ltd on behalf of the Estate of Vita Sackville-West:
  Knole and the Sackvilles (© Vita Sackville-West 1922)

Harold Nicolson

The Land (© Vita Sackville-West 1927)
Passenger to Tehran (© Vita Sackville-West 1926)
12 Days in Persia (© Vita Sackville-West 1927)
The Letters of Vita Sackville West to Virginia Woolf (© Estate of Vita of Sackville-West 1984)

I am also indebted to Adam Nicolson for letting me draw on Nigel Nicolson's work. Extracts from *Portrait of a Marriage* (© Nigel Nicolson 1973), *Vita and Harold: The Letters of Vita Sackville-West and Harold Nicolson* (© Nigel Nicolson 1992), and *Long Life* (© Nigel Nicolson 1998) and are reproduced with the permission of Curtis Brown Group Ltd on behalf of the Estate of Nigel Nicolson.

I am grateful to Anna Sander, archivist at Balliol College, Oxford, for her help in making available, and for permission to quote from Harold Nicolson's diaries prior to 1930.

The extract from Harold Nicolson's *Why Britain is at War* (Penguin Books 1939) is reproduced by kind permission of Penguin Books Ltd.

Quotations from *Harold Nicolson, Volume I* (© James Lees-Milne 1987) and *Harold Nicolson Volume II* (© James Lees-Milne 1988); from *Harold Nicolson* (© Norman Rose 2005); and from *Dreadnought* by Robert K. Massie (Pimlico 1993) are reproduced by kind permission of the Random House Group Ltd.

Quotations from *Diplomacy* by Harold Nicolson (1963) and from *Sir Harold Nicolson and International Relations* (© Derek Drinkwater 2005) by permission of Oxford University Press.

The extract from *Chips: The Diaries of Sir Henry Channon*, edited by Robert Rhodes James (Weidenfeld & Nicolson 1967) is reproduced by permission of Sheil Land Associates Ltd.

The quotation from *Constantinople: City of the World's Desire, 1453–1924* by Philip Mansel (© Philip Mansel 1995) is reproduced by permission of John Murray Press.

Extracts from *Curzon's Persia*, edited by Peter King (Sidgwick & Jackson 1986); from *The Proud Tower* (Papermac 1980) and *August 1914* (Papermac 1994) by Barbara Tuchman; from *Curzon* by David Gilmour (Papermac 1995); and Harold Macmillan's *Blast of War* (1967) are reproduced by permission of Macmillan Publishers.

Extracts from *Vita* by Victoria Glendinning (Weidenfeld & Nicolson, 1983); from *The Duff Cooper Diaries*, edited by John Julius Norwich (Phoenix 2006); and from Winston Churchill's *The Second World War, II, Their Finest Hour* (Cassell, 1949) are reproduced by permission of Orion Publishing Group.

Acknowledgements

I am grateful to Professor David Cannadine and to *London Review of Books* from permission to quote from the article 'Rose's Rex'.

Quotations from Harold Nicolson's *Observer* review of George Orwell's *1984* and Roy Hattersley's obituary for Kenneth Harris in the *Guardian* are both reproduced with consent.

Every effort has been made to contact and acknowledge copyright holders of texts quoted. If this has been unsuccessful, copyright holders are invited to contact the publisher directly.

Preface

I knew about Vita Sackville-West before I knew about Harold Nicolson. I was brought up in the Kent and Sussex borderlands, not too far from Sissinghurst and I went there with my parents in the early 1960s. I barely remember the visit, though I do remember a tea shop in Sissinghurst village. I cannot tell whether this was before or after Vita's death, but it was her name I knew first because of Sissinghurst, because of the garden. And because of Knole, which we passed whenever we went to see my mother's brothers and their families who populated the south-eastern edges of London. And because of my Latin master, Mr Williams, who used *The Land* as an illustration of the immense and long-lasting influence of *The Georgics*.

> A green, wet country on a bed of clay,
> From Edenbridge to Appledore and Lympne
> Drained by the Medway and the Rother stream
> With forest oaks still hearty in the copse.

Vita was writing about my home, and when literature binds itself to a particular place or region the effect is powerful and enduring. But even then I could see that the work was essentially (if intentionally) backward-looking – *The Land* was published four years after *The Waste Land*. Her novels, too, while popular in their day and technically competent, suffered by comparison with Lawrence, Forster, Huxley, Waugh, Powell – writers of her own or a slightly later generation who were simply that much more adventurous.

Nonetheless, Vita Sackville-West was a figure on my literary landscape, her presence on the skyline reinforced by the geographical connection with home. So that when I eventually came to read Harold Nicolson's work – some years later, while studying literature in Newcastle-upon-Tyne – I saw him against the background of her. It took me a while to understand that he was the more interesting character and the more original writer, whose work had more to offer to later generations. One of the obstacles was Bloomsbury, of whom I shall have more to say later. Bloomsbury did not always see the world outside their confines clearly. They were very wrong about Harold, but I did not immediately see that.

I went on to live in Morocco, where Harold's parents had been based during his adolescent years, and then to join the Diplomatic Service. If that created a link, it was wholly coincidental, and if I picked up his lesser-known writings here and there or works by his contemporaries, works which mentioned or reflected on him in some way, it was out of general interest. Only much later when I was working in Oslo did the interest turn into a project. I had to write a c.v. and, with no forethought that I can remember, I found myself adding a line to the effect that I hoped to write a biography of Harold Nicolson. Even then, I did not begin writing for another five years, until the summer of 2008. By then I was in Milan. My wife was not enamoured of diplomatic life and preferred to spend her time restoring the house we had bought in Scotland and working in the wonderful garden there – which gave me both the stimulus and the opportunity, and, I suppose, suggests another link with Harold, although again it was no more than coincidental. I finished writing four years later, by which time I was a bed-and-breakfast proprietor in Kirkcudbright.

As Harold Nicolson wrote in several of his introductions, this book makes no great claim to original research. Circumstances did not permit it, and, in any case, there are few new facts to be discovered. I have corrected a few minor errors and explored Harold's family background in a little more detail, but my main concern has been with interpretation. I have relied mainly on published and internet sources, plus a few visits to key locations – though I was also able, courtesy of Balliol College, to consult the manuscripts of Harold's early diaries. Previous biographies by James Lees-Milne and Norman Rose have been vital, as has Victoria Glendinning's biography of Vita, and, of course, Harold and Vita's diaries and letters. Lees-Milne's two-volume work is not uncritical, but it is friendly and it was written by someone who knew and shared the social world that Harold inhabited in the second half of his life. Norman Rose's book, published in 2005, looks at Harold from a later and more detached perspective. Rose's more thematic approach suggests a much more enigmatic character.

Yet I felt there was still a story to be told, a character to be uncovered and seen in his proper historical perspective – and by that I mean in relation to the huge historical and cultural movements which were shaping Europe and the world during his lifetime, not simply the list (impressive though it is) of people he knew or had dinner with at one time or another. I felt that Harold's motives and his decisions needed to be probed more, and that in order to do this effectively, his background and his early life needed to be looked at in more detail – not least because of the importance he evidently attached to it. I have also tried to show his and Vita's homosexuality for what it was, an important factor of their lives which, at one point, provoked a crisis, but in no sense a dominating factor.

I had a lot of help in the process of writing and putting this book together. Above all, I would like to thank Peter Winnington for his incredible editor's eye and his invaluable help preparing the text for publication, and Stan Calder, who read the text chapter by chapter as it came off the computer. Damian Leeson and Stephen Pern also read and made suggestions. And, of course, Jennifer, Ezra and Adam, who had to put up with constant mutterings about 'Harold' this and 'Harold' that for the whole four-year period. I have dedicated this book to my brother, Michael, whose knowledge of the period was phenomenal and who was always at the end of the phone to answer queries about the livery of Southern Railway locomotives or cinema-going in the 1940s. Sadly, he died before he could see his contributions in print.

Laurence Bristow-Smith
Kirkcudbright, July 2014

1 Nicolsons

Harold Nicolson had a highly developed sense of history. One of his great strengths as a writer was to understand and communicate how the past informs the present. His diplomatic and historical studies such as *Peacemaking* and *The Congress of Vienna* were explicitly intended to draw lessons from past events which could be applied to present and future situations. His biographies have a greater historical purpose than the mere chronicling of the subject's life. *Lord Carnock* and *Curzon: The Last Phase* are part of a trilogy (together with *Peacemaking*) looking at changes in diplomatic theory and practice. *George V* is a biography, but also a study of constitutional monarchy. For Nicolson, the past was more than just facts: history had to be tempered with imagination. When researching his books he would go to key locations – houses, towns, gardens – in order to soak up the atmosphere, to see what his subject saw, to feel what his subject felt, to gain a sense of direct connection with the past. It was this impulse which led him, while in Athens researching *Byron: The Last Journey*, to stand in front of the statue of Byron outside the National Gardens, take off his hat, and explain to the shade of the poet exactly what he was doing there.

This sense of history undoubtedly came from his family and his family background. Three of his best books – *Lord Carnock*, *The Desire to Please*, and *Helen's Tower* – are books of family history. The last two, in fact, are the beginning of a never-completed series of studies in autobiography and family history to be called *In Search of the Past*. There is also, in much of his work, a sense that history and identity are linked: that the interaction between individuals or families and the great events of the outer world in some way creates or conveys identity. So it is worth looking at the family from which he sprang and how family history would have presented itself to him as a boy – the names and locations; the family traditions that he would have been brought up to believe; the stories of his parents' and grandparents' lives that he would have heard as a child. These things are more than just facts: they help explain how the adult Harold Nicolson looked at and understood the world about him.

By most people's standards the Nicolsons were an ancient enough family. As far as anyone can tell, the family which became Clan Mhic Reacail (or MacNeaceil or MacNicol) and was later anglicised as Clan Nicolson, seems to be descended from Scandinavian – most probably Norwegian – raiders who stopped raiding and began to settle on the Isle of Lewis in the ninth century. Somewhere in the thirteenth century, they arrived on the Isle of Skye and settled in the north-eastern part of the island, the area now known as Trotternish. Most of the region consists of a stubby, dramatic, north-pointing peninsula: a wild and rugged landscape where human settlement, and what little cultivable land there is, are confined to a thin coastal band. South of the peninsula, the district stretches beyond the impressive natural harbour of Portree as far as Loch Ainort; it is bounded on the west by the River Snizort. The precision of these borders, which are still recognised by the local population to this day, reflects the extent and importance of ancient land ownership.

Once they reached Skye, Clan Mhic Reacail put down roots. They farmed; they fished; they undoubtedly fought; and they quite probably sat on the Council of the Lord of the Isles in the fourteenth century. By Skeabost Bridge, near where the River Snizort reaches the sea, is St Columba's Isle. Local tradition holds that twenty-eight Clan Nicolson chiefs are buried there, which – even allowing for shorter or curtailed lifespans – represents a considerable period of continuous occupation. At Bile, dominating the northern side of the entrance to Loch Portree, is a massive crag known as Nicolson's Rock and further up the loch, just on the edge of Portree itself, is the bracken- and bramble-covered site of Scorrybreac or Scorrybreck. A traditional, stone-built clan stronghold, Scorrybreac was probably begun in the fourteenth century and remained the home of the Clan Nicolson chief for some six hundred years – until the nineteenth century when the impact of the Highland Clearances forced the then chief, Norman Nicolson, to emigrate to Tasmania.

Harold Nicolson visited Portree and Scorrybreac in 1938, shortly after his son, Nigel, had bought the Shiants, a group of uninhabited islands between Lewis and Skye. Even then, nothing survived of Scorrybreac beyond traces of collapsed walls under the vegetation, but Harold was deeply moved by the place and felt a tug of belonging. At the same time – and this is highly characteristic – he balanced such romanticism against a more reasoned assessment of his position.

> It is strange how excited I am by my first view of Skye. Before going to bed I gaze at the sunset behind the mountains and watch the sea-gulls wheel, and think perhaps my ill-adjustment to English life has been due to this Celtic strain. I agree with Nigel that nothing is so ridiculous as the Sassenach who pretends to be a Highlander. Yet deep in me is a

dislike of the English ... my joy at knowing that by origin I belong to these solemn proud hills is certainly not anything but deeply sincere.[1]

He was wrong – or so it seems – to speak of 'this Celtic strain'. In his *Clan History of the Nicolsons of Skye*, David Sellar says: 'it seems likely that ... the Nicolsons are of high Norse descent.... Although a Gaelic origin has sometimes been claimed for the clan, the older and better view is that the Nicolsons are of Scandinavian descent.'[2] A Scandinavian origin certainly seems more appropriate for the rulers of lands which, until 1266, owed allegiance to the Norwegian crown.

Harold was also wrong about his 'ill-adjustment' and his sense of Englishness. Whatever his heredity, he was English through and through.

An alternative version of the family's origins – and one to which Harold alludes in the opening pages of *Lord Carnock* – suggests that Clan MacNicol originated around Assynt in what became Sutherland. When the male line died out at the beginning of the fourteenth century, the MacNicol lands passed through marriage to Torquil MacLeod of Lewis. The remnants of the MacNicol clan then removed themselves to Skye and to Scorrybreac.[3]

This second version – which would, it is true, allow more room for a Celtic strain – is less convincing as an account of the origin of such a widespread and important clan, and the story may perhaps describe the fortunes of a secondary branch of the MacNicols. At this distance, of course, it scarcely matters, except insofar as Harold was sufficiently interested to know and record these family traditions when writing about his father. Indeed, he was sufficiently interested in his genealogy and its implications to exaggerate. It is one thing to state the probability of Norse descent, but quite another to claim, as Harold did, that the Nicolsons 'could trace their ancestry to the ninth century on emigrating from Norway.'[4] To be able to claim such a solid historical pedigree was useful when, as a married man, he needed to balance, if not compete with, the weighty and fully-documented ancestry of the Sackvilles.

The Nicolson baronetcy originated with Thomas MacNicol, who left Scorrybreac for Edinburgh in 1570 and anglicised his name to Nicolson.[5] At the beginning of *Lord Carnock*, Harold says that Thomas 'acquired property and riches, bought and embellished the house of Carnock and the estate of Tillicoultrie, and in 1637 purchased a baronetcy of Nova Scotia.'[6] The transaction may have been mercenary, but it was also a recognition of social and economic status.

The hereditary Order of Baronets was the idea of King James VI and I. In 1611, he instituted the Baronetage of England, which, reduced to essentials, granted a title to two hundred men of good birth who were willing to help pay for an army to pacify Ireland. In 1619, the Order was extended to Ireland. Then in 1625 Charles I instituted a third creation, the Baronetcy of Nova Scotia, originally intended to benefit one hundred and fifty men, again of good birth, who were willing to offer 2,000 marks to transport six settlers to Nova Scotia and maintain them for two years. Over time, all three orders outstripped their original size and purpose.

Thomas Nicolson's baronetcy, dating from 16 January 1637 and named for the property he had acquired at Carnock, near Dunfermline in Fife, was a relatively early one. Twice in the course of its history the direct male line failed and the title passed to a cousin. On the second such occasion, in 1806, Harold Nicolson's great-grandfather succeeded as Major General Sir William Nicolson, ninth Baronet. While the title may have passed down the generations, the Scottish estates that went with it disappeared at an early stage. Aristocratic though they might have been in terms of lineage, neither Harold nor any of his immediate forbears belonged to the landed classes – unlike the Sackvilles – which meant that they had little or no income beyond what they earned.

Harold begins *Lord Carnock* with a sketch of his father's character.

> Arthur Nicolson, to the depths of his being, was a shy man. Beneath the high spirits of his early manhood, as beneath the courteous urbanity of his later years, was concealed an inner core of self-repression, diffidence and almost morbid reserve. These disabilities were due to his sufferings and humiliations as a child.[7]

Children can misjudge their parents and Harold may well be overstating the case here. There is no doubt that Arthur Nicolson was a reserved, intensely private man – many of his class and generation were – but his reserve may not have been as intense or as morbid as his son suggests. His early years certainly left him with a legacy of unhappiness and self-doubt to overcome, but he overcame it with conspicuous success, exercising, in the course of his later professional years, a not insignificant influence on European, even world, history.

His parents were Captain Sir Frederick William Erskine Nicolson, tenth Baronet, and Mary Clementina Loch, the only daughter of a Scottish MP, James Loch of Drylaw. They were married in 1847. Mary Nicolson bore three children in quick succession – Clementina, Frederick and, in September 1849, Arthur – before dying in July 1851. Arthur was less than two years old.

The family lived in London, in a small and by all accounts grim and unwelcoming terraced house in William Street, just off Lowndes Square in Knightsbridge.[8] Two years after his wife's death, in December 1853, Sir Frederick Nicolson left England for the Far East, commanding the thirty-six-gun frigate, HMS *Pique*, apparently leaving his children in the care of a housekeeper or governess. At some point, the children were rescued by their maternal grandfather with whom they then lived either in Albemarle Street in Westminster or in the tiny village of Golspie in the far north-east of Scotland. Harold ascribes the need for rescue to the circumstances of Sir Frederick's second marriage, in 1855, to Augusta Cullington, whom he describes as 'a tart'.[9] However, the precise sequence of events of is not clear.

In August 1854, in somewhat strange circumstances, following the suicide of his commanding officer, Rear Admiral Price, Sir Frederick led an unsuccessful attack by British and French forces on the Russian city of Petropavlovsk. In the spring of 1855, he took part in a second attack on the same city. By 1856, HMS *Pique* had become part of the British naval force involved in the Second Anglo-Chinese War, sailing between Shanghai and Fuzhou. It seems, therefore, that Sir Frederick's unfortunate second marriage must have taken place in the Far East – though how, and where, and exactly what the lady in question was doing in the region remain a mystery, unless her profession did, indeed, involve following the fleet. In any event, it seems unlikely that a marriage taking place so far from England and two years after his departure would have brought about the sudden need to remove his three children from William Street. It is more probable that they were taken into their grandfather's care at some time shortly after he left England in 1853.

In *Lord Carnock*, Harold Nicolson says that his grandfather returned from the Far East having committed 'some error of judgement at Petropavlovsk' which resulted in him being unable to obtain any further sea-going appointment.[10] It is undeniable that Sir Frederick did, indeed, show poor judgement before Petropavlovsk in 1854 – he chose a poor landing beach and trusted information from an American deserter with the result that two hundred men died in the failed assault. However, in the five years between Petropavlovsk and his return to England in 1859, he seems to have tried hard to redeem himself. He took a prize off Cape Clasett; he led a successful attack on the forts on the northern shore of the Peiho, near Tientsin (Tianjin); he made a diplomatic visit to Japan; and he safely conveyed Lord Elgin from Hong Kong to Peiho (surely not a duty to be given to a captain in disgrace).

His children, meanwhile, were being brought up by their maternal grandfather. Arthur Nicolson told Harold that he could

> remember the sooted smell of the curtains in Albemarle Street ... watching the hats and bonnets in the street below. He remembered seeing Queen Victoria prancing on a black horse, the scarlet of her riding habit slashed by the blue of the Garter, and how the Guards, bearded from Inkerman, raised their bearskins to her upon bayonets. He remembered talk of Alma, of Balaklava, of the China Wars ...[11]

It seems that only in 1861, after his return to England and the subsequent death of his unacceptable second wife, were the children returned to Sir Frederick's care.

The Admiralty did not forget and, following his return from the Far East, Sir Frederick was effectively removed from the active service list. Under the system as it then existed, any captain who lived long enough would eventually become an admiral as those above him in the Navy List slowly died off. Sir Frederick eventually obtained flag rank, but he never again went to sea, remaining resentfully in William Street, where 'for forty years, he nursed a grievance against the Admiralty,' attended meetings of the Thames Conservancy Board and, according to his grandson, read 'several thousand French novels.'[12]

Arthur Nicolson began his education at a private school in Wimbledon before being sent to the Royal Navy's training ship, HMS *Britannia*. Harold suggests that this move took place in 1861, when Arthur was twelve,[13] but this seems unlikely. The *Britannia* did not accept cadets until they were thirteen years of age and there is no record of his presence there until 1864, when he would have been approaching fifteen. However old he was, life on board the *Britannia* would not have been easy. An old three-decked sailing ship, originally built in 1820, she had been turned into a training ship at Portsmouth in 1859 and migrated down the coast, arriving in Dartmouth in 1863, and later giving her name to the shore-based Royal Naval Training College. By the time she reached Dartmouth, *Britannia* was little more than a hulk. Cadets slept in hammocks in conditions so overcrowded and insanitary that there were frequent outbreaks of sickness and disease. Winter and summer, cadets were roused at five in the morning and their day, a mixture of physical training and courses of instruction in the basics of seamanship, lasted up to fourteen hours.

Nevertheless, Arthur did well and, in 1866, graduated third in his year, but with the clear conviction that he was not cut out for the Royal Navy.

One can only imagine the scenes in the house in William Street. Arthur Nicolson left no direct account of his father, but Harold's description in *Lord Carnock* and *The Desire to Please* seems likely to reflect his views – 'a choleric and egotistic man';[14] 'a fierce and selfish old man with a raucous voice';[15] 'a voice which wounded and alarmed';[16] a man who 'interfered with the liberty and the feelings of his children.'[17] *Britannia* must have furnished Arthur with sufficient self-confidence to defy Sir Frederick, for he won the argument and in the summer of 1866 went to Rugby School.

By the time Arthur Nicolson arrived at Rugby, Thomas Arnold, the school's great and reforming headmaster, had been dead over twenty years, but Rugby remained one of the top schools in the country. Rugby's radical revision of the traditional curriculum – among other things, introducing prefects, and putting a new emphasis on sport and fair play – had reshaped the public-school system and had an impact on the values of the nation as a whole. The school's reputation could hardly have stood higher. Arthur, however, did not succeed. His final report categorised him as 'an absolute failure.'[18] Once again, one can only imagine the 'thunderous gloom' of William Street.[19]

In *Lord Carnock*, Harold relates the bizarre and unverifiable story that, during his last year at Rugby, Arthur was beaten up and kidnapped. The main outcome of the incident appears to have been that his uncle, Henry Brougham Loch, took an interest in him, securing him both a place at Brasenose College, Oxford, and, later, his nomination to the Foreign Office. By 1867, when his interest in Arthur Nicolson began, Henry Loch had already had a remarkable career at the centre of Queen Victoria's expanding Empire. He started life in the Royal Navy, but, like Arthur, did not care for it. (Was this a point of sympathy with his nephew?) He joined the British East India Company and the Bengal Light Infantry; he fought in the Anglo-Sikh War and the Sutlej Campaign; he raised and commanded a force of Bulgarian cavalry during the Crimean War; he was attached to Lord Elgin's mission to China and was present at the capture of Canton during the Second Opium War; he returned to China with Lord Elgin in 1860, was captured by the Chinese and subsequently released. It is much more likely to have been Henry Loch's career than his father's that inspired Arthur Nicolson's interest in imperial and world events.

Unfortunately, Arthur was no more successful at Brasenose than he had been at Rugby. There were problems with the College authorities; there were debts; and it was considered better for all concerned that he should sever his connection with the University without taking a degree. The situation in William Street was 'thunderous in the extreme.'[20]

With characteristic irony, Harold Nicolson writes in *Lord Carnock*: 'On leaving Oxford, Arthur Nicolson began to study seriously.'[21] And the irony is reinforced by the fact that the same could be said of Harold himself. Certainly, Arthur Nicolson changed after leaving Oxford in 1869. Perhaps he was happier working by himself, studying French in Switzerland and German in Dresden, rather than being confined within an institution. Harold claimed that it was during this period that his father learned the habits of application and concentration that remained ingrained in him for the rest of his life. Arthur was away from home for almost a year before being called back, in July 1870, to take the Foreign Office entrance exam. His whole working life in the Foreign Office and the Diplomatic Service was to be dominated by the rise of Germany, so there is a further irony in the fact that he almost did not get back in time because of the outbreak of the Franco-Prussian War, which led directly to the establishment of the German Empire.

Helped by a German friend, who smuggled him onto a military train with '*Nach Paris*' chalked on the compartment door, he reached London, sat his papers and – much to his own surprise – came first in that year's competitive exam. Less than a month later, he started work in the French Department as an unsalaried junior clerk. From that moment, he had a career which he found fulfilling and satisfying. He also joined an elite group which would accept and look after him. Both aspects were important. Of course, it was not all plain sailing and there were times when he almost felt he had had enough of diplomacy, but, as his character dictated, he persisted. The decision to join the Foreign Office was one he never regretted.

The first inkling of professional success did not make life at home any easier. In 1867, Sir Frederick had married for a third time, to Anne Crosse who, unfortunately, proved to be an alcoholic. Arthur was concerned for the welfare of his sister, Clementina, who was still living at home. This caused a rift with his new stepmother and with Sir Frederick, who sided with his wife – which was doubly unfortunate because, under the system as it then existed, new entrants to the Foreign Office received no salary for the first two years. Arthur was dependent on his father for money. Very little was forthcoming.

However, release was on the horizon. In 1872, although only twenty-two, Arthur Nicolson was made Assistant Private Secretary to the Foreign Secretary, Lord Granville. This gave him his first taste of being at the centre of things in his own right. In 1874, he was offered a transfer from the Foreign Office to the Diplomatic Service and a tour of duty in Berlin as Acting Third Secretary. It was to be thirty-five years before he lived in

England again, and when he returned he was Head of the Foreign Office.

This was the world of Harold's father and grandfather, the source of family stories and anecdotes. Harold would have understood that he came from an ancient, aristocratic, but unlanded family. The lack of a family estate was something he might sometimes regret, especially when he compared himself to his wife and her family, or to his Oxford and Foreign Office peers, but its absence had led to a tradition of public service among the Nicolsons which was at the root of Harold's character. Service abroad of one form or another was not uncommon in Victorian times, but the Nicolsons had been soldiers, sailors and administrators, men who travelled and who were familiar with distant places, for three or four generations – and there can be little doubt that they entered and committed themselves to public or imperial service because they were landless and needed to earn their money and their place in society.

All this meant that the Nicolson family had a history of being at the centre of things, of being close to military and political events which went to shape Britain, the Empire and even, in Arthur Nicolson's case, the world. This, in turn, greatly influenced Harold Nicolson, both intellectually and emotionally. It created an expectation and a need which had important implications for the choices he made during his life, but it was a need that Vita could never understand, either intellectually or emotionally.

In his writing, Harold is always seeking out political or historical reference points. It is as if, for him, an individual only truly exists when defined in relation to political and social events of recognised significance. This, for example, is how he chooses to remember his German uncle, the husband of his father's elder sister, Clementina:

> In a pension at Interlaken, she met an elderly German widower of the name of Beemelmans. She was herself at that date over thirty years of age. Much to my grandfather's fury, and to my father's regret, she married this gentleman, who at the time held some minor post in the German Railways. They lived in a new quarter of Strassburg, where they owned a dim, trim little house, the front door of which bore a white enamel plate 'Ministerialrat Beemelmans'.... Herr Ministerialrat Beemelmans is not to me a vivid figure. He died some years later and my recollection of him is blurred. I can recall only a round, guttural and tobacco-laden person.... Yet ... he had himself been the very first German soldier to enter Strassburg. He had been present at the siege of Paris. He remembered the burning of St Cloud; and he would recount how the cannon fired and the projectiles made a wide arc in the air and

then descended with a heavy pounce upon the squares and streets of the French capital.[22]

It is easy to see the point at which Herr Ministerialrat Beemelmans catches Harold's imagination. That individuals are defined by public events or public attitudes is a concept which underlies almost everything he wrote and much that he did in pursuing his own public career.

On a more immediate and personal level, Nicolson family history taught Harold about the distinction between personal and public existence. Harold claims that Arthur Nicolson's experiences at the hands of his father implanted in him a reserve which limited his ability to communicate his emotions and feelings to his children. Why his reaction to his upbringing should have taken such a form is not clear. We know that during his time at Oxford, and even during his early years in the Foreign Office, Nicolson enjoyed something of a wild youth, including a love affair with a married woman.[23] As he grew older, so he grew quieter – though in his later years some of his quietness may well have been due to the pain of the arthritis, from which he suffered so severely. Yet he was never an unsociable man. He fulfilled the representational duties associated with his diplomatic role with notable success: in St Petersburg, the Nicolsons 'became extremely popular in Russian society.'[24] In the things he did and the letters he wrote to his wife, there is a dry wit and an appreciation of the absurd which does not necessarily fit with the idea of deep reserve. Nor was he unassertive. King Edward VII was an acknowledged expert on all questions of uniform and official decorations, yet Arthur was prepared to argue and even defy his Sovereign over the question of the badge of his Nova Scotia Baronetcy and its precedence over the Order of the Bath.[25]

Only on a personal level, where emotional matters were concerned, did his reserve, a kind of emotional secretiveness, take over. He seems to have feared the consequences of allowing himself to display emotion. As he wrote to Harold – and as Harold might well have said himself – 'I do so hate rows.'[26] If Arthur Nicolson suffered from the all-too-clear expression of his father's feelings, such as they were, Harold suffered from the reverse. Arthur Nicolson's feelings for his children went deep, but they were rarely expressed openly. In this, of course, he was typical of his generation. Harold summarised the values which his father absorbed during his formative years.

> He was taught on all sides that manliness and self-control were the highest aims of English boyhood: he was taught that all but the most material

forms of intelligence were slightly effeminate: he learnt ... to rely upon action rather than upon ideas. Under such a system the higher sensibilities of the mind and soul were apt to become submerged if not sterilised.[27]

In later life Harold reflected that 'we were always strangers to our parents.'[28] Letters and diaries again suggest that he may have been overstating the case, but, equally, it is clear that much was felt that was not expressed.

In going through his father's papers after his death, Harold was amazed to discover how worried his parents had been about him as a child. They thought him 'mercurial' and incredibly lazy.[29]

Harold was more obviously outgoing and gregarious than his father. He enjoyed people and he enjoyed socialising, but despite this, and despite his immense personal emotional honesty, he too had his own particular reserve – a dislike of displaying or expressing emotion; a hatred of emotional situations and rows – which stayed with him all his life. Like father, like son.

2 Hamiltons

If the descent of the Nicolsons was dominated by their title and their sense of public duty, that of Harold Nicolson's mother's family – the Hamiltons – was dominated by Protestantism and land. Like the Nicolsons, the Hamiltons came originally from Scotland, though they were a lowland clan of Anglo-Norman origin, with estates spread across the Lothians, Lanarkshire and Ayrshire. One branch of the family became the most powerful family in Scotland after the Stuarts, with many titles and a Dukedom. The branch from which Harold Nicolson was descended was decidedly less grand.

Hans Hamilton was born in 1536, the illegitimate son of Archibald Hamilton, from Raploch in Lanarkshire. In 1563, having received a good education and taken orders, he and his wife Janet moved to Dunlop in Ayrshire where he became the village's first Protestant Minister. The family were clearly not poor, but neither were they in any sense prominent. It was their eldest son, James Hamilton, born a few years previously in 1559, who engineered a change in the family fortunes.

James Hamilton began life as an academic. He was educated at St Andrews University and worked as a teacher in Glasgow. In 1587, he moved to Dublin and founded 'The Free School' before becoming one of the first Fellows of the new Trinity College in 1593. His career then took a political turn. He became an agent for King James VI of Scotland, first in Ireland and then in London at the court of Elizabeth I, where he was involved in the negotiations leading up to James' accession as King James I of England in 1603. Eventually, after a complicated passage of being in and out of favour at court, he was created an 'undertaker' – being one who undertook, against certain conditions, to settle and regenerate lands in Ireland granted by the King. In 1606, under the terms of what is now known as the Hamilton and Montgomery Settlement, James Hamilton was granted lands in Ulster, in the area of Southern Clandeboye, stretching from Bangor to Killyleagh and down both sides of Lough Strangford. In 1609, he was knighted and, in 1622, created Viscount Clandeboye. Between these two dates, in 1613, he settled in the twelfth-century castle of Killyleagh where, eight generations later, Harold Nicolson's mother, Mary Catherine Rowan Hamilton, was born.

James Hamilton was clearly a man of great academic and political ability, but he was also an extremely pious man, devoted to the Protestant cause and a strong supporter of Presbyterian worship among the settlers he brought across from Scotland. His legacy, above and beyond the lands which passed down to his descendents, was the creation of the Ulster Scots and a great strengthening of the Protestant Ascendancy. His son, also named James, raised 'a regiment of Foot and a troop of Horse' for the Royalist cause during the Civil Wars and, in 1647, three years after his father's death, was elevated to the rank of first Earl Clandeboye by a grateful Charles I. He was forced to submit to Cromwell's Commonwealth in 1649, but managed to keep the family estates intact.

However, the family did not maintain its new prominence. In *Helen's Tower*, Harold Nicolson relates at length the Byzantine story of how Lady Alice, the wife of the generally weak-minded second Earl Clandeboye, destroyed her husband's will and induced him to sign another, naturally more favourable to herself, before poisoning him. These events took place in 1675. The second Earl's cousins, who knew he had intended them to inherit, took Lady Alice to court, starting legal proceedings which were to last over twenty years, during which time the estate and its revenues were impounded. In 1700, the court found for the two descendents of the original Hamilton cousins, but the consequences of the judgement, modified by a subsequent will, were Gilbertian in their absurdity.

Each property must be divided ... into exactly equal halves. They went so far as to draw a mathematical line across Killyleagh Castle itself, by which the Keep went to the nephew, whereas the courtyard and the Gate House with attendant battlements were accorded to the daughter.[1]

The Gate House half of the inheritance, which included the two-thousand-acre Clandeboye Estate, passed by marriage to the Blackwood family, while the castle itself remained in the possession of the Hamiltons, creating endless trouble between the two families. This ludicrous division of the Killyleagh property continued until 1847, but the important aspect of the story as far as Harold Nicolson is concerned is that it was brought to a resolution by Lord Dufferin.

His full title was Frederick, Fifth Baron and First Marquis of Dufferin and Ava; his family surname was the incredibly cumbersome Hamilton-Temple-Blackwood; and he was Harold Nicolson's uncle by marriage, having married Hariot Rowan Hamilton, elder sister of Harold's mother. It was on his coming of age – and some years before his marriage to Hariot – that Lord Dufferin decided to hand back to the Hamilton family those parts of the Killyleagh Castle and estate which he had inherited through the Blackwood line, thus ending the absurd division of the property. His romantic stipulation was that 'the Hamiltons were to pay to the Lord and Lady of Clandeboye an annual tribute in the shape of a golden rose and a golden spur each alternate year.'[2]

Lord Dufferin, the subject of *Helen's Tower*, was one of Harold Nicolson's heroes, uniting all those aspects of the aristocratic world which Harold enjoyed, appreciated and quite probably envied. Dufferin had a distinguished ancestry, which brought him a connection with the playwright Richard Brinsley Sheridan, an impressive title, and large inherited estates. At the same time, he combined a larger-than-life romantic approach to the world with an extremely successful public career. He was very much at the centre of things.

At the age of thirty, before entering public life, he made an adventurous voyage to Iceland, Jan Mayen Island and Spitzbergen, writing a successful and still entertaining travelogue, *Letters from High Latitudes* (1856), on his return. He then went on to fill, one after the other, a scarcely credible list of high public offices – Under-Secretary of State for War; Under-Secretary of State for India; Chancellor of the Duchy of Lancaster; Paymaster General; Governor General of Canada; Ambassador to Russia; Ambassador to the Ottoman Empire; Viceroy of India; Ambassador to Italy; and, lastly, Ambassador to France.

Harold Nicolson

James Lees-Milne summarises Harold Nicolson's relations with his father as 'consistently respectful, admiring and affectionate, without being intimate.'³ Respect is certainly the keynote of *Lord Carnock* – the most emotionally committed piece of writing in the book is that part of the Epilogue contributed by Vita – though it is equally true that, writing a book about his father, Harold would have striven for an objectivity he might not have felt. But respect is rarely the basis for emulation. There appears no evidence that Harold ever considered any other career than the Diplomatic Service. Why should that be? His father was a diplomat, but so was Lord Dufferin. If we are searching for role models for the young Harold Nicolson, role models for a choice of career and, indeed, for an approach to life which combined a successful public career with a romantic temperament, then Lord Dufferin appears a more likely candidate than Lord Carnock.

> The brilliance of his attainments, the glamour of his parentage, the awe which he inspired, were softened by an almost feminine sensibility, by the perfect conjunction of strength and gentleness; by the fact, ultimately, that he was the kindest man that ever lived.⁴

Harold never wrote like that about his father.

Harold saw Ireland, his Irish heritage and his Irish connections through romantic, rose-tinted spectacles, not least because it was his mother's background and he was devoted to his mother. Ireland was a place of emotion. In *The Desire to Please*, the family are on holiday when his mother is recognised by 'a scare-crow woman', known as 'Mad Meg', whom she had known as a child.

> Meg flung herself from the carriage and fell backwards into the ditch shouting affection at my mother. 'My darlint,' she screamed, 'my little darlint.' ... We all wore different expressions. My father looked embarrassed but amused. My sister was still gasping from the paroxysm of fear that had assailed her. I felt disgusted and disturbed.
>
> My mother behaved most strangely. She was still half-laughing and half-crying and her hat had been twisted to one side by Meg's attempts at an embrace ... what did hats matter now that one was back at Killyleagh, that one was fifteen again, and that Mad Meg had jumped to kiss one after thirty years?⁵

The different reactions of the members of the family are brilliantly drawn, but the Irishness of Harold's mother triumphs because Ireland somehow allows for the expression of those emotions which, in the world of the Nicolsons, would remain buried in diffidence and reserve. And, in the book as in life, there is a level at which this version of Ireland comes to represent the more emotional relationship Harold Nicolson had with his mother.

Ireland also had another function. Ireland and Irishness was a club, another group to which Harold tried to attach himself. It is normal to want what you do not have. Harold had a nomadic childhood in Persia, Hungary, the Ottoman Empire, Bulgaria, Morocco. It gave him an experience of the world that informed his whole life. At the same time, simply because his life had taken that path, he longed for roots and stability; he longed to come from somewhere, to belong somewhere. Ireland became an image of a place he could have come from, a place where he could have belonged – although in reality he was no more Irish than he was Scottish. This feeling, of course, was closely related to his sensitivity that the Nicolsons 'have been for many generations a landless tribe,'[6] a sensitivity later heightened by close association with Vita and the Sackvilles. The Hamiltons and the Blackwoods certainly had land and they had the easy superiority that went with it.

The Ireland of Harold's childhood – the estates of the Hamiltons and of Lord Dufferin, Clandeboye House, Killyleagh Castle, Shanganagh Castle south of Dublin where his grandmother lived – was the Ireland of the Protestant Ascendancy. It was, or appeared to be, a timeless world, where men

> would touch their hats as the carriages crackled by ... the curate propped his bicycle against one of the stone cannon balls at the entrance to the house; and at 11.15 each morning the butler would enter the library bringing cake and Marsala, the London newspaper and the English mail.[7]

The politics, the violence, the starvation, the great religious divide – these things were unknown to him as a child. In *The Desire to Please*, he charts the process of understanding, first as an awareness of 'Catholics' as 'a forbidden subject ... something aloof and hostile beyond the warm orbit of my family life';[8] and then, when he was eighteen, learning that

> my mother's forbears had behaved in no way better than Edmund Spenser. They had behaved even worse, since they had been more successful.... Not only had the Hamiltons been as greedy as any of the undertakers, but they had profited by their loot. All except one.[9]

The Hamiltons were loyalists. All except one. Their lands and their wealth came from the Crown and from the Protestant settlement in the seventeenth century. Harold Nicolson's mother was herself a loyalist. The exception was her great-grandfather, Archibald Hamilton Rowan: 'We do not talk about him much ... we are rather ashamed of him in a way.'[10]

Hamilton Rowan was born in 1751, to all appearances the next in the respectable lineage of the Hamilton family. However, he became involved with the Irish cause, reversed his surname, threw over the traces of his upbringing and became 'a rebel'. In 1790, he joined the United Irishmen, and in 1792 was arrested for seditious libel, being eventually convicted and imprisoned two years later. Even in Newgate Prison, he continued to plot the overthrow of British rule and had to escape and flee to France to avoid a charge of High Treason. In France, he was arrested and imprisoned as a British spy, before being released on the intervention of Robespierre himself. In 1795, he fled to the United States, living on the edge of poverty, until, in 1801, a conditional pardon from the British Government allowed him to travel to Hamburg to be reunited with his family – and also with his income which he had been unable to enjoy whilst on the run. In 1803, he was granted a full pardon and returned to Killyleagh where he became a respectable citizen, though one who continued to follow liberal, but legal, political interests. He died in 1834, having outlived all his Irish radical companions.

This is the story which lies at the heart of *The Desire to Please*. Why did Harold choose to write about Hamilton Rowan? The story has a romantic appeal. Harold always fancied himself a rebel – though on less grand a scale than Hamilton Rowan – even though the belief does not stand up to examination. Here was a great-great-grandfather who was a rebel; whose life was full of action and controversy. Harold's treatment of the man and his life is essentially romantic, at times close to sentimental. He tries to balance this against the historical narrative of the times, but in the end romance triumphs.

> From the towers of his castle he could look down upon the prosperous little town and out over the wide stretches of the Lough to where the sunshine struck the distant Scottish hills. His wife and daughters were around him. Three of his sons held commissions in His Majesty's forces. ... Gradually he was forgiven even by the Anglo-Irish aristocracy.... He was assuredly more fortunate than many.[11]

Harold Nicolson asks why Hamilton Rowan broke the family mould and behaved as he did, but comes up with no definite answer beyond the suggestion that '"Ireland" glimmered for him as a land of heroes and martyrs – of castles, battlements and fairies – as the land of the incalculable and the unexpected.'[12] Harold's identification with and affection for Ireland had much the same basis.

3 Childhood

It was Lord Dufferin's diplomatic career that led to the meeting of Arthur Nicolson and Catherine Rowan Hamilton. Arthur Nicolson finally escaped from the oppression of his father and the gloom of William Street at the beginning of 1874, arriving in Berlin as Third Secretary in the Embassy. Two years later, as a result of complications arising out of a love affair, he was posted to Peking as Second Secretary. Another two years and he was back in Berlin, applying himself energetically to studying the German political scene. At the end of 1879, he transferred to Constantinople, where he served under three Ambassadors in quick succession – Sir Henry Layard, the excavator of Nineveh; George Goschen, later Chancellor of the Exchequer and First Lord of the Admiralty; and then Lord Dufferin.

During the hottest months of the year, the British Embassy in Constantinople moved to its summer quarters at the small bay of Therapia on the western shore of the Bosphorus, twelve miles north of the city. It was here that Lord and Lady Dufferin arrived, accompanied by Lady Dufferin's younger sister, Catherine, in June 1881. In *Lord Carnock*, Harold Nicolson gives a full account of the romantic circumstances under which his parents first came to know one another – dinner under the magnolias, after-dinner theatricals, moonlit expeditions on the Bosphorus.[1] The wedding took place on 20 April the following year in the chapel of the main Embassy in Pera, that part of Constantinople which overlooks the Golden Horn from the north. There was a naval escort; Lord Dufferin gave away the bride; *Lohengrin* was played; and the whole was conducted 'in circumstances of the greatest diplomatic ceremony.'[2]

The pace of life for the newly-wedded couple was anything but relaxed. In October 1882, following the British occupation of Egypt, Lord Dufferin was appointed High Commissioner in Cairo. He took the Nicolsons with him and it was there, in January 1883, that Catherine Nicolson gave birth to their first son, Frederick. Shortly afterwards, however, both she and Lady Dufferin contracted typhoid. They recovered and returned to Constantinople that April, followed some weeks later by Arthur and Lord Dufferin. The Nicolsons remained at the Constantinople Embassy less than a year. In March 1884, they transferred to Athens where, almost as soon as they arrived, their second son, Erskine, was born, and where Arthur acted as Chargé d'Affaires. Athens lasted barely a year and the family were off again, this time to Persia where they arrived in April 1885.

Tehran, which was to feature largely in Nicolson family mythology, was then a city contained within a long circuit of walls pierced by twelve gates. Outside the walls, an open, dusty plain stretched away in three directions, while to the north rose the Elburz Mountains. The British Legation was in the northern part of the city, in its own walled compound. Lord Curzon, writing just a few years later, described 'a fine gateway, upon which Her Majesty's initials are carved in stone ... a large wooded enclosure ... a dense growth of trees, interspersed with winding pathways and runnels of water . .. [concealing] the main building of the Legation, as well as four other substantial detached houses accommodating the various secretaries.'[3] The main Legation building had been designed by a British architect and featured a special, modern cast-iron roof structure, though it remained loosely oriental in style. The detached houses were less attractive, constructed of grim yellow brick and variously described as resembling Victorian rectories, a public school without the boys, the precincts of Wormwood Scrubs, and a Victorian lunatic asylum.[4] In one of these, on Sunday 21 November 1886, Harold George Nicolson was born.

As at Constantinople, there was also a summer Legation, in the village of Gulahek, about ten kilometres north of Tehran in the foothills of the Elburz and conveniently close to the Shah's summer residence of Sultanetabed. The Gulahek compound was even larger than that in Tehran and correspondingly more rural and relaxed. The Minister had a fine, Georgian-style Residence, while the staff had cottages scattered among the trees, smaller but more private and more attractive than the yellow brick horrors in Tehran. Gulahek was much preferred by Arthur and Catherine Nicolson and also – forty years later – by Harold.

In the mid-1880s, the Foreign Office was watching Persia and its ruler, Shah Nasr-ed-Din, with a degree of nervousness. To the north, Russia had extended its territory and its influence up to the Afghan border. Britain, ever fearful of a threat to the Indian Empire, was determined to resist any further expansion. In March 1885, just a month before the Nicolsons' arrival in Tehran, Britain and Russia had come close to war over the status of the Panjeh Valley in western Afghanistan. If the Shah fell under Russian influence, he might well allow Russian troops to cross Persian territory and

Childhood

threaten the western border of the India. And the Shah was caught between fear of the Russians and dislike of the British, who had thrown him out of Afghanistan thirty years previously. Diplomatic persuasion, including a trip to Britain where he had received the Order of the Garter from Queen Victoria, had so far held the balance. Arthur Nicolson's task was to keep things that way at a time of heightened Anglo-Russian tension and, consequently, increased Russian pressure on the Shah. He did it and did it well for three years – for most of which he was acting as Chargé d'Affaires – even concluding an agreement that the Shah would not sign up to any secret deals with the Russians without informing the British. It was a key period in his career. 'You are now, my dear Arthur,' wrote Lord Dufferin, 'one of the marked men of the service.'[5]

Harold would have known nothing of this – he was only sixteen months old when the family left Tehran – but he would have heard much about Persia during his childhood. He would have heard about his birthplace. He would have known that his parents were happy there; that his father found the country beautiful and the people charming; that he had done well at the Legation and been awarded first a CMG and then a KCIE as a result.[6] In 1925, Harold was offered a choice between going as Counsellor to Peking or to Tehran – his father had, of course, served in both. Harold chose Tehran, partly because he believed 'Tehran would be the one Vita would dislike least', but also because 'his father was loudly persuasive.'[7] Family memories played their part.

Just how much Harold could be influenced by parental stories is illustrated by the incident which occurred when the family left Tehran. Arthur Nicolson had been appointed Consul General in Budapest.

> On the journey with his wife and three baby boys across the Russian steppes the last carriage of their train caught fire. The story was so often referred to in the Nicolson family that for years, until his mother pointed out that he was only a year-and-a-half old at the time, Harold believed that he vividly remembered every detail of the incident.[8]

Any consideration of Harold Nicolson's life between his arrival in Budapest in 1888, aged not quite two, and his own departure for Persia in 1925, when he was not quite forty, has to take into account the autobiographical aspects of *Some People*. It is easy to assume that *Some People*, with its accessibility, humour and first person narration, is factually accurate, but from its first appearance in 1927 the book has had the capacity to confuse. Ostensibly, it is a series of essays about people the author has known during his life. Virginia Woolf's view was that 'by the end of the book we realise that the figure which has been most completely and most subtly displayed is that of the author,'[9] suggesting that the work was a kind of autobiography. However, Harold's son, Nigel, quotes his father as saying: 'The idea ... was to put real people in imaginary situations, and imaginary people in real situations.'[10] *Some People* has to be treated with caution. The question of Miss Plimsoll is a case in point. In *Some People*, Harold introduces her as his governess and describes her character in some detail; and she reappears in *Helen's Tower* and *The Desire to Please*. The name is clearly contrived, but he undoubtedly had a governess or series of governesses. Whether the Miss Plimsoll who appears in his work is a fictionalised portrait of a real person, a composite of several governesses, a literary device which allows him to dramatise certain aspects of childhood and the relationship between children and adults, or a mixture of all these, is unclear. And the evidence is contradictory.[11]

Budapest was the location for Harold's first memories. In *Some People,* he claims to remember the main railway station decked in black, violet and gold in mourning for the death of Crown Prince Rudolf at Mayerling in January 1889. He would have been just over two. He remembered a nursery maid called Anna who 'had a sewing machine and used to eat raw bacon on a green plate'[12] – the kind of detail which does not smack of invention. He certainly remembered the British Consulate in Andrássy Street and the ceremony of inspecting the dining table with his mother before an official diplomatic dinner. He remembered his mother reading to him, his glass of milk at bedtime, reciting the Lord's Prayer and then, when the light had been turned out, the dreadful night terrors – inspired by Herr Geverts who kept the sausage shop on the corner and who, Harold believed, crept into his bedroom in the dark.[13] He also remembered lying in his upper storey bedroom suffering from typhoid.

Persia had been what we might now call a developing country. The Austro-Hungarian Empire was quite the reverse. Budapest was one of the great cities of Europe, with trams and factories – both of which Harold remembered – and a huge construction programme, including the newly-opened Hungarian Royal Opera House, further down Andrássy Street, and the then still-unfinished Parliament Building, the biggest in the world. Politically, however, the Empire was in the long slow process of decay. The end was still twenty-five years away, but Arthur Nicolson saw and reported the symptoms which would eventually lead to disintegration: the way in which the Magyar ruling classes treated the ethnically diverse populations of outlying provinces – the Croatians and Serbs, Ruthenians and Slovaks;

Childhood

the rigid and racially-based social stratification. Arthur disliked the excess of pomp and ceremony, being 'smothered by uniforms'[14] – something he perhaps transmitted to Harold – and was only too glad when, in 1892, he was asked to return to Constantinople as Secretary to the Embassy.

It was in the interval between these two tours of duty (or postings as the Foreign Office refers to them) that Harold and his mother visited 'Uncle Dufferin' and her sister, 'Aunt Lal', in Paris, where Lord Dufferin was Ambassador. This was the visit so vividly described at the beginning of *Helen's Tower*. It was a world in which the aristocracy ruled and an army of servants oiled the wheels; when the telephone was only just becoming common currency; where the horse remained king and motorised transport was an eccentric rarity. One of the best portraits of the age and class in which Harold was growing up is contained in the first chapter of Barbara Tuchman's *The Proud Tower*.[15] Her analysis of the role of the horse in the society of the day is particularly interesting.

> The English gentleman was unthinkable without his horse.... The man on horseback was the symbol of dominance, and of no other class anywhere in the world was the horse so intrinsic a part as of the English aristocracy. He was the attribute of their power.... [The] horse was still as inseparable from, and ubiquitous in, upper class life as the servant, though considerably more cherished. He provided locomotion, occupation and conversation; inspired love, bravery, poetry and physical prowess.[16]

In *Helen's Tower*, there is a photograph of Harold Nicolson on horseback, taken in Bulgaria in 1895, when he was nine. Wearing a kind of Tam o'Shanter, gaiters, whip in hand, he looks very much the part and very much at ease in it.[17]

To the modern reader, the much-quoted description of the footmen at breakfast with their powdered hair,[18] or the even more poignant description of guests arriving for dinner at the Embassy in rue du Faubourg Saint-Honoré could just as easily come from the seventeenth century as from the end of the nineteenth.

> I could see across to the porte cochère, under which a slow and jingling procession of carriages was passing in. Carriage after carriage fronted me with two lamp-lit eyes, and then blinked sideways as it turned on the cobbles of the courtyard. When the carriages approached the carpeted steps leading to the front door, the footman upon the box would swing

downwards, holding a basketed mud-guard wherewith to protect the skirts of his mistress from any contact with the wheel. Each coachman carried a tall whip in his hand, and many whips shone with silver in the light of the lamps.[19]

But for Harold Nicolson this was real. This was his childhood. He was sensitive and observant, and these were the things he remembered and recorded about his early years. His life spanned a period of immense political, technological and social change, but it was these childhood experiences which informed and shaped his perspective on the modern world.

Like the Austro-Hungarian Empire, the Ottoman Empire was decaying, but it was medieval not modern decay. Turkey was 'the sick man of Europe'[20] and the Western Powers surrounded the patient, jostling for influence and concessions. The Sultan ruled from the great palace of Yildiz, surrounded by huge exotic gardens, by his women and by his eunuchs. His rule was despotic and violent. The court was subject to elaborate, theatrical rituals such as the *selamlik* – once witnessed by the seven- or eight-year-old Harold – in which the Sultan, accompanied by his ministers, the diplomatic corps, soldiers and marching bands, made his weekly progress to and from the Hamidiye Mosque, which was all of fifty metres from the palace gates.[21]

> 'The whole system,' [Arthur] Nicolson complained despairingly to Lord Rosebery, 'is rotten to the core. The Sultan ... calling up his Sheikhs, astrologers and attendants at all hours to try and get some solace and comfort from some new terror which seizes him ... his palace is the haunt of all that is despicable and depraved.'[22]

If Harold, in later life, followed his father in feeling an affection for Persia and its people, he shared with him also a dislike for the Turks bordering on contempt.

However reserved Arthur Nicolson may have been, however little emotion was actually communicated between father and son, there can be no doubt that Harold was shocked in the summer of 1894 when his father returned from a yachting trip dangerously ill. Harold speaks of 'ptomaine poisoning.'[23] Acute sickness was followed by severe gout.

> For six weeks he was unable to walk, and for three months he was on crutches. He emerged from this ordeal with shoulders prematurely rounded and bowed, and persistent arthritis which thereafter gave to his small frame an increasingly crippled appearance.... He would dress

himself and be carried into the next room. Propped in a chair, his face in perspiration from the agony of his limbs, he would sit there arguing with Said Pasha.... The experiences of those four months aged him by many years.[24]

Although written thirty-five years later, the words make it clear that Harold was moved by the weakness and physical change he saw in his father.

In the autumn of 1894, Arthur Nicolson, still suffering from the aftermath of his illness, was moved from the pressured environment of Constantinople to serve as British Agent and Consul General in the Bulgarian capital of Sofia, which the Foreign Office no doubt expected to offer less stressful surroundings. Bulgaria was a new country, carved from the decaying Ottoman Empire by the Russians in 1878 and placed, by international agreement, under the rule of Alexander of Battenburg. The trouble was that the Russians, having created this new country, expected to control it. The Bulgarians had other ideas. They elected Stefan Stambolov to lead a government which espoused policies far too liberal for Tsarist Russia. Alexander not only showed signs of siding with his liberal government, he also greatly expanded his country's borders and conducted a successful war against the Serbs, Russia's great regional ally. In 1886, the Russians organised a coup. Alexander was deposed, but the Bulgarians under Stambolov's leadership fought back, maintaining their independence and electing Ferdinand of Saxe-Coburg-Gotha as their new King. Ferdinand began with liberal sympathies, but Russian pressure was too much for him and he soon turned against Stambolov and the liberals. By this time, however, Stambolov was seen across Europe as a patriotic hero, especially in countries such as Britain and Austria-Hungary which viewed Russian expansion with deep suspicion. So that when, in July 1895, Ferdinand had him assassinated – hacked to death with curved Turkish-style swords, known as yatagans – there was international outrage. Arthur Nicolson received personal instructions from Queen Victoria that he was to attend the funeral and place a wreath on Stambolov's coffin. But the funeral itself was disrupted by gunfire and mounted police with drawn swords.[25]

Harold was eight years old. He noticed things. In a small town such as Sofia, political violence must have been much more evident than in a metropolis like Constantinople. In *Some People*, he tells how Stambolov's fingers were hacked off during the fatal attack and how his widow then preserved them in vinegar and placed them on public view in her window, presumably as a protest against the regime and a rallying point for opposition. Harold, fascinated but forbidden to view the grisly display, tricks Miss Plimsoll into passing the house. She is horrified and Harold is punished.[26] It is a curious tale. Nowhere else in his life or his work does Harold show any particular fascination for the gothic or the macabre. At the same time, the story rings true. It is too bizarre to invent, but more persuasively it shows Harold as actively mischievous. Almost all the other governess anecdotes show him, rather passively, failing to live up to her expectations – which does not fit with the memories of his parents and others. One assumes he just wanted to see for himself, to check the reality of what he had been told, but there is also the implication that he was not unfamiliar with and certainly not repelled by the consequences of violence.

The Stambolov incident happened during Harold's last few days in Sofia, so that whatever its impact might have been, Bulgaria had no time to strengthen its hold upon him. After only ten months, Arthur Nicolson was on the move again, this time to Tangier as British Minister to Morocco.

Between postings, the family spent the summer of 1895 on the Kent coast at Walmer Castle. Lord Dufferin was still in Paris as Ambassador, but in 1892 he had also been appointed Lord Warden of the Cinque Ports.[27] The position was a sinecure in the gift of the monarch, offered as a reward to senior public servants or military leaders, and it brought with it the right of residence in Walmer Castle, one of Henry VIII's coastal defences. The Nicolsons, with no home of their own in Britain, were happy to spend the summer there. Harold found himself in yet another environment rich with historical associations: he played on the battlements where Pitt the Younger and the Duke of Wellington had walked. Walmer had the advantage of being within easy range of Folkestone, where Harold's two elder brothers were already at school. And it was to Walmer that Arthur Nicolson invited his father, now eighty, to spend some time with the family. The invitation led, after twenty-five years, to a *rapprochement* between them. Harold gives his perspective on the reunion in *Lord Carnock*.

> He sat there on the bastion at Walmer looking out to sea. His grandchildren (three singularly scrubby little boys) were climbing on the cannons. Life adjusted itself. Sir Frederick Nicolson, as he sat there in the sun, sang a little Spanish tune which he had heard off the Barbary coast in 1839. His grandsons left their cannons and gathered round him.... He said he would now sing them a song in German. He sang, in a correct but bronchial voice, 'Im wunderschönen Monat Mai.' They were much impressed.[28]

It had already been decided that Harold should join his brothers at their preparatory school, The Grange, in Folkestone, but before being sent there he was allowed to accompany his parents to Tangier. Arthur Nicolson's new appointment as Minister was a significant step up in his career. The previous twenty years had seen much of Africa carved into colonies by the European powers, but Morocco had retained its independence. This was a state of affairs Britain wished to see continued, not least because Morocco controlled the southern coast of the Straits of Gibraltar – and the Straits controlled access to the Mediterranean, which was essential for Britain's imperial supply lines, to Malta, Egypt, the Suez Canal and to the Indian Empire beyond. In 1895, Morocco was a backward country, though not necessarily a poor one. There was natural wealth which could be exploited and great agricultural potential. The country's nominal ruler was the fourteen-year-old Sultan, Abd El Aziz, but effective power was wielded by the Grand Vizier, Bu Ahmed – power, at least, over that half of the country which was not in more or less permanent tribal revolt. Sooner or later, Morocco was bound to cause trouble on the international scene. Arthur Nicolson's job was to delay the inevitable for as long as possible without getting Britain in any way militarily or politically involved.

The importance of the issues at stake was reflected in the manner of his arrival. The family stayed with the Governor of Gibraltar, Sir Robert Biddulph, in his official residence, the Convent. Arthur met the senior naval and military officers in the colony and dined beneath the immense display of heraldry which dominates the Convent's dining room. Gibraltar was an imperial hub. It would have been busy and noisy. The new dockyards were under construction and the navy would have been much in evidence. It was the Royal Navy, in the form of HMS *Bellona*, a modern light cruiser commissioned only the previous year, which conveyed him and his family across the Straits to Tangier.[29] As Her Majesty's Envoy Extraordinary and Minister Plenipotentiary left the ship, the *Bellona* fired her guns in salute and there came an answering salute from the shore.

In *Some People*, Harold makes great play of Miss Plimsoll's infatuation with all things naval, and his own failure to share the interest or live up to her expectations. In this version of events, the crossing to Tangier, during which he is sick into a canvas bucket, represents the moment when 'she must have realised ... that my heart was not of oak.'[30] But *Some People* is not always to be taken literally and it is difficult to imagine a nine-year-old boy who would not be impressed by the modernity of the *Bellona*, with its six guns, twin funnels and long, low, steel hull,[31] or with the booming salutes in honour of his father. Once again, Harold – whether or not he had any concept of the political dimension of his father's job – must again have had a sense of being at the centre of things; that his father had an important and, above all, acknowledged public position.

Arthur Nicolson was to stay in Tangier nine years. They were important years for his career: maintaining Britain's position while the balance of interest and advantage among the other European powers became increasingly complicated and tense. They were important years, too, for his family: his fourth child, and only daughter, Clementina Gwendolen (known as Gwen) was born in July 1896. And for his youngest son, they were crucial. In October 1895, within a few weeks of the family's arrival in Tangier, Harold took the steamer from Gibraltar to Southampton, returning to England to attend school for the first time.[32] By the time Sir Arthur Nicolson (he succeeded to the title on his father's death in 1899) left Tangier to become Ambassador to Madrid in January 1905, Harold was already beginning his second term at Balliol College, Oxford.

Of necessity, Harold saw Morocco only during the school holidays – he calculated that he made thirty-six journeys by steamer across the Bay of Biscay during his school years – but he loved the country and it left a mark on him. He loved the colours, the smell of spices in the narrow streets of the old town or *medina*, the almost gratuitous exoticism. He remembered a society quite astonishingly primitive, especially given its proximity to Europe. There was no electricity and no gas – candles and oil lamps were the only forms of lighting. There were no proper roads and no wheeled vehicles of any kind. For the ordinary people, the mule with panniers slung over its back was the main means of transporting goods. Harold, the son of the English 'Bashador',[33] rode a horse and remembered going out in the evenings on horseback to visit friends, with a servant walking ahead of him carrying a lantern. When his mother went out to evening parties, she was carried in a sedan chair. Sir Arthur's progress around the country was marked by 'a man with a great silken standard [who] rides in front of me, and ... a special escort of 12 who never leave me – rather a bore.'[34] Other memories were less picturesque. Harold recalled standing on an upturned wooden tub to peer over the legation wall into the Muslim cemetery where the victims of a cholera epidemic were being buried to the accompaniment of tears and wailing.[35] If the Persia he had heard his parents talk about and the Constantinople of his early memories were essentially medieval, Morocco offered a glimpse of an even older civilisation. In a *Spectator* article, written nearly fifty years later, Harold suggested that the shadowy streets of Tangier and the flickering oil lamps gave him an experience of what life would have been like in the Rome or Athens of the ancient world.[36]

Throughout his life, Harold retained an affinity for the ancient world and classical literature, but – as in this case – his response was imaginative and emotional rather than scholarly or academic (as his third-class degree would demonstrate).

What was he like, the nine-year-old boy who arrived at the Grange Preparatory School in Folkestone in October 1895? Even by the standards of the late Victorian era when many of the children of the upper and upper-middle classes were connected with some part of the Empire through the army, navy, politics or commerce, Harold was a cosmopolitan child. Born in Persia, he had lived in Hungary, Turkey, Bulgaria and – if only briefly – Morocco, though never in England. Indeed, he probably knew Ireland better than England as a result of visits to his mother's family at Killyleagh and Clandeboye. Privilege, too, was something the Victorian upper classes took for granted, but the son of a senior diplomat would probably have lived in more privileged and grander surroundings than many of his new schoolfellows.

In *Some People* and *Helen's Tower*, the picture that Harold draws of himself as a child is one of Alan Bennett-like embarrassment and inadequacy, constantly failing to live up to people's expectations or doing the wrong thing – letting his balloon float to the ceiling in the main hall of the Paris Embassy;[37] not knowing what a quarterdeck was and being thus unable to salute it.[38] There is clearly an element of dramatic and humorous effect in this. By his own account, he was nervous in an imaginative sense. In Hungary, he was terrified of Herr Geverts, the sausage shop owner. In Walmer, he feared 'the giant ghost of the Duke of Wellington (to say nothing of that of Mr Pitt).'[39] In Gibraltar, while staying in the Convent, he believed he saw 'about to spring upon me ... a huge black figure with outstretched hands ... draped in chains'[40] – it turned out to be a statue of Lord Heathfield, holding the keys of Gibraltar. At the same time, he could be physically courageous, when riding his horse, dancing along the battlements at Walmer Castle, or climbing round an upper-storey cornice of the Tangier Legation to surprise Miss Plimsoll.[41] And he could be mischievous, even defiant, as shown by the incident of Stambolov's fingers; or when, in Constantinople, he and his brothers refused to build a hut with Miss Plimsoll; or, again, when he locked Miss Plimsoll in the schoolroom and threw the key into the garden.[42] However, such childhood misbehaviour is not necessarily the same as the rebelliousness which Harold, mistakenly, liked to see in himself in later years. Mischievousness could take dramatic form.

> One day during a reception at the Legation Harold burst into the drawing-room disguised as a runaway black slave girl, and in a flood of gibberish appealed for protection to the visiting French Minister, 'a most lugubrious person who wore black gloves,' according to Sir Arthur himself, who used to relate the story with much relish.[43]

Harold's parents considered him 'mercurial', 'lazy', and 'comical', and they worried about him.[44] Lady Dufferin (Aunt Lal) thought him spoilt,[45] and he certainly was his mother's favourite. He was probably quite a handful.

Only one thing strikes a discordant note, and that is Harold's statement, quoted earlier, that 'We were always strangers to our parents.' Was this really true? The children of aristocratic Victorian families were brought up by governesses and sent to boarding school at a relatively early age. But there is nothing in the family anecdotes which emerge from *Lord Carnock*, *Helen's Tower*, *The Desire to Please* or *Some People* to suggest a damaging lack of parental engagement. Lady Nicolson seems always to have been there – to show him the table during their diplomatic progress across Europe,[46] to calm his fears that Paris in 1892 might be bombarded as it was in 1870,[47] to shepherd him back to bed after his night terrors. Even Sir Arthur, for all his reserve, seems to have had some level of communication with his son. His reaction to Harold's impersonation of a slave girl is hardly that of a remote Victorian father. Nor does the anecdote related by James Lees-Milne suggest a lack of domestic warmth.

> Once when summoned to his father's study because of a misdemeanour he boldly swung open the door, and, pretending to be one of the footmen, asked, 'Did Sir Arthur ring for coffee?' Sir Arthur was so amused that he forgot to administer punishment.[48]

4 School

The Victorian preparatory school is one of the unexplained mysteries of British social history. From all over Britain and from all corners of the Empire, parents sent their children to educational establishments – often expensive – where their children lived in Spartan conditions and were frequently bullied and beaten by their contemporaries or by their masters. A generation earlier, Kipling and Churchill had suffered agonies at their prep schools, while Asquith had merely hated his. A generation later, George Orwell, Evelyn Waugh, Cyril Connolly, John Betjeman and Jocelyn Brooke were among those who published accounts of the ill-treatment and unhappiness of prep school life. And the memories did not fade. Half a century after leaving the Grange, Harold Nicolson wrote to Jocelyn Brooke that 'the regime of old Hussey [the headmaster] seems to have been perpetuated by his successor.... I can see that you were just as cold and miserable there as I was myself.'[1]

Accustomed to a warm North African climate, to elegant and spacious surroundings, Harold had to acclimatise himself to the cold (the Grange was inadequately heated), to poor food (Harold was appalled, years later, to learn that the headmaster had amassed a respectable sum of money from economies made at the boys' expense), and to what he referred to as 'the bleak unhallowed dormitory of my private school.'[2] And when the first shock was over and school had become more familiar, it simply became desperately monotonous. Harold's elder brother, Frederick, claimed they were 'at their desks from 8 a.m. till 9 p.m.'[3]

The school had been chosen by Sir Arthur on the basis of its high moral tone and the boys were constantly lectured on the need to maintain this abstraction. They were also constantly beaten. There is no evidence that Harold ever actually asked to be taken away from school, but no one reading the letter to his mother that survives from 1896 could fail to be aware of the subtext.

> Hussey ... spanked me for missing a music lesson and said he would cain me next time. On Monday at 12½ he cained me, then next at 2, and he cained me and found out it wasn't my fault he said that next time I ought to be cained he would let me off.... Your *loving, loving, loving* son Harold.[4]

Harold later claimed to have been beaten sixteen times while at the Grange.[5] Even Hussey's staff admitted he was a bully.[6]

Harold hated Hussey and he hated the Grange. He hated the four years he spent there. He looked forward ceaselessly to the holidays when he would return on the P & O steamer to Gibraltar and then cross to Tangier. On other occasions, when there was either not enough time or not enough money for him to return to Morocco, Harold would cross to Ireland to stay at Killyleagh, Clandeboye, or, more often, at his maternal grandmother's house, Shanganagh Castle at the foot of the Wicklow mountains. There he would dream of belonging to Ireland, of a more settled, less nomadic existence. Even thirty years later, in one of his radio talks, Harold could recreate the intensity of his and his brothers' longing for the holidays.

> At this moment your sons are sitting in their bare little rooms at school, and as they gaze up at their calendars ... 'twenty days,' they think, 'till Christmas.' And at the thought a little fish, a little herring of excitement, begins to jump and writhe within their souls.... In a few minutes the bell will ring for lights out. They will snuggle into their cold little beds. 'Nineteen days,' they will think before they fall asleep.[7]

Holidays at Shanganagh may have had another influence on Harold. His grandmother, Catherine, was a lady of considerable force of character and independent opinions. She was an early champion of political rights for women. She believed in the value of higher education for women and for the lower classes. Nor was she morally outraged by the reputation of Parnell's lover, Katherine O'Shea, whom she pointed out to her grandson. And she lived until she was ninety-nine. At school, Harold began to express his own views on political issues, views which were often the opposite of most of the other boys'. He publicly supported the Boers during the Boer War. He spoke up for Dreyfus during the great French scandal of 1899. At this stage, he was probably doing no more than championing the underdog, but it marked him out from his schoolfellows and led to some mild bullying. There were a number of occasions during later life when Harold appeared to court this kind of situation, turning himself into a martyr for no obvious good reason.

If the prep school regime aimed – through some perversion of muscular Christianity – to create strength of character through suffering, it certainly failed in Harold's case. Both he and his brother, Frederick, gained notoriety for being untidy. Harold's written work was 'disgustingly untidy' – though he was generally academically keen and 'really good at Greek.'[8] Neither then nor at any later stage in his school career did he have any aptitude for sport. And though he mocks the importance of school sports in *Some People* – 'the physically gifted enjoy for a short space of years a prominence of which it would be ungracious to deprive them'[9] – it is clear that this was another weight he had to carry. He does not appear to have made any particular friends and he does not seem to have impressed any of the masters. In his diary, he states that he was 'so unhappy', contradicting *Some People*, where he says 'I was not in the least unhappy, only absent-minded.'[10] All in all, he emerged from four years at The Grange oppressed by 'fear and a sense of failure.'[11]

Harold did, however, emerge from the Grange with the habit of books.

For the rest of his life, he was never without a book. Books, the sense of public duty that he inherited from the Nicolsons and his love for Vita were perhaps the three great shaping forces of his adult life. The Nicolson household was clearly literate, though not necessarily literary. Before he went to school he had read 'Froggy would a-wooing go' and

> a book, which I read three times, called *The Angel of Love*.... It was all about consummate virtue in nursery life. Virtue, so far as I can recollect, triumphant. I loved that book. No work has had so profound an influence upon my development.[12]

Presumably, in a cold and hated prep school environment, he read to escape. Neither then nor later, would he have seen this as important. His philosophy of reading is set out with complete clarity in 'How to Read Books'.

> The main point ... about reading is to read. The first thing to do is to make absolutely sure that you really do like reading. The thing is supposed to be, and often is, a pleasure: there is no reason why it should be elevated into a duty. You should begin by reading ill-written books and those which your literate friends decry. Well-written books often require some effort on the part of the reader, and, if you are only just beginning, this effort is sheer waste of time.[13]

This advice to a later generation appears to be based solidly on personal experience.

> Then there was Scott, whom my father wished me to like, and Dickens, who was my mother's special favourite. I loathed – I still loathe these authors. I read G. A. Henty and Merriman and Marion Crawford and Marie Corelli and Anthony Hope. These are the great masters to whom I owe my initiation to literature. And then later there came Wilde and Pater and Swinburne. And finally Beerbohm. All of these, except of course the last, are authors whom I condemn today.... There was a book also by Mr Lewis Hind ... called *The Education of an Artist*. It was a soppy sort of book about a young man who strolled, all philistine, into the gallery at Antwerp and forty minutes later undulated out of that gallery a confirmed aesthete, having been converted by a little drawing of St Anne visiting a Cathedral.... I had the pleasure, many years after, of expressing my gratitude to Mr Hind ... and, my word, was he surprised.[14]

And somewhere, quite probably early in his life, Harold Nicolson learnt about irony.

Folkestone, in those days, was a modestly fashionable resort on Kent's chilly east coast, but The Grange was nowhere – an undistinguished prep school with a spurious reputation for a high moral tone. By contrast, Wellington College, where Harold arrived in January 1900 on his return from Christmas holidays in Morocco, was very much somewhere. Victorian morality was still to the fore – Norman Rose tells how the first headmaster, E. W. Benson, placed 'wire entanglements ... along the top of the dormitory cubicles to prevent any illicit toing and froing'[15] – and the school may not have had the hallowed traditions of Eton or Harrow, but it was very much at the centre of things.

Among Harold's fellow pupils was Prince Alexander of Battenburg, the son of Princess Beatrice, Queen Victoria's youngest child. In May 1900, following the relief of Mafeking, Queen Victoria herself came to visit her grandson. It was forty years since Arthur Nicolson had seen the great Queen from the windows of his grandfather's house in Albemarle Street. She was now only a day or two short of her eighty-first birthday and had less than a year to live, but the British Empire was at its zenith and she was still its symbol. Harold, for all his pro-Boer sympathies and supposed rebelliousness, caught hold of the mudguard of her carriage and ran, cheering, all the way to the gate of the school grounds. The incident was important enough for him to record it in detail in *Helen's Tower*.[16]

Conceived as a memorial to the Duke of Wellington and built in a broadly (if eccentrically) classical style by John Shaw, Wellington College from the first enjoyed royal favour. Queen Victoria laid the foundation stone in 1856 and performed the opening ceremony three years later, while Prince Albert became its first President. It was originally intended as a school for the orphaned sons of army and East India Company officers. By the time Harold arrived the intake had broadened considerably, but it remained a school where the next generation were prepared for the task of running the Empire, its ethos thus reflecting the Nicolson view of the centrality of public service.

In *Some People*, Harold's presentation of himself at Wellington is again of a boy who fails to fit in; whose character inevitably leads him to disappoint those who take an interest in him. Again, there is a degree of perfectly reasonable dramatic characterisation in this. At the same time, Harold's failure to be any good at sport pursued him and quite clearly did lead to him being a figure of fun. 'Games remained of paramount importance' at Wellington.[17] His lifelong poor physical coordination meant that he could barely kick a ball in the right direction. Worse still, he failed even to be interested in sport – an attitude beautifully dramatised in *Some People* where Harold and Reggie Cooper, sit on the boundary absorbed in conversation and cherries, completely oblivious to the result of the annual cricket match against Charterhouse.[18] This hindered his rise through the school hierarchy (although he did eventually reach the dizzy heights of dormitory prefect) and seems also to have reinforced his sense of inadequacy – 'Altogether I am a fool and I'll never get on in the world.'[19] Naturally uninterested in sport himself, there is nonetheless a sense that, at this age at least, he accepted at face value the general consensus of the age and of the public school system: that those who were good at games were those who would be successful in later life. His deeply ironic commentary on this idea, encapsulated in the figure of J. D. Marstock in *Some People*, is an adult's not a schoolboy's perspective. At the time, it hurt.

In *Some People*, Harold claims that at Wellington 'I was not unhappy.'[20] In a letter to his parents just before leaving school in 1903, he wrote that it was 'funny to think it is nearly over and how happy and unhappy I have been.'[21] In an article in *The Listener*, he claims 'it is not that I was ever unhappy at Wellington; it is that I was bored there as I have never been bored in all my life.'[22] Harold's *Diaries*, however, present a somewhat darker picture. In contrast to his attitude to Balliol, which became an object of affection and a source of pride in later life, Harold claimed to have 'no affection for the school whatsoever and no pride in it.'[23] Returning to dine with the Master during the Second World War, he felt the 'old sadness' settle on him immediately – 'I must have been *very* unhappy there for the mood to return to me after forty years.'[24] On his sixtieth birthday, Harold looked back on the day he left Wellington as the beginning of the rest of his life.

> I have had forty years of happiness, from the day when as a little boy I walked down to the station at Wellington College with a surge of freedom in my heart. Since that hour of liberation I have had a wonderful succession of delights and interests.[25]

Whatever his attitude to school at the time and however he presents himself in *Some People*, Harold was not unsuccessful academically. He was bad at maths, particularly algebra, and disliked the maths master, Mr Elton, but he was always good at languages – particularly Latin and Greek – and he claimed to derive his love of the classics from his years at Wellington, and in particular from the then Master, Dr Pollock.

If Lord Dufferin was the first of the heroes which populate Harold's life,

Dr Bertram Pollock was the second. Pollock was a clergyman – destined to become Bishop of Norwich – a classicist, a disciplinarian, and something of a social climber, who had been appointed Master of Wellington at the very young age of twenty-nine in 1893. Under its first Master, the Reverend E. W. Benson, Wellington had a reputation for strict discipline. By the time Harold arrived, Pollock had removed the more excessive measures – including the 'wire entanglements' and the system of elaborate night-time dormitory patrols – but discipline was maintained by a system which regimented the boys' contacts and their activity.

> We were not allowed to consort with boys not in our own house: a house consisted of thirty boys, of whom at least ten were too old and ten too young for friendship; and thus ... my training in human relationships was confined to ten boys who happened to be more or less my contemporaries. In addition masters took pride in feeling that not only did they know what any given boy should be doing at that particular moment, but they knew exactly what the said boy would be doing at 3.30 p.m. six weeks hence. We had thus no privacy and no leisure.[26]

It was this aspect of life at Wellington which led Harold to feel 'a grievance against it for having retarded my development.'[27]

Norman Rose has pointed to the social dimension of Pollock's regime – 'he conscripted two princes, three dukes, three earls, three bishops, six baronets, and a former prime minister to serve as its governors.'[28] At the school's inception, Prince Albert had wanted it to steer away from the traditional classics-based curriculum, placing more emphasis on modern languages and science. He wanted the school to embody the view of the future which underpinned the Great Exhibition of 1851. Fifty years later, however, the difference had been eroded and Wellington's curriculum was not vastly different from that of other major public schools. 'Dr Pollock was too olympian, too unconcerned to bother with reforming the school curriculum.'[29] Aristocratic endorsement was what counted and Dr Pollock supplied it, thus maintaining the school's position in what was, in the end, a highly competitive and lucrative educational marketplace.

Harold, with his diplomatic background and his experience of social and cultural nuances, could spot a snob when he saw one. In his *Spectator* article, 'Corporal Punishment', he tells how Mr Elton, the hated maths master, arrived late for class one morning, explaining, by way of apology, that he had been kept by the Duke of Connaught. Harold 'whispered the one word "snob".' He was overheard and 'beaten as I had never been beaten before.'[30]

Harold did not, however, see the snobbishness in Dr Pollock, because Pollock had become his hero.

In fact, in his first three years at school, he did not see much of Pollock at all. The Master kept himself aloof from the younger boys, the sense of distance enhancing his authority and mystique. Until the Upper Sixth, Dr Pollock was

> a remote and rather alarming mystery; my feelings in regard to him were a mixture of fearful curiosity and religious awe; there was something emotionally magnificent about him, something theocratic. His tall slim figure billowed in a silken gown as he glided rapidly through the cloisters.... The other masters cowered visibly at his approach; they seemed, when standing behind him, to become moth-eaten and affable and unimportant.[31]

This, from *Some People*, though not factually inaccurate, is both a partial and an ironic view. In reality, Pollock was self-confident to the point of arrogance. He was professionally and socially ambitious and perfectly capable of manipulating school life to serve his own ends. His contempt for the teaching staff – 'If all the staff resigned today, I could easily supply all their places tomorrow'[32] – contrasts starkly with his treatment of the Upper Sixth, and there was a reason for this.

Once boys reached the Upper Sixth, they came under Pollock's personal tuition. He was a man of great ability, and the Upper Sixth received the full force of his charm and ability. He taught them Latin and he taught them well, with the aim of instilling not just knowledge but understanding. He challenged the assumptions on which their previous educational experience was based. Lessons would take place sprawling 'on pine needles in his garden' or 'beside his fire on the floor ... [where] he would give us coffee, strong and redolent, and granulated sugar and little cakes; the two footmen would appear with the Georgian silver and Wedgwood cups.' As Pollock plainly understood, 'the contrast with the scrubbed boards and chipped enamel of school life spread a sense of Olympian ease and privilege.'[33] This was, of course, excellent psychology. At the pinnacle of their school career, the boys were suddenly treated like adults. The changed surroundings of their lessons reconnected them with the world that most of them would have known at home. Pollock knew that this was the period on which they would effectively be judged by their parents and their peers. After this, they would go on to university and to forge their careers. He wanted his place in their particular pantheon to be secure.

Harold, for one, was convinced. He fell heavily under the Master's influence, telling his parents that 'He is the most fascinating man I shall ever meet.'[34] But his claims that 'until I came into direct contact with Doctor Pollock I learnt nothing serious from Wellington'[35] and 'if I have since understood in any way the meaning and the purposes of culture, my understanding is due entirely and absolutely to Dr Pollock,'[36] both need to be seen in the context of the J. D. Marstock chapter of *Some People*. In this chapter, the Harold character reaches a new stage of understanding and maturity, and also a closer relationship with the Master, with the realisation that Marstock, whom he had previously admired as the epitome of public school values, is not capable of making the leap to the deeper level of cultural understanding that Dr Pollock is offering. It is a dramatisation of a young man's entry into the world of the educated elite and, as such, subject to Harold's characteristic layers of irony. At the same time, both statements are absolutely typical of the way he responded to his heroes. In life, he was immensely loyal to his friends, although he was objective enough to recognise and sometimes record their faults and weaknesses. In his writing and in his political views, he strove for objectivity, balancing cause and effect, merit and blame with great assurance. Faced with one of his heroes, however, objectivity disappears: the romantic side of his nature asserts itself and he sees only what he wants to see. With Dr Pollock, he saw the intelligence and the humanity and their connection to a refined and elegant lifestyle. He also – another key characteristic – immensely enjoyed being admitted to the inner circle around the Master. He failed – or did not want – to see Pollock's other side.

Harold was thirteen when he arrived at Wellington and seventeen when he left. As far as one can tell from his letters, his relationship with his parents through these years out remained open and affectionate. He would tease his mother about buying him a panama hat for his birthday or whether there would be young ladies to flirt with at Christmas. Nor did he feel the need to hide his views on political personalities or events – calling Lord Roberts, Britain's Boer War commander and a school governor, a 'little beast'. And when he talks about his character, his hopes and fears for the future; when he thanks his parents for spending so much money on his education, he seems a normal, sincere and affectionate son.[37]

These were also the years of puberty when we might expect him to have discovered something of his sexual orientation. Norman Rose has said that 'it is as certain as anything can be that he experienced his first homosexual adventures at Wellington.'[38] One can only agree. James Lees-Milne, who, in researching his biography, had the advantage of his long friendship and many conversations with Harold, wrote more obliquely that 'in spite of ... absurd precautions, Satan flourished at Wellington like a green bay tree.'[39] Harold himself wrote of the regime at Wellington in *Some People* that

> the vices which this system was supposed to repress flourished incessantly and universally, losing in their furtive squalor any educative value which they might otherwise have possessed.[40]

He was preparing to follow in his father's footsteps by going up to Oxford, although he was trying for Balliol College rather than Brasenose. Whether the choice of Oxford was Harold's or his parents' is not clear. Sir Arthur's university career was hardly a model for emulation, but Harold's farewell letter from Wellington suggests that he was increasingly impressed by his father's intellectual stature – 'In reading through Father's letters I see how clever he is & I wish I could be like him.'[41] In September 1903, he took and passed the written entrance examinations, known as Responsions, in Latin and Greek. In October, he had to go up to Oxford for his *viva voce*. It was a highly traditional format. He was faced by three dons who asked him to translate one of the odes of Horace. He was nervous. He stammered. He made a few mistakes and felt intimidated by the dons who laughed at him. But he passed and was able to enjoy the thought that he was 'a commoner of Balliol.'[42] He was still one month short of his seventeenth birthday.

This was a considerable achievement and he recognised the fact. He also recognised the support he had received from some of his teachers – the Reverend Kempthorne, known as 'Kemp', his housemaster; O. T. Perkins, the Upper Sixth Greek master; and, of course, Dr Pollock. At the same time, repeating the pattern which emerged at the Grange and would recur throughout his life, Harold's consciousness of his own success was undermined by self-doubt.

> In work I have succeeded above my expectations, yet I should not say I was at the top of the tree.... I shall be sorry to say goodbye to Pollock, Kemp & to Mr Perkins. They have all done their best for me & I don't think I shall ever forget it. I am beginning to see that brain counts for little but that character counts for everything, & it is not a pleasant thought as my character is weak and easily influenced.[43]

Why did he see himself as weak and easily influenced? Was it just that he did not fit in and was bad at games? Was it guilt at a few early homosexual experiments in the dormitory? Or was it the feeling – which he never grew out of – that he wanted everyone to like him, that he hated having to stand up to disapproval or unpopularity? And, above all, why was he prepared to accept the conventional wisdom that character counted for more than brains?

He left Wellington in December 1903 and spent the next couple of months in Tangier.

5 Weimar

Harold met all the entry requirements for Balliol except age. The College authorities judged him too young and would not accept him in residence before the autumn (or, in Oxford terminology, Michaelmas) term of 1904. It was decided that he should spend the intervening months in Weimar, learning German and continuing his study of the classics. Both the language and location suggest the influence of Sir Arthur Nicolson, who spoke German well and had enjoyed his two tours of duty in Berlin in the 1870s. It may also be that the decision had already been made that Harold should try for the Diplomatic Service, for which languages were essential, and that this was early preparation.

Weimar, where Harold arrived at the end of February 1904, was one of the great cultural centres of Europe. It had been Goethe's home for nearly sixty years until his death in 1832, and his works were performed and studied there with an almost religious intensity. Bach had lived there, as had Liszt, Wagner and Berlioz, and both the concert hall and opera house (for the construction of which Goethe was responsible) held busy and popular seasons. The city was also home to one of Europe's greatest libraries, named for Duchess Anna Amalia of Saxe-Weimar-Eisenach, which held – and, indeed, holds – a Goethe collection, a Shakespeare collection, a Faust collection, and many thousands of musical books and manuscripts. The six months Harold spent in Weimar marked the beginning of his love for the German language and German culture – a love which survived two world wars and, half a century later, led to him receiving *Das Grosse Verdienstkreuz mit Stern* (the Cross of Merit with Star), an honour given by the Federal German Government to those who have rendered particular service to Germany.[1]

Harold stayed with the Reverend F. E. Freese and his wife in their flat in Prellerstrasse, just five minutes' walk from the Theaterplatz and the city centre. Freese, who appears to have been recommended to Sir Arthur by a Diplomatic Service colleague, was acting as chaplain to Weimar's British community. His role in relation to Harold was a combination of host, tutor and social mentor. Harold liked the Freeses and their flat and enjoyed having Freese as a tutor. Every day, he worked at his German, making rapid progress, and then worked at Latin and Greek, translating at least one hundred lines from the main texts on which he would be required to work at Balliol. He was less keen on the social aspects of life in Weimar – especially the British community.

By 1904, political differences and tensions had begun to emerge between Britain and an increasingly assertive German Empire, but Germany was still seen by many, if not most, British people as Britain's natural partner in Europe, particularly in a cultural context. Victorian and German respectability were well matched and there was a British community in most sizeable German cities. Weimar was no exception and the Freeses, by virtue of his position as chaplain, were at the centre of it. The resident British population seems to have been a mixture of *nouveau-riche* middle-class families trying to acquire culture for themselves and their offspring, and the impoverished gentility who found life cheaper on the continent. Harold damned both. In his letters home, he is critical of the superficiality of their manners and their underlying lack of knowledge. He disapproves of the women, particularly the young women, for their mixture of coyness, flirtatiousness and ignorance.[2]

These letters from Weimar do not show him in a particularly good light – or perhaps one should say they show him as a more or less a normal teenager who has escaped from school and home and wishes to demonstrate the fact. He tries to be worldly-wise and sophisticated, but his judgements are brash and shallow and his tone too often mocking. The letters are lively enough and show that he was already a keen observer of people, but they lack his later ironic tone. One senses that he is writing with an eye to his audience, seeking parental approval of this new grown-up self.

The exception is the letter he wrote to his mother for her birthday.

> I do wish I could be at Tangier ... & be able to kiss you and tell you how I love you more than anything in the whole world. I can't think what I should do if you died. I think I should kill myself.... I wish I could go back and be eight years old again when I had you all to myself & could sit on your knee all day without your feeling tired or other people saying it looked silly.[3]

Harold Nicolson

This contrasts so completely with the tone and content of the other Weimar letters that one suspects that he may have been lonely or homesick. He always loved his mother deeply, and these gushing, somewhat embarrassing sentiments show how much, at this stage of his life, he still needed her affection and approval – though there is nothing to suggest that it was ever withheld. Once again they throw into doubt Harold's later assertion that 'we were always strangers to our parents.'

One slightly odd aspect of Harold's period in Weimar, to which both James Lees-Milne and Norman Rose draw attention, is his attitude to music. He was never a musical man. He loved literature and he had a strong, educated – if ultimately conventional – taste in the visual arts, but music rarely features in his letters, diaries and articles. Yet at Weimar he claimed to have been to the opera at least twenty-five times. The programme for the season included several of Wagner's works – not usually regarded as the place to begin one's musical initiation – and a new opera, *Buddha*, by the composer Max Vogrich, who was known to the Freeses and to whom Harold was introduced. It is also probable that he saw and heard works by Richard Strauss, who was at the height of his fame, a German national hero, whose stirring romanticism had the capacity to appeal to a seventeen-year-old. After he joined the Foreign Office in 1909, Harold's letters and diaries still record the occasional evening at the opera and the odd concert – *La Bohème*, he told his parents, was 'thrilling' and *Tristan und Isolde* 'wonderful'[4] – but such entries soon cease. It seems strange that music should have featured so prominently in his life for such a short time. Did he take an interest for social reasons? Because the Freeses were interested? Because he could peer at the Grand Duke and Grand Duchess of Saxe-Weimar in their special gilt and velvet box? Or because Weimar's musical society was preferable to the British community? He apparently met an American lady, a Mrs Phillips, who had been taught by Liszt and known Wagner 'intimately'. Perhaps, as James Lees-Milne suggests, there was nothing else to do.[5] In any event, whatever importance music held for him soon disappeared so completely that Norman Rose has speculated that he may have become tone deaf at some subsequent stage.[6]

Despite Harold's well-publicised – indeed self-publicised – sporting inadequacy, and despite the fact that at a relatively early age he began to put on weight and became a slightly plump or portly figure, he was not as a young man unathletic or unphysical. He always enjoyed riding, and during his early years at the Foreign Office – the same period when he was watching *La Bohème* and *Tristan* – he played golf and tennis. When he was posted to Constantinople in 1913, he took up sailing, something he enjoyed off and on for many years. His final weeks with the Freeses showed that he was not only capable of sustained physical effort, but that he also enjoyed it.

Having first asked permission from his parents, presumably for financial reasons – he was always sensitive about the amount his education was costing them – he accompanied the Freeses on a walking and climbing tour in Switzerland. They spent a month based in the village of Champex, overlooking the lake of the same name, and exploring the surrounding mountains. Some of their excursions lasted two or three days, sleeping in huts on the mountainside, and, on one occasion, they kept walking well into the night because the moonlight was so bright. Although defensive when questioned by an Oxford man about his sporting preferences – 'I shrivelled up at once into my shell'[7] – Harold actually revelled in the physicality of the experience. He felt fit; he felt well; and he felt competent.

The Reverend Freese, an experienced climber, must have felt some confidence in Harold's abilities, for he included him in a party to climb le Grand Combin on the Swiss-Italian border. Le Grand Combin is a 4,314 metre (14,153 foot) peak, these days classified as a Grade Two climb, surrounded by glaciers and with a reputation for poor ice conditions. They reached the summit without serious difficulty, but on the way down the whole party, still roped together, slid down part of the icefall. Some of them were injured, but it could have been much worse. Harold was triumphant. He had some experience of academic success, but a physical achievement like this was something new. He wrote to his parents in great detail – with hand-drawn maps of the route and notes on climbing conditions – telling them what had happened, and insisting they should not worry. Yet his youth still showed through. With an arrogance both teenage and would-be aristocratic, he dismisses their guide's panicky reaction to the accident on the grounds that 'it is breeding that tells more than anything else in this sort of thing.'[8]

The party returned to Weimar via Berne, where they visited the main tourist sights – the cathedral, the clock tower, the bear pit – and went swimming in the River Aar. Above the main portal of Berne Cathedral, Harold saw for the first time Erhard Küng's magnificent fifteenth-century sculptures of the Last Judgement, including those illustrating the parable of the Wise and Foolish Virgins. Although at the time he did no more than make some smart remarks, suggesting that some of them looked like his young sister, Gwen, the sight haunted him and the parable became a reference point to which he returned more than once in his writings.[9] At Weimar, he said goodbye to the Freeses and took the train for Calais. Three days later, he arrived at Clandeboye, the house of his now widowed Aunt Lal. He would spend a month there with his family, who were taking their summer leave from Morocco, before going up to Oxford.

6 Oxford

In the second week of October 1904, the Nicolson family returned from Ireland to London. Sir Arthur and Lady Nicolson, together with their daughter, Gwen, returned for what was to be their last period of residence in Tangier. Harold took a train from Paddington to Oxford for his first term at Balliol College.

It is astonishing just how much we know about that day. We know that, like so many people who are nervous, he packed early. He had his hair cut, allowing the barber to give his scalp a friction rub. This left a heavy scent of *violette de Parme* and, when he arrived in College, an unfortunate impression. We know that he took a four-wheeler to Paddington, piling his luggage on the roof; that he bought a first-class ticket and a newspaper to read because he was so nervous; that as the train pulled into Oxford he kept putting on his gloves and hat and then taking them off again. We know that he was concerned not to look like a freshman; that he made his way through a station crowded with undergraduates in search of a horse-drawn hansom cab; that there were no cabs to be had and that he had to take the station bus with a commercial traveller in a white tie, who immediately spotted him as a new student and asked if he been to Oxford before. We know that the commercial traveller got off at the Mitre, leaving Harold to go on up Broad Street to Balliol, where he was so concerned to project an image of experience that he was annoyed that the ostler thought he might not recognise his College. We know that on arrival he spoke to Hancock, the Head Porter, invoking the name of Lady Carnarvon; that Hancock was delighted and gave him directions to his rooms; that he crossed the Garden Quad and turned a corner where he found a door with his name painted on it in white and that beyond the door was his sitting room where a fire was burning in the grate and a kettle on the hob. We know the precise orientation of the rooms, the view from his sitting room onto the Garden Quad and the view from his bedroom onto St Giles. We have a description of every piece of furniture and where it was placed; every picture on the walls and where it was hung.[1]

We have this information because Harold recorded it in his letters and because it remained in his memory for the rest of his life. Going to university is, in its own way, a rite of passage, part of the transition to independence and manhood and he certainly saw it as such. His nervousness shows. His first letter from Oxford is markedly less assertive in tone than the Weimar letters – though the teenage brashness and arrogance quickly reasserts itself. He undoubtedly wanted his parents to know that he appreciated the opportunity that he was being offered. But to Harold Balliol was more than a rite of passage or an educational opportunity, it was a place to belong – the first of many that he would seek out during his life. It was a club, a closed society, which he desperately wanted to accept him as a member. He knew already the aphorism 'once a Balliol man, always a Balliol man.' His worry was that the inadequacies and insecurities he felt inside himself would prevent him from being accepted. Hence, his concern – remembered in a speech he gave at Balliol in 1930, twenty-six years later – that the waft of *violette de Parme* would damage his reputation before he had one.[2] His diary entry for that day in 1930 gives an image of how he saw himself on arrival at Oxford. He hopes that his speech 'may have done some good perhaps to one or two shy young men like myself, who feel they are doomed to failure.'[3]

And of course, as he was well aware – though it would have done nothing to make him less nervous – Balliol had another, greater significance. The College stood for history and for privilege, two things guaranteed to appeal to Harold. Balliol men were an elite. They saw themselves as such and the British establishment of the time apparently agreed. Oxford, founded in 1167, is Britain's oldest university and Balliol, founded somewhere around 1263, claims to be Oxford's oldest college – though the claim is disputed by Merton and University College. By the time Harold arrived, Balliol could point to well over six hundred years of continuous, independent existence. Harold, with his strong sense of history, would have been aware that he was walking in the footsteps of men who had influenced the thought and the literature of the nation – men such as John Wycliff, Sir Thomas More, John Evelyn, Adam Smith, Arthur Hugh Clough and Matthew Arnold. Perhaps Sir Arthur had also pointed out that the last three Viceroys of India – the Marquess of Lansdowne, the Earl of Elgin, and Lord Curzon – had all been Balliol men. Lord Dufferin, unfortunately, had been at Christ Church.

Despite its long and distinguished history, Balliol's star was still in the ascendant, largely because of the influence of Benjamin Jowett. Jowett died in 1893, having been a member of the College for fifty-five years, and Master for twenty-three. He was not a great academic, although his translation of Plato was much acclaimed in its day, but he was a great reformer. He demanded commitment on the part of the Fellows and tutors to their academic and pastoral responsibilities. Equally, he expected more commitment and harder work on the part of Balliol undergraduates. He made it his business to know every undergraduate personally and devoted all his energies to the College: he made land available for a new Hall and a cricket ground; he made scholarships available to those who could not otherwise afford a Balliol education; he took undergraduates on long vacation reading parties which were carefully designed to further their education and strengthen their loyalties to himself and to the College. Jowett was not a liberal and was only progressive insofar as progress, for him, meant the return to a solid moral basis for life and work at Balliol College. He was at once a theologian and a highly practical man. He saw the essence of his work as the production of highly-educated and moral Balliol graduates who would go out and do good in the wider world. This spirit lived on after Jowett's death in 1893, not least in the sense of loyalty to the College and its ideals shared by 'Balliol men' in later life, a fellowship which became increasingly important to Harold as he grew older.

Jowett reformed the spirit and the organisation of Balliol, but, even in later years when he was also Vice-Chancellor of the University, he did not attempt to reform the curriculum. In academic terms, the Oxford that Harold joined was very backward-looking. He was studying Greats, Oxford's traditional classics course and the basis of a university education for many generations of English gentlemen. For the first three terms (or trimesters), he would concentrate on Latin and Greek language and literature. The following six terms would concentrate on Greek and Roman history and philosophy with an additional component of English literature. Harold would always defend the value of his traditional, classical education – 'Latin and Greek are perhaps a luxury form of education, but they are a luxury which pays every time'[4] – although such a defence says as much about his views on society as about the value of the subject itself.

To some extent, Greats played to his strengths. He was always good at languages, and his analytical abilities were evident throughout his life – in his Foreign Office memoranda, his parliamentary speeches and books such as *The Congress of Vienna* and *George V* which involved the synthesis of huge amounts of material. What other options did he have? Neither Law nor Divinity would have suited him, nor would Natural Sciences. English was largely confined to philology and texts from before the fourteenth century – though a more modern option, including texts up to the end of the eighteenth century had recently been added. History might have been a possibility, but it is doubtful whether he gave the matter any thought. Greats was the traditional subject for the sons of the aristocracy and prospective members of the Diplomatic Service.

Whether or not he looked for an alternative, Harold's choice marks him as a traditionalist. In the late Victorian and Edwardian eras, the value of a classical education was held to be timeless, but timelessness was running out. Particularly at Oxford and Cambridge, the university system – for all its many positive moral and academic qualities – had become rigid and complacent, unable or unwilling to respond to social change. The nineteenth century had seen rapid scientific and technological development sweep across Europe. In Britain, however, these changes were not reflected in the university system. Scientific research remained, by and large, the preserve of the wealthy amateur who brought his results to one or other of London's learned societies – the Royal Society was the most prominent, but the Geographical, Geological, Chemical and Physical Societies all played their part. Nor had the British universities expanded to keep pace with a population which almost doubled between 1851 and 1901. The result was that, by 1913, Britain, with a population of 45 million, had only 9,000 university students and produced only 350 first- or second-class graduates in science, technology and mathematics put together. Germany, with a population of 67 million, had 60,000 students and produced 3,000 graduate engineers alone.[5] It was a failure of imagination which would have immense consequences. Harold, at Balliol, would have been untroubled by such matters, but he was to spend the rest of his life watching the destruction and disintegration of a society which had based itself on the traditional values inherent in the kind of education he received. That is the subtext of much of his writing.

Harold began by throwing himself into his work – attending sixteen lectures a week – and into College life. Undergraduates were expected to take up some kind of sport, so he took up rowing, finding that the

> boat was wet and heavy, the loofah on which I sat was wet and light, the oars were dripping and enormous, and I myself incompetent and damp. A man on the bank would ... say things to me through a megaphone which were sharp and rude.... I felt that ... Nature had never, even in her wildest moments, intended me to be an oar.[6]

He gave up after two terms. Rowing was not for him, but he quickly fell in love with Oxford and succumbed to the Balliol mystique. His letters home soon show a return of his snobbishness and censoriousness, at times so strong that it suggests a fear of those who are different from him. He dislikes Rhodes Scholars,[7] colonials, 'niggers and atheists', female undergraduates, accents, university slang (though he is using it himself within a few weeks). He tells silly stories about Rhodes scholars – 'It is said that they keep their money in gold bricks under their beds.'[8] Of course, times and attitudes were different – and James Lees-Milne quotes a contemporary, L. E. Jones, who suggests that Harold was far from unique in his attitudes[9] – but it is apparent that Harold was still very immature. It is embarrassing even now to read the account of his first encounter with Edward Caird, Master of Balliol and Professor of Moral Philosophy, whose *Collected Works* run to twelve volumes, including erudite studies of Comte, Kant, Hegel and the theology of the Greek philosophers. Caird was 'an awful old fool & I could kick him. He is like a Scotch Meenister & very dull and stupid. He said "Vera glad to see yer Meester Nicolson," shaking hands like an elephant would.'[10] However, Harold seems to have got on well with his tutor, Cyril Bailey, and he formed an enduring friendship with another Balliol tutor, F. F. Urquhart, universally known as 'Sligger' because of his sleek, well-groomed appearance.[11] Urquhart took Harold under his wing, and his influence probably did more to nudge him on the road to maturity than any other factor in his Oxford life.

Urquhart's mere presence at Balliol was a testimony to Jowett's reforming spirit. In 1571, the Test Acts demanded that all members of the university subscribe to the Church of England and the Thirty-Nine Articles. The Acts remained in force for three hundred years, through the turbulence of the Civil Wars and the Restoration and through the two hundred years of conservative Anglicanism which followed. In that time, nearly all members of the university had to take holy orders and remain unmarried. Only in 1871 were the Test Acts repealed, allowing non-conformists and others to become Fellows. On his election to a Balliol Fellowship in 1896, Urquhart became the first Roman Catholic Fellow at Oxford since the Reformation.

Urquhart was the embodiment of what Jowett wanted from a Fellow. He was not a great intellectual, nor a great academic, but he had a genius for education in the broadest sense of the word. History was his subject and he was conscientious, if uninspiring, in the performance of his academic duties. He also played a reluctant role in the administration of the College, eventually becoming Dean. But his real contribution was made during the breakfasts and the long evenings of conversation in his room which he shared with generations of students, treating them as adults and steering them gently towards maturity.

Urquhart himself was slim, athletic and handsome, and enjoyed the company of handsome young men, especially if they were intelligent and well connected. He even liked photographing them, but there is a general consensus that even if his inclinations were homosexual they never took physical form.[12] Indeed, he was generally considered emotionally cold, a nineteenth-century celibate. Harold, immature and gaffe-prone (at least in his own estimation) quickly became one of Urquhart's favourites and responded by elevating Urquhart to the hero status shared by Lord Dufferin and Dr Pollock. Although there is no direct evidence to support the idea, the advice Harold gave to his son, Nigel, when he was about to enter Balliol thirty years later may well have derived from Urquhart.

> Balliol does not care overmuch for the extent of a man's knowledge: it cares dreadfully for his state of mind. Remember what they want to find out is whether you are *intelligent*, not whether you are *learned*. They judge intelligence by the extent to which you avoid saying something stupid, rather than by the extent to which you manage to say something bright.[13]

Certainly, Urquhart's methods were oblique enough. When he died, his biography was written by Cyril Bailey, Harold's Latin tutor. Harold gave it a favourable review, noting that Sligger

> suggested to young men that they would grow out of their affectations and attain their own realities ... that their failings and even their vices were unimportant and that they must surely possess inside themselves an inner core or energy and righteousness.[14]

This is all rather abstract. A more practical illustration is given in *Some People*, in the chapter dealing with 'Lambert Orme', whom Harold identified as based on the writer Ronald Firbank. Harold portrays himself as a gauche, unimaginative young student, painfully out of his depth when faced with Orme's flamboyant exhibitionism. At first antagonistic, then gradually impressed and attracted, his view is suddenly reversed again when Urquhart declares Orme 'absurdly childish'.

> A few days later Sligger, most subtle of dons, presented me with a copy of *Marius the Epicurean*. I found it on my table when I came back from the river: there was a note inside saying, 'I think you had better read this.' ... By this homeopathic treatment I was quickly cured.[15]

Harold was something of a late developer, but, however it was achieved,

Urquhart was certainly a major influence on his character, guiding his taste and giving him the self-confidence he lacked. The friendship – for Urquhart treated his chosen undergraduates as fully adult friends – lasted from 1 November 1904, only a couple of weeks after Harold arrived in College, when Urquhart asked him to lunch, until Urquhart's death in September 1934.

During the Christmas vacation of 1904, Harold paid a brief visit to his maternal uncle, Fred Rowan Hamilton, in Surrey, then returned to Wellington to visit Dr Pollock, staying – a badge of his new status – in the Master's Lodge. Most of the vacation, however, was spent in Paris, lodging with a family called Dumas and improving his French. This seems to confirm that the decision had been taken that he would to try for the Diplomatic Service when he graduated, though how much the decision was his own and how much influenced by Sir Arthur it is impossible to say. Paris had its moments. He saw Sarah Bernhardt in *Phèdre*. He witnessed a traffic accident in the place de l'Opéra and saw the victim 'with blood bubbling from his noise and mouth.' He dined with Urquhart, who was passing through Paris, on New Year's Day. He even tried to shock the Dumas' maid by pretending to be drunk but the joke backfired when Dumas *père* opened the door. On the whole, however, he seems to have been bored and lonely. The regime of working at his French in the morning – Pasteur Dumas 'repeated his sentences very slowly three times, so that Harold could not fail to understand' – and then going into the Louvre to work his way round the galleries palled after a while. Paris itself was noisy and full of traffic and the Dumas family, while perfectly pleasant, were dull.[16] On the way back to Oxford, he stayed with Reggie Cooper, his one friend from Wellington days. The only lasting result of the vacation was Harold's moustache. Grown in the first instance to make him look older, it lasted the rest of his life.

His regime of hard work and exercise seems to have begun to break down in his second term. Oxford offered social opportunities denied to him during his nomadic childhood and in the restricted world of Wellington. He started to make friends: with Hughe Knatchbull-Hugessen ('Snatch'), later Ambassador to China, Turkey and Belgium, and a KCMG; with Arthur Bertie ('Tata'), who also joined the Foreign Office and received an MC and DSO in the First World War; with John Melville, Lord Balgonie ('Jack'), soon to succeed to two Scottish titles, Earl of Leven and Earl of Melville, before dying in a hunting accident. He also started to enjoy himself. He bicycled on a tandem across to Blenheim Palace to go skating on the lake. He went swimming in the River Cherwell. He went riding in the park at Wytham Abbey, Tata Bertie's home. He raced down to London to see a rather silly musical comedy called *The Earl and the Girl* which he feared his mother would find vulgar. He played roulette, won £3 and then lost it again.[17] He wrote letters to his mother reassuring her that he still loved her.[18] He wrote to his father asking for £10 to buy a horse.[19] All in all, he was behaving like a normal undergraduate.

There were other moments when undergraduate high spirits took on a more arrogant complexion and pushed acceptability and decency to their limits. Such stories may have been exaggerated in the remembering or the telling, but one wonders how Harold would have looked back on them in maturity. On one occasion he is supposed to have driven through Oxford in a horse-drawn coach, spraying people with soda siphons and throwing bananas at cyclists. On another,

> He was elected to one of three Balliol societies, namely the Brackenbury, which was recruited from the raffish and sophisticated members of the College. At his first meeting a member moved a vote of censure against a workman who had the indecency to throw a fit outside the College gate. There was much joviality in the debate that ensued.[20]

In January 1905, Sir Arthur Nicolson took up a new appointment as Ambassador to Spain and it was to Madrid that Harold went for his Easter vacation that year. He found his father politically once again at the centre of things. Just a month earlier, in March, Kaiser Wilhelm had landed in Tangier and announced that he considered the Sultan an independent sovereign. This somewhat gratuitous announcement – Germany had no real interests in Morocco – had provoked an international crisis.

The nine years that Sir Arthur had spent in Tangier had seen Morocco gradually becoming more important as a focus for international attention. Now, suddenly, it was a flashpoint. Britain's interests in Morocco were trade and making sure that the passage of the Straits of Gibraltar was in no way threatened by whoever controlled Morocco's northern shore. France hoped to round off its colonial conquests in North Africa by including Morocco and Britain had recognised French interests in the country in the Anglo-French Entente of April 1904 – in exchange for a free hand in Egypt. Spain held two small but profitable colonies on the north Moroccan coast – Ceuta and Melilla – which it did not want to see threatened. Moreover, Spain too was bound to France by a treaty, signed in October 1904, agreeing to divide up northern Morocco between them. The Kaiser's sudden descent on Tangier aimed to stir up Moroccan nationalism, confound French ambitions and drive a wedge between France and her allies. The international atmosphere that Easter was tense. 'The Germans,' Sir Arthur wrote, 'have during the last few days been endeavouring to win over Spain by two methods. The Emperor has been exceedingly courteous and gracious and despatched effusive telegrams to King Alfonso, while his Ambassador (Herr von Radowitz) has adopted another method by assuming a threatening and overbearing attitude.'[21] Sir Arthur's role was to persuade the Spanish to stand firm and resist German pressure. For Harold, as an aspiring diplomat, it must have been a fascinating time.

Even in the early twentieth century, dynastic marriages could still play a part in strengthening political resolve, and a significant portion of Sir Arthur's time during his brief period as Ambassador to Spain was taken up with preparations for the marriage of King Alfonso XIII to Princess Victoria Eugénie, the daughter of Princess Beatrice, Queen Victoria's youngest daughter and thus niece to King Edward VII. The marriage did not take place until 31 May 1906, by which time Sir Arthur had left Spain, but preparatory discussions began in the summer of 1905. That Easter, before the discussions started, Harold was able to see the young king in action. The Diplomatic Corps was invited to the Royal Palace to attend a ceremony called the Repast of the Poor. Sir Arthur was given a very grand seat in front. Harold, who had tagged along, was 'hustled politely but firmly into a sort of fold or pen.'

The ceremony involved the Cardinal of Madrid, the Queen Mother, Spain's twelve most senior grandees, twelve specially selected beggars and, of course, King Alfonso. The king's role was to wash and kiss the feet of the beggars and then serve them an elaborate eight-course meal, the menu for which was passed round to the diplomatic corps and spectators when they arrived. However, with an absurdity of ritual worthy of Gormenghast, the beggars were not allowed to touch the food set before them. Rather, the plates were passed out of the hall by a chain of footmen and sent off to be sold for charity. The whole ceremony was conducted to the sound of Gregorian chant and the smell of incense. The king was only eighteen – just six months Harold's senior – and Harold clearly empathised with him, especially when the palace's aged and infirm major-domo spilt a basket of oranges which rolled all over the floor of the hall. The king laughed uncontrollably.

Alfonso XIII was king from birth, but was forced into exile with the proclamation of the Second Spanish Republic in April 1931. Harold gave a radio talk expressing sympathy for the king, as an individual if not as a monarch, and recalling in immense detail the ceremony he had witnessed almost exactly twenty-six years previously. The whole scene made a deep impression on him. Just as in his childhood in Tangier, he believed he had caught a glimpse of life in ancient Greece and Rome, so, that day in Madrid, he felt that he had caught a glimpse of the era of Philip II and Spain at the height of its imperial grandeur which had survived into his lifetime.[22]

Harold's meeting with Ronald Firbank also took place that Easter. Firbank came with a letter of introduction and there is no need to doubt the factual basis of the lunch and subsequent horse ride described in *Some People*.[23] Harold probably exaggerates their respective behaviours to heighten the contrast between their characters, but there is no doubt that he did find himself caught between antagonism and attraction towards Firbank's aesthetic affectation and camp style. It is unlikely that the relationship between Harold and Firbank ever took physical form. In the end, and partly through Urquhart's influence, Harold's 'Kipling side' triumphed and he never himself adopted such an openly camp style, but that did not mean an end to the fascination. Over the years, a number of his friends and lovers were men whose behaviour was much more overtly homosexual than he felt comfortable with himself.

In *Some People*, Harold draws a contrast between his own rooms and those of Lambert Orme/Ronald Firbank.

> He had painted [his room] a shiny black: there were grey sofas with petunia cushions: there was a Coromandel cabinet with blue china on the top and some hardstone stuff inside. It was not in the least like the room of an undergraduate: it made me at first rather ashamed of my own room with its extracts from 'the hundred best pictures', its photographs of the charioteer of Delphi, and its kettle-holder with the Balliol arms.... I was entranced by that little *gîte* at Magdalen: by the firelight flickering on the yellow books, by the Manet reproductions ...[24]

This is fictionalised because Firbank was not at Oxford at all but at Trinity Hall, Cambridge, yet the meaning is clear. For Harold, as for so many undergraduates before and since, Oxford was a period of awakening: there is a curious echo of this passage in *Brideshead Revisited*, in the way Charles Ryder sees his rooms before and after his meeting with Sebastian Flyte. Harold's awakening – whatever it consisted of – did not necessarily make him popular. James Lees-Milne quotes Sir Charles Clay, a contemporary of Harold's at Balliol and later Librarian of the House of Lords, as suggesting that Harold was 'a negative character' while at the College, and 'a late developer.'[25] In *Some People*, Harold claims that 'looking back at Balliol I realise that during those three years I was wholly abominable. That Balliol should have shared this opinion indicates its admirable sense.'[26] There is undoubtedly some dramatic exaggeration here. It is true that Harold did not distinguish himself at Balliol; at the same time, there is no evidence that he was ever in trouble with the College authorities – and in that sense, at least, he did better than his father.

Sligger Urquhart continued to give Harold encouragement. In the summer of 1906, Harold received an invitation to join one of his famous reading parties at the Chalet des Mélèzes (later known as the Chalet des Anglais) in the Haute Savoie Alps. The chalet was a very special place for Urquhart and an invitation indicated both confidence in the recipient and admission to Urquhart's inner circle – an honour which Harold would greatly have relished. Situated 1,000 metres above the small town St Gervais-les-Bains on the slopes of a mountain called Le Prarion, which butts onto the Mont Blanc massif, it had originally been built by Urquhart's father. On his death, it passed to Urquhart's elder brother, David, from whom Urquhart bought it in 1896, leaving it as a bequest to Balliol College on his death. Every year from 1891 until 1931, with the exception of 1907 (when it was being rebuilt after a fire) and the First World War years, Urquhart would invite parties of ten or twelve undergraduates, mainly from Balliol but also from other colleges, to spend two weeks reading and walking in the mountain air.[27] It was far from luxurious. There was no heating beyond open fires, no electricity and, in the early days, no running water. Mornings were spent in reading and study; afternoons were spent walking in the mountains. Food was basic and chores were shared. Nonetheless, invitations were greatly prized. Everyone who went there seems to have remembered long, inspirational after-dinner conversations beneath the clear Alpine skies.[28] This was Harold's second experience of the Alps in two years. No doubt, he found the regime at Chalet des Mélèzes both more intellectual and more Spartan than his stay at Champex with the Freeses, but he left no detailed record of his two weeks there. What we do know, however, is that he went straight from these isolated, tranquil surroundings to the heart of metropolitan St Petersburg.

The Moroccan crisis of 1905 had led to a major international conference in the Spanish town of Algeciras the following year. Germany had two major objectives: to prevent France from achieving any kind of diplomatic success in relation to Morocco and, if possible, to create tension between Britain and France. The fact that neither objective was achieved and that the Anglo-French Entente was, in fact, strengthened as a result of the conference represented a conspicuous success for the leader of the British delegation, Sir Arthur Nicolson. His success was recognised in the form of a GCMG,[29] formal thanks from the British and French Governments, and personal letters of congratulation from both King Edward VII and the Prime Minister, Sir Henry Campbell-Bannerman.[30] Even at such a moment, the inner man could emerge in a letter to his wife: 'People are very good to me, aren't they? And sometimes I feel I am a humbug.'[31] Harold inherited that strain of inner self-doubt.

In London, the Moroccan crisis and the Algeciras Conference increased the sense that Germany posed a threat to the existing international order and to Britain's position in the world. The new Liberal Government under Campbell-Bannerman felt an increased urgency to conclude an agreement with Russia, which was already formally allied to France. A new Ambassador with a mandate to negotiate was appointed. Sir Arthur Nicolson arrived in St Petersburg on 28 May 1906 to find Russia in chaos. Nineteen hundred and five had been a year of revolution and uprising. First Bloody Sunday; then a general strike; then the Tsar's October manifesto promising constitutional reform; then a repudiation of those promises. In March 1906, the Tsar ordered the formation of an Imperial Duma, or parliament; then he curtailed its authority so drastically as to render it almost powerless. In May, he appointed a new government and, the same day, formally opened the Duma, which immediately called for electoral, political and land reforms. The Tsar and his government refused any concessions and there was total deadlock. It was at this point that Sir Arthur arrived.

A lull in the chaos allowed him to begin negotiations on the subject of Tibet, which had long had the potential to disrupt Anglo-Russian relations, but in July came more trouble. The Duma was in chaos; there were fears of a peasant uprising; there was a massacre of Jews and mutiny by a regiment of guards. On July 22, the Duma was dissolved, martial law declared and Pyotr Stolypin, formerly Minister of the Interior, became Prime Minister. Anarchists and agitators took advantage of the situation. There were strikes, mutinies and calls for resistance, but the new government won through, despite British and international condemnation of the repressive measures taken along the way. It was at this point that Harold arrived.

Paris and St Petersburg were the grandest, the most imperial of Britain's Embassies. In St Petersburg

> the British Embassy was an immense though low-storeyed house, washed in blood red.... The reception rooms were on the top floor and the staircase (scarlet and white) ran up to them through a series of pile-carpeted landings graced with Empire statues.... The saloons above

were large and hung with red, blue, and yellow damask. There was a large white ballroom, and a large oval dining-room in which the candles were swathed in mauve.[32]

The Diplomatic Staff was large and included both Military and Naval Attachés. The Embassy Staff was a small army – a Steward, a Groom of the Chambers, chefs, butlers, valets, a mounted escort supplied by the Russian authorities, 'footmen, coachmen, porters, housemaids, moujiks.'[33] Sir Arthur, a small, slightly fidgety man, whose personal tastes were anything but grand, worked in a 'large room, with white bookcases and dark red walls, from which the portraits of former Ambassadors glowered upon the vast Sheraton writing table and the leather armchairs.'[34]

Harold was impressed by the grandeur, but within days of his arrival, he experienced at first hand the other side of Russian political life. A group of revolutionaries bombed Prime Minister Stolypin's house. Sir Arthur was close to Stolypin and immediately sent Harold round to see if there was anything that could be done to help.

> In the trees that lined the canal-side opposite the villa were entangled the lace curtains of the upper bedrooms; the whole front of the house was blown in; and in the roadway were two landaus tilted sideways with their horses lying in a pool of blood. They were carrying stretchers out from the garden and loading them into ambulances. I felt very sick and hurried away.[35]

Twenty-five people were killed, though Stolypin himself survived.

That August was the first of a number of visits Harold made to St Petersburg. He called it 'that slip-shod and tragic capital'.[36] Nonetheless, Russia and the Russians made a great impression on him. He remembered the sights and sounds and smells of the capital. The scale of St Petersburg was

> set by the Neva, widest and swiftest of town rivers, which, after tumbling under the Troitzky Bridge, swelled out into a great estuary dwarfing the quays and palaces which line its banks. At midnight in June it would still swirl under a faint sun, and on December afternoons at two o'clock the lamps were lit upon their wooden trestles and the horse-trams would creep slow and black across the wide and untidy surface of the ice.... [Across] the river ... the chimneys of the Putiloff works belched heavy smoke.... From my balcony, as I read *Crime and*

Punishment, I could see the slim spire ... designed for the prison fortress of Peter and Paul. It rose like a long gold needle above the baroque steeple, a thing of gaiety and grace.... [The] peculiar stench of Russia (which arises I am told from the fish-oil with which the sheep-skins are treated) ... pervades the Russian continent from Vladivostok to Reval.[37]

He witnessed the immense contrasts of St Petersburg society: the fabulous displays of wealth on the part of the Grand Dukes and Duchesses, and the beggars squatting on the quayside. He was introduced to (and claimed to be bored by) the diplomatic *demi-monde* who would 'hang about in the ballrooms of Embassies.... Outside, the coachmen in quilted coats waited till dawn while icicles gathered on their beards.'[38] He even took Russian lessons.

These experiences gave Harold a view and an understanding of the Russian people, their character and psychology – 'that sense of oppression and secrecy, which is the bane of Holy Russia'[39] – which informed his journalism and his broadcasts during the 1930s and 40s, particularly his coverage of the Paris Peace Conference in 1946 when his views were often at odds with those of the official British delegation.

One experience which Harold declined during his first visit to St Petersburg was the opportunity to spend three weeks at Yalta with Prince Félix Yussupov, who had ambitions to go to Oxford and, indeed, did so in 1909. Yussupov, a year younger than Harold, later became a Russian hero when he and the Grand Duke Dmitri lured Rasputin to the Yussupov family's Moika Palace, shot him, poisoned him and pushed his body into the freezing Neva. In the summer of 1906, however, Félix Yussupov was young, spoilt and effeminate – he was already known to be fond of cross-dressing. Harold disapproved – much as he had disapproved of Ronald Firbank's camp exhibitionism – and preferred to stay in St Petersburg. It was a decision he later regretted.[40]

Back at Oxford, Harold moved out of College, sharing lodgings with 'Snatch' Hugessen and another friend, 'Crooked' Pemberton, who later became a Clerk to the House of Lords and an Inspector of Schools. Although now in his third year, Harold somehow never managed to become a senior figure in College life or in any of the many College societies. He found himself looking with a kind of distant longing at a new generation of undergraduates, younger than him, but somehow more confident and more worldly-wise. These included Patrick Shaw-Stewart, Julian Grenfell, Charles Alfred Lister and Edward Horner, key members of a Balliol grouping which became known as the 'Corrupt Coterie' – 'exuberant beyond the patience of dons' – all of whom were to die in the First World War.⁴¹ Of this group, Ronald Knox, the theologian, Catholic convert and intimate friend of Harold Macmillan and Evelyn Waugh, was the only survivor. Harold knew these people, but he never felt accepted by them or belonged to their group.

He returned to St Petersburg to spend Christmas with his parents. No doubt he spent some time studying for his exams, but he was already thinking beyond university. On the way back to Oxford, he spent a few days in Paris – making his first acquaintance with Jeanne de Hénaut, who will reappear shortly – and then in Frankfurt, inspecting establishments and families where he might work on his languages before sitting his Foreign Office exams.

The Easter vacation was spent at Blois in the Loire Valley, again improving his French. The town appealed to his historical sense: the connection with Joan of Arc, the famous eighteenth-century stone bridge across the Loire, the massive château with its one hundred bedrooms – though in general he seems to have found the Renaissance châteaux of the Loire too ornamented and elaborate for his taste. He stayed with the family of a Professor Gervais, just on the edge of the town. As on previous occasions, he found French family behaviour slightly *bourgeois*. His letters, however, are less judgemental in tone than previously, except in one area where we catch a glimpse of Harold the traditionalist and an odd lack of self-awareness.

Even as a young man, Harold was never particularly religious, contenting himself with keeping up appearances. Religion features only rarely in his writings and journalism, and when it does, as in his essay 'The Edwardian Week-End', his perspective is one of observation and interest rather than belief.

> With fervour would these Edwardians sing the psalms and the hymns, with reverence would they listen to the stories from the Old Testament. The smell of leather and wet mackintosh would permeate the damp little church. Every now and then an umbrella would tumble from a pew. The final benediction descended upon bowed heads.... They walked back to luncheon under dripping trees.⁴²

He would attend church if social circumstances dictated, even leading prayers when, during his diplomatic career, his role as Chargé d'Affaires required it. He enjoyed the language and the poetry of the King James Bible but, faced with organised religion, could become quite indignant – 'As always when I hear sermons I want to contradict,' he wrote to Vita on one occasion. 'I am glad the Christian religion is in decline.'[43] He described himself as 'a good pagan'.[44] At Blois, however, he was shocked by the family's anti-clericalism (itself a squarely traditional attitude among the French middle-class). Writing to his parents at the end of April 1907, he thought it 'absolutely revolting' when Professor Gervais's seventeen-year-old daughter claimed that Christ was the illegitimate son of a Roman centurion.[45]

He returned to Oxford for his final term, but he had not done enough. He got a Third. It was a bitter disappointment. He should have done better. He could have done better. He knew that he had not worked hard enough.

The onset of middle age often stimulates nostalgia. During the 1930s and 40s, Harold returned on several occasions to the subject of undergraduate life, always with the suggestion that, however intelligent and hard-working the new generation of undergraduates might have been, they were having less fun than he and his contemporaries had.

> What was lacking in us was brain and will. We did not think the right sort of thoughts, and even when we thought them correctly, we went out to a music hall and drove back in a cab. We lacked a sense of purpose. Now none of the younger generation lack a sense of purpose.[46]
>
> [Modern] undergraduates ... are not able today, as we were able, to have their meals in their own rooms or regularly invite guests to breakfast or to luncheon. When I look back on my university years those meals – those heavy breakfasts and uproarious luncheons – glimmer for me as the happiest of all occasions.[47]

And yet he was not happy at Balliol. It may have been teenage depression. In his *Spectator* article 'Tzarist Russia', he speculates that 'the depression which [St Petersburg] caused me was due perhaps to the circumstances that I at the time was passing through the gloomy period of my later 'teens.'[48] In *Some People*, he states that 'I never learnt to cope with Balliol until after I had left it.'[49]

In later life, his attitude changed. As time passed and the wound of his third-class degree healed, nostalgia for his pre-war youth and corrective memory set in. He became affectionate towards – even downright sentimental about – Oxford and Balliol. Returning to speak at the St Catherine's dinner in 1930, he told the assembled Fellows and students 'how unhappy I was at Balliol and why ... and how fond I am of it now.'[50] Twelve years later, returning to Balliol to give a talk on Anglo-French relations, he spoke of 'those dear buildings' and 'dear Oxford.'⁵¹ By 1953, when awarded an Honorary Fellowship at Balliol, he claimed that 'of all honours this earth can give, that is the one I most desire.'⁵²

7   Preparation

Harold's situation on leaving Oxford was not as bad as his father's had been. He had passed through school and university without obvious difficulty and without troubling the authorities, but, equally, without conspicuous success. He clearly had already the inclination and the capacity to study, if not yet the necessary discipline. Where he most resembles his father is that it was only after leaving Oxford – in Harold's case with a disappointing degree – that he stepped up a gear and found the purpose and the application he needed.

In the August of 1907, Harold returned to St Petersburg for a short break. Sir Arthur was too wise and too sympathetic to make Harold suffer the kind of parental disapproval he had suffered at the hands of Sir Frederick Nicolson forty years previously. James Lees-Milne suggests that 'in spite of his affection for his youngest son [he] did not have a high opinion of his abilities ... was not surprised by his only getting a Third in Greats and certainly did not expect him to pass the Diplomatic Examination.'¹ This may have been true, and yet Sir Arthur must have had some faith in Harold. For all his senior ambassadorial rank, he was not a rich man. He would hardly have agreed to fund the next two years of nomadic study – during which Harold moved between families in France, Germany and Italy, working on his languages, studying political and diplomatic history and preparing for the dreaded exam – without some hope that his son might in the end succeed. Perhaps he remembered his own early failures.

Harold was to return to England in October. In the meantime, life in St Petersburg continued to veer wildly between extremes. In June 1907, the second Duma was dissolved and a new electoral law imposed by imperial decree. There was uproar. On August 16, Sir Arthur called on Prime Minister Stolypin and found him in a garden 'surrounded by a high palisade and triple rows of barbed wire entanglements, beside armies of mounted and foot gendarmes.'² There were fears of strikes and revolution. Spies and secret police were reported everywhere. At the same time, at the British Embassy, night after night, the porter would don a gold-laced uniform and huge beadle hat. He would thump with a gold mace upon the floor as the guests arrived. They would stream up the scarlet staircase between a double row of hired footmen standing like zanies in their powder and state liveries.... The women carried tiaras on their heads and were dressed by Worth and Paquin. The men wore diamond stars upon their breasts, and their shirt-fronts were slashed by blue or scarlet ribbons.... There would be orchids and printed menu cards stamped with the royal arms in gold.[3]

It was in this atmosphere, strange, contradictory and full of suspicion, that an incident occurred which Harold, though claiming to be much embarrassed, narrates at length in *Lord Carnock*.

He awoke one night to hear the sound of surreptitious movement in the the Embassy archive room, which was next door to his bedroom. He woke his father, who decided to stand guard at the head of the staircase, while Harold went off to wake Neville Henderson – 'Attaché to the Embassy ... a young man of courage, beauty and immense muscular development.' Harold and Henderson returned through the warren of passageways so as to approach the archive room from the opposite direction. Unfortunately, Sir Arthur had not kept to his own battle plan. Henderson heard a movement in the darkness and leapt forward.

> There was a shout, a crash, a gurgle. 'Animal,' yelled Henderson, 'je vous tiens.' [Harold] rushed to the switch and turned [the light] on. He observed his father struggling violently in the hands of Neville Henderson, who had grabbed him by the throat. There followed an embarrassed and somewhat perfunctory search of the Chancery.... It was found that a large brown cat had been locked in ... and was trying to get out.... Next evening, Nicolson ... told the story to his Austrian colleague. In a few hours it was known all over St Petersburg and beyond.[4]

This is another of those instances which cast doubt of Sir Arthur's reputation for reserve. Henderson himself, it should be added, accepts the general accuracy of Harold's narrative but claims that he was too agitated to speak any language but English.[5]

On the evening of 31 August 1907, Sir Arthur, in his carriage and accompanied by his mounted bodyguard, drove to the Russian Foreign Ministry where he and Foreign Minister Izvolsky (also spelled Isvolsky) formally signed the Anglo-Russian Convention. The Convention was the culmination of the negotiations which Sir Arthur had been conducting since his arrival in St Petersburg. It 'was not a treaty of alliance; there were no military clauses; the words 'war', 'aggression', and 'defence' did not appear. Its professed purpose was to eliminate friction between two empires at three points in the Middle East and Central Asia.'[6] The three points were Persia, Afghanistan and Tibet, and the issues were long-standing and deep-rooted, with their roots in Russian expansionism and British paranoia about the security of her Indian possessions. Continual manoeuvring for position by the two Empires had led to scores of minor incidents and most observers were convinced that a major, violent clash was only a matter of time. Moreover, the whole tenor of relations between the two countries militated against an agreement. Queen Victoria had described the current Tsar's father, Alexander III, as 'barbaric, Asiatic and tyrannical,'[7] a characterisation which British public opinion would have accepted as applying to the nation as a whole. Even the conservative end of the British political establishment regarded Russian absolutism as extreme.

The conclusion of the Anglo-Russian Convention was thus a considerable diplomatic achievement, for which Sir Arthur again received the personal congratulations of King Edward VII and the Foreign Secretary, Sir Edward Grey. It represented a significant step in the realignment of the European powers. Harold was able to watch at first hand as his father carefully and with immense patience conducted negotiations which were at the very centre of the world stage.

> Nicolson adopted the methods of a humane and highly skilled dentist dealing with three painful teeth. He would work for a bit on Afghanistan, proceeding delicately but firmly; at the first wince of pain he would close the cavity with anodynes, cotton wool and gutta percha, and proceed, at the next sitting with Tibet. He was enabled by these methods to win the entire confidence of M. Isvolsky, and gradually to bring his three tasks to a state of simultaneous readiness without at any moment having jabbed the nerve.[8]

Harold left St Petersburg for London in October 1907 and for the next two years led a wholly nomadic existence. After a few weeks in London, he went to stay in Paris. From Paris to Frankfurt; from Frankfurt on to Torre Péllice in Piedmont; then on to Turin, Blankenburg, Paris again, back to London, St Petersburg for Christmas and New Year, Hanover, Hildesheim, Wiesbaden, Siena, and Paris yet again, before returning to London to sit his Diplomatic Examination in August 1909. It was an intense period, one in which Harold grew and matured. He was already well travelled, but his experiences during these two years added greatly to his understanding of people and cultures at a very different level from that provided by his diplomatic childhood.

In Paris, he stayed in the sixteenth *arrondissement*, at 174 rue de la Pompe, half way between the Trocadéro and the Bois de Boulogne, in an apartment belonging to Jeanne de Hénaut. Jeanne was already a legend and gained subsequent immortality as the subject of one of Harold's best (and also more factual) pen portraits in *Some People*.[9] 'She believed sincerely that God had granted to her the mission to coach young Englishmen for the Diplomatic Service.'[10] From among her many successes, she would elevate a select and aristocratic few – Robert Vansittart, Lord Moore, Lord Colum Edmund Crichton Stuart – to serve as beacons of linguistic ability and breeding for her current students. Harold, despite being a brilliant linguist, claimed never to have featured in this pantheon. It was his misfortune to have studied with Jeanne at the same time as Lord Eustace Percy, whom she regarded as sufficiently regal in all respects to be her candidate for King of France should the monarchy ever be restored.

The apartment was on the fifth floor and reached by way of an aged lift. It was small, accommodating only three students at a time, with Jeanne's mother obliged to use the cubicle-like drawing-room as a bedroom. It also smelt of the fish which Jeanne boiled up to feed to her cats. The surroundings were shabby, even squalid. Furniture in the rooms was basic – Harold's had a bookcase, a table, a bed, a brass lamp and a tin bath. Meals were frugal and the regime geared only to work. Life under these circumstances was itself an education to the upper-class young Englishmen who lodged there.

Harold had first met Jeanne and her mother in January 1907 when investigating places where he might study. His letter to his parents begins with the mother.

> The old Madame is such a very dirty, grimy, smelly old thing that it requires an amount of courage to grasp her by the hand. She is just like an old Irish woman, and wears a little fur cape which I would not let [my dog] even sniff at.... Her daughter, on the other hand, though equally dirty, is like Cleopatra would have been if ugly. She is frankly pagan, and suggestively oriental, and wears a sort of thing between a tea-gown and a dressing-gown, ending in a ruff under her chin. Her hair is a wig which looks like horse-hair.... She has the blue of a much-shaved moustache on her upper lip, and the laugh of a fat man – while her eyes are like lumps of black coal which suddenly light up when she speaks.[11]

For all these strictures, he and his fellow students fell rapidly under Jeanne's spell. In part, it was her eccentricity. She smoked hand-rolled cigarettes almost continuously. Her religion was a bizarre personal mix of theosophy and Buddhism. She insisted on using green ink to record her pupils' most brilliant compositions. She had an openly combative and contemptuous relationship with her mother: '*Figurez-vous, messieurs,*' she concluded, pointing at her mother as if at some particularly revolting specimen in a medical museum, '*ça, a dansé avec Alfred de Musset.*'[12] In part, it was her genius as a teacher: 'She knew instinctively just the sort of phrasing and idiom which would convey to the examiners the impression that one possessed *toutes les aisances de la langue française.*'[13] But much of the hold Jeanne exercised over those young Englishmen who came into her orbit was based on sheer willpower: an absolute belief that the discipline she imposed would lead her students to success; an absolute belief that their success and elevation to her aristocratic pantheon was the true purpose of her life.

Harold made several visits to rue de la Pompe during his two years of preparation for the Diplomatic Examination and went to see her in 1919 after the First World War when he was working in Paris. In the end, he came to see her combination of eccentricity, pride and determination as the embodiment of the French character – '*C'est bien elle: c'est bien la France!*'[14]

Harold experienced a different, more obviously ascetic, discipline in Torre Péllice, where he went to learn Italian in the spring of 1908. Torre Péllice is a small, ancient and isolated town, sitting in the rocky Val Péllice, at the foot of the mountains separating Piedmont from Hautes-Alpes. In the twelfth century, it became the home of the Waldensian Church. The Waldensians believed in poverty and austerity, surviving centuries of persecution and eventually becoming allied to the Presbyterian churches. The austere atmosphere survived. Harold lodged in a college for Protestant pastors, working under the personal supervision of the director, Professor Falchi, and living in a huge barn-like room scattered with odd bits of furniture. He stuck it for a few weeks, but at Easter he escaped to Turin to visit the immensely wealthy Mazzuchi family, a connection made at Oxford. 'Three sybaritic days in a Papist household'[15] provided both a contrast and a necessary relief from the austerity of Torre Péllice. The bathroom, he wrote to his mother, 'made me feel like Poppaea.'[16]

Three months during the summer of 1908 were spent in Saxony, at Blankenburg, a small, elegant white-painted town in the foothills of the Harz Mountains. Here, Harold stayed with Herr Baumeister Ehrlich and his wife and experienced yet another kind of life, which, forty-five years later when he came to write *Good Behaviour*, he used as an example of that peculiarly Germanic 'type of civility – *Gemütlichkeit*.'[17] Herr Ehrlich had retired from his architectural practice in Leipzig and built himself a pleasant Tyrolean-style villa 'with wide eaves and a long balcony running outside the windows of the bedroom floor.'[18] The Ehrlichs lived comfortably, their daily routine punctuated by four clearly defined meals – *Morgenkaffee* at eight o'clock, *Mittagessen* at one o'clock after which Herr Baumeister retired to bed, *Nachmittagskaffee* at four o'clock, and *Abendessen* at seven p.m. Sometimes, in the early evening, Harold and Herr Ehrlich would walk into the town and drink a bottle of wine. Engaged, as ever, by a historical connection, Harold was fascinated when Herr Ehrlich told him

> about the Franco-Prussian war; or how he had acquitted himself at the battle of Weissenberg and how he had been wounded at Mars-la-Tour. He would tell me about his student days and the girl he had known at Nordeney and how, when the Crown Prince Frederick visited Leipzig, it had been he who had handed him upon a velvet cushion a golden key.[19]

Then, after the evening meal, Frau Ehrlich would play the piano and sing or read plays or poems, while her husband sat in his armchair with a cigar. Under other circumstances, or later in his life when he had absorbed more of Vita's attitudes, Harold might have been prepared to find the Ehrlich household dull or *bourgeois*. As it was, he was charmed by the way they supported each other, and chose to use them as an example of German decency, benevolence, and gentility.

From Germany, Harold went for a further spell at rue de la Pompe, and then, in the autumn, returned to London, where he lived in the comfortable but impersonal circumstances of a 'gentleman's chamber' at the St James's Club in Park Place, Mayfair. As well as languages, the Diplomatic Examination included papers on political science and Harold commuted daily to Hampstead where a private tutoring establishment, or crammer, provided the necessary input. He also looked up old friends. He spent a weekend with 'Crooked' Pemberton,[20] and it seems to have been in this period that he revisited Tata Bertie's home at Wytham Abbey where he met Winston Churchill for the first time – 'only thirty-four and already a member of the Cabinet.'[21] In time, Churchill was to become another of Harold's great heroes – a position he did not necessarily relish.

Before returning to spend Christmas and New Year of 1909 in St Petersburg, Harold wrote to his parents asking to be 'guaranteed against' a long list of things:

(1) (a) hash (b) curry (c) Irish stew (d) mince (e) ragout (f) cold mutton (g) pork in any form (h) English potatoes (i) Dutch cheeses...
(2) The use of the word 'couch' for sofa, 'serviette' for napkin
(3) The casual reference to the younger sons of peers as 'The Honourable'
(6) The leaving of long black hairs in the bath...
(12) Any undue affection on arrival...
(14) Any discussions as to my health
(15) – or my underclothes...
(17) – or to the date of my departure[22]

It is a cheeky letter. It shows Harold as snobbish, fussy, and slightly irritated by family habits – as one might expect from any twenty-two-year-old, eager to establish his own adult status – and offers a glimpse into Nicolson family life.

One small portent of the future occurred during the Christmas vacation. Oscar Browning, the writer, historian and wit, was visiting Russia and stayed for a few days at the Embassy. Thirty years previously, Browning had been dismissed from his post at Eton partly as a result of his relationship with the young George Nathaniel Curzon, which was held to be excessively close, though apparently non-sexual. Browning had gone on to become a Fellow of King's College, Cambridge – from which, in 1908, he had just retired. He had maintained his friendship with Curzon, even travelling to India during Curzon's Viceroyalty, and was inclined to trade heavily on the connection. That Christmas, Harold heard a great deal about the man who was to play an important part in his life in the years following the First World War.

In January 1909, Harold returned to Germany, staying with 'old Frau Bürgermeister Lahmeyer of Hanover, with her two dear daughters Lilli and Ermine' and then with 'little Herr Heindt of Hildesheim, one of the few Germans whom I have ever seen to smoke a long pipe with a painted porcelain bowl.'[23] From Germany, he returned to Italy, but this time to Siena where his experience was wholly different from Torre Péllice.

He began in gloom. Via Stalloreggi, where he stayed, was a narrow, paved street between tall houses. Arriving 'at night, after a long journey... before a house with gratings like a Moorish prison... to enter a stone hall like the Escorial,' Harold sensed and disliked an underlying medievalism. But the next morning 'there was sunshine behind my shutters... on the table coffee and rolls... brown roofs and blossoms from the window.'[24] It was a vision of Italy and Harold, like so many before and since, fell deeply in love.

Every morning he walked across the Cathedral square, down some steps and knocked at a sinister little door of the house of his teacher. Don Orlandi, a delightful old priest, lived in cool rooms smelling of violets and incense.... And every evening Harold would pass through the red gates [of the city] into the hush of the country outside. He would read Shelley and Carducci, about whom he was wildly enthusiastic, as about all things Italianate and Tuscan. 'Even the cuckoos here speak with a Tuscan accent.'[25]

Siena remains a remarkable city. Like many hill towns in Tuscany, it is probably of Etruscan origin, but its days of glory were in the thirteenth, fourteenth and fifteenth centuries. It grew rich on the wool industry and became Europe's first banking centre as a way of developing its trade. Its great buildings – the Palazzo Publico, the Torre Mangia and, above all, the Duomo – and the artists of the Sienese School who filled them with masterpieces stand at the end of the medieval era looking forward to the Renaissance. In wealth and commerce, in art and architecture, as a centre of learning, Siena briefly approached its great rival Florence. But the two cities became enemies rather than rivals and fought continually for over three hundred years until 1555, when Siena was finally forced to surrender its independence. It rapidly became, and remained, a backwater, so that the city Harold saw retained much of its early Renaissance appearance and atmosphere.

Had he been born fifty years earlier, Harold would have gone on the Grand Tour. As it was, Siena was his first real cultural immersion in Italy. A love affair with Italian culture was almost obligatory for a classically-educated Englishman of Harold's age and class. Greece and Rome remained predominant, but the Renaissance was seen as essentially a rediscovery of the principles underlying the art, literature and philosophy of the classical world – and the Renaissance meant Italy. As a consequence, generations of educated Englishmen travelled to Italy believing they were getting as close as they could to the spirit which underpinned their education.

Harold loved Italy and came to speak Italian well, but he never developed the same empathy with Italy and the Italians as he did with the French and the Germans. At the same time, he believed firmly that 'the intellectual and aesthetic benefits conferred upon the world by Renaissance Italy can be compared only to those bequeathed by Greece and Rome.'[26] With his background and his education, it was inevitable that he would see things that way: where educational and cultural values were concerned, he was very much a traditionalist. The values he absorbed in his youth might flex, but they rarely changed.

Harold returned briefly to Jeanne de Hénaut in Paris and then to his political crammer in Hampstead. In June 1909, he had a formal interview before a Foreign Office board, chaired by the Permanent Under-Secretary, Sir Charles Hardinge, his father's predecessor as Ambassador in St Petersburg and soon to be Viceroy of India. Success would result in a technical nomination as Attaché which would allow him to sit the exam. Failure would mean humiliation and the waste of two years' hard work. He passed and returned to his political crammer until August.

The Diplomatic Examination was a major undertaking and Harold was very nervous. He sat three papers in French (translation, composition and an oral), three in German, and three in Italian. He also sat papers in English composition, English précis, French 'critical questions', modern German history, Roman history, and political science.[27] He went back to St Petersburg to wait for the results. They arrived by telegram on 22 September 1909. Harold had come second, behind Lord Eustace Percy, but ahead of his friend Tata Bertie. Both Harold and Eustace Percy had scored higher marks than had ever previously been achieved in the examination. There was jubilation in the Nicolson household – 'what unwonted excitement for this official domicile – my father casting off his ambassadorial dignity and behaving like a schoolboy – and my mother in tears of joy.'[28]

The rest of the process was a formality. Harold had to be accepted by the Civil Service Commission, which involved form-filling and a medical. He gave his two heroes, Dr Pollock and Sligger Urquhart, as referees. The medical found that he was 5 feet 10½ inches tall and weighed 10 stone 8 pounds.[29] He wore a small moustache, and reading glasses when required. The bureaucracy rumbled on. Eventually, 'I was told by the Civil Service Commission to "put myself at once into communication with the Foreign Office with a view to entering upon my duties there".'[30]

8 Office

In 1868, George Gilbert Scott completed a new government office building exactly opposite No. 10 Downing Street. The huge, Italianate complex was designed to accommodate four departments of state – the Home Office, the Colonial Office, the India Office and the Foreign Office. The Foreign Office occupied that quarter bounded by Downing Street and Horse Guards Parade on one side and St James's Park on the other. It was through the

Horse Guards Parade entrance that Harold Nicolson, wearing a new, subdued tie and clean boots, arrived to take up his duties on 19 October 1909.[1]

Harold was joining the Diplomatic Service, which in those days was technically separate from the Foreign Office, and separate again from the Consular Service. Recruits to the Diplomatic Service could expect a period of training in London before being sent off overseas, where they would spend most of their careers. The case of Sir Arthur Nicolson, who left England in 1874 and moved from one Embassy or Legation to another for thirty-five years before being asked to return to London, was not at all unusual. In practice, of course, there was a degree of interchange between the two services – although each time an officer moved from one to the other he was subject to formal transfer procedures. After only three months, Harold recognised 'mutual suspicion and secretiveness' between the two services.[2] Not until 1943 was the formal integration of the two organisations proposed – something which Harold welcomed in one of his *Spectator* articles.[3]

The theory, insofar as there was one, seems to have been that the interview which screened candidates before the Diplomatic Examination ensured that they had the requisite personal skills and were sufficiently presentable to join the Service. The examination itself tested their linguistic, intellectual and analytical skills. What new recruits, such as Harold, lacked, and what their first few months in 'the Office' were supposed to give them, was a grounding in how the system worked. They would open incoming correspondence, register it in heavy leather-bound ledgers, look out and attach related papers and the relevant files, tie the resulting bundle with special linen tape and place it on the desk of the senior officer responsible. They would receive and decipher incoming telegrams from Consulates, Legations and Embassies around the world (known as 'posts' in the Foreign Office). They would file, cross-reference and, in a world before photocopiers, hand copy important documents. They would learn the jargon of their trade and talk of despatches (usually extended assessments of the political situation written by Ambassadors, Ministers or other Heads of Post overseas), of telegrams (cipher communications between London and posts, giving instructions or reporting developments of immediate interest), and of minutes (the Civil Service term for written communications within one's own department). They would watch information flow up and down the Foreign Office's somewhat rigid hierarchy, through the layers of clerks to the Head of Department, to the Assistant Under-Secretary and, ultimately, at the apex of the pyramid, to the Permanent Under-Secretary of

State, also referred to as the Head of the Foreign Office. Harold spent his first days in the Foreign Office in the China Department, where he misspelt Bangkok while copying a document and was later given the immense responsibility of drafting a letter about a typewriter to be sent to Japan.[4]

It was what Harold wanted, but it was hardly a brave new world and he was quickly bored. The hours, however, were undemanding – he arrived at ten thirty in the morning and never seems to have had to work late – and he was able to compensate for boredom at work with an active social life. Previously, he had spent only short periods in London when cramming for the Diplomatic Examination, but now he was free to play the young man about town. He was a new face, well-travelled, personable, intelligent, enthusiastic and amusing. Moreover, he came from a good family and his father, as Ambassador to Russia, although rarely seen in London society himself, held a significant social position. The friends with whom he spent his time came from similar, or grander, backgrounds. There was Reggie Cooper from Wellington; Tata Bertie from Balliol; Gerry Wellesley, a diplomat and later seventh Duke of Wellington; Gerald Villiers, on the Foreign Office staff; Gerald Tyrwhitt, later fourteenth Baron Berners, the writer, composer and general eccentric; Alan Lascelles, known as 'Tommy', who became Private Secretary to George VI and Elizabeth II. Harold also became close to Archibald Clark Kerr, later Ambassador to Russia during the Second World War and first Baron Inverchapel. They were a gilded generation.

Very often, they simply ate together in restaurants or in the clubs – Harold's was the St James's, which he had joined a couple of years previously – chatted and gossiped. At other times they would go to the theatre – everything from *The Merry Wives of Windsor* with Ellen Terry and Beerbohm Tree to the latest musical hit, *The Dollar Princess*, which opened in September 1909 and ran for 288 performances. Harold saw three of them. As mentioned earlier, apart from Weimar, this seems to have been the only time in his life that Harold took a serious interest in music, with visits to the opera and the ballet. It was also the period of his life when he took most interest in sport – particularly golf and tennis – but sport was connected with another great institution of the time: the country house weekend.

In the years before the First World War, there were some 'two hundred great families who had been governing England for generations ... everyone knew or was related to everyone else.'[5] These families would have a London house and at least one house in the country, where it was customary to ask groups of important or entertaining guests for weekend parties. With the opening of the season, for those who could take the time – and there were many (though not including junior Foreign Office clerks) – there were also shooting parties which might last a week or ten days. The days passed according to an elaborate etiquette. Ladies wore hats, even at breakfast. In the afternoon, they wore elegant tea gowns with high necklines and long, flowing sleeves. At dinner, they would wear low necklines and almost no sleeves, while men wore full evening dress. In the early hours, guests retired to their rooms where a brass frame on the door contained a card with their name on it. Originally, such gatherings were termed Friday-to-Monday parties. Harold, in his snobbish youth, objected to his parents using the term 'week-end',[6] though he became reconciled to it later.

His magazine article, 'The Edwardian Week-End', is a minor masterpiece of observation and also gives a glimpse of Harold's contradictory character.[7] It is Harold in his role as the would-be pricker of pomposity, yet his attitude is ambivalent. He gently satirises the rigidity of the etiquette and the dress, the quantity of food and the complexity of the menu, the vapidity of the conversation – 'Colonel Westmacott, you simply must tell us about the Zambesi…. Oh, Clara! Is it really true that dearest Evy has got to go to Nauheim?' But for all that, it is clear that he understands these Edwardian rules and forms of behaviour from within. He gains a frisson of enjoyment from the fact that 'tea was served in the blue gallery' and that 'after tea there would be bridge tables in the red drawing room.'[8] He claimed that the demise of such parties meant that 'the war has not been fought in vain. We have been released from false and exacting pretensions.' But he also had to admit: 'I do not regret that I was also young enough to touch the fringe of Edwardian luxury.'[9] In fact, in the period after joining the Foreign Office, he played a full part in 'Friday-to-Monday parties', staying at Kirtlington Park in Oxfordshire, recently purchased by the Earl of Leven and Melville; at the Vyne in Hampshire, home of the Chute family; at Stratfield Saye, home of the Duke of Wellington; and, of course, at Knole near Sevenoaks, home of the Sackvilles. And the experience was useful, allowing him to meet on equal terms 'distinguished elder statesmen like Balfour, writers like Henry James, and artists like Sargent.'[10]

On 6 May 1910, King Edward VII died. It was a defining moment in the history of the British Empire. Edward was Queen Victoria's son, the 'Uncle of Europe', a close relation of most of Europe's ruling families. At the same time, he was his own monarch. His reign had seen the end of Britain's tradition of splendid isolation and a realignment of relationships with the continental powers. His passing marked the end of an era and left Britain facing a new and very different world. The funeral took place on 21 May. In attendance were nine kings ... five heirs apparent, forty more imperial or royal highnesses, seven queens ... and a scattering of special ambassadors from uncrowned countries. Together they represented seventy nations in the greatest assemblage of royalty and rank ever gathered in one place ... the sun of the old world was setting in a dying blaze of splendour never to be seen again.[11]

Harold's slightly surreal duty was to shepherd the Haitian delegation attending the funeral. His letter home shows him to have been torn between his emotional response to the funeral and a slightly snobbish fear that the Haitians, who in the parlance of his age he refers to as his 'niggers', might embarrass him with their lack of *savoir faire.*

They appeared in full and flamboyant uniforms with silver-handled umbrellas in their hands which I only managed to persuade them to relinquish by pointing to the sun quivering on the brasswork of the motors in the courtyard.... Slowly the big long funeral train slid in ... then the whole platform was flooded with Kings.... [Then] came a double line of Grenadiers carrying the coffin. The guns began to fire in the distance. Between each shot there was a dead silence.... Afterwards we were given an excellent lunch, but I was ashamed of my niggers who overate enormously.[12]

The end of another era was approaching. In June, Sir Arthur Nicolson was offered the post of Permanent Under-Secretary at the Foreign Office. He did not want to leave Russia, but the Nicolson sense of public duty triumphed – 'if it is put to me that the public service requires my coming [to London] I could not refuse.'[13] He rejoined the Foreign Office on 1 October 1910 after thirty-five years overseas. His arrival in London naturally affected Harold's position in the Office – not necessarily for the better.

Sir Arthur Nicolson was an immensely successful Ambassador, but he did not really have the temperament to be Permanent Under-Secretary – 'I am too easy-going in a way, and I always trust to men all cordially joining in keeping the machine going.'[14] In much the same way, thirty years later, Harold would see himself as lacking the 'power and drive' to be a successful minister.[15] As Head of the Foreign Office, Sir Arthur was directly responsible to the Foreign Secretary, Sir Edward Grey. He also had to manage important relationships with the Office's two dominant and very different personalities: Eyre Crowe, the Head of Western Department and William Tyrrell, Grey's Private Secretary. It was not an easy task.

Sir Arthur, with his many years of experience, was a man of decided views. He desired to avert a European war, but believed this could only be done through strength. Strength meant maintaining the Entente with France and Russia and, when necessary, standing up to what he saw as the German menace. If war came, then it came, but war was better than humiliation. These views were strongly supported by Eyre Crowe, who had responsibility for policy towards Western Europe. Sir Edward Grey was less willing to make such a clear commitment. He believed that war could only be justified as an absolute last resort. He also felt his position to be complicated by what Parliament would accept. William Tyrrell was devoted to Grey. He did everything he could to spare the Foreign Secretary unnecessary complications and worries and consequently took on more responsibility that was usually associated with his position. He was by nature a negotiator and a conciliator and, as such, his advice tended to oppose the more direct approach to the European balance of power favoured by Nicolson and Crowe. As a result, Nicolson felt his authority undermined by a man who was, in theory, very much his subordinate.

The antipathy between Sir Arthur and Tyrrell had begun while Sir Arthur was still Ambassador in St Petersburg, but naturally worsened with his return to London. Sir Arthur had clearly made his feelings known at home and Harold had apparently absorbed them, for Harold reported that his first encounter on his first day in the Foreign Office was with 'that little beast Tyrrell.'[16] For Tyrrell, it was enough that Harold was Sir Arthur's son: he encompassed father and son in the same dislike. This was unfortunate, for Tyrrell was married to Sligger Urquhart's sister and might, under other circumstances, have become Harold's ally. As it was, the tension between him and Sir Arthur continued for five years until he moved to the Home Office in 1915. But ten years later, when Tyrrell, in his turn, became Permanent Under-Secretary at the Foreign Office, he found himself in a position to have a significant and, as it happened, negative influence on Harold's diplomatic career.

Throughout his first year in the Foreign Office, until they returned from St Petersburg, Harold continued to write to his parents frequently. His letters are informative, impatient, and affectionate – and again give the lie to his claim that he was a stranger to his parents. The relationship was open enough for him to tell them that he was thinking about marriage – not with a specific individual, but, in an oddly abstract way, as something he would like to happen. In part, this seems to have been a vision (a very conservative one) of domestic bliss – 'I do like matrimony ... what a joy in the evenings ... to fly back to a big chair, a book and a little cuddly wife who wouldn't talk.'[17]

In part, it seems to have been a reaction to his nomadic life – 'I wish I could get married.... I hate this vague sort of luggage life.'[18] But he did not tell his parents that during the first few months of 1910, he was actually unofficially engaged to Lady Eileen Wellesley, sister of his friend and Foreign Office colleague, Gerry Wellesley. It seems to have been a desultory sort of relationship: Harold visited Apsley House, the Wellesleys' London home, on a number of occasions, and the two of them enjoyed walking together in the country during weekends at Stratfield Spey. But his diary suggests no passionate attachment and records no dramatic break up.

Something else that Harold did not tell his parents, something he kept very much to himself, was that, concurrently with his half-hearted pursuit of matrimony, he was having a series of affairs with young men – one called Greg and another referred to as 'Uppie'.[19] There was also Archie Clark Kerr. They first met in Berlin at the very beginning of 1910 when Harold was returning from his last visit to St Petersburg, and soon became close friends. Over the next three years, the two of them spent much time together, going to the theatre or the ballet, motoring round England in Harold's old and unreliable car – which he actually called 'Green Archie' – or rushing off to the south of France. Harold was obviously emotionally attached to him, and remained so for a number of years, but not (and this was a sign of things to come) in a way that affected his feelings for Vita. Three years later, just before their marriage, he told Vita that 'it is odd the affection that I have for [Archie], and he for me for that matter. He is the only one of my friends I am really sentimental about.'[20]

What are we to make of this? How far did Harold understand his sexuality at this stage of his life? Did he realise the extent of his homosexual leanings? It is certainly true, as Norman Rose points out, that the conventions of the age and his class would, in any event, have required him to marry and raise a family,[21] but if he regarded marriage solely as a protective front, he would hardly have been in such a hurry. Cloyingly domestic though his vision of marital harmony may sound today – 'I am sure it is the sort of life in which one's shaving water would always be hot, and one's breakfast adequate'[22] – there is nothing forced or dissembling about it. And Harold was, above all, an honest man. We can never be sure, but it is likely that he was just taking his fun where he could find it. If challenged, he might well have said that homosexuality was an amusing experiment, but that it was, in the end, simply a phase which would pass when marriage came along.

9   Courtship

On Wednesday, 29 June 1910, Harold Nicolson lunched with the Wellesleys at Apsley House at Hyde Park Corner. Eileen Wellesley, his unofficial fiancée, who had theatrical tastes, was wearing an eighteenth-century style dress in the manner of Kitty Clive. Later, they all went on to dine with Mrs Annie Stanley – whom Harold knew from St Petersburg, where her husband, Captain Sir Victor Stanley, had been Naval Attaché at the Embassy. Lord and Lady Sackville had also been invited, together with their eighteen-year-old daughter Victoria Sackville-West, who had officially 'come out' as a debutante earlier that month. Victoria was known as 'Vita', to avoid confusion with her mother who had the same Christian name. After dinner, the whole party went to the Adelphi Theatre in the Strand to see a Sherlock Holmes thriller, *The Speckled Band*, which Conan Doyle had recently adapted for the stage.

In Harold's diary, this day of intense social activity is compressed into a terse two-line entry.

> Lunch Apsley House. Lady E. in her dress as Kitty Clive. Dine Mrs Stanley. Sackvilles there. On to *The Speckled Band*.

Years later, he added a comment in red ink: 'This was the first time I met Vita.'[1]

Vita's version is more detailed.

> He arrived late at a small dinner-party before a play, very young and alive and charming, and the first remark I ever heard him make was, 'What fun,' when he was asked by his hostess to act as host. I liked his irrepressible brown curls, his laughing eyes, his charming smile and his boyishness.[2]

She took the initiative by inviting Harold to Knole, the Sackville family home near Sevenoaks in Kent, the following weekend. A Shakespearean masque was to be staged in Knole Park in aid of the Shakespeare Memorial Theatre Fund. Ellen Terry was performing, so was Eileen Wellesley, and so, too, was Vita herself, playing Portia in a costume borrowed from Ellen Terry. In the event, the performance was rained off, but there was lunch in the Great Hall for a distinguished array of guests, including H. H. Asquith, the Prime Minister, who had come down from London specially for the event. Harold was persuaded to stay overnight and was shown round the house and gardens by Lady Sackville the next morning.

He saw 'Vita West', as he calls her in his diary, on two further occasions that July, at a dinner and then at a ball given by the Strathmores, the parents of Elizabeth Bowes-Lyon, at their house in Lowndes Square. On 6 August, he was back at Knole for a second weekend, but Vita was in bed with flu. He returned the following Thursday, when Vita's friend, Rosamund Grosvenor, was also there. Again, he stayed overnight. On 5 November, Vita wrote him an odd little note, the first surviving example of some 10,500 letters that they wrote to each other over the next fifty years.

> My dear Mr Harold,
> I have been asked to 'ask a man' to dine on Thursday with Mrs Harold Pearson and go to a dance, so would you like to come? I promise you won't be made to dance!... Come to tea tomorrow at 6 South Street with the Rubens lady, who is here and tells me to ask you....
> Yours very sincerely,
> Vita Sackville-West[3]

James Lees-Milne calls this an 'ungracious little note.'[4] Perhaps it is, but it can also be interpreted to suggest that they had already discovered certain areas of common understanding – that the rest of the world's entertainments did not have to be taken at face value; that Harold disliked dancing – and were beginning to share common references – 'the Rubens lady', so named for her appearance, was Rosamund Grosvenor.

Later that same month, the Sackvilles headed south for the winter. Vita's illness in the summer had been diagnosed as pneumonia rather than flu and it was held advisable for her to spend the winter somewhere warm. They rented a huge, white-painted villa – Villa Malet – overlooking a secluded bay just west of Monte Carlo. Harold was invited to join them. He spent Christmas Day with his parents in London. On Boxing Day he set off for Paris, where he met Archie Clark Kerr and the two of them travelled south by train to join the Sackvilles, arriving on New Year's Day 1911.

They stayed ten days, apparently spending much of their time looking for places to play golf. Vita was attracted by Harold's 'exuberant youth combined with his brilliant cleverness.' What Harold thought is not recorded. There was no hint of romantic attraction in his behaviour towards her – hardly surprising given that he was emotionally, and quite possibly physically, involved with Archie. According to Vita, they 'fell into a rather childlike companionship ... he was the best actual *playmate* [she] had ever known.' When he left to return to London, Harold said goodbye 'without any apparent regret' and Vita was 'rather hurt.'[5] And that could, quite easily, have been the end of the relationship. They neither saw nor corresponded with each other for nine months, during which time a lot happened in both their lives.

Back in London, Harold found he had only two weeks in which to prepare for his first overseas posting: he had been appointed Attaché to the British Embassy in Madrid. Attaché was the lowest grade of diplomatic officer overseas: his duties would be filing, record keeping, coding and decoding, but it was a start. He arrived in Spain at the beginning of February 1911.

The Ambassador in Madrid was Sir Maurice de Bunsen, a man of immense experience, who had served in Tokyo, Siam, Constantinople, Paris and Lisbon before arriving in Madrid in 1906 as successor to Harold's father. He went on to become Ambassador to the Austro-Hungarian Empire in the days leading up to the outbreak of the First World War. Sir Maurice was a grand figure, very much in the traditional mould of the British diplomatist. In the five years of his Ambassadorship, he made himself popular at court and won the confidence of King Alfonso XIII and Queen Victoria Eugénie by his personal mediation when Spain and France were in dispute over the ever-troublesome subject of Morocco. No doubt, Sir Maurice took some degree of special interest in the son of his immediate chief in London. Certainly, Harold seems to have been invited to certain court functions, a privilege not offered to every Attaché.

> I have observed ... regal impassivity [and] hierophantic inattention, in the ceremonial of the Spanish Court. Alfonso XIII was young and naturally exuberant; Queen Victoria Eugénie was beautiful and urbane. Yet when, at an official reception, they would seat themselves upon the great thrones of Aragon and Castille, raised high upon a dais, each step to which was flanked by a golden lion pawing a golden globe, they would assume an expression of being unaware that there were people around them.... The grandees of Spain were grouped behind them; the diplomatists, embassy by embassy, were aligned with their backs to the windows.... [The] Ministers, the officers of State and finally the members of the Cortes filed in slow procession, bowing to their sovereigns as they passed. These salutations were not returned. The eyes of Alfonso and Victoria Eugénie continued to gaze with languid inattention at the floating clouds.[6]

This description and Harold's memory of the Repast of the Poor, quoted earlier, offer an interesting comment on the nature of Harold's underlying humanity, and give an indication why he was never at ease with Spain and Spanish culture. He saw in the forms and ceremonies of the upper levels of whatever society he was observing clues to the inner health of that culture. What he saw in Spain was not ceremony, but oppressive ritual – ritual from which human purpose and logic had been removed. In both instances, he saw the human qualities of the individuals involved being suppressed or overpowered by the prescribed ritual behaviour.

One might have expected his first overseas job and acceptance by both Embassy and Ambassador to have given Harold a little more self-confidence. However, writing to his parents after six months in Madrid, he claims to be 'the most utter failure socially ... excellent at making friends but hopeless at making acquaintances. I think it's a question of indolence, and still more of modesty.'[7] The mature Harold was anything but a social failure and anything but indolent. Is this just a young man's lack of self-confidence or something more? It is a confused letter, possibly a little depressed. He was not often depressed – it was something from which his usually high spirits preserved him – but he was clearly not happy in Madrid and it may be that this letter was a veiled plea for help. Certainly, very soon after writing it, he became ill. His posting was cut short and he was sent home to England. He never returned to Spain. Many years later, he admitted to James Lees-Milne that the illness was gonorrhoea: 'It all came from Spain and the effect of Andalusia and a desire to establish my sex.'[8]

An interest in marriage, an unofficial engagement, friendship with Vita, and then his first – and, apart from his marriage, only – recorded heterosexual relationship, with, one assumes, a prostitute: Harold was clearly asserting his heterosexuality. What we can never know is how self-conscious or how deliberate was that assertion at this stage.

Back in England, he underwent five weeks of treatment. Probably worse, he had to explain to Sir Arthur Nicolson – as both father and Head of the Foreign Office – the exact nature of his illness. He also confessed to Sligger Urquhart. Both took the matter philosophically. On 12 September 1911, Harold was formally transferred back to the Foreign Office. He cannot have been feeling particularly happy with life, but it was characteristic that he should bounce back quickly.

While he was still convalescent, he revived his contact with the Sackvilles. Vita, who, like most people, knew that he had been ill, but not the cause of his illness, remembered him that September as 'a rather pathetic figure wrapped up in an Ulster on a warm summer day, who was able to walk round the garden with me.'[9] Before long, however, he was back at work, lunching and dining with the familiar crowd of Foreign Office colleagues – Archie Clark Kerr, Tata Bertie, Reggie Cooper. In November, he was at Knole for another weekend and Lady Sackville speculated that he might be in love with Vita. That same month, the Foreign Office apparently forgave him his Spanish indiscretion and told him that he had been nominated Third Secretary pending an overseas posting.

He was at Knole again for Christmas and New Year, very much the friend of the family, playing golf with Lord Sackville and Walter Rubens (the husband of Lord Sackville's mistress) and helping Vita paint her sitting-room. He had also become a favourite with Lady Sackville and it was to her that he confessed that he was in love with Vita. She encouraged him, noting in her diary that both she and Lord Sackville found Harold 'very *sympathique*', but she was worried about his lack of money.[10]

On New Year's morning 1912, while he was still at Knole, Harold learnt that he had been appointed Third Secretary to the Embassy in Constantinople. Vita 'hoped he would propose ... before he went away ... but felt diffident and sceptical about it.'[11] Suddenly, the tempo accelerated. Harold was committed to spending two weeks at Clandeboye with his family, which he did, returning to London to make preparations for Constantinople – and, incidentally, to spend an evening with his friend 'Uppie'. On 18 January, there was to be a ball at Hatfield House, the seat of the great Cecil family since the beginning of the seventeenth century. Harold and Vita were planning to go, but the day before came the news that Sir John Murray Scott, Lady Sackville's long-time admirer, companion and benefactor, had died of a heart attack.

Harold arrived at the London hotel where the Sackvilles were staying uncertain whether Vita would be allowed to attend the ball. In the end, it was agreed that the two of them and Lord Sackville should go as planned. Vita was relieved because 'by then I was sure that Harold meant to propose to me and I knew I should say yes.'[12] So they went. Harold kept out of Vita's way until after midnight to avoid the dancing he so disliked. Then he came to find her and they escaped upstairs. Harold recalled that they found an attic and sat on a guest's hat box.[13] Vita remembered that he 'was very shy and pulled all the buttons one by one off his gloves.' He proposed and she accepted. Harold did not kiss her, but they sat together, 'bewildered over supper,' talking about having a flat in Rome.[14]

Harold was invited down to Knole on 20 January to say goodbye. He seems to have stirred Lady Sackville's motherly and emotional side: she told Vita that she wanted to help him in his career. Lord Sackville was less impressed. He did not think Harold rich enough or aristocratic enough for his daughter – she had several other admirers who were both. But they agreed that Vita, who was not yet twenty, was too young to marry. Lady Sackville took Harold into the Chinese Room and laid down conditions. He and Vita could not be officially engaged for a year and a half. They might communicate with each other, but not in the manner of engaged people and not using words such as 'Dearest' or 'Darling.'[15] Harold and Vita, a little confused by the whole business, spent all their time together walking in Knole Park 'at great speed through wet grass.'[16]

Harold returned to London with a farewell note from Vita which read: 'I love you. Goodbye.' He told his parents how things stood and, on 24 January 1912, took the train for Paris, the first leg of his journey to Constantinople. Before leaving, Harold sent Vita an early twentieth-birthday present – her birthday was not until 9 March. It was a battered sixteenth-century statue of Saint Barbara, which Harold had brought back with him from Spain. Lady Sackville thought it was 'dismal looking'[17] but Vita loved it from the moment she saw it. She wrote Harold a thank you letter which he opened on the train: 'He' – she got the gender wrong to begin with – 'is quite lovely, and has a gloriously flat nose.'[18] 'Barbara', as she was known in the Nicolson family, 'became a symbol of their marriage, accompanied them from house to house, even in Persia, and is still at Sissinghurst.'[19]

10 Vita

As Ambassador and as Permanent Under-Secretary at the Foreign Office, Sir Arthur Nicolson's advice was listened to by Cabinet Ministers, by the Prime Minister, and by the King, even when it came to the declaration of the First World War. Socially – even after retirement – he would be invited to the great houses of the nation and for some years he was invited by King George V to Balmoral, where he would go on picnics with Queen Mary and her children, among them, of course, the future Edward VIII and George VI. Although, in the terms of the age, relatively well born, Sir Arthur owed this position and what little wealth he had to his professional abilities, not to birth, family tradition, land or inheritance. His situation was not unique, but nor was it usual for someone in his position.

In 1895, the year in which Arthur Nicolson was posted to Morocco and Harold first went to school, Lord Salisbury became Prime Minister for the

Vita

third time. He was a Marquess. His Cabinet included another Marquess, a Duke, the son of a Duke, an Earl, a Viscount, three Barons, two Baronets and a squire with a nine-hundred-year pedigree. There were only six commoners, and one of those was the Prime Minister's nephew.[1] Of course, things were changing. By 1911, when Harold met Vita, Asquith was Prime Minister. The son of a wool merchant and mill owner, he was of more modest origins than any previous holder of the office, but his Cabinet included three Earls, a Viscount and two Baronets. The landed aristocracy still held far more wealth and power than anyone else.

Because of his father's profession and position, Harold was brought up among members of the governing elite. At Oxford and in the Foreign Office, he must have been conscious that his friends and colleagues – Tata Bertie, Tommy Lascelles, Eustace Percy, Gerry Wellesley, Archie Clark Kerr – were all from backgrounds which were more aristocratic, more landed and richer than his own. And it is noticeable that the two families to which Harold tried to attach himself – the Wellesleys and the Sackvilles – fit that ancient, landed and wealthy profile.

If Nicolson family tradition liked to claim descent from Viking raiders in the ninth century, Sackville tradition – on much stronger grounds – traced their family back to the Norman Conquest and the Domesday Book. The Sackvilles came to prominence in the sixteenth century with the figure of Sir Thomas Sackville, who became Baron Buckhurst and, later, first Earl of Dorset. Thomas was not only a writer – co-author of *Gorboduc* and a contributor to the *Mirror for Magistrates* – he was also a property magnate and an investor in the burgeoning iron-foundry business. He became Lord Lieutenant of Sussex, Lord High Treasurer, Chancellor of Oxford University, and a very rich man. His importance to subsequent generations is that through him, as a grant from his remote cousin, Queen Elizabeth I, Knole House came into the Sackville family.

Thomas Bourchier had one of the longest tenures as Archbishop of Canterbury on record – thirty-two years from 1454 to 1486. He spent thirty of those years building Knole. On his death, it passed with his office to his successor, John Morton, and to his successors. In 1537, Henry VIII took it from Archbishop Cranmer and kept it for the crown. In 1566, it passed to the Sackvilles and remained in the family through the generations, as Vita's forbears managed the estate and fulfilled their appointed roles as Members of Parliament, Justices of the Peace, and Lords Lieutenant of the County with the occasional foray into the higher levels of government.

Knole is more than just a house, it is a huge complex of buildings, described by Vita in *The Edwardians* as 'a mediæval village with its square turrets and its grey walls, its hundred chimneys sending up blue threads up into the air.' It has a Green Court, a Stone Court with a Jacobean colonnade, a Water Court, and four other courts. The complicated roofscape is decorated with leopards. There is a Great Hall, a Great Staircase, a chapel – hung, in Vita's childhood, with Gothic tapestries – a Brown gallery, a Cartoon Gallery, and a Leicester Gallery. The dining room used by the Sackvilles was the Poet's Parlour, used by Pope and Dryden, Congreve, Wycherley and Rochester. There are enormous staterooms, including the King's Bedroom, prepared for King James I, and the Venetian Ambassador's Room with the bed intended for James II. The whole complex covers some six acres (2.4 hectares) and is set in a beautiful wooded and landscaped deer park of a thousand acres (400 hectares).[2]

All this – the history, the buildings, the park, the intense Englishness of it all – was part of Vita. It defined one side of her character and populated one half of her imagination. By the time she was born, the family had been living in Knole for well over four hundred years. As a little girl – an only child, who mixed very little with other children – she would wander through this warren of history, where there were

> magical things ... ancient carved bosses, grotesque faces in the woodwork; a door-stopper called 'Shakespeare', a square little man of a size to look at a three-year-old eyeball to eyeball ... and above all the heraldic leopards.... At the top of the great house, right under the vast acreage of roof and chimneys [were] long attics, which give access to the roof ... stacked with discarded paintings, statues, furniture and carvings, stowed away there by successions of Sackvilles.... Here Vita would retreat, to play and prowl and dream and rummage in trunks and chests.[3]

There were gardens, too, at Knole. 'History,' says Vita's biographer, Victoria Glendinning, 'spilled over from the house into the garden.'[4]

> First accounts for the garden proper appear to date from the reign of Henry VIII ... when, in 1543, Sir Richard Longe was paid 'for making the King's garden at Knole.'[5]
>
> The white rose which was planted under James I's room has climbed until it now reaches beyond his windows on the first floor.... The soil is rich and old. The garden has been a garden for four hundred years.[6]

This is the origin of one Vita – the sensitive Vita who wrote *The Land* and *The Garden*; the rooted Vita for whom Knole would always be the most important place on earth; the aristocratic Vita who could write to Harold 'I'm not "cultured" (how dare you!), but essentially primitive; and not 1913, but 1470';[7] the English Vita whose outbursts against the Germans, even fourteen years after the war, were vitriolic – 'I wish you shared my Kentish interests instead of shaking the blood-stained hands of Germans in London.'[8]

But there was another Vita, reflecting the other side of her heredity. Her grandfather, Lionel Sackville-West, the fourth son of George Sackville-West, fifth Earl de la Warr, was brought up conventionally enough, although not at Knole, but at Bourn Hall in Cambridgeshire. He was educated at home, joined the Diplomatic Service and served in Lisbon, Naples, Stuttgart, Berlin and Turin before arriving in Paris in time for the Franco-Prussian War of 1870. He continued to rise in his profession, becoming British Minister to Argentina, Madrid and, ultimately, in 1881, to the United States.

It was while he was a young attaché in Stuttgart in 1852 that his life took an unconventional turn. He took a trip to Paris and fell in love with a Spanish dancer. Her real name was Victoria Josefa Durán y Ortega; her stage name was 'Pepita'. She was the daughter of a barber from Malaga and a gypsy, and, at the time Lionel met her, she was married to her former dancing teacher. Lionel was not her first lover, but he became her last. They never married – Pepita was a strict Roman Catholic and would not consider divorce – but the relationship lasted nearly twenty years and they had five children, of whom Victoria Josefa Dolores Catalina, Vita's mother, was the second, born in Paris in 1862. Pepita left the stage and Lionel established the family in a villa in Arcachon, just south-west of Bordeaux, under the name of West. They lived there, quietly but comfortably, with Lionel visiting whenever he could take leave, until 1871 when Pepita died. Lionel, who left for Buenos Aires the following year, arranged for the children to have a good Catholic education, with the result that Victoria and her two sisters spent seven years in a Paris convent. For Victoria, who had inherited in fair measure her mother's independence of character, it was a miserable time.

In 1880, Lionel 'acted with decision and courage.'[9] The children were told the truth about their parents' relationship and brought to England to meet their aristocratic relations at Knole. The Sackvilles appear to have accepted the situation with surprising calmness, and the children were taken under the wing of Lionel's sister, the Countess of Derby. In 1881, Lionel was appointed as Minister to Washington. The position had an important social dimension and he was unmarried, so he took Victoria with him. As a result, just two years after leaving her French convent, 'Lionel's illegitimate and inexperienced daughter was a diplomatic hostess presiding over his parties and making a huge success of it.'[10]

Victoria presided over the British Legation for seven years. She was 'exceptionally pretty with big blue eyes and the thick dark hair, hip-long, that she had inherited from Pepita.'[11] In 1888, a minor scandal put an end to Lionel Sackville's tenure in Washington and to his diplomatic career. Victoria was naturally apprehensive about returning to England, but, at this crucial point in the story, Lionel's elder brother, Mortimer, first Lord Sackville, died childless, leaving Lionel as his heir. Lionel inherited Knole and, at the age of only twenty-six, Victoria moved with apparent ease from hostess at the British Legation in Washington to being mistress of the great house in Kent, a role she was to fill for the next thirty years.

In Washington, Victoria had received and rejected twenty-five proposals of marriage – or so she claimed, for she had a tendency to dramatise and exaggerate – among them Charles Hardinge (later to chair the Foreign Office board which interviewed Harold), millionaire businessmen, senior diplomats, even, according to one account, the President of the United States, Chester Arthur.[12] Yet within months of coming to live at Knole, she had fallen in love and was talking of marriage with a man five years younger than herself, who had only just left university. The man she chose – for, given her age, character, and experience, one assumes that she made her own decision – was the eldest son of her father's younger brother, William, and thus her first cousin. Confusingly, he, too, was called Lionel Sackville-West.

The young man had another thing is his favour. Lionel senior was only sixty-one and could be expected to live for a few years yet. His two sons were, of course, illegitimate. They had been well treated and settled on an estate in Natal Province in South Africa, but they could inherit neither title nor land. It was possible, though unlikely, that Lionel senior might marry and father a son, but on the assumption that he did not, his brother William and then Lionel junior were the heirs to Knole.

It was not – or not solely – a mercenary match. There were a few rumblings in the Sackville family about first cousins marrying, about Victoria's Spanish blood and her Catholicism, but the wedding took place at Knole in June 1890. Victoria and Lionel immediately 'embarked on a sexual idyll ... they made love on the library sofa, in the bath, in the park and on a fur rug that excitingly charged Victoria with static electricity. She recorded it all in her diary – where, when, how and how often.'[13] She became pregnant the following year and Vita was born, after a long and extremely painful labour, in the early hours of Wednesday 9 March 1892.

The idyll did not last. The extreme pain of her labour – 'I was suffering so much that I begged them to kill me'[14] – had a permanent mental, if not physical, effect. Lionel wanted a second child, the all-important male heir, but Victoria had no wish to repeat the ordeal of childbirth. By the time Vita was eight, Lionel had embarked on a relationship with Lady Camden, the first in the series of mistresses which was to last the rest of his life. By the time Vita was twelve, Victoria had put an end to any further marital sex life on medical grounds. She did not herself take lovers in the technical sense, but she did have admirers: prominent men, such as Sir John Murray Scott (known as 'Seery') and Edwin Lutyens ('McNed'), whom she leaned on for advice and emotional support. Vita, a solitary child in the corridors of Knole, loving her father dearly but closer in character to her mother, watched and tried to understand.

When Lionel senior died in 1908, Victoria felt the loss intensely. She and Lionel junior became Lord and Lady Sackville, but their situation was complicated by the fact that her elder brother, Henry, was mounting a challenge to the inheritance. His claim was that Pepita had never been married to her dancing-master husband, but had been secretly married to Lionel senior. This would make him legitimate and thus he – and not Lionel junior – would be rightful heir to both the title and to Knole. The case had been hanging around for years, costing more and more money (a lot of which Seery lent to the Sackvilles) and eventually came to court until 1909. Lionel junior won his case and was confirmed in his inheritance, but the true cost was not financial. More damaging was the stress, the insecurity, and the public exposure. Vita knew what was going on. There were no secrets at Knole and her mother loved telling her life story, but it was quite another thing to have newspapers exposing the intimate history of the lord and the Spanish dancer: a tale of sex, money and inheritance.

Vita hated being in the public gaze, but she revelled in the story of Pepita, whose biography she wrote some thirty years later. Pepita came to represent the other side, the non-Sackville side of her character. This was the romantic Vita, who responded with such intensity to all things Spanish and Italian, who never ceased falling in love; the rebellious Vita, who longed to scandalise English society with her cross-dressing and her lesbianism; the independent Vita, who resented what she saw as the yoke of marriage; the sexually aggressive Vita, who took and discarded lovers at will. Many of the struggles and conflicts of her life were rooted in her attempts to balance or reconcile the two sides of her character.

When she met Harold, Vita was young and immature. Brought up largely at Knole, she was educated by private tutors and by her governess and then at a day school just off Park Lane in central London. She spoke French and Italian, but her real education came from obsessive reading which, from the age of twelve, she combined with obsessive writing. She wrote 'her daydreams ... in the sententious style of Scott and Dumas ... [the] day-dreams of a highly literate, romantic adolescent, fired by her environment.'[15] At fourteen, she was writing a novel about her ancestor the fourth Earl of Dorset, *The Tale of a Cavalier*; then she wrote *The King's Secret* about Charles II. She wrote three plays in French, one of them in verse. She wrote a novel in French, *Richelieu*. At seventeen, she wrote a verse drama on the tragic life of the poet and forger of medieval poetry, Thomas Chatterton, which she had privately printed. An only child growing up in an intensely romantic and historic house with which she had an intensely romantic relationship, it was almost inevitable that she should become a writer.

Harold's proposal to Vita in January 1912 was curiously sexless. He did not even kiss her. We know that he was not lacking in sexual experience with young men and that he had had a heterosexual encounter in Spain. Perhaps he was still uncertain – though not, apparently, particularly anxious – about his sexuality. Vita was a playmate, but in moving relations onto a more formal footing was he to some extent in awe of her and her background? Vita herself was not completely without experience of sexual matters. One summer at Seery's shooting lodge in Scotland, she had received a declaration of love from a farmer's son who had then masturbated in front of her. From the age of sixteen, she had repeatedly been the subject of unwelcome attentions, amounting to attempted rape, on the part of her godfather, the Hon. Kenneth Hallyburton Campbell. She never told anyone at the time and we only know because she wrote to Harold about it over thirty years later. She herself suggested that 'perhaps it accounts for much.'[16]

Vita's adolescent years were characterised by intense, emotional relationships with two friends – Rosamund Grosvenor and Violet Keppel (later Trefusis). Her largely solitary childhood seems to have intensified her responses to friends when she did eventually find them. She recorded Violet's first avowal of love and her own clumsy attempt to say 'Darling' in response; her disturbed feelings when Violet, leaving for Ceylon, kissed her.[17] Recalling the year 1911, when Harold was in Madrid, Vita was later to write:

> I want to be frank. I have implied, I think, that men didn't attract me, that I didn't think of them in what is called 'that way'. Women did. Rosamund did.... I don't remember very clearly, but the fact remains

that by the middle of that summer we were inseparable, and moreover were living on terms of the greatest possible intimacy ... [although] the thing did start in comparative innocence. Oh, I dare say I realized vaguely that I had no business to sleep with Rosamund ... but my sense of guilt went no further than that.

Anyway I was very much in love with Rosamund.[18]

This sounds like a first lesbian affair. James Lees-Milne refers to it as 'a passionate affair which, on Vita's part, was purely physical, for Rosamund ... soon bored her.'[19] In one part of *Portrait of a Marriage*, Vita talks of her 'physical passion' for Rosamund. In another, she says 'we never made love.'[20] Victoria Glendinning, who as Vita's biographer has weighed the evidence, says that Vita and Rosamund 'shared a diffuse and sentimental sensuality, but never, then or later, did they technically "make love". They did not think of it.'[21]

Such innocence may not sound credible today. In the end, it does not matter. What is important is that, at the time Harold proposed and she accepted, there was a duality in Vita's approach to her emotional life which was similar to his. She certainly did not think of herself as a lesbian – she later claimed to have had no knowledge of homosexuality at this age – and, as we have seen, it is doubtful that Harold actually thought of himself as homosexual, though his knowledge and experience of sexual matters were well in advance of hers. However, they had both already developed a capacity for close emotional and sexual (or quasi-sexual) relationships with their own sex, and neither of them appears to have seen this as a barrier to normal relations with the opposite sex. Where she and Harold differed was in the intensity of her sexual nature, and in her capacity to become confused and to generate confusion for those around her where emotional and sexual matters were concerned.

11 Constantinople

When the Nicolson family left Constantinople in the autumn of 1895, Harold was a boy of eight. When he returned in January 1912, he was a twenty-five-year-old adult and a Third Secretary at the Embassy with a certain status of his own. When the Orient Express stopped in Sofia, he was met and embraced by Zacchari, the British Legation servant, who had known him as a child. At the Turkish border, he was met by a member of the Embassy staff who travelled with him on the train, dealt with his luggage and saw him through all the necessary formalities. The train reached the shoreline of the Sea of Marmora, passing through the Walls of Theodosius and round Seraglio Point beneath the great Topkapi Palace. It arrived in Sirceki station, Constantinople's European terminus, where he was met by a horse-drawn carriage and driven across the Golden Horn by way of the old Galata Bridge. Once on the Pera shore, the carriage wound its way up the hill to the grand portals of W. J. Smith and Sir Charles Barry's 1851 Embassy building, set amid its lawns and gardens, where Harold's parents had been married almost thirty years before.

The Ottoman Empire had changed radically since Arthur Nicolson had been Secretary to the Embassy in the 1890s and the process of decay and disintegration was to accelerate during the two-and-a-half years of Harold's tenure as a Third Secretary. The combination of weakness, despotism and corruption identified by Arthur Nicolson had led to the rise of the Young Turks, a revolutionary movement with its origins among students and military cadets, which demanded reform of the Turkish administration. They were suppressed and persecuted by the secret police until, in July 1908, a group of young officers took to the hills in Macedonia. The revolt spread; the army – long unpaid – mutinied; and Sultan Abdul Hamid caved in. He granted the civil liberties that he had suppressed for the past thirty years and promised parliamentary elections.

It was an almost bloodless coup. The Ottoman Empire became a constitutional monarchy, but success had been too easy. The Young Turks were themselves divided; the new liberal environment allowed the formation of a Muslim faction which demanded the implementation of *sharia*; the Sultan fought back politically; the new government was compromised. In 1909, a Young Turk army from Salonica descended on the capital, forcing the abdication of Abdul Hamid and setting his more liberal brother, Mehmed Reshad, on the throne. A degree of political stability was established, but it was too late to arrest the disintegration of the Empire. Italy, which had rather lost out in the great European dash for a colonial empire, quite cynically declared war in September 1911 and invaded the provinces of Tripolitania and Cyrenaica, the area we now know as Libya. Turkish troops fought back, but the Italians were able to establish a naval blockade along two thousand kilometres of coastline.[1] In November, Italy claimed effective suzerainty over the whole area and moved its attention to the Aegean. The war was still under way when Harold arrived in Constantinople.

As if internal problems and Italian aggression were not enough, the

Ottoman Empire was also under pressure from the Russians, who wanted control of their access through the Turkish Straits from the Black Sea to the Mediterranean; from the Germans, who sought to increase their political influence through schemes such as financing the Baghdad railway; and from the new Balkan nations who were constantly stirring up their client populations in the hope of carving more territory for themselves out of what was left of European Turkey. The role of the British Ambassador to the Sublime Porte, as the court of the Ottoman Sultan was formally known, was to try and maintain British influence in these trying times. Sir Gerald Lowther, who had succeeded Sir Arthur Nicolson in Tangier in 1905 and was then posted to Constantinople in 1908, did his best, but he was hampered by the fact that he was not an Ottoman expert – this was his first experience of the region – and by the fact that he was not in a position to offer any practical, that is military or financial, help.

To some extent, Harold's life in Constantinople resembled his experience of St Petersburg two or three years previously. The Empire seethed and tottered, but the busy social life of the expatriate and diplomatic communities was wholly unaffected. On his return from Constantinople in 1914, he rapidly became known throughout the Foreign Office for his ability to produce concise but perceptive analyses of complex political situations – an ability which was to become the hallmark of his later books, diaries and radio talks – so it is strange how little attention he appears to have paid to the political situation in Constantinople. He coded and decoded the telegrams that flashed back and forth between London and the Embassy. He learnt Turkish. But otherwise, he seems to have given himself up to pleasure.

> The young secretaries accompanied the Ambassador to the golf course, rode with the Counsellor's wife by the Sweet Waters, went to fancy-dress balls and concerts, or merely ambled through the bazaar looking for Persian drawings and carpets. In view of Harold's later contempt for games, it is odd to learn that he constantly played golf, had lessons in squash rackets and dancing, and was even elected secretary of the Polo Club.[2]

Harold does not seem to have been particularly short of money during his first months in Constantinople. Polo is a notoriously expensive sport and he kept his own horse, called Bottle. Shortly after his arrival, he also bought a small yacht from the son of the Russian Ambassador and taught himself to sail.

Harold Nicolson

The boat features in an anecdote concerning 'Lambert Orme' in *Some People* which Harold later told James Lees-Milne was based on actual experience of Ronald Firbank.[3] Firbank arrived in Constantinople and sent a note to Harold saying he had 'descended' at the Pera Palas Hotel.[4] The Pera Palas, originally built for European travellers arriving on the Orient Express, was a few minutes' walk from the British Embassy. It was very much *the* European hotel in Constantinople and just the kind of place where Firbank would have wished to be seen. In reality, Harold seems to have visited Firbank and found him 'ridiculous.' In the *Some People* version he alters the story, presumably for dramatic effect, so that they never meet. In any event, an arrangement was made to go sailing on the Bosphorus the next morning. Harold waited for his guest until eventually a man turned up with a note from Firbank saying: 'Today is too wonderful ... let us keep today as something marvellous that did not occur.' Harold left a note saying 'silly ass' and went sailing 'indignant and alone.' He returned home to find his sitting room full of lilies which Firbank had brought round.[5] The incident is dramatised to undermine Harold's no-nonsense sensibility, but it contains an essential truth in that Harold, for all his other qualities, never appreciated whimsicality. Oddly, this passage, like that cited earlier involving Firbank and the decoration of his undergraduate rooms, also finds an echo in *Brideshead Revisited*, where Sebastian Flyte fills Charles Ryder's rooms with flowers as an apology.[6]

In April 1912, the real world intruded when Italian torpedo boats blockaded the Dardanelles and disrupted shipping, creating a particular problem for Russia, half of whose exports passed through the Straits.

Harold continued socialising and sailing. He soon found, however, that the waters of the Bosphorus and the Sea of Marmara, with their strong currents, unexpected squalls and unpredictable, deflected winds were not the safest place for an inexperienced sailor. His diary for 7 May records 'sail in a gale out to Marmora and am nearly drowned.'[7]

June was an eventful month. Harold's old schoolfriend Reggie Cooper arrived to join the staff at the Embassy and, at the end of the month, Harold met Pierre de Lacretelle, who became the main source for the composite character of the 'Marquis de Chaumont' in *Some People*. Lacretelle was a dark and willowy young Frenchman who had arrived in Constantinople to work for the Ottoman Bank. He was the same age as Harold, had been born in Sofia, where his father had been attached to the French Legation, and had experienced the same kind of nomadic childhood. Unlike Harold, however, he was heir to an enormous fortune, having become the sole heir to a rich and eccentric aunt by agreeing to be baptised. Harold's annotation to his own copy of *Some People* describes him as 'one of the most brilliant people I have ever known.'[8]

Harold was immediately attracted. James Lees-Milne's account sounds as if it was drawn from Harold's own memories. In July, Harold and Pierre

> spent a week tacking up and down the Bosphorus, dawdling on the sun-baked shores of the Black Sea, dallying in a low-ceilinged room in Therapia, and all the while reciting and talking about French poetry, while the water lapped against the walls outside and steamers hooted in the distance.[9]

Against this background of dalliance, Italian torpedo boats returned to the Dardanelles. The Straits were closed, again cutting Russia's main trade route to the outside world. Russian exports collapsed and there was a run on Russia's main banks.

Meanwhile, Harold and Vita continued to write to one another in the terms prescribed by Lady Sackville. They discussed aspects of their relationship. Harold was obviously worried that he was a (relatively) poor man marrying a rich heiress. Vita reassured him that 'I am *not* rich, and even if I was, it couldn't possibly jar.... So don't worry.'[10] She confessed to the intensity of her passion for Knole and to the fact that she used to hate her cousin Eddy Sackville-West because he was the one who would inherit the great house and the park which she loved so much. She confessed – ironically in view of later developments – to being 'atrociously jealous' and claimed – again ironically in view of the future – 'I will always be ready to go to dinner parties if you want me to ... and look nice, and you won't be ashamed of me.'[11]

During the course of this first separation, one can sense Vita growing up. Her letters become less guarded. She tells Harold that she does not want to marry that autumn because 'this is the first year I have lived at all ... and begun to make friends.'[12] She pays less attention to her mother's restrictions on their correspondence and, at one point, begs him to write to her in more open, intimate terms – what she calls 'a totally post-Hatfield letter.'[13] And there is more irony in the fact that this particular letter was written at the height of Vita's involvement with Rosamund and while Harold was dallying with Pierre de Lacretelle on the shores of the Bosphorus.

Harold wrote to Vita, but he also wrote regularly to 'My Dear Lady Sackville'. He recognised from the beginning that she was a powerful figure in Vita's life – indeed, she was to remain a powerful and often troublesome figure in both their lives right up to her death in 1936. She wrote to him as

'My dear Boy' and appeared to encourage his pursuit of Vita, but then, for a while at least, her enthusiasm cooled as she saw Vita being circled by other, richer and more aristocratic suitors – Patrick Shaw-Stewart, Lord Granby and Viscount Lascelles.[14] She had by this stage met Sir Arthur and Lady Nicolson. The Nicolsons were nothing if not respectable but Lady Sackville – remarkably, given her own background – was hugely condescending. She was charmed by Sir Arthur, 'a dear', but found Lady Nicolson 'deadly dull' and dismissed them both as 'very ugly and very small and unsmart looking.'[15] Her immense self-centredness meant that she could never understand Harold's professional obligations. She pressed him to pull strings or make excuses in order to get his leave brought forward so that he could join Vita in Paris. Even her goodwill could create difficulties: she decided to cultivate Sir William Tyrrell on his behalf, which can hardly have improved relations with a man who already disliked both Sir Arthur and his son.

It was probably just as well that Lady Sackville had another problem facing her at this time, the outcome of which was to have a major impact on Harold and Vita's future. The Sackville inheritance case had been settled in 1909, but now, only three years later, Lady Sackville was back in court in another sensational case centring on a disputed will. Her admirer, Seery, had died in January 1912 and left the bulk of his fortune – £150,000 in cash and an apartment in the rue Laffitte together with contents valued at £350,000 – to Lady Sackville. Within days of his death – in fact, on the very day that Harold left for Constantinople – the Scott family announced that they were to contest the will. The result was another headline-grabbing squabble between society families which rumbled on, taking its toll in terms of stress and emotional outbursts from Lady Sackville, until it eventually came to court in June 1913.

Harold returned to England for two month's leave in August 1912 and was invited down to Knole for the weekend. Arriving at his parents' the day before, he found a note from Vita telling him to arrive at eleven o'clock and come to her room 'the back way, through the stables and the Great Hall' because she did not want to meet him in front of all the other house guests.[16] This must have sounded encouraging, but the reality of the weekend was not so pleasant. Two of his rivals – Viscount Lascelles and Patrick Shaw-Stewart – were also present. So, too, was Rosamund, who, if not an actual rival, was certainly an emotional distraction for Vita, as well as someone to cling to when she could not make up her mind about the men who were circling her. Vita paid no special attention to Harold, but he appeared to take this calmly. The same guests assembled the following weekend when Vita and Rosamund acted a play called *The Miracle*. Again, Vita paid

Harold no special attention. 'She told her mother she would like to "live alone in a tower with her books," then she threw up her arms and said, "Oh! Mama, I really don't know what I want!"'[17]

Harold played a waiting game. He was her companion and not someone who pressured her to make a decision. It seems to have paid off because on 1 September he recorded, 'Things smiling.'[18] Then, whether to relieve the pressure or as some kind of personal celebration, he dashed across to Paris to spend a couple of days with Pierre de Lacretelle at the Astoria Hotel, where he was also introduced to Jean Cocteau. From Paris, he went to Clandeboye for a brief family holiday, but he was back at Knole before the end of the month.

Whatever private reservations Lady Sackville may have had – the fact that Viscount Lascelles was heir to Harewood House and had £31,000 a year from property alone had made a deep impression on her – Harold's star was now definitely in the ascendant. He was introduced to other members of the Sackville family. Lord and Lady Sackville agreed that the engagement might be considered official and Harold and Vita might write to each other without restrictions. He was also invited to call Lady Sackville by her family name – 'Bonne Mama'.

This last point may seem minor, but it had considerable significance. The Sackville-Wests were an exclusive clan and one feature of their exclusivity was an elaborate family slang – *Bonne Mama* or *BM* for Lady Sackville; *mar* for something young or sweet or vulnerable and, by extension, for Vita herself; *bedint* for something vulgar or middle-class. Use of this slang marked admission to the inner circle and was a definite honour. For Harold it was a sign of the acceptance by a group – or, in this case, a family – something which was always so important to him. He used Sackville slang in his letters to Vita and to his sons for the rest of his life.

Harold's leave was rapidly approaching its end. Down at Knole again for the last weekend in September, he took decisive action. As they walked in the garden on a west Saturday, he kissed her and called her his wife. 'He kissed me! I love him,' she wrote in her diary, 'But I want so much to see R[osamund] again.'[19] They were better matched than they knew.

In April that year, Vita and Rosamund, chaperoned by a governess, had spent a few days in Florence to assuage what Vita called her Wanderlust.[20] Now they wanted to go back, so it was agreed that they would travel with Harold as far as Bologna, where he would leave them to return to Constantinople. The parting – the first of many they were to experience – upset them both. Harold's diary reads: 'A dreadful day. Say goodbye at early morning.'[21] Vita recovered more quickly because she had Rosamund and, as she later wrote, 'I was never so much in love with Rosamund as during those weeks in Italy and the months that followed.... We motored all over Italy, and I think it was our happiest time.'[22] In addition, Viscount Lascelles arrived in Florence the day after Vita and Rosamund. Vita did not treat him kindly. She nicknamed him 'Misère' and, in letters to her father, ridicules his appearance at a fancy dress ball which they all attended at the Villa Medici in Fiesole. At the same time, she appreciated his extravagance in the shops.[23] Harold travelled on to Venice where he picked up the Orient Express, returning to Constantinople and an entirely different world.

The Balkans were on the edge of chaos. The treaty ending the Italo-Turkish war was signed at Ouchy in Switzerland on 15 October, just after Harold's return to the Embassy,[24] but the war proved disastrous for both parties. The Turks had been forced to sue for peace and obliged to surrender Tripolitania and Cyrenaica. The Italians had spent so much more than originally anticipated that the government found itself in financial difficulties; they also found themselves facing persistent resistance among their new North African subjects which involved more costly military excursions and was not finally suppressed until 1931. As far as Turkey was concerned, it was not just the terms of the treaty which caused problems. Her military and institutional weaknesses had been exposed as never before. The hungry, young nations of the Balkans saw their opportunity. Bulgaria, Greece, Serbia and Montenegro formed a loose grouping known as the Balkan League, issued an ultimatum which they knew the Turkish Government could not possibly accept and, on 17 October 1912, declared war.[25] That same day, Harold watched the Sultan make his weekly visit to the Hamidiye Mosque, the *selamlik* ceremony he had seen with his father twenty years previously. On this occasion however, the Sultan travelled by water

> enthroned under a canopy in the stern of the State caique, 100 feet long and painted white and gold ... manned by twenty-six picked rowers. Salutes were fired ... as the Sultan passed up the Golden Horn to the Sweet Waters. There he drank tea ... while the famous Ertogrul band played sentimental airs, and the diplomatic corps strolled through the flowery meadows.[26]

The war marked the end of an era and the end of Turkey's pretensions to be a European power. Three Bulgarian armies swept down from the north towards Constantinople. The Turkish army consisted of 185,000 men and 750 guns but it just collapsed. By 1 November, there were rumours in

Constantinople that the Bulgarians were approaching the city. By 3 November, they had reached the Catalca line, earthworks and fortifications 22 miles (35 kilometres) to the west. By 15 November, they controlled all of Thrace with the exception of Adrianople (Edirne) and were ready to begin their assault on Constantinople itself. Elsewhere, the Serbians drove towards the Adriatic coast and, together with the Montenegrins, moved against Turkish forces in Macedonia. Greek forces entered Salonica and immediately began turning mosques back into the churches they had been before the Ottoman conquest. Albania declared independence. 'Provinces which had been Ottoman for five centuries were lost in five weeks.'[27]

The whole of Europe was alarmed. Sir Gerald Lowther and his staff in the Embassy were in the diplomatic front line and working under constant pressure. Telegrams and despatches flew back and forward between Constantinople and London, reporting on the situation and trying to make sense of Turkish policy. Harold's letters and diaries say little about his own role in the crisis. Later, he would develop a reputation for responding well to pressure, but during this period he apparently awarded a CMG to the wrong Consul and there was an incident when four important despatches, typed by a volunteer British resident and addressed to the Marquess of Crewe, Secretary of State for India, were returned because they began with the salutation 'My Dorl'.[28] Presumably, they should have been checked by somebody. Certainly, Harold learnt a lot about the complexities of Balkan politics and geography which would serve him well later on. By the time of the Paris Peace Conference in 1919, he was regarded as an expert on the region and his advice was sought by everyone from the Prime Minister downwards.

Pressures were mounting outside the Embassy as well. The advance of the Bulgarian armies was preceded by a tidal wave of refugees, on foot or driving ox-carts, seeking safety within the city walls. Sultanahmed, the area around the Blue Mosque, was turned into a refugee camp. Cholera broke out within days and the sick were taken into Aya Sofia for treatment. Huge numbers of wounded Turkish soldiers needed help and both the Fatih Mosque and the German Embassy were turned into hospitals. Lady Lowther worked alongside other diplomatic wives to coordinate Red Cross aid.

As soon as it looked as if Bulgarian armies might reach the city, the foreign powers decided to send warships to Constantinople to protect their subjects. The light cruiser HMS *Weymouth*, detached from the Mediterranean fleet, was the first to arrive – an arrival dramatised in Harold's 1921 novel, *Sweet Waters*.

> The sound of a gun crashed suddenly against the windows. And then another. Lukacs put a trembling cup upon the table.
>
> Tenterden's voice broke in upon the silence: 'There is no need,' he said, 'to be alarmed. It is a British cruiser. She is saluting the Turkish flag.'[29]

HMS *Weymouth* was followed on 11 November by the armoured cruiser HMS *Hampshire* and by 14 November there were fourteen foreign warships moored in the Bosphorus. On 17 November, the Bulgarian forces began their assault on the Catalca lines. In *Sweet Waters*, Harold describes 'a strange, muffled thudding' and the way in which 'large windows shook and trembled at the sound of the guns.'[30] On 18 November, in a joint military operation involving countries which would be at war in less than two years, 2,700 foreign sailors and marines deployed in the Pera district, north of the Golden Horn where most of the embassies were located and where the majority of the foreign community lived. But that proved to be the day when the crisis broke. The Bulgarians failed to carry Catalca and although hostilities continued in a desultory fashion for another two weeks, an armistice was concluded on 3 December, leading to a conference of the European powers the following week. 'Peace negotiations decided on,' wrote Harold. 'How dull!'[31]

On the day that the windows shook in Pera and the Bulgarians stormed the Ottoman defences at Catalca, Vita wrote in her diary: 'I cannot, I cannot leave everything for him – at least I don't think I can.'[32] But Harold had no idea of her reservations, and on Christmas Day she received a letter suggesting that they should announce the wedding when he returned on leave in April and marry in September. In the event, Harold did not return until June. Those six months were a difficult period. He was quite clear what he wanted, but Vita was elusive and changeable, swayed by every new experience and new emotion.

On 14 January 1913, Harold wrote to Vita about the possibility that he might be posted to Vienna if his father was appointed Ambassador there. He knew she would not like it because of its snobbishness, but he made the best of it. The point was, however, 'that we've jolly well got to go.'[33] Vita had celebrated New Year acting the part of a Persian Caliph in the Great Hall at Knole with Rosamund, Violet Keppel and her father in attendance and in front an audience of peers and Cabinet ministers. Of course, diplomacy would be boring. Like Lady Sackville, she could never comprehend his – or anyone else's – sense of duty. 'But I love you, little Harold, so what are we to do about it?'[34] It was at best a two-edged reply. Then there was a period when she did not write at all. Harold was upset and wrote an emotional appeal. Her response was logical – 'It is this long delay and separation which upsets our apple cart.... I do see it is worse for you, much worse'[35] – but not particularly warm or reassuring.

At the end of March, Vita went to Spain. She accompanied Mrs Mary Hunter, sister of the composer, Ethyl Smyth, who was to surface at intervals during Harold's career. Vita was full of romantic illusions. Spain was the land of her grandmother, Pepita, and Pepita – whom she knew only through her mother's partial and almost certainly exaggerated descriptions – was the embodiment of free, bohemian, liberated womanhood. Mary Hunter, if not liberated, was at least outrageous and her behaviour also encouraged Vita to see Spain as a land of freedom. She saw Pastora Imperio, one of the great flamenco dancers; she saw gypsies singing and dancing and then shared a meal with them; she saw Juan Belmonte, the greatest matador of his day. It was tourism, of course – though she scorned tourists in search of 'local colour' – but Vita often mistook transient elations and emotions for permanent states of mind. She wrote to Harold that she was 'a different being' who could '*never* go back to that humdrum existence.'[36]

Harold's existence was anything but humdrum. In Constantinople, there had been a revolution. Returning from Tripoli where he had been fighting the Italians, the Young Turk leader Enver Pasha was appalled at the weakness of the government which, at the London Conference, seemed ready to cede Adrianople, Turkey's second city, to the Bulgarians, even though it was still in Turkish hands. He led an attack on the Sublime Porte, shot the Minister of War and forced the resignation of the Grand Vizier. Harold saw him the following day and described him as looking 'cocky'.[37]

Turkey tore up the ceasefire and fighting resumed. Harold went to the front on at least two occasions. He visited a field hospital, 'dressed up as a doctor with a red crescent and a fez.' He saw the filthy conditions in which the wounded were treated, men who 'sobbed when they were moved, and when their coats were taken off they screamed.'[38] He saw terrified Turkish officers who had run away from the fighting. He helped the wounded onto a steam launch which dodged Bulgarian spotlights and took them back to Constantinople: 'I found a red crescent officer and handed the wounded over to him. Then I jumped into a cab.'[39] This is much more risky and adventurous behaviour than one usually associates with Harold, but they were not the kind of risks or adventures to appeal to Vita – 'sometimes I think you are really quite happy there with your ... wars, and I am not by any means all-important.'[40]

Vita returned from Spain via Italy, where she stayed with Violet Keppel and her mother at Ravello. It was the beginning of the end of her affair with Rosamund and a first indication of her future involvement with Violet. Back at home, she fell into an anticlimactic depression. At first she wanted to marry Harold as soon as possible in order to get it over with. Then she swung in the opposite direction. She sent Harold a letter which has not survived, apparently calling off the engagement. Harold was not naturally assertive in personal relations. This is what Vita means in her 1920 narrative, which forms the basis of *Portrait of a Marriage*, when she says: 'Some men seem born to be lovers, others to be husbands; he belongs to the latter category.'[41] However, when Harold did assert himself, she jumped. Or, as Victoria Glendinning puts it: 'on the occasions when Harold took positive action, [she] responded almost gratefully, as if that was what she had been waiting for.'[42]

On this occasion, he sent a telegram – in French, so the clerks and delivery boys at Sevenoaks Post Office would not understand – asking for a yes or no answer. Was he to take her letter seriously? 'No,' she replied, 'Don't believe a word of it.'[43] The telegram was followed by an impassioned letter, a cry from the heart of unusual intensity – 'I feel I should kill you.... And Vita, I was coming back so soon – only six weeks – and I had planned it all out so. Oh Vita really really I get so angry.'[44] And that was it. Vita responded – 'something snapped, and I loved Harold from that day on; I think his energy in sending me a telegram impressed me.'[45] Assertiveness had worked: the marriage was on.

Harold left Constantinople just in time, taking a boat to Marseilles. While he was at sea, war again exploded in the Balkans. It was less than two months since the Treaty of London had been signed, but the victors had already fallen out amongst themselves. Bulgaria suddenly attacked Greece and Serbia. Romania also joined in, attacking Bulgaria from the north. Enver Pasha saw his opportunity and, with Bulgarian forces occupied elsewhere, the Turkish army went on the offensive, recapturing large swathes of the territory it had just lost. This time, Bulgaria sued for peace and the war was formally ended by the Treaty of Bucharest in October 1913.

None of this was important enough to recall Third Secretary Nicolson from his leave. Harold landed at Marseilles and moved on to Avignon where he read in the English papers that the court case brought by the Scott family against Lady Sackville, disputing Seery's will, had started the previous week. He hurried to London, arriving on 3 July, in time to support the family and to be in court when Vita was called to give her evidence. It was a difficult time for the Sackvilles. Naturally enough, Lord Sackville found the whole business humiliating. Lady Sackville was magnificent in court, but suffered intense emotional reactions afterwards. When the *Daily Sketch* noticed Harold's presence in court and forecast that an engagement would be announced soon, she reacted furiously, complaining publicly that the announcement was 'unauthorised'.[46] Then, on 7 July, the court found in her favour: Seery's generous bequests were not the result of 'undue influence'. She was acquitted; she was vindicated; she was rich; and all objections to the marriage suddenly evaporated.

12   Marriage

The engagement was announced on 5 August 1913 and the wedding fixed for 1 October. Lady Sackville gave Vita an allowance of £2,500 a year and went on a spending spree. She took Harold and Vita in her Rolls-Royce to stay with her friend Mrs Heneage at Coker Court, a beautiful fifteenth-century manor house in the village of East Coker near Yeovil, which they were to borrow for the beginning of their honeymoon. On the journey there and back, Lady Sackville bought them furniture. Back in London, she helped them choose a ring and a wedding dress and showered presents on Vita.

There was a strange interlude towards the end of August. Lady Sackville had a new admirer, William Waldorf Astor. He invited her to holiday with him at Interlaken in Switzerland. She accepted on condition that she might bring Harold and Vita with her. It was not quite clear whose morals were being protected by whom – 'The two pairs of chaperones left each other discreetly alone all day and reunited for dinner before withdrawing to their four strictly separated bedrooms.'[1] Harold and Vita were happy together, but still more friends than lovers. After ten days, he had to return, first to Buxton in Derbyshire where he stayed with his parents and then to London and the Foreign Office. Vita wrote that 'the whole place is littered with coffee cups'[2] – another piece of Sackville slang, meaning things that reminded her that Harold had been there.

Vita and Lady Sackville returned via Paris. Again, Lady Sackville behaved with lavish generosity, buying Vita an elaborate trousseau and then presenting her with a magnificent string of emeralds and diamonds. Was this deliberate on the part of Lady Sackville? Nothing could have done more to emphasise Harold's – or the Nicolsons' – financial position relative to the Sackvilles. Was this her way of indicating that Vita would be the dominant partner in her marriage to Harold, as she herself had been in her marriage to Lionel? Or, with her own marriage breaking down, was she simply seeking to bind her daughter closer to her? In that, she certainly succeeded. Vita's affair with Rosamund had melted away. Now, she was swept up in admiration for her mother. Lady Sackville's magnificent performance in court, her suffering, her vindication, and now this huge, theatrical display of generosity was the kind of romantic drama that Vita understood. She loved her father – and hated the rift that was daily growing between her parents – but it was with her mother that she identified. Harold knew something was wrong – 'I feel you do not care nearly as much for me. There are heaps of signs that you don't.'[3] All he could do was to wait.

Why was Vita getting married at all? She had no real idea what she wanted. Her emotions swept her first one way and then the other. Why did she accept Harold? Why did she go through with it? Harold certainly offered her a way out from the pressures and expectations of London society, from the attentions of suitors whom she did not necessarily care for, and from her own indecision. Harold, at least, knew what he wanted. He had waited. He had not sought to pressure her. True, he had not told her about his homosexual affairs, but then she had not told him about her relationship with Rosamund Grosvenor. In sexual matters, although Harold was the more experienced, they both seem to have been remarkably naïve. Even though she was not able to analyse it until later, Vita already felt the division between physical passion and companionship which was to characterise their relationship. As Nigel Nicolson puts it: 'Vita was always in love. I do not know of any moment when she was not longing to see or hear from the only person who could satisfy that longing.'[4] Harold was that person for only a brief period, the first few years of their marriage, but he was always her companion. Perhaps, even at this early stage, Vita sensed that he would accept her and love her without challenging her essential nature. Whichever way she looked, Harold seemed the answer – 'Harold was like a sunny harbour to me.'[5]

The marriage of the Hon. Victoria Mary Sackville-West to Mr Harold George Nicolson took place in the chapel at Knole on 1 October 1913. It was a grand affair and the press were interested – Vita's social position and her recent appearance in court meant that 'Kidlet' (one of Seery's nicknames for her) was news. The guest list was long and distinguished, though only twenty-six family members could fit into the chapel, which was decorated with white flowers from Knole's extensive greenhouses. The Bishop of Rochester presided. The bride wore cloth of gold and a veil of gold Irish lace which her mother had worn at the coronation of the Tsar. Lord Sackville gave his daughter away. By Harold's side at the altar stood his eldest brother,

Freddy, as best man, wearing the full dress uniform of the Fifteenth Hussars.

The event was not without its tensions. The bride had cried for an hour the night before 'at the prospect of leaving Knole and giving up my liberty.'[6] Rosamund underwent tortures of jealousy as she counted the wedding presents and acted as one of the bridesmaids – the other was Harold's sister, Gwen. Violet Keppel did not attend but sent a sarcastic letter of congratulation. Olive Rubens, Lord Sackville's mistress, sang an aria from Gounod, while her husband played the organ. Although no ripple appeared on the surface, Harold was aware of an undercurrent of feeling – the Sackvilles looking down on the Nicolsons because they were unsmart and not active in London society. Lady Sackville herself did not attend. She was, by her own account, stricken with period pains and confined to bed. Perhaps she could not bear to see her daughter married; perhaps she could not bear not to be the centre of attention. One can only speculate.

And in the middle of all this was Harold. He left no record of his thoughts or reactions on his wedding day. James Lees-Milne offers the best assessment: Harold probably enjoyed it 'because he enjoyed most things. Besides, he felt that he had won through.'[7]

After the reception, a huge affair with four duchesses and the band of the West Kent Yeomanry, Harold and Vita escaped by train, first up to London and then on to East Coker and Coker Court. On the train, they drank champagne from a thermos flask. It was nine o'clock by the time they arrived. They ate dinner and Harold, presumably nervous, sat on talking about his admiration for Lord Dufferin for so long that Vita had to remind him that he had a wife.

The honeymoon lasted a month. They spent three days at Coker Court. Returning to London, they were obliged to spend the night in separate houses – Harold with his parents in Cadogan Gardens, Vita at the Sackville's house in Hill Street. 'A regrettable arrangement,' was Harold's comment.[8] The next day they crossed the Channel and headed south, via Paris and Milan, to Florence. They visited the Uffizi and the Duomo. Harold attempted, without any great success, to paint watercolours. They travelled the countryside, visiting – among other places – Volterra where, in the way of newly-weds, they fantasised about buying a castle called Rocca Silliana, supposedly built by Sulla around 100 BC during the First Civil War against Marius. It was a dream that appealed to Harold's classical education and Vita's romantic spirit. They were happy, but Vita nursed a secret guilt. The cottage where they were staying was the one where she had stayed with Rosamund when their affair was at its height eighteen months previously.

After ten days in Florence, they travelled by train to Brindisi where they were joined by Harold's valet, Wilfred Booth, Vita's maid, Emily, and their heavy baggage. They took ship for Alexandria. Lady Sackville, in her heavy-handed manner, had arranged for them to spend ten days as guests of Lord Kitchener in Cairo.

Kitchener, in 1913, was sixty-three and a legendary figure. He had served throughout the Levant and the Middle East. He had avenged the death of General Gordon at the Battle of Omdurman in 1898. He had been brutal but successful in the Second Boer War. He had been Commander-in-Chief in India where he clashed with Lord Curzon and engineered Curzon's resignation and fall from grace. Now, he was British Agent in Egypt and Consul General in Egypt and the Anglo-Egyptian Sudan. Egypt was formally part of the Ottoman Empire, ruled by a Khedive appointed by the Sultan in Constantinople, but this, as all the world knew, was a polite fiction. Kitchener ruled Egypt and the Sudan as a representative of the British Government. Lady Sackville certainly exerted her influence to obtain an invitation for the newly-weds in a way that Sir Arthur Nicolson would never have done, but it must be doubtful whether Kitchener would have agreed if the groom had not been the son of the Head of the Foreign Office.

Harold left no record of his impressions of Egypt or of Kitchener. Vita's account, given in her book *Passenger to Tehran*, makes it clear that the visit did not begin well. Dinner on the evening of their arrival was formal in the extreme. Kitchener was pompous about Egyptian art – 'I can't ... think much of a people who drew cats the same for four thousand years' – and then outraged when Vita's mongrel, Mikki, was found trotting around the Residence. Things improved the next day, however, when Kitchener took them to the zoo 'as pleased as a child with the baby elephant which had been taught to salute him with its trunk. The ice was broken.'[9] They did the tourist things – the pyramids, Luxor, Karnak – and they went sailing on the Nile. Vita was particularly impressed by the sight of Harold in action, talking regional politics with Kitchener.

By this time, they were both eager to reach Constantinople. The journey, via Piraeus, left them 'bored and impatient.'[10] When they arrived, on 3 November, they were met by Harold's colleagues – including Gerry Wellesley, Vita's Uncle Bertie (an inspector in the Ottoman Public Debt Office) and a number of Ottoman officials, described by Vita as 'people in beautiful clothes who kissed Harold's hands.' Harold, again, left no record of the occasion, but Vita was 'impressed how popular he was with everyone ... [and] astonished at his constant sweetness.'[11]

They quickly found somewhere to live. Harold called it their 'little blue house'[12] but it was, in fact, a large, wooden villa in the Turkish style in the Cihangir district of Beyoğlu, about a mile from the Embassy. The view was stunning, from Aya Sofia and the Topkapi Palace on Seraglio Point across the entrance to the Bosphorus to Scutari and the Asian shore. The garden at the back of the house, which fell away steeply towards the Bosphorus, was south-facing and caught the sun for most of the day. This was where they conducted their first experiments in creating a garden, a series of terraces dropping away down the hillside. As a garden, it had no time to mature for they lived in the house for less than eight months, but it was the beginning of a shared interest that was eventually to lead to Sissinghurst.

Harold was only a Third Secretary, but with his salary and Vita's generous allowance, they lived in some style. The house was large – they had a bedroom and a sitting room each, plus guest bedrooms, a dining room, drawing room, smoking room and staff quarters. They employed a total of seven staff, including Wilfred, Emily, 'a beautiful Montenegrin ... footman, and a chef like a Greek god'[13] as well as a twelve-year-old Negro boy. Harold worked at the Embassy. Vita kept house, gardened and – something she never did again – took part in the round of visits, teas, receptions and dinners which were expected of a diplomat's wife. When they were together, they would go sailing, decorate the house, or go shopping in the bazaars. Vita liked Constantinople more than she had expected. She liked the house; she liked Harold's friends; and she was very much in love with Harold. It was diplomacy she hated; and she resented the hold it had on him. Later, when they were back in England, he recalled how, when he came home late from the Embassy, he would be 'soundly snubbed.' Vita would 'go on writing ... refusing to turn round.'[14]

Harold appears to have been busy at work. While he had been away, Sir Gerald Lowther had left and Sir Louis Mallet had taken over as Ambassador. Mallet was an experienced diplomat, trusted by the Foreign Secretary, Sir Edward Grey, and much admired by Sir Arthur Nicolson. Unfortunately, like his predecessor, he was new to the region and did not speak Turkish. This put him at a disadvantage, especially compared with his German colleague, at a time when fall-out from the Balkan Wars was beginning to spread to Europe as a whole. Adrianople had been recovered, but Turkey was still weak, disorganised and at risk from its predatory neighbours. The government, beset by the Ambassadors of the European powers clamouring for influence, asked for British assistance in reorganising the navy, French assistance with the police force and, unfortunately, German assistance with the army. On 14 December 1913, General Otto Liman von Sanders arrived in Constantinople with sixty German officers. He was quartered in the War Ministry and given command of the Turkish First Army Corps. This was more than the Russians could accept. They protested strongly. The French joined them. Sir Louis, too, protested, though he was instructed to keep the British protest within bounds, so that the Turks did not take offence and throw themselves completely into the arms of the Germans. In the event, the Turkish Government crumbled under pressure and von Sanders became Inspector-General of the Turkish army rather than an actual commander. Nonetheless, he did a great deal to modernise the Turkish army in a short time; and he impressed Enver Pasha, who, spurred to action by the evident weakness of the government, effectively appointed himself War Minister and negotiated the secret agreements which were to bring Turkey into the First World War on the side of Germany and Austro-Hungary. Tensions within the diplomatic community continued to rise. Diplomatic colleagues who had co-operated so closely less than a year before when the city was threatened by the Bulgarians, now regarded each other with suspicion, uncertain whether they should accept each other's invitations.

The week before Christmas, Dr Maclean of the English Hospital confirmed that Vita was pregnant. She was 'pleased, but Harold was most pleased.'[15] In his usual extrovert way, he wanted to tell everyone. Vita, always a more private person, insisted the news be kept to themselves and their parents. She even tore up a letter which he wrote to Lady Sackville. The letter he wrote to his own parents is more circumspect – 'Vita says I may tell you of our great secret and you will guess what it is.'[16] Here, as elsewhere, one senses a division between them. For Harold, reality existed in relation to the outside world, whereas for Vita life took place on some kind of inner plane, to which she could control access. But such moments were few. On the whole, they seem to have been very happy.

Social life carried on as before. Gerry Wellesley had broken off his engagement to Violet Keppel and now had a new fiancée, Dorothy Ashton, known as 'Dottie', who came out to visit. Lord Sackville, together with Olive and Walter Rubens, visited in April 1914, with Rosamund arriving a few days later. Olive Rubens reported that Harold and Vita adored each other and were 'radiantly happy.'[17]

The idyll continued when they left Constantinople on leave in June 1914, so that Vita could be at home for the birth, due at the beginning of August. As Vita wrote, 'the correct and adoring young wife of the brilliant young diplomat came back to England in June. I remember a divine voyage by sea from Constantinople to Marseilles, through the Aegean, a second honeymoon.'[18] If there is an ironic tone to that first sentence, it is because the quotation is taken from Vita's 1920 narrative, written after the climax of her affair with Violet and during a period when she felt differently about herself. At the time, she was genuinely happy and Harold's letters to his parents convey the same impression.

They met Lady Sackville in Paris and stayed, at her expense, in the luxurious Hotel Edouard VII in avenue de l'Opéra. Harold had gently discouraged his mother-in-law from visiting Constantinople, relaying messages through Lord Sackville that Vita was 'irritable because of her state.'[19] This may have been true, but if he was anticipating trouble from Lady Sackville, he was right. The first signs appeared in Paris, where she complained of feeling excluded and unwanted because Harold and Vita were 'so wrapped up in each other and so happy.'[20]

They arrived at Knole and Harold went off for three days' sailing on Lord Sackville's yacht, *Sumerun*. He wrote almost every day to 'my own darling wife.' Vita missed him. She grew nervous and wrote him a letter in case she should die in childbirth. Again, for all her later barbed comments about the early years of her marriage and about being 'thoroughly tamed,'[21] there is no doubt about their mutual happiness at the time.

> We shall have had nearly a year of absolutely unmarred perfect happiness together.... There hasn't been a single cloud the whole time, and at least you will never have the torment of feeling that we might have made more of each other because that would not have been possible.[22]

13 War

On the afternoon of Sunday, 28 June 1914, the Foreign Office received a telegram from Mr Jones, the Vice Consul in Sarajevo:

> According to news received here Heir Apparent and consort assassinated by means of an explosive nature.

The Head of the Foreign Office was not an admirer of Archduke Franz Ferdinand. 'I met the Austrian Heir Apparent at Windsor,' he had written to his youngest son the previous November. 'A sly and stupid man.'[1] His initial assessment was that 'the tragedy which has recently occurred at Sarajevo will, I hope, not lead to further complications.'[2] His hope was not fulfilled.

Harold Nicolson

At the time, Harold Nicolson left no record of his reactions to the coming of the First World War. In the Introduction to *Lord Carnock*, written some fifteen years later, there is a passage where he attempts to distinguish between the 'causes' of the war, which he sees emerging from four hundred years of history (1500–1900), and the 'origins', which he confines to period immediately prior to the war (1900–1914). In terms of the 'causes', he blames England for the long 'predatory period' when it built up vast possessions across the globe and for then failing to realise that a 'young and hungry' Germany would want to do the same. In terms of the 'origins', he finds Germany culpable – though less so than Austria or Russia. It is a curiously unsatisfactory piece of writing which does not convince. One can understand that, having been personally involved in the Peace Conference in Paris, and having witnessed the signing of the Versailles Treaty which included 'that ignorant and disgraceful paragraph', the War Guilt Clause, Harold would wish to distance himself from the simplistic notion that Germany alone was to blame for the war. On the other hand, the division between causes and origins is too broad and too abstract, and the notion that nations necessarily follow the same process as they move towards maturity is itself simplistic. The whole argument is forced. It smacks of the political correctness of another age.

Nor does the argument fit with Harold's otherwise logical exposition of the position that his father had arrived at in 1914; a position which, in all probability – and the language in the second paragraph supports the assumption – reflected his own views at the time.

> He thought that German sea power was dangerous because it was backed by preponderating military power on land. He thought that, relying on the latter, she would 'dominate the Continent' ... that Germany by threatening France or Russia with her army could force those countries into neutrality, if not into an alliance. That the defection or subjugation of France and Russia would mean not only that our naval forces in the Mediterranean and elsewhere would be inadequate, but that Russia would be in a position to menace us in Central Asia.... The nightmare which haunted Nicolson was a continental coalition which would ... place England in a position where she would either have to face a disastrous war or capitulate to German dictation.
>
> I do not think that, given the circumstances, any British public servant could have thought, and therefore advised, any differently. It was quite obvious that Germany believed in force, and that only by force could she be restrained. I am honestly unable to conceive how a man,

placed in Nicolson's position, could have risked any other diagnosis....
Even today ... we cannot say for certain that his diagnosis was wrong.[3]

For nearly a month following the assassination of Franz Ferdinand, it looked as if Sir Arthur's hope might be realised. International reaction was slow. It was not until 23 July that Austria delivered its ultimatum to Serbia. Only then did events begin to accelerate. Sir Edward Grey described the ultimatum as 'the most formidable document that has ever been addressed from one state to another.'[4] He was under no illusion that 'we are within measurable, or imaginable, distance of real Armageddon,' but he still hoped that Britain might be able to avoid getting involved.[5] The British Government machine swung into action. All Foreign Office leave was cancelled. Harold was called up to London and given a desk in the department dealing with Eastern Europe. Grey attempted to call a conference of the European powers. He woke King George V in the middle of the night and got him to send a personal message to Tsar Nicholas II. It was all to no avail. Germany mobilised. On 1 August, Germany declared war on Russia. German troops moved into Luxembourg and took up position on the French border.

How much did Harold see or know of this process? He must have heard something from his father. In *Lord Carnock*, he describes the tension between Sir Arthur and Sir Edward Grey. Grey desperately hoped to avoid Britain becoming involved in a European war. So did Sir Arthur, but not at the expense of national honour. There was no treaty of alliance with France, merely an Entente and subsequent 'conversations' on military and naval matters. Sir Arthur believed that we were honour-bound to support France. And Harold, had his opinion been asked, would probably have said the same, but he was merely a junior clerk.

The German Government sent an ultimatum to the Belgian Government demanding free passage for its troops so they could attack France. Belgium resisted and King Albert appealed to Britain for help. There was a treaty with Belgium. On 3 August, Sir Edward Grey rose in the House of Commons and gave one of the greatest of all parliamentary speeches. It was a triumph, but, for Grey, it represented failure. He returned to his office where Sir Arthur 'congratulated him on the success of his speech. Sir Edward did not answer.... He brought his fists down with a crash upon the table. "I hate war," he groaned. "I hate war."'[6] The British Government sent an ultimatum to Germany to withdraw its forces by midnight Berlin time on 4 August.

That evening, for a brief moment, Harold suddenly took centre stage in world events for the simple reason that he was the most junior member of staff available in the Foreign Office at the time. The incident has been related elsewhere, but it deserves repetition.

The German Government was not expected to reply to the ultimatum. Consequently, Grey had drafted a brief letter confirming that 'His Majesty's Government consider that a state of war exists between the two countries as from today 11 o'clock p.m.' for delivery to Prince Lichnowsky, the German Ambassador.[7] With the letter were included passports for Lichnowsky's family and household, a diplomatic signal that he was expected to leave the country forthwith. The Foreign Office was working under pressure, preparing telegrams containing the same message for despatch, when the moment came, to Colonial and Dominion Governments, Embassies, Legations and Consulates around the world. A Private Secretary from 10 Downing Street – James Lees-Milne's account emphasises the fact that he was 'hatless', as if only great urgency could excuse such sartorial dereliction[8] – brought news that Germany had declared war on Britain. The text of the message to Prince Lichnowsky would have to be changed to read 'the German Empire having declared war upon Great Britain.' It was duly altered and delivered personally to the Ambassador by the hand of the Assistant Head of Eastern Department. Only then came further news that Germany had not declared war. An intercepted wireless message to German shipping had been misinterpreted. The original text of the Lichnowsky letter had been correct after all. The Foreign Office had sent the German Ambassador an incorrect declaration of war.

Harold's task was to retrieve the incorrect version and substitute the correct one. The German Embassy was in Carlton House Terrace, only a short walk away. Harold crossed Horse Guards Parade and the Mall, which was crowded with people caught up in the tension and the excitement, waiting to know if war would be declared. He rang the bell at the side door of the Embassy which was eventually answered. It was past eleven o'clock. The Ambassador had gone to bed with strict orders that he was not to be disturbed. Harold insisted. He had an urgent communication from the Foreign Secretary. Eventually, he was admitted and escorted to the Ambassador's bedroom where the Ambassador was 'reclining in pyjamas.' Harold explained his errand.

> Prince Lichnowsky indicated the writing table in the window. 'You will find it there,' he said. The envelope had been but half-opened and the passports protruded. It did not appear that the Ambassador had read the communication or opened the letter.... He must have guessed its signifi-

cance from the feel of the passports and have cast it on his table in despair. A receipt had to be demanded and signed. The blotting pad was brought across to the bed, and the pen dipped in the ink.... Prince Lichnowsky turned out the pink lamp beside his bed, and then feeling that he had perhaps been uncivil, he again lighted it. 'Give my best regards,' he said, 'to your father, I shall not in all probability see him before my departure.'[9]

Before turning out his own light, Harold wrote to Vita – 'Such a busy Harold. Such a mémoire-full Harold.'[10]

The next day, 5 August, Harold managed to leave the office in time to spend the night at Knole. At ten o'clock, Vita went into labour. Harold called the doctor and stood waiting in the dawn for him to arrive. The following morning, he had to return to the Foreign Office. Vita's labour continued until half past four that afternoon when she gave birth to a son.

Harold and Vita's happiness was diluted by a sudden burst of anger from Lady Sackville. First, she was angry at not being allowed to see Vita for some hours after the birth, then because Vita did not ask to see her again that evening. She left for London the following day and when she came back all she would do was abuse Harold for taking Vita away from her. There had already been disagreement over the godparents. Some months earlier, Lady Sackville had asked Lord Astor to be godfather. No one else had been consulted and, on Lord Sackville's objection, she had been obliged to withdraw the invitation. Now Harold – rather tactlessly, it has to be admitted – asked Olive Rubens to be godmother. Next, there was trouble over the child's name. Harold and Vita had intended to call the child Benedict, but Lady Sackville, following Sackville tradition, insisted on Lionel and threatened to disinherit Vita. In the end, to keep the peace, they agreed on Lionel Benedict with Rosamund, Olive Rubens and Violet Keppel as godmothers, and Baron Bildt and Kenneth Campbell (Vita's godfather) as godfathers. But after the christening there was another row because Harold and Vita were calling the child Benedict (or 'Detto', short for 'Benedetto') in daily life.

She was menopausal. Her husband was in love with Olive Rubens. Her own love affair with Baron Bildt had come to nothing. Her brother, Henry, had recently committed suicide. There were many reasons for Lady Sackville's discontent with life, but that did not make it any easier for Harold and Vita to bear. And it was Vita who bore the brunt. During the week, Harold spent the nights in London, either at the Sackville's house in Hill Street or with his parents in Cadogan Gardens. He was simply too busy to get away – which did nothing to endear the Foreign Office to Vita.

Then came another row. Lady Sackville started making accusations against Harold's father. Harold, usually the mildest of men, was always sensitive about his family in relation to the Sackvilles. He was also under pressure at work and concerned about Vita's slow recovery from Benedict's birth. This time, he exploded and was so rude to Lady Sackville that he felt obliged to apologise later. He persuaded Vita to leave Knole and stay with his parents in London. Vita agreed, but it was a short term solution. She was never at ease with Harold's parents and they both knew that she would find Cadogan Gardens cramped after Knole, so they rented a house of their own, 182 Ebury Street in Belgravia, where they lived for most of that winter, occasionally going down to Knole for weekends.

The war changed the course of Harold's career. There was no thought of his going back to Constantinople. Telegrams were sent to the Embassy and the Nicolsons' belongings were put into storage beneath a staircase in the main building – they were retrieved, intact, and sent back to England in 1919. On 1 October, he was formally transferred back to the Foreign Office and appointed to the new War Department, created by merging the Eastern and Western Departments which had previously looked after European affairs. The War Department was headed by George Clerk, later to become Lord Curzon's Private Secretary and eventually Ambassador to Paris, who reported upwards to Sir Eyre Crowe who reported to Sir Arthur Nicolson. Clerk and Harold had known each other in Constantinople and were to work closely together throughout the four years of the war. Although very different characters, they became good friends. Clerk was 'in all respects the typical old-fashioned diplomatist, tall, slender, faultlessly dressed, wearing spats, an eye glass.'[11] Harold found him 'appreciative and encouraging and stimulating. He never snubs one for being uppish.'[12] Clerk quickly recognised the quality of Harold's work and, instead of being jealous, publicly acknowledged Harold's value to the War Department and to the Foreign Office as a whole.

It seems likely that Clerk was also responsible for Harold being exempted from military service, which happened in December. Vita was, of course, delighted. Harold kept only the scrappiest of diaries during the war years so there is no direct information about his feelings. James Lees-Milne, again with the benefit of his conversations with Harold, suggests that he was unhappy when diplomatic colleagues such as Gerry Wellesley and Reggie Cooper were able to enlist, and that he was prey to the somewhat conventional sentiment of wanting to test himself, to discover whether or not he was a coward. Objectively, it is hard to fault the Foreign Office's decision. Harold was of obvious value in London and, given his lifelong lack of practical ability, would in all probability have made a poor warrior.

Domestic life settled into a routine. Harold worked at the Foreign Office, often quite late into the evening, and went home to Ebury Street. Vita would have liked him to come home earlier – she came to accept but could never understand Harold's sense of duty and obligation – but they were still extremely happy together. They dined with friends. They moved in London society. By March 1915, Vita was pregnant again. That same month, they discovered and bought Long Barn, which was to be their home until they bought Sissinghurst fifteen years later.

Long Barn is situated on the edge of the village of Weald, which gives its name to that swathe of Kent which Vita loved above all other areas and which features so powerfully in her long poem, *The Land*. Like Knole, Long Barn is built of dark, purple-red brick fired from Wealden clay, but it is older, probably dating from the fourteenth century. A local tradition has it that William Caxton was born there. The purchase price was £2,500. The house, and the land that went with it, were immensely important to Harold. Vita loved its age – and the fact that it was only a couple of miles across the fields to Knole. For Harold, Long Barn represented ownership and the land that the Nicolsons had never had. He was twenty-eight. He had never owned a house before. He had never even lived in a house owned by his parents. It was his first attempt at putting down roots. They moved in on 10 April and, almost at once, set about planning and developing the garden. Vita's creativity expressed itself in the planting. She revelled in the plants themselves, in the details of colour, shape and name which later came to inform her poetry. Harold was the planner: it was a more formal, architectural pleasure. He created, but he also controlled, stamping his ownership on the place.

The domestic idyll continued. 'We are more in love than ever,' wrote Vita that summer, 'I thank God that I have known absolute happiness.'[13] And as a footnote to their happiness, Harold's valet and Vita's maid decided to marry. Relations with Lady Sackville were restored. Her way of expressing affection was generosity: she bought them a Rolls-Royce and paid for a chauffeur. The only cloud was that Lord Sackville and his regiment, the West Kent Yeomanry, were on their way to Gallipoli.

Then tragedy struck. Harold and Vita's second child, a boy, was stillborn. One can only guess at Harold's reaction. Lady Sackville describes him as 'very dejected.' Vita was ill for a month. Her letters to Harold are questioning and desperate, but it is clear that only he could give her the support she needed – 'Oh Harold I wish you were here.... Harold I want you so badly.'[14]

They sought solace in other things, particularly developing Long Barn. There was an old barn, probably as ancient as the house itself, in the field adjoining. Its timbered structure was taken down and re-erected as an additional wing to the main house. Harold drew up most of the plans himself – it was a considerable project and part of his new enthusiasm for ownership. When he needed advice or assistance, he was able to turn to Edwin Lutyens, arguably Britain's greatest architect. Lutyens was Lady Sackville's new favourite and new companion, and, later, when the rows began again, would act as an intermediary between her and the Nicolsons.

Building work made Long Barn uninhabitable for the time being, so they lived in Ebury Street, spending Christmas and weekends at Knole and walking across the fields to inspect progress. In March, Vita was twenty-four. Harold gave her a field which ran along the boundary of Long Barn. Lady Sackville, still in generous mood – and not to be outdone by her son-in-law – bought them the adjoining farm so there would be no risk of the land being built on. She also lent them the money to buy the house in Ebury Street, which, up to that point, they had been renting. Harold's dreams of ownership and belonging were suddenly fulfilled. Eighteenth-century Ebury Street (where Mozart had lived for a few months in 1764) was 'stern and prim'; Long Barn was 'the cottage all untidy and tinkly'[15] – although the cottage in question had seven bedrooms and four bathrooms. Harold had a natural ability to move with ease between the two different worlds these homes represented.

In Sackville slang, the word *mar* originally meant young or vulnerable. It became Lord Sackville's pet name for Vita, and one which Harold adopted. At this time in their relationship, Harold and Vita began to refer to themselves as 'the mars' in the third person. It was a game they played: it drew them together after the stillborn child and emphasised their youth. Also at this time, Vita began to call Harold 'Hadji', a name coined by Sir Arthur, which in Arabic is the title given to someone who has completed the pilgrimage to Mecca. How this came to be applied to Harold one can only speculate, but the sense of Harold being on a journey or some kind of quest throughout his life is not inappropriate. Both pet names were to last the rest of their lives. By the early summer of 1916, Vita was pregnant for a third time.

There was still a war on. It occupied Harold during the day and absorbed him intellectually, but it had surprisingly little impact on the rest of his and Vita's life. There were concerns about the price of petrol, worries about Lord Sackville, and about friends and colleagues at the front, but there was no shortage of money or food, and no shortage of labour at Knole or for the work on Long Barn. Vita was not remotely interested in the war and referred to the time Harold spent at the Foreign Office as 'lessons'. One wonders how he coped: by day dealing with the political realities of a continent tearing itself apart; in the evening faced with a wife and mother-in-law who seemed to see the war largely in terms of personal inconvenience. Just occasionally, something would bring the truth home. In December 1916, Winston Churchill and his wife, Clemmie, stayed at Knole; his account of what really happened during the Dardanelles campaign the previous year brought the whole company to the verge of tears.

Harold continued to work in the War Department with George Clerk. It is difficult to reconstruct precisely what his role was. His diary is little more than a list of lunches and social engagements and he never mentions official business in his notes and letters to Vita. In the early stages of the war he was still very junior and would have had no policy input, but it is clear that from the beginning his area of expertise was considered to be Eastern Europe and the Balkans. By early 1915, it had become apparent that the war was not going to be over in a few months. The Foreign Office began a new wave of diplomatic activity preparing the ground for the collapse of the Ottoman and Austro-Hungarian Empires and the emergence of a number of new nation states across the Balkans and the Middle East. Secret agreements were reached with Russia, promising that she would be allowed control of the Turkish Straits – the Bosphorus and the Dardanelles – which gave her navy and merchant marine access to the Mediterranean, as long as British and French interests in the region were adequately protected and compensated. This was followed by the negotiations leading to the Treaty of London in April 1915, by which Italy agreed to enter the war on the side of Britain and France. The Italians drove a hard bargain – demanding not only those Italian-speaking provinces of Austria which bordered Italy (*Italia Irridenta*), but also Adalia Province on the Turkish mainland and islands of the Dodecanese. Harold seems to have had some peripheral involvement and to have shared the Foreign Office view that Italy's behaviour was outrageous.

Sir Arthur Nicolson had never been happy as Head of the Foreign Office. He had twice tried to escape back into diplomacy – as Ambassador to Vienna or to Paris – but had been thwarted by the international situation and the outbreak of war. Now, nearly sixty-seven and crippled with arthritis, he wanted nothing so much as to retire. Sir Edward Grey agreed that Lord Hardinge, returning from six years as Viceroy of India, would be a suitable replacement. The return of a Viceroy was a full-dress ceremonial occasion and Harold was asked to act as his father's official representative. At the end of April, he found himself standing on the platform at Victoria Station, flanked by a guard of honour and surrounded by hordes of top-hatted and formally-dressed officials, waiting for Lord Hardinge's train to arrive. He told Vita that he felt underdressed and insignificant.[16] On 20 June 1916, Sir Arthur retired from the Foreign Office and was elevated to the peerage as Lord Carnock. It was forty-six years since, on the eve of the Franco-Prussian war, he had returned to London to sit his Foreign Office exams. Harold appears to have benefitted from the new regime and was given more responsibility. He was asked to write a paper on the situation in the Balkans, which he submitted at the end of November 1916, and to examine ways of mobilising support for the party of the pro-British Prime Minister, Eleftherios Venizelos, in schism-ridden Greece.

The birth of Nigel Nicolson at the Ebury Street house in the early hours of 19 January 1917 allowed Harold and Vita to put memories of their still-born son behind them. This time Vita's labour was short, only four and a half hours, and there were no complications – either medical or with Lady Sackville. For the moment at least, Lady Sackville was behaving well and seemed to be taking an interest in Harold's career. When George Clerk lunched at Hill Street, she seemed delighted to hear about Harold's success and all previous tensions seemed to have been forgiven and forgotten.

Once Vita had recovered from the birth, she and Harold decided to move back to Long Barn. The house was fully habitable now; they had two children; and Vita wanted to help her mother manage Knole and the estate where the effects of conscription and rationing were now beginning to bite. Harold commuted daily when he could – but otherwise stayed with his parents at Hill Street or at his club in St James's. On those evenings when he stayed in London, he often saw Archie Clark Kerr, who had been posted back to the Foreign Office the previous December. He also saw Reggie Cooper, who had reached the rank of Colonel, and was on leave from the Western Front. He met Osbert and Sacheverell Sitwell, although they never became close friends. He spent a lot of time with Edwin Lutyens, fascinated by the great work Lutyens was planning for New Delhi. Throughout his life, however busy he was, Harold always found time for friends.

The tempo of his professional life was increasing. The change of government in December 1916 brought new personalities. Arthur Balfour was now Foreign Secretary and Lord Robert Cecil his deputy. Harold submitted advice to both of them and seems to have begun to earn respect for his political perception and his sometimes heterodox views: 'I suggest peace with Austria against everybody's views, and instead of just turning it down [Clerk] sends for me to discuss it all.'[17] At the beginning of August, Pope

Benedict XV launched a set of Peace Proposals which were despatched to the Heads of State of all the world's major powers. Benedict was genuinely horrified by what he termed 'the suicide of Europe'. Since his coronation, just a month after the outbreak of war, he had been actively promoting humanitarian relief and made numerous appeals for peace. His August 1917 proposals went further and attempted to give concrete form to his moral position. There were seven key points: a cessation of hostilities; disarmament; acceptance of international arbitration; the evacuation of occupied territories; freedom of the seas; the renunciation of indemnities; and an examination of the right to nationhood of certain ethnic groups. Harold was given a week to assess the implications for Britain and its war aims.

He claimed – mistakenly as it turned out, though perhaps understandably because it was what all the Allied Powers believed at the time – that the Pope's proposals had been inspired by contact with Germany. He dismissed the seven points as a basis for substantive negotiations: they were too vague on points which both sides would inevitably interpret in their own favour. What, for example, was meant by freedom of the seas? What exactly constituted an occupied territory? The French would claim Alsace-Lorraine was occupied territory. The Germans would say it was part of Germany. What about obligations under treaties entered into since the outbreak of war, such as Britain's agreements with Russia and Italy in 1915? It was a peace initiative from a genuinely good man, but it was essentially backward-looking and, despite three years of gruelling and destructive warfare, no one wanted a return to the *status quo* of 1914. In particular, President Woodrow Wilson, having led the United States into the war on the side of the Allies in April 1917 against considerable domestic opposition, was determined that it should lead to a positive change in the international environment. His negative response effectively torpedoed the Pope's initiative and neither Britain nor any of the other major powers bothered to respond. Harold's analysis, however, attracted praise from Lord Hardinge, Lord Robert Cecil and Eyre Crowe.

Very shortly afterwards, he was given another important task. He was seconded to work with Sir Mark Sykes on the issue of how to respond to pressures from the international Jewish community for the establishment of a Jewish homeland. From a British Government perspective, the issue was part of the problem of how to deal with the expected collapse of the Ottoman Empire. For more than half a century, British policy had been to prop up 'the sick man of Europe' as a counterweight to Russia. Now, with Turkey allied to the Central Powers, that policy had to be revised, if not reversed.

Sir Mark Sykes was only seven years older than Harold, but he had already been a soldier, an author, a politician and an honorary attaché at the Embassy in Constantinople. At the beginning of the war, Kitchener had drafted him into the War Office to advise on Middle Eastern affairs. Lloyd George, who became Prime Minister in 1916, recognised his value and appointed him as one of two political secretaries to the Cabinet. What he lacked in formal training and linguistic knowledge, he made up for in charisma and long experience of the region. Harold, who combined experience of Turkey with a good knowledge of the Balkans and a solid Foreign Office background, was an obvious foil.

The British Zionist Federation was established in 1899 to coordinate the campaign for a permanent Jewish homeland and its leading spokesman was Dr Chaim Weizmann who eventually, in 1949, became the first President of the State of Israel. Born in Russia and educated in Switzerland, Weizmann became a British citizen in 1910 and made a significant contribution to the war effort as Director of the Admiralty Laboratories. He first met Arthur Balfour as early as 1906, but it was when they met again in 1914 that Weizmann convinced him that the Jewish homeland should be in Palestine, rather than some location with which the Jews had no historical connection – Uganda had been suggested at the time. Balfour became Foreign Secretary in 1916, by which time Britain was seeking an acceptable post-war structure for the Ottoman provinces of the Middle East and trying to buy the support of interested and potentially useful parties. The Jewish lobby and the Zionist Federation became correspondingly more important, and Mark Sykes became their main line into government.

Sykes and Harold were allocated two rooms in the basement of the Foreign Office which

> had been fitted up as an air-raid shelter for the Prime Minister, who would nip across from Downing Street when the Zeppelins approached. They had been repainted in vivid suffragette colours and furnished with armchairs, tables, a sofa, and a harmonium on which, it was said, Mr Lloyd George would, when the bombs fell, play Welsh hymns.[18]

From this unlikely setting emerged the Balfour Declaration which, it is not overstating the case to say, proved one of the most important government documents of the twentieth century. The text was read to the House of Commons on 2 November 1917 and also contained in a letter to Lord Rothschild, dated the same day, for onward transmission to the British Zionist Federation:

> His Majesty's Government view with favour the establishment in Palestine of a national home for the Jewish people, and will use their best endeavours to facilitate the achievement of this object, it being clearly understood that nothing shall be done which may prejudice the civil and religious rights of existing non-Jewish communities in Palestine, or the rights and political status enjoyed by Jews in any other country.

Thirty years later, writing for *The Spectator*, Harold recalled Sykes's character and their respective roles in their brief partnership.

> Sykes was a man of abundant energy, imagination, zest and knowledge; he was not, however, a trained official. He did not possess for files and minutes that reverence which the British civil servant so easily acquires. ... [He] had a talent for scribbling caricatures and comic drawings which were accurate and quick; his first reaction to any new idea was to illustrate it rapidly in his green ink; he was apt to use official papers for this pastime.... My only function was to see that Sykes drafted his minutes and memoranda in proper form.[19]

Leaving Harold's customary self-deprecation to one side, the meaning is clear: Harold was Sykes's minder and responsible for keeping him within bounds. And when he adds 'the Balfour Declaration was not some sudden opportunist statement made at a time of difficulty; it took weeks to draft, and every word was scrutinized with the greatest thought and forethought,'[20] it strongly suggests that, while he did not himself originate the policy, he was responsible for its formal expression on paper.

By the time Harold was writing in *The Spectator*, the world had moved on. He admits that 'developments which ought to have been foreseen were not foreseen' and that, with hindsight, the Declaration would have been drafted differently. But he maintains that Britain had kept the promises made in the Declaration: 'We never promised a Jewish State. All we promised was "a" National Home "in" Palestine; and that promise was explicitly conditional on the maintenance of the rights of the Arabs.'[21] There may be an element of self-justification in this, but it is not just splitting hairs. This is the precision of language required by international law and international agreements. And it is worth recalling that in 1917, when the Balfour Declaration was published, the Jewish lobby expressed disappointment that Palestine was not designated 'the' national home for the Jews. As a writer, Harold came to enjoy a great reputation as a stylist and that reputation rests to a significant degree on the precision in the use of language which he acquired at the Foreign Office.

Harold can certainly be accused of being anti-Semitic. It was a not uncommon attitude in the first half of the twentieth century; it was part of a cultural legacy which he never seriously challenged; and yet he was consistently pro-Zionist. Taking his cue from Mark Sykes, he never saw Zionism and Arab nationalism as mutually exclusive. He saw both as movements which could help fill the vacuum necessarily created when the Ottoman Empire collapsed – and that was something he saw as profoundly desirable.

> Long residence at Constantinople had convinced me that behind his mask of indolence, the Turk conceals impulses of the most brutal savagery.... The Turks have contributed nothing whatsoever to the progress of humanity.[22]

Whatever its later history in terms of interpretation and implementation, there is no doubt that the intention behind the Balfour Declaration was sincere; that Balfour himself and others around him believed that it would contribute to solving immediate problems in the Middle East and the historical problems of the Jewish people. That it did not is one of the great tragedies of the twentieth century. Balfour certainly recognised Harold's contribution. It was shortly after his 2 November speech to the House of Commons that he introduced Harold to his brother Gerald as 'young Nicolson, my staunchest adviser.'[23]

Despite a rising reputation and praise from the highest levels of the Foreign Office hierarchy, Harold was still fretting at being kept in London. He was formally exempt from military service. If he could not enlist, perhaps he could be sent abroad somewhere. What about Rome? He arranged for Gerry Wellesley to sound out George Clerk. Clerk was appalled – 'the whole war department would collapse.' And even if he could be persuaded to let Harold go, Lord Hardinge 'would never hear of it.'[24]

Praise for one's efforts is always welcome, but there is something in Harold's reaction to the praise he received that smacks of insecurity. Whenever he received a compliment, he would tell Vita – though he knew she would not be interested – as if he wanted her to know that important people thought he was clever and useful; that Nicolsons were not, after all, inferior to Sackvilles. The higher up the Foreign Office or government hierarchy the praise originated, the more he valued it. It mattered immensely what people thought of him, and we return to the idea of the self being defined in relation to the public body. Praise from the Foreign Office hierarchy meant that Harold was accepted by the club. He belonged.

14 Revelation

Portrait of a Marriage, both as a successful book and as a BBC dramatisation, has had an immense and largely distorting impact on perceptions of Harold and Vita's marriage. The book consists of a passionate, moving and revealing narrative written by Vita about her love affair with Violet Keppel-Trefusis,[1] and a series of contributions from Nigel Nicolson which put the larger frame of their life and marriage around the turbulent emotions of Vita's story. Yet it must be remembered that Vita was writing in 1920, only a few months after the climax of her affair. Had she written it twenty-five years later, her tempestuous relationship with Violet would certainly have stood out, but it would have stood out as one among many. As it is, her narrative is factually accurate, but not always emotionally so. It tells only one side of the story and, despite her pleas for forgiveness, it is not always fair or, indeed, accurate in its assessment of the role Harold played.

Harold could never have written a narrative like Vita's. He did not take his affairs that seriously: they were exciting; they were light-hearted; and they were fun. Vita's were soul-searing passions which took over her life. Nor would his temperament have allowed him to do so. All his life, he found it extremely difficult to be open about sexual matters. By the time he reached middle age, there were a few friends with whom he could discuss his sexual preferences without fear or embarrassment, but it was a closed circle. As he grew older, letters to Vita or to those same close friends might include an allusion to his sexuality or that of people around him, but it was all very coded and oblique. And in his public writings, he generally sought to avoid the whole issue. Of course, as a good Victorian, Harold was brought up to believe that although certain things might be done, they were not to be publicly discussed, but there were practical reasons for his reticence as well. Male homosexuality was illegal. Prosecutions were rare, but public exposure was enough. Society would find its own way to punish offenders, as would the Foreign Office.

Both Harold and Vita were principally homosexual in their orientation. Once they realised and understood the fact, it helped shape their lives and their marriage. Her account was written after that realisation. Nigel Nicolson's narrative was written after their deaths when it was possible to look back on the way they made their marriage work. When Vita wrote, 'I have implied, I think, that men didn't attract me, that I didn't think of them in what is called "that way",'[2] she was speaking after the event. There is plenty of evidence that, for the first few years of their marriage, she was attracted to Harold and they were sexually compatible. In Constantinople, shortly after their marriage, Vita wrote an unpublished novel, *Marian Strangways*, and while it is dangerous to read too much into fictionalised accounts of real events, the heroine's sexual initiation is full of positive imagery and the awakening of 'primitive instincts.'[3] Vita had three children in less than three-and-a-half years, and it is clear that she still wanted Harold physically after Nigel's birth – 'Come up and peep in at my door, and if I am asleep kiss me and creep away like a little mouse; and if I am not asleep kiss me all the same, and then stay with me.... I lay [sic] and wait for you with as much thrill as though you had never told me you loved me till yesterday.'[4]

What Harold had concluded about his sexuality by the time he married, we can only guess. He may have thought that marriage would 'cure' his homosexuality. There is some evidence that his sex drive was less intense than Vita's. She apparently told her mother that Harold 'too quick and too sleepy' and that he was 'physically cold.'[5] Harold angrily took her to task:

> I've got a grievance against you – why did you tell BM the most intimate things about you and me? It's all right telling her things about yourself – (though I think that very unwise) – but it is bad luck on me to tell her things about me, which are at once repeated to Ozzie[6] and via him *urbi et orbi*.[7]

Faced with these accusations, Harold read Marie Stopes' *Married Love*, which was published in 1918, and found why 'Hadji goes to sleep and Mar doesn't. I find I am the *rule* and not the exception.'[8] But this all happened slightly later, when sex had become an issue between them. If Harold was sometimes an unsatisfactory lover, there is nothing to suggest that, for the first four years of their marriage at least, it was a major problem or that their sex life was anything but mutually satisfactory.

Was it inevitable then that Harold and Vita's homosexuality should emerge at some point? It must have been probable – even though their love was intense and sincere. As Victoria Glendinning says, 'every role that Vita played, she played thoroughly.' And, for a time, until other forces intervened, she was content to be 'conventional in her marriage ... [and] conventional in the social life they built up.'[9] She even wrote to Harold that she liked arranging his shirts. If it had been left to her to be the catalyst of change, how soon would it have come?

And was it inevitable that their homosexuality should emerge in such a sudden and disruptive manner? Again, it must have been probable, especially given Vita's – rather than Harold's – temperament, and perhaps also because the society around them was in the grip of violent change and self-doubt. Such speculations are ultimately fruitless, but they serve to emphasise that the eventual nature of their relationship was not a foregone conclusion. For four years, their married life had been extremely happy, but whatever they understood about themselves – and it does not appear to have been much – they knew very little about each other. The process of discovery was about to begin and it was Harold, not Vita, who was to be the agent of change.

It was not until the second half of 1917 that the effects of the war began seriously to affect the lifestyle of the English upper classes. In August 1916, Harold and Vita were invited to a weekend party at Cold Overton Hall in Rutland. So lavish was the hospitality that even Vita's social conscience was aroused – 'caviare, quails stuffed with *pâté de foie gras*, peaches, tuberoses and malmaisons; bath salts; Rolls-Royces at the station. (I seem to have heard something in London about a war?).'[10] A year later, things were very different. At the beginning of 1917, the Germans resumed unrestricted submarine warfare, a decision which brought the United States into the war on the side of the Allies, but also resulted in the loss of over six million tons of shipping that year. Britain was hard hit. More and more men were called up, with consequent labour shortages. Food rationing meant that, at Knole, there were times when the only meat available was venison from the deer in the park. The war hit home in other ways, too. On 2 October, Harold and Vita, returning home, were unable to reach the house in Ebury Street because a bomb had fallen close by. They decamped to Hill Street where they celebrated the appearance of Vita's first commercially-published work, *Poems of West and East*.

And yet still, somehow, the rich managed to retain something resembling their pre-war social life. Towards the end of October 1917, Harold and Vita were invited to Knebworth House, home of the Lytton family. Victor, the second Earl of Lytton, was Parliamentary Under-Secretary at the Admiralty. His sister, Emily, had married Edwin Lutyens and Lutyens had subsequently remodelled much of the interior of the house and parts of the formal gardens. Among the guests, the arts were represented by John Lavery, the painter; his beautiful American wife, Hazel; and Osbert Sitwell, just beginning his literary career. Politics were represented by Sir Louis Mallet, Harold's former Ambassador from Constantinople, and Sir Horace Rumbold under whom Harold was to serve in Berlin from 1928 to 1929. Edward Marsh spanned the two – at the time, he was Private Secretary to Winston Churchill, then Minister of Munitions, although he is better known today as a patron of poets such as Rupert Brooke and John Betjeman.

At some stage during the Knebworth weekend, Harold contracted a venereal infection from another man. It would, of course, be fascinating to know from whom. It was probably another of the guests, for in the years which followed Harold expressed quite particular views on sex and class.

> He was in a way mystified by the partiality of the younger generation for what he called the lower orders. Possibly because of his fairly starchy Victorian upbringing he did not relish their company though he undoubtedly had commerce with them in Berlin. Even these encounters made him uneasy, and their recollection was distasteful to him.... He actually admitted to Raymond Mortimer that 'the idea of a gentleman of birth and education sleeping with a guardsman is repugnant to me.'[11]

But this is not conclusive. Later distaste for 'the lower orders' could easily derive from an infection caught in the servants' hall.

Harold's doctor insisted that he tell Vita as there was a possibility that he had passed it on to her and that she, too, might need treatment. It all depended on the results of medical tests. On 6 November, therefore, Harold was forced to tell Vita what had happened, which necessarily involved confessing to his homosexual affairs. We cannot know whether this was his first homosexual fling since their marriage or whether there had been previous incidents: Victoria Glendinning identifies a teasing tone in his letters to Vita when he mentions male friends such as Archie Clark Kerr.[12] It scarcely matters. What is clear is that Vita had absolutely no idea of his homosexual leanings. She was shocked and angry – both by his confession and by the fact that she might be at risk from the infection.

Vita took herself off to stay with a woman friend in Oxford. Harold wrote to her three times a day. They are panicky, disjointed letters: a mixture of embarrassment, guilt, fears for their health, attempts to elicit sympathy, attempts to offer reassurance. But the thing he fears most is her reaction.

> I am so flight[13] about it. It will be such an awful business if the report is not satisfactory. I simply *dread* it. Darling if you hated me today, how much will you hate me if [the infection] really does come?... Darling I shall be so wretched about it if it goes wrong. I shall know what you suffer and it will be my fault, my fault: – and that eats into my brain like some burning acid.... Dear one – let's face it together and bravely.'[14]

Even if things go right, – and there is nothing in our fears, I have exposed you to things you hate and loathe and of course you cannot help rather hating me for it.... Darling if the worst comes to the worst I fear we will have a bloody time ahead. You will have to have treatment – and it may last a fortnight.[15]

Harold's enforced confession marked the beginning of a change in their relationship, though it was not immediately apparent, even to them. The relationship itself would be tested and would survive, but the image they had built up for themselves as the perfect, young married couple – 'the mars' – began to unravel.

Vita did not develop an infection. Harold was cured by January, but forbidden by his doctor to resume sexual relations with his wife until six months from the date of the original infection, which he calculated, would take them to 20 April 1918. Vita returned home and they took up their life together, in all but the sexual sense. Vita was writing *Heritage*, which was to be her first published novel, and would read Harold instalments. They worked together in the garden at Long Barn. They had weekend parties with friends such as Ozzie Dickinson, Edwin Lutyens, and the Wellesleys; modest literary celebrities like Maurice Baring and Hugh Walpole; and some of Harold's Foreign Office colleagues who, like him, were considered too valuable to be released for military service. A good-looking, well-connected couple, they were regular and welcome guests at the dining tables of London society hostesses such as Lady Cunard and Lady Colefax. Everything seemed normal again.

At the Foreign Office, Harold continued to work under pressure. The war news was not good. By the end of 1917, the number of U-boats hunting in the Atlantic had reached record levels and, despite minefields and the adoption of a convoy system, they were still managing to sink more than 300,000 tons of Allied shipping every month. Since the Ebury Street incident, Harold also seems to have been worried by the prospect of Zeppelin raids. These raids generated far more fear than actual damage – there were only eleven over London in the whole of 1917 – but for a population to whom aerial bombardment was a wholly new concept, they were profoundly unsettling.

Harold was preoccupied with Persia, whose territorial integrity and political goodwill had long been recognised as crucial to the security of Britain's Indian Empire. In 1912, the Anglo-Persian Oil Company completed the construction of the world's biggest oil refinery at Abadan and in 1913 began producing significant quantities of fuel oil and other products. Winston

Churchill, by then at the Admiralty, insisted on a partial nationalisation of the company so as to secure supplies for British naval operations in the Gulf and the Indian Ocean. In a series of memoranda at the beginning of 1918, Harold recognised the growing economic importance of Persia and its oil reserves. Any agreement with the Persian Government, he argued, would have to be based on persuasion and conciliation, not on threats of force which, at a time when British forces were overstretched elsewhere, were obviously unrealistic. Harold's views were noted and approved and eventually fed into the controversial Anglo-Persian Agreement of 1919.

In January, the Prime Minister wanted to know what the prospects were for an Allied military victory in 1919 or thereafter. He asked the Chief of the Imperial General Staff, who, before responding on the military issues involved, asked the Head of the Foreign Office what political or diplomatic developments might affect Germany and its allies during the period. Harold was asked to give his assessment. In his self-deprecating way, he made light of it – 'apparently we are thought to be endowed with prophetic gifts'[16] – but this was recognition at the highest level. The result was a ten-page position paper, submitted to the War Cabinet on 10 March 1918, entitled 'The Consideration of Future Political and Diplomatic Developments.'

Harold maintained that Germany was in a stronger position than at the end of 1916 and in no danger of economic or military collapse. Stalemate on the Western Front, the success of the U-boat campaign in the Atlantic and the collapse of Russia meant that Germany had everything to gain from prolonging the war. If Germany were to launch another major attack against Britain, it was more likely to be eastward towards India. Germany was relatively stronger than its allies, so the British resources should be concentrated on preventing Germany from achieving a military victory, while at the same time political and diplomatic efforts should be made to detach Germany's allies one by one. Turkey would prove the most difficult, but if the political cost could be borne, it might be achieved. Bulgaria might be bought off by guaranteeing her possession of those parts of Macedonia which she had been promised under the Treaty of London in 1913. Austria-Hungary was, in Harold's view, the weak link and should be the political target. The Emperor Franz Joseph had died at the end of 1916, having held the empire together for sixty-eight years. The new Emperor, Charles I, was known to wish for peace and, in any case, his Empire was both exhausted and being torn apart by the ethnic divisions which had been papered over for so long.

Harold's paper is an impressive, closely-argued piece of work. As it rose through the Foreign Office hierarchy on its way to the War Cabinet, his arguments were endorsed and praised, first by his immediate superior, Lancelot Oliphant; then by Lord Hardinge, the Permanent Under-Secretary; and then by Lord Robert Cecil, the Under-Secretary of State. When Lord Hardinge called him in to offer congratulations, Harold was delighted and recorded every word in his diary: 'You know, really it represents a very able view of the situation. I can't think how you managed to concentrate so many ideas in so small a space.'[17]

As it turned out – and though it did not affect his reputation – Harold and all those who endorsed his views were mistaken. A matter of days after Harold submitted his paper, the Germans launched their Spring Offensive. The German High Command had chosen to gamble on an all-out attack on the Western Front before large numbers of United States' troops could be deployed in Europe. The attack began at Amiens before dawn on 21 March 1918 with the biggest artillery barrage of the war. Over 1,100,000 shells were fired in the first five hours. The Germans broke through and drove the front line back sixty kilometres towards Paris before they could be held. Harold had two weeks' leave at the end of March. Working in the garden at Long Barn, he and Vita could hear the sound of the guns eighty miles away.

Harold went back to work at the beginning of April. The date when they could safely resume sexual relations was approaching and there is no doubt he was looking forward to it. But on 13 April, Violet Keppel invited herself to stay at Long Barn. On 18 April, Harold did not manage to get away from London. Vita and Violet

> dined alone together, and then ... from ten o'clock until two in the morning – for four hours, or perhaps more – we talked.
>
> Violet had struck at the secret of my duality; she attacked me about it, and I made no attempt to conceal it from her or from myself.... Then when I had finished, when I had told her how all the gentleness and femininity of me was called out by Harold alone, but how towards everyone else my attitude was completely otherwise ... she told me how she had loved me always, and reminded me of incidents running through years, which I couldn't pretend to have forgotten.... I was infinitely troubled by the softness of her touch and murmur of her lovely voice. She appealed to my unawakened senses.[18]

Can it be coincidence that this happened just before the crucial 20 April date? It seems unlikely. Circumstances certainly favoured Violet in her pursuit of Vita at that particular time, but if it had not been Violet, then the likelihood is that it would have been someone else. Vita's *Portrait of a*

Marriage narrative is an intensely romantic piece. It was written when she was still more than half in love with Violet and attributes to Violet much more influence over the course of their affair than was in fact the case. It was Harold's confession, not Violet's declaration, which had opened the floodgates of self-realisation for Vita. She could not admit it at the time, but, much later, towards the end of her life, she wrote that:

> There was once a time when Violet and I were so madly in love and I hurt you so dreadfully.... I think it was partly your fault, Hadji. You were older than me, and far better informed. I was very young, and very innocent. I knew nothing about homosexuality. I didn't even know such a thing existed – either between men or between women. You should have told me. You should have warned me. You should have told me about yourself, and have warned me that the same sort of thing was likely to happen to myself. It would have saved us a lot of trouble and misunderstanding. But I simply didn't know.[19]

Vita and Violet concocted a plan to go off to Cornwall together. Harold, stuck in London writing a memorandum about Holland and hoping that when he got away on Saturday they would 'have a nice holiday together and get ourselves to each other,'[20] was told only at the last minute, and then only because Vita wanted help. Harold obligingly wrote to Hugh Walpole asking if he knew somewhere for Vita and Violet to stay. His tone suggests he is not best pleased, and he seems already to be making excuses for them: 'They have a sudden desire to see the sea.'[21] Walpole offered the loan of his rather primitive cottage on the cliffs above Polperro and the two women set off for Cornwall on 27 April. The famous love affair had begun.

15 Violet

Vita and Violet's departure for Cornwall marked the beginning of a two-year crisis in Harold and Vita's relationship. We know now that their relationship survived; that it was shaped and strengthened by what happened, by what they learnt about each other and themselves; but there was nothing inevitable about it at the time. The challenge for the biographer is not only to convey the uncertainty, unhappiness and worry Harold felt as a result of Vita's behaviour, but also to follow in parallel the story of his professional life, which saw him at the centre of world events, working immensely hard and shouldering major responsibilities. That he coped at all is a minor miracle – or perhaps it was the intensity of his workload that allowed him to cope, allowing little time for introspection.

Harold knew from the first that something was wrong. He and Vita had spent brief periods of time apart before, but this was different. She had never gone away without him. He was hurt and he was worried. On the day she left, he wrote her six letters.

> All this is not very cheery for a young husband who has just been deserted by his wife, and whose two infant sons are marooned in some distant village in charge of a hard-featured stranger.[1]
>
> But I get angry when I think of you going away quite gratuitously like that – just for a whim.[2]

It is an indication of Harold's character, and a measure of his understanding of Vita's, that his letters are not just emotional appeals or statements of feeling. They are full of images expressing his state of mind, images which he knew were more likely to appeal to her poetic imagination more than plain words – even though they had no immediate effect.

> So if you see that the 'body of an unknown man – stout and middle-aged with plentiful curly hair and a snub nose' has been picked up at Wapping Stairs, you will know it's me.[3]

In one letter, which constantly repeats the refrain, 'Oh solitude! Oh *pauvreté*!' he describes minute by minute his long, lonely evening.

> But can one (a deserted and suicidal husband) eat alone at 8.05 p.m.? No! So I pick up *The Statist* and read a very brilliant little article on 'River Drainage and Navigation in Ireland'. And by then it is 8.10.
>
> So by then I go upstairs. And I order soup, and they bring me soup, and I eat it. And by then it is 8.13. And they bring me cold dead salmon with jellified mayonnaise. And again I eat it and it is 8.15.[4]

In the meantime, he continued to work on Holland.

Vita returned from Polperro after a week, but then stayed in London only briefly before decamping to Long Barn. Harold was working on the complex issue of whether the United States should declare war on Turkey. In his letters to Vita from the Foreign Office, he meditated on the nature of his masculinity – 'I suppose I am too cultured and *fin de siècle* to impose my virility.'[5] From Long Barn, Vita replied that she preferred his 'gentleness and patience' and blamed their problems on 'Wanderlust ... the longing for new places, for movement, for places where no one will want me to order lunch, or pay housebooks.' She denied that Violet was at the root of the problem or that there was any need to be jealous of her. Violet simply saved her from 'a sort of intellectual stagnation and bovine complacency.' It was Harold she wanted to go off with when 'the bloody war' was over.[6]

How much of this was true? Perhaps Vita and Violet had not yet made their decision to run away together, but the affair was undoubtedly more serious than she was admitting. And what did Harold believe? He certainly did not like Violet. James Lees-Milne identifies an unexplained incident in June 1917, almost a year previously, when Harold had written to Vita: 'Damn that little too-too [French *toutou*, meaning 'lapdog', implying that Violet is a bitch] – it hates me & misses no opportunity of letting me down.'[7] He knew and saw that when Vita came to London, more often than not she chose to stay with Violet at the Keppels' house in Grosvenor Street rather than at Ebury Street. He must also have sensed that her attitude towards his work had hardened. He was 'tied to a beastly office' and she confessed openly that 'if only I can keep you I am afraid I don't much care what happens to the war, if only it would stop.'[8] She said she wanted to go away with him at the end of the war, but she was attacking all that he believed in and all that he had been working for since 1914.

In July, Vita and Violet disappeared to Polperro again, this time for three weeks, leaving Nigel and Ben at Knole. Harold remained at the Foreign Office, assessing the political and diplomatic impact in the Balkans of American involvement in the war.

He understood from very early on in the crisis the dilemma that he faced. Vita, egged on by Violet, was responding to the Latin side, the Pepita side, of her heredity. Everything had to be passionate and dramatic. The word 'adventure' appeared frequently in Vita's vocabulary and the novel she wrote at this time was called *Challenge*. This was an area where he could not go. He was not adventurous in the sense of wishing to break social bounds and shock.

> Goethe (like Hadji, Shakespeare, Leonardo da Vinci, Michelangelo – and unlike the secondary geniuses such as Byron, Christ, Alfieri and de Musset) had no sense of adventure. He had a certain feeling for escapades, but that is a different thing.[9]

The fact that in September 1918, when Lord Denman's committee looked at the suitability of civil servants for military service, he was again classed as 'indispensable' cannot have helped his case. He had every right to be flattered when 'Mr Balfour, whose opinion was solicited, stated that he did not know how Mr Nicolson could be replaced: that, indeed, he had no hesitation in saying that it would be almost impossible to do so,'[10] but Vita did not care about Mr Balfour.

He understood how he appeared to Violet and how Violet made him appear to Vita, but he could only be the man he was. So he chose, with customary irony, to play up the reliable, unadventurous side of his nature.

> Violet in her clever way has made you think I'm unromantic.... Oh dear! How can an impoverished middle-aged civil servant cope with so subtle an accusation? You see, if I was orfully rich I could have a valet and an aeroplane and a gardenia tree, and it would all be very Byronic – but not being rich, or successful, it is just 'poor little Hadji, he's such a darling and *so* patient.'[11]

What do you do when your wife is having a passionate, all-consuming affair with another woman? Harold's tactics were those he had employed before they were married, when Vita was surrounded by other suitors. He emphasised his love, his patience, his understanding. He let her know she had hurt him.

> Darling, what do your odd unconvincing bursts of affection mean? What does your intermittent and (alas) so convincing coldness mean? Little one, I am not a fool. I can forgive and forget anything, and understand a good deal.
>
> But can't you tell me? Can't you write it to me? What has happened? You see it isn't *me* – and so it must be *you*.[12]

Just occasionally, he allowed himself a little temper – usually directed at Violet – though he invariably apologised for such crossness later.

> Little one – I wish Violet were dead: she has poisoned one of the most sunny things that ever happened. She is like some fierce orchid, glimmering and stinking in the recesses of life and throwing cadaverous sweetness on the morning breeze. Darling, she is evil and I am not evil. Oh, my darling what is it makes you put her above me?[13]

What he did not do was rant, threaten, or issue ultimatums. He was a diplomat, a conciliator. He even suggested that Vita should get a cottage in Cornwall where 'she can go ... when she wants and be quite alone and have whom she wants.'[14] His accusations and his challenges were, usually, low key and often not even explicit. What he offered was not openly stated, but implied in his regular, undemanding assertions of love. Such patience was natural to Harold, but it may also it may have been conditioned by Vita's forgiving attitude to his own homosexual transgressions. He stood for stability and he believed – he had to believe – that it was stability Vita would seek when the affair had run its course. The danger, of course, was that it might not run its course: it might just become permanent.

That September marked the turning point of the war and, with the possibility of victory, the demands made on Harold by the Foreign Office increased even further. The German Spring Offensive had finally run out of impetus with the failure of the Champagne–Marne attack in July. Maréchal Foch, the Supreme Allied Commander, ordered a counter-attack which began at Amiens on 8 August. The attack began well, but slowed. Foch drove his troops on until, on the night of 31 August, the Australian Corps of the British Fourth Army crossed the River Somme. By 2 September, the Germans had retreated to the Hindenberg Line, from which they had launched their great offensive in March. It was the beginning of the end, and not only on the Western Front. Bulgaria, an area of special interest to Harold, was on the point of surrender.

Earlier in 1918, the Bulgarian Government had brought back a liberal former Prime Minister, Aleksandar Malinov, an opponent of Bulgaria's alliance with Germany, to try and negotiate peace. He failed and Bulgaria fought on. On 15 September, the Allied forces based in Salonika under General Franchet d'Espèrey launched an offensive known as the Battle of the Vardar. On 26 September, the Bulgarians surrendered. Harold received the news from the War Office and immediately began drafting terms for an armistice – withdrawal from occupied parts of Greece and Serbia; immediate demobilisation; the surrender of all weapons and *matériel*; the release of prisoners. The terms were agreed with other Allied Governments and signed, with remarkable speed, on 29 September. Harold also wrote an assessment of the political situation in the Balkans following Bulgaria's surrender, which he delivered on 28 September. 'The Balkan Situation and Observations' again found favour with Mr Balfour.

At the same time, perhaps because of his previous work with Sir Mark Sykes, Harold was also asked to consider certain aspects of Middle East policy. On 19 September, the Egyptian Expeditionary Force under General

Allenby attacked the Turkish Yilderim Army Group under their German commander, Liman von Sanders. The Battle of Megiddo took place along a line between the River Jordan and the coast some fifty kilometres (thirty miles) north of Jerusalem and lasted five days. It was the last major engagement of the war to involve Ottoman forces. For five days, they were driven steadily northward. Then they scattered. Damascus fell within days and then, a week later, Beirut. The Ottoman Empire had been decaying for years. Now it was disintegrating.

The speed of victory and the sudden need to exercise control over vast areas of former Ottoman territory created political problems. In May 1916, Sir Mark Sykes had negotiated a secret treaty with the French diplomat, François Georges-Picot, which anticipated the end of the Ottoman Empire and agreed that its Middle Eastern provinces should be carved into spheres of influence. Only when the end came did it become apparent that the Sykes-Picot Agreement ran contrary to promises made by the British High Commissioner in Egypt, Sir Henry MacMahon, to the Sharif of Mecca, Hussayn bin Ali – promises which had actually persuaded the Arabs to join the war against their Ottoman overlords. Harold was summoned to talks with the Chief of the Imperial General Staff, Sir Henry Wilson, and then spent the afternoon in discussions with the Foreign Secretary and Lord Robert Cecil. The risk was not just diplomatic embarrassment, but a real possibility that the Arab revolt might turn against British and French troops in the region. Sir Eyre Crowe began negotiations with the Quai d'Orsay and, by November, an Anglo-French Declaration was published, papering over the cracks and apparently promising self-determination for the Arabs. Harold, meanwhile, was despatched to Rome on quite another matter.

The weekend before he left, however, Harold demonstrated his independence by going, alone, to a weekend house party at Westwood Manor in Wiltshire. Did Vita care? She wrote him a reassuring letter: 'I know, as I know the sun will rise tomorrow, that I love you unalterably.'[15] But was it true? As soon as he left for Rome, she embarked on a bizarre transvestite adventure. Dressed as Julian, she paraded through London with Violet as her girlfriend, and then they spent a night as man and wife in an Orpington boarding house. Harold knew nothing of this.

The imminence of victory also meant that Italian attitudes to the Balkans, and to Turkey where the 1915 Treaty of London had promised her territorial concessions, became crucial. British policy was to create some kind of Balkan Federation to counterbalance German influence. The Italian Government had issued a statement, designed to undermine Austria and appease Slav opinion, in favour of the creation of what was to become the Kingdom of Yugoslavia. In Rome, Harold, now clearly considered a Balkan expert, held meetings with the Ambassador, Sir Rennell Rodd, and his staff to get a better understanding of the Italian position. What he learnt was to be vital to his work during the Paris Peace Conference. He also met and fell under the spell of the charismatic Greek Prime Minister, Eleftherios Venizelos – which was to prove something of a mixed blessing. And when not working, he was able to spend some time sightseeing with two old friends, Gerry Wellesley and Gerald Tyrwhitt (now Lord Berners, following the death of his father the previous month), both of whom were attached to the Rome Embassy.

As it happened, Gerry and Dottie Wellesley were soon to return to London and had agreed to rent Harold and Vita's house in Ebury Street, but there was work to be done on the house first and so, on their return, Harold and Vita were forced to stay with his parents in Cadogan Gardens. Vita was never happy at close quarters with the Carnocks, and in her current rebellious mood the arrangement was never going to last long. Moreover, unknown to Harold, Violet was inciting her against his parents – 'that horrid bedint house ... such dowdy surroundings ... will draw the warmth from your body ... will curb your vagrant gypsy spirit.'[16] They also went to stay in Brighton, where Lady Sackville had bought three houses on the seafront and, with the help of Edwin Lutyens, knocked them into one. Ben and Nigel were staying there with their nurse, but Vita went to London almost every day to be with Violet. Harold was so concerned that he confided his worries to Lady Sackville.

But what did he know? He knew that Vita and Violet had known each other since they were thirteen and eleven respectively; that Violet had always been in the background as Vita's friend; that they had holidayed together in Scotland and Italy. He knew that Violet's childhood had been a strange one – her mother had been Edward VII's mistress, a fact which Violet's father (who was probably not her biological father) had had to accept. But when Harold had met Vita, it was Rosamund who was in the ascendant; Violet had slipped away, partly because she was living abroad. He knew that she had reappeared in their lives after their return from Constantinople, acting as Ben's godmother and staying at Knole and at Long Barn. He knew that he did not care for her. He knew that in April 1918, she had suddenly reappeared in their lives and rapidly become the dominant force in Vita's life; that there was a passionate relationship between them which was causing Vita to neglect him and to neglect their children.

But there was much more that he did not know, both about Violet and

Violet

about the relationship with Vita. He would not have known that they had adopted revolutionary names for each other – Lushka for Violet and Mitya for Vita (when she was not being Julian). He would not have known about Vita's transvestite antics and he would not have known of the intense passion that poured out of Violet in letters and phone calls. It was a passion which may have begun in a romantic desire for gypsy freedom, but which ended in selfish, even violent, possessiveness. It combined love for Vita with a desire to shock and scandalise the rest of the world, and, ultimately, to destroy Harold and Vita's relationship in order to possess Vita for herself. On this last point, Violet herself was quite specific, though not to Vita.

The war was coming rapidly to a conclusion. On the Western Front, the Germans were being pushed steadily backwards. On the Italian Front, the Battle of Vittorio Veneto began on 24 October. Resistance crumbled with surprising speed and on 3 November Austro-Hungarian forces signed an armistice. In Germany, a naval mutiny spread to the shore and civil unrest engulfed the whole country. On 9 November, the Kaiser abdicated and fled to Holland. Meanwhile, Paris had been chosen as the location for the Peace Conference and Harold had been told he would be part of the British delegation. He was to be a member of the team working on the terms of the peace treaty for Austria, Italy, Turkey and the entire Balkan Peninsula. On the day that the Kaiser abdicated, Harold wrote to Vita asking whether she wanted to come with him to Paris or whether she would rather go off somewhere with Violet. Had Vita told him that she and Violet intended to go to abroad as soon as the war ended? Or had he guessed?

In *Peacemaking*, Harold claims that on 11 November 1918 he was working on the Strumnitza enclave – an extreme example of Balkan obscurity which borders Greece, Macedonia and Bulgaria. Needing to go to the Map Room, he happened to look in on the Chief Clerk's office, which overlooked Downing Street, at the moment when the Prime Minister, Lloyd George, appeared on the doorstep of Number 10 to announce the end of the war.

'At eleven o'clock this morning the war will be over.'
The crowd surged towards him. Plump and smiling he made dismissive gestures and then retreated behind the great front door. People were running along Downing Street.... There was no cheering. The crowd ... surged around the wall of the Downing Street garden.... [Lloyd George] went towards the garden door and then withdrew. Two secretaries who were with him urged him on. He opened the door.... He waved his hands for a moment of gesticulation and then again retreated. The crowd rushed towards him and patted feverishly at his back.... Having

regained the garden enclosure, Lloyd George laughed heartily with the two secretaries who accompanied him. It was a moving scene.[17]

Harold did not feel the need to join the crowds in the street. In a letter to Vita written on the actual day – which differs slightly from his later *Peacemaking* account, suggesting that the crowd was, in fact, cheering wildly and singing 'God Save the King' – he says that he carried on with his work feeling

> oddly responsible. I feel that what I do [drafting peace terms] is likely to be accepted and that one tracing of my pencil in this familiar room on my own familiar maps may mean the fate of millions of remote and unknown people.
>
> I feel, almost an impulse 'God guide me to the right.' I feel quite solemn about it.[18]

He continued his exploration of what kind of settlement might be possible in the Balkans. He had a long interview with Venizelos, who was in London lobbying for Greece to receive key Greek-populated areas of the now collapsed Turkish Empire. He was also required to produce a paper on Romania.

Violet had been stirring things with Lady Sackville, who began quizzing both Harold and Vita about the state of their marriage and why Vita wanted to go to France. Vita simply lied. Harold settled for half-truths. Whether he knew it or not, there were now tensions between Violet and Vita. They were rowing about going to France, and they were rowing also about Violet's 'attachment' to Major Denys Trefusis of the Royal Horse Guards. Trefusis was a romantic figure – tall, handsome, decorated for his bravery at Ypres and the Somme – and he wanted to marry Violet. Violet had certainly been writing letters to him every bit as passionate as her letters to Vita, but at this point she was simply using him to make Vita jealous. They left for Paris on 26 November, spending their first few days in an apartment lent to them by the German-American writer Edward Knoblock – who was restoring a Regency villa not far from Brighton and had thus become friendly with Lady Sackville. Once out of sight of Harold and her family, Vita's transvestite impulse reasserted itself. She wandered the streets of Paris dressed as Julian or sat in cafés in the guise of a wounded soldier. Harold knew only that she was in Paris with Violet; he had no idea how long they would be there or where they intended to go next.

On 2 December, Harold was required to stand by while Lloyd George met the French Prime Minister, Clemenceau and the Italian Foreign Minister, Sonnino. The meeting, which took place in London, did not seem decisive at the time, but the conclusion it reached – to investigate how much the defeated Central Powers could be expected to pay in reparations – was to have far-reaching implications. Three days later, he was writing an angry letter to Vita:

> You have stayed in Paris nearly a week without a word to me as to when you were going south or where. The result is that I haven't the least idea where to get hold of you. You really are quite *hopeless* about such things, and I put it all down to that swine Violet who seems to addle your brain. Oh you little idiot, I should shake you if you were here.[19]

The following day, he was more loving: 'It gets no better my ache for you. ... And then I want you in another way as well, and that makes me restless, and nervy.'[20] By the next day, he had decided on an alternative solution. He wrote that he was going to spend the weekend with Victor Cunard. His letter is not explicit, but given Victor Cunard's reputation, the statement that Violet was 'not the only string to our bow' can have left Vita in little doubt that his intention was to begin a homosexual affair.[21]

Victor Cunard was the nephew of Sir Bache Cunard, the shipping magnate, whose wife, Lady Emerald Cunard, was one of London's leading society hostesses. It was probably at one of her lunches or dinners that Victor and Harold had met. Victor was different from most of Harold's lovers in that he was much younger – aged twenty to Harold's thirty-two – and he was obviously, at times outrageously, camp. In associating with him, it was Harold who was now courting notoriety and drawing attention to his sexual orientation. He even invited Victor to Knole, where Lord Sackville took an immediate dislike and dismissed him, euphemistically, as unconventional. Even this, one suspects, was calculated on Harold's part. However unhappy Lady Sackville was about Vita and Violet's liaison, she still reported everything that happened at Knole to her daughter. Harold's actions were obviously aimed at Vita: to show that she was not the only one who could have an affair – although he never intended or pretended that it would threaten their relationship. Whether he intended it to be seen as a turning point, marking an acceptance of his homosexual nature as she had apparently accepted hers, is less certain, but that is what it became. Harold's heterosexual life was effectively at an end.

Vita and Violet moved from Paris to Avignon. Using the same hysterical tactics she had used to force Vita to go to France in the first place, Violet now made Vita promise to stay in France until January. They moved south to Monte Carlo. Harold had no idea what was going on. He had not expected her to stay away so long. He certainly expected her back by Christmas, which he spent at Knole with Ben and Nigel. It cannot have been fun: at least half his time was taken up acting as peacemaker between Lord and Lady Sackville whose relationship was strained to breaking point. Then Vita sent a telegram to say she had run out of money. Though she did not tell him, she and Violet had lost money gambling and did not have enough to pay their bill at the Hotel Bristol when they left. Victoria Glendinning suggests that they may actually have been asked to leave after another transvestite incident when Vita, as Julian, danced with Violet at the hotel's *thé dansant*.[22] Harold cabled £130. It was her money, but it was also appreciably more than his annual take-home pay of £86.

Immediately after Christmas, Harold was called back to London. The Paris Peace Conference was due to open in Paris in just over two weeks and President Wilson was arriving for preparatory talks with the Prime Minister and the Foreign Secretary. Harold was required to stand by in case his advice was required. It was not, and he went back to Knole for the weekend, taking Lord Berners with him. Berners, who was shortly to leave the Diplomatic Service to concentrate on composing modernist music, was not only seriously eccentric – at one stage he had a pet giraffe – but also both homosexual and effeminate. His presence at Knole irritated Lord Sackville (though not Lady Sackville, who adored him) and can only have confirmed suspicions about Harold's sexuality which he seemed no longer concerned to deny.

New Year's Eve was spent at Knole, but on 1 January, Harold and Lord Berners returned to the Foreign Office. That evening, they dined together and went 'on to a show.'[23] On 3 January, Harold took the boat train from Charing Cross station to Dover and crossed to Calais. At Calais Maritime he met Eustace Percy, who, Harold noted in his diary, was taking his wife, Stella, with him to Paris. They had taken a flat in avenue d'Iéna. Harold would be staying by himself in Room 89 in the Majestic Hotel.

16   Peace

The Paris Peace Conference was a monumental undertaking in every sense. The world had been at war for over four years. Some sixty million men had been mobilised. Over eight million soldiers had been killed, seven million permanently disabled, and another fifteen million seriously injured. Estimates of the number of civilians who died from the war, or the effects of the war, vary between five and ten million. Four Empires – the German, Austro-Hungarian, Turkish and Russian – had collapsed, and vast swathes of territory on three continents had changed hands. It was the victors – the 'Allied and Associated Powers' – who gathered at Paris with the task of drawing up a series of treaties which would settle outstanding disputes, redraw the map of Europe and the Middle East, and create an international framework to resolve international disputes without recourse to war.

It was a daunting task, beset with endless complications, and Harold came to see the choice of Paris, 'that shell-shocked capital', as 'a grave initial blunder.'[1] Of the original Allies, Russia was in the grip of a civil war and did not attend, so proceedings were dictated by the Council of Five (Britain, the United States, France, Italy and Japan). The defeated powers (Germany, Austria, Hungary, Bulgaria and Turkey) were not admitted to discussions. Germany had surrendered on the basis of President Wilson's 'Fourteen Points', but not all the victors understood or accepted what this meant. The Fourteen Points first saw the light of day in January 1918 in a speech to the Unites States Congress. Then they were supplemented by 'Four Principles' (February 1918) and 'Five Particulars' (September 1918). Harold was among many who, in January 1919, believed that these various criteria, the Fourteen Points in particular, would provide the basis for an equitable international settlement and 'took it for granted that on them alone would the Treaties of Peace be based.'[2] But neither Woodrow Wilson's idealism nor his political abilities were able to cope with the actual situation on the ground in post-war Europe, or with the Byzantine complexity of relationships and past agreements among those countries which found themselves on the winning side.

Two examples, in both of which Harold was involved, illustrate the complexity of issues where there was no absolute right or wrong and where the Conference was forced to balance political realities against moral arguments – or, failing that, simply duck the issue. In 1916, the Sykes-Picot Agreement had effectively promised France control over Syria after the war in return for British control over Iraq. At the same time, the British High Commissioner in Egypt had assured the Sharif of Mecca that Britain would support the establishment of an Arab kingdom with its capital at Damascus. The 1918 Anglo-French Declaration had papered over the cracks, but in Paris the issue flared up again.

Mr Lloyd George stated that if Damascus, Homs, Hama and Aleppo were included in the sphere of direct French administration, then the British would have broken faith with the Arabs. Lord Allenby ... expressed the view that 'there would be trouble, even war.' M. Pichon said that France could not release Great Britain from the terms of a solemn agreement.... President Wilson ... said it was a matter of complete indifference to him what France and Great Britain had decided in the form of a Secret Treaty; they had since accepted the Fourteen Points: they were thus obliged, whatever their previous engagements, to consider only the wishes of the populations concerned.[3]

But what did the population want? The French produced an expert who claimed that the population wanted a French mandate. Emir Feisal, the son of the Sharif of Mecca, claimed the contrary. President Wilson suggested the establishment of an American-led Commission of Enquiry. The King-Crane Commission started work in June 1919 but did not report until the end of August by which time President Wilson had withdrawn and the United States had more or less lost interest in the Peace Conference. The Commission found that the population was not only opposed to a French mandate, but also to the Balfour Declaration which committed Britain to establishing a homeland for the Jews in Palestine. The report was 'a highly inconvenient document'[4] and was consequently lost to view. In the end, that November, British forces withdrew from Damascus, leaving the Arab army to face the French, who took over by force – their *de facto* control later being legitimised as a League of Nations mandate.

The case of Italy was even more complex. The 1915 Treaty of London, which brought Italy into the war, had been a piece of political expediency at a time when the Allies were under intense pressure.

> Sir Edward Grey was so disconcerted by Italy's conduct that he retired to the country on a plea of illness. The Permanent Under-Secretary [Sir Arthur Nicolson], in his first conversation with the Italian Ambassador, allowed himself an expression which savoured of somewhat contemptuous realism. 'You speak,' said the Ambassador, 'as if you were purchasing our support.' 'Well,' said the Under-Secretary, 'and so we are.'[5]

The Treaty promised Italy

> territories which would place under domination some 1,300,000 Jugoslavs, some 230,000 Germans, the whole Greek population of the

Dodecanese, the Turks and Greeks of Adalia, all that was left of the Albanians, and vague areas of Africa. It was not, therefore a Treaty which was in any consonance with the principle of self-determination or the doctrine of the Fourteen Points.[6]

It was undoubtedly the most important and far-reaching of the Secret Treaties signed during the war. However, so much had happened between 1915 and the opening of the Conference that there was a general feeling that in many, if not most, respects it had been superseded. The Italians, out of understandable motives of self-interest, insisted on its validity, so negotiation on the basis of the principles of the Fourteen Points was required to ensure an equitable solution. 'The Italian problem thus became ... the test case of the whole Conference.'[7] All might have been well had President Wilson stuck to his guns, but as early as January 1919 he agreed that Italy should be given the South Tyrol and its 230,000 undeniably German-speaking inhabitants. The principle of self-determination was thus breached from the first. The President's concession was apparently made as a result of 'insufficient study,' but it was a gift. It allowed Italy a defensible negotiating position on other, potentially more damaging, aspects of the London treaty; so that when it came to the intricacies of the Adriatic problem, which involved not only the claims of Italy but also those of Greece and the composition of the nascent Yugoslav and Albanian states, the President found 'he had already discarded his ace of trumps.'[8] Other states, Britain and France included, were quick to realise that self-determination was not an unbreakable rule and 'demoralisation spread through Paris like a disease.'[9]

The Paris Peace Conference was, we know now, a failure. It did not secure peace. Indeed, it actually created resentments, imbalances and instabilities which led directly to 1939. In his 1933 study, *Peacemaking*, Harold Nicolson analyses how that failure came about. *Peacemaking* is not a book with mass appeal, but it is central to his *oeuvre* in that, by juxtaposing his thematic analysis of the workings of the Conference with his diary of what was happening at the time, it shows him working out empirically his philosophy of how diplomacy should and should not work. As with so much of his historical writing, he uses his analysis of the past to point morals and messages for the future. The book was, in fact, reissued in the middle of the Second World War, its didactic purpose explicitly reinforced by a new introduction listing twelve key lessons 'which negotiators of future peace treaties can learn from the errors and misfortunes of their predecessors.'[10]

For all that, Harold travelled to Paris on 3 January 1919 not only in an optimistic, but in an almost noble frame of mind.

I lunched that morning between Calais and the Gare du Nord, with the conviction that I was embarking upon a task for which I was qualified by protracted study, by high ideals, and by a complete absence of all passion and prejudice.... We were journeying to Paris, not merely to liquidate the war, but to found a new order in Europe. We were preparing not Peace only, but Eternal Peace.[11]

Harold – together with Eustace Percy and the Australian-born brothers Allen and Rex Leeper – found himself a member of the advance guard of a British delegation which was eventually to number 207 people. For the duration of the Conference, the British occupied two adjoining hotels on avenue Kléber. For reasons of security, the Majestic, where they lived, was staffed 'from attic to cellar with bright British domestics.'[12] The Astoria, where they worked and kept their maps and documents was, bizarrely, given the potential for security leaks, staffed entirely by French nationals. Sir Maurice Hankey, Secretary to the Cabinet in London and Secretary to the British delegation in Paris, took the Villa Majestic, opposite the hotel, and the Prime Minister and Foreign Secretary took apartments in nearby rue Nitot. The delegation set up its own printing press and established a telephone system linked directly to London. They had cars and motorcycle messengers at their disposal and there was a daily aeroplane from Buc, just south-west of Paris, to Croydon. For Harold, who loved this kind of purposeful organisation, the whole set-up 'hummed with the frictionless efficiency of a British Department of State.'[13]

The Peace Conference would not formally begin until 18 January, but there was a lot of ground to be prepared. Harold began by calling on the American delegation, which was established in what had formerly been Maxim's Restaurant. The Americans would have a great deal of influence in the inevitably protracted negotiations which lay ahead and it was important to Harold to understand how far their views on the Balkans and South-East Europe coincided with those of the British delegation. From his diaries, one senses not so much a difference of view but a difference in approach. The British delegation was made up of professionals, like Harold himself, whereas the Americans were more often academic experts with less diplomatic knowledge.

Paris was full of all sorts of people wanting to air their views. Apart from the Americans, he had a long discussion with Také Jonescu, the former Prime Minister of Romania. He talked with a Transylvanian poet called Goga, and with another Transylvanian called Virgil Tilea, who was to become Romanian Minister in London in the period before the Second

World War. He had more discussions with Venizelos on the future of Greece, and he discussed the future of Central Europe with Edvard Beneš, the Czechoslovak Foreign Minister. He talked with other members of the British delegation: a War Office expert on railways, and an expert on the treatment of the French-speaking minority in Canada, from whom Harold hoped to pick up ideas that might be applied to ethnic minorities in the new European states, such as Poland, Czechoslovakia and Yugoslavia. His diary entries are full of obscure place names and details of competing territorial claims. A record of one pre-Conference meeting with the American Balkan experts reads:

(1) Bulgaria. Stern justice. Macedonia, Ishtib and Kochana, with alternative railway. Difficulty of Gostivar–Monastir line. Serbo-Bulgarian frontier little change. They do not believe in that Pirot–Widin nonsense. Much opposed to the cession of Western Thrace to Greece and incline to give Struma frontier to Bulgaria, compensating [sic] Greece in Asia Minor. Dobruja – 1913 line without Silistria and with certain minor modifications.[14]

What impresses is not just the depth of his knowledge but the intensity of his commitment.

Gradually, the Majestic filled up. Sir Eyre Crowe arrived. Now Assistant Under-Secretary of State, Crowe had long been one of Harold's heroes and was to be his 'beloved chief' for the duration of the Conference[15] – 'It is a joy to be working under someone so acute and precise.'[16] Harold was not alone in admiring Crowe. Balfour leaned heavily on his advice during the Conference and he even attracted compliments from the notoriously ill-tempered French Prime Minister, Clemenceau. A supporter of Sir Arthur Nicolson's strong stance on German expansionism in the years leading up to the war, Crowe wanted a 'fair' peace, believing that another war would only be avoided by re-establishing a balance of power which took into account the concerns of all interested parties. Harold adopted his view completely. The area where they differed was the League of Nations. Crowe – rightly as it turned out – saw the Covenant which established the League as no different from any other treaty. Harold took a more idealistic view and, when the Conference finished, actually accepted a seven-month secondment to the League's International Secretariat.

Lord Hardinge also arrived in his designated role as 'Organising Ambassador.' The Conference consisted of a Supreme Council, a Council of Five, a Council of Ten, a Council of Relief, and a Food Council, as well as a raft of regional and national committees. Lord Hardinge was the British presence on the body tasked with making this complex structure work and ensuring that the myriad political, military and social issues which the Conference set out to resolve were brought before the right bodies in the correct sequence. Hardinge clearly had his eye on Harold and on 10 January invited him to dinner. Harold, apparently in assertive mood, suggested reform of the Diplomatic Service and pointed out that, after ten largely successful years, he was still a Third Secretary with a take-home salary of only £86 per annum. 'I ... *made* my opportunities,' replied Hardinge. Harold's concluded that, 'we may not rise very quickly in actual rank or salary, but any energetic person is given important work from the start.'[17]

Activity and job satisfaction were all very well, but privately he was depressed. Communication with Vita had all but dried up. That same day, he had written one of the angriest letters he was ever to write to her. Could that perhaps explain his assertiveness over dinner?

> Of course, I know it is a lot to ask – but you might at least send me a post-card.... I know that your dirty little friend must chaff you about it a great deal, and that you must feel I am a tie and a responsibility. But try and remember that I am alone here, and anxious to settle about a flat which I can't do till I hear from you.... Damn! Damn! Damn! Violet. How I *loathe* her. I refuse absolutely to see her.... I feel I should lose my head and spit in her face.[18]

For Harold, who was a great believer in the value of good manners, this is strong stuff, and although he immediately wrote a more loving letter, apologising for his outburst, there is no doubt that his anger was real, and it was to endure, beneath the surface, for the next few months. The flat to which he refers had been found for him by Eddie Knoblock, with whom he had dined on a couple of occasions – even in Paris, busy as he was, Harold made time for a social life. The plan was that he and Vita should move in as soon as she came to join him. But when would that be?

A week later, he was writing to Vita about Comte Jean de Gaigneron, 'a nice friend for Hadji as he knows all the clevers',[19] from which she would have understood that this was Harold's new lover. During this period, it seems that an outburst of anger was often followed by the appearance of a new boyfriend. De Gaigneron's physical appearance and his snobbishness feature in *Some People* as attributes of the Marquis de Chaumont, although Harold made it clear that he drew on a number of sources for de Chaumont's character, including Pierre de Lacretelle. De Gaigneron himself had recently returned from military service in Morocco where he had been on the staff of Maréchal Lyautey. His aristocratic background and a minor artistic talent – he painted stylised oils of Arab scenes – gave him an entrée to Paris's intellectual circles, where he introduced Harold. He was also promiscuously homosexual. His involvement with Harold was short-lived and physical rather than emotional, though they remained on friendly terms for many years.

In the meantime, Harold was working on Cyprus and on Albanian railways. His diary also relates a comic chase across Paris in the wake of the Foreign Secretary trying to track down the location of a meeting between the Lloyd George and President Wilson. They found it and, eventually, after a wait of two-and-a-half hours, Harold was introduced to the President who questioned him about the population of Fiume.

H.N. hopefully 'Oh yes – do you mean with or without the suburbs?'
P.W. 'Yes, there is a suburb called Ashak or something.'
H.N. 'Susak. Well, the figures are, the figures are …' pause … 'I have got them here.' (Scrubble in my pouch: quite rapid production of statistics; read them out impressively).
P.W. 'So I thought – and the line between Fiume and Ashak is a small one.'
H.N. 'A mere rivulet, Mr President, one cannot possibly separate the two.'
P.W. 'So I gather. But the Italians tell me that if one tries to pass from Fiume to Ashak one is certain to be murdered.'
H.N. 'Oh, but Mr President …'
P.W. 'Waal! I guessed he was talking through his hat …'
This is called 'giving expert advice.'[20]

Preparations continued. Harold was under pressure, working simultaneously on Hungary, Italy, Albania, the Serbs, Bulgaria, Greece, Romania and Czechoslovakia. Meanwhile, the world's political leaders were struggling to agree strategies for dealing with the world's press and bridging linguistic gaps – 'French furious at English being accepted as a diplomatic language,' Harold noted.[21] Eventually, on the afternoon of 18 January in the Salle de l'Horloge at the Quai d'Orsay, the Peace Conference was opened by President Poincaré and the first plenary session chaired by Prime Minister Clemenceau. At the end of this opening session, Harold overheard Jules Cambon, whom his father had known in Madrid and who had been French Ambassador in Berlin in the years before the war, saying '*Mon cher, savez-*

vous ce qui va résulter de cette conférence? Une improvisation.' Harold marked the old man down as a cynic, but Cambon was right.[22]

With the Conference under way, Harold's days became a round, though not a routine, of meetings of national committees, interviews with politicians, discussions with experts, and drafting position papers. He worked long and he worked late, but he still managed to broaden his acquaintance outside his professional sphere. On 26 January, he was visiting the home of ballet designer and artist Etienne de Beaumont, where Jean Cocteau was reading his new poems inspired by aeroplanes and aviation, *Le Cap de Bonne Espérance*. Among others gathered were Paul Painlevé, the former French Prime Minister, and novelists Paul Adam and André Gide. Harold walked home through the snow with Cocteau.

Such evenings were played out against a background of growing personal unhappiness. Vita had kept him informed of her whereabouts by telegram but had not written for a month. Now he received a letter from Cannes, where she was in bed with a cold. Dated 27 January, it managed to be self-pitying, insensitive and irresponsible at the same time.

> It is dreadful of me not to write to you.... But as I've often said to you in talking, it's so difficult for me to write to you when I'm staying with V.; it seems to me indecent.... It is indecent for me to write to you under these circumstances, oh, do, do, do try and see it!
>
> Darling, I do hope you liked being in Paris ... but I am anti your conference because it has spoilt the exchange, and I hadn't yet changed any of my English money hoping it would go up!...
>
> Hadji ... Oh, nothing. But so many things, all the same.
>
> I'm lonely, and have got a cold and wish I hadn't come here ...[23]

Worse was to come. He vetoed a suggestion that she should stay longer in Cannes and they agreed that she would join him in Paris in the first week of February. He had arranged to take over the flat for that date, but she let him down at the very last moment. He was devastated.

> I am feeling crushed, and sore, and sad today – because it's Sunday – and I had been packing some things to take round to the flat. I packed them so tenderly as if they were bits of you, my saint – and I was so happy, so happy.
>
> And then your letter came – and it was so dark and grim and horrible. I have never been so disappointed in my life....
>
> But all the sun has gone from Paris – which has become a cold, grey

meaningless city where there is a Conference going on somewhere.... I
feel you are slipping away, you who are my anchor, my hope, and all my
peace.[24]

He tried to cheer himself by socialising. He dined with Cocteau, with
Prince Antoine Bibesco, the Romanian diplomat and writer, and with
Bibesco's fiancée, Elizabeth Asquith, a daughter of the former British Prime
Minister. He lunched with Edwin Lutyens, and with the artists Augustus
John and William Orpen. But then there were problems at Knole with the
boys. Ben, in particular, seems to have been difficult and destructive and –
whether as cause or effect – had been badly treated by his nurse. Neither
Lord nor Lady Sackville could cope. Both wrote to Harold telling him that
Vita must come home, but Vita remained stubbornly in Cannes. Removed
from Knole, the boys went to stay at Cadogan Gardens with the Carnocks,
but the house was too small and Ben had to go and stay with a family friend
in Hampstead. In the end, they were resettled at Knole with a new nurse,
but, as Harold wrote on 8 February, it was 'really too bloody having these
worries on top of all I have to go through in the way of work.... Good God,
how this Violet business has poisoned our life.'[25] His feelings were raw and
the next day his anger broke through again.

> I have torn up the rest of this letter.... I don't want to write to you at
> present much – as I don't want to say things which I shall regret.... Only
> day and night there is a voice in my ear, 'She lied to you! She broke her
> promise to you....'
> What frightens me so, is that I feel now I don't *want* to see you.[26]

But, being Harold, his feelings quickly swung back again and his letters
become more pleading and affectionate.

Deliberately or not, Vita had placed him in an impossible position. He
knew where she was, but not what she was doing and very little about her
state of mind. Nothing that he wrote to her seemed to make any difference,
yet he was receiving angry letters from Lady Sackville and sad letters from
Lord Sackville, both of whom obviously thought he was failing to exercise
sufficient marital authority – even though they of all people should have
realised how resistant Vita was to authority. Yet they of all people should
have realised how resistant Vita was to authority. At the same time, London
gossip about Vita's behaviour was reaching fever pitch, helped rather than
hindered by Lady Sackville's attempts to demonise Violet. The stalemate
lasted for another month.

Harold Nicolson

Harold was constantly busy. The chapter in *Peacemaking* comprising extracts from his diaries between 6 February and 9 March is titled 'Committees'. Harold was technical adviser – 'whatever on earth that may mean'[27] – to the Greek Committee and was then given a similar role on the Czech Committee. He also sat on or chaired a number of sub-committees. These looked in detail at ethnic distribution, mineral wealth, industrial centres, transport corridors and a range of other factors and then drew the precise lines of the new international frontiers. Of course, no one country could be discussed without reference to its neighbours. Greece and the nascent Czechoslovakia had frontiers with almost every other country in south-east Europe. Added to which, Greece was claiming the Dodecanese and territory on the Turkish mainland around Smyrna. All this, combined with Harold's acknowledged expertise on the region as a whole, meant that he was consulted on almost all issues concerning Central and South-East Europe and Asia Minor – certainly more widely than his official position and his rank (still a Third Secretary) would normally suggest.

He continued to operate on easy terms with a range of extremely senior people: Lloyd George; A. J. Balfour; Sir William Tyrrell; the Canadian Prime Minister, Sir Robert Borden; the Greek Prime Minister, Venizelos; the Romanian Prime Minister, Bratianu; the Czech Foreign Minister, Beneš. He seems to have been something of a power-behind-the-throne. The British representative on the Czech Committee was to be Sir Joseph Cook, Premier of New South Wales. Harold had to coach him on his role and, when the first meeting of the Greek Committee came around was less than fulsome in his principal's praise.

> I go down with Sir Joseph Cook. His attitude is one of benevolent boredom, but from time to time he gives a smile of contempt indicative of the fact that although he may be ignorant of geography as of the French language, yet he represents a young and progressive country, whereas we others are 'effete'.[28]

Yet Harold's skill and persistence got things done – 'At 4.30 full Czech Committee. We decide on what I trust is a good line in Silesia.... The whole thing will be fixed up by my sub-committee on Friday.'[29] His letters and diaries are full of technical and geographical detail, and also of sharply-observed sketches of Conference life.

> Greek Committee. Asia Minor. The Americans state their views in opposition to Greek claims. We state ours in favour. The Italians, when

asked, say, first that the question is not within our terms of reference, and then, when beaten on that point, say that they have no instructions and can't say when they will get them. The French produce a line more or less like ours.... I can't understand the Italian attitude.... They obstruct and delay everything – and evidently think that by making themselves disagreeable on every single point they will force the Conference to give them fat plums to keep them quiet.[30]

He was certainly working extremely hard. There are frequent diary entries on the lines of 'work all day with the Americans';[31] 'Work all day, telephoning three times to London';[32] 'Czechs all morning ... Czechs all afternoon.'[33] Even when he had flu, he spent the 'whole afternoon poring over North Epirus maps.'[34] The twenty-third of February was 'a holiday. With Allen Leeper and Rhys Carpenter to the Forêt de St Germain. A sense of spring in the black twigs.'[35] It was his only day off in six weeks. Presumably, it was around this time that he told Balfour that he was 'feeling stale,' provoking the incident narrated some years later in the article 'Cure for Overwork', which contains not only Balfour's eccentric but apparently effective prescription for the condition – a prescription involving *foie gras*, champagne and detective stories – but also a superb character sketch of the man himself.[36]

On 17 February, Mark Sykes was taken ill in his room at the Hotel Lotti in rue de Castiglione. He died just two days later. Harold felt 'glum and saddened.' He recognised that the Sykes-Picot Treaty had been a mistake, but valued Sykes' human qualities: the combination of 'push and perseverance ... enthusiasm and faith' with a personality that was 'boisterous, witty, untidy, fat, kindly, excitable.'[37] Sykes' death was just one of tens of millions worldwide caused by the Spanish flu epidemic which lasted from 1918 to 1920. Although often overshadowed or underestimated because it overlapped with the last months of the First World War, the epidemic undoubtedly killed many more people than the war which had just ended. It was particularly severe in France, where over 400,000 died, and must have provided an unspoken background to life in Paris during the Peace Conference. Both President Wilson and Maréchal Joffre caught it, but survived. It can only have been another worry at the back of Harold's mind.

As ever, despite work and worries, despite complaints that he was kept busy until one a.m. and found himself coming home 'dead to the world',[38] Harold contrived to have a social life and to move among that odd mixture of aristocrats and artists which characterised Parisian society in the aftermath of the war and into the 1920s. On 2 March, he dined at the Ritz in place Vendôme at the invitation of the Romanian Princess Hélène Soutzo. Among the other guests was Marcel Proust. The story of their encounter is worth repeating because it shows Harold's skills of observation and characterisation at their best. Not a word is wasted.

> Proust is white, unshaven, grubby, slip-faced. He puts his fur coat on afterwards and sits hunched there in white gloves. Two cups of black coffee he has with chunks of sugar. Yet in his talk there is no affectation. He asks me questions. Will I please tell him how the Committees work? I say, 'Well, we generally meet at 10.0, there are secretaries behind....' '*Mais non, mais non, vous allez trop vite. Recommencez. Vous prenez la voiture de la Délégation. Vous descendez au Quai d'Orsay. Vous montez l'escalier. Vous entrez dans la Salle. Et alors? Précisez, mon cher, précisez.*' So I tell him everything. The sham cordiality of it all: the handshakes: the maps: the rustle of papers: the tea in the next room: the macaroons. He listens enthralled, interrupting from time to time – '*Mais précisez, mon cher monsieur, n'allez pas trop vite.*'[39]

They met again, once more in the opulent dining rooms of the Ritz, at the end of April. They discussed homosexuality – for which Harold, with his customary reticence in sexual matters, uses the French term '*inversion*' – but there was no meeting of minds. Harold suggested it was

> a matter of glands or nerves. He says it is a matter of habit. I say, 'surely not.' He says, 'No – that was silly of me – what I meant was that it was a matter of delicacy.' He is not very intelligent on the subject.[40]

Work continued. After three months together, the delegation was acquiring a sense of identity. On 15 March, there was a dinner for all those who had been educated at Balliol. Those present comprised sixty percent of the non-military members of the delegation – an odd and perhaps instructive sidelight on the delegation and on the British Government machine in which Harold was included and to which he was so deeply committed. 'We feel proud,' Harold noted.[41]

That same evening, Vita arrived in Paris, having for the moment broken away from Violet. She was on her way back to England to see the boys (whom the Nicolsons referred to as 'the babies', despite the fact that Ben was four) – pressure from Harold and from her parents having apparently told at last. She stayed three days in Paris, but she did not join Harold in the Majestic, preferring to stay with friends. They had not seen each other for three-and-a-half months and there had been some turbulent passages in that time. Clearly, there were things to discuss – not least, one suspects, how they were going to manage their now acknowledged homosexual inclinations in the context of their marriage. Whatever was said, their three days together seem to have been a success. Harold was naturally forgiving and conciliatory and, in the way of their relationship, was writing to her even while she was still in Paris, again presenting himself as her anchor in a troubled world: 'I want you to think: "Well, whatever I do, there is one person who I need never consider, who will always understand – and that is my fat, red-faced, bourgeois, sentimental but *so* loving Hadji".'[42]

This approach was natural to Harold, but it was also very astute, for he realised that Vita's return to London would not be painless or straightforward. She was 'scolded' by her father, who normally doted on her. She was subjected to storms of anger from her mother. She felt guilty about the children – 'it appears that no day has passed without [Ben] asking for me.'[43] Then, when she went to Brighton, where the boys were staying, she saw Violet's engagement to Denys Trefusis announced in the newspaper. She had known it was coming. She was even complicit in the arrangement – 'we both thought she would gain more liberty by marrying'[44] – but it still came as a shock. Later, she claimed that 'I felt like suicide after those four wild and radiant months',[45] which may have been a true reflection of her state of mind, but certainly ignored the true nature of her relationship with Violet, whose passionate and jealous temperament was capable of extremes of ecstasy and anger, but did not allow for unalloyed radiant bliss. And Violet, despite her engagement, was still begging Vita to run away with her – 'Fly, fly, fly, fly with me now.'[46]

Throughout this difficult period, Harold occupied the centre ground. Whatever he felt in himself – and he was surely much less certain than his letters suggest – to Vita he is tolerant and gentle and understanding. He wants to shield her from unhappiness; he is sympathetic to how she must feel seeing Violet's engagement announced; he will fight her battles for her. He even wrote Violet a letter of sympathy and understanding. But when necessary he could also be firm: he does not expect Vita to break with Violet, but he will not allow her to go away with Violet for any extended period.[47] He avoids presenting himself and his vision of their life together as exclusive or in any sense an opposite. As he put it a couple of months later, just before Violet's wedding – 'Why do you imagine there is nothing between eloping with Violet and cooking my dinner?'[48] All this, of course, made it easier for Vita to turn to him when she felt threatened or isolated. Not that she told him everything, but at least the dialogue continued and, whatever it cost him privately, Harold continued to be the voice of love and reason, like water dripping on a stone.

As if an extended marital crisis and work on the Greek and Czech Committees were not enough, Harold found himself, on 1 April, whisked off on an expedition to Budapest in company with his Foreign Office colleague Allan Leeper and the South African General and member of the Imperial War Cabinet, Jan Smuts. Such was Harold's standing in the delegation that Smuts had actually argued with the Foreign Secretary and insisted on his presence.

Central Europe was in limbo. It was nearly five months since Austro-Hungary had sued for peace. The old Empire had collapsed and everyone was waiting for the emergence of a clutch of new nation states. There was massive inflation, unemployment, shortages of food and of housing. The imperial administration had lost any semblance of authority and was crumbling, but, until the word came from Paris, there was nothing to take its place. The Hungarians, provoked by tactlessness on the part of the French Military Mission and fears of Czech, Romanian and Yugoslav encroachment, took matters into their own hands. On 21 March, a Soviet Republic was proclaimed in Budapest under the leadership of Béla Kun. Smuts' ostensible task was to meet Kun and see whether he could be induced to agree to the line proposed for the new border between Hungary and Romania. He was also tasked to assess whether or not Kun could be used as a channel of communication to the Soviet Government in Moscow – which, with the Bolshevik Revolution only eighteen months old and suffering military intervention on behalf of its White Russian opponents by the countries who were now running the Paris Conference, was understandably hostile and inaccessible.

Smuts' team set off from Paris in a special sleeper attached to the Paris–Bucharest express. They arrived in a snowy Basel the next morning, where the Archbishop of Split joined the train, 'rustling stiff silk in the corridor of the wagon-lit.'[49] Then on to Vienna, where Harold was acutely conscious of the impact of the war.

> My first sight of an enemy country.... [Vienna] has an unkempt appearance: paper lying about: the grass plots round the statues are strewn with litter: many windows broken and boards nailed up. The people in the streets are dejected and ill-dressed.... I feel that my plump, pink face is an insult to these wretched people.[50]

The Bolshevik headquarters in Vienna was chaotic, reminding Harold of a refugee camp, but he managed to extract both a safe conduct for Smuts' mission and an interpreter. Their sleeper was attached to a special train for the overnight journey to Budapest and Harold awoke the next morning in the city's Ostbahnhof, where Béla Kun and his officials arrived to welcome them. The Hungarians had reserved rooms for them at the Hungaria, the city's most luxurious hotel, but Smuts refused to leave the station and negotiations took place on the train. Smuts interviewed Kun, while Harold was left with the Foreign Commissar who began by showing off his knowledge of Hume, Mill and Spencer, before moving on to the benefits of Bolshevism for Central Europe and the triumph of the machine – 'I ask him what machine? He makes a vague gesture embracing the whole world of mechanics.'[51] Harold was not impressed.

In the pauses between rounds of discussions, Harold and Allen Leeper escaped from the station and were driven around Budapest. Their minders offered them tea at the Hungaria. It was

> a put-up job carefully staged to impress us. The foyer of the hotel is full of people having lemonade and coffee at little tables. An orchestra plays Hungarian tunes. It has all been arranged to show us that even under Bolshevism Buda Pesth remains the gayest city in Central Europe. But two serious mistakes have been made. In the first place there are Red Guards at all the doors with fixed bayonets. And in the second place they omitted to tell the people at the tables that they must make conversation with each other.... It is quite clear that these huddled silent people have been let out of prison for the afternoon in order to fill the foyer of the Hungaria.[52]

Harold had known Budapest as a child in the 1890s and had passed through on his way to Constantinople before the war. Now, it seemed even sadder than Vienna. As far as he could see, the only result of the revolution was 'a universal sadness and shabbiness.'[53]

By the Saturday evening, after a day-and-a-half of negotiations, Kun had gone as far as he could in agreeing to the Allied proposals. But Smuts was not in negotiating mood. He brought matters to a polite but firm end: 'They stand in a row upon the platform, expecting him to fix the time for the next meeting. And as they stand the train gradually begins to move. Smuts brings his hand to the salute. We glide out into the night ... [leaving] four bewildered faces looking up in blank amazement.' Smuts had determined that Kun, as a communist propelled to power by a nationalist movement, was of 'no importance or seriousness and that he is not capable of giving effect to any treaty.'⁵⁴ It was a wholly correct assessment. Béla Kun's regime lasted one hundred and thirty-three days.

Harold thoroughly enjoyed the trip, though he was depressed when he returned to Paris to find 'how little has been agreed since we left. In fact I see no progress at all.'⁵⁵ Yet, in another sense, it may have had an unfortunate influence upon him. The trip turned Smuts into another of Harold's heroes. The progression is visible in the *Peacemaking* diaries. To begin with, Smuts is 'very reserved'. Then he is 'silent, dignified, reserved.' In negotiations with Kun, he is 'friendly', courteous', but retains 'a tremendous dignity'. By the time they are on the return leg to Paris, Smuts has become 'delightful, telling us stories of the Veldt with a ring of deep homesickness in his voice. A lovely man.'⁵⁶ By the end of April, Harold and Smuts were dining together and talking about religion and anthropology. Harold found him 'simple and intricate', terms of approbation in his vocabulary.⁵⁷ A later age remembers Smuts as an imperialist in the traditional mode, a friend of Churchill and a man whose segregationist views paved the way for South Africa's apartheid system, but, in reality, he is not so easy to categorise. He actually fought against the British during the Boer War and he was a passionate advocate of both the League of Nations and, later, the United Nations.

Harold, too, was a believer in the League. He had arrived in Paris with a theoretical bias in its favour, and his subsequent experiences of the selfishness, duplicity and fallibility of the Powers had reinforced his belief in the need for an international solution to international problems. So that when, on 8 May, he was asked by Sir Eric Drummond, the former diplomat who had been chosen to be the first Secretary General of the League, whether he would like to help set up the new organisation, Harold was delighted and accepted.

Two months later, Harold was summoned by Lord Hardinge who had heard about his decision to work for the League and was both surprised and disappointed. He wanted Harold to be his Private Secretary. Would Harold turn down the League and accept? Harold declined. But why? By almost any standards, it was a bizarre decision, almost career suicide. To be Private Secretary to the Head of the Foreign Office was and remains a fast track to promotion and to an ambassadorial post. The appointment was a logical progression from the work Harold had been doing in Paris and recognition that he had been doing it well. So why did he turn it down? In the letter he wrote to Vita describing the interview, he says, 'I murmured something – "interest", "hope", "the new Europe".' But the rest of the letter is almost childishly facetious, ending in a flourish, 'You can never say again that I am ambitious!'[58] Yet Harold *was* ambitious: he enjoyed being at the centre of things and exercising influence in what he considered a good cause – which is precisely what he was turning down. The letter seems to be laying claim to some kind of idealism, yet idealism was never Harold's strength. He was always too ready to compromise and see everybody's point of view – unless he was under the influence of one of his heroes, whose views he so readily adopted as his own. Ten days before his interview with Hardinge, Harold had dined with Smuts and discussed the issue of when and how conscience should rule a man. Smuts said he had agreed to sign the Versailles Treaty 'against his conscience.' Yet for Harold, he still remained 'a splendid, wide-horizoned man – for whom I have the deepest admiration.'[59]

For the moment, however, this was in the future. Following his return from Budapest, Harold's professional and personal life continued at an intense pace. He struggled with the Americans over the Greek frontier of Northern Epirus. He plotted with Arnold Toynbee, who represented the Treasury, to resist a Greek enclave around Smyrna on the Turkish mainland. And then, in the middle of April, he managed to fly home and spend Easter at Long Barn with Vita and the boys. It was the first time for nearly six months that the family had been together. By 23 April, he was back in Paris, accompanied for a short while by Vita. Almost at once, Orlando, the head of the Italian delegation, walked out in a huff and the Japanese delegation also threatened to leave. There were arguments about Italy's position in the Adriatic, Greek claims in Anatolia, Czech claims along the Hungarian border. On 14 May, Harold found himself closeted with Lloyd George, Clemenceau and President Wilson explaining the situation in relation to the Greeks, the Turks and Asia Minor – an issue for which he was not actually responsible. The following day saw the publication of Vita's first novel, *Heritage* (Harold insisted on calling it 'Celery'), which was generally well received. But this was overshadowed by the final breakdown of Lord and Lady Sackville's marriage. Lady Sackville could not endure the continuing presence of Olive Rubens at Knole. Lord Sackville would not ask her to leave and he would not beg Lady Sackville to stay. Lady Sackville left, never to return. The break-up had long been inevitable, but for Harold and Vita, particularly Vita, it was yet another emotional strain.

By the beginning of June, events in Paris were moving towards some kind of *dénouement*. The peace treaty with Germany had taken shape. Harold was pessimistic. He saw the terms imposed – massive financial reparations and the infamous 'War Guilt' clause by which Germany accepted responsibility for the war – as unjust and offering the Germans no hope for the future. The Germans made a string of counter-proposals which Harold had to help translate. At the same time, there were the inevitable objections to the frontier lines and the plebiscite plans drawn up by the Conference. Harold and his colleagues worked ceaselessly trying to resist or accommodate objections from the Serbs, Czechs, Hungarians, Romanians and Greeks, all of which called for detailed knowledge of the geography and demography of the region.

As if this were not enough, Vita was in a tailspin. Violet was due to be married on 16 June. Vita knew she had the power to stop the marriage if she chose to: Violet was writing her desperate letters, begging for a sign. Vita was caught between her love for Harold, a primitive feminism, and an adolescent desire to shock polite society:

> O Hadji, I never ought to have married you or anybody else ... you are the dearest and sweetest and tenderest person in the whole world.... Women ought to have the same freedom as men when they are young. It's a rotten and ridiculous system at present.... O Hadji, if you knew how it would amuse me to scandalise the whole of London! It's so secure, so fatuous, so conventional, so hypocritical, so whited-sepulchre, so cynical, so humbugging.[60]

She feared that she simply would not be able to control herself when the moment came.

Despite all the pressures upon him, Harold responded calmly, treating the problem almost as a diplomatic one. He wrote every day. He was firm and decisive where action was needed, urging her to come to Paris at once, but understanding and supportive where her emotions were concerned. And it worked. In the end, after a nightmare journey during which she read and re-read Harold's letters 'until they almost lost all sense,'[61] she arrived at Gare du Nord on 14 June. Harold met her and they spent the weekend together at Versailles. The fact that the Conference had sent its formal response to the German counter-proposals just hours before her arrival allowed him to take a day off.

Harold had to return to work on the Monday, leaving Vita to watch the clock until she knew that the wedding had taken place. Bizarrely, Denys and Violet passed through Paris the next day on their way to St Jean de Luz on the Côte Basque. There was a huge emotional scene between the three of them – Harold appears to have kept out of the way – in which Violet told Denys that she had never cared for him and had wanted to run away with Vita, but it ended in an anti-climax. Violet and Denys went on to St Jean de Luz and the following weekend Harold and Vita went to look for a house in

Geneva, where Harold thought he would be sent with the League of Nations.

Harold arrived back in Paris on Monday 24 June – Vita returned to England – to find that the German authorities in Weimar had accepted the terms of the treaty and agreed to sign. The ceremony took place in Versailles in the Galerie des Glaces at three o'clock on the afternoon of 28 June 1919, which was, whether by accident or design, the fifth anniversary of the assassination of Archduke Franz Ferdinand. Conscious of history in the making, Harold recorded the event in some detail in his diary ('It will amuse Ben and Nigel') and in a letter to Vita. At first, he was excited. Soldiers were posted along the road to Versailles. Cavalry in steel-blue helmets lined the avenue up to the Château. Gardes Républicains stood on every step of the grand staircase. In the Galerie des Glaces, it was 'like a wedding: no applause, but not what you would call silence.' Clemenceau presided. The moment came. The Gardes Républicains drew their swords, silence fell and the German representatives were escorted into the hall. Clemenceau said: 'We are here to sign the peace.' The Germans signed. The Allied delegations filed past the table 'like candidates filing past the Bishop at confirmation,' signing one after another. Then it was over. The Germans 'were led from the room in silence.' Clemenceau said: *'Messieurs, le traité est signé. La séance est levée.'*[62]

> *'Oui,'* says Clemenceau, *'c'est une belle journée.'* There were tears in his bleary eyes.
> Marie Murat was near me and had overheard. *'En êtes-vous sure?'* I ask her. *'Pas du tout,'* she answers, being a woman of intelligence.[63]

It was dignified and it was historic, but in the end it was another anti-climax. Harold did not believe – and nor did many of those present – that the Treaty of Versailles was just or that it would guarantee European peace.

He went back to the Majestic where he was given 'free champagne at the expense of the tax-payer.' He had come a very long way since, as the office junior, he had been sent to retrieve the incorrect declaration of war from Prince Lichnowsky's bedroom. His views on the Peace Conference would take more coherent shape in the future, particularly in *Peacemaking*, but even at the time he knew it had failed to achieve what it set out to and would create problems in the future. Even the champagne tasted bad. He went to bed 'sick of life'.[64]

17   Crisis

The signing of the Treaty of Versailles was an event of both political and symbolic significance. Germany was the acknowledged leader of the Central Powers; Germany was held responsible for the war; and, by the Treaty, forced to admit it. In the public mind, therefore, the signing of the Treaty represented a form of closure: peace was assured and the guilty had been punished. It was only once the Treaty had been signed that the Allied Powers felt able to stage their victory parade through Paris. Harold had felt the ceremony in the Galerie des Glaces to be anticlimactic, and to be 'most painful' in the way it stigmatised the German representatives,[1] but he had no such reservations about the unashamed triumphalism of thousands of allied soldiers marching through Paris.

The Hotel Astoria commanded an impressive view of place de l'Etoile and the Arc de Triomphe. Harold had pressed Vita to come and join him for the occasion. Predictably, she had declined. She dismissed anything to do with the Conference as political, and thus not for her. On the morning of 14 July, he went up to the roof to watch.

> The Astoria waved with enthusiasm while the British Grenadiers came from under the arch, and behind them hundreds and hundreds of British regimental flags – stiff, imperial, heavy with gold lettering, 'Busaco' 'Inkerman' 'Waterloo' – while the crowd roared with enthusiasm, and our own Tommies on the roof yelled 'Good Old Blighty', and Douglas Haig passed with his generals at the salute. Mar would have sobbed.... Hadji pretended to be looking at the programme – but he was rather weepy too. I have never had such a patriotic feeling. I never felt less League of Nations. There they were, the flags of British regiments ... emblematic of our past victories of which this is the most glorious, the most democratic and the most final.[2]

With the German Treaty signed, the glamour departed from the Conference. President Wilson returned to the United States. Clemenceau, Lloyd George, Balfour and the new Italian Foreign Minister, Tittoni, all returned to their domestic responsibilities. The Japanese delegation also departed, leaving the Conference to be directed and decisions taken by a Council of Four – the United States, Great Britain, France and Italy – each represented by a senior civil servant. In Britain's case the civil servant in question was Harold's hero, Sir Eyre Crowe. Yet the work of the

Conference was far from finished: treaties still had to be concluded with the remaining Central Powers and their allies – Austria, Hungary, Bulgaria and the Ottoman Empire.

These changes increased rather than diminished Harold's workload. He sat on seven committees or sub-committees dealing with an immense range of issues – from access to the coal mines on the Czech-Polish border and control of the northern Adriatic to the Albanian frontier with Yugoslavia and Greek claims in Thrace and Anatolia. He was very much at the centre of things. Usually, his stance on important issues was considered and logical. As ever, he was a conciliator. The Teschen coal mines, for example, were in what was ethnically Polish territory, but they were essential to the Czech economy. Harold proposed and intrigued for a compromise under which Poland retained sovereignty over the region but the Czechs were allowed access to the coal and the transport infrastructure. The final solution was a more cumbersome partition of the region, but nonetheless its origins lay in Harold's proposals. He boasted to Vita about '*how* clever, how dishonest, how deeply Machiavellian' he had been.[3]

With the Teschen issue resolved, Harold managed to escape from Paris for a few days. He and Jean Cocteau travelled to the village of Offranville in Normandy, in the hinterland of Dieppe. Their friend, the painter Jacques-Emile Blanche, had designed and painted a war memorial for the local church – a remarkable sixteenth-century building featuring an impressive twisted spire and dedicated to St Ouen, a seventh-century Archbishop of Rouen. It was the briefest of visits, but Harold was delighted to be in rural France, among ordinary French people. Their directness and simplicity, even the way in which they coped with the aftermath of the war, were a world away from the sophistications of Paris.

Harold left Cocteau at Dieppe and crossed to England for two days at Long Barn with Vita. There is no documentary evidence of what passed between him and Vita that weekend, but James Lees-Milne says that Harold 'believed that those two days with Vita had averted a breakdown of their marriage,'[4] an assertion presumably based on his conversations with Harold.

He flew back to Paris and, in the days that followed, showed his growing skill and influence by engineering an important diplomatic compromise. The controversial 1915 Treaty of London had given the Italians possession of the city of Trieste. They were now demanding Fiume (nowadays Rijeka), together with the Istrian peninsula and a number of Adriatic islands – Cherso (Cres) and Lussino (Lošinj) – and as much of the Dalmatian and Albanian coastline as they could get. The Americans, for a cocktail of reasons including President Wilson's earlier misjudgement over the South

Tyrol, were strongly opposed to any further concessions to Italy. The French were indifferent. Harold, conscious of the strategic importance of the northern Adriatic coast, backed the American position, but worked for a compromise. It was a struggle, but, eventually, the Italians and Yugoslavs were persuaded to agree that Fiume should become a 'free city' under the protection of the League of Nations, and it was so designated under the Treaty of St Germain-en-Laye, the formal peace agreement with Austria, signed on 10 September 1919.

Unfortunately for Harold's diplomatic achievement and for the future of the region as a whole, two days after the signing of the Treaty, the Italian poet-adventurer, Gabriele d'Annunzio, made a complete nonsense of the peace process by marching into the city with two thousand supporters. This started a chain of events which involved the city being bombarded by the Italian navy, a fascist coup and, ultimately, annexation by Mussolini's Italy. In less than four years, Harold's fears about the future control of the northern Adriatic were fully realised.

Where Harold's judgement became less reliable was in dealing with Greece: not because he saw or understood the issues with less clarity, but because he lost his customary detachment. Eleftherios Venizelos, the Greek Prime Minister, was well known for his charm and charisma. From their first meeting in Rome before the end of the war, it was evident that Harold had fallen under his spell. By the time the Peace Conference was under way, he was writing gushingly (and foolishly) to his father: 'I can't tell you the position that Venizelos has here! He and Lenin are the only two really great men in Europe.'[5] The Allied Powers owed Venizelos a debt in that he had brought Greece into the war on their side, yet it was plain to many that his expansionist territorial demands were storing up trouble for the future. Harold was instructed to present Venizelos with a joint British-American proposal on the division of Thrace which fell far short of what Venizelos wanted.

> It was very painful. I simply loathed it – and it was like letting Venizelos down. He was very indignant, and stormed for an hour. It was *bloody*. We then went away and I got [Balfour] to agree that we could not force a settlement on Venizelos. But I hardly slept all night ... and at 9.0 I went round again to see V. and suggested a possible compromise. He had not slept either, and there were tears in his eyes. I then went to Tardieu [of the French delegation] and got him to agree, and then to [Balfour] who also agreed.[6]

Harold's compromise offered Venizelos far more than the original proposal, but Venizelos was not satisfied, kept up his campaign and, in the end, was rewarded with a kind of success. The Treaty of Sèvres, eventually concluded between the Allies and Turkey in August 1920, gave Greece almost all the territory he had been demanding. But by then it was too late and the Turkish nationalist revival was under way. It would be the Treaty of Lausanne in 1923 which finally settled the borders of Greece – and once again Harold would be part of the British negotiating team.

It was not so much what Harold did that pointed up his weakness, but the way he did it. 'I don't care if you do laugh,' he wrote to Vita the following year. 'He *is* my hero, dear old man in his skull cap and his charming Christ-like smile.... I'd chuck anything for what V represents. You see, he is *winged reason*. He is as sane as any man, and yet his sanity soars.'[7] Venizelos was his hero and with his heroes he became emotionally involved. He could not bear to disappoint them. On this occasion, Balfour was merely amused, but others in the Foreign Office – and, later on, his political colleagues in the House of Commons – came to see a weakness of judgement in this form of uncritical attachment.

Harold was working under such pressure – often twelve hours a day – that he was unable to take his summer leave. He did manage to snatch another weekend at Long Barn at the beginning of September, but it was not a great success. He had toothache and Vita was depressed. She was under pressure from Violet for the two of them to go away again. Harold again showed his diplomatic skill. Whatever he felt inwardly, he must have known it was no good forbidding Vita to do anything. He knew she was writing another novel, to be called *Challenge*, a thinly-disguised version of the Harold-Vita-Violet triangle and set among the Greek islands, so he suggested they should go to Greece and even offered to use his connection with Venizelos to make sure they were properly looked after. Then he hurried back to Paris, at Balfour's insistence, in order to be there for the signing of the Treaty of St Germain-en-Laye with Austria on 10 September.

As had happened previously when Vita made a bid for what she called freedom, Harold found his own quiet way of retaliation. Just a week later, he was writing to her from Paris that

> I have got such a funny new friend – a dressmaker, with a large shop in the rue Royale, and a charming flat at the Rond Point (where I spent the *whole* of Saturday night – sleeping on the balcony).... Mar would like my new friend, I think – very attractive ...[8]

The new friend was the fashion designer Edward Molyneux who, over the next thirty years, would design clothes for most of the royal houses of Europe as well as for many of Hollywood's leading actresses.

In October, Harold was at last able to take some leave. He returned to Long Barn and spent a few days with Vita before she and Violet left for Paris and the south of France. Vita left him a letter '*packed* with love' to read when she had gone. 'Nothing,' she wrote, 'in this world could ever alter my love for you, I KNOW THAT.'[9] Harold could have been forgiven for thinking that they had reached some kind of mutual understanding and equilibrium. In fact, the next six months were to be the most difficult of their forty-nine years of marriage.

On 19 October, two days after Vita's departure, Harold went up to London to begin his secondment to the League of Nations, working at Sunderland House in Curzon Street. His role was to help in the organisation of the League's International Secretariat, and the expectation was that he would move to Geneva to oversee its formal establishment. But in London his problems pursued him. Lady Sackville had never been discreet or considerate of others. Her own marriage had broken down and now she was spreading rumours about Harold and Vita's: Vita was bewitched; Harold was weak; Violet was the one to blame. And Vita had made things worse by telling her mother 'the most intimate things' about their marriage which Lady Sackville was now passing on to her friends. Mercifully, the League wanted him to return to Paris, where he longed to 'drench myself in work.'[10]

But Paris did not help. He arrived and returned to his room in the Astoria only to discover that Vita, knowing that he was in the city, had quite deliberately left for Carcassonne without seeing him. Worse, she had left no address and instructions that he should not write. He was hurt and sent her, *poste restante*, a rebuke which, in context, has a stately quality.

> What a cruel contemptuous thing to do. If you think you can treat me like [Violet] treats [Denys Trefusis] you are wrong. I shan't allow my life to be wrecked. I have done all a man could to meet you and understand you, and you go out of your way to wound me.[11]

Being Harold and having given his warning, he reverted again to being the supportive and understanding husband. He offered sensitive and practical criticisms of the manuscript of *Challenge*. He arranged for Vita and Violet to travel to Greece on a Greek naval cruiser in company with Venizelos – although the trip had to be abandoned because of an assassination plot.

The situation rapidly became a repeat of what had happened at the beginning of the year. The two women remained in Monte Carlo, gambling at the Casino and playing tennis. Vita wrote her novel and at least once indulged in her transvestite games. Harold remained in Paris, working, worrying, and calling on her to join him.

On 1 December, he wrote masterfully that he wanted her in Paris within the week. Two days later, he told her that

> I fear I am going downhill without you – and I get so awfully depressed that I drink too much, and I spend my time with rather low people, but I am ashamed to go into society, so I live in the demi-monde and I don't like it much.[12]

Precisely who the 'low people' were is not recorded. As before when deserted, Harold was making it clear that he could manage without her sexually, but he was also clearly asking for sympathy. He did not get it. Vita's response was muddled, at times aggressive and at times verging on the hysterical – despite her claim that it was 'sober fact and truth.' She repeatedly expressed her love for him but at the same time blamed him for failing to realise or take seriously the real nature of her relationship with Violet.

> you talked of 'wild oats.' You talked of me being away as a holiday. You write of V. as Mrs Denys Trefusis – don't you realise that that name is a stab to me every time I hear it? Yet you write of her as that as a joke.[13]

As for resuming their sex life, that was 'impossible'. Could he not see that? She would travel up to Paris on 15 December and 'when I come back this time, V. and I [will] give each other up for ever' – though she neither came back when she promised nor gave up Violet.

Harold's situation was getting desperate. His emotions were all over the place. For a moment, on 8 December, he thought she might have abandoned him for good. The next day, she was 'frank and splendid' and he understood 'what you are sacrificing for me.'[14] Nor were things improved by the fact that Lady Sackville had now joined him in Paris, ranting and raving about Vita's behaviour and threatening to cut her off without a penny. Worse still, he had a huge and very painful abscess on his knee which required an operation.

When Vita did eventually arrive in Paris, on 18 December, there was a *rapprochement*. She looked after him while he recuperated and they both regained a degree of stability. They spent Christmas and New Year together

– although she stayed in a different hotel – and were happy. Harold received a letter from Lord Curzon, who had succeeded Arthur Balfour as Foreign Secretary, telling him that he would receive a CMG in the New Year's Honours list in recognition of his work during the Peace Conference.[15] He was delighted and surprised. He had certainly worked hard and proved himself extremely effective, but at thirty-three, he was still young to receive such an honour. Almost as important, as far as Harold was concerned, was the letter of congratulation he received from his father. Whatever the state of his personal affairs, Harold's professional standing at the end of the year, despite having turned down the offer to be Lord Hardinge's Private Secretary, could hardly have been higher.

Vita's stability did not survive reunion with Violet. She returned to Knole on 2 January 1920 to be with the boys, who had not seen either of their parents since October. Harold was to follow two weeks later. He was looking forward to a break and longing to be with his family. On 8 January, she wrote him a loving letter, calling him 'my precious boy,'[16] but as soon as she saw Violet again she became, in Harold's graphic phrase 'like a jellyfish addicted to cocaine.'[17] By the time he returned to England, far from giving Violet up, Vita had decided to go off with her for good. On 16 January, she met Harold, still hobbling on sticks following his operation, at Victoria Station and they went to his parents' house in Cadogan Square. After dinner, she told him that she and Violet intended to leave together the next day. There was a scene. Harold refused to let her go. Lady Carnock hugged her and begged her not to go. Vita fled. The next day, she took Harold to see Violet in Grosvenor Street. There was another scene, and, in the end, it was agreed that nothing would happen for at least a fortnight, until Harold's leave was over and he returned to Paris.

Those two weeks were spent at Knole with the boys as a family holiday. Harold did not mention the subject of Vita and Violet's elopement once. Such forbearance, such self-control seems scarcely credible, but it was characteristic. Before their marriage, when Vita was being circled by wealthy admirers, Harold had played a waiting game. He was doing so again. He seems to have understood – or hoped – that stability and endurance were things which Violet could not offer. He offered calm. He appealed to the English side of Vita: the gardener, the scion of Knole and its hundreds of years of history. Did he also know that during their last trip Vita and Violet had rowed constantly? Did Vita tell him that she was being worn down by Violet's unreasoning jealously? He certainly knew their relationship was passionate and dramatic; that Violet's appeal was to Vita's Pepita ancestry, to her would-be rebellious, gypsy self. And he was surely astute enough to realise that the very intensity of the relationship would cause it to burn itself out sooner or later.

Previous biographers of both Harold and Vita have quoted at length from the remarkable exchange that took place at the end of Harold's leave. Vita's emotional outpouring, seeking reassurance and certainty, was written within hours of Harold leaving Knole to return to Paris. The exchange is worth quoting again because of the light it sheds on both their characters and on the balance of their relationship at the time.

> Hadji, Hadji, I feel lonely and frightened. There is so much in my heart. ... Oh Hadji, the reason why I sometimes get you to say things, to say you would miss me, is that I long for weapons with which to fortify myself; and when you do say things, I treasure them up, and in moments of temptation I say them over to myself, and I think 'Then he *does* mind, he *would* mind, you *are* essential....'
>
> So I fish and fish, and sometimes I catch a lovely little silver trout, but never the great salmon that lashes and fights and *convinces* me that it is fighting for its life.... You just say 'Darling Mar!' and leave me to invent my own conviction out of your silence.[18]

Harold replied two days later from Paris.

> You see, what appeal can I make except that of love? I *can't* appeal to your pity – and it would be doing that to let you see what I feared and suffered. It would be ridiculous to appeal to your sense of duty etc. – that's all rubbish. So what is there left but appeal to love – my love for you and yours for me? And how can *that* appeal be anything but inarticulate? How can I formulate in words how I love you?... But you must feel and see it – and all you have done and sacrificed shows that you have felt it.
>
> I know that you think sometimes that if you left me I should recover in a year or two and not be unhappy. I think you are so wrong there. You see, you would have ruined my life – I mean my inside life – and all the joys you had given me would be stinking corpses. I should mind acutely and permanently. It would poison my heart and ruin my character.[19]

For all his mildness, Harold comes across as very male. He is loving, but logical. He is reassuring, but not to the point of hyperbole. He exposes his tactics. He exposes his fears. Where Vita is swept along by her own passion, Harold retains his self-control and his ability to stand outside himself. Vita ends: 'My darling, my darling, I shall love you till I die, I *know* I shall.' Harold ends: '*What* a hopeless letter!'

Back in Paris, Harold picked up the threads of his work with the League, working on the seemingly interminable and insoluble problem of who should control which parts of the northern and eastern Adriatic coast, and also on the new complexities of returning large numbers of prisoners of war across international borders which did not exist when they were captured. He was still hoping that Vita would join him, assuring her that his new hotel, the Alexandre III in rue Montaigne, was comfortable and clean and that she would be able to write. But Vita had gone to Lincoln, ostensibly to research her new novel, *Dragon in Shallow Waters*, a bizarre and sensational story set in the Lincolnshire fens. She told Harold she was there and staying at the Saracen's Head. She did not tell him that Violet was with her and that they were again planning to elope. Yet her letters are full of hints and clues – 'some latent honesty within me will not allow me to write when the future is uncertain and when I know that any day I may cross the Channel on that desperate voyage.'[20]

The events of the next few days have been described by Lady Sackville as 'quite like a sensational novel' and by Norman Rose as 'a French farce.'[21] Certainly there is an adolescent quality to the events themselves and to the emotional currents surrounding them. Violet and Vita fled to Dover, Vita – by her own account – trying to persuade Violet to return to Denys. For some reason, Violet crossed by herself to Calais, leaving Vita to follow the next day, but then as soon as Violet had gone, Vita met Denys who had driven down to Dover in pursuit. Denys refused to leave her, following her back to the dingy room in the King's Head which she had taken for the night and pacing up and down until she finally told him where Violet was and what their plans were. Bizarrely, they then agreed to travel together, so that neither one should reach Violet first. At this point, Vita, now alarmed by the irrevocable step she was taking, wrote Harold an almost desperate letter, in which her own emotional turmoil is mirrored by the tempestuous weather in the Channel outside. But Harold did not receive it. Alarmed by her earlier letters from Lincoln, he had left Paris and was on his way to England to look for her. When she and Denys took the ferry for Calais on the morning of 10 February in the teeth of one of the worst storms that winter, Harold was actually crossing in the opposite direction.

Vita and Denys met Violet – who was in a state of nervous collapse – in the buffet of the Gare Maritime in Calais. The next day the three of them travelled to Amiens where Denys, in despair, gave up and returned to England, determined that he would never see Violet again. A matter of hours later, when the two women had found themselves a hotel, Violet's father, Colonel Keppel, appeared, determined that they should not slip away. He was, according the Vita, 'pompous, theatrical and unimpressive.'[22] They could barely restrain their laughter. Unable to achieve anything himself, he sent a telegram to Denys, suggesting that he return.

Meanwhile, Harold had met Denys in London and been told what was happening. Thanks to his war experience, Denys was a pilot, and Mrs Keppel, desperate to separate Violet and Vita if at all possible and nothing if not well connected, had borrowed a two-seater plane so he could fly to Amiens. Lady Sackville persuaded Harold to go with him and on 14 February the two husbands flew across the Channel. Their reunion, if such it can be called, with their wives in the hotel in Amiens was 'absurd and childish'. Vita wrote later that:

> Harold said we would be starved out by having someone always with us till we gave way – it was all undignified and noisy to a degree, and I hated it, and was rude to Harold, and he said a lot of silly things that showed him in a wrong light.[23]

What happened next is almost incomprehensible from a twenty-first century point of view. Harold asked Vita: 'Are you sure Violet is as faithful to you as she makes you believe?' Vita, by her own account and in the euphemistic terms of the age, asked Denys whether he had been 'really married' to Violet and asked Violet whether she had 'belonged' to Denys. Denys refused to answer. Violet said that she had. Vita went 'half mad with pain and not understanding' and tore herself away.[24] Harold took control and the two of them fled to Paris.

It was an extraordinary *dénouement*. Denys and Violet had been married since the previous June. Had Vita made Violet promise that she would not consummate her marriage? She was a married woman who had had three children. How could she make such a demand? In *Portrait of a Marriage*, Vita suggests that Violet *was* technically still a virgin.[25] Had Denys agreed to this before the marriage? Again, there is a sense of naïvety in the emotional and sexual triangle which, given both Vita and Violet's family backgrounds, is surprising to say the least. Why did it all matter so much? Or was Vita actually looking for a way out? In her biography of Vita, Victoria Glendinning suggests that 'no wife who has decided to leave her husband for ever sends daily messages in case he should be worried. She was still asking to be stopped, whether she knew it or not, and at last, at Amiens, he stopped her.'[26]

Harold Nicolson

Whatever the explanation, the crisis was over. Vita and Violet met briefly in Paris where Violet tried to explain, but Vita felt hurt and deceived. They separated. Violet went to Bordighera, while Vita stayed for a short while in Paris with Harold and then, at the end of February, returned to England. Harold took some leave and he and Vita went to London social gatherings and to the theatre as if nothing had happened.

On 20 March, with Harold's full consent (though he still worried), Vita travelled to Avignon to meet up with Violet and the two of them went on to Bordighera, San Remo and Venice. They had been parted for six weeks and the magic had gone. They fought continuously. That summer, back in England, they met in restaurants and theatres, but there was no peace between them. Violet was demanding what Vita could not now give. There was to be a last trip abroad together at the beginning of 1921, but the affair gradually tailed off.

It had lasted two years and was the defining period of Harold and Vita's relationship. It had put Harold under immense emotional stress and at times pushed Vita close to madness. Harold, with his decency, patience and good manners, had won through. But what precisely had he won? What was it that he wanted or needed so badly? There is no doubt that he loved Vita deeply all his adult life. As he grew older, he was inclined to play down the sexual element in their attraction. When, in June 1929, he and Vita were invited to give a broadcast discussion of marriage on the newly-incorporated BBC, Harold stated that 'sex lasts a short time, from three weeks only to three years.' His own sexual need for Vita lasted longer than that – she was still, verbally at least, fending him off during her affair with Violet – but after Violet their sexual relations ceased. In part, this may have been because Vita feared another infection scare, but more important seems to have been a mutual acceptance of their sexual orientations. It was not that sex was unimportant to them. They both had numerous lovers. Harold's were all male and the relationships, with one notable exception, were lighthearted, sexual flings which would mature easily into friendship. Vita's, with one exception, were all female, but her relationships were intense and passionate often to a point where she could not sustain them, and they frequently ended in upset and recriminations.

Theirs was not primarily a sexual love, yet it was a genuine love, more than merely platonic companionship. In the same 1929 radio broadcast, Harold tries out the metaphor of marriage as a car running on pneumatic tyres – 'one must learn that punctures are inevitable, that they are reparable, and that (if one is cheerful about it all) they are somewhat amusing.' It is a little complicated – he was never a technical man – but it does lead to a clear statement of what he believed marriage should be and how it should work:

> I think the secret of a successful marriage is the capacity to treat disasters as if they were incidents and not to magnify the incidents into disasters. Marriage is a continuous process and not a static condition. It is a plant and not a piece of furniture. It grows, it changes; it develops.[27]

Marriage, then, was for the long term; and the goal Harold and Vita set for themselves was an emotional interdependence which allowed for physical and intellectual independence. After, and even during, the dramas of Violet, they recognised in each other the best chance of achieving that end. Violet was a very real individual, but she was also a testing ground for every aspect of Harold and Vita's relationship. Norman Rose suggests that 'the Trefusis affair confirmed Vita's dominance in her relationship with Harold. She not only held the purse-strings, but also the emotional strings.'[28] This is only partly true. If Vita gained Harold's acceptance of her sexual nature and freedom, he gained her acceptance of his – which, at Knebworth, had triggered the whole, long, train of events. Vita emerged from the Trefusis affair with her identity and personal independence established, but Harold had his moral authority confirmed. Her adventurousness was accepted, but it took place within an agreed framework of values, some liberal, some traditional, which were Harold's – that combination of trust, confidence, support and respect which is so clearly demonstrated in their letters. It certainly helped that they were both highly literate individuals who could express and analyse their emotions when the other was not present. The written word was essential to both of them. It was through their letters rather than through conversation that they communicated complex emotional messages, maintaining and developing their relationship. It was not an untrammelled idyll: there were stresses and strains and rows as between any couple – and there were a number of occasions when Vita in particular did not tell Harold the whole truth – but once the Trefusis crisis was over, the marriage was never going to fall apart.

Yet it cannot end there. Harold was more than just emotionally dependent on Vita: the marriage had social, financial, and professional implications as well. What might have happened to Harold if Vita *had* finally and permanently eloped with Violet; if there *had* been a formal separation or even divorce? In a strictly professional sense, Harold had little to worry about – he had established his worth at the Foreign Office during the war and subsequently at the Peace Conference – but the position was more complicated than that.

Although the social upheavals that came in the wake of the war were bringing in a spirit of greater tolerance, British society at the beginning of the 1920s could be very unforgiving of sexual scandal. Adultery, at least among the upper classes, was widespread and tolerated as long as it did not become public knowledge. Male homosexuality was known to exist: it might be tolerated in certain – mainly artistic – circles, but it remained illegal. 'Buggers' and 'sodomites' were regarded by most of the British population with abhorrence. Female homosexuality, by contrast, was barely acknowledged and certainly not understood. Harold had already taken a number of risks by associating with the likes of Victor Cunard and Jean de Gaigneron who made no attempt to conceal their orientation. The danger for him was that any public exposure of the sexual nature of Vita and Violet's liaison – and as it was London was buzzing with gossip – might have backfired and exposed his own homosexuality. Exposure would certainly have ended his career and, for that reason if for no other, Harold would be extremely anxious to avoid divorce or any public attention of that kind. To fight, as he did, to maintain the form of his marriage, adapting its inner structures to suit his own and Vita's sexual preferences, was in his professional and social as well as his personal and emotional interests.

Sexual matters aside, separation from Vita would have had a major impact on Harold's lifestyle and social position. Vita did hold the purse-strings. He had, in the traditional phrase, married money, and he had also married into the landed aristocracy. True, Vita would not inherit Knole, but it was her money that had made Long Barn possible. His only income was his Foreign Office salary, which might just have allowed him to rent a small flat in London; he stood to inherit little from the unlanded Lord Carnock, whose estate would, in any event, be divided between his three sons. Harold was not a mercenary man. He was immensely generous to friends, helping people who were in difficulties, paying the bill in the restaurant, ordering the best food and the best wine. At the same time, he was a dreadful manager of money and worried constantly about being hard up. It would be unfair to suggest that money was in any sense a major factor influencing his behaviour during the period of Vita and Violet's affair, but he would scarcely have been human if he had not thought about it.

For all that, Harold comes out of the story well; better than Denys Trefusis who comes across as terribly weak. If it was a combination of sensational novel and French farce, it had at least the virtue of a traditional, happy ending. The hero got the girl and they lived – in their own very particular way – happily ever after.

18 Author

By the end of February 1920, only days after the crisis at Amiens, Harold had engineered himself back from Paris to the League of Nation's London headquarters – which did not formally transfer to Geneva until that October. He understood that Vita was suffering emotionally and wanted to be there to support her. Commuting from Long Barn to Curzon Street was obviously preferable to being in Paris while Vita pined by herself in Kent. Equally, although the relationship between the two women had passed the peak of its intensity, they were still seeing each other and spending time together. It was better for him to be on hand in case there were any signs of a revival.

In London, he was at once given a new task. The Soviet Union had not been represented at the Paris Conference. This was hardly surprising. The Bolshevik regime was regarded as a international pariah and the Allied countries which made up the Council of Five had all intervened – indeed, in 1920, were still actively fighting – on behalf of White Russian forces seeking to reinstate the Tsar. The Bolsheviks retaliated by sponsoring coups in European states, such as that led by Béla Kun in Hungary and the abortive Spartacist coup in Germany in 1919. The League of Nations now wanted to send a commission to the Soviet Union. The aim would be to make contact with the Bolshevik Government, explore opportunities for mediation, and, depending on the results, indicate that Soviet membership of the League might not be a complete impossibility. Harold, with some experience of pre-war Russia and some knowledge of the language, was to prepare terms of reference and background material for the commission.

He clearly expected it to be a long process. He brought his secretary, a Miss Williams, back from Paris and set to work. On 3 March, he received a letter from the Foreign Office notifying him that he had been promoted to the rank of First Secretary and, when he communicated the news to his family, was again cheered to find how well his father thought of him. Domestically, there was a problem with Vita's novel, *Challenge*. The central relationship between Julian and Eve was all too obviously that between Vita and Violet. Ostensibly, it was Lady Sackville and Mrs Keppel who saw the danger of scandal and persuaded Vita to withdraw the book from publication. In reality, Harold seems to have manipulated the situation so that he got what he wanted without appearing to be the prime mover. He must have been nervous when, on 20 March, Vita left to join Violet in Avignon, but appears to have hidden it as best he could. He carried on working on the

Soviet Union and then took a few days leave at Long Barn, working in the garden with Lady Sackville, who had clearly enjoyed the crisis and was currently his ally.

It was Greece and Turkey which, three weeks later, drew him back to Paris. In a bizarre echo of what had happened in February, he was setting off for France just as Vita was returning to England and they again managed to be on steamers crossing the Channel in opposite directions at precisely the same moment. Once in Paris, Harold found that little progress had been made on the issues he had been dealing with two months previously. As far as Greece was concerned, the terms he had agreed with Venizelos the previous August still stood, but they had leaked and so strengthened a revival of Turkish nationalist sentiment. A new Ottoman parliament in February had passed the *Misak-ý-Millî*, or National Oath, which called for self-determination and the safeguarding of the Turkish homeland. In March, Allied forces under British leadership tightened their grip on occupied Constantinople in order to keep the Straits open and protect the Armenian population. At the beginning of April, the Ottoman parliament was dissolved, but, within days of Harold's return to Paris, the nationalists under Mustafa Kemal (later to be known as Atatürk) had set up a provisional government in Ankara and signed an agreement with the Soviet Union for the supply of arms. What were the Allies to do? Should they negotiate with the legitimate but discredited and powerless government of the Sultan or with a bunch of nationalist revolutionaries who had made a pact with the Soviet devil? Could the League intervene? Harold worked alongside the League's Secretary General, Sir Eric Drummond to see what could be done. It was a thankless task.

By May, back in London again and with the current phase of the Turkish crisis apparently past, Harold was looking forward to some leave. For many years, Lord Sackville had kept his yacht, *Sumerun*, on Southampton Water and had spent part of the summer sailing off the south coast of Devon and Cornwall. This year's cruise had already started and Harold was due to join Vita and her father on board at Falmouth, but at the last minute a sudden crisis in Persia intervened. It was another immensely complex situation. In 1919, British forces had, with the reluctant acquiescence of the Persian authorities, garrisoned parts of northern Persia to prevent a Russian invasion – and thus safeguard British interests in the oil fields in the south. However, when the British gave refuge to defeated White Russian forces fleeing from the Russian Civil War, Soviet forces landed at the Caspian Sea port of Anzali. The British, under orders not to fight on Persian soil, retreated. The Soviets captured the strategically important city of Resht and set up a Soviet-style republic in the province of Girlan. The already weak government of Sultan Ahmed Shah appealed to the League. Britain, France and Italy supported the Shah but – while understandably terrified of the apparently irresistible spread of the Soviet revolution – they had no political appetite for another war. For Sir Eric Drummond, who again insisted on having Harold as his right hand man, it was another mission impossible.

Neither in Turkey nor in Persia did the League manage to achieve anything concrete or decisive – indeed, it is difficult to see what could have been achieved. Harold's secondment came to an end on 31 May and he returned to the Foreign Office. On the whole, it had not been a great success. It would be an exaggeration to say that he was disillusioned, but his enthusiasm for the League certainly diminished after he worked for it. Of course, the period had been largely overshadowed by personal considerations, but equally the League had kept moving him from job to job rather than giving him a role which offered a consistent focus for his talents. The most important thing that happened during his secondment was that he began to write his first book.

The impulse seems to have come from a colleague, and subsequently friend, Michael Sadleir, who, like Harold, was first a member of the British delegation in Paris and then seconded to the League Secretariat. In civilian life, however, Sadleir was director of Constable, the publishers. Their conversation took place on the stairs of the Majestic Hotel at the height of the Paris Conference when Harold was working twelve hours a day, advising statesmen and chairing committees. Harold was not so much bored as expecting to be bored. He had become so used to being frantically busy, he would not know what to do with himself when the pressure eased. Of course, this was also the time when Vita and Violet's affair was at its height, so there may have been an element of not daring to look down into the void, but one senses something more. Harold was not prepared to drift. The young man who, eight or nine years previously, had lounged around on the banks of the Bosphorus and given himself up to the social life of Constantinople's diplomatic community had changed. His ambition might not always run along traditional lines, but he wanted recognition. And he wanted to achieve something that was important to him on a personal level.

For a publisher to suggest that someone write a book is not particularly original, but Harold was struck by the idea and took it seriously. Vita understood. He must have discussed it with her while he was convalescing from his knee operation that Christmas, for in January 1920 she was urging that he '*must* write the Life of Verlaine.... I can't imagine anybody who could do it better.'¹ She supported the idea from the start. She was far more interested in him being a literary success than a diplomatic one, and just as Harold always supported her over her writing, so she would always support him over his. There was never any literary jealousy between them; nothing, indeed, except mutual praise and encouragement and, when it was necessary, judicious and constructive criticism.

Harold would have been introduced to the poetry of Paul Verlaine either at school or, perhaps more likely, at Oxford. James Lees-Milne has dated his first scholarly interest in the poet to 1910, when he read both Edmond Lepelletier's biography (published just the previous year) and then Verlaine's own *Confessions*.² Lees-Milne also draws attention to the fact that Harold quoted Verlaine in a letter he wrote to Vita at the beginning of 1915 – a quotation which, with hindsight, seems stunningly apposite to their post-Violet relationship.³

> *Je fais souvent ce rêve étrange et pénétrant*
> *D'une femme inconnue, et que j'aime, et qui m'aime,*
> *Et qui n'est, chaque fois, ni tout à fait la même*
> *Ni tout à fait une autre, et m'aime et me comprend.*⁴

For someone who was effectively bilingual, with a strong interest in French culture and history, and of progressive rather than radical literary sensibilities, Verlaine was not a particularly surprising choice. As Harold's characteristically low key opening paragraphs point out, there was plenty of source material available and he had the added advantage of there being no biography in English of the poet.

Harold always wrote fast. By 15 May, when Vita was still sailing with her father off Cornwall and while Harold was waiting for the leave that had been cancelled because of the Persian crisis, he noted that he had written 16,000 words. By July, he was far enough advanced to send what he had written to Michael Sadleir at Constable. Sadleir agreed to publish the book on fair, though not generous terms, and Harold was launched on his new career as a writer.

The moment his secondment to the League ended, the Foreign Office sent Harold back to Paris once again for what was to be a tumultuous summer. The Treaty of Trianon, the formal conclusion of peace terms between the Allies and the new state of Hungary, was signed on 4 June. Harold was only peripherally involved, although certain aspects of the treaty were to come back and haunt him later. He was more concerned with the Treaty of St Germain with Austria, which, although signed the previous September, needed modification before it could be ratified and become effective. While Harold was steering the necessary negotiations, which were complicated by continual delaying tactics on the part of the Italians, his hero, Venizelos, made what even Harold admitted was 'a false move.'[5] Venizelos made public the terms of the Treaty of Sèvres which the Allies had agreed to impose on Turkey. The Sultan's protests only emphasised his powerlessness and 'brought many thousand troops to the Kemalist cause.'[6] There were conferences at Hythe, on the Kent coast, and at Boulogne, but no progress was made. In June, with the covert encouragement of Lloyd George, the Greeks launched a series of attacks in Anatolia and then in Thrace with the aim of forcing the Turks to accept the treaty. Harold, for all his pro-Greek sentiments, was not convinced this was the best policy.

Despite the distractions of the Turkish conflict, Harold managed to get agreement on all the outstanding Austrian issues and the Treaty of St Germain was finally ratified on 17 July, becoming legally effective a week later. It was another notable success, although the fact that the Italians were distracted by events in Albania probably helped. A sudden and successful Albanian military offensive had put paid to any idea of establishing an Italian protectorate over the territory. The two sides rapidly signed an agreement and the Albanian issue, a legacy of the 1915 Treaty of London and one which had involved Harold on numerous occasions, came to a swift and unexpected conclusion. Three weeks later, the Greeks having defeated Turkey on the battlefield, the Treaty of Sèvres was also signed. The Greeks got everything they wanted. Italy took Rhodes and the Dodecanese. Armenia became independent and the Straits were placed under international control. The Treaty was humiliation for Turkey and, from the first, the nationalists refused to accept it. It was never going to last.

Caught up in the momentum of these events, Harold did not get back to England or spend as much time with Vita as he would have liked. As ever, letters were their main channel of communication. She was upbeat about his diplomatic success and on the progress of *Verlaine*, which he was evidently showing her chapter by chapter as he wrote. He felt able to tease her about her 'Amazonian theories' which would have women remain unmarried and live in 'truculent virginity.'[7] At the same time, he knew she was depressed. There was little he could do. Vita still felt the pull of Violet, who wrote frantic, emotional letters. It was under these circumstances – struggling with her emotions at a time when Harold, the fixed point in her emotional universe, could only get back from Paris for the occasional weekend – that she began to write the confessional narrative which, fifty years later, became the core of *Portrait of a Marriage*. As Victoria Glendinning says, the writing itself was 'a symptom of recovery.'[8] Vita was on the mend. She and Violet might make two or three more brief trips away together and give Harold a few unsettling moments, but 'the great adventure' was fading fast.[9]

By the early autumn of 1920, Harold was back in London and working at the Foreign Office. Greece and Turkey were still his staple diet. It was a conflict in which both Lord Curzon, the Foreign Secretary, and Sir Eyre Crowe – Harold's 'beloved chief', who had become Head of the Foreign Office on the retirement of Lord Hardinge – took a close interest. The stakes were high. The slow crumbling of the Ottoman Empire and consequent instability in the Balkans had been a key factor in events leading up to the outbreak of war. Many people, including Harold, saw a larger and stronger Greek state as one way of ensuring stability in the region, but Greece was now opposed not just by the weak remnants of Ottoman power, but by the emergent and wholly unpredictable Turkish nationalist movement under Mustafa Kemal.

Over the next two years, until the Lausanne Conference in November 1922, Harold was responsible for keeping track of the political and military balances within and between the two countries, and for drafting position papers which recommended the policy he saw as most advantageous to British interests. His problem was that the situation changed so rapidly and so radically that he was constantly having to revise both his analysis and his recommendations. It was a period during which he matured professionally and grew in confidence, justifying over a longer timescale and at the higher level of First Secretary the good opinions he had earned during the intense and pressured atmosphere of the Paris Conference. Harold enjoyed working hard and would always follow up any idea that caught his attention. Of course, there were times when he moaned about his job, but his interest in foreign affairs and his commitment to his official duties never slackened. At the same time, he seems to have recognised that the Foreign Office alone was not enough, for this was also the period in which writing became not just an additional activity but a second career: he published two books – his study of Paul Verlaine and a novel, *Sweet Waters* – and wrote a third, *Tennyson*, which was published in March 1923.

The Treaty of Sèvres marked the political high point of Greek diplomatic success. Within a matter of weeks, in one of those bizarre incidents which sometimes alter the course of history, King Alexander was walking in the gardens of the Greek royal family's summer palace at Tatoi when he was bitten in the leg by a pet monkey. The wound became infected and he died of blood poisoning. Alexander had been on the throne since 1917, when his pro-German elder brother, Constantine, had been forced to flee the country (though, crucially, he had not formally abdicated). Alexander had supported Venizelos when he had brought Greece into the war on the side of the Allies and their fortunes had become inextricably entwined. Now, with Alexander dead, Venizelos, despite his achievements in winning new territory for Greece around Smyrna and in Thrace, was significantly weakened. He lost the election on 14 November, overwhelmed by a tide of resurgent, traditional royalist sentiment, and three days later he fled the country. It seemed certain that King Constantine would be recalled. How should Britain react?

On 20 November, Harold submitted a paper to Sir Eyre Crowe advising that Britain – and also France – should oppose the return of Constantine, even to the point of imposing political and economic sanctions, if necessary. He based his argument on Constantine's pre-war support for 'the Hohenzollerns' and on the inefficiency and corruption which had characterised his first period on the throne – although there is no doubt that Harold's views were influenced by his personal sympathy for Venizelos. Crowe noted that if the Greek nation wanted Constantine back, then it was not for Britain to oppose their wishes.

The following day, Harold finished the manuscript of *Verlaine* and seems immediately to have begun what was to become *Sweet Waters*. Moving without pause from one project to the next was to become a regular occurrence throughout his writing life. Five days later, he was writing excitedly to Michael Sadleir about his plans for 'a splendidly psychoanalytical obscene novel.'[10] There are a few fragmentary traces of psychoanalysis and one sees where the obscenity might have fitted in, but it is fair to say that the published text of *Sweet Waters* bears little relation to this original description.

The new Greek Government called a plebiscite, which overwhelmingly supported the restoration of Constantine, who was back on his throne two weeks later. On 20 December, Harold submitted another paper, just a month after his last one. Constantine's return had to be accepted. Britain's aim was to create stability in an unstable region, but the situation was complicated by the attitude of her allies. Italy, for reasons of her own in the Adriatic, wanted a weak Greece. France, suspicious of British influence in Greece, saw her best opportunity for the future in backing the new Turkey of Mustafa Kemal. In these circumstances, Harold argued, stability was best served by supporting Constantine as long as he accepted the conditions of the Treaty of Sèvres, which, he pointed out, were in any event highly favourable to Greece. It was, as both Crowe and Lord Curzon acknowledged, a thoughtful proposition. The only problem was that Constantine effectively abandoned Sèvres by declaring himself in favour of continuing the Greek offensive in Anatolia.

For the first time since 1917, Harold and Vita spent a family Christmas with the boys in Kent, but he was quickly recalled to London. On 8 January 1921, he submitted a paper drawing attention to the Greek advance in Anatolia. If Sèvres was to be maintained, he suggested, Britain had to support Greece, even if it meant opposing French interests. Crowe was not convinced. Anything as radical as Harold was proposing would have to wait until after a conference in Paris, scheduled for later that month – and it would require the agreement of Lord Hardinge, now Ambassador in Paris, which was unlikely to be forthcoming. The very next day, the situation changed again. Turkish nationalist forces under Ismet Pasha (later the first Prime Minister of the Turkish Republic) came up against Greek troops at the first Battle of Inönü. It was not a major engagement but it was significant. It was the first time the Greek advance had been checked and it was the first time that Turkish nationalist military forces had been able to prove themselves in battle.

While Harold was following the twists and turns of the war in Anatolia, Vita and Violet made one last trip abroad. The original plan had been to go to Spain, but Harold had objected. He understood the different strands of Vita's character and the way she responded to different stimuli. Spain would have brought Pepita to the surface again. They compromised on the south of France. Vita travelled down to meet Violet at Nîmes and the two of them went on to Hyères, just to the east of Toulon.

No sooner had Vita departed than Harold was again called upon to draft another memorandum. The issue now was Smyrna. The Treaty of Sèvres gave Greece a protectorate over an enclave of Turkish territory around Smyrna. After five years, a plebiscite was to be held to decide whether the territory should formally become part of Greece or revert to Turkey. This arrangement had become a *cause célèbre* for the Turkish nationalists; and the French, seeking political advantage, were now offering them support. Britain had traditionally supported Greece – Lloyd George, indeed, had encouraged the Greek invasion – but now found Greece led by the unpalatable King Constantine. This was an extremely awkward position and Lord Curzon was looking for an escape route. Harold was asked to suggest ways in which the Smyrna chapter of Sèvres could be modified to allow for a compromise with the Turks.

It was a measure of his growing confidence that he did no such thing. His memorandum, submitted on 18 January, was actually a list of reasons why

Sèvres remained the best basis for British policy and should *not* be modified. Greece, he argued, was winning the war on the ground and unlikely to withdraw from Smyrna just because Britain and France asked them to. The nationalist Turks would only be encouraged to make even more demands. And the French would see Britain's change of policy as an opportunity further to undermine British power and prestige in the region. Sir Eyre Crowe was convinced. Lord Curzon was not. The following day, he sent for Harold, explained the situation, and required Harold to go away and do what he had been asked to do in the first place. It had been a high risk strategy on Harold's part, although one motivated by conviction. Curzon does not appear to have been angry, as a lesser man might have been, at being disobeyed. The incident may even have been the beginning of the odd friendship that grew up between them. Curzon, as his biographer David Gilmour makes clear, 'had no use for yes-men.'[11]

Harold crossed to Paris on 23 January 1921 and the Conference began at the Quai d'Orsay the following morning, but the war between Greece and Turkey was pushed into the background by the question of German reparations, and nothing was achieved beyond an agreement to hold a further conference in London in a month's time. Harold was impressed by Curzon's ability to synthesise the complexities of the situation in his opening speech and by Lloyd George's oratory, but one detects also a slight shifting of his priorities. On the way across to Paris, he was preparing an article which he had apparently been commissioned to write on the Civil Service.[12] Then, on 27 January, he went to a lunch hosted by Maréchal Foch. Among the guests were Lloyd George, Curzon and the new French Premier, Aristide Briand. Normally, Harold would have been fascinated by conversation and the relationships between such eminent men. On this occasion, however, he seems to have been more interested in his neighbour, the Comte de Fels – himself an interesting combination of diplomat and writer – who owned and edited *La Revue de Paris*.[13] By the end of the meal, the Count had been persuaded not only to review *Verlaine* but also to offer Harold the chance of writing an article.

That same afternoon, Harold went off to see his old hero, Venizelos, who was in bed in the Majestic Hotel propped up on pillows. Even in exile, Venizelos remained a figure to whom Harold responded emotionally. Sir Eyre Crowe certainly understood this and was prepared to make use of the relationship when it suited his purposes. On this occasion, he had chosen Harold as the most suitable person to inform Venizelos officially of the forthcoming London Conference, which, on the face of it, seemed likely to be damaging to Greek interests. As things turned out – and despite its sometimes detrimental impact on Harold's judgement – his close relationship with Venizelos was to pay dividends as the balance of advantage around the Aegean continued to swing back and forth and Venizelos continued his roller-coaster career.

Harold returned from a week in Paris knowing that the next month would be spent going over the Graeco-Turkish issue yet again in preparation for the London Conference. Vita had not returned from Hyères and had not written, which made him cross. A week later, he wrote her a sharp letter, which mixes ridicule – 'Well really, Fatushka (or whatever it is)' – with quite unusual assertiveness – 'And please also realise that this is definite. I shall be more angry than I have ever been if you do not come back on that date.'[14] There is a clear change in his attitude: he is no longer worried about whether she will return, but rather about the practicalities of when and how. Or at least that is how he presents it – one wonders whether he was really quite as sanguine as the letter suggests. Certainly, a letter from Denys Trefusis announcing that he had had enough and was intending to separate from Violet gave him a jolt. This was just the kind of action which risked inflaming Violet's anti-male sentiments and carrying Vita with her. Harold went to Dottie Wellesley for advice. Even though Gerry Wellesley had abandoned the Foreign Office for architecture after the war, the two families remained close and, over the year since Amiens, Dottie had become increasingly friendly with Vita. For Harold, at the time, it was a logical choice, but one which would come to carry an ironic significance, first when Dottie became Vita's lover and then later when the Nicolsons were called on to offer support as the Wellesleys' marriage fell apart.

As so often when concerned about Vita, Harold sought solace among his male friends. He spent the weekend of 12–13 February at Oxford. He saw Sligger Urquhart and commented unfavourably on the way in which the patrician quality of Balliol had become diluted in the post-war world. Most of the time, however, he spent with Eddie Marsh, who was still Winston Churchill's Private Secretary, and Marsh's particular friend, the composer Ivor Novello. There were also two younger figures: Victor Cazalet, who became MP for Chippenham in Wiltshire; and Henry 'Chips' Channon, who also became an MP but is principally remembered for his diaries, which often overlap with Harold's but are written from a different, more socially ambitious viewpoint. All one can say is that it was a strongly homosexual cast.

The next few weeks were a kaleidoscope of activity which saw both Harold's fortunes and the political fortunes of the Greeks and Turks fluctuating wildly. He arrived at work to be told that the Government of the

Kingdom of Serbs, Croats and Slovenes (the original name for what, in 1928, became Yugoslavia) wished to award him the Order of St Saba in recognition of his work at the Peace Conference. Foreign Office regulations prevented him accepting, but it was nonetheless a boost to his ego. On 17 February, together with his colleague D'Arcy Osborne – who served as Minister to the Holy See throughout the Second World War and, later, became Duke of Leeds – he submitted a paper outlining suggested policy and procedure for the following week's conference. The line proposed was a kind of pro-Greek *realpolitik*. Sèvres would have to be modified, but the Greeks had at least fought the war as Allies, whereas the official Turkish Government had been allied to Germany and the nationalist alternative was in league with Soviet Russia. Qualified support for Greece accorded better with Britain's long-term interests. Lord Curzon approved and even passed Harold a morsel of praise for a second paper on the possibility of rewarding the Greeks in Eastern Rumelia at the expense of the Bulgarians in recompense for concessions in and around Smyrna.

The Conference duly opened on 21 February amid the portrait-hung corridors, gilt mirrors and crimson carpets of St James's Palace. Harold was there, cheered by a telegram from Vita that she would be returning the following weekend, and watching events carefully. The first problem was the Turks. They were militarily weak but not at all conciliatory, demanding the restitution of all the territories they had lost to Greece since the war and reparations on top. The second was Lloyd George. Having previously been more pro-Greek than Curzon, he now showed signs of ignoring the Foreign Office's balanced approach, reversing his position entirely and bending to accommodate the French and Italians who saw more advantage in supporting the rising tide of Turkish nationalism. The third was Dmitri Stancioff, the Bulgarian Minister in London, who had got wind of the possibility that Greece might be compensated at the expense of his country and came to Harold to lodge an indignant – and largely justified – protest. Harold was thrown into dejection. All he had worked for seemed about to be thrown away. After a week of meetings and negotiations, the Allies agreed among themselves and offered a series of modifications to Sèvres which were roundly rejected by both Greeks and Turks alike. On top of which, Vita had delayed her return.

That was not all. For the duration of the London Conference, Harold appears to have been living in a grubby rented room with a gas ring in Bentinck Street, behind the Wigmore Hall.[15] It seems an odd choice and it was certainly an arrangement he found depressing. Ebury Street was rented out and his conference commitments did not allow him to commute from

Long Barn. Beyond that, one can only speculate that he felt he could not afford a hotel and that his other options, the Sackvilles' house in Hill Street and the Carnocks' in Cadogan Gardens were unavailable. Whatever the case, it was from this rented room that Harold emerged, somewhat depressed, at the beginning of the second week of the London Conference to be told by his Foreign Office colleague, Robert Vansittart, that Winston Churchill was making 'a frightful row' over a conversation Harold had had with the leader of the Greek delegation. Harold had apparently warned the Greeks that the British did not expect the Turks to be conciliatory and that it would therefore be in Greek interests to be as conciliatory as possible. Presumably, given Harold's sympathies, this was done to help the Greeks, but it could equally have been interpreted as an attempt to engineer a positive outcome to the Conference. The worst he had been was indiscreet. The Greeks, however, had been even more indiscreet and Harold's comments had leaked out. It is difficult to see why Churchill, as Secretary of State for Air – shortly to become Secretary of State for the Colonies – should have felt so involved or been so angry, but he was and he even raised the matter with Lloyd George.

Of course, it is never a good idea for a civil servant to upset a member of the Cabinet, but Harold had been in the Foreign Office long enough to know that, intense as such moments can be, they invariably pass over. In *Sweet Waters*, which Harold was writing at just this time, Tenterden, the Chargé d'Affaires, says to a junior member of staff: 'Well, we're all indiscreet at intervals ... try and make your intervals as long as possible.'[16] Yet Harold could not take his own advice. Praise elated him; criticism invariably cast him into the depths. Coming on top of the events of the previous week, this comparatively minor incident sparked an outburst of self-pity.

> So even my personal position has gone wrong now. No home. No affection. No money. No happiness. Oh Vita, Vita, what have you to answer for. I simply long to get abroad and away from them all. What a bloody thing it is to have such a thin skin! Last week was the worst week I have ever gone through. I am a harmless happy creature by nature. If only I didn't care for her it would help. But I love her so.[17]

As James Lees-Milne points out, Harold's current predicament had nothing to do with Vita[18] – beyond the fact that she was not there to comfort him. In his diary Harold is frequently honest enough to acknowledge his own weaknesses, but this entry leaves one feeling that it was written with the expectation – or hope – that Vita would read it before too long.

The London Conference dragged on until 4 March, by which time Lloyd George had returned to his pro-Greek stance and the Turks gave at least the appearance of accepting the settlement offered to them. It was typical of so many of the meetings and conferences with which Harold was involved in the years after the First World War. The experts toiled to produce a policy, but negotiations were compromised not only by intransigence on the part of the principals but also by internal disagreement among the British negotiators – as between Curzon and Lloyd George – and by conflicting interests among the Allied Powers. In the end, the London Conference achieved nothing. Sir Eyre Crowe summed up the general view when he 'put his head in his hands' and said, 'I hate the Balkans.'[19]

After many changes of plan, missed trains and general confusion, Vita arrived back in London on 9 March, the Wednesday after the end of the Conference. She and Harold immediately went down to Knole to see Ben and Nigel and stayed overnight, so Harold was at Knole on the morning of 10 March when *Paul Verlaine* was published and the first reviews appeared.

Paul Verlaine is not, and was never intended to be, an academic study. It is rather a literary biography. The narrative of Verlaine's troubled life is balanced by extensive, illustrative quotation from the poems and Harold never loses sight of the fact that it is the poetry that makes Verlaine's life of interest. Using a narrative technique that contains strong visual and often impressionistic elements, he attempts to reach an understanding of Verlaine's character by reconstructing his emotional state in certain key moments or passages of his life. In this, one can detect the influence of Lytton Strachey, whose *Eminent Victorians*, published less than three years previously, began the process of creating a more accessible, more psychological and more honest framework for biography. There is no doubt that in *Verlaine* and in his subsequent books on Tennyson, Swinburne and Byron, Harold benefitted from Strachey's example – he was quite open about his admiration for Strachey's work – but, while present, the influence is far from overwhelming and it would be a mistake to see Harold as a mere imitator of Strachey's method, as Virginia Woolf was later to claim.

The literary establishment at the beginning of the 1920s was much smaller than it is today and much more homogeneous. It was largely in the hands of Oxford and Cambridge graduates who would have seen Harold as one of their own. A first book from someone of Harold's background, provided it was tolerably well written and did not seek to upset too many established reputations, could expect a reasonably warm welcome and *Verlaine* was generally well received. The *Morning Post* praised his knowledge of French poetry (which was, in fact, somewhat patchy) while the

Bookman, more perceptively, caught a glimpse of the craftsman and stylist which Harold was to become. The veteran critic and writer, Edmund Gosse, in the *Sunday Times* was also welcoming.

Harold's attitude to Gosse, whom he knew from the lunch and dinner tables of Lady Cunard and Lady Colefax, is both characteristic and revealing. Gosse was over seventy by the time *Verlaine* was published. He knew or had known everyone from George Eliot to Thomas Hardy and André Gide. He had been responsible for launching Ibsen onto the English stage. In his day, he had been able to make or break literary reputations, but by the 1920s that day had passed. Gosse belonged to the pre-war world and his good opinion was not something young writers particularly sought or cared about. For Bloomsbury, notably Virginia Woolf and Lytton Strachey, he became a figure of fun: a pompous old man regaling the world with irrelevant anecdotes of literary figures from a bygone age. Harold saw things differently. He respected Gosse. He saw the old man's stories of the life in 1880s (which often included imitations of Carlyle, Browning, Swinburne and Tennyson) as a valuable link with the literary past. When Gosse died in 1928, he wrote an appreciative obituary for the *Nation*, a weekly paper actually owned by a group which included the Bloomsbury stalwart, John Maynard Keynes. While it is possible to dismiss Harold's attitude as simply conservative and old-fashioned, he can equally be seen as demonstrating both a literary and critical judgement independent of the current fashion and a sense of historical continuity.

Not all the reviews were favourable. Remarkably, in view of what is generally said about him, the *Times Literary Supplement* accused Harold of 'vulgarity'.[20] The *Observer*, by contrast, complained of his 'superiority' of tone and that he was unsympathetic towards Verlaine.[21] Faced with criticism of this kind, Harold's response was predictably thin-skinned, displaying the same tendency to over-react as he did when criticised at the Foreign Office. 'Unjustified', 'atrocious' and, 'malicious' are the words which pepper his diary.[22]

Writing in 1944, twenty-three years after the publication of *Verlaine*, the American writer and critic, Edmund Wilson, suggested that 'it was priggish to be shocked by Verlaine, as Nicolson obviously was, and to dismiss him with a sharp tone of reprimand.'[23] The charge comes as part of a broad-based attack on Harold's character and attitudes which needs to be seen in the context both of its time and Harold's later work. As far as *Verlaine* is concerned, it seems harsh. It was natural to Harold, both personally, in terms of his character, and strategically, in terms of what it might reveal about his own (and Vita's) sexual inclination, to be reticent in writing about sexual matters. He is not explicit about the homosexual bond between Verlaine and Rimbaud, but no one reading the book – especially the extract from *A Season in Hell* and Harold's subsequent commentary on the impact of Rimbaud's exhortations on Verlaine's imagination[24] – can be in any doubt about the sexual nature of their relationship. Nor does Harold go into graphic detail about Verlaine's *ménage* with Esther Boudin and Eugénie Krantz, but he says enough for the reader to understand the situation with complete clarity – 'They were neither of them young women: they were both greedy for money: they were both rather slatternly and dishonest. … It is no use pretending that their life together was anything more than a sad and filthy farce.'[25] This is neither priggish nor shocked. A degree of ironic detachment may dilute his sympathy at times, but the tone throughout is frank and realistic rather than judgemental.

Verlaine is very much a first book and also something of a young man's book. The opening pages are almost defensive, as if Harold were explaining to himself why he is writing. There are some structural oddities: having chronicled the last, tragic meeting between Verlaine and Rimbaud, Harold breaks off the main narrative to sketch the rest of Rimbaud's life, apparently more because he is enjoying the story than because it adds anything to an understanding of Verlaine. And the terminal essay on Verlaine's literary reputation, while making Harold's literary purpose clear, has a formal, academic tone which sits oddly with the rest of the book. There are one or two passages of broad, dinner party generalisation, including one about the French, which show Harold at his Victorian best – or worst – and jar on modern ears: 'they have patriotism but no public spirit, foresight but no vision, wit but no humour, personality but not individualism, discipline but no order…. They have none of our cheerful and blundering intuition.'[26]

For all that, *Verlaine* remains worth reading. The strangeness of Verlaine's early years, the compulsions of his affair with Rimbaud, the failures of his middle years and the slide into overproduction and degradation are set in the context of French culture and French society which Harold understood so well. There are some vivid descriptive passages – such as Verlaine's disastrous fight with Rimbaud and the picture of his domestic arrangements at the end of his life – and there are a number of sharply perceptive or wryly-expressed observations, the first of those characteristic Nicolson touches which Vita referred to as the 'Hadji bits.'

19 Balance

Vita's return from France in March 1921 marked a turning point in her life, and in Harold's. He continued to divide his time between the Foreign Office, his writing and an active social life, but the atmosphere of their relationship changed. It was not just that he was delighted to have her back, that she was actually there and that they could begin to share things again. It was the fact that relations between them were no longer strained by the presence of Violet in the background. Vita seems to have made a conscious decision to draw a line under that phase of her life. She had not touched her *Portrait of a Marriage* narrative since the previous October. Now, she abandoned it, leaving the events of that spring in Hyères unrecorded. She added just one final paragraph in which she speaks of her 'great unhappiness which I try to conceal from poor Harold, who is an angel upon earth'; of her sense of guilt that she has come through 'safe secure and undamaged save in my heart,' whereas Violet 'may not choose to live'; and of 'Violet's doom, which she herself has consistently predicted.'[1] It is a melodramatic and unconvincing conclusion. Just as there are times in Harold's diary when he seems to be writing in the hope of being read, so here one senses that Vita is writing in the hope that Harold might read her words and offer her sympathy.

Whatever her feelings, Vita's actions betrayed no sign of lasting unhappiness. She returned to life at Long Barn and in London and slipped into what for her and Harold was to become their own particular version of normality. Their marriage acquired the sense of balance that it had so conspicuously lacked over the previous three-and-a-half years – ever since Harold had been forced into confessing his homosexuality in November 1917. They attended London society dinners hosted by Sibyl Colefax. They dined out with friends, such as the Wellesleys. They attended the wedding of Harold's Foreign Office colleague, Allen Leeper – just the sort of function that Harold enjoyed but which, under Violet's influence, Vita would have scorned. At the end of May, they went on holiday together, something they had not done for some years, spending two weeks aboard Lord Sackville's yacht, *Sumerun*, during which they crossed to Cowes in the Isle of Wight and then cruised westward along the south coast, stopping off in Dartmouth, Fowey and Falmouth. They were able to share their literary interests: *The Dragon in Shallow Waters* had just been published to popular acclaim and Harold was putting the final touches to *Sweet Waters*. At the end of the holiday, they travelled back to Long Barn to spend the last few days of Harold's leave together. Harold sent his manuscript to Michael Sadleir at Constable. A couple of weeks later, Vita came up to London to join Harold for lunch with Jan Smuts, who was now Prime Minister of the Union of South Africa. For Harold to lunch with Smuts and enjoy listening to the already legendary South African holding forth on President Wilson's role in the Peace Conference, the failings of the current generation of British politicians and life in the South African bush was to be expected. Far stranger, and again an indication of the change in her and in their relationship, was that Vita should agree to accompany him and apparently enjoy the occasion.

The centre of the Nicolsons' life was Long Barn, which in the first half of 1921, as if to demonstrate that a sense of permanence had returned to their residence there, acquired both a generator to provide electric light and a tennis court. Long Barn was where Harold returned every evening when his workload allowed and where Vita returned to her writing with a new fluency. They began to receive an increasing number of visitors. There were Harold's Foreign Office colleagues, such as his new favourite Charles Cradock-Hartopp. There were his Whitehall connections, such as Eddie Marsh and Jack Wodehouse, another of Churchill's Private Secretaries, who had represented Britain at polo in the 1920 Antwerp Olympics. There were artists, such as Augustus John, who arrived with his mistress, Eve Fleming, mother of the writers Peter and Ian Fleming; and Ronald Balfour, best-known for his illustrations for *The Rubaiyat of Omar Khayam*. There were numerous literary connections: Hugh Walpole, the novelist; Jack Squire, editor of the *London Mercury*; John Drinkwater, the poet and playwright; Algernon Blackwood, in whose tales of supernatural or paranormal forces Vita had developed an interest; Clive Bell, with whom Harold, in particular, developed a friendship quite divorced from Bell's role in Bloomsbury. And there were other friends such as Harold's one-time lover, Victor Cunard, and, of course, Gerry and Dottie Wellesley.

Meanwhile, at the Foreign Office, Harold's energies were being absorbed in a new set of problems which had been thrown up by the various peace treaties. The latest was the Burgenland: a thin, irregular strip of land which, historically, had belonged to the Hungarian part of the Austro-Hungarian Empire, but which the Peace Conference had allocated to the new state of Austria on the grounds that a 1910 census had shown a large German-speaking majority. The Hungarians formally agreed to the transfer when they signed Treaty of Trianon on 4 June 1920, but nothing was done until the Treaty was finally ratified a year later. In the meantime, a number of Hungarian landowners opposed to the transfer had organised bands of militia armed with rifles and hand grenades to resist the change of sovereignty. The Austrian authorities, in an attempt to avoid provoking violent resistance, attempted a low key approach and made the disastrous, if understandable, decision to send in the gendarmerie rather than troops. They were immediately driven back and further incursions were discouraged by snipers deployed along the border. Coordinating the Foreign Office's response to what was a stand-off rather than a crisis, Harold worked with his French colleagues at the Quai d'Orsay, putting pressure on the Austrian Chancellor to accept Italian mediation. And, in the event, mediation worked. Under the Venice Protocol, signed in October 1921, Hungary withdrew its snipers and allowed Austria to occupy the Burgenland with the proviso that a plebiscite should be held in certain key areas. Voting took place in December and early in 1922, Austria was confirmed in its possession of most of the Burgenland, while the important town of Ödenburg (today's Sopron) remained within Hungary. On the map, the solution looked a trifle messy, but it represented a clear victory for the principle of self-determination.

Harold's other problem in the summer of 1921 was Albania. It was to continue to occupy him right up to the end of the year, but, unlike the Burgenland, no definitive solution was to prove possible. Faced with the incredible complexity of ethnic distribution in the Balkans, the Peace Conference had failed to settle the issue of Albania's borders and the whole region remained politically unstable. The previous summer, Albanian forces had enjoyed a notable success against Italian troops around the port city of Vlorë, securing an agreement which – for the moment, at least – removed the threat of an Italian takeover. But the Serbs had taken advantage of the situation and invaded from the north. In July 1921, they set up a puppet state, the Republic of Mirdita, based on the northern city Rëshen. The Balkans had caused enough trouble and none of the Allies wanted to see further instability in the region. The first thing to be done was to offer reassurance to Albania's numerous ethnic minorities. The second was to address the fundamental issue of the borders themselves. Harold's role was to draft a proposed line of approach which the Italians would accept. This he did, earning praise from Lord Curzon. He then contributed to a 'Declaration Concerning the Protection of Minorities in Albania' which was issued by the League of Nations on 2 October. As an acknowledged expert on Balkan affairs with experience of the issues surrounding Albanian independence that went back to the 1915 Treaty of London and beyond, he was the natural choice to go to Paris in November when the issue was brought before the League of Nations. A committee was formed

Balance

to look again at the Serbian-Albanian border, chaired by General Maxime Weygand, the French military commander who had presented the terms of the armistice to the German commander in the railway coach at Compiègne in 1918. Harold's expertise was important in putting together a formula which both sides could accept. It was a small success for the League. Although Albania remained internally unstable, there were no further encroachments on its boundaries until the Italian invasion in 1939.

Harold revelled in this kind of work. He had a natural curiosity and an equally natural ability to research and marshal facts, to assess political and personal pressures and put them in their proper context. The subject barely mattered: it was the process he enjoyed. In the Foreign Office, knowledge and understanding, even of the most obscure issues, was a part of being at the centre of things. The same skills underpin many of Harold's books, notably his biographical works and historical surveys, but in the Foreign Office their application was practical: they helped shape government policy and guide its implementation through diplomatic action. And in the Foreign Office, Harold's abilities also ensured that he received regular helpings of praise from Eyre Crowe, Lord Curzon and others in the hierarchy whose approval he sought: something which, despite his manifest experience and success, he continued to need in order to maintain his self-confidence.

The ease with which Harold manages his facts and his material can also be misleading. When *Verlaine* was published, the *Morning Post* credited him with a greater knowledge of French poetry than he in fact possessed. And the modern reader, faced with Harold's easy and persuasive style is apt to assume that he was a greater expert on art, letters, poetry or manners than he really was. In October 1921, Harold spent three weeks in Italy with Vita and the Wellesleys. James Lees-Milne draws attention to diary entries which show that, though he might respond to the aesthetic qualities of a particular object or work of art, he was not necessarily well informed about artistic matters, nor inclined to make the effort to learn – 'We stop at Marina and look at some Domenico frescoes. Are they Domenico? And who was Domenico?'[2] Where he did respond, where he became curious and observant, was when an item or, more often, a place had historical or literary connections. He was more interested in visiting the house on the Spanish Steps where Keats died, or Castel Gandolfo, with its links to papal history and to the Latin League, than he was in examining the contents of art galleries or looking at architecture from an abstract point of view. This is not to suggest that he was lacking in artistic appreciation – though he had gaps in his awareness like anyone else – but rather to reiterate that, for

Harold, people, places and things were in the main defined by their connection to an outer, social or historical world, not by their inner or aesthetic qualities.

Vita, Gerry and Dottie left for Italy at the beginning of September. Harold joined them in Rome a month later. When he arrived, he found that Vita and Dottie had taken themselves off to Split and Dubrovnik and not yet returned. (Did he have a moment of private worry that history might repeat itself?) Gerry whisked him off to see Gerald Berners, who had left the Foreign Office but remained in Rome pursuing his musical interests, at his flat in Via Varese. They went on sightseeing expeditions in Berners' Rolls-Royce. They visited Frascati and Castel Gandolfo and picnicked in the hills overlooking Lake Albano. It was very much a boys' day out. Harold christened their chauffeur 'William the Adonis'[3] and they were accompanied by the young Prince Philipp of Hesse. Philipp was a great-grandson of Queen Victoria, English-educated and a talented interior designer. He was also bisexual. Berners had just introduced him to Siegfried Sassoon with whom he was to have a two-year relationship before marrying Princess Mafalda, the daughter of the Italian King, Victor Emmanuel III. He was destined to become an odd, tragic figure. Impressed with Italian fascism, he returned to Germany to join the Nazi Party and became an active collaborator in Hitler's euthanasia programme, but then he fell from grace and was imprisoned in Dachau and later Niederdorf concentration camps.

That night, Harold retired to his room in the Hotel Inghilterra, a sixteenth-century palazzo just a stone's throw from the Spanish Steps. At midnight he was woken by a rattling at his door and found Vita, returned from her trip with Dottie. For the next ten days, the two couples continued their holiday in Rome, seeing the sights, meeting friends and making occasional excursions. The Castel Gandolfo trip was considered such a success that it was repeated, this time with both Philipp of Hesse and Siegfried Sassoon, whose company Harold particularly enjoyed. They lunched *al fresco* under a vine and played games with paper boats in a stream, before returning to dine together in Rome. It was one of the high points of a holiday which otherwise seems to have been characterised by a degree of tension – there were squabbles about architecture in Venice and a row about Tiepolo in Munich. They all blamed Gerry because he insisted on organising intense programmes of cultural activity and expecting everyone else to follow his lead, but the true cause lay with the Wellesleys' marriage which, as Harold and Vita both knew, was not was going at all well. Harold returned to the Foreign Office on 24 October and picked up the threads of the Albanian crisis. The next day, *Sweet Waters* was published.

Nineteen twenty-one was the year of *Women in Love* and *Crome Yellow*. It was also the year of Sheila Kaye-Smith's *Joanna Godden*, Georgette Heyer's *The Black Moth* and John Galsworthy's *To Let*. *Sweet Waters* was not in the front ranks of the avant-garde, but nor was it in any sense backward-looking. If there is a suggestion of Jane Austen in Harold's highly developed sense of irony and the way the mature hero ultimately gets the girl, in other ways the novel is very much of its time. The narrative moves between something approaching stream of consciousness and detached, even distant, third party description depending on what aspect of character or story he is seeking to emphasise. And Harold's interest in defining the relationship between the individual and his social and historical context – a preoccupation of many later twentieth-century novelists – marks the novel as a product of the period after the First World War.

Sweet Waters is the story of a young woman, Eirene Davenport, growing to maturity and finding love. It is also an intensely nostalgic novel. The evocative descriptions of Constantinople's tree-lined streets and squares, the cafés and restaurants, the steamers passing up and down the Bosphorus, all draw on Harold's memories of living in the city before the war. And the descriptions of a Turkish field hospital under Bulgarian attack in the novel's final stages are drawn from Harold's personal experiences during the First Balkan War. The sense of nostalgia may also be linked to Harold's memories of his engagement and the early years of his marriage. James Lees-Milne has pointed out how Eirene, with her beauty, awkwardness and uncertainty, resembles Vita, and that her self-centred, manipulative mother could be Lady Sackville.[4] After three years of intense marital stress, Harold could well have been looking back to more tranquil times.

Harold himself features in the novel in two guises. There is an ironic self-portrait in the figure of Angus Field, the sad, ineffectual junior clerk at the British Embassy (whom he described to Michael Sadleir as 'a little sodomitic cad'),[5] who writes bad poetry and is a totally hopeless lover. Then there is an idealised self-portrait in Hugh Tenterden, the commanding diplomatic hero, who is always in control and always judges correctly. Tenterden's character also bears a noticeable resemblance to that of Jane Austen's Mr Knightley.

To the modern reader, *Sweet Waters* may have something of the air of a costume drama – suitable perhaps for a Merchant-Ivory style adaptation – but it remains atmospheric and very readable. When correcting the proofs, Harold had been nervous about the book. 'One goes down and down the page,' he wrote to Vita, 'and it flops and one flops, and there comes nothing but despair when one turns over.'[6] When publication day came, however, the reviews were generally favourable and the book sold three thousand copies in its first three months.

All in all, 1921 ended well for the Nicolsons. Violet had disappeared from their lives. They were back together and there was a sense of permanence about their relationship – Vita gave Harold eight acres of land adjacent to Long Barn for his birthday. They had established a mutually-agreed and acceptable basis for their marriage which would never seriously be challenged. Vita had published a novel, *The Dragon in Shallow Waters*, and a collection of poems, *Orchard and Vineyard*. Harold had published *Verlaine* and *Sweet Waters*. Vita was engaged on a book of short stories, *The Heir*, and a volume of family history, *Knole and the Sackvilles*, both of which would be published in 1922. Harold was still enjoying life in the Foreign Office, immersed in the apparently endless struggle between the Greeks and the Turks. There was even a degree of harmony in their relations with Lady Sackville – with whom Harold, Vita and the children spent Christmas at Brighton.

That September, Harold had written excitedly to Vita that he was about to begin a new book, though he had no idea what it was to be about. Then he added:

> Oh, darling, how lucky we are both of us to write books and to love each other so very much and with such confidence (not in fidelity, darling – don't get that into your head) but confidence in each other's respect and love.[7]

20 Tennyson

Harold did not actually decide on the subject of his next book until that December when, after a day working in the garden at Long Barn, he announced that it was to be a biography of Tennyson. Many years later, when he was a regular columnist for the *Spectator*, he produced an article entitled 'Writing Books'[1] in which he sets the biographer and historian apart from the novelist. The main difference, in his view, is that the biographer and historian need to absorb and arrange large amounts of existing material. He advises that

> The intending biographer ... should first purchase a very large, and if

possible a loose-leaved, notebook. He should then acquire the most detailed standard work upon his subject. He should then devote much time and trouble to summarising in his notebook the facts and comments contained in the standard work. If he does this carefully, legibly and methodically ... he will then after much toil have before him the main outlines of the narrative.... Thereafter he will read all available works and documents bearing on his subject, and will insert in his notebook all the additional material he requires.... He can then discard all works of reference and use his notebook as the sole quarry.[2]

It is a methodical, if pedestrian, approach. Assuming that Harold followed his own advice, it seems to have served him well, for having decided in December that he wanted to write about Tennyson, he completed his basic research in just three months. His diary records that he started writing on Good Friday 1922, which was 25 March.

It was a busy period in other ways. During January, Harold and Vita continued to enjoy a shared social life which, in retrospect, has an authentic 1920s quality to it. Accompanied by the Wellesleys, they went to the cinema, still silent in those days – though the first shot of the film they saw, *The Great Adventure*, actually featured a trumpeter sounding a fanfare. *The Great Adventure* was a costume drama, set in the seventeenth century and filmed at Knole, and it starred Lady Diana Cooper, the wife of Harold's Foreign Office colleague, Duff Cooper, who was to play an important role in the Munich crisis and in Churchill's wartime government. The Nicolsons also dined with the Colefaxes, where they met Aldous Huxley, who was basking in the notoriety of his first novel, *Crome Yellow*, which actually satirised the kind of society he was now moving in. They also attended the première of Edith Sitwell's *Façade* with William Walton's music.

> The recitation took place in an ordinary London drawing-room with a curtain cutting off the re-entrant end. On the curtain was painted a huge futurist face with a large hole for the mouth. Through the mouth was fixed a megaphone and through the megaphone came the voice of Edith [who] recited some twenty poems from *Façade*, with forced emphasis on the metre.[3]

At the end of January, Vita went off to Sicily with Dottie Wellesley. At some point, either now or perhaps later in the year, their close friendship developed into an affair. Harold knew what was happening, but appears to have been relaxed about it. This affair was of a wholly different character from that between Vita and Violet. Vita's emotions were intense and Dottie's dependence on her was increased by the fact that her marriage to Gerry was slowly falling apart, but the relationship never reached the pitch where Harold felt undermined or threatened. There were certainly times when it became an irritation, but he knew now that, intense as Vita's emotions might be, she would soon be ready to move on.

In Vita's absence, Harold went alone to an evening party at Buckingham Palace. Viscount Lascelles, who had been one of Vita's more insistent suitors in 1912, was about to marry Princess Mary, George V's only daughter, and it was the custom to put the wedding presents on display. For Harold, the evening was chiefly memorable because he had the opportunity to talk to Ellen Terry, whom he had last seen playing Mistress Page opposite Beerbohm Tree's Falstaff ten years before. Ellen Terry had known Tennyson over a period of nearly thirty years. She had met him in 1864 when just seventeen, during her brief marriage to the painter, G. F. Watts. He had written his tragedy, *The Cup*, with her in mind. She had heard him recite his own works many times, and she had attended his funeral service in Westminster Abbey in 1892. 'He was very kind,' she told Harold. 'Very vain and very gruff. But so simple.... Just vain and simple. Like a child.'[4] Harold pressed her for

> an exact imitation of the Laureate's recitation. The words, I said, did not matter: what I wanted was the tune. She was very gracious; she boomed off at once into the trochaics of *Locksley Hall*, swaying increasingly upon the red settee to the motion of the verses, stamping finally with her little feet ... then I knew exactly how Tennyson recited *Locksley Hall*.[5]

This kind of direct link to the literary past was important to Harold. Like his conversations with Edmund Gosse, it gave him a sense of historical continuity and, in this case, a strong sense of Tennyson the man, which he pursued in April when he spent a week in Cambridge and Lincolnshire. In Cambridge, he concentrated on Tennyson the poet, studying the manuscripts held in Trinity College, but in Lincolnshire he visited the places which were background to Tennyson's youth: Somersby Rectory, where the Tennyson children lived with their timid mother and their melancholic and often drunk father; Mablethorpe, the seaside town where they spent childhood holidays, where Tennyson and his brother Charles shouted their poems at the sea. Harold was always sensitive to the interplay between character and place and Somersby, in particular, affected him deeply:

The sense of Somersby ... an island of green-sand in a waste of chalk, coddling down among its elms and hedgerows with the grey curve of the wold above it and the darkening flats beyond; the sense that here the gentler beauties of Nature come as some rarer and more exclusive privilege; that the gifts of warmth and scent and colour, the song of birds and the sound of running water have a more detailed, more concentrated significance.[6]

For Harold, this was the foundation of the man who became the poet.

In the meanwhile, at the Foreign Office, it was back to the Greeks and the Turks. After the failure of the London Conference the previous year, the Greeks had continued their advance into Anatolia. By August, they were within forty kilometres of Ankara, but were halted at the Battle of Sakarya. The battle lasted twenty-one days and, although in military terms it was essentially a draw, the Greeks were left so short of men and *matériel* that they had to withdraw. A stalemate ensued. By 1922, the Allies had had enough and, in March, proposed an armistice – a proposal on which Harold was consulted. But Mustafa Kemal would have none of it. His nationalists were growing stronger by the day and, under a treaty signed the previous year, they were receiving increasing amounts of military supplies from the Russians. The stalemate took on a diplomatic as well as a military dimension.

During May, his days continued to be full of Greeks and Turks, or, for a little variety, the impact of the recently-signed Treaty of Rapallo between Germany and the Soviet Union on the new states of Central Europe. In the evenings and at weekends, he worked seriously on *Tennyson*. In 'Writing Books', he warns the aspiring biographer 'of dark days when his book would grow stale to him as the sound of his own voice ... that there would come moments when his material, however carefully arranged, would become disorganized and flap round him in confusion like a colony of rooks.'[7] This clearly did not happen with *Tennyson*. Harold wrote like a man possessed. According to his diaries, between 2 and 18 May, he wrote four full chapters, over one hundred and thirty pages of printed text, reading extracts to Vita and Dottie, who was staying with them at Long Barn, as he went along. But there was one key location he had not visited.

At the end of May, Harold and Vita left Long Barn in a heat wave and joined Lord Sackville on board *Sumerun*, which was at Dover. As soon as they were on board, the weather broke and they sailed down to Southampton in stormy weather. From Southampton, they crossed to Yarmouth. Harold and Vita walked the four miles to Freshwater Bay and up

Bedbury Lane to Farringford, the Georgian manor house which Tennyson had purchased in November 1853 and where he spent the greater part of his last forty years. Farringford did not impress Harold in the same way that Somersby had. He writes of 'the valley ... hiding the secretive little house, jumbled into the damp hollow among its cedars and chestnut trees',[8] whereas in reality Farringford is a large Georgian manor house – at that time still set in a substantial estate – sitting in the shadow of what is now known as Tennyson Down. But the visit did enable Harold to understand what Farringford meant to the poet and, much aided by his conversations with Gosse, he produced a brilliant, atmospheric description of what it felt like to visit Tennyson there in the 1860s.

> The honoured but appreciative guest arriving before sunset in a cab from Yarmouth pier; the momentary glimpse of the poet over the hedge mowing the lawn in spectacles and black sombrero ... the parlour maid and the very late Gothic of the drawing-room window; the evening sun on the cedar outside.... Mrs Tennyson rising, gentle and nervous ... and then, slowly framed in the doorway, the dark bulk of the Laureate ... a deep growl of acknowledgement, if not of greeting, would proceed from the mass of his tangled mane and beard ... in a crisis of embarrassment one would pass into the dining room ... the Laureate would embark with grunt and growl upon some broad Lincolnshire story ... and with the conclusion would come ... a loud appropriate guffaw.... Gradually ... the ice would melt, and with the port a certain geniality, heartening but still very insecure, would descend upon the occasion.[9]

After Farringford, Harold felt able to work on the opening section of his book – 'The Tennyson Legend' – which draws together the threads of his thesis that Tennyson was essentially a genuine, lyric poet beset by the complications of his age, his circumstances and his character. But his leave ended and, returning to the Foreign Office at the beginning of June, he found himself immersed again in the ever-recurring problem of Italian claims in the Adriatic, and in particular along the Dalmatian coast.

Harold simply did not trust the Italian delegation to deliver their side of any agreement that might be reached and said so. Lloyd George wished to be conciliatory. Harold drafted a paper which might best be described – in Foreign Office parlance – as cautious. Lloyd George was furious and claimed that the Foreign Office were deliberately obstructive. Negotiations continued. The Italian delegation did try and renege on their commitment to withdraw from the Dodecanese, proving Harold right. He drafted another paper. If the Italians behaved as they proposed, Britain would feel able to withdraw from its commitments under the troublesome 1915 Treaty of London. The Italians were furious and walked out.

Caught at such a point, Harold cuts an impressive figure. As a Foreign Office official, he was completely on top of his subject, equipped not only with the facts to argue with the Prime Minister, but also with the courage and authority to do so. As a private individual, he was writing, at immense speed, a literary biography which would soon achieve the status of a classic. And in his spare time, he was either gardening at Long Barn or offering tacit support to Gerry Wellesley by staying at Portland Place as the Wellesley marriage drifted slowly onto the rocks.

Harold finished *Tennyson* and sent the manuscript to Constable on 28 August, just in time to be summoned back to work to manage the fall-out from a massive Turkish offensive which had broken the stalemate in Anatolia. His diary comment – 'Greeks utterly beaten in Anatolia, poor darlings'[10] – was no less than the truth and it happened with incredible speed. The Greeks continued to be pushed back; the Turks swept down the Menderes Valley and on 8 September, just two weeks after the beginning of the offensive, Turkish troops reoccupied Smyrna. It was the end of the war, but not the end of the suffering. Turkish soldiers massacred thousands of Greeks and Armenians and, whether by accident or design, Smyrna burnt for four days, killing thousands more and leaving large parts of the ancient city as smoking ruins.

21 Curzon

Mustafa Kemal and his nationalist forces were in triumphant mood. They had driven the Greeks into the sea. Now they turned north with the aim of forcing Allied troops to evacuate Turkish soil. Two agreements allowed Allied troops the right to occupy Constantinople and a thin strip of territory on either side of the Dardanelles and the Bosphorus: the 1918 Mudros Armistice, which ended the fighting between the Allies and the Ottoman Empire, and the subsequent Treaty of Sèvres, which formally ended the war. This 'Neutral Zone' existed to ensure that the Straits remained open to all ships of all nationalities, but to Kemal and his nationalists the Allied presence was simply evidence of Turkey's humiliation. The crisis which followed – the Chanak crisis – was fast-moving and dangerous, with implications for the British Government, the British Empire, relations among the Allies, and for Harold.

On Friday 15 September 1922, before retiring to Hackwood, his country house, for the weekend, Lord Curzon made it clear to the Cabinet that any attempt to hold the Dardanelles by force would be foolish and would end in failure. Once Curzon had departed, however, Lloyd George, who had always disliked the Turks, egged on by a belligerent Churchill, then Secretary of State for the Colonies, decided that the Turks must be kept out of Europe even if it meant war. The Prime Minister's office issued instructions and Harold, who was expecting a visit from a member of the Greek Embassy at Long Barn that weekend, was authorised to say on a strictly private and confidential basis that Britain would hold the Dardanelles by force if necessary, with or without French assistance. The following Monday morning, as a result of a press statement authorised and signed by the Prime Minister, Harold found this same policy, expressed in aggressive terms, announced in the British press. He felt he had been made a fool of. Worse, he thought the new policy disastrous. It was a decision made on political grounds, but made without regard to the resources required to enforce it – resources which simply were not there. Foreign Office officials were astounded that a statement of such importance should have been issued without their having been consulted. And Curzon, as one might expect, was furious.

The situation worsened almost immediately. The French and Italians began withdrawing their forces from the southern shore of the Dardanelles, including the important city of Çanakkale; and the Dominions, led by Canada, let it be known that this was not a cause for which they were ready to go to war. Harold, whose responsibility had technically been for Greece rather than Turkey, was drafted into the team dealing with the crisis. On 21 September, Curzon met President Raymond Poincaré in Paris and (after a meeting which quite literally reduced him to tears) obtained limited French support. On 22 September, Turkish nationalist forces took control of Çanakkale. Two days later, Kemal and his confident, victorious troops entered the Neutral Zone to be confronted by General Charles Harington whose defences consisted of 'but three hundred rifles and a single strand of wire.'[1] To everyone's amazement – and to the disappointment, even anger, of the more aggressive members of the Cabinet – there was no violence. Was Kemal daunted by the prestige of the British Empire? Did he believe that Britain really would fight? In any event, he withdrew his troops from the Neutral Zone and agreed to a formal meeting with Harington ten days later in the town of Mudanya on the southern shore of the Sea of Marmora.

On 29 September, Harold was called into the Foreign Secretary's office to advise Curzon on the whole issue of the freedom of the Straits – which was the fundamental reason for the British military presence on the Dardanelles and the Bosphorus. This was not an encounter to be taken lightly. Curzon was a man who studied the issues before him. He was an expert on the Near and Middle East. He had travelled in Greece and Turkey before Harold was born and in Russia, Persia and Afghanistan before Harold was at school. Harold, however, knew his subject.

In the event of a Russian threat to India, Britain wanted to be able to send warships through the Straits to carry the fight to Russia in the Black Sea. Russia, for defensive reasons, was equally keen to see the Straits closed to foreign warships, though open to the commercial traffic which was essential to her economy. Traditionally, Britain's fear had been that a strong Russia would pressurise a weak Ottoman Empire into closing the Straits. Now, with the Turks resurgent, it was Mustafa Kemal who had the power to close the Straits against Britain or Russia or both, as he chose. From a British point of view, the underlying situation had not changed. Britain was not interested in controlling the Straits, only in obtaining the passage of warships in the event of a Russian threat. Lord Curzon listened and, somewhat condescendingly, dubbed Harold 'able'.[2]

The victorious nationalist Turks were now apparently able to challenge the world's greatest imperial power on the Straits, while the Greeks had collapsed. King Constantine was deposed in a military coup. The future was unclear, but it was obvious that Venizelos could soon once again become an influential figure and the Foreign Office suggested that Harold should re-establish contact with him. News of the Greek revolution encouraged the Turks who again advanced on British lines in the Neutral Zone. The Mudanya talks began on 3 October. The atmosphere was tense. Mustafa Kemal demanded that Turkish troops be allowed to cross the Dardanelles and occupy Eastern Thrace. The French Commander, General Charpy, agreed; General Harington refused. Kemal issued an ultimatum. Curzon raced across to Paris for the second time in as many weeks for discussions with Poincaré ('that horrid little man').[3] A formula was agreed: the Allies would occupy Eastern Thrace pending a peace conference which would replace the defunct Treaty of Sèvres. Charpy and Harington were authorised to put these terms to Kemal, making it clear that there would be no further concessions. Kemal agreed and war was averted – but then he had got the promise of everything he wanted without fighting, and he had driven a wedge between his opponents.

The Armistice of Mudanya was signed on 11 October. Two days later,

Harold was told by his old friend Lancelot Oliphant, now the Assistant Secretary overseeing Central Department, that the conference would open in the Swiss city of Lausanne on 20 November and that he was to be part of the Foreign Office delegation. In the intervening six weeks, Harold watched as the participating countries turned themselves upside down. In Greece, the Revolutionary Committee formally requested Constantine's son to take the Greek throne as George II. They also, much to Harold's delight, asked Venizelos to be the Greek delegate at Lausanne. In Italy, the blackshirts of the National Fascist Party marched on Rome and forced King Victor Emmanuel III to hand over power to his new, if unelected, Prime Minister Benito Amilcare Mussolini. In Turkey, Mustafa Kemal finally brought the Ottoman Empire to a long-overdue end, deposing Sultan Mohammed VI and establishing a Turkish Republic. The fact that the Sultan eventually fled Constantinople on board the British battleship HMS *Malaya*, just before the Lausanne Conference opened, did nothing to relieve Turkish suspicions of Britain's intentions. And in Britain, Lloyd George ceased to be Prime Minister when the Conservative Party withdrew from the Coalition Government which he had led since 1916. Domestic reasons were paramount, but the Chanak crisis did not help – it was clear that his aggressive pro-Greek interventions and his refusal to listen to the advice of his Foreign Secretary had made a difficult situation worse. A general election on 15 November gave the Conservative Party a substantial majority and the new Prime Minister, Andrew Bonar Law, had just time to confirm Curzon in his position as Foreign Secretary before Curzon left for Lausanne on 17 November.

At school – Eton, naturally – Curzon's contemporaries had taken it for granted that he would be in the Cabinet before too long. Indeed, one friend was supposed to have gone so far as to extract 'a promise that Curzon would appoint him Chancellor of the Exchequer when he became Prime Minister.'[4] Yet even at school, the duality of Curzon's character had been recognised. He was intellectually brilliant, a leader, a great organiser, a man of deep and powerful emotions. At the same time, he could be arrogant, obstinate, self-centred, cold, and capable of arousing deep-rooted opposition, even hatred. At the time of the Lausanne Conference, Curzon was approaching sixty-four. His career, like his personality, had been brilliant but flawed. He had travelled widely and written a number of impressive works on Russia, Persia and Central Asia. He had risen rapidly through the ranks of the Conservative Party to become, in 1899, arguably the greatest but certainly the most magnificent of all Viceroys of India. Yet he had resigned and left Calcutta as a result of an unedifying squabble with

Kitchener, and then spent ten years in the political wilderness. During the First World War, Curzon's talents had proved too valuable to ignore and he had served in the Cabinet in several different capacities before Lloyd George appointed him Foreign Secretary 1919.

Harold, with his Foreign Office background, would have known of Curzon all his life. Neither his appointment nor his resignation as Viceroy would have gone unremarked in the Nicolson household. Moreover, Curzon, too, was a Balliol man and, though he left no great mark upon the College, his presence there (from 1879 to 1882) was still remembered by some during Harold's undergraduate years and still regarded as a source of pride. Nearer to home, during a debate in the House of Lords, Curzon had savagely criticised the 1907 Anglo-Russian Convention, which Sir Arthur had done so much to shape and to negotiate. This may go some way towards explaining Harold's initial antipathy towards Curzon: he was always very protective of his father's reputation. Drafting his memoranda in 1918, Harold had been critical of the government, and particularly Curzon who understood the region, for their lack of a forward policy on Persia. He maintained a hostile attitude when Curzon took over at the Foreign Office. He called Allen Leeper's appointment as Curzon's Assistant Private Secretary 'a bloody job';[5] he found Curzon unpredictable, likely to change his mind and his policy without warning; he wrote of Curzon as 'caddish and disloyal.'[6] And when Curzon came into conflict with Viscount Allenby, then High Commissioner in Egypt, over whether or not Egypt should be recognised as a sovereign state, Harold was not so much supportive of Allenby as critical of Curzon whose handling of the matter, according to Harold, marked him as 'a coward' and 'a shit.'[7]

This attitude towards Curzon may also have been a kind of pre-emptive hostility, based on a fear that Curzon would dislike him. Like so many others, Harold seems – at least at first – to have seen Curzon as the epitome of stiff, shockable, diplomatic formality.

> Coming out of his room in the Foreign Office just before Christmas, whom did [Curzon] meet but young Harold Nicolson, with a pipe in his mouth! Curzon nearly had a fit, and dropped his stick. Harold confided in Vita that this was the most awful thing to have happened. He drew a sketch of the situation to emphasise what a *faux pas* he had committed.[8]

There is an element of exaggeration in this – Harold was always inclined to see himself as more of a rebel than he really was – and there is no evidence that Curzon ever disliked him. He had always been complimentary about

Harold's drafts and he certainly did not object to his inclusion in the Lausanne delegation.

Just a month after the Allenby episode, in March 1922, Harold and Robert Vansittart, Curzon's Private Secretary, went to see Curzon in his London home at Carlton House Terrace with a proposal they hoped might break the Greek-Turkish deadlock. Curzon, who suffered from curvature of the spine and was frequently in pain as a consequence, was resting in bed. Although his first priority was, no doubt, the Greek proposal, Harold's ever-observant eyes wandered round the room.

> Pink and white wallpaper; maple washing stand with cheap wash basin – cornflowers; Pears soap; a thin rather scruffy shaving brush; maple dressing table; half empty bottle of hairwash; a large stained wooden hairbrush; a glass electric light shade above it all; by his bed a red silk-and-brass reading lamp; on the wall cheap etchings of Belgian cathedrals; photographs of Lady C and the children in cheap blue frames; a washing bill on the mantelpiece; an old Gladstone bag and a green suitcase in the corner; a brass bed with a pink silk eiderdown and in it the Marquess in a flowered dressing gown. His spine was hurting and he winced as he bent over to write.[9]

This entry into comparative intimacy with Lord Curzon seems to have marked the beginning of a change in Harold's attitude. It was a repeat of the pattern of his relationship with Smuts, but on a larger scale. As Harold got closer to Curzon, so he came to understand him better. Soon, as he confesses in the famous 'Arketall' chapter of *Some People*, Lord Curzon's personality became 'almost an obsession' to him.[10]

Although *Some People* contains exaggerations and compressions, it clearly illustrates the mixture of admiration and affection which characterised Harold's new relationship with his chief. The 'Arketall' chapter contains a version of the description of Curzon's bedroom quoted above, but adds:

> My eyes wandered round the room in mute surprise. They returned finally to the figure in the bed.... 'You are observing,' he said, 'the simple squalor of my bedroom. I can assure you, however, that my wife's apartments are of the most unexampled magnificence.' And at this his shoulders shook with that infectious laughter of his, that rich eighteenth-century amusement.[11]

Later, Harold describes Curzon's return from his first meeting with Mussolini:

> He paused at the doorway of his apartment and surveyed it. 'How ghăstly!' he sighed.... 'How positively ghăstly,' he repeated.... [We] pulled up the least diminutive of the sixteen armchairs.... He sank back, sipped at a brandy-and-soda, sighed deeply, and then embarked on a narrative of the Vevey conference.
>
> Ah, those Curzonian dissertations! No small thing has passed from my life now they are silenced.... The precise marshalling of detail, the sense of conscious continuity, the sense of absolute control. The voice rising at moments in almost histrionic scorn, or dropping at moments into a hush of sudden emotion; and then a flash of March sunshine, a sudden dart of eighteenth-century humour, a pause while his wide shoulders rose and fell in rich amusement. And all this under a cloud of exhaustion, under a cloud of persistent pain.[12]

Later still, when Curzon had steered the Lausanne Conference to a successful conclusion, Harold wrote exuberantly to Vita:

> When I thought he was wrong, he was right, and when I thought he was right, he was much righter than I thought. I give him 100 marks out of 100 and I am so proud of him. So *awfully* proud. He is a great man and one day England will know it.
>
> But you see Britannia *has* ruled here. Entirely against the Turks, against treacherous allies, against a weak-kneed cabinet, against a rotten public opinion – and Curzon has *won*.... And it was just due to [him] sitting there solid and *grand seigneur* and amused and brutal.[13]

Curzon, in short, had joined the ranks of Harold's heroes, and it is easy to see why. He was an aristocrat from a landed background; he had the certainty and complete self-confidence that Harold always envied; he was also, apparently, a man of means. The fact that Curzon depended on his wife's and latterly his daughters' money was not widely known – although if he had not insisted on maintaining an opulent and aristocratic life style of the kind which, by 1922, already belonged to a bygone age, such dependence would not have been necessary.

Then, of course, whether in the Foreign Office, as Viceroy or in the War Cabinet, Curzon had lived his professional life very much at the centre of things. He also appealed to Harold's sense of continuity. He had heard

Gladstone and Disraeli speak in the House of Commons. He had stayed with Lord Derby, who had been Disraeli's Foreign Secretary. He had read out loud to Queen Victoria the telegram announcing Kitchener's victory at the Battle of Omdurman. He had known Oscar Wilde. He had even, in 1884, visited Tennyson, and stayed overnight at the poet's house at Aldworth in Surrey and, when in 'good form', would give an imitation of Tennyson reciting 'Tears, Idle Tears'. It was, Harold remarked, 'far more effective than any other imitation that I have heard.'[14] Harold's fascination with Curzon would find an outlet not just in *Some People*, but more significantly in *Curzon: The Last Phase*, his study of Curzon's character and diplomatic practice during his years as Foreign Secretary.

22 Lausanne

The main body of the Foreign Office delegation which left London for Lausanne on 17 November 1922 consisted of Sir William Tyrrell, Assistant Under-Secretary and thus effectively number two in the Foreign Office after Sir Eyre Crowe; Allen Leeper, Curzon's Assistant Private Secretary; and Harold, the acknowledged expert on the Balkans and the Greek-Turkish conflict. Once in Lausanne, they were reinforced by Sir Horace Rumbold, the British High Commissioner in Constantinople, and Admiral Sir Roger Keyes, the Naval Adviser. Now, more even than during the Peace Conference in Paris, Harold could claim to be at the centre of things. Another member of Curzon's retinue was 'a very drunk and incompetent valet called Tivendale', immortalised by Harold as Arketall.[1] Contrary to the picture painted in *Some People*, however, it appears that Curzon was neither tolerant of nor amused by Tivendale's behaviour – which included telling the hotel that he had orders to taste every bottle before it was served because the Foreign Secretary was terrified of poison.

Curzon always travelled in the style befitting a British Foreign Secretary, let alone a man who had once been Viceroy of India. The South Eastern & Chatham Railway attached a special Pullman car to the afternoon boat train from Victoria to Dover Maritime for his use.[2] On the cross-channel steamer, he was provided with a cabin conveniently adjacent to the gangplank. Once in Calais, where he was greeted by both the British Consul and a French diplomatic representative, another special carriage awaited courtesy of Les Chemins de Fer du Nord. When he arrived in Paris at Gare du

Nord, a Rolls-Royce belonging to the British Embassy transported him smoothly to the Ritz Hotel. It was a stately progress.

The next day, which was Saturday, Curzon, with Harold and the rest of his staff in attendance, met Poincaré and the French delegation in the Quai d'Orsay's Salle de l'Horloge, the room in which the opening session of the 1919 Peace Conference had been held. Previous meetings between Curzon and Poincaré had been less than amicable but on this occasion relations between the principals remained polite, while relations between the two delegations were positively good, something Harold was to emphasise as a major contributory factor to the success of Lausanne. After five hours of talks, a common position was reached on all the main points at issue, a communiqué issued and a telegram despatched to Mussolini suggesting that he should join them in Lausanne.

The next morning the delegation was transported, again by Rolls-Royce, to the Gare de Lyon where a special three-coach train awaited them. Poincaré and the French delegation had one coach; Curzon and the British delegation had the second, while the third, this being France, was a special dining car. The day was divided between work and lunch. Before leaving London, Harold had drafted a detailed memorandum on procedure for the Conference which Curzon had approved. Now, as the train headed for Switzerland, he was able to discuss and modify his ideas with the Quai d'Orsay's influential Director of Political Affairs, Jules Laroche. The joint scheme which emerged from their cooperation was to give Curzon an important advantage in managing the Conference.

They stopped at Pontarlier, just short of the Swiss border, where a message from Mussolini awaited them. He would not come to Lausanne, but he would meet Curzon and Poincaré for dinner at Territet, less than an hour beyond Lausanne. Harold was fascinated and delighted by the contrasting ways in which this message was received.

> whereas M. Poincaré regarded the proposal as an insult, Lord Curzon regarded it as highly romantic. He was delighted by the boyish naïveté of the request.... M. Poincaré, who had none of Curzon's humour or romanticism, fretted at one end of the presidential train. Curzon, at the other end, was back at Balliol, laughing heartily.... In all solemnity he sent a message along the platform to M. Poincaré to the effect that the real motive of Mussolini was not so much to humiliate France and Great Britain as a certain awkwardness about appearing at Lausanne. His last visit to that lake-side city had ended in his being expelled by the police. M. Poincaré took this message seriously.[3]

In the end, the two statesmen decided to continue to Territet, while Harold, Allen Leeper and the lesser functionaries, including Tivendale, got off at Lausanne with instructions to settle into the hotel and make preparations for the next day's meeting. Emerging from the station, they found themselves faced with the magnesium flashes of cameras and the cheers of an enormous crowd: the Swiss had organised a full scale civic reception led by the Mayor of Lausanne. Tivendale raised his bowler and there followed a moment of comic misunderstanding until Harold stepped forward and explained that Lord Curzon would be arriving later.

They were staying in Ouchy at the Hotel Beau Rivage, where Curzon was expected to arrive before midnight. Harold and Allen Leeper were waiting for him in the lobby when through the door came 'a small brown gentleman in a brown suit and very white shirt-cuffs. He carried a brown bowler in his left hand and his right was thrust in his waistcoat.'[4] It was Mussolini. Apparently appeased by the willingness of Curzon and Poincaré to accept his invitation to dinner, he had decided to join the Conference. The following morning, when the three were due to resume their discussions, Mussolini again sought to demonstrate his importance by arriving 'deliberately late' by some thirty-five minutes.[5] When he did arrive, he 'shot into the room like a brown thunderbolt, stopped short, clicked his heels, bowed and exclaimed, *"Je vous salue, Messieurs."*'[6] Harold thus gained a glimpse of Mussolini just over three weeks after the March on Rome which had brought him to power, but the new dictator does not seem to have left a very deep impression. In *Curzon: The Last Phase* – written, it should be remembered, long before Mussolini threw in his lot with Hitler, and in which Harold is prepared to describe Poincaré as 'that ghastly civil servant'[7] – he says only that Mussolini seemed 'a shade embarrassed by being thus confronted at his first diplomatic conference by such giants of the profession [and] chafed uneasily against his stiff white cuffs, rolling important eyes.'[8] In his 1943 *Spectator* article, 'The Fall of Mussolini', Harold remembered a man who 'strutted horribly through the corridors of the hotel,' but who otherwise 'did not ... seem a formidable figure: he seemed bewildered, flustered, uncomfortable and most anxious to please.'[9] In the event, Mussolini's diplomatic inexperience meant that he simply agreed with the points made by the British and French delegations – '"*Je suis d'accord*" was the most important thing that he said.'[10] As a result, the three Allied powers began the Conference with the advantage of a common position.

At four o'clock that same afternoon, the opening ceremony of the Lausanne Conference took place in the Casino de Montbenon. President Robert Haab of the Swiss Confederation gave an official welcome to representatives from eleven countries: official delegations from Britain, France, Italy, Turkey, Greece, Romania, Bulgaria, Yugoslavia,[11] the Soviet Union, and Japan, and a team of observers from the United States. Curzon and all the other speakers struck an equally correct note – the only exception being Ismet Pasha, leader of the Turkish delegation, who made a series of sulky accusations. Proceedings were then adjourned until the following day. Among the accredited press correspondents, representing the *Toronto Star*, was the young Ernest Hemingway. He and Harold did not meet. One can only imagine the conversation they might have had.

The real business of the Conference began the following morning in the Hotel Château d'Ouchy, just a couple of hundred metres along the elegant Quai de Belgique from the Beau Rivage, and it continued for two-and-a-half months until 4 February 1923. Although Curzon and his team left Lausanne without a treaty – it was eventually signed in July 1923 after a second, much smaller conference – the negotiations and, in particular, Curzon's conduct of the negotiations, were regarded as a triumph for the Foreign Secretary and for Britain. The Freedom of the Straits to both commerce and naval ships of all nations was assured; a wedge was driven between Turkey and the Soviet Union; the future of the Mosul region (which Turkey claimed but which Britain regarded as part of Iraq) was referred to League of Nations arbitration; and, as a result, Britain's heavily dented prestige in the Balkans and the Near East was restored. The French and Italians signally failed to achieve any of their objectives and also failed to gain credit with the Turks, whom, prior to the Conference, they had been assiduously cultivating.

Curzon's triumph, of course, was not achieved alone. Harold was now thirty-six (his birthday coincided with the Conference getting down to its first working session in the Château d'Ouchy) and had been a First Secretary for three years, so that while he was still some way from the most senior ranks of the Foreign Office, he was by no means the office junior, and his contribution to the success of Lausanne was considerable. In the first place, it was Harold – with later modifications from Laroche – who drew up the procedural plan for the Conference which allowed Curzon to take control from day one, creating three principal committees and appointing himself Chairman of the most important, the Territorial Committee. Harold was the acknowledged expert on the whole question of Freedom of the Straits, and the 'Straits Convention', which was accepted by Ismet Pasha on 20 December in the face of Russian opposition. In the end, this was probably the most important achievement of the Conference, not just because it secured free passage for both commercial and naval traffic, but because it allowed Curzon to exploit differences between the Turkish and Russian delegations and ultimately bring Turkey to a position where she decided to align herself with the western powers rather than the Soviet Union. But this achievement itself rested on work by Harold, Sir Roger Keyes, and his French counterpart, Admiral Lacaze, whose behind-the-scenes activities identified the cracks which Curzon was able to prize open.

As during the Paris Conference four years previously, Harold showed himself a very able committee man. He was the British representative on three 'Sub-Commissions' as Curzon termed the bodies which were subsidiary to the Conference's three committees. Two of these dealt with demilitarisation – of Eastern Thrace and of certain strategically important Aegean islands – and both were chaired by General Weygand, with whom Harold had collaborated on Albanian issues at the League of Nations the previous year. The third was the Sub-Commission for Prisoners of War and Cemeteries. This was the one that caused Harold genuine grief. He was not a particularly religious man, but he had a strong sense of honour and of national pride, so that when the Turks

> had the impudence to say that they must be allowed to dig up our graves at Gallipoli and put them all in one cemetery ... I simply saw red. I told them that it was incredible that a beaten country could raise such a question. Then they climbed down but they did not climb down far enough and I refused to go on discussing. Really they are quite, quite mad – and if they want war they will get it. I feel I won't speak to them again. I told them that the British Empire would never, NEVER evacuate Gallipoli until our graves were safeguarded.[12]

Such anger was unusual.

Another of Harold's strengths which proved valuable to Curzon's conduct of negotiations was his experience and understanding of the Greeks and his relationship with Venizelos. Greek aggression in Anatolia had done more than anything else to stimulate the rapid growth of Mustafa Kemal's nationalist movement, but by the time of Lausanne the Greeks had been defeated on the battlefield and were in the throes of revolution at home. Venizelos, leading the Greek delegation at the request of the new, military government, was in a 'position of impotence', wholly reliant on the Allies to help him salvage something from the Conference. But the weakness of the Greek position did not prevent them from causing problems.

Harold considered Venizelos 'the only delegate of [Curzon's] own standard',[13] but Curzon did not care for him. On occasion, he was prepared to admit that Venizelos was 'impressive',[14] but for the most part Harold felt that 'for some odd reason, he hates Venizelos.'[15] Harold's affection for the old man was undiminished, but privately he was forced to admit that 'V. is not quite the man he was.'[16] As negotiations progressed, it became necessary to extract concessions from the Greeks. Curzon's method was to exploit Harold's relationship with the former Greek Prime Minister and make him carry messages: 'Well, go to your friend Venizelos and get him to agree.' Harold loathed 'trying to extract from Venizelos concessions of which I disapprove,' but Curzon recognised that he was 'able to manage the Cretan' and made him continue.[17]

Within days of the opening of the Conference, the Greek Government managed to complicate and weaken their position still further. The ruling Revolutionary Committee put Dimitrios Gounaris, the former Prime Minister, and a number of others whom they held responsible for their country's defeat on trial for high treason. The trial was rapid and at dawn on 28 November, within hours of the verdict – indeed, before it was made public – Gounaris and five others were shot by firing squad. International reaction was immediate and the British Minister was withdrawn. For Harold, it was the last straw. The Greeks had let their Allies down 'first politically by getting rid of Venizelos; then militarily by being beaten by the Turks; and now morally by this business.'[18] Curzon, too, was outraged and told Venizelos to stay away from the next session of the Conference, but his immediate problem was how to avoid the Turks taking advantage of the situation. This he did, in his own inimitable style, by inviting Dr Fridtjof Nansen to address the Conference on the issue and the condition of Greek refugees expelled from the Turkish mainland.

The crisis in Athens gave rise to an odd situation which seems to have had an impact on Harold's later career. There are several versions of events and it is difficult to be certain what happened, but the end result seems to have been that the animosity which Sir William Tyrrell had felt for Sir Arthur Nicolson was now extended in full measure to include Harold. The issue at stake was the safety of Prince Andrew of Greece. Remotely connected with the British Royal Family (as the nephew of Edward VII's Queen Alexandra), Prince Andrew was among those court-martialled by the new government and there were fears that he, too, might be executed. Among those attending the Lausanne Conference was Sir Gerald Talbot, the British Naval Attaché in Athens. According to James Lees-Milne, as early as 23 November – before the executions – Harold had discussed with Tyrrell the possibility of sending Talbot back to Athens to remove Prince Andrew. When the news of the executions came, however, it was left to

Harold to take the initiative and send Talbot back because Tyrrell was drunk and 'incapable of action'.[19]

That Tyrrell had a drink problem was known throughout the Foreign Office and that Sir Eyre Crowe arranged for Tyrrell to come home from the Lausanne Conference is a fact. Harold claimed that he kept knowledge of Tyrrell's drinking from Lord Curzon, but informed Crowe who then brought Tyrrell home under the pretext that his wife was ill. Norman Rose points out, quite correctly, that Curzon must have known about Tyrrell's drinking and also draws attention to Curzon's low opinion of Tyrrell as expressed in a letter to Lady Curzon – 'a small man. He has no knowledge of reading or width of view ... he could not grapple with big situations or make a good Ambassador.'[20] This raises the possibility that Tyrrell may have been sent home simply because of poor performance, albeit perhaps exacerbated by drink. Rose also notes that others have claimed that Tyrrell returned from Lausanne as a result of a nervous breakdown – and it is true that the death of his two sons had caused him to have a nervous breakdown in 1915 and continued to trouble him deeply[21] – though such a claim does not, of course, rule out the possibility of alcohol abuse.

The evidence is inconclusive and complicated by the fact that Harold apparently did not record his version of events until some years later – after he had left the Foreign Office.[22] Nonetheless, Harold believed that the fact that he witnessed Tyrrell dead drunk and the fact that Curzon publicly thanked him in Tyrrell's presence for his actions over Prince Andrew created a resentment which lasted for the rest of his diplomatic career. The full effect of this would only become apparent when Tyrrell succeeded Crowe as Head of the Foreign Office in 1925.

Sir Gerald Talbot's mission was successful. Prince Andrew was banished rather than executed. He and his family were forced to abandon most of their possessions and flee the country on board the light cruiser, HMS *Calypso*. The youngest member of the family, only eighteen months old at the time and carried on board in a cot made out of an orange box, was later to become Prince Philip, the Duke of Edinburgh.

Curzon also made use of Harold's abilities and personality in other ways. Neither his position nor his rather stiff outward persona made it possible for him to communicate informally with those attending or surrounding the conference. If Alexander Stamboliski, the Bulgarian Prime Minister, or Ion Duca, the Romanian Foreign Minister were granted an audience with Lord Curzon, they would inevitably convey their message in the most formal, diplomatic manner. Over lunch or a drink with Harold, they would be more relaxed. The nature and underlying reason for their position, together with potential negotiating points, would become clearer. Similarly, Harold was able to communicate with members of the press in an off-the-record manner which would not have been possible for Curzon. At times, this was enjoyable – Harold's old friend Pierre de Lacretelle was covering the Conference for the French weekly *Journal des Débats* and they would occasionally lunch together, though they did not resume any closer relationship. At other times, it was more difficult. Curzon was furious to find that the English sculptress, writer and general adventuress, Clare Sheridan, was representing the *New York World*. Sheridan's pro-Bolshevik, anti-establishment stance would never have endeared her to Curzon, but she had also caused immense trouble and generated troublesome anti-British propaganda during the Chanak crisis and he refused to see her, even though she managed to interview Mussolini and Ismet Pasha and lunch with the Russian delegate, Chicherin. Curzon told Harold to get rid of her and he certainly tried – to the point where Vita claimed to be worried he might fall in love with her[23] – though in her memoirs Sheridan only remembers Sir William Tyrrell and Sir Roger Keyes, both of whom she seems to have been able to charm.[24]

Despite his obvious authority within the British delegation and his obvious contribution to the success of Curzon's diplomacy, there is at times an odd sense of immaturity in Harold's attitudes. In Paris, he was kept up late by Curzon drafting a telegram for the Foreign Office and then had to walk from place Vendôme to the British Embassy in rue du Faubourg Saint-Honoré at two in the morning in order to send it. In Lausanne, during Conference sessions, he describes sitting behind Curzon and having to run errands for him. Such irritating tasks are part of normal diplomatic life, but Harold seems positively to have enjoyed being Curzon's dogsbody. And there were two occasions during the Conference when Harold acted against Curzon's wishes, drawing up the terms of a full treaty rather than a draft treaty, as he had been instructed. On the first occasion, he got away with it, claiming that it was the sensible thing to do.

> The Marquess leaned forward in his chair and his eye glared. 'You thought that, did you? You thought that.' Then he flung himself back. 'Well, I suppose you were right.' This is a moral victory. Of course he'll blame me if things go wrong and take the credit for himself if it goes right. But I still WON.[25]

On the second occasion, a few days later, Curzon was less forgiving and told Harold that any failure to achieve a treaty would be largely his fault.

Harold was so upset that he immediately sent a telegram to Vita begging her to come and visit him. It was, in the words of James Lees-Milne, 'a case of the little schoolboy, reprimanded by the headmaster, turning to his mother for consolation.'[26] Indeed, there is something childish in both his triumph and his distress. He was an acknowledged expert in his field; his political judgement was excellent; yet there remains a sense of emotional immaturity, an acute sensitiveness to criticism, an over-identification with his favourite causes and individuals that, as a First Secretary within range of forty, he should have grown out of.

Harold remained fully committed to the Foreign Office and to the task in hand. He told Vita that Lausanne was 'far more interesting than the Paris Conference as one has the feeling that it may break down at any moment.'[27] During the ten weeks he spent in Lausanne, he worked regularly from his nine o'clock morning meeting with Lord Curzon until eleven p.m. or midnight, weekends included. Yet even under this strenuous regime, he managed to find time for a personal life.

For the first month at least, he was correcting the proofs of *Tennyson*. He had asked Eddie Marsh to look over the manuscript for him. It was a sensible choice. Beyond the fact that they had known each other for years – ever since 1909, when Marsh and the writer Maurice Baring had called at the Embassy in Moscow with a letter of introduction to Sir Arthur – Marsh was an experienced reader of manuscripts. Moreover, he was an established and recognised patron of the arts, who knew everyone in the literary world and had used his influence on behalf of writers such as James Elroy Flecker, Rupert Brooke, and Siegfried Sassoon. It is easy to underestimate how much Harold wanted to succeed as a writer. Three books in three years represented a huge effort. He had courted Gosse to make sure that *Verlaine* got a good reception. Marsh's association with *Tennyson*, acknowledged in the 'Introductory Note', would certainly do the book no harm. The problem was that there was a lot to correct. Marsh saw, and Harold acknowledged, that the book had been written too fast. But that was the way in which Harold approached life. Even while still correcting the proofs of *Tennyson*, he was reading everything he could find about Byron in preparation for his next project.

Christmas was spent in Lausanne and on Christmas Day there occurred the incident dramatised in *Some People*, when Tivendale the valet danced drunkenly with the lady guests in the ballroom of the hotel and was duly sacked. His departing gesture, the following morning, was to hide all Lord Curzon's trousers, causing a brief period of panic among those attending upon the Foreign Secretary until they were discovered under his bed.

Lausanne

The Conference was suspended over New Year 1923, so Harold, Allen Leeper and one or two other members of the delegation decided to visit Gstaad, which even then was both an expensive and exclusive resort. The journey, on the narrow-gauge Montreux–Oberland Bernois railway, is one of the most spectacular in the world, but Harold, bizarrely, claimed to have read Byron all the way. The next day, after a fancy dress ball at the Palace Hotel which he did not particularly enjoy, Harold showed himself uncharacteristically sporting and went skiing. He was careful at first, but then grew overconfident.

> The houses of the village rushed up to meet me: it was like coming down in an aeroplane: I thought how right you had been to warn me against winter sports: and where I had put my Will: and whether I had been good enough to Mummy: and then just as my whole life began to rise before me, I saw that a barbed wire fence was also rising to meet me. I flung myself on my back and there was a shower of snow and skis and Hadji – and I came up crash against one of the supports of the fence.

He was 'wet, frightened, bruised and hungry' but there was no permanent damage done.[28]

Vita arrived on 12 January. They had been apart for eight weeks. Harold was longing to see her, not only on his own account, but, as he admitted, because he was snobbish and wanted to show her off.[29] Despite the demands of Harold's conference duties, they managed to spend some time together. They visited the Château de Chillon near Montreux: Vita was fascinated by its medieval history under the Counts of Savoy; Harold was more interested in the fact that Byron had visited in 1816 and written his great romantic poem, 'The Prisoner of Chillon', as a result – it had actually been written in the Auberge de l'Ancre which, renamed the Hotel d'Angleterre, was next door to the Beau Rivage where they were staying. They spent time reading each other's work: Vita let Harold read and make suggestions for her new novel, *Grey Wethers*; he read aloud extracts from the revised manuscript of *Tennyson*. Then there were official dinners: those with Lord Curzon went well because he admired both Vita and her writing; those with members of the Turkish and Japanese delegations were unbearably stiff and formal.

When Vita left on 21 January, Harold was miserable, but in the aftermath of her departure he made an important decision: he would buy a typewriter. It was a significant departure.

Henceforth nearly all his letters to [Vita], and those to his friends which were not dictated, were typewritten by himself. He never learned to use all his fingers, and when he was in a hurry the result was often erratic. His portable typewriter became his indispensable companion which he treated almost as a human being. It (and there was a succession of them) was always referred to by him and his secretaries as 'Tikki'.[30]

The end of Lausanne came quickly. On 23 January, Lord Curzon, in a performance Harold recorded with relish and in some detail in *Curzon: The Last Phase*, demolished the Turkish position on Mosul. The following day, he informed the French and Italian delegates that he intended to present the Turks with a treaty on 31 January with a deadline for agreement of 4 February. Suddenly, news leaked out in Paris that the French Government, at the instigation of Poincaré, was on the point of reaching a separate agreement with the Turks. Even the French delegation at Lausanne was outraged and protested to the Quai d'Orsay. Pierre de Lacretelle came to Harold's aid and supported the British position, publishing a scathing attack on Poincaré's policy. Curzon, however, kept his nerve and presented his treaty as planned. The French backed down. The Turks demanded extra time. Curzon refused. Riza Nur, Ismet Pasha's deputy, tried to wheedle Harold into negotiating a separate peace.

> The public school spirit assails me. 'Excellence,' I answer, *'l'Empire Britannique ne conclut pas de paix séparée.'* 'But there are precedents,' he leers. *'Nous nous foutons,'* I answer, *'des précédents.'*[31]

The pressure was intense. The points which Ismet Pasha could not accept seemed small, but still he could not bring himself to sign. At 9.15 on the evening of 4 February, Lord Curzon and the British delegation left the hotel for the station where the Orient Express was waiting. Would the Turkish delegation relent at the last moment?

> Bompard [of the French delegation], fussy and out of breath, dashes up the staircase. 'No good,' he says. *'Nous partons,'* I say to the stationmaster. Slowly the great train slides into the night.[32]

In the end, it did not matter. The formal agreement would come later. What mattered was that Britain's objectives had been achieved: there would be no war with Turkey and no war in the Balkans. Curzon's triumph was recognised and acknowledged across Europe, even by the governments which he had outmanoeuvred – though not, as Harold pointed out, by the *Daily Mail*.³³ When his train arrived at Victoria Station, the massed ranks of the Cabinet were waiting on the platform to greet him as a public demonstration of approval. Lausanne was undoubtedly Curzon's finest diplomatic hour, and, in all probability, Harold's also.

23 Bloomsbury

On 14 December 1922, while Harold in Lausanne was exulting that Lord Curzon's 'expert tactics' had succeeded in detaching the Turks from the influence of Moscow,¹ Vita went to a dinner party in London where she met Virginia Woolf. It was a meeting which was to have an immense impact on both their lives and also, not always positively, on Harold's. The dinner was given by the writer and art critic, Clive Bell. It was held at his house in Gordon Square in Bloomsbury and it marked Vita's introduction to the Bloomsbury Group with its complex characters and their even more complex relationships. Vita had been introduced to Bell the previous year by Lady Sackville, but it was only on the publication of his book, *After Cézanne*, in July 1922, that she wrote to him, expressing admiration for his work and inviting him to Long Barn where he met Harold. The two men came from very different backgrounds – Bell was the son of a wealthy engineer and coal mine owner – and they held very different views about life and art. In his first major work, *Art*, published in 1913, Bell famously claimed: 'To appreciate a work of art we need bring with us nothing from life, no knowledge of its ideas or affairs, no familiarity with its emotions,'² whereas possibly the dominant theme of Harold's work is the importance, even the necessity, of seeing life, individuals and art in their historical context. Nonetheless, they recognised in each other an openness and an enthusiasm in their approach to life which formed the basis of a friendship which endured until Bell's death in 1964.

Over the years, the Bloomsbury Group has developed a kind of mystique, its members seen as a small, enlightened coterie, dedicated to setting their lives and their art free from the moral and social restrictions of the age. At the time, of course, it was less clear cut. In the much smaller, literary and artistic world of the time, Bloomsbury's members may have been known, individually or collectively, for their advanced social views and their advocacy of the *avant-garde*, but neither their views nor their work were credited with the significance they have since acquired.

Harold and Vita were aware of Virginia Woolf as a writer – it was Vita's expression of admiration for the recently-published *Jacob's Room* that led Clive Bell to bring her and Virginia together. They were aware also that she had a history of severe mental problems. Harold's first question on hearing that Vita had dined with Virginia was an ungracious 'Did she look very mad?'[3] Both women, however, immediately scented the potential in each other, although, of the two, Vita was initially the more interested. Immediately after that first Gordon Square dinner, she wrote to Harold: 'Darling, I have quite lost my heart.'[4] Less than a month later, she was writing of 'her *darling* Mrs Woolf' whom she loved 'with a sick passion.'[5] A couple of days later, she confessed, 'Oh dear, how much I love that woman.'[6] Harold does not seem to have been over-concerned. He was more worried about Violet who had reappeared in London and telephoned Vita. He was also concerned about Vita's relationship with Dottie Wellesley which he feared might cause gossip or be cited as a cause of the breakdown of the Wellesleys' marriage, so he may even have welcomed the new friendship as a distraction. Virginia was more cautious. She was impressed, even awed, by Vita's aristocratic pedigree, her command and her self-assurance – 'the supple ease of the aristocracy' – but she had reservations. Vita was 'florid, moustached … a grenadier; hard; handsome; manly; inclined to double chin.' Nor was Virginia prepared to admit Vita as an intellectual equal: she lacked 'the wit of the artist.'[7]

It was a wet Sunday afternoon a couple of weeks after Harold's return from Lausanne when he and Vita dropped in on Leonard and Virginia Woolf at Hogarth House, their home in Richmond-on-Thames. The initiative was Vita's. Harold may not have been on the top of his social form: they had just been to visit his parents and he was worried about his father, now seventy-three and never a strong man, who had developed heart problems. Whatever the circumstances, the encounter was not a success. Virginia's diary, which provides the only record of the meeting, is uncompromising. She recognised that Vita – 'a pronounced Sapphist' – was sexually interested in her (though the relationship did not become sexual for some considerable time) and was honest enough to admit that she was attracted by Vita's aristocratic background. But when it came to Harold, he was 'simple downright bluff; wears short black coat and check trousers, wishes to be a writer, but is not I'm told & can believe, adapted by nature.'[8]

A month later – on 15 March, the day *Tennyson* was published – things went even worse. The occasion was another Gordon Square dinner. Using the collective 'we judged' (which appears to include Clive Bell, Duncan Grant and Lytton Strachey), Virginia's diary describes Vita and Harold as 'both incurably stupid.' She dismisses Harold as 'bluff, but oh so obvious' and suggests that Vita took her conversational cue from Harold, having nothing of her own to say – which, given Vita's character, seems unlikely.[9] And where Virginia led, other members of Bloomsbury apparently followed. James Lees-Milne records that 'Lytton Strachey was rude to Harold at their first meeting.'[10] Lees-Milne also says that

> When Maynard Keynes sent him a copy of [*Tennyson*] to review for *Nation and Athenaeum*, Lytton replied, 'I'm sorry to say that I can't face Lord Tennyson. Harold N's book is so disgusting and stupid.'[11]

Virginia also claimed to have thrown *Tennyson* on the floor 'in disgust'.[12]

Whatever the merits of its members and their works, Bloomsbury judged others harshly. Their criteria could be rational and intellectual, but could equally be personal, flawed or simply prejudiced. Even then, Virginia's judgements, based on clothes and external appearance seem so superficial, so un-Bloomsbury, and the terms used ('stupid', 'obvious' 'in disgust') seem so shallow, even childish, one has to ask why Bloomsbury was initially so hostile to the Nicolsons and to Harold in particular. It would be a mistake to regard the Bloomsbury Group as necessarily homogeneous, but its members did share certain broad, unifying ideas and attitudes. One of these was to set their face against 'Society', which, in general, they regarded as philistine and unintellectual. And Society was what they saw Harold and Vita as representing.

Their judgement on Vita was, after a time, reversed. 'Virginia,' writes Vita's biographer, 'shared her circle's scepticism about Vita's writing and her intellect, but she was fascinated by her as a woman.'[13] It was a fascination, as Virginia herself admitted, which mixed the romantic and the snobbish. She saw 'a high aristocrat ... virginal, savage, patrician', with Knole in her background and an ancestry stretching back to the Norman Conquest.[14] She came to recognise both the passion and the very independence that she had first denied, that mixture of Spanish blood and an aristocratic indifference to what the rest of the world thought. Led by Virginia, Bloomsbury accepted Vita because she was an aristocrat. They saw her sensitivity and her rejection of convention as all the more remarkable in someone from such an aristocratic background – failing to see the extent to which she was able to rebel *because* of that background. Vita herself had few intellectual pretensions and may well have been flattered by their interest.

For her, the main draw was undoubtedly the attraction of Virginia. She might find the conversation of other members of the group, such as Roger Fry, stimulating, but her temperament remained resolutely individual. She might defend Bloomsbury against claims that it was 'devitalised and devitalising', but she would never really belong.[15] And she was never going to side with Bloomsbury against Harold: she never forgave Strachey for his attitude and his behaviour.

Vita was one thing, but neither Virginia Woolf, nor Bloomsbury in general, was equipped to appreciate Harold. He represented Society in a different guise. Vita was an aristocrat, but Harold was a man-about-town. In the weeks and months following his return from Lausanne, he threw himself into the London social whirl. He was regularly invited to Lord North Street by the Colefaxes, whose society dinners for the great, the good and the famous were as far from Bloomsbury as it was possible to get. He attended a ball given by Lady Curzon at Lansdowne House, the London home of Gordon Selfridge, founder of the department store. He dined with Churchill, temporarily out of office and out of Parliament, and with other senior politicians. He dined with Foreign Office colleagues and friends at his new club, Buck's, although he was also a member of the Marlborough. He stayed at Sherfield Court, the Wellesleys' country house in Hampshire – Gerry insisted on having traditional weekend parties despite the rift in his marriage. He stayed at Gerald Berners' house at Faringdon near Oxford. This was the Society Bloomsbury had set its face against. Worse still, Harold was a diplomat, working for the Foreign Office. The whole business of politics and managing the relationship between states, which to Harold was of fundamental importance, was anathema to Bloomsbury. Lady Sackville had at one time objected to diplomacy as being socially beneath Vita. Bloomsbury saw it as intellectually beneath them. Diplomacy and the Foreign Office represented the establishment.

The mistake, of course, was to take Harold at face value. He was a pipe-smoking, moustached man who wore conventional clothes and worked for the Foreign Office. As such, his judgement could be dismissed out of hand. In 1929, Vita showed Harold a collection of poems called *King's Daughter*. Harold advised against publication. Coming after *The Land*, which had brought Vita a huge reputation, he thought the poems too slight. Virginia's reaction was revealing but hardly literary: 'And why,' she wrote to Vita, 'should you attach any importance to the criticism of a diplomat?'[16]

Virginia's friendship with Vita lasted nearly nineteen years, but she never really accepted or understood Harold. When *Byron: The Last Journey*, was published, she would not allow its quality. When it was praised by

Clive Bell and Desmond McCarthy, she wrote to Lytton Strachey that they had 'drunk too many glasses of [Harold's] champagne to be trusted.'[17] She was less self-assured when on unfamiliar ground and on her first visit to Long Barn was patronising rather than hostile, describing Harold as 'trusty & honest & vigorous.'[18] But where Harold's profession was concerned, her hostility, expressed in regular asides in her letters to Vita (and influenced no doubt by her own insecurities and her fear that Vita would be swept off to some far distant diplomatic post), never slackened. On one occasion, she even wrote to Vita that Harold ought to be doing 'a man's work' in England 'instead of a flunkey's in Berlin.'[19]

Harold, for his part, must have known or sensed much of this, but he was not by nature confrontational and, whatever he felt, would never have let his feelings show – not least, because he understood that for Vita this was a 'soul-friendship.'[20] Although he might worry and would later warn Vita that she did not have '*la main heureuse* in dealing with married couples,' he accepted that 'you are probably very good for each other' and did nothing to intervene.[21] He genuinely admired Virginia's writing. In 1961, when interviewed by the *Observer* for his seventy-fifth birthday, he claimed that of all contemporary novelists, she was the one who had done most to extend his awareness of the world. He enjoyed a perfectly amicable social relationship with the Woolfs – though it was perhaps a diplomatic one, maintained for Vita's benefit, and he preferred Leonard to Virginia. When asked by Vita about his feelings towards Virginia, he hedged and said only that he would never forget 'how she was kind to me when I was smarting from Lytton's rudeness.'[22]

Harold did not share many of Bloomsbury's values and they could not share many of his. He certainly believed in intellectual honesty and was always ready, over a glass of wine or after dinner, to enjoy a conversation about life and art – though he disliked discussing sexual matters and was shy of discussing his emotions except with a small number of close friends. But he also believed in duty and public service; he valued the process of constitution and government; he could be moved by patriotic emotion – as he had been watching the Victory Parade in Paris in 1919. This was what he called his Kipling side, and here Bloomsbury could not follow him. The fact that the majority of Bloomsbury had taken a pacifist stance during the war was another point of divergence. Nor was Harold's versatility a recommendation. He moved with alarming ease between Society, diplomacy, politics, literature, history, journalism and gardening. Bloomsbury saw him as shallow. He saw Bloomsbury as 'a narrow but stimulating lot.'[23]

It would be a mistake to overstate the extent to which philosophical differences affected normal social activity. In the period between that rainy Sunday visit to Richmond at the beginning of 1923 and Harold's departure for Persia in November 1925, Bloomsbury did constitute a part of his crowded social life. There were numerous dinners and discussions, evenings spent in Gordon Square or at Long Barn deep in conversation about art and literature. And he did make friends among Bloomsbury's members. He was on good, though not close, terms with John Maynard Keynes, whom he had first met as a Treasury representative in Paris in 1919. Clive Bell has already been mentioned. Desmond McCarthy, the critic and editor, became a trusted and loyal friend, and then there was Raymond Mortimer with whom Harold developed one of the closest and deepest relationships of his life. But the fact remains that Harold was inevitably an outsider, much further from belonging even than Vita. All his life he sought to belong, to join, to become an insider, but with Bloomsbury it was not possible. Nor is there any evidence that he wanted it to be. Between Harold and Bloomsbury there could be no meeting of minds.

24 Byron

Harold's involvement with Bloomsbury and its members is interesting, even revealing, but the cultural significance now attached to Bloomsbury should not obscure the fact that they represented only a small part of his extraordinarily busy life. He was, in effect, following two careers simultaneously, achieving a measure of success in both and doing so without any apparent strain. Although he did finally choose to leave diplomacy to become a full-time writer and journalist, the decision to do so was taken for personal reasons and as a response to personal pressures. There was never any suggestion of a conflict between his two roles or any suggestion that he could not cope with the pressure. Harold thrived on activity.

The first major event following his return from Lausanne was the publication of *Tennyson*, which, Virginia Woolf's and Lytton Strachey's strictures aside, was generally very well received. It was also more widely reviewed than his previous books, an indication that his reputation in literary circles was growing. A couple of the old guard – Tennyson's friend, Willingham Rawnsley, and the President of Magdalen College, Oxford, Sir Herbert Warren – did not appreciate Harold's picture of the great man, but, if anything, this boosted his reputation, particularly among the younger generation of reviewers. Possibly the review which meant most to Harold was that by Edmund Gosse, which appeared in the *Sunday Times* at the end of March 1923. In one sense, Gosse was the old guard personified for he had visited and talked poetry with Tennyson half-a-century before, but Gosse applauded what Harold was doing. He understood that, in examining Tennyson's inner life and setting him against the background of his age, Harold was not attempting to undermine him either as man or poet. Rather, Harold was trying to show that Tennyson's poetic genius was all the more impressive because it sprang from a personality which was subject to doubt, depression and the usual run of human emotions; that the beauty of Tennyson's language and his greatness as a poet did not necessarily rest upon a profound or coherent philosophical position. Harold's insight was to see that Tennyson was the man he was, and to like him for it.

It was on reading *Tennyson* that Virginia Woolf claimed that Harold was 'due to Lytton'[1] – and it is possible that Strachey's hostility stemmed from seeing Harold as a mere imitator. Harold never denied Strachey's influence and it is certainly present in his method and in some of the descriptive passages, but there is a fundamental difference in what Strachey achieved in *Eminent Victorians* or *Queen Victoria* and what Harold was attempting in *Tennyson*. Strachey was selecting detail from a huge wealth of material in order to isolate and highlight the essential characteristics of an era. Harold was seeking a kind of unity, drawing together disparate impressions and ideas about one man in order to explain his character and its relation to his poetry. Certainly, *Tennyson* marked a step forward for Harold as a writer in a technical sense. Despite – or perhaps because of – the speed at which it was written, the book is stylistically and structurally more coherent than *Verlaine* and its central thesis far more clearly defined. Sligger Urquhart regarded the book as a masterpiece, though he nit-picked on some of the detail, and James Lees-Milne argues that 'in this book the authentic, wholly mature Harold Nicolson emerges.'[2] Unfortunately, we have no record of Lord Curzon's reaction.

In the meantime, life at the Foreign Office was comparatively quiet. Harold was concerned with preparations for the second Lausanne Conference. Neither Curzon nor Harold would be going: Britain was to be represented by the British High Commissioner to Constantinople, Sir Horace Rumbold (whose title would change to Ambassador once a formal peace with Turkey had been signed). Nonetheless, there were position papers to be prepared and to be approved by Curzon, paving the way for what has been rightly regarded as the most successful of the many post-war treaties. Once the Conference began on April 23, however, work slackened sufficiently for Harold to put in a major effort on Byron.

As with Verlaine, Harold's interest in Byron went back a long way, probably to his schooldays at Wellington. Time had drawn a discreet veil over the accusations of adultery, incest and sodomy which had pursued Byron during his lifetime and caused him to leave Britain for good in 1816. He was lauded not only as a great poet, but also as an idealist who threw himself whole-heartedly into the struggle for Greek independence, though it cost him his life – a role which, in the intensely classics-oriented world of the British public school system, was sufficient to ensure him heroic status. Byron was required reading for those competing for Foreign Office entry and Harold, during his own period of 'cramming', had studied *Don Juan*. For a twenty-two-year-old, his response to both the emotional and technical aspects of the poem was impressive.

> Harold detected in the first canto of *Don Juan* a sort of dance rhythm, and in the concluding couplet a sort of breakdown of emotion. *Don Juan* was, he observed, the cleverest of all English poems, in that it was addressed to a wide audience, to lovers of verse and those not in the usual sense lovers of verse at all; if Byron did not bring a new idea into the world, he quadrupled the force of existing ones.[3]

Yet, when it came to writing *Byron: The Last Journey*, it was not the poetry to which he was responding: the poetry barely features at all. It was Byron's intense, larger-than-life personality which attracted Harold. As with *Tennyson*, he rejected the traditional view of his central character. Byron, Harold argued, was not a clear-sighted, idealistic hero who 'went to Greece inspired solely by Philhellenic enthusiasms.' Rather, he was a man who knew 'diffidence, irresolution, perplexity, and fear.'[4] Even in his own lifetime, Byron's reputation was such that by throwing himself into the cause of Greek independence he 'lifted [it] from the muddied by-ways of party politics, and rendered it at once an enterprise, a novelty, an excitement, and a very emotional romance.'[5] In practical terms, Byron accomplished nothing at Missolonghi beyond his own death, which Harold saw as tantamount to suicide, but

> by that single heroic act he secured the liberation of Greece. Had Byron, as he was urged, deserted the Hellenic cause in February 1824, there would, I feel convinced, have been no Navarino: the whole history of South-eastern Europe would have developed differently.[6]

Byron was still a hero, but a hero of a different kind, one who overcame his doubts and insecurities – more complex, more troubled, in a sense more modern.

Two other reasons may well have influenced Harold's choice of Byron as a subject at this time. The first was the fact that 1924 would be the centenary of Byron's death. Harold's inability to manage his finances meant that he was chronically hard up – in April 1923, he wrote to Vita about his 'black and haggard poverty.'[7] He needed money and he very much wanted to be a successful writer. A book to coincide with the Byron centenary would be useful on both counts. The second was Harold's love affair with Greece, which almost certainly pre-dated his fascination with Byron. Wellington College and Dr Pollock had provided him with a traditional, English, classics-based education, imparting a love of the classics which stayed with him for the rest of his life. And Greece was the heartland of the classics. In that sense, *Byron* is an imaginative response to the traditional relationship between a well-educated Englishman and Greece. But it is more: it is also a celebration of the role that one Englishman was able to play in securing Greek independence from the Turks. During the tortuous negotiations in Paris, throughout the vicissitudes of the Greek campaign in Asia Minor and, again, during the negotiations at Lausanne, Harold had consistently espoused the Greek cause. There is no doubt that Harold, with his strong sense of historical continuity, was to some degree identifying with Byron's struggles on behalf of the Greeks. It is for that reason, as much as because of the personal relationship, that *Byron* is dedicated to the man whom Harold saw as the true Greek leader of his age: Venizelos.

Harold followed his now established mode of composition. In October 1922, while still in London and preparing for the Lausanne Conference, he began reading all the available source material and making detailed notes. He continued – when not following the dictates of Lord Curzon, serving on committees, correcting the proofs of *Tennyson* or skiing – throughout the time he spent in Lausanne and then on his return to England. He also made a trip to Nottinghamshire to absorb some Byronic atmosphere at Newstead Abbey. Byron inherited Newstead, together with the title of sixth Baron Byron of Rochdale, in 1798 when he was ten, but he did not live there until 1808 when he came down from Cambridge. At that time, the Abbey, parts of which date back to the thirteenth century, was largely in ruins, with only a few small habitable rooms. Byron seems to have done little to improve the situation, using the Great Hall for fencing and shooting practice and allowing a tame bear and a wolf the run of the house. In fact, he lived there only intermittently before selling the estate in 1818 to relieve his financial problems. Harold saw his writing table and his bed, and some of his personal possessions, such as boxing gloves and swords, but Newstead did not make the same kind of impact on his imagination that Tennyson's childhood home, Somersby, had made.

Just as Harold was ready to start writing, an event occurred which brought home just how unstable and violent a region the Balkans remained, even a hundred years after Byron's death. Alexander Stamboliski, the Bulgarian Prime Minister, was deposed by a military coup, tortured and beheaded. Stamboliski, while not an uncontroversial figure, was a Bulgarian patriot who had been imprisoned for his opposition to Bulgarian support for Germany during the war. He had represented Bulgaria at the Paris Peace Conference and again at Lausanne. Harold's reaction, in a letter to Vita, is revealing, beginning with his personal feelings but ending with a touch of professional detachment.

> He was like a great bison with little furtive red eyes and a great massive frame. His hands were like large dimpled hams, and he painted his face, and roared like a bull and all his buttons came undone. He was a fine man, in a capricious way, and I can't help being sorry.... I hate the idea of someone whom I knew and abused and worked with and rather liked, lying in some dusty roadway with his tongue cut and his hair clotted with blood.
>
> What swine the Balkans are! My pig farm. But how glad I am that they are my own speciality.[8]

The first draft of *Byron* was written at a speed which, even by Harold's standards, was remarkable. It was written at Long Barn; begun on 29 June and completed on 26 July – 110,000 words in thirty-three days. Harold seems to have intended to spend the rest of the summer going over the manuscript and revising it, but his plans were interrupted by a sudden international crisis in – of course – the Balkans.

Two long-standing problems, both of which had involved Harold, now coincided. The first was Italy's determination, dating back to the inevitable 1915 Treaty of London and before, to gain more territory along the Adriatic coastline. The second was Albania, which had emerged from the Balkan Wars as an independent state, but without established or agreed borders. The northern borders were established in the aftermath of the 1913 London Conference, but the southern border with Greece was a more complex problem. A plan to send a commission to investigate on the ground had been overtaken by the outbreak of the First World War, and it was not until

1923 that a commission, under the auspices of the Conference of Ambassadors of the Allied Powers, still sitting in Paris, was actually sent. On 27 August 1923, four members of the commission, the Italian General Tellini and three of his staff, were murdered at Janina on the Greek side of the proposed frontier. The area was known to be lawless and the Greek Government had already protested to the Albanian authorities about the depredations of 'Albanian brigands.' There was certainly no reason to suppose official Greek involvement, but, within two days of the killings, the Italian Government had sent a Note Verbale holding Greece responsible for the outrage and demanding, among other things, a payment of 50 million lire. The Greek response was conciliatory, while naturally enough rejecting any responsibility for the deaths and the demand for compensation. But Mussolini was not listening. Even before he received the Greek response, the Italian battle fleet set sail from Taranto. On 31 August, only four days after the killings, Italian warships bombarded Corfu town, killing twenty civilians. Italian troops landed and occupied the island.

A full-scale international crisis had blown up in less than a week. Newspapers speculated about 'the new War.'[9] At the Foreign Office, Harold was so occupied following the twists and turns of Britain's response to the situation that he could not get back to Long Barn and had to stay in London almost all the time, 'sometimes at the Automobile Club, and sometimes with Gerry in Portland Place, and sometimes even in the office.'[10] Greece appealed to the League of Nations: Britain supported the appeal. Italy insisted the matter be handled by the Conference of Ambassadors: Poincaré supported Mussolini, and Britain fell into line. By mid-September, the Ambassadors gave their judgement, to all intents and purposes supporting Italy, obliging Greece to apologise and pay compensation. Despite this rapid diplomatic victory, Mussolini showed no inclination to abandon Corfu. It was only on 27 September when the Italian navy realised that it could face a confrontation with the British Mediterranean fleet that Italian troops were actually withdrawn. It was a depressing episode: force and the threat of force were the victors.

In his diary, Harold was critical of both Curzon and Sir William Tyrrell. They 'only backed the League because they felt, ignorantly, that it was a way out of the difficulty. When they realised it was not a way out but a way deeper in, they tried to back out without saying so.... Tyrrell because he is for an arrangement at any price; Curzon because of his inordinate vanity.' Even at the time, Harold saw the events of September 1923 as marking the beginning of the end for the League of Nations, a judgement which commentators and historians have upheld ever since. His judgement was based on his idealistic belief in the League – 'we had a chance of calling the new world into being in order to redress the balance of the old'[11] – and also on his eternal love of Greece. He was right, but he failed, perhaps unusually, to appreciate the *realpolitik* of the European situation. No one was really going to risk war with Italy over Corfu. Italy was an essential partner when it came to dealing with Germany, which was suffering from hyperinflation, mass unemployment and on the verge of complete social collapse. France and Belgium had occupied the Ruhr that January in pursuit of reparations and were anxious to keep debate on their actions within the Conference of Ambassadors. They did not want to give Mussolini a stick to beat them with. And then there were Anglo-French relations, which had been strained, to say the least, in the run up to Lausanne. Curzon wanted to get things back on track: as far as Britain was concerned, France was simply more important than Greece. Was it just because the situation involved his beloved Greece that Harold failed to see the broader perspective? Or was he actually becoming more idealistic?

Despite his criticisms, Harold remained captivated by Curzon's eccentricities. On one occasion, in the early stages of the Corfu crisis, Curzon visited Paris for talks with Poincaré. On his return

> Tyrrell, Allen and I went to Victoria to meet him.... First came a procession of red boxes and the green baize foot-rest. Then slowly and majestically came the Marquis. The reporters got out their notebooks. The photographers set flame to their magnesium. The detectives detected. The crowd crowded.
>
> 'Where is Nicolson?' said the Marquis, but the rest was lost in a burst of cheering from the crowd.... 'Nicolson?' he exclaimed again.... I pulled myself together for the instructions which were to settle the fate of Europe.
>
> 'I have been reading *Grey Wethers*,' said the Marquis – 'magnificent book. The descriptions of the downs are as fine as any in the language. Such power! Such power! Not a pleasant book, of course! But what English!'[12]

Such incidents can have done little to endear Curzon to his other subordinates, nor Harold to his colleagues.

For two weeks Harold was so busy that he had no time to keep his diary but then, when the crisis was over and rather than take a break, he threw himself straight back into the social and literary whirl. On the evening of 20 September, he and Vita accepted an invitation to attend the first night of

James Elroy Flecker's poetic drama *Hassan*. It seems to have been a strange evening. Harold had met Flecker once when they were contemporaries at Oxford but had no particular admiration for his work: when he came to write of Swinburne, he was to say that 'the blood-stained sensuality of *Poems and Ballads* appears to have served but little purpose – to have led at its best to Flecker, and at its worst to Wilde.'[13] Flecker had died in 1915 but his widow, Helle, had worked hard to promote his work, receiving support in her efforts from Eddie Marsh. To succeed in getting *Hassan* staged at His Majesty's Theatre with music specially composed by Delius and conducted by Eugene Goossens, and with actors of the calibre of Henry Ainley and Cathleen Nesbitt in the main roles, was a considerable achievement on her part. The performance went well, but Harold, whether through overwork or empathy with Mrs Flecker, found the after-performance supper profoundly depressing. She

> had of course expected the Ritz and photographers, and auratum lilies, and a few well-chosen words.... She got nothing of the sort ... a ham sandwich, and a glass of banana cup, and a little desultory conversation from such inadequates as myself, and a gentleman from the disposals board, and Eddie Marsh.... The claret cup splashed upon the cloth and sprinkled little pink banana discs.[14]

What would Bloomsbury have said?

25   Affair

A week later, having settled nine-year-old Ben at his preparatory boarding school, Summer Fields, on the Banbury Road just outside Oxford, Harold took some leave. But he did not take a rest. After lunch on Friday 28 September, he took the boat train from Victoria, crossed to Calais and went on to Paris where he picked up the Orient Express, arriving in Athens before lunchtime on the Sunday. This was to be a Byron trip and it is characteristic of the way Harold approached his research that his first visit was not to a library or a museum, but to the elaborate piece of statuary outside the National Gardens which depicts the allegorical figure of Greece crowning Byron the poet-hero with a wreath of laurels. Here, Harold took off his hat and explained to the poet why he had come. Of course, it was piece of self-conscious eccentricity, but it does illustrate Harold's need to develop some kind of personal connection with the subjects of his biographies. It was something he did with all of them – with the exception of George V – but it was more acute in the case of Byron, because of his hero worship. Indeed, a few months later, this same tendency led to an odd, comic incident while he was lunching – perhaps lunching rather well – at the Marlborough Club in Pall Mall.

> And beyond the lavatory is the little room in which they keep the sofa which was Byron's at Missolonghi.... The room was quite dark – lit only by the embers of a very economical fire. The lights were unlit.... I clasped the wooden parts of the sofa.... Byron, Missolonghi, Missolonghi, Byron. I repeated the words, since that (I believe) is the psychic thing to do.... I thought myself INTO Byron. And then a gradually a sort of strange, unknown feeling came over me.... It was absurd but something white and phosphorescent began to glimmer opposite against the curtains.... It really did: it emerged quite definitely, darling, as a FACE.... You *know* I don't make things up: and I *swear* to you that at that moment I saw the face of Byron looking at me.... Then I got frightened and dashed to the electric light switch. I turned on the light. There was a bust against the curtains with a brass plate underneath – WINIFRED EMERY BY ALBERT TOFT.[1]

In Athens, Harold stayed mainly with his friend and colleague Charlie Hartopp, but on a couple of occasions he drove out to spend the night with Charles Bentinck, the Chargé d'Affaires, who had a villa in Kephisia just outside the city. Harold disliked Kephisia, largely, it seems, for aesthetic reasons: the villa had 'oleanders and a gramophone and a shower bath which sighs at one when one pulls the handle because the water has run out,' and the toilet had 'a japanned tin pail to help one out ... and a horrid little bristly brown brush.'[2] He remained in Greece for just over two weeks. He had several long talks with Shirley Atchley who had been attached to the British Legation for many years. Officially, Atchley was a translator, but his main value was his encyclopaedic knowledge of Greece, its language and dialects, its history and politics, even its flora and fauna. In the cool surroundings of the library of the British School, Harold became fascinated by the memoranda sent to Byron by one Frank Abney Hastings, a British naval officer who had fought at Trafalgar but then taken service with the nascent Greek navy. He offered sound technical and tactical advice on how the Turks could be beaten at sea, but, visionary though Byron was in some ways, he could not cope with the idea of steam-powered ships and ignored Hastings' letters. Harold felt he had caught a glimpse of how Byron's story might just have taken a different turn.

He drove out through the pine forests to Marathon and gazed across the strait to the mountains of Euboea. He drove south to Sounion (or Sunium) to visit the Temple of Poseidon which Byron visited in 1811 and which features in *Don Juan*. He travelled to Patras and crossed by boat to Missolonghi, which he decided was 'exactly and very squalidly what it was in 1824.'[3] At Missolonghi, he was helped by the local headmaster: he had known the boatman who, as a boy, had ferried Byron across the lagoon. Together, they identified the location of the house in which Byron died and mapped out its structure. Harold may have been researching Byron's love affair with Greece which ended so tragically, but, in doing so, he was also celebrating his own love affair with the country and its culture. His classical education was never far from the surface. He had been trained from an early age to respond to Greece and all things Greek and he did so quite passionately. The Greek landscape was the most beautiful he had ever seen, and as for Athens, 'my violet-crowned Athens ... it beats Rome hollow.'[4]

On 15 October, Harold set off to join Vita in Florence. He took the overnight ferry from Piraeus to Brindisi, and from Brindisi the overnight train to Rome. On the journey, whether as a break from Byron or for some other reason, he read *The Three Musketeers*, an uncharacteristically swashbuckling choice. In Rome, he went to visit Gerald Berners, but found, in addition to Berners, Osbert and Sacheverell Sitwell, with whom he was never wholly at ease. On the last leg of the journey, his travelling companion was Geoffrey Scott, whose wife, Lady Sibyl, owned the Villa Medici in Fiesole where Vita was staying. Harold had been separated from Vita for nearly three weeks and was longing – 'aching' was his word[5] – to see her again, but their reunion was to be more complicated than he imagined.

Geoffrey Scott was an Oxford-educated writer and architectural historian. While still an undergraduate, he met Mary Berenson, who was married to the influential American art historian Bernard Berenson, and was quickly drawn into the artistic and intellectual circle which the Berensons created at I Tatti, their villa in the hills outside Florence. Scott began to make a reputation for himself with the publication of *The Architecture of Humanism* in 1914. It was through Berenson that he met Lady Sibyl Cutting, the widow of an American diplomat, whose wealth had enabled her to buy the Villa Medici, one of the oldest and certainly one of the most beautiful of the Renaissance villas which surround Florence. They married in 1918.

Harold Nicolson

Vita had met Geoffrey Scott as long ago as 1911 when she was travelling in Italy with Rosamund Grosvenor and he had been working temporarily at the Embassy in Rome. Then she met him again with Harold in 1921 during their Italian holiday with Gerry and Dotty Wellesley. His reappearance in their lives in the summer of 1923 may have had a Bloomsbury connection – he was good friend of John Maynard Keynes, whom he had met at I Tatti in the years before the First World War – but however it came about, he soon became a regular visitor to Long Barn and, that August, he and Vita had taken a trip to the Lake District together.

One can only imagine how Harold, with his sense of history and continuity, responded to the Villa Medici. Built in the 1450s by Michelozzo di Bartolomeo for Cosimo the Elder, its design reflected early Renaissance principles of proportion and balance. It was intended from the first as an intellectual retreat, a home for Cosimo's Platonic Academy; and under Cosimo's grandson, Lorenzo the Magnificent, it continued to be a meeting place for the philosophers, poets and artists who inhabited the Florentine court. In 1772, it was bought by Margaret Walpole, widow of the second Earl of Orford, and had passed ever since through the hands of the English community in Florence. William Beckford, the author and art collector, had visited; so, too, according to one story, had Thomas Jefferson during his years in Europe. In these surroundings, high on the hillside overlooking Florence and the valley of the Arno, Harold sat every morning for a week working on his manuscript.

In the afternoons, there were calls to be made among the English and American community: on the Berensons, of course, at I Tatti, but more important as far as Harold was concerned, on Mrs Janet Ross, who lived in Castello Poggio Gherardo, reputed to have been the setting for Boccaccio's *Decameron*. Mrs Ross was now eighty-five but in her youth she had been close friends with George Meredith and John Addington Symonds. She had known Tennyson, and she had also known Teresa Guiccioli, Byron's mistress from 1818 until he set off on his journey to Greece in 1823. While staying at the Villa Medici, Harold also met and talked with Lady Sibyl's daughter by her first marriage, Iris Cutting, who was shortly to marry the Marchese di Val D'Orcia. In later life, as Iris Origo, she was to become a writer with more than a passing interest in Byron: *Allegra* (1930) is a biography of Byron's daughter, Clara Allegra, and *The Last Attachment* (1949) is an account of Byron's relationship with Teresa Guiccioli.

It should have been an idyllic few days, but it proved a testing time. Vita had embarked on *The Land*, her long, narrative poem describing and celebrating the annual cycle of the Kent countryside. Geoffrey Scott was working on *The Portrait of Zelide*, a biography of the eighteenth-century Dutch writer, Isabelle de Charrière, which was to become his best-known work. Under the influence of the Villa Medici and the Tuscan autumn, their intense literary friendship became a full-blooded sexual affair – 'On a hillside, one lovely evening, when the moon rose above a sea of olives, [Geoffrey] took her in his arms.'[6] Harold knew what was happening, as did Lady Sibyl, but neither sought to interfere.

For Harold, this was a matter of honour, even loyalty. The 'open' character of Harold and Vita's marriage which impressed or shocked, according to taste, when *Portrait of a Marriage* was published in 1973 was not, as some have assumed, an anticipation of ideas which became current (though far from widely-practised) in the 1970s. It was rather a continuation of accepted practice among aristocratic families in the late nineteenth century. Barbara Tuchman, writing of the period between 1890 and 1914, suggests that:

> As long as the partners in these ... infidelities did nothing to provoke a public scandal ... they could do as they pleased. The overriding consideration was to prevent any exposure of misconduct to the lower classes. ... Within the closed circle of the ruling classes the unforgivable sin was to give away any member of the group; there must be no appeal to the Divorce Court, no publicity that would bring members of the class into disrepute.[7]

This was the theory and the accepted practice with which Vita, in particular, had grown up, and which fits, in large measure, the story of Lord and Lady Sackville. In Harold and Vita's case, however, it was qualified by an overt understanding that their sex lives and sexual preferences would never be allowed to threaten their emotional relationship. And yet, when it happened with Geoffrey, Harold did not find it so easy. It is often difficult in biography to give a precise interpretation of a letter or a communication, but it is a reasonable assumption that in 1921 when Harold wrote to Vita that they were lucky 'to love each other so very much and with such confidence (not in fidelity, darling – don't get that into your head) but confidence in each other's respect and love,'[8] he was not thinking of heterosexual infidelity.

Nigel Nicolson, following Lady Sackville, suggests that Harold 'knew about the affair from the start, and in a curious way was rather pleased.'[9] This does not seem borne out by his state of mind over the next few weeks. He left Fiesole on 28 October, feeling 'very depressed,'[10] and returned to London via Pisa, Genoa and Ventimiglia, seeking out the places where

Byron lived or stayed during his time in Italy. At Monte Carlo, uncharacteristically, he took time out to gamble at the Casino. Returning to the Foreign Office, his mood remained depressed. Vita followed him home, but for the moment at least she was completely taken up with Geoffrey. 'My love and tenderness,' she wrote to him, 'are a bank on which you can draw unlimited cheques.'[11] She told Lady Sackville that 'she missed Geoffrey atrociously ... [that] he is very passionate. ... She is sure Harold doesn't mind.'[12] Harold may, as James Lees-Milne suggests, have 'realised that this gentle and civilised man would never rob him of Vita's enduring affection,' but he is surely also correct is saying that 'the spectacle cannot have been agreeable for him to witness at close quarters.'[13]

In the meantime, Harold got on with his life. He finished *Byron*, enlisting Desmond MacCarthy's help for the final revisions, and took the manuscript round to Constable, glad to be rid of it. He toyed for a while with the idea of writing about Pope but gave it up – possibly, as he claimed, because he was out of sympathy with the eighteenth century and disliked Pope's character or, more likely, because he was simply not in the mood. He worked on an odd commission – writing a miniature article for a miniature book which was to be placed in the library of a special dolls' house being built for Queen Mary by Edwin Lutyens. Harold and Vita spent New Year at Knole with Ben and Nigel, Lord Sackville and Olive Rubens, Dottie Wellesley and her son, Valerian. Harold's end-of-year diary entries frequently contain a kind of summary or judgement on the previous twelve months. On this occasion, one senses just a little uncertainty about Vita.

> I have been well in health and spirits; my piles and constipation better; very happy with my darling Viti and my two boys; not really distressed at the approach of middle age and the consequent extension of my figure and thinning of my hair. Viti also I think has been happy.[14]
>
> I decide and resolve to be less irresponsible, not to have claret for luncheon, and to suffer fools more gladly. I don't know what Viti decides.[15]

Harold's end-of-year summary also includes the revealing statement: 'I have not made any very exciting new friends, but I have not lost any old ones.'[16] So much for Bloomsbury.

Vita met Geoffrey again on his arrival in England on 10 January 1924. They dined together at the Berkeley Hotel. The following day was Friday and Geoffrey was invited down to Knole for the weekend. Harold and the boys were there as well. The next thing was an invitation to meet Lady

Sackville at White Lodge, her home in Brighton. Harold went back to work.

On 15 January, he joined the crowds lining the Mall to watch the royal procession on its way to the State Opening of Parliament and he noticed how the twenty-year-old Prince of Wales seemed much more popular than King George V. It was an incident Harold must surely have remembered in later years when the Prince of Wales had become the exiled Duke of Windsor and he found himself writing George V's official biography. That same evening, he attended a strange and oddly melancholy dinner at Lord Curzon's London house in Carlton House Terrace. There had been a general election the previous December. Stanley Baldwin's Conservative Government had lost its overall majority and, although he remained leader of the largest party and had been invited by the King to form a new government, it was obvious that his administration was limping towards its end. Curzon knew he would be out of office within a matter of days and the dinner was one of thanks and farewell to those senior members of the Foreign Office who had supported him during his four-and-a-half years as Foreign Secretary. In the event, although Curzon did his best to be genial, the evening was a failure. The dining room was magnificent in red and gold, but 'I sit at the end of the long table,' Harold wrote, 'and see a perspective to right and left of civil service faces.' Everyone knew that Curzon had been desperately disappointed in May the previous year when, despite his success at Lausanne, Stanley Baldwin, not he, had been chosen to succeed Bonar Law as Prime Minister. Everyone realised that this was probably Curzon's farewell to public office. As a consequence, 'everyone [felt] rather shy ... conversation [was] hushed and stilted.' And the atmosphere was not helped by the fact that the food was bad. With the coffee came 'a certain imminence upon us, a certain feeling that someone, somehow should make a speech.' But nobody did and the evening ended early. The guests filed out, shaking hands with their host in what Harold described as 'a sorry ceremonial.'[17]

Waiting for the change of government, the Foreign Office was becalmed. Harold was dealing with yet another issue left over from the endlessly troublesome 1915 Treaty of London. Mussolini was pressing for Britain to cede to Italy the territory of Jubaland, at the time the north-eastern province of British East Africa, today the southernmost part of Somalia. Curzon was willing to agree, but in return he wanted Italy to give up the Dodecanese islands. Curzon, not without reason, distrusted Italian territorial ambitions and saw a strong and continued Italian presence in the eastern Mediterranean as a both a potential source of trouble and a threat to the freedom of the Straits. In the end, he bowed to advice from Harold and Sir

Eyre Crowe and left the matter to be dealt with by Ramsay MacDonald and the incoming government.

Harold saw a lot of Curzon during his last few days in office, lunching alone with him and Lady Curzon. There can be no doubt that he was something of a favourite with them both. During the final phase of negotiations with the Turks, while Curzon and Harold were still in Lausanne, Duff and Diana Cooper had been skiing in St Moritz and had dined with Lady Curzon. She had said that 'Curzon was very pleased with Harold Nicolson, who would probably replace Vansittart' as Principal Private Secretary to the Foreign Secretary[18] – an opinion she now repeated to Harold. Curzon must have said something.

On 22 January 1924, Ramsay MacDonald became Britain's first ever Labour Prime Minister. The world was changing. 'Today 23 years ago dear Grandmama [Queen Victoria] died,' George V wrote in his diary. 'I wonder what she would have thought of a Labour government!'[19] Harold was in sympathy with the changes, not least because Labour was more inclined to support the League of Nations, but he recognised from the first that the new Prime Minister would take a while to get used to the ways of the Foreign Office – 'a rather urgent paper which I sent in on Wednesday has still not been returned. This marks a great difference from the Curzon days.'[20] MacDonald took office as Prime Minister, Foreign Secretary and Leader of the House of Commons, a huge burden which led to squabbles with Crowe as to which duties he could and could not delegate to his Foreign Office deputy, Arthur Ponsonby. Ponsonby was not a particularly happy choice as Under Secretary of State. He had served in the Diplomatic Service in the 1890s, subsequently becoming an MP. He had also been one of the leading voices opposing British participation in the First World War. Harold considered him a 'moth-eaten little man' whose attempts to be friendly were rather pathetic.[21] Duff Cooper, who was Ponsonby's Private Secretary for his first two weeks in office, recorded that 'it is impossible to dislike [him] but the people that he sees and that are his friends and the views he holds are equally disgusting.'[22]

Harold was not appointed Principal Private Secretary to Ramsay MacDonald. The job went to Walford Selby, the Assistant Head of Central Department. The decision sent Harold into an orgy of self-deprecation. In his diary, he admits that he wanted the job and was 'disappointed and mortified' that it had gone to somebody else. He speculates that Crowe and Tyrrell regarded him as 'not wholly safe nor temperamentally sound.'[23] James Lees-Milne suggests that Harold assumed that his superiors knew about his homosexuality and 'like most normal Englishmen of their generation and upbringing, assumed that homosexuals, however brilliant they might be, were emotionally unstable people not to be relied on under stress and in crisis.'[24] That is certainly possible, but, looked at dispassionately, there were a number of obvious, operational reasons for choosing Selby over Harold. He was senior to Harold, having been in the Service longer; he had been a First Secretary longer; and his professional experience was broader. He had been Sir Edward Grey's Assistant Private Secretary before the War; he had served in the Grenadier Guards; he had more experience of front line diplomacy than Harold, having served in Berlin, the Hague, and Cairo, where, as an Arabic speaker, he had worked alongside Allenby during the negotiations which ended the British Protectorate. That the appointment was a good one is not really open to question: Selby served five Foreign Secretaries and held the position for eight years. More interesting is Harold's apparent failure to understand his own position, his own worth, even his own character. Ever since his posting to Constantinople at the beginning of 1913, his work had centred on Turkey, Italy, Greece and the Balkans. There had been times when he had been allowed or encouraged to look at the broader spectrum of British policy, but essentially he remained a specialist, an expert in an important but comparatively narrow field. He had proved himself able, even brilliant. His mercurial intelligence allowed him to take a fresh look at established policies and argue his case cogently in papers which would go all the way up to the Prime Minister. The issue was essentially one of character. Harold's very brilliance and originality meant that he was simply not the right person to hold the hand of a new and wholly inexperienced Foreign Secretary.

In the meantime, Vita was constantly with Geoffrey Scott, at Knole, at Long Barn, at the flat he had borrowed in Hanover Terrace, at the Sackville house in Hill Street, where they shared a room. Lady Sackville was 'shocked that he shows so much proprietorship over her.'[25] At a lunch given by Lady Sackville on 1 February, she noted that Harold said nothing and 'put it down to G.S.... At the best, he can't like it and his pride must suffer.'[26] Lady Sackville may well have been right, but hurt pride, especially in relation to Vita, was not something Harold would ever have admitted. It was a matter of integrity. He had promised Vita freedom within their marriage and freedom she should have, whatever the cost to himself. He was probably worrying about gossip, which was beginning to circulate. Although it was gossip of a very different order from that which circulated during Vita's affair with Violet, any discussion of his wife's sex life could still raise questions or lead to inferences about his own. And not a little of the gossip originated with Lady Sackville who, despite a genuine if muddled concern for Vita's well-being, was, as Victoria Glendinning accurately judges, 'incapable of discretion'[27] – another reason to remain quiet at lunch.

Harold understood better than anyone else – arguably better than Vita herself – that the very intensity of her affairs meant that they were inevitably short term, but Geoffrey did not. Geoffrey believed, or hoped, that this was the real thing; that it would last. In mid-February, he returned to Italy, resigned from his translating job at the British Embassy in Rome and wrote to Vita proposing he should spend six months of the year in England with her and six months in Florence with his wife. Vita had already begun to find him emotionally demanding, but this level of commitment and this level of planning for the future frightened her. She began to cool. Her letters to him became shorter and scrappier. Victoria Glendinning notes:

> Vita's cooling towards Geoffrey gave Harold the confidence to approach her again sexually. On 10 March he wrote in his diary: 'Vita nuova.' She wrote in hers: 'Hadji. My God!' The experiment may not have been repeated often, but Vita told a relieved [Lady Sackville] that 'she really thought she could not be really madly in love with anyone, as she was so fond of Harold. She said she got *des béguins* which lasted two or three days and she got over them easily.'[28]

Two or three months might have been nearer the truth, but in essence what she said was correct. Harold knew that he could never compete in terms of passion and intensity, but his experience had taught him that, that if he waited, if he was there when he was needed, she would return. And he was right.

In the Foreign Office, the advent of a new Labour administration and a new Prime Minister meant an opportunity for new starts, in particular with the French. Disagreements over the French occupation of the Ruhr and over Turkey and the Balkans meant that Anglo-French relations had been stormy. Nor had the antipathy between Curzon and the French Prime Minister helped matters. Harold, having taken over from Walford Selby as Assistant Head of Central Department, drafted a letter for Ramsay Macdonald to send to Poincaré expressing the view that, although they might disagree on some of the details, the two countries were in substantial agreement on the broad principles of foreign policy. MacDonald sent the letter through diplomatic channels and also arranged that it should be published in *The Times* and the *Manchester Guardian*.

MacDonald seems quickly to have realised Harold's usefulness – at least, when Harold put in an application for leave at the beginning of March, MacDonald rejected it on the grounds that he wanted to reopen negotiations with the Italians over the future of Jubaland and Harold would be needed in London while the discussions continued. In fact, as things turned out, the planned holiday – a trip to Spain by car with Vita and Dottie Wellesley – would never have materialised. Lord Carnock, who was becoming increasingly frail, had a series of heart attacks and Harold did not want to risk being away from London at such a time. The three of them spent a long weekend in the Welsh borders instead, much to the annoyance of Lady Sackville who wanted them to help her pack up the Sackville house in Hill Street which was being sold.

Byron: The Last Journey was published on 25 March. It was widely reviewed and, though there were one or two dissenting voices, the overall verdict was positive. *Byron* was agreed to be an entertaining read. Harold's biographical approach to his subject was inevitably – and quite justifiably – compared with Lytton Strachey. Virginia Woolf, predictably, championed Strachey, finding *Byron* 'tawdry and melodramatic.'[29] Oddly, it was John St Loe Strachey – Lytton Strachey's uncle and also one of London's most experienced journalists, having been editor of the *Spectator* for thirty-six years – who understood that it was not a competition. He saw how Harold was building on Lytton Stachey's method, developing it and taking it forward to the point where it allowed him more freedom to probe his subject's character and psychology.

Byron was a celebrity and his later years are heavily documented. Harold selected and marshalled his information effectively so that the book presents a clear and well-argued view of Byron's last journey and its tragic end. It remains an informative and entertaining read, and yet, for a man who became revered as a master of English prose, it is an extraordinarily uneven book, quite possibly – again – because of the speed at which it was written. In the early stages, Harold's desire to inject life and colour into his reconstruction of events sometimes simply overreaches itself. The description of Lord and Lady Blessington arriving in Genoa; Lady Blessington's speculations on Byron's character and person; Byron's meditations on the situation in which he finds himself as he waits to leave Genoa; his self-analysis and apparent premonition of death as the brig *Hercules* leaves Leghorn for Greece[30] – these are episodes where Harold is at best lavishly embroidering his material, at worst indulging in unjustified speculation. They read almost like passages from a historical romance. Such lapses in literary judgement are rare in Harold's writing and they stand in stark contrast to the balanced historical approach he adopts in a chapter such as 'The Greek War of Independence.'[31] In the same way, *Byron* is stylistically uneven. It veers between a familiar, conversational tone – 'Leigh Hunt was Shelley's fault entirely: Shelley was like that, he let one in for things.'[32] – to solid, academic formality – 'The lure of Greece, which, to those whom it has not assailed, appears but as the emotional indulgence of the scholar or the visionary, possesses for its victims a reality which is not temperamental merely, but organic.'[33] The effect of these mixed messages is both confusing and distancing, to the point where Harold's long-time supporter, Edmund Gosse, writing in the *Sunday Times,* accused him of taking a sarcastic approach to his subject matter.

Byron certainly consolidated Harold's reputation as a biographer. It also marked the beginning of a change of direction. Harold's interest in history is evident in both *Verlaine* and *Tennyson*, most obviously in the weight given to the historical context and the way it is interwoven with the development of his subjects' personal lives. *Sweet Waters*, too, depends for its success on the interaction between the character's lives and actual, accurately described historical events. No account of Byron's last journey would be possible without a full exposition of the historical and political forces in which he became embroiled and which his life and, according to Harold, his death played a part in shaping. In *Byron*, however, one senses historical events for the first time taking centre stage, offering the first clear indication that, although his work might take biographical form, Harold was at heart a historian rather than a biographer.

The decision to write a book on Byron in time for his subject's centenary proved both commercially and professionally astute. Not only did the book attract a good deal of attention, leading to very satisfactory sales, but so, too, did Harold himself. He made his first tentative steps on the road to literary celebrity. He was invited to the ceremony to mark the hundredth anniversary of Byron's death on 19 April. It took place at Hyde Park Corner in front of the poet's statue: fifty-seven tons of Greek marble supposedly representing Byron and his dog, Boatswain, sculpted by Richard Belt in 1880 (although according to John Trelawney, Byron's eccentric and adventurous friend who had been with him in Greece, it looked nothing like Byron at all). It was a very formal occasion. The Greek community and Greek diplomatic representatives were seen to lay wreaths and make speeches in honour of a man who, as James Lees-Milne points out, would have hated the whole thing.[34] After the wreath-laying, Harold was invited to an equally formal lunch, with more speeches, at which Stanley Baldwin was the guest of honour.

His evening engagement was a total contrast. Jack Squire, who was connected with a number of educational programmes in the working class areas of London, had arranged for him to give a lecture on Byron in a bookshop in Bermondsey. Bermondsey was then a rough and run-down district on the edge of the Surrey Docks, so Harold's lecture was given to an audience which consisted in large measure of dockers and labourers. He acquitted himself well and enjoyed the experience. It was a small beginning, but it was a beginning. His next lecture, a few weeks later, was delivered at a much more prestigious venue – Central Hall, Westminster – and more were to follow in the course of the year.

Harold had actually tried to make a much more significant contribution to the Byron centenary. He had 'put up a minute to the PM suggesting that the Elgin marbles be returned to Athens.' If Harold had wanted to demonstrate the intensity of his pro-Greek sympathies to the new government, he could hardly have chosen a better way, and no one can accuse him of not being foresighted. But his initiative was, in his own words, 'not a success and [caused] bad blood.'[35] However, compensation came the following month. Venizelos, who had just finished his fourth stint as Greek Prime Minister, arranged for him to be awarded an Honorary Doctorate by the University of Athens. He was, justly, very proud of the honour.

Geoffrey returned to England in June, and came immediately to spend the weekend at Long Barn, but the affair was past its zenith. In his absence, Vita had reinstated Dottie Wellesley as her companion and confidante. She had also re-established contact with Virginia Woolf who had now moved back to Bloomsbury from Richmond and had asked Vita to write something for the Woolfs' Hogarth Press. Dottie and Virgina were also invited to Long Barn that weekend. What did Harold make of this strange cast, drawn together by their passion for Vita and by Vita's passionate nature? All we have is Virginia's description of him sitting sleepily in front of the fireplace while Geoffrey told stories for the amusement of herself and Dottie. Sensing that he was losing Vita, Geoffrey had written: 'I sometimes think you react to people by the amount of passion or suffering they *display*.'[36] A year or so later, Harold confessed to Vita that he disliked Geoffrey 'because he is more emotional than I am, and you are impressed by emotion.'[37] They were both right.

Harold was not passionate. He disliked displays of emotion. Victoria Glendinning's view is that

> What disappointed Vita in Harold was his absorption in his work and in books at the expense of what she called 'life'. Her absorption in both her

own work and her own life could often exclude him for a while; it was understandable if he did not always spring to attention on the occasions when she would have liked him to – but it widened the gap between them. Long Barn, 18 April 1924: 'H. had the day off but didn't take much notice of Ronnie [Balfour] and me as he is deep in [reading about] Jane Carlyle. The dead mean more to him than the living, I think. Ronnie and I went for a moonlight walk after dinner, but he wouldn't come.'[38]

Harold's ability to absorb himself in his work and his books, his seeming detachment from life, may not always have made for harmonious domestic relations, but it did make it possible for him to cope, to survive, when Vita's emotional and physical passions led her off – temporarily – in a new direction.

Vita was trying to distance herself from Geoffrey. In one sense, it was a repeat of Violet: she had been swept away by someone with a possessive and demanding nature, but when she found the whole thing too much for her to cope with, she turned back to Harold. Shortly after that weekend at Long Barn in June 1924, the two of them went on holiday to the Dolomites. If her affair with Geoffrey continued, in intermittent and desultory fashion, into 1925, that was largely because Geoffrey would not end it and Vita did not know how to.

For Vita, the affair was an adventure, her first and only sexual affair with a man. It left no scars and when it was over she got on with the rest of her life. Geoffrey was not so lucky. Lady Sibyl had tolerated previous infidelities on his part, but Vita proved the last straw. At first she was hysterical, then depressed. Faced with the wishful possibility, which Geoffrey must have communicated, that Vita might become a permanent feature in his life, she sought solace elsewhere. In May 1925, she told Geoffrey that she wanted a divorce so that she could marry the writer and critic, Sir Percy Lubbock. Geoffrey wrote to Vita that it was possible she might be cited in divorce proceedings, but urged her not to tell Harold. This only proved how little he understood her, for when Vita was in trouble – what Harold called her 'muddles' – it was to Harold that she immediately turned. Harold would offer her sympathy without blame, and Harold would write to Geoffrey asking him to stay away. Geoffrey was distraught. He was also poor, having up to that point lived on Lady Sibyl's money. His finances revived a little when *The Portrait of Zélide* won the James Tait Black biography prize, but his life never did. Lady Sibyl's divorce action went through in 1926 without mentioning Vita. Geoffrey moved to New York where he died of pneumonia in 1929.

26   Policy

Vita's decision to go on holiday with Harold in July 1924 was not the end of Geoffrey, but it was a clear statement that the end would come. Harold understood that and so did Lady Sackville who, volatile as ever and having forgiven them for not helping her close up Hill Street, suddenly showered them with gifts, apparently as a reward for Vita's decision. She effectively gave them the Ebury Street house by saying that she did not want the loan she had given them repaid; she offered £500 a year towards its upkeep; she offered £200 a year towards Ben's school fees; and she offered to pay Harold's supertax. Her diary entry – 'They are *delighted*, bless them'[1] – seems somewhat superfluous.

The holiday was to be a walking tour in the Dolomites, an idea which appealed to Vita's gypsy fantasies and her love of the outdoors. Harold, more prosaically, wanted to lose weight. They had taken a kind of practice walk through Sussex and Hampshire the previous July, but this was a more ambitious undertaking. Hiking was just becoming popular – though it was only in the 1930s that it became a fashionable mass movement – and when Harold and Vita set off from the small town of Dobbiaco (Toblach) in the Puster Valley, just south of the Austrian-Italian border, with their canvas-and-leather rucksacks and wooden walking sticks, they were the very image of between-the-wars hikers. They began well, even reaching the top of the 2,239 metre (7,343 feet) Pordoi Pass, west of Cortina, but Vita found the paths too steep and too rugged and then the weather broke, so they ended their holiday with a couple of sybaritic days in Venice. They also found time to write. Vita wrote most of her novella, *Seducers in Ecuador*, her response to Virginia Woolf's request for something that the Hogarth Press could publish. Harold wrote a piece on Byron commissioned by the *Nation and Athenaeum*, a weekly magazine controlled by John Maynard Keynes and Leonard Woolf (suggesting that not all Bloomsbury was as hostile to *Byron* as were Virginia and Lytton Strachey). And when they returned home, Harold found another commission waiting for him: this time from what might be seen as the other side of London's literary divide. Jack Squire, whose politics were right of centre and whose *London Mercury* was a competitor to the *Nation and Athenaeum* (Bloomsbury mocked the coterie of young writers surrounding the *Mercury* as 'the Squirearchy'), wanted a book on Swinburne for Macmillan's 'English Men of Letters' series. Was Harold interested?

Harold Nicolson

On his return to the Foreign Office, Harold was plunged into the month-long London Reparations Conference which ended with the adoption of the so-called Dawes Plan, an agreement to reduce and reschedule Germany's immense reparation payments. Then, at the beginning of September, he was asked to replace Miles Lampson as Head of the Foreign Office's Central Department. In theory, the move from Assistant to actual Head of Department – and Central Department was one of the Foreign Office's most important – was a significant step up. It should have been a Counsellor's appointment, but Harold was not formally appointed Counsellor until he was posted to Persia at the end of 1925. He was young for the appointment – not yet thirty-eight – so it may have been a temporary promotion. European security was by far the most urgent issue, so Harold certainly had the expertise for the job, whereas Lampson had spent much of his career in the Far East. Even if it was only a temporary promotion, he stayed in the role until he left for Persia and acquired – at least while Sir Eyre Crowe was still in charge – a powerful voice in shaping Britain's European policy.

The whole thrust of British diplomacy and British policy towards Europe was to avoid another war, but that presupposed an understanding of where the threat came from. With hindsight, we know that the threat came from Germany, but in the 1920s this was far from clear. In February 1924, at Ramsay MacDonald's request, the Foreign Office had conducted a review of European policy. Harold, while culturally a strong Francophile, was among those who argued that France's determination to control the Rhineland meant that it, too, posed a potential threat to European peace. Uncertainty led to a string of proposals for pacts, treaties and protocols with which Harold was closely involved. Britain's position was complicated by a reluctance to make formal commitments to the League of Nations – although MacDonald, like Harold, was a supporter – and by the fact that any European commitment also had implications for the Empire and the Dominions. Faced with these difficulties, Harold began to urge the government to decide precisely what kind of European policy it wanted. In September 1924, he proposed

> the establishment of arbitration machinery as a basis for a system of European public law. Certain of the British distaste for alliances, he argued that Britons might agree to defend this new system (with penalties for violation such as financial and economic blockade, as well as naval, though not military force). Such a modus operandi, he stated, might prove an effective alternative to prevailing governmental and

public unwillingness to embrace the League of Nations as a vehicle for ensuring European security.[2]

Although conceived in the context of MacDonald's 'Geneva Protocol' initiative which failed, Harold's ideas did have an influence on government policy and became part of the thinking underlying Britain's approach to the Locarno Treaty in October 1925.

If work consisted in large measure of agonising about the future, one particular weekend looked to the past. The Nicolsons' holiday had been a success and that autumn, as in the aftermath of the Trefusis affair, they were again seen together in society – and very much not the kind of society of which Bloomsbury approved. On the evening of Friday 26 September, Vita drove them both down to Hackwood House, the magnificent seventeenth-century mansion near Basingstoke, rented since 1907 and renovated by Lord Curzon. It was to be an aristocratic house party in the pre-war style and on a pre-war scale – a last glimpse of the old order. The drive from the gates to the house ran for over half a mile through parkland and past artificial lakes. In the grounds alone, Curzon employed a staff of eighteen. The house itself had been modernised by adding bathrooms, central heating and electric bells in the bedrooms, but it still required an army of footmen and butlers, maids and chambermaids, cooks and potboys. The public rooms were of almost vice-regal splendour with 'rare Flemish tapestries ... family portraits and ... a pair of magnificent silver chandeliers fashioned to [Curzon's] own design out of various gifts he had received when he was Viceroy of India melted down.'[3] Dress for dinner was white tie and tails. Ladies wore long dresses and their jewels. Guests lined up in the old-fashioned manner to enter the dining room, each man with a lady on his arm. Dinner consisted of seven or eight courses. Harold enjoyed talking with the former Duchess of Marlborough, now Madame Jacques Balsan, but found Mrs Ambrose Dudley boring. The ladies retired, leaving the gentlemen to port and cigars. When the gentlemen emerged, there was coffee and conversation and perhaps some word games – Curzon discouraged cards after dinner.

The mornings were leisurely – Harold read and made notes for *Swinburne*. Lunch was a less formal production than dinner, but still a formidable meal. After lunch, there were walks to see 'the macaws & the little birds & the woods & the water garden & the avenues.' Curzon, Harold noted, was 'in delightful form.'[4] Then dinner again. So the weekend passed, until Monday morning when Vita motored home and Harold was able to return to London 'by train with the rest of the house-party in reserved carriages.'[5]

Ten days after this excursion into what was already a bygone age, MacDonald's government was defeated on a motion of no confidence and the country was faced with a general election. Harold had come to like MacDonald and, in his diary, left a sympathetic pen portrait of what it was like to have a meeting with him.

> He sits there puffing a pipe and very dour and sad and disillusioned. He waggles his leg with impatience, perplexity or despair, and yet he does not seem to wish to hurry the conversation.... Rather tentative are his remarks and very Scotch in sound. He flares up once at the thought of Mussolini. His eyes give a sudden flash.[6]

We know now that the brief Labour Government of 1924 was a constitutional government like any other, but there were many at the time who had genuinely feared that a Labour Government would lead to revolution. Harold, who saw MacDonald in action facing the hostility of Tory businessmen and others viscerally opposed to Labour's ideas, believed that the Prime Minister was a fundamentally honest and sincere man. In Harold's view, he was head and shoulders above anyone else in the Labour Party, but at the same time he could be dangerously naïve, expecting others, particularly Lords Rothermere and Beaverbrook who controlled newspapers such as the *Daily Mail* and the *Daily Express*, to behave with an honesty and sincerity equal to his own. And at work he could be frankly disorganised, creating embarrassing situations which reflected badly on the Foreign Office. MacDonald's decision to be both Prime Minister and Foreign Secretary had given him an enormous workload which Harold and others in the Foreign Office did their best to manage and make bearable. It was a shock, therefore, to find out, apparently from Lord Carnock, that MacDonald had been privately extremely critical, accusing the Foreign Office of being 'lazy, incompetent and ignorant.'[7] Harold was deeply offended and his faith in MacDonald badly shaken. Harold's attitude to the Foreign Office was an odd mixture of traditional institutional loyalty and something very close to gratitude. He was quite ready to criticise the Foreign Office and quite ready to listen to criticism voiced by colleagues – he knew the Foreign Office to be an imperfect organisation – but would always resent and react strongly to external criticism. Even later in his career, when writing for newspapers or speaking in Parliament, he would always spring to its defence. The Foreign Office, for all its faults, had accepted him; it had given him a sense of purpose and a sense of community, so he would defend it.

Policy

Polling day was 29 October and Labour was anticipating a modest defeat, but with just four days to go the campaign was thrown into confusion by the publication of the so-called Zinoviev letter. Apparently written by the Chairman of the Comintern to the Central Committee of the British Communist Party, the letter implied that Labour's policies, such as normalising relations with the Soviet Union, were somehow bringing revolution in Britain that much nearer. Had it been published in the *Daily Mail* alone, the electorate might have been less ready to believe it was genuine, but, through a bureaucratic blunder for which Eyre Crowe was personally responsible, it was also published officially by the Foreign Office, making its authenticity much more difficult to deny – and leading to more bad blood between the Office and MacDonald. The incident undoubtedly influenced the result and when Baldwin's Conservatives took office on 4 November 1924 they did so with a substantial majority.

Harold took leave again during November. Following his usual method, he had spent the last three months reading everything he could find about Swinburne and making copious, detailed notes. Now, he settled down at Long Barn and began to write with his usual speed. By the time he returned to work, he had a first draft of over half the book. Vita was writing *The Land* and, when they were not writing, they worked in the garden together. It was a quiet time at Long Barn, without visitors, further evidence of the calm that had returned to their relationship. Only when Harold returned to work at the beginning of December was there a sudden flurry of tension. Vita went to Paris to spend a few days with Walter Berry, a lawyer and ex-diplomat who had been close to both Henry James and Marcel Proust. Berry, with the very best of intentions, sought to create an amusing dinner party for Vita and invited Violet Trefusis. It was over four years since the crisis in their relationship, but the prospect of seeing Violet again made Vita panic: she felt 'sick at the idea.'[8] Harold also panicked. On the day of the dinner, he wrote to her twice and sent a telegram.

> I do so dread that woman. Her name brings back all the aching unhappiness of those months, the doubt, the mortification and the loneliness. I think she is the only person of whom I am frightened – and I have an almost superstitious belief in her capacity for causing distraction and wretchedness.[9]

In the end, of course, it came to nothing.

Shortly after the New Year, Harold and Vita made their second visit in recent months to The Wharf in Sutton Courtenay in Oxfordshire to stay with the Asquiths, whom they knew well. The Asquiths had been visitors to Knole in the years before the First World War, and they had known Lord Carnock when he was Ambassador to St Petersburg. The Wharf was small by comparison with Hackwood – Asquith had had it built in 1913 on the site of an old pub – and weekends were consequently that much less formal. Harold was fond of Asquith, who, despite a political career that had lasted nearly forty years, disliked talking shop at the weekend. He was also devoted to Margot Asquith, with whom he would sometimes lunch when she was in London. Although popularly seen as outspoken, gaffe-prone and vain (and, in some quarters, suspected of lesbian inclinations, despite her five children), Margot struck Harold as 'brave, affectionate, [and] loyal.' He added a slightly uncharacteristic comment, which at once mirrors Bloomsbury and seems directed against them: 'The love which hangs above her house gives it a spirituality which is different from the ghoulish intellectualism of other circles. Both V and I feel it is a real privilege to go to the Wharf and come away with an added sensitiveness to life.'[10]

One of the things he liked about Margot was her directness and her spontaneity. In an echo of his relationship with Gosse, he liked the way in which her stories of people she knew or had known were accompanied by gestures, imitations and acted-out conversations. The last time he had seen her, it had been Kitchener. On this occasion, it was King George V, whom she had accused of not enjoying himself: 'The King was taken aback. Finally, and quite simply, he said, "Yes, I know: but, you see, I don't like Society: I like my wife."' It was characteristic of Margot that her likes and dislikes should be spelt out with great clarity: Edward VII was 'German and coarse'; Queen Mary was 'hard and stupid and sly' and loathed her children.[11]

By the New Year, the new government was having to face up to the same problems as the old one. Harold's fears that Curzon would return as Foreign Secretary and would ask for him as Private Secretary had proved groundless. (Harold remained fascinated by Curzon as an individual but had seen all too clearly the demands he could make on those closest to him.) Baldwin had appointed Sir Austen Chamberlain as Foreign Secretary. Harold was never completely at ease with Austen Chamberlain and distrusted his judgement, but, as he was to discover, they were at least in general agreement about the need to engage with European problems – in contrast to a large faction in the Cabinet, led by the newly-appointed Chancellor of the Exchequer, Winston Churchill, who at this stage favoured standing back and avoiding any foreign commitments. On 22 January 1925, Chamberlain called a meeting for 'all senior members of the Office … to discuss the future of the British Empire.' Everyone had their say and nothing was decided, but the meeting left Harold with a clear sense that 'the real problem, which no one would face, is, "Have we got a Dominion or a Downing Street Foreign Policy?" The two things are very different and cannot well be fused without trouble.' [12]

The next day, Harold circulated a paper dealing with Anglo-French relations. Although he had been warned the previous autumn by General Wauchope, the Head of the Control Commission, that Germany was already seeking to evade certain conditions of the Versailles Treaty – in particular, refusing to destroy industrial plant which could be used to manufacture artillery and heavy weapons – it is clear that, at this stage, he still saw the French as the biggest threat to European peace. French fears of Germany were real, logical, hereditary and justified – and there was nothing Britain could do to remove them. Moreover, there was a sense in which French fears of Germany acted as a counterbalance to any potential French conflict with Britain. It was a depressing picture, but – unfortunately – an accurate one.

A month later, on 20 February, Harold submitted his response to Chamberlain's request for a further review of European policy. 'British Policy Considered in Relation to the European Situation' was, and remains, a brilliant analysis of the difficulties facing British policymakers at the time.

> All our late enemies continue full of resentment at what they have lost; all our late Allies are fearful of losing what they have won. One half of Europe is dangerously angry: the other half is dangerously afraid.... Fear begets provocation, armaments, secret alliances, ill-treatment of minorities; these in turn beget a greater hatred and stimulate a desire for revenge, whereby fear in intensified, and its consequences are enhanced. The vicious circle is thus established.

Russia, Harold argued, was not at that stage a major factor in determining British European policy: her fate and her future were still too uncertain. Germany, however, was. Germany would almost certainly regain its economic and military strength and seek to overturn those aspects of the Versailles Treaty which it regarded as unjust or humiliating. This would inevitably strengthen the nervousness, insecurity and hostility already evident in France's policy towards her larger neighbour, driving the French to 'expedients which in the end [would] only provoke the German revenge of which she stands in terror.'[13] This ingrained, historical opposition between the two major European powers was not the kind of dispute that the League of Nations had been set up to deal with, nor was there any point in looking to the United States for help or mediation. This was not a question of altruism, but of self-interest. Britain's days of splendid isolation were over. Its security and the security of its interests in the Dominions and the Empire were inextricably bound up with European security. And the key to European security was France. The best way to proceed, Harold concluded, was to recognise this and establish a new entente between Britain, the Dominions and the Empire (shortly to become the Commonwealth) and France which would bolster French security.

It was not an optimistic document, nor did it offer a recipe for European peace, but it was a clear and realistic response to a difficult and potentially dangerous situation. Crowe was impressed. So was Austen Chamberlain – so much so that he ordered Harold's paper to be circulated to the King, members of the Cabinet and all the Dominion Prime Ministers. A slightly edited version was also published in the main British newspapers on 2 March.

For reasons which remain unclear, Harold was never happy with his paper, or with the reaction to it. He even used the incident to cast doubt on Chamberlain's judgement. Yet the 20 February memorandum marked the high point of Harold's influence within the Foreign Office and on British foreign policy. He was a respected member of a small group which would play a crucial part in shaping Britain's relationship with the rest of the world. If the eventual form of the Locarno Treaty later that year did not completely follow Harold's recommendations – most notably in that it was a wholly European treaty and left to one side the position of the Empire and the Dominions – it certainly showed that Britain was ready to make European commitments; that the idea of splendid isolation was finally dead.

27 Change

On 2 March 1925, the day on which his views on European security appeared in the newspapers, Harold had lunch with Lord Curzon. It was to be their last meeting. On 5 March, while dressing for dinner at Christ Church College, Cambridge, Curzon suffered a major haemorrhage of the bladder. On 9 March he had an operation. He rallied a little, but gradually weakened and died in the early hours of Friday 20 March. Harold was deeply moved.

He and Vita attended the funeral service in Westminster Abbey, which was full to overflowing. The Archbishop of Canterbury officiated and the pallbearers included Baldwin, Churchill, Lord Salisbury (who would shortly take over Curzon's role as Leader of the House of Lords) and Asquith. The hymns included Curzon's favourites – 'Abide with Me' and 'Nearer, My God, to Thee.' After the service, Curzon's coffin was taken by special train from St Pancras to Derby and then to the family estate at Kedleston. The next day, Harold was among a smaller group of mourners who made their way up to Kedleston for the burial. This time the Archbishop of York, Cosmo Lang, officiated and the hymns were 'Rock of Ages' and 'Now the Labourer's Task is O'er.'

Even in death it seemed, Curzon had the capacity to create work for those about him. St Loe Strachey had asked Harold to write an article for the *Spectator* about Curzon, which he did, dwelling on Curzon's personal qualities and the fact the 'sense of national loss ... [and] outburst of national homage' at his death came, tragically, too late: a 'posthumous understanding of a man who imagined always that he was misunderstood.'[1] He showed the text to Lady Curzon, who approved, before it was published. Then there was the issue of who should write Curzon's life. Jonathan Cape, the publishers, asked Harold. This was certainly an honour, but Harold was not keen. Cape asked Lord Ronaldshay, but Lady Curzon was not happy with the choice and begged Harold to reconsider. Harold, who was fond of Lady Curzon, was obliged to explain gently that his position in the Foreign Office was a significant complication to writing a political biography of a man who had so recently been Foreign Secretary, and, in any event, there was so much material to read and assess he simply did not think he could manage the task. So Ronaldshay it was. Curzon's much later biographer, David Gilmour, judges that if Harold had agreed, the resulting work 'would have gained in flair but lost in diligence.'[2] And then there were Curzon's unfinished writings. Gilmour also says that 'George Curzon was almost incapable of owning or inhabiting a piece of property without attempting to write a book about it,'[3] and at his death there were at least five books, either in manuscript or note form, which the executors asked Harold to have a look at. This was another call on his time, and not one which he felt offered much in the way of reward. In the end, he edited *Bodiam Castle* – a short and evocatively illustrated history of the castle in Sussex which Curzon bought in 1917 and left to the nation on his death. It was published in 1926.

Although Harold did not write Curzon's official life, he did, nearly ten years later, write his own memoir. *Curzon: The Last Phase* is a diplomatic rather than a personal testament, the final part of Harold's diplomatic trilogy, but its concluding pages show just how well Harold understood Curzon's essential duality: the formal and forbidding public figure who was also a private man, happiest among the warmth and humour of a small circle of friends. Curzon was, after all, one of Harold's heroes.

> The impression left upon the memory of those who were closest to him during the last year of his life was not the impression of an unhappy or embittered man. It was an impression of genial humour triumphing over personal mortification and physical suffering. It was the impression of a man who knew that his own failure would endure as a fine legend long after the successes of politicians, less significant than he, had been forgotten.... It is the memory, not of a self-pitying egoist, but of a genial philosopher; of George Curzon gazing with admiration across the orchids of a dinner table towards the gentle splendour of his wife's beauty; of George Curzon stumping happily among the Siberian iris of the Hackwood water-garden; of his teasing the macaws in the conservatory; of his generous approbation of Ramsay MacDonald's diplomatic successes; of young faces, at a dinner table, laughing at his stories.[4]

Easter 1925 was spent in Italy, first on Lake Como, where Harold ate too much and suffered as a result, then in Venice. He tried to make progress with *Swinburne*, which pressure of work had caused him to neglect; Vita went sightseeing with Geoffrey Scott; and Ben, aged eleven, who had come on holiday with them, fell under the spell of Venice, Italy and Italian art. Years later, when editor of the *Burlington Magazine*, he would claim that his decision to become an art historian dated from this trip.

On 28 April, while Harold was still on leave, another of his heroes, Eyre Crowe, died. He was just sixty. His death changed both the Foreign Office and Harold's attitude towards it. Crowe had held senior positions dealing with European policy for nearly twenty years and had seen eye-to-eye both personally and on policy matters with both Sir Arthur Nicolson and Harold. He had been an exponent of a highly practical and pragmatic diplomacy. With his death, Sir William Tyrrell took over as Permanent Under-Secretary. Tyrrell, as Harold makes clear in *Lord Carnock*, was a very different personality.

> Sir William Tyrrell was intuitive, conciliatory, elastic, and possessed a remarkable instinct for avoiding diplomatic difficulties. Sir Eyre Crowe was ... industrious, loyal, expert, beloved, obedient, courageous ... [and] believed that in the conduct of public affairs it was essential that every-

thing should be recorded in writing without ambiguity. Sir William Tyrrell relied on the spoken rather than the written word.... Sir Eyre Crowe believed in facts; Sir William Tyrrell believed in personal relations; the former relied on lucidity; the latter on atmosphere; the minutes of Sir Eyre Crowe were precise and forceful; the conversations of Sir William Tyrrell were intangible but suggestive.[5]

The Tyrrell–Nicolson feud had its roots in distant pre-war days, and the fact that Harold, on joining the Foreign Office in 1909, maintained his father's hostility towards Tyrrell, presumably out of loyalty to his father, clearly did nothing to improve matters. Then there was the Lausanne incident. Harold may have seen Tyrrell drunk in Lausanne and Tyrrell may have resented it. Tyrrell may have felt that Harold went behind his back to Curzon. He may have felt that Harold was Curzon's favourite and resented it. Whatever the case, there was a current of ill feeling between them to which Harold, with Crowe gone, suddenly felt exposed. From having been very much at the centre of things, he suddenly felt 'rather out of it personally' and blamed Tyrrell. He was convinced that Tyrrell was turning Chamberlain against him; that his views were being ignored; and that others were getting the praise and attention that he used to get. This may have been true. It may be that Tyrrell, as Harold had feared when not offered the job as MacDonald's Private Secretary, regarded him as temperamentally unsound. Yet, it is worth recalling how sensitive Harold could be to criticism. If Tyrrell had been critical, Harold was quite capable of overreacting and, indeed, he was certainly overreacting to something. Within days of returning to work to find Tyrrell as Head of the Foreign Office, he suddenly decided that he was 'not really interested in Foreign Politics'[6] – which was nonsense. And as regards Chamberlain, it is worth noting Harold's hostility. In his diary, he several times refers to the Foreign Secretary as a fool and an ass. It would not be surprising if this attitude had got back to Chamberlain, whether through Tyrrell or through someone else.

However it came about, by the end of May 1925 Harold had become disillusioned with his work and 'bored with the FO.'[7] As a consequence, during the summer, he seems to have immersed himself in everything except the Foreign Office. *Swinburne* had made only intermittent progress since the previous November. In January, he had recorded a conversation with Gosse about Swinburne's sex life – how he liked being whipped and was excited by pain; how, despite active encouragement from the actress Adah Isaacs Menken, he remained a virgin – but, fascinating though this was, it was not material he could use, nor did it move composition forward. Now, he returned to his manuscript with determination, working mainly at Long Barn where Vita was in the process of completing *The Land*. By the end of August, *Swinburne* was all but complete.

Harold's social life was never exactly dull, but even by his standards that summer saw a sudden burst of visits, parties, meetings with friends and new acquaintances. Bloomsbury played a significant part in these engagements. Vita's *Seducers in Ecuador*, written at the request of Virginia Woolf and published by the Hogarth Press at the end of 1924, had found favour with Bloomsbury – 'They imagine they have "discovered" you,' he wrote to Vita, perhaps a little sourly[8] – and this drew Harold and Vita closer to the social orbit of the members of the group. It was not all easy going – Virginia Woolf records a couple of stiff dinners involving Vita, and one occasion, at a party hosted by the young George Rylands, when Harold squabbled with Lytton Strachey[9] – but that summer the Nicolsons saw the Woolfs regularly until Virginia's depression returned. They socialised with Duncan Grant and Vanessa Bell, with Clive Bell and Roger Fry. They dined with Bertrand Russell and Lady Ottoline Morrell. Harold also met Roger Senhouse, later to become Lytton Strachey's partner, and the writer and critic Francis Birrell.

There were many non-Bloomsbury engagements, too. The Asquiths' daughter Elizabeth Bibesco stayed at Long Barn and upset everyone by behaving badly towards Dottie Wellesley. She became involved with another visitor to Long Barn, a young landscape painter and poet called Ian Campbell-Gray, who had painted a somewhat unsatisfactory portrait of Harold. Then there was Ethel Smyth, the composer and campaigner for women's rights, who, despite her deafness, came to listen to the nightingales. Harold remained fond of her, though she proved a demanding guest. He dined with Lady Ribblesdale, another of the great society hostesses of the era. He also became friendly with Archibald MacLeish, the influential American poet, who was at that time living in Paris as part of the American artistic diaspora.

There were house parties in the traditional manner, the grandest being when Harold and Vita were invited to Blenheim Palace by the Duke and Duchess of Marlborough. Among the twenty guests were the former King and Queen of Portugal, Winston Churchill (the Duke's cousin) and a number of other Conservative politicians – the Duke himself having been a junior minister under Salisbury and then under Balfour. Harold met Frederick Lindemann, who was to become Churchill's scientific adviser during the Second World War. Vita enjoyed talking to the Duchess, who was a keen gardener. It was such a grand occasion that there was a fête on Saturday afternoon and then a full scale ball in the Hall after dinner that evening. A week later, Harold went alone to Chartwell, Churchill's house on the outskirts of Westerham in Kent. The house was a nineteenth-century red-brick mansion which had been extended and modernised by Philip Tilden, a disciple of Lutyens. Churchill was in raptures about the result. Harold was not persuaded about the house, but was happy to see Churchill in such good and enthusiastic form. Apart from the Churchill family, the only other guest was Brendan Bracken. They had not met before but Bracken would become an important figure in Harold's parliamentary life in the years leading up to and during the Second World War. His first impression was that Bracken was 'a most self-confident and I should think wrong-headed young man.'[10]

The real compensation for Harold's disillusion with the Foreign Office during that summer – and just possibly one of the reasons for it – was a thirty-year-old writer and critic called Raymond Mortimer. They had first come across each other in 1918. Raymond, whose Oxford career had been interrupted by the war, had served at a hospital in France before being brought back to use his excellent French in the Foreign Office's Cypher Department. No friendship developed at that stage: not least because Raymond saw Harold through the eyes of his subordinates who felt that he talked down to them. After the war, Raymond returned to France to pursue his ambitions as a writer, but the need to earn a living brought him back to London where his literary temperament naturally brought him into the orbit of Bloomsbury. It was in this context that he and Harold met again.

Harold and Vita gave a dinner at the house in Ebury Street on 31 January 1924 to which Raymond was invited. Harold's reluctance to commit to paper details of his emotional or sexual life makes it difficult to chart the progress of the relationship. Raymond's name appears with increasing frequency in Harold's diary – they dined together, went to the theatre together, Raymond came to stay at Long Barn – but it was only in June 1925, when Vita told Harold that she was in trouble over her relationship with Geoffrey Scott and might be cited in his divorce case, that Harold confessed to her that his friendship with Raymond had become an affair.

By that time, the relationship had become deep and mutual. Harold wrote to Vita 'please realise that it is *not* important – but only important enough to emerge from an emotion to an attitude – and as such implying deception on my part if concealed.'[11] He was underplaying his feelings, but he was being a good deal more honest than she had been over Violet. For the next two years, his relationship with Raymond could be termed passionate; by 1927 it had begun to evolve into a deep and enduring affection. Harold's management of the situation and of his emotions during those two years is both revealing and characteristic. His first concern was to avoid any possibility of getting into a false position with Vita. And this was important. Vita never had a moment's fear or doubt about Harold's feelings for her, or about the future. She was able to regard the attachment benevolently and to become extremely fond of Raymond herself. His second concern was that Raymond should understand the rules of engagement from the beginning. He did not want Raymond to resent 'my ties and my surroundings' (Vita, the boys, Long Barn), but he did not conceal his difficulties: he told Raymond, 'I never realised that I would find it difficult to reconcile my desires & my duties.'[12] There is no doubt about the strength of his affection or the influence Raymond exerted – 'everything is conditioned in its importance by reference to you'[13] – but, with clear memories of Violet, he makes the boundaries explicit. He might like them to go off together 'for weeks on end,' but it is not going to happen. Yet, he concludes, that need not spoil the relationship.[14] All Harold's honesty and strength of character is encapsulated here. Emotion is tempered by reason, but not crushed or denied. There must have been a risk that Raymond would be offended, would find this approach cold or emotionally compromised, but Harold would not deceive him or hold out false expectations. And it worked. Thirty years later, Raymond was to write:

> I have never loved anybody else so profoundly nor has any other friend been so consistently and patiently and imaginatively affectionate, thoughtful and appreciative. When I have been horrid to you ... it has been from unconscious jealousy (I now perceive) because I knew I could not be so important in your life as you in mine.[15]

The balance had shifted. Work had often sustained Harold at times of emotional stress; now a new and exciting emotional direction was compensating for unfulfilling work. And then, suddenly, on 23 September everything changed again. Walford Selby, Austen Chamberlain's Private Secretary, asked if he would be prepared to accept a Counsellor's post in either Peking or Tehran.

Harold was surprised by the offer, though he should not have been. He had been a First Secretary for five-and-a-half years. Counsellor was a significant promotion. Now thirty-eight, he was still young for the rank, but he had certainly proved himself. He was out of sympathy with the current Foreign Office leadership – and they, quite probably, with him – but they could not deny his achievements or his ability. His dissatisfaction with his work must surely have communicated itself. A posting as Counsellor would solve both problems as well as being a logical career move. It was a logical career move in other ways as well. Harold had, after all, signed up for the Diplomatic Service not the Foreign Office and, though interchange between the two was increasing, he had worked abroad for only three years – six months in Spain and two-and-a-half years in Constantinople – in a career that had so far lasted sixteen. He needed foreign experience.

Harold's first instinct was to refuse on the grounds

(1) That we can't dump the children anywhere. (2) that Ben requires constant looking after by either V. or me if he is not to go off the rails. (3) that we can't afford it if V goes backwards and forwards. (4) that with both father and [Lady Sackville] ill, we can neither of us go so far away. On second thoughts, however, I realise (1) that it is a mistake ever to refuse a job. (2) that it would mean promotion... (3) that I can't hope to stay here for ever and might get something far worse. (4) if that if V. stays at home in the summer it won't be so bad. Decide to consult Oliphant and father.[16]

Peking, Harold felt, was out of the question. Tehran was a possibility – 'of all the foreign posts it would be the one Vita would dislike least.'[17] He had evidently not considered the possibility that she might choose not to accompany him, but only visit. The following day, Lancelot Oliphant, whom Harold had known since being drafted back into the Foreign Office in 1914, told him unequivocally that he should accept. Harold lunched at Cadogan Gardens with his father, who was equally clear in his advice. Walford Selby was pressing, suggesting that further promotion might follow after a year or so.

Harold told Vita that same evening. She was, he recorded, 'rather dismayed.'[18] He dined with Raymond and told him. The two of them then went on to see an adaptation of Michael Arlen's *The Green Hat*, which had just opened at the Adelphi, starring Tallulah Bankhead, in the hope that it might cheer them both up. That weekend, Harold and Vita went to stay with Dottie Wellesley at Sherfield Court. Raymond was the only other guest. The four of them studied maps of Persia.

The next week the appointment was settled and it was agreed that Harold would leave on 4 November. Lancelot Oliphant gave Harold lunch and some advice – 'He must... be guided by his head and not by his heart.'[19] For Harold, who, despite his own best intentions, had become sufficiently sentimental to attach Raymond's tie to his own blue pyjamas ('I can't tell you how nice it looked.'[20]), this was probably useful advice. More importantly, Oliphant had been in touch with his cousin, Sir Percy Loraine, who was currently the Minister in charge of the Legation in Tehran. Loraine had written to the Foreign Office expressing pleasure and gratitude at Harold's appointment.

The month that followed was full of preparations and farewells. There were suitable clothes to be bought. He could expect to be away from England for the best part of two years and western-style tailoring was not to be relied on in Tehran. He went to Moss Bros, whose reputation had increased since it became known that King George, seeking to ensure that ministers would be correctly dressed at court, had recommended them to members of Ramsay MacDonald's government. He also visited Saville Row and Jermyn Street. There was a medical where he was inoculated against typhoid and cholera and given prophylactics against malaria. He reviewed his will and visited his publisher. There were briefings by numerous members of the Foreign Office, including Tyrrell, who said very little, and by Austen Chamberlain, who made it clear that Sir Percy Loraine and his views had the Government's full backing.

Harold's broad spectrum of social connections necessarily meant a large number of farewells. The Asquiths gave him lunch. Lady Curzon gave him lunch and a pair of Lord Curzon's diamond and sapphire cufflinks. Edmund Gosse organised a drinks party and made such an affectionate speech that Harold felt quite moved. The Colefaxes gave him dinner. He said goodbye to Dottie and to Gerry Wellesley (separately) and to Geoffrey Scott.

Then there was the family. He dined with Lord and Lady Sackville (separately) and visited those relatives it was possible he might not see again: his mother's brother Freddy and her sister Aunt Lal, widowed for over twenty years and now well over eighty. He and Vita spent an evening at Cadogan Gardens with his parents who managed to be both proud and tearful.

The boys had loomed large in his initial rejection of the idea of going abroad and his farewell to Ben, in particular, was emotional. Ben, just turned eleven, had been at boarding school for two years by that time. Initial difficulties with bullying had been overcome and he seemed to be enjoying his work and showing a strong interest in art. He and Harold had grown closer during their recent trip to Venice, and Harold was aware how much he needed parental contact and supervision. At their parting, outside Summer Fields School while a car waited for Harold, Ben cried, and the next day wrote a letter: 'My dear Persian Prince, Oh Daddy I thought about you all last night and felt what a pity it was for you to go to Persia.'[21] Nigel, approaching nine, was less emotional. The letter he wrote, which was sent ahead with a number of letters from Vita, so that Harold would receive them *en route*, was more literary and imaginative in its approach, encapsulating the difference in character between the two boys – 'It must be funny to leave Long Barn for two years.... But it will be lovely to come home to find the new garden blooming with lovely flowers, and your room will be a *"fête de fluers"* [sic] arranged by Mummy who will have roses in her hair.'[22]

Harold spent the weekend before his departure at Long Barn with Vita and Raymond, who had acquired the nickname 'Tray'. It was sunny, late-autumn weather and they walked in the garden together. Back in London, on his last evening, there was a supper party given by Christabel MacLaren, a Bloomsbury connection described by Quentin Bell as 'a lady of great wealth but of diminutive intellect.'[23] The party seemed unreal after the merry-go-round of the last month. Raymond cried when they said goodbye. Harold wrote to him: 'It was almost unendurable saying goodbye to you this evening.... Dearest Tray, you are so much to me.... Anyway, you know that there is someone in the world to whom you are of supreme importance.'[24]

On the morning of 4 November, before leaving Ebury Street, Harold and Vita wept in each other's arms. Despite, or even because of, their various affairs – Vita's with Geoffrey Scott and now Harold's with Raymond – parting for any length of time was becoming increasingly difficult and increasingly emotional, for both of them. It may sound strange that two intelligent people, both capable of their own forms of detachment and with no sexual bond between them, should suffer in this way, but there is no doubt that they did. Indeed, their reaction to parting and separation was to reach such a pitch that it eventually became a major influence on Harold's career.

Vita drove him to Victoria Station. It was, he wrote, 'an agonising farewell. Feeling absolutely wretched.'[25]

28 Journey

When Arthur Nicolson took up his posting in Tehran in 1885, he travelled with his wife, two small sons and a nurse. It was an epic journey. They travelled by sea, first from Athens to Constantinople and then onward through stormy weather and rough seas along the Black Sea coast of Turkey to Trebizond and Batoum (Batumi), just inside the Russian border. From

Batoum, they took the newly opened railway, which wound its way up through tunnels and over unconvincing bridges to Tiflis (Tiblisi) and then down, following the Kura Valley, to Baku on the Caspian coast. At Baku, they boarded a filthy Caspian steamer which took two days to reach Resht on the northern coast of Persia. From Resht, they travelled by caravan, moving only at night because of the heat. The women and children travelled in litters, Arthur on horseback. It took five days to traverse the Elburz Mountains by way of the gorge of Sefid Rud and then another two to cross the sweltering open plain and reach Tehran.

Forty years later, Harold's journey, though not without its discomforts and inconveniences, had no such epic quality. He took the Southern Railway boat train from Victoria to Dover Maritime, where he crossed by Channel steamer to Calais. From Calais to the Gare du Nord took less than four hours. At the Gare du Nord, he took a cab to the Gare de Lyon, where he boarded that evening's Simplon Orient Express for Trieste, arriving at midnight the following day, some thirty-six hours after leaving London. By the time he reached Trieste, he had written four highly emotional letters to Vita, telling her how much he missed her, and broken down in tears at least twice. He had also written one very affectionate letter to Raymond; chatted with the son of a former Master of Balliol College who was now Minister of Education in British-administered Iraq; ogled a male steward who came to deal with his luggage; written the first words of 'MY NEW BOOK';[1] and tried to read A. N. Whitehead on relativity. It was an efficient progress.

It was raining heavily when Harold boarded the aging but stately Lloyd Triestino steamer, SS *Helouan*, and it continued to rain for the next twenty-four hours as they sailed south through the Adriatic. The weather matched his mood. He wrote to Vita that 'when night falls ... a wave of home-sickness comes over me.... I have not had the spirit yet to go on with MY NEW BOOK.'[2] *Swinburne* had been delivered to the publishers before he left England and Harold knew that in Persia it would be impossible write another poetic study or biography. He needed a subject that did not require the same degree of research. The first glimmerings of what was to become *Some People* seem to have come to him and the first ideas been sketched out before he left England; but it was as he walked the rainy decks of SS *Helouan* (respecting the privacy of the King of Mesopotamia who was walking in the opposite direction) that the book developed in his mind. The *Helouan* called at Brindisi, crossed to the Albanian shore and called briefly at Corfu Town – which must surely have brought back memoirs of the Corfu incident just two years previously. The weather cleared and the next morning, ever the classicist, he was up at dawn to watch the light come up behind the mountains of the Peloponnese. A couple of hours later, there occurred the odd incident which he recorded in a letter to Vita and then reproduced in the opening scene of the 'Miriam Codd' chapter in *Some People*.

> 'Excuse me, sir,' said a gentle voice behind me, 'what is that lovely island?' It was an old lady in a blue veil reading a Tauchnitz Hergesheimer. 'That, madam,' I replied, 'is the island of Cythera, or Kythera, in modern Greek Cerrigo.' 'Oh, indeed!' she said. 'It was the centre,' I explained, 'of the cult of Aphrodite.' She ignored that remark. ... She looked vaguely at Cythera. 'So that is Cyprus,' she murmured.[3]

As James Lees-Milne makes clear, although this incident was factual, Harold never saw the old lady again and the rest of the Miriam Codd story is pure fiction – and a warning not to take *Some People* too literally.[4]

Alexandria, where the *Helouan* arrived and where Harold disembarked on 9 November, had grown in size since his honeymoon visit with Vita in 1913, but its character remained unchanged. An American resident, Jasper Brinton, wrote in 1926 that 'the harbour is the same as always, lively, interesting and cosmopolitan. Two British battleships to remind one who owns Egypt. The dock the same swarm of noisy humanity.'[5] Charlie Hartopp, last seen in Athens but now posted to Cairo, sent a local messenger who supervised Harold's disembarkation, looked after his luggage and accompanied him on the journey to the Egyptian capital.

Britain had given up its Protectorate over Egypt in 1922 and declared the country a constitutional monarchy under King Fuad, but Britain did not give up control of the Suez Canal, of the Sudan, or of Egypt's foreign policy. Independence was thus heavily qualified. The British maintained a significant military and diplomatic presence (of which Charlie Hartopp was a part) and, although there continued for many years a three-way tussle between the King, the largely nationalist parliament, and the British, the real power in the land – at least in 1925 – was the British High Commissioner. The current High Commissioner, appointed earlier that year, was Sir George Lloyd, shortly to become Lord Lloyd of Dolobran. Lloyd came from a wealthy steel-manufacturing family, but had given up the security of the family firm for the world of public affairs. In 1905, through the influence of writer and traveller Gertrude Bell, he had obtained a post as Honorary Attaché at Constantinople. In 1910, he returned to England and stood successfully for Parliament, but maintained his Middle Eastern interests. During the War, he had served at Gallipoli and with

T. E. Lawrence in Arabia. Thereafter, through a combination of influence, ability and an intensely conservative outlook, he had worked his way up to reach one of the great imperial proconsular posts.

Harold had met Lloyd in Constantinople before the War and did not particularly care for him. Nevertheless, the High Commissioner's views were an important factor in Middle Eastern politics and Harold made an official courtesy call. Lloyd immediately asked him to dinner.

> It was a formal and chilly meal. The guests were herded together and then lined up in order of precedence ... [their] names were shouted out as though they were on parade. Harold was allotted Lady Lloyd, whom he piloted into the dining room behind her husband, stalking solemnly, in vice-regal isolation. The bowing, curtseying, the pomp and drinking of the King's health prevented relaxed conversation and enjoyment, in spite of Harold's fondness for Lady Lloyd. It was precisely the proconsular manner of life he detested.[6]

It was certainly unfortunate that Harold should have suffered this extreme example of diplomatic formality on his way to Tehran where his role would, of necessity, involve a certain amount of formal entertaining, but his attitude was not quite as simple as James Lees-Milne implies. Weekend parties at Hackwood or Blenheim, which were hugely formal, provoked no such protest or antipathy on his part. On this occasion, however, as sometimes happened when he felt ill at ease or uncertain of himself, Harold played up his supposed rebelliousness, condemning the whole lifestyle rather than the particular occasion. He was ready enough to enjoy the pomp and grandeur of a formal occasion when it suited him – or perhaps when he felt more in sympathy with his host. He was certainly far more out of sympathy with its unregulated, bohemian opposite.

Whatever Harold's feelings, Lloyd was nothing but cordiality and invited Harold to accompany him on an official tour of inspection. On the day in question, Harold walked from Charlie Hartopp's flat to the High Commissioner's Residence, but from that moment the day was transformed into an imperial progress of the grandest kind: at a time when Egypt's perennial political crisis was slightly worse than usual, Lloyd felt the need to impress upon the Egyptians the full might and majesty of the British Empire. The Lloyds, their *aides-de-camp* and Harold set off in a Rolls-Royce and a Daimler at great speed, escorted by police cars and motor bikes. Policemen lined the route holding back the Cairo traffic, which even in 1925 was dense and undisciplined. The entire Egyptian Cabinet were at the station to greet the Lloyds as they and their entourage boarded a special train for Alexandria. Harold had a saloon all to himself and was offered a kipper for breakfast by a white-coated waiter. On arrival in Alexandria, the Lloyds went off for an audience with the King. Harold and Robin Furness, the Oriental Secretary at the High Commission and a specialist in all things Egyptian, escaped from the proconsular circus and went for a swim.

Back on the train, Harold lunched with the Lloyds as they chugged slowly westwards towards the edge of the desert and heard, in detail, the substance of Lloyd's conversation with the King. They transferred to cars, this time with a Camel Corps escort which rather slowed their progress. Eventually, they reached Burg El Arab, a model settlement created by the legendary Wilfred Bramly, or Bramly Bey, one-time Governor of Egypt's Western Desert Province. Burg El Arab encapsulated the problems faced by Egypt and by Sir George Lloyd. Intended as a settlement for the Bedouin, who might thus be induced to defend rather than menace Egypt's western desert borders, it had started well, but with independence in 1922, the nationalists condemned the whole idea. It was seen as 'unpatriotic, an intolerable gesture towards the Bedouins, who were traditionally Egypt's enemies. Official difficulties were thrown in its way, funds were cut off' and the town was left 'silent and empty.'[7] Lloyd was an old-fashioned imperialist, who believed that the purpose of the Empire was to improve the lot of its subject races. He was an enthusiast and a supporter of Bramly, but faced with the deep-seated, historical divisions of the Arab world he was powerless.[8]

Harold left Cairo on 15 November. He took the train from Cairo's Ramses Station to the Suez Canal and crossed by ferry to El Qantara on the eastern bank. He took an overnight train which rumbled slowly along the coastal plain to Gaza, Ashquelon and Lydda (Lod) where it began to twist and climb into the Judean hills, reaching Jerusalem before lunchtime. His first stop was the house of Ronald Storrs, another of those semi-legendary British figures who populated the Middle East in the first half of the twentieth century. Storrs had been Oriental Secretary in Cairo (he had shown Harold and Vita round the city during their honeymoon visit in 1913), served with the Egyptian Expeditionary Force in Baghdad and Mesopotamia and was now Civil Governor of Jerusalem and Judea. Harold's second stop was Thomas Cook's office where he was told that he could not immediately get a place on a Nairn Brothers' convoy across the desert to Baghdad.

There followed five days of conflicting advice and changing plans. Field Marshal Lord Plumer, the High Commissioner for Palestine, advised him to fly. Ramleh aerodrome told him to try the Egyptian airmail flights. The RAF at Ramleh advised against flying at all and he was back where he started. When not pestering the Nairn office at the Allenby Hotel and fretting at the delay, Harold explored Jerusalem, 'the most poignant city in all my wanderings.'[9] Despite its cultural and religious importance, it was still small and undeveloped. He visited the Holy Sepulchre and the Ecce Homo convent. He and Ronald Storrs walked the five miles to Bethlehem, which, in those days, was a walk through open country, brown hills and olive groves. Eventually, he managed to get a seat for Baghdad.

Jerry and Norman Nairn were New Zealanders who had served in Palestine during the War and stayed on in the region to run a garage which turned into a transport business. By 1925, they had a fleet of battered Buicks and Cadillacs running a more or less regular twice-weekly service across the Syrian Desert between Jerusalem and Baghdad. The journey took less than two days, but the convoys were not escorted and the Amman–Baghdad leg could be dangerous. Earlier in the year, a convoy carrying bullion had been ambushed and robbed, and one of the drivers killed.

Harold's convoy 'hooted out of Jerusalem' at 9.30 p.m. on 20 November. The road dropped over a thousand metres in a series of tight bends into the Jordan Valley where they passed through the city of Jericho. They crossed by the Allenby Bridge into Transjordania, where the road deteriorated and they bumped along until somewhere after midnight when they arrived in Amman. They ate and slept in bell tents inside a barbed wire enclosure on the edge of the town. It was Harold's thirty-ninth birthday and before going to sleep 'by the light of the flickering candle,' he opened a birthday letter from Vita which he had carried with him from England.

Harold was woken at five in the morning, drank tea and climbed into a 'large sort of charabanc which held six people' – four passengers and two drivers. They set off just as dawn was breaking. Harold told Vita that the 'wide sad downs' outside Amman were like the country near Rottingdean on the Sussex coast. They hit the open desert: the road was shale, then sand, then 'lava boulders'. They stopped for lunch, then sped along 'for over two hundred miles over a hard tennis court at 60 miles an hour.' They drove on as darkness fell: 'We had done 400 miles and passed only one human being, and he was dead – a dead man by the roadside with his guts disarranged by vultures.' Then, as if to emphasise the wisdom of Harold's decision not to fly, they 'pulled up with a jerk in front of an extraordinary jumble of white wood and aluminium ... a wrecked aeroplane *de luxe* ... we lit a fire from the wreckage and had supper.' They drove on through the night. Just before dawn they met a British armoured-car detachment camped on the edge of the desert. By lunchtime, they had reached Ramadi, where there was an RAF base, and crossed the Euphrates. Another two hours, and by mid-afternoon they were entering Baghdad and pulling up outside the Hotel Maude.[10]

Harold had only a few hours in Baghdad. He called on the British High Commissioner, Sir Henry Dobbs, whose unenviable role was to try and administer Britain's League of Nations mandate in such a way as to 'build a sovereign but compliant Iraqi state.'[11] At the High Commission he also found letters waiting from Vita and from Sir Percy Loraine in Tehran. Then he went to see Gertrude Bell, whom he had first met in Constantinople and who was now Dobb's Oriental Secretary – an unusual appointment for a woman in the 1920s and indicative of her immense knowledge of and influence in the Arab world. Thus briefed on the view from Iraq, he took a comfortable, if slow, overnight train from Baghdad to the railhead at Khamkin (Khânaqin), just short of the Persian border but still some 650 kilometres (400 miles) from Tehran.

The last leg was frustrating and uncomfortable. A convoy of vehicles belonging to the Eastern Transport Company set off for the Persian border. Harold was crammed into a small Dodge with two members of the Persian Imperial Bank, an orderly from the Legation in Tehran who had been sent to meet him, and an Irish driver. There was no room for his legs and he was freezing cold. There were predictable delays caused by passports and customs, and the car was 'so rotten that we crawled and crawled'. The driver drove into a hole in the road which bent the front axle and broke the exhaust pipe. They feared an ambush: this was Kurdish country and the Kurds, never a docile people and full of resentment at not being given their own homeland after the war, were given to acts of violence which would now be called terrorism. The convoy arrived at Kermanshah, the first night's stop, five hours late. Harold stayed with the British Consul and his wife, the Cowans, 'on a camp bed in their drawing room, too small for me, hard, and incredibly cold.'

The next day, the damage to the car meant they could not leave until afternoon. The road, Harold told Vita in one of his odd, English comparisons – perhaps intended to convey a sense of familiarity and persuade her that a visit to Persia would not be all bad – was 'just as good as the road from the village to Sevenoaks.' It was the car that was the problem. Harold's reaction to the delay and the mismanagement was – perhaps surprisingly – a caricature of the Imperial Englishman abroad. He stormed and he fretted and he fumed. Kermanshah was 1,500 metres (nearly 5000 feet) up and in the middle of the Zagros Mountains, but, Harold wrote to Vita, 'this hanging about... destroys the pleasure I should get from the amazing beauty of the scenery.'[12]

That day, even more squashed by the presence of another passenger (another bank manager), they made it as far as Hamadan, still 360 kilometres (220 miles) from Tehran. Harold was offered the hospitality of the British Vice Consul, who lived in an old-style Persian house with a courtyard and poplar trees. He was warmer and more comfortable than he had been at Kermanshah, but he still fretted – especially the next morning when the car, expected at six o'clock did not turn up until nearly ten. There was snow on the road as they crawled up and over the Aveh Pass, but they reached Qazvin, still 150 kilometres (almost 100 miles) short of their destination, with only a couple of punctures to delay them.

On Thursday 26 November, just over three weeks after Harold had left England, they left Qazvin for Tehran. The road 'ran perfectly straight across the plain ... a stream of animals and vehicles flowed along it, dejected, dilapidated, with merchandise for the capital; droves of donkeys, huge caravans of camels ... carts drawn by men, two in front and two behind, who sweated and crawled onward.'[13] They were approaching Karaj, perhaps just fifty kilometers (thirty miles) from Tehran, when the car's back springs collapsed and they had to walk into the town. At least there was a telephone which allowed him to call for rescue. A little while later a car appeared bringing, in the best British tradition, cold beer and cold partridge to mitigate the discomfort. Harold and his fellow passengers were sitting in the courtyard on a caravanserai and still eating when a red-coated Legation guard 'comes in, salutes and says that the Minister is there. I dash out and find Percy [Loraine] in the yellow Legation car. Bundle my things in and do the last 25 miles in comfort – while an amazing sunset turns the hills to scarlet.'[14]

29 Legation

In 1925, Persia, like the rest of the Middle East, was going through a period of radical change. Since the end of the eighteenth century, the country had been ruled by the Qajar Dynasty. It was with the most powerful and longest-ruling Qajar Shah, Nasr-ed-Din, that Arthur Nicolson had in 1886, the year of Harold's birth, negotiated an agreement that Persia would not enter any secret agreement with the Russians without first consulting the British

Government. Nasr-ed-Din, an impressive figure – reformer, moderniser, autocrat, painter and poet – who had ruled for forty-nine years, was assassinated in 1896. Since then, Persia had lost its way. The authority of both the monarchy and the government had been weakened – not least by public disclosure of the fact that Sir Arthur Nicolson's diplomatic triumph, the 1907 Anglo-Russian Convention, which divided the country into Russian and British spheres of influence, had been negotiated, agreed and signed without a word being said to the Persians themselves. By the time Nasr-ed-Din's great-grandson Ahmad was placed on the throne in 1909, at the age of eleven, central authority was crumbling.

After the war, during which Persia was effectively occupied by British, Russian and Turkish forces, Britain had sought a treaty with the shaky regime of Ahmad Shah. The 1919 Anglo-Persian Agreement recognised and reaffirmed Persia's right to be considered a sovereign state – though its main purpose (and in this it drew on Harold's Foreign Office paper of 1917) was to secure the favourable position of the Anglo-Persian Oil Company which provided vital supplies for British naval and other forces operating in the Middle East. However, the agreement was never ratified. When Soviet forces crossed the northern Persian border and attempted to set up a Soviet-style republic based on Resht (the crisis which involved Harold during his period of secondment to the League of Nations), the Persian Government fell. New nationalist ministers were less keen on the agreement with the British and, in any case, the country was dissolving into anarchy. Then, in February 1921, one Reza Khan, commander of the Persian Cossack Brigade, seized power in a rapid *coup d'état*. Initially, he took command of the army and made himself Minister of War, but it was not long before he took control of the government, suppressed both nationalist unrest and tribal rebellion, and established his authority over the country as a whole. By the time Harold arrived, Reza Khan was the undoubted ruler of Persia.

Many years later, Gladwyn Jebb, Harold's colleague at the Legation – a young man Harold considered to possess remarkable eyelashes, 'great beauty and ... a gentle charm'[1] – portrayed Tehran as 'an almost completely medieval town, surrounded by a deep ditch and large mud wall, or ramparts.'[2] Jebb's description was imaginative rather than historically accurate. Tehran's city walls – some eighteen kilometres (eleven miles) in circumference – were actually built in the 1870s during the long reign of Nasr-ed-Din, though they may have looked medieval. Nasr-ed-Din had also begun the process of modernising the city, so that even in 1892 Lord Curzon could write of

> shops ... with glass windows and European titles. Street lamp-posts built for gas.... Avenues, bordered with footpaths and planted with trees.... A metalled and watered roadway ... broad, straight streets that conduct into immense squares and fringed by the porticoes of considerable mansions ... a city which was born and nurtured in the East, but is beginning to clothe itself at a West-End tailor's.[3]

The pace of westernisation slowed under the weaker regimes which followed and stalled altogether during the disruption of the war years. During Harold's time

> the town was like a vast garden, or rather a collection of gardens, centring round the bazaar, a huge rabbit-warren of a place.... Near the bazaar there was a tumble-down palace and a central square or *Maidan*, surrounded by rather unimpressive nineteenth-century buildings of which the most imposing were those of the Imperial Bank of Persia, then firmly under British control, and of the Anglo-Persian Oil Company.[4]

There were some cars and horse-drawn trams and a surprising number of bicycles, but the majority of the population travelled on horseback, by cart or carriage, with donkeys and camels used as pack animals.

The Legation compound, a short distance north of the *Maidan* on what is now Firdowsi Avenue, was large and beautiful, with spreading plane trees, lawns, tanks and water features, all tended by an army of gardeners. At its centre was 'a low building occupying three sides of a court, and terminating at one end in a campanile, or clock-tower, of Byzantine design. On one side is the Chancellery; in the centre are the reception rooms and Minister's quarters ... [opening] onto a lovely garden, where swans float on brimming tanks and peacocks flash amid the flower-beds.'[5] Harold's house was quite another thing. It was not the one in which he had been born, though it was more or less identical. Outside, it was of ugly yellow brick. Inside, it was featureless, badly designed and appallingly furnished. There was a Foreign Office tradition that diplomats arriving in post were offered the chance to buy some of their predecessor's furniture in order to save the effort and expense of shipping such possessions round the world, but Harold was so appalled at what he saw that he refused to buy anything except the essentials. He sacked all the servants except the cook, Taghi, and announced that he was prepared to camp until his own furniture arrived from England. Worse still, the house was on the eastern side of the compound, close to the main gate and the guardhouse, with no private garden. If Harold wanted to sit out of doors, he had to do so in full view of the traffic coming in and out of the gate – and, given the size of the Legation community, there was always someone coming or going.

Like many of the more remote Embassies and Legations, the British Legation in Tehran was a self-contained world. There were red-coated mounted messengers (known as *gholams*), a small detachment of British soldiers and a troop of Central India Horse, providing both security and polo ponies. There were interpreters and translators, typists, secretaries, archivists, dragomen, cooks, servants, gardeners. There was a doctor, a Consul General, and an Oriental Secretary, who stood between the local staff and the diplomats, offering advice on linguistic and cultural matters. This enormous and complex organisation supported a superstructure consisting of a Military Attaché and four diplomats: a Third Secretary (Gladwyn Jebb); a First Secretary (Christopher Warner); a Counsellor (Harold); and, at the top of the pyramid, His Majesty's Envoy Extraordinary and Minister Plenipotentiary, Sir Percy Lyham Loraine.

Loraine traced his family back to a Norman knight. His family had obtained their Northumbrian estate, Kirkharle Hall, in the early fifteenth century and he himself was twelfth Baronet in direct succession. He was tall, with a slow, formal, superior manner. He dressed immaculately, enjoyed hunting and shooting, and kept black retrievers – even in Persia. His one (slight) splash of eccentricity was to drive around in a yellow Vauxhall tourer. He was, in short, everything that a traditional English gentleman should be. Loraine's appointment as Minister in 1921 came as a result of Lord Curzon's personal intervention. Curzon realised that if anyone could appeal to Persia's new ruler, who was an odd mixture of the arrogant and the insecure, proud at what he had achieved yet conscious of his humble birth and lack of education, it would be someone of Loraine's appearance and character. By the time of Harold's arrival, Loraine had been Minister for four years and his ascendancy was complete. It was obvious to Harold from the first that Reza Khan 'adores Percy – and Percy is rather pleased with himself (and with justice) at having backed a winner from the start.'[6] Loraine had established a position for himself in Reza Khan's counsels which enabled him just to listen or to offer advice on issues of policy, whether foreign and domestic, without causing offence and without incurring jealousy on the part of the members of Reza Khan's government. No other diplomat had anything approaching Loraine's influence. It was a notable achievement and one which had been recognised by both the Foreign Office and the Foreign Secretary – a fact to which Harold should have paid more attention.

Loraine accompanied Harold on a round of calls, introducing him to senior members of the government and other important Persians. They met the Sheikh of Mohammerah, 'a sort of feudal despot who tried to fight Reza Khan and got the worst of it.'[7] They met the former Governor of Khorassan, who was smoking a water pipe with a diamond mouthpiece. On 3 December, they called on the Foreign Minister. Harold was enjoying himself. His letter to Vita is chirpy and interested. The Persian Foreign Office was 'rather a jolly old building with a courtyard and a fountain and the most heavenly picture running right across the top of the staircase.' The meeting room had 'a wallpaper of yellow chrysanthemums and red damask curtains.' The Foreign Minister himself was 'a copper-coloured man, or rather bronze-coloured.' The meeting began slowly and Harold realised that 'what took 5 minutes at home must take two hours here ... by easy flatulent stages one passed on to more serious business.'[8] On 10 December came the all-important call on Reza Khan, who was to be proclaimed Shah by the Persian parliament or *Majlis* later that week. Harold would be responsible for continuing the relationship when Loraine left Persia and it was important to get off to a good start. To begin with, Reza Khan 'looked cross and tired and dirty,' but gradually relaxed and eventually 'laughed a great deal – and for the rest of the interview was simple and jolly and with a certain force and dignity ... he told me to come and see him as often as I liked when he was Shah.'

Even though the meeting went well, Harold was not 'sure about' the future Shah. It was something on which he came to disagree profoundly with Loraine. Harold's accounts of this and subsequent meetings with the Shah contain a flippancy, a patronising tone and a tendency to dwell on the Shah's odd or uncouth physical appearance.

> I told him how we hoped he would make a nice good kind Shah. He was pleased by these assertions, and relaxed.... Suddenly he took his hat off – disclosing a tiny little shaven head.... He looked more of a scallywag than ever....'[9]
>
> Coarse red hands. Rather coarse nose. Fine chin. Clipped moustache turning up at the ends. Unshaven. Bushy eyebrows. Fine but rather bulging eyes ... the dominant impression [is of] a non-commissioned officer in the Cossack brigade: coarse humour, ungainly manner, latent brutality.[10]

There is more to this than Harold's normal close observation. It almost enters the realm of caricature: the stage Englishman meeting the archetypal foreigner. Harold obviously regarded Reza Khan as an upstart with imperial pretensions. Of course, his writings express sentiments which he was far too professional and too well mannered to display, but his feelings nonetheless influenced his views and his judgement. He could never quite take the Shah seriously – either as an individual or as a wielder of political power – and his opinion of the Shah was to contribute to his difficulties with London later on.

Just two days later, Harold and Loraine attended the crucial meeting of the *Majlis*, which was sitting as a Constituent Assembly. Its proceedings were long, complicated, ritualistic, legalistic and beset with all sorts of bizarre interruptions and delays. Harold wrote a detailed account to Vita.

> They were discussing whether it mattered that Reza Khan's mother was a Circassian and not a Persian. They got terribly tied up in knots over this discussion and the President kept on ringing his little bell rather aimlessly. Then a funny little man in a black turban and a dressing gown got into the tribune and said it didn't matter what his mother was so long as she was Moslem. They had never thought of that and were so pleased with the idea that they all clapped their hands.... Then some soldiers turned a hose on the awning from outside ... because of the dust: only ... the water made a noise like a machine gun and descended in a cascade on the heads of the groups of gendarmes who were standing in the far corner. The Constituent Assembly simply loved that part & they laughed and clapped their hands ... everybody was quite happy & shouted jokes & went across & talked to each other. And the reading began again. When it was over three servants advanced in awful solemnity carrying two soup tureens and a silver basin. They handed the soup tureens round the Assembly & each member threw in a little bit of paper.

Of course, this was intended to amuse, but the tone is patronising, suggesting that this sort of foreign nonsense should not be taken too seriously. Yet this was, after all, the debate which ended 130 years of rule by the Qajar dynasty and passed the resolution offering Reza Khan 'the Imperial Throne of Iran.'[11] Would he have written in such a vein about the proceedings of the House of Commons?

Three days later, Reza Khan took the oath of allegiance before the *Majlis*. Loraine, Harold and the rest of the diplomatic, consular and military staff of the Legation were all present in full uniform. Harold noted that Reza Khan read the oath with difficulty – but that in itself was progress because he had been illiterate a year previously. He also forgot to swear on the Koran and had to be reminded. After the short ceremony, the members of the Constituent Assembly, the new Shah's entourage, the country's military leaders, the aristocratic and wealthy elite of Tehran, the British Legation staff and the rest of the Diplomatic Corps all returned to the Golestan Palace for a formal reception. Whatever Harold may have felt about Persia's new ruler, it was evident that the country had just taken a new direction.

Professionally, Harold had made a good start, and he was making good progress with his knowledge of Persian. At the same time, he felt that he did not quite fit in. Social life in Tehran was extremely limited, especially during the four or five months of the year when snow on the western mountains deterred or prevented visitors from attempting the route. Contacts with the expatriate community or other diplomats were largely a matter of duty. The Legation staff was large but there were only a few people with whom Harold felt at ease. He got on well with Gladwyn Jebb. He liked Christopher Warner, finding him both efficient at work and personally attractive (though the relationship remained purely professional). He liked the Military Attaché, Colonel Fraser, and his wife. The problem centred on Percy Loraine.

Harold was not shy in any conventional sense of the word. He was not an uncritical believer in hierarchies – he certainly did not accept the standards and values of those above him on account of their position. Yet there was clearly something about Loraine and Loraine's capacity to judge him which unnerved Harold, which brought out a latent lack of confidence. Harold was not a bohemian; he was not a rebel; yet neither was he rigid or oldfashioned in his standards of behaviour. Loraine was. Moreover, this was the first time in his career that Harold had been called upon to fulfil a representative role, as a leader of both the Legation and the British community. Loraine had far more experience of this kind of role and a clear, if oldfashioned, view of how it should be done. Not for nothing had Loraine been christened 'Ponderous Percy' by the Legation staff.

Thus when it became clear that Loraine regarded Harold's top hat as not up to standard, and expected him to dress 'in grand clothes' rather than 'pottering in an old suit,' he accepted the criticism and asked Vita to send him what he needed with all speed.[12] He was aware that Lady Loraine thought he – and, when she visited, Vita – were 'odd.' He was sensitive, though more stubborn, in the face of her view that he should entertain the British community: 'I'm damned if I will,' he wrote to his parents.[13] He found that, in this small world, his habits and behaviour were scrutinised and discussed.

My pipe, I find, has labelled me with my colleagues as 'an original'. The fact that I only brought out 250 visiting cards and not 5,000 has served me the epithet of a '*faiseur de paradoxes*'. It does not make for my popularity.... The Persians on the other hand like me very much indeed.[14]

It took time for Harold and Loraine to develop confidence in each other. This seems to have been a question of character rather than professional ability. Gladwyn Jebb's memoirs show how much Harold's reputation had preceded him – 'his spectacular efforts at the Peace Conference ... dazzlingly urbane and already quite famous'.[15] Loraine had clearly known all this when he welcomed the appointment, but the reality was different. He soon came to feel that Harold did not conduct himself with sufficient formality. He was shocked to find him walking to the shops and carrying home the things that he had bought, instead of having someone carry them for him. He was shocked when Harold's shoelaces came undone – as they had a habit of doing – at official functions. Harold was obviously aware of Loraine's feelings and told Vita that his new chief 'is ... rather pomposo, and justifies it by the old bromide, "But these sort of things mean so much to Orientals."'[16] In the end, even if their views diverged on certain key issues, notably the Shah, Harold came to respect Loraine's achievement, and he was extremely grateful for Loraine's generosity and support. Loraine seems to have been cooler. On his return to London in July 1926, he clearly did not stand up for Harold in the Foreign Office, and he was highly critical of *Some People* when it appeared the following year.

Outside work, life in Tehran could hardly have been more different from life in London. Harold had bought his predecessor's horse and whenever possible rode out across the dusty plain, exploring the countryside. His preferred companion was Gladwyn Jebb (who also had failed to establish himself in Loraine's good graces). Sometimes, their trips involved shooting snipe, woodcock, chukar and quail. If they were after bigger game, such as gazelle, they borrowed one of the Legation's three Fords. On longer trips, they might spend a night camping in one of the abandoned villas and palaces which lay scattered and crumbling across the south-facing slopes of the Elburz. Otherwise, he read – Greek in the morning, novels or poetry in the evening – wrote his diary, wrote letters, studied Persian and kept himself to himself. He missed Vita; he missed Raymond Mortimer; he missed his sex life – but he was not precisely lonely, for Harold, despite his gregariousness, could be very self-contained. In a letter written after Vita's visit in the spring on 1926, he tried to explain how he felt.

> Don't think, my dearest, that I'm unhappy. Only sort of suspended neutral feeling. You see this sort of life is really what I like best: Work, riding, hot weather, reading, writing, bathing. But it seems to have no point without you. I get through the days quickly, contentedly, mechanically – but it is only when something ... jerks me into being myself again and not a machine that I realise how automatic and perfunctory is my existence.[17]

Sex was much on Harold's mind. For the most part, it was an abstract consideration. Raymond, he found, was writing an article on 'alternatives to chastity' which came to the conclusion that 'the best life is marriage plus liaisons', a conclusion apparently based on his observations of and respect for Harold and Vita's manner of conducting their marriage.[18] The article was never published because Leonard Woolf, for whom it was written, thought it was too open about sexual matters and could be construed as encouraging what the world saw as immorality. Musing on Persian men in a letter to Clive Bell, Harold wrote that they were 'oleaginous and pimpled like the Greeks. It is a strange and stimulating thought that the two civilisations that have gone the whole hog on sodomy should be peopled by males with whom to sleep would be an experience both glutinous and prickly.'[19]

When male visitors arrived, Harold's first reaction was to determine their sexual potential and to inform Raymond or Vita. Patrick Buchan-Hepburn, later an MP and later still Governor General of the Federation of the West Indies, arrived in August 1926. Harold found him quite beautiful but insipid. On a fishing trip which required them to share a tent, Buchan-Hepburn

> made it quite clear to me that he wasn't one of that sort. I had already made it quite clear that I was. I think he was a little nervous, Jebb not having arrived and there being champagne and only a few camels to appeal to if I lost my head ... I have already read Patrick the parts in this letter which refer to him. He clearly thinks you must be just as odd as me.[20]

This is all very amusing but it was sailing close to the wind. They may have been in a remote valley beneath Mount Demavend in northern Persia and not in London, but the revelation of Harold's homosexuality – had Buchan-Hepburn chosen to make it – would have been just as damaging. In the end, neither Persia nor visitors yielded the kind of sexual adventure Harold appears to have been hoping for.

30 Visit

If Harold's new life lacked excitement, it did offer a number of quiet compensations – it was protected; it was healthy; it offered a sense of belonging and community; it ran according to routine and the diplomatic bag schedule; work was neither demanding nor stressful; and whatever certain individuals might think of him, he had a recognised professional and social position. Christmas Day was spent quietly – first at lunch with the Legation doctor and his family, then walking through the bazaars and gardens of north Tehran with Gladwyn Jebb. On New Year's Day, he held a (very) small drinks party for Christopher Warner, Gladwyn Jebb and the Vice Consul, Jack O'Dwyer, and woke the next morning with an appalling hangover. Life continued. The first real excitement of 1926 was the arrival of Vita at the beginning of March.

For Vita, the most important thing since Harold's departure had been the fact that her relationship with Virginia Woolf had taken physical form. She hinted as much rather than said so directly in her letters to Harold. He read the signs, understood, and promised not to be jealous, but he did issue his clear, if low key, warning that she had not *'la main heureuse* in dealing with married couples.' He seems to have been more concerned that she should be secretive about her work: she did not tell him that she had decided to call her long poem *The Land* and refused to tell him what Virginia thought of it. Her private life continued to be incredibly complicated. She was still close to Dottie Wellesley; Geoffrey was still in love with her, though she now found his presence something of a trial; Dorothy Warren, a connection of Ottoline Morrell's, was in love with both Vita and Geoffrey. Vita herself was concentrated on Virginia Woolf. 'I am,' she wrote, 'reduced to a thing that wants Virginia.... I just miss you, in a quite desperate human way.'[1] Yet even in the midst of her discovery of Virginia, she could write to Harold: 'Oh darling, I do love you SO AWFULLY. It doesn't get any better as time goes on. I hoped it would. But it doesn't.'[2] She had learnt from previous experience. Harold was her emotional bedrock and she would do nothing to imperil that. Virginia, like so many others over the years, could not understand how their relationship worked. 'What's six weeks with Harold to him,' she wrote, a few days before Vita's departure, 'compared with four months without you to us?'[3]

Vita said goodbye to Virginia at a farewell dinner given by Clive Bell in a Bloomsbury restaurant called The Ivy. The following day, 19 January, was Nigel's ninth birthday. It was also the day on which he was to due to join his brother Ben at Summer Fields preparatory school on the outskirts of Oxford. Vita, accompanied by Raymond Mortimer, took both boys to the circus before driving them on to the school and saying goodbye. The next morning, she set off for Persia.

Vita's journey took five-and-a-half weeks. For most of that time she had Dottie Wellesley as travelling companion. As far as Cairo, they followed the same route as Harold. Then, after a few days sightseeing in Luxor and the Valley of the Kings, they took a British India Steam Navigation Company ship, SS *Rajputana*, for Bombay calling *en route* at Aden. In Bombay, they were met by Edwin Lutyens who conducted them northwards by train. They visited the great, deserted city of Fatehpur Sikri. They visited the Red Fort at Agra and the Taj Mahal, which had been restored by Lord Curzon during his viceroyalty. They visited New Delhi and inspected Lutyens' great project. It was fascinating – and recorded in a series of wonderful letters to Virginia – but all a little too much. By the time they arrived back in Bombay, Vita had a sprained ankle, a sore throat and a recurrent fever. Dottie returned to England via Egypt, while Vita embarked on SS *Varela* for Basra via Karachi and a series of ports up the Persian Gulf. The journey gave her time to recover.

From Basra, where she was looked after by the British Consul and his wife, Vita took the train to Baghdad – passing a sign at a station which said 'Change for Bablyon.'[4] In Baghdad, she visited Gertrude Bell who gave a dinner for her, took her to tea with the King and helped her choose a dog, a Saluki called Zurcha which was to prove irredeemably stupid. Leaving Baghdad on 27 February, Vita took the slow train to Khamkin where she joined a convoy of cars 'caked in mud, with bent mud-guards, and the words "TRANS-DESERT MAIL" barely legible on the bonnet' for Tehran.[5] The journey as far as Kermanshah was potentially dangerous, but the driver refused an escort offered at the Persian border post because it would slow them down. At one point, a horseman rode straight at the car. The driver put his foot down and the horseman swerved away. 'That's their trick,' the driver said.... 'If I'd pulled up there would have been four or five of them round us in a minute.'[6] Vita wrote to Virginia that she had 'been attacked by a bandit': it was a slight, if pardonable, exaggeration.[7]

In the meantime, Harold and a driver had set off from Tehran on 27 February in one of the Legation Fords. They reached Qazvin without difficulty the same day, but when they turned south towards Hamadan they met fresh snow on the mountains and a journey which should have taken a day took more than two. At Hamadan, they were still a full day's drive from Kermanshah through some very rugged country. Harold was getting more and more anxious about Vita's safety and insisted they press on. Eventually, despite the front springs of the Ford collapsing along the way, they limped into Kermanshah at six o'clock on the third day. Harold renewed his acquaintance with the Cowans at the Consulate and waited.

> 6.30 passed, and then 7 and I found the suspense intolerable. Only a fortnight earlier a car had been held up by brigands outside Kermanshah and both the occupants had been shot. By eight o'clock I could bear it no longer and went into the consulate garden.... But the night seemed empty of everything except my own anxiety. They told me dinner was ready. I could eat nothing. Then the man came in and said quite casually that a motor was coming up the drive.... I could make out two huddled figures inside ... and there was my Vita all in furs with a new dog on her knee. We almost cried with excitement. And we talked and talked and talked. She had seen Egypt and Delhi and Agra but we talked about the garden at Long Barn and about Ben and Nigel.[8]

They started for Tehran the next morning, spending two nights on the road and talking all the way. The excitement was genuine: there can be no doubt that they had missed each other terribly and were overjoyed to see each other again. Only one small incident marks a difference between them. Harold was devoted to Vita, never sought to hide it and did not care who knew it. Vita was more cautious, more given to compartmentalising relationships. Writing to Virginia, knowing how Virginia felt about Harold and that she did not fully understand their relationship, Vita downplayed the importance of the reunion in Kermanshah – 'Met Harold, with letters in his pocket – two letters from Virginia which I read first.'[9]

Vita stayed in Persia for two months. If not precisely unhappy in Tehran by himself, Harold was certainly much happier with her there. He had enjoyed discovering the country by himself or with Gladwyn Jebb, but her presence gave everything a new purpose and a new meaning. Weekends allowed them to escape from legation life to explore the valleys and the foothills of the Elburz Mountains. Vita's visit coincided with the Persian spring and there were flowers everywhere, many of which she had never seen before, in the woods and valleys, in the overgrown gardens of ruined villas, even in the desert. They developed a particular affection for Doschan Tapeh, 'a high sudden hill, starting up out of the plain,' where Nasr-ed-Din Shah had built a palace with vast, open views in three directions across the North Persian Plain to the mountains beyond. At the foot of the hill was 'a walled-in square, symmetrically planted with trees, where [the Shah had] kept his wild animals.' The hillside was 'full of sage and the wild lavender with the big pink flower,' while the ruined palace retained 'traces of its former splendours' and there was a mysterious room papered with upside-down illustrations from the *Illustrated London News* of 1860.[10]

During the week, there were diplomatic duties. As the wife of the Counsellor at the British Legation, Vita had a role to play, paying calls on other wives in the British and the diplomatic community, even presenting the hockey prizes. There were lunches and dinners to give and attend, including an immensely formal dinner at the Persian Foreign Ministry in honour of the Shah's birthday, when Harold wore diplomatic uniform and again demonstrated his capacity for awkwardness on ceremonial occasions by getting his sword caught between his legs. The experience confirmed Vita in her view that 'I don't like diplomacy, though I like Persia.'[11] Harold was by her side throughout, immensely proud of her. 'Vita in Persia,' he told Clive Bell, 'is a lovely sight. Slow and imperturbable she moves with her long slim legs; slowly and imperturbably she receives the unveiled admiration of the Persian notables.'[12] Vita's natural bearing and aristocratic lineage may well have helped raise Harold's stock in the eyes of Sir Percy Loraine, who was very much influenced by such things – although the elevation was not to last.

When it came to social life, Gladwyn Jebb was the only member of the Legation staff with whom the Nicolsons felt any intellectual affinity and he became a lifelong friend. He was easy company and would join them on their weekend excursions, disappearing early in the morning to shoot snipe or antelope and then rejoining them later in the day. Otherwise, there were evenings with Prince Mirza Firouz,[13] a member of the deposed Qajar family and a Francophile of a high order who liked to reminisce with Harold about life in Paris and their mutual friend, Jean Cocteau. There was Elizabeth Daryush, the daughter of Poet Laureate Robert Bridges and a significant poet in her own right. Born and bred in Oxford, she had recently married Ali Akbar Daryush, a Persian civil servant, and returned to Persia with him. Harold and Vita liked her, but felt her rather a sad, lonely figure who would be happier in Boar's Hill (to which she eventually returned).[14] Archibald MacLeish turned up, having been asked by the League of Nations to investigate opium production, and spent a lunch telling them of his passion for the work of Virginia Woolf and T. S. Eliot. Interesting though these isolated figures and events were – and though neither Harold nor Vita expected Tehran to be London – they only served to emphasise the scarcity of real companionship. The difference was that while Harold had an official position and could find distraction in his work and his absorption in

Persian life and culture, Vita was regarded as his spouse and forced into a supporting diplomatic role (two things she seriously disliked). She enjoyed Persia and while she was there she accepted and played out her role, not least in order to support Harold, but she missed England and she missed the stimulation of Virginia and of Bloomsbury. She wrote a lyrical and perceptive travel book based on her experiences – *Passenger to Tehran* – but Vita was not by nature as adaptable as Harold. It is obvious from her letters to Virginia that Persia was an experience, a holiday, but not, as for Harold, a commitment (however temporary). It was a difference in temperament and in approach which was to exert increasing pressure on Harold over the next four years.

About half way through Vita's visit, Raymond Mortimer arrived in Tehran after a somewhat adventurous journey during which 'he fell over a precipice and was fired on, but survived.'[15] Harold had originally wanted to delay Raymond's visit until Vita had returned to England, but had relented because he did not want to hurt Raymond's feelings – 'that poor little Pippin,' as he called him.[16] Vita did not mind: she told Virginia that Raymond 'is very happy, and as good as gold: scribbles away and gives no trouble.'[17] The three of them appear to have gone everywhere together without any tension or embarrassment. Nothing could better illustrate the combination of love and unselfishness in Harold and Vita's relationship.

At dawn on 18 April, the three of them set off, again in one of the Legation's old Fords, for Isfahan. They had meant to leave three days before but had been delayed by an unseasonal snowfall. Vita drove, but they took a mechanic with them just in case. Leaving Tehran, they passed wheat fields and red cliffs, a huge, shimmering salt lake, an oasis, quicksands and a swamp. They climbed up to another plateau, passing snow peaks and carved valleys. That night they stopped in Dilijand and stayed in a huge and echoing empty room lined with teapots, provided by the village headman. The next day they crossed a great arid plain, reaching Isfahan in the early evening. There, they joined Sir Percy Loraine and Gladwyn Jebb who were making an official visit to the region. Together the British party was conducted round the great sights of the city – the Hall of Forty Columns, the great Madrasseh and the carpet weavers. On the way back, they stopped overnight in Kum (Qom) – these days usually referred to as a holy city, to Vita it was no more than a 'sacred village'[18] – but it was not the cities that left the deepest impression: it was the vast yet endlessly varied landscapes of the Persian plateau. For Harold, they became his standard of comparison especially when, some years later, he sought to describe the landscapes of the western United States.

For four years, Loraine had supported and guided Reza Khan's efforts to bring order to Persia after years of anarchy and civil war. He had seen his favourite consolidate his authority, accept the inevitability of a monarchy rather than a republic, win over the influential mullahs and the powerful feudal landowners and be formally proclaimed Shah by the *Majlis*. One major event remained: the coronation. And in Persia, the coronation would be more than a formality: it would be seen – by ordinary people, by the clergy, by the nobility and by defeated warlords – as a public demonstration of the new Shah's power and authority. British interests, as interpreted by Loraine, demanded that the coronation should be both splendid and successful.

For Harold, this meant tremendous and largely pointless urging of Persian officials to make sure that everything would be ready for the great day – Persian attitudes to preparation being very different from English ones. Vita, however, was plunged into a quite fabulous situation. First, in Lady Loraine's absence, she was asked to supervise redecoration of the hall, known as the Museum, in the Golestan Palace in which the coronation would take place – 'I go down there and put on an apron, and mix paints in pots in a vast hall, and wonder what the Persian is for "stipple".'[19] Then, invited to choose which of Persia's state treasures should be displayed on the great day, she and Lady Loraine were taken to see the Crown Jewels. 'It was simply the Arabian nights,' she wrote to Virginia.

> I am blind. Blinded by diamonds.
> I have been in Aladdin's cave.
> Sacks of emeralds were emptied out before our eyes. Sacks of pearls. Literally.
> We came away shaking pearls out of our shoes. Ropes of uncut emeralds. Scabbards encrusted with precious stones. Great hieratic crowns.
> All this in a squalid room, with grubby Persians drinking little cups of tea.[20]

In the meantime, Tehran was filling up with 'barbarians who have ridden in from the mountains for the coronation, and who parade the streets on their wild ponies, dressed to emulate the plumage of peacocks – huge turbans of silk and furs, wide sashes ... stuck with silver-mounted weapons of every description.'[21] Harold's account of the great day, in a letter to his parents, is characteristically downbeat, but does suggest that the Shah rose to the occasion.

We drove there in State – a thing I particularly abominate. I never did like amateur theatricals, and I loathe bumping along a street surrounded by escorts. My friendly profile does not lend itself to such pro-consular antics and the collar of my uniform cuts cruelly into my chubby neck. Then we arrived.... Loraine springs rigidly to attention while they play God Save the King. Lady Loraine bares her head as do the devout after receiving Holy Communion, and I get hot and uncomfortable, longing with a homesick passion for my pipe.... Under Vita's orders this vast railway station has been painted a simple apricot. It looked very well. So did Vita. She wore in the centre of her black toque the emeralds which Nasr-ed-Din-Shah had presented to Mummy.... Slowly the Shah, dressed in a blue mantle embroidered with pearls, slouched up the aisle and climbed on to the throne.... He sat on it – rigid, theocratic, rather superb – this Cossack Trooper, the Ruler of the World, the King of Kings.[22]

Harold's run of unfortunate incidents at formal occasions continued the next day. The Shah had decided to give a party in the gardens of the Palace, complete with fireworks and champagne, to celebrate his coronation. Harold and Vita had been dining at the Opium Commission and were just about to go on to the party when the trousers of Harold's diplomatic uniform split across the seat. Safety pins and his tail coat 'hid what might otherwise have seemed ungainly.' This was followed by another misadventure when Vita discovered that she had lost the large central emerald from her chain. Harold went in search of it and eventually found 'the Prime Minister and the Minister of Public Works anxiously going round the Peacock Throne trying to fit into it an emerald which had been found lying at its feet.'[23] He reclaimed Vita's property and they went home.

It was time for Vita to return to England. A few days after the coronation, she, Harold and Raymond set off for Resht. They were accompanied by General Arfa of the Persian army and his English wife, Hilda, with whom Vita was to travel as far as Moscow. They passed Qazvin and descended into the valley of the Sefid Rud or White River, staying overnight at the Hotel Fantasia in Rudbar. It was a different Persia here: fertile, lush and steamy. Vita noted that the country and the houses could at times be compared with Devon or Hampshire. At the port Enzeli (Bandar-e-Anzali), just outside Resht, on the morning of 5 May, Vita and the Arfas boarded a Caspian steamer for Baku. For Harold, the parting was devastating. He had prepared for it by giving letters to the Arfas to give to Vita *en route*, and by sending letters ahead to Moscow, but he could not prepare himself.

> When I closed your bedroom door at Rasht, I stood for a moment on the landing with a giddy agony, which made the whole house swing and wobble.... We stopped for lunch by the roadside, and put the water-bottle to cool under a spring. I went to wash a fork.... I crouched there, holding the fork in the stream – tears pouring down my face. I went up behind the rock and leant against it and shook and shook with sobs.[24]
>
> I flung myself on the bed in an agony of suffering as I have never known. I walking up and down in the dark saying, 'Vita, Vita, Vita, Vita!', with tears splashing on the dark floor.... This morning I broke down completely.... Oh my dear, we can't go through this again.[25]

For Vita, it was the same.

> Oh my dear, God keep you safe. Life is empty and silent. I feel light-headed with pain. Never, never, never again. I cannot bear it.... I simply can't live without you.[26]

It is all too easy to take the cynical view and suspect that these emotions are exaggerated in the recording, but that does not seem to have been the case. Raymond Mortimer, who returned with Harold to Tehran, was appalled at what they were putting themselves through and wrote to Vita to tell her so in no uncertain terms.

> I have never seen anyone so wretched as Harold.... It seems to me imbecile to put yourselves in such a situation, and really make me rather angry.... I'd give anything to have a relationship with someone like Harold's with you, and it infuriates me to see it made a cause of suffering instead of happiness.... Because he is made wretched by [these partings] himself, he feels in some way that it is all right, which is mysticism and nonsense.[27]

And yet, as Nigel Nicolson points out in *Portrait of a Marriage*, there was nothing imperative demanding that she return home. Ben and Nigel were at school. Lady Sackville could be ignored. Virginia 'could come alive in letters.'[28] Why then return? One reason has already been given. Unlike Harold, and despite her passionate response to Spain and Italy, Vita was never truly happy outside England. These lines from the closing passage of *The Land*, were written in Tehran on 23 March.

> I saw the round moon rise above the pines,
> One quiet planet prick the greening west,
> As goats came leaping up the stony crest....
> That moon, that star, above my English Weald
> Hung at that hour, and I not there to see;
> Shining through mist above the dew-drenched field ...
> Then all my deep acquaintance with that land,
> Crying for words, welled up.²⁹

The other reason lies deeper in Vita's character. She understood that their present situation was not tenable, but there was a level at which she remained the indulged only child of Knole, not selfish so much as unreflecting. However much she loved Harold, it never seriously occurred to her that she might be the one required to make the sacrifice. In Tehran and also later in Berlin, Harold appears to have anticipated – or hoped – that Vita would at some stage join him for longer than just a visit. It was not to be and deep down he must have known it. Vita's rootedness was something he had to, and did, accept as a fundamental part of their relationship, yet there were times, especially in these middle years, when he could have been forgiven for feeling that most of the compromise was on his side.

31 Chargé

Shortly after Vita's departure, *Swinburne* was published and the first reviews began to trickle through to Tehran via the diplomatic bag. The best was by Gosse in the *Sunday Times*, a ringing endorsement of Harold's status in relation to his generation of writers, suggesting that *Swinburne* was his most original work to date. This was more generous than accurate on Gosse's part. Other reviews were mixed: some hostile, suggesting Harold was being unfair to his subject; others appreciative without being enthusiastic.

Swinburne died in 1909. More than a century after his death, it is perhaps difficult to understand why Harold's thesis that he was a flawed and formulaic poet, who never outgrew his youthful enthusiasms and never recovered from a severe nervous breakdown in 1879 brought on by various forms of excess, should have proved even mildly controversial. It is a judgement few would now contest. Even Gosse, whose *The Life of Algernon Charles Swinburne* had appeared in 1917 and taken a much more reverential view of

the poet's achievement, admitted that he was at least partly won over by
Harold's arguments. In his day, however, Swinburne was regarded as one of
the poetic greats and regularly nominated for the Nobel Prize, hence his
inclusion in Jack Squire's English Men of Letters series, which consisted of
critical studies of major English poets. Harold contrived to suggest that
Swinburne might not be a major poet, but, unfortunately, his concentration on Swinburne's poetic technique, dubbed 'painstaking' by Raymond
Mortimer,[1] does not make riveting reading. From *Verlaine* to *Tennyson* and
then to *Byron*, Harold's work had shown a gradual progression away from
poetry and towards history. In that sense, *Swinburne* represented a step
backwards. It is not a bad book. It is neither inaccurate nor unfair.[2] It is just
not very interesting. This ability to fix upon only marginally interesting
subject matter was to recur later in Harold's writing career.

Several reviewers noted mistakes in detail and stylistic oddities – presumably the result, as ever, of the speed at which Harold wrote. His attention to
detail and to grammar was now, and was to remain, under much closer
scrutiny than previously. This was Raymond Mortimer's *métier* and, though
Harold might on occasion grumble that Raymond was 'like a spaniel snorting for truffles; the truffles in his case being incompetence on the part of
others,'[3] he could not say that Raymond was wrong.

Raymond stayed on in Persia for two months after Vita's departure. To
judge from letters to Vita and to Clive Bell, he and Harold settled into an
easy companionship, punctuated by friendly arguments based on their
respective roles as creator and critic – Raymond 'couldn't (damn him!) have
written the book himself – being a lazy cove, and sits there all comfortable
and says little destructive things.'[4] Raymond was there to calm Harold
when he worked himself into a state about Vita's safety on her journey
home, which coincided first with disorder in Russia and then with a revolution in Poland (Vita, needless to say, came through both unscathed). Their
only serious disagreement came just before Raymond was due to return
home and in the context of Sir Percy Loraine's departure.

Loraine had been in Persia since December 1921. His task had been to get
the measure of Persia's new ruler and to proffer the hand of British friendship, provided that British interests were protected and advanced. In this,
in the view of the Foreign Office, he had been extremely successful and he
was now to take a step up the diplomatic ladder and become Minister at the
British Legation in Athens. He would leave on 2 July. His successor, Robert
Clive, would not arrive until November, so there would be a four-month
interregnum, during which Harold would be Chargé d'Affaires.

Lady Loraine left at the end of May, to the private relief of Harold, who had never warmed to her and found Sir Percy much more relaxed and approachable when she was not there. A few days later, with the summer heat settling upon the city, the Legation moved to its summer quarters at Gulahek on the slopes of the Elburz. Raymond went off to visit Shiraz in company with the American writer and traveller, Vincent Sheean. Harold's shoelaces again came undone in the presence of the Shah during a call at the summer palace at Saadabad. There was a political crisis which meant that Mostofi al Mamalek became Prime Minister for the sixth time. Loraine, accompanied by Harold, made a round of farewell calls, formally taking his leave of the Shah on 28 June. It was a strange encounter which may well have sowed the seeds of the despatch Harold was to write a few months later. There was a bond, even a friendship, between the two men, but Loraine would not allow the relationship to stand in the way of his duty. He lectured the Shah on corruption and delay in the Persian administration and on Persia's international obligations (which included repaying a loan from Britain). The Shah liked – even admired – Loraine, but to Harold at least it was evident that personal admiration was not going to translate into a willingness to act in accordance with Loraine's wishes.

On 30 June, Harold hosted a farewell dinner on behalf of the Legation staff and senior members of the British community, or 'colony' as it was known in Tehran. It was a production number in the imperial style. A durbar tent was erected on the lawn; 'a balalalalalalaika orchestra' played; Chinese lanterns hung from the trees. 'We had soup, trout, cutlets in aspic, turkey and an apricot ice.' After the dinner, there was a party in Harold's house with another band, 'heaps of drink', and dancing, which lasted until two in the morning. But it was Harold's speech of tribute to Loraine at the conclusion of the dinner which sparked the disagreement with Raymond. By Harold's own account it was 'a nice English-public-schoolboy sort of speech ... quite moderate and devoid of undue sob stuff. But I admit it was rather an Empire builder's speech.' It was clearly a speech appropriate to the circumstances – Loraine 'replied very slowly and with some emotion' and Harold concluded that 'the colony were impressed by my noble uplifting patriotic sturdy homily.' Raymond, however, was 'really angry about it ... he hates the Kipling side in me.' Harold was 'rather crushed by this attack' – and no wonder.[5] It was as if Bloomsbury had landed in Gulahek to challenge him, for Raymond's attitude was very much the Bloomsbury attitude towards Empire and establishment.

Harold's problem – one which dogged him all his life – was that he belonged to both worlds; he could see both sides of the argument. He detested the coldness and formality of the proconsular lifestyle he had experienced with the Lloyds in Cairo. He hated emotional dishonesty. In his letters to Vita, he mocks (albeit tongue firmly in cheek) the 'empty life' of his diplomatic activities and hopes his future biographer will recognise his 'noble and incessant activities in the cause of life and literature.'[6] At the same time, his age, upbringing and profession made him a child of the Empire. It was his professional duty to give speeches to the British community in praise of Sir Percy Loraine and traditional British values whether he believed it or not. In point of fact, he did believe in the practical superiority of British civilisation – it was the attitude inherent in his response to the Shah and to the antics surrounding the debate in the *Majlis* on the Shah's accession. Indeed, the experience of Persia was having its effect: 'I am becoming immensely imperialist,' he wrote to his parents. 'I don't like war – because it mars people. But I like dominion when it is exercised ... with perfect calm.'[7] Yet such imperialism as he possessed was never even remotely militant. His attitude to the Empire evolved over time, but it remained essentially pragmatic – 'so long as we have an Empire, our policy is bound to be imperial.'[8] Harold recognised the force of the Bloomsbury argument, but to him it was both idealistic, in that it ignored the historical reality of the Empire and its achievements, and arrogant in its assumption of moral superiority.

At dawn on 2 July, Sir Percy Loraine shook Harold's hand and climbed into his yellow Vauxhall tourer. In a display of imperial deference, which presumably outraged Raymond Mortimer, the entire Legation staff turned out in full uniform and lined up to bid him a formal farewell. The mounted escort formed up under the plane trees – Central India Horse in front, Legation messengers behind – and Loraine drove slowly away, accompanied by his escort to the point where the main road left Gulahek village. Technically, Harold was not Chargé d'Affaires until Loraine left Persia, but in reality the responsibility was his from the moment the yellow Vauxhall drove out of the compound.

And he enjoyed it. He enjoyed being in charge. He enjoyed the trappings of the position – the tiled floors and high ceilings of the Gulahek Residence; the Legation car and liveried chauffeur; the salutes of the Indian cavalry at the Gulahek compound and the Persian guard at the Golestan Palace. But responsibility brought demands also, and Harold was to learn much over the next four months. Seventeen years in the Foreign Office had put him at the centre of some of the most important political events of the time; he had come up with any number of imaginative solutions and bold recommendations; but he had never previously had to take the final responsibility.

The first lesson came within hours of Loraine's departure with news from Khorasan in the north-east of the country. The army, fuelled by 'an explosive combination of ideological opposition to the regime and severe material grievances relating to pay and conditions,'[9] were in revolt and were marching on Meshed, the regional capital, encouraged, even perhaps accompanied, by Russian troops. The danger was that the Soviets might encourage the formation of a breakaway republic as they had at Resht in 1920. Loraine was Minister until he crossed the frontier, but if Harold thought of recalling him, he swiftly decided against it. He sent a low-key telegram to the Foreign Office alerting them to the revolt and warning that, although contained at present, it had the potential to spread. He showed equal confidence when it came to analysing the political situation and giving London his views. The contents of the first diplomatic bag to leave Tehran following Loraine's departure showed a distinct change of tone, less trusting of Reza Shah and altogether more pessimistic about the future of Persia and Anglo-Persian relations. It was a theme Harold was to develop with increasing conviction, but his confidence was not appreciated in the Foreign Office.

The position brought other responsibilities, too, not always agreeable. That summer saw a series of religious visitors – two English ladies from the Church Missionary Society to whom Harold was obliged to offer accommodation for three weeks; Bishop Thompson, the Anglican bishop in Persia, who gave Communion to the Legation staff; another, larger group of missionaries to whom Harold gave dinner. To Harold, who disliked organised religion and disliked proselytising religion even more, these visits were something of a trial, yet his letters make the most of the comic possibilities of the situation – his servant bringing champagne and toast for the bishop to celebrate Communion; his dog Henry howling throughout the sermon; his longing to contradict the bishop's confused analogies between life and a football match with Christ as a referee; Henry being petted by the missionaries and exposing 'what, for his age, is a fine sexual organ.'[10] His judgements might be sharp, but he had a softer side, too. The English missionary ladies were just *so* English: as they tried to make sense of Persia, 'one could see the poor little sparrow-mind fluttering back to the rectory drawing-room.... I was touched by this, and went to be bed ... trying to feel more hospitable about them.' It was, he supposed, in a reference which, however ironic, would again have horrified Raymond, 'the white man's burden.'[11]

Raymond left just two days after Loraine, another dawn departure, but this time from the recently constructed airstrip just to the west of Tehran. He and Vincent Sheean had decided to fly to Moscow. Air travel was a risky business, which added an extra dimension to an already emotional parting, but once Raymond had gone Harold found himself settling into an easy routine, which, although it must have varied day by day, is worth recording because it demonstrates his capacity for self-discipline.

> He woke at 6 o'clock, and read Greek books till 7, when he had his tea. At 7.10 he shaved, and at 7.20 bathed. At 7.30 he had breakfast, and at 8 wrote his daily letter to Vita. Between 8.30 and 9.30 he wrote his book. From 9.30 to 6 o'clock he worked in the Chancery. From 6 to 7.30 he rode, usually with Gladwyn. From 7.30 to 7.40 he had a hot bath. At 8 he dined, and at 9.30 went to bed.[12]

Gladwyn Jebb was a great support, both as friend and colleague – Harold promoted him Acting Head of Chancery – but he was also the occasion of another lesson in responsibility. Jebb was responsible for ensuring that all necessary action had been taken on the telegrams and other papers coming into the Legation before they were filed, or in Foreign Office parlance 'put away.' By his own admission, this activity took place when not playing tennis, bathing, riding or playing polo.

> Drowsily ... one evening I 'put away' a highly important telegram from the Government of Iraq in which we were desired to inform the Persian Government that a rebellion ... was impending on the Kurdish border. Only a few days later, when a chaser came in, was this error discovered, whereupon Harold nobly insisted on ... informing Baghdad that the paper had been disregarded entirely through his own fault. Luckily the rebellion never took place, but I had a great lesson ... in the duty of any senior to assume responsibility for the misdeeds of his junior.[13]

Life for the Legation staff at Gulahek may have been relaxed, but for the Shah and for Persia, the summer of 1926 was punctuated by rebellion and rumours of rebellion. By the usual logic of the Foreign Office, Harold received a telegram congratulating him on the way in which he had dealt with the Khorasan episode – though in fact he had done nothing more than have several inconclusive conversations with the Foreign Ministry. A more serious outbreak of dissent in the Kurdish areas in the east of the country was eventually defeated and the figurehead, Salar-ed-Dowleh Qajar, brother of the late Mohammed Ali Shah, forced to flee to British-controlled Iraq – which led to Harold receiving a formal protest from the Shah alleging that the British had supported the revolt. Trouble then flared in Persian Baluchistan on the border with what is now Pakistan, again stimulated by

Salar-ed-Dowleh. The Government of India saw a threat to British interests, particularly to the Duzdap railway, a commercially important and British-owned, cross-border link. The Foreign Office told Harold to issue a written ultimatum making it clear that if the Shah did not act, the Government of India would send in troops to secure the railway. Harold protested that this would offend the Persians, encourage the Russians and lead to Britain being dragged before the League of Nations. In fact, he protested twice, but was told to get on with it. Ignoring his instructions, he visited the Foreign Minister at home and delivered his message over tea in the course of a long and rambling Persian conversation. It was all a bit of a muddle, for the Foreign Office suddenly recognised the force of Harold's objections and changed its mind, while at the same time the revolt collapsed, as much because of disagreements among the rebels as because of Persian Government intervention. Nonetheless, Harold had shown a capacity for decisive and independent judgement.

Throughout his period as Chargé, Harold wrote regularly to Lancelot Oliphant in the Foreign Office giving his interpretation of events and developing his theme that the Shah should not be considered a reliable partner in pursuing British interests. This correspondence culminated in his despatch, 'Anglo-Persian Relations,' dated 30 September 1926, which upset the Foreign Office and, Harold claimed, seriously damaged his career. Harold had certainly never kept his views a secret. He told his parents that the picture Loraine painted for the Foreign Office of a stable Persia was 'fanciful'.[14] In a letter to Loraine – with whom he maintained a correspondence after the latter's departure – Harold states unequivocally that

> we see differently about the Shah. You feel that he is something reliable and solid. I think him infinitely untrustworthy and sly. Again, you believe somewhere in the Persians. I think them the most contemptible race on earth. You believe in good relations as something positive: I only see them as something negative.[15]

He had written in similar terms to the Foreign Secretary: 'A policy of friendliness and non-intervention is by far the least troublesome policy we can adopt, but it is a negative policy.'[16] It is clear that on his return to London, Loraine had meetings with the top echelon of the Foreign Office and the Foreign Secretary during which he discussed Harold's pessimistic view of Anglo-Persian relations while giving his own more positive (one commentator has used the term 'self-congratulatory'[17]) assessment of the situation. In any event, the tenor of Harold's despatch did not come as a surprise. His mistake, in writing it, was to misjudge the character and temper of his own organisation and then, not for the first time, to overreact to criticism.

A despatch is a formal communication from the head of a diplomatic mission overseas addressed to the Foreign Secretary and thus normally reserved for consideration of major bilateral or international policy issues. There was no reason why Harold should not have written a despatch – though it was perhaps unusual for a Chargé of such short duration to make such a comprehensive appraisal of the state of relations with his host country. What was more unusual – and counter-productive – was to make a direct attack on the policies of a Minister who had left post less than three months previously, who was bound to see it, who had the support of the Foreign Secretary, and whose cousin was the Head of Eastern Department and thus the arbiter of Middle Eastern policy. Where the Foreign Office was wrong was in failing to realise that things could change: that Loraine's policy, which had been correct four years previously, was no longer applicable, and that a great deal had happened even in the three months since he had left Tehran.

What did Harold actually say? He suggested there was a need 'to review the present state of Anglo-Persian relations.' He examined the tripartite role in which British foreign policy had cast Persia: as a buffer against Soviet aggression and the spread of communism; as a rampart defending the western border of the Indian Empire; as a strategic base and source of oil to support British ascendancy in the Gulf. There was, he suggested, 'a prevailing uncertainty' in British policy. It was 'illogical and confused' and needed clarification. The Shah's actions in closing the Soviet border had weakened the economy of the northern provinces and, paradoxically, driven them into increasing dependence on illegal Russian trade and illicit Russian money. Elsewhere, the army was in a state of mutiny; the tribes were in revolt; the entire government machine was corrupt and incompetent. In these circumstances, 'the policy of creating a stable and self-dependent Persia, capable of maintaining herself unaided, must be regarded as somewhat chimerical.' But Harold reserved his strongest criticism for the Shah, whom he doubted had 'the intellectual or moral calibre necessary for his high functions'. The Shah was 'secretive, suspicious and ignorant... wholly unable to grasp the realities of the situation or to realise the force of the hostility which he has aroused.' His 'internal policy is apparently to discredit all possible rivals' and his foreign policy 'to bribe his enemies and to abuse his friends.' Britain's policy of good relations and non-intervention was not yielding positive results. Britain was increasingly unpopular and Russian influence was strengthening. The implication was that

Loraine's efforts over the previous five years had been wasted and British policy misguided. And yet, Harold ended with his own illogical conclusion, stating that he did not 'for one moment advocate any change in the policy at present being pursued'; he was merely doubting 'its productive value.'[18]

Like *Byron* and *Swinburne*, this despatch may well have suffered from Harold's habit of over-rapid composition. Lancelot Oliphant wrote a covering minute which accompanied the despatch up the chain of command to Sir William Tyrrell and the Foreign Secretary, describing it as 'not altogether logical.' If Harold did not agree with the basis of British policy and did not think it would be effective, then why did he not advocate change? Whether, as Oliphant also claimed, the despatch was 'unduly alarmist' is quite another question.[19] On the face of it, the evidence was there. No one could deny that the country was in a state of constant, if sporadic, upheaval, or that corruption was rife. The Shah himself went on whisky and opium binges. His ministers were all terrified of him. His first reaction on hearing of the Khorasan revolt had been to strike his Court Minister, Teymourtash, round the face. And this same Teymourtash had been on 'secret' missions to Moscow, sounding out the price of Russian support. It was the lack of secrecy surrounding these missions that had stimulated the sudden wave of pro-Russian and anti-British feeling which Harold had detected and communicated to the Foreign Office. Yet neither Oliphant nor Tyrrell were prepared to countenance this questioning of a policy which Loraine had implemented and they had loudly endorsed.

Austen Chamberlain's reaction was both different and more intelligent. He disagreed with Harold over the value of 'good relations' which he saw as a prerequisite for the achievement of British policy goals. He disagreed about the Shah, whom he believed (correctly as it turned out) had the capacity to survive. But what Chamberlain glimpsed was that Harold had written the kind of speculative paper that he would have written when in London and removed from the actual practice of diplomacy. Now, of course, Harold was part of the practice he was analysing, and his criticisms were seen as partial, even, in some quarters, self-promoting. Chamberlain's assessment of the situation was absolutely clear: 'If I were Mr Nicolson I would feel discouraged not to receive a reply. If Mr Nicolson were a fool I should remove him. As he is certainly not a fool, I infer that, away from daily contact with us, our intentions are not as clear to him as to us. Let us make them clear.'[20] The fact that Chamberlain's recommendations were ignored – Harold received neither a formal reply nor any clarification of government policy – suggests a personal quality to the dispute. Tyrrell, we know, had never cared for Harold; Oliphant had been open and helpful to date but his attitude changed, quite possibly as a result of discussions with Loraine. Certainly, Loraine took the whole matter personally and thought Harold guilty of ingratitude.

Official communications between Tehran and London were sent by diplomatic bag and took at least ten days to make the journey, so Harold could not have expected a considered response for at least a month. In the event, it was with the arrival of Loraine's successor, Robert Clive, at the beginning of the November, that he discovered the degree of criticism which his despatch had aroused. His reaction, as so often when criticised, was at once defiant and immature. In a letter to Raymond Mortimer, he ranted that he had 'merely tried to tell the truth & diminish some of the cant in which we endeavour to hide our impotence & lack of purpose ... [but] they don't like the truth at the FO. They like to be told that everything is going quite splendidly.'[21] Harold as rebel is never convincing. This was the man who would later tell the House of Commons, 'I thank God that I possess the Foreign Office mind.'[22]

By the beginning of October, the mornings were becoming chill and the evenings darker. Harold gave the order to close up the Gulahek compound and move the Legation back to Tehran. This depressed him. He enjoyed the rhythm of life at Gulahek, the outdoor life and the ability to go for long rides on the magnificent Bay Rum, which he had bought from Loraine. Winter meant long, dark evenings when he would miss Vita that much more. He also knew that he would soon have to give up his position and powers as Chargé, which added to his depression.

Robert Clive and his wife, Magdalen, arrived on 5 November. Harold drove out to Karaj on the Qazvin road to meet them. They had a picnic lunch by the roadside and then drove in convoy on towards Tehran. As they swung into the Legation Compound, the whole staff, lined up in full uniform, came to the salute or doffed their caps in a mirror image of Loraine's departure. Clive shook hands with everyone and moved into the Minister's quarters which Harold had just vacated. Harold was surprised to find himself resentful at having to give up the reins of power and, at the same time, ashamed at such resentment. He returned to his yellow brick house by the gate.

Clive could not have been more different from Loraine. Although distantly related to Clive of India, he did not regard his ancestry as a matter of importance. In life and in dress, he was broadly conventional and formally correct, but where Loraine was vain and ponderous, Clive was intellectual and analytical. Harold, who had been dreading the arrival of someone he might dislike, was hugely relieved and, for the few months they worked together, they got on well without ever being close. With Magdalen Clive, things were different – at least initially. Harold began by being unusually censorious: he disliked her voice ('a sort of brave whine'); the way she called Clive 'Daddy'; and her meanness, which was 'simply terrifying'. By Christmas, however, he had changed his mind, having, rather oddly, predicted that he might in the letter which originally detailed his dislike.[23]

Clive's first duty on arrival was to tell Harold that he would not be receiving a reply to his despatch and that Tyrrell and Oliphant did not appreciate or agree with his pessimistic views. Yet before the end of the year, Clive was reporting to the Foreign Office that he agreed with Harold. His first interview with the Shah was marked by a barefaced lie about the purpose of Teymourtash's recent visit to Moscow – which the Shah claimed was to finalise a fisheries treaty. He made the correct noises about friendly relations with Britain, but in such a graceless manner that Harold concluded he had been on an opium binge. Worse was to follow. The Shah agreed to recognise the sovereignty of Iraq, but the next day attached impossible conditions to the offer. He reneged on a contract to allow Imperial Airways aircraft *en route* for India to land and refuel on Persian territory. He raised yet more difficulties in order to stall debt repayments to Britain. He even arranged to have a member of the *Majlis* shot. Loraine's house of cards was already wobbling.

> By the end of 1927, however, it became clear to the British in Tehran that Reza Shah 'is one thousand times worse than Ahmad Shah in his love of money and land, and in the short two years that he has been proclaimed Shah, he has amassed a huge, huge fortune.' Eventually, the Foreign Office turned to share Nicolson's assessment of Reza. By 1932 they referred to him as 'a dull savage of the sergeant-major type,' and a year later a 'bloodthirsty lunatic.'[24]

Time would prove Harold right on the main issues. Time would also have dealt with the reaction in the Foreign Office to his despatch – which was a question of ruffled feathers rather than a career-damaging furore – but he was not prepared to wait. With the arrival of the news that his views had aroused criticism in London – and also, perhaps, with the arrival of Clive as Minister – Harold's attitude to life in Tehran seems to have changed. Political issues feature less in his diaries and correspondence, while books and literature, although always present, suddenly feature more.

He wrote appreciatively of *Passenger to Tehran*, which he thought was '*absolutely first class*' because there was 'nothing second-hand' about it: 'all those emphatic landscapes have been given a personal interpretation.'[25] He was genuinely excited by *The Land*, which had been published on 30 September. It was not just the fact that Vita was receiving immense public recognition, but the poem itself. 'I don't mean to exaggerate,' he wrote, 'but it has added a pleasure to my life.... Of course naturally I want it to be a public success. But intrinsically I don't care. I simply know that it *is* part of English literature.'[26] Virginia Woolf, accurately, saw *The Land* as the product of a 'natural traditionalist,'[27] which, of course, is precisely why it appealed so strongly to Harold. It also worked for him because his responses to the natural world, sharpened by his experiences in Persia, were so often mediated through literature, so he would gallop on Bay Rum while shouting out passages from *The Land* to the wind across the Persian plain. Some of the *aperçus* in his letters – 'why is a fine autumn morning more *silent* than a fine spring morning?'[28] 'the sound of a dry leaf pattering on a tin roof, the trail of smoke against the umber plain'[29] – suggest a sensitivity which may owe something to his immersion in the poetic world of Vita's poem.

The Land led him on to other modern poetry. He read Osbert Sitwell; he read the poems as well as the novels of Thomas Hardy; he read T. S. Eliot and admired his intellect; but he reserved his greatest praise for the work of Paul Valéry which he not only enjoyed for itself, but also because it sparked all sorts of theories and ideas about the relationship between poetry, economic prosperity and national prestige. He also developed an idiosyncratic, but at the same time assertive, appreciation of Omar Khayyam and Fitzgerald's translation which he considered should have been more openly homosexual. It was not possible 'seriously [to] imagine that the tulip-lipped, cypress-waisted moon-faced *tapettes* of the quatrains [were] anything better than little bugger-boys from the bazaars.'[30] There was nothing new in Harold reading poetry and writing to Vita about it, but there was a sense of renewed interest, a new urgency in the way he wrote.

At the same time, Harold was clearly restless and discontented, more so now than in the summer of 1925 before it was suggested he go to Tehran. He seems to have lost confidence in himself and his abilities. He convinced himself that Vita would find him boring after her immersion in the highbrow society of Virginia and Bloomsbury. When he finished *Some People*, he chose to send it to his usual publisher, Constable, rather than the Woolfs' Hogarth Press (Leonard Woolf had suggested they might publish something by him) because he felt they would regard it as insufficiently serious. Even then, he told Michael Sadleir at Constable that he was 'a little ashamed of the book.'[31] He told Clive Bell it was 'idiotic'[32] and his parents that it was 'silly.'[33]

Another incident which sheds light on Harold's state of mind coincided with the new Minister's first official reception for the Legation's Persian contacts. Harold's spaniel, Henry, had had to be put down and Harold, a life-long dog lover, was understandably upset. But when he heard that Henry's body had been thrown on the rubbish heap outside the Russian Embassy next door, he 'absolutely saw red' and was, in his own words, 'transfigured with rage.' His anger was such that it frightened his servant who was 'sent ... out with lanterns and a man to rescue that poor little corpse and bury it decently. ... It is things like this,' he concluded, 'that show one what savages these people really are. I walked back to the Reception, and looked at all those polite frock-coated people with a feeling of loathing.'[35] An Englishman's sentimentality about dogs is something few other nationalities can comprehend, but the uncharacteristic intensity of Harold's anger and his utter, unqualified condemnation of all Persians suggest a classic case of expatriate stress.

And then, on 21 November, he turned forty. Always sensitive to age, it was, he decided, 'a black day.'[35] 'I simply hate it,' he wrote to his parents, 'All that I care for is youth and energy and striving.'[36] When it came to the end of the year and his customary review of the preceding twelve months, he was no happier, noting that he had put on weight and lost a lot of hair. All in all 1926 had been 'a bloody year.'[37] Looked at dispassionately, the only real reason for such a verdict can have been his fall from grace with the Foreign Office.

32   Return

Vita left London for her second visit to Tehran on 28 January 1927. This time the journey would take only ten days. She was going via Moscow, travelling with Dottie Wellesley and Leigh Ashton, the expert on Chinese art who later became Director of the Victoria and Albert Museum. In Moscow, where Vita took the opportunity to visit Lenin's mausoleum and file past his embalmed corpse, they were joined by Gladwyn Jebb's sister, Marjorie, and a Miss Elgood who was going to join the Legation staff as a secretary. The party left Moscow early on 2 February 'in an over-heated train with hermetically sealed windows,'[1] arriving nearly three days later at Baku. They boarded a Caspian steamer, which reached Bandar-e-Anzali, the port of Resht, on the morning of 6 February. Harold was on the quayside waiting for them, having spent two days driving up from Tehran, the second day through a snowstorm.

Once again, Harold and Vita were overjoyed to be reunited and the whole party drove in two cars back to Tehran via Qazvin. Vita spent the journey happily rediscovering the beauty of the Persian landscape – 'it seemed from the first as though I had never been away.'[2] Within days of arriving in Tehran, she received the news that *The Land* had been awarded the prestigious Hawthornden Prize. It was public recognition of her status as a poet: Harold was delighted, as was Vita herself, though she knew that Virginia and Bloomsbury would not approve. There was horse-riding; there was sight-seeing; but Vita's happiness did not last. By her account, Harold seems to have bounced back from his black mood: being the man he was, reunion with Vita and the company of Dottie and Leigh Ashton was probably enough to cheer him up. It was Vita who, before the month was out, was depressed by the 'fear of Hadji continuing in diplomacy. The FO says he will have to come back in Sept. for another year. God help us! I had expected to find him disgusted with exile and social duties, but it is quite the contrary.'[3] Her reaction was to mobilise her Bloomsbury allies. To Raymond Mortimer, she wrote: 'we'll see what we can do to keep Harold in England, though he's being very stubborn about it so far – and more determined than ever to be an Empire-builder.'[4] And to Virginia: 'I can't bear there to be a third year of this business. But Harold is in a very Empire-building frame of mind. Enormous skill will be necessary to get him out of it.'[4] It is not clear what, in practical terms, she meant by Harold's Empire-building frame of mind, but it is clear that the fundamental divergence of opinion, which had always existed between them, about the value of Harold's work as a diplomat had come to the surface.

Vita was in a mood to apply silent pressure and, according to her biographer, 'her silences were thunderous.'[5] Harold crumbled. On 12 March, there appears in his diary the much-quoted passage:

> Wake up in the morning with conviction that I shall chuck the diplomatic service. I had been fussing and worrying about this problem for months, and then this morning I woke with a calm and certain conviction as if it had come to me from outside. Write to Cadman by bag asking him to give me a job.[6]

This does not ring quite true. He had been dissatisfied and stressed ever since Clive's arrival and news of the Foreign Office's reaction to his despatch, but this is the first mention of leaving the Diplomatic Service. The new element can only have been pressure from Vita, based on her apparently intensified dislike of diplomatic life.

> The Union Jack floats languidly over the guard house, a flute player passes in the street, at midday the muezzins let out a yell. There, across the way, are the Consulate and the Chancery, with all their paraphernalia of government – providing security for us who doze in the sun and speculate on subtleties....You can't imagine – you who collect letters six times a day out of the wire mouse trap at the foot of your stairs – you can't imagine the enormous importance of THE POST in this place. It is the only thing which punctuates our otherwise eventless weeks. Thus the servant rushes in with a beaming face to say 'The post has come!' ... The post has come; that is, there has been no storm in the Caspian; the ship has not been wrecked; the motor has not gone over a precipice; the pass has not been blocked by snow; the bridge has not been carried away by a flood. The post has come![7]

But if Harold was prepared to write to Sir John Cadman, Chairman of the Anglo-Persian Oil Company, then her battle seemed won.

A posting to the Legation in Tehran in the 1920s normally lasted for three to four years with a period of home leave in the middle. Harold had been in Tehran for some sixteen months and his leave was due. The original plan had been to leave with Vita at the end of March and to return in September. Now it seemed, he would leave with Vita but not return. In Tehran, at least, Harold did not keep his intentions secret. He told Clive, who, in his own particular reserved manner, rather than saying a formal goodbye, wrote an affectionate letter of farewell which was handed to Harold on his departure. He told his Legation colleagues, who saw him off, and he told his household, including Taghi, who cried and hid in the house as Harold drove away. But he did not tell the Foreign Office.

The Nicolsons left Tehran at dawn on 23 March, together with Dottie Wellesley and Marjorie Jebb. They travelled in two cars – a Dodge driven by Vita and Harold's dilapidated old Ford, which was piled high with luggage and driven by Garne, the English chauffeur. With Garne was Harold's valet, whose name, variously spelt Bogher or Bagh'er, was 'unless very carefully pronounced ... apt to arouse horror and dismay among the members of the British colony.'[8] Their departure from Persia, however, was by an extremely circuitous route. Harold, as a student of the ancient world, wanted to see the ruins of Persepolis and of Pasagardae, the capital of Cyrus the Great. They drove south, through Isfahan towards Shiraz, dogged by breakdowns, accidents and primitive or eccentric accommodation, but it was worth it. Both cities left indelible images in his mind. In particular, his first sight of the tomb of Cyrus – a white, limestone box with a pitched roof, like a bathing hut, set on a stepped pedestal, isolated on its plateau but surrounded by wild asses idly grazing on wild thyme – was a moment he would never forget.

The party returned to Isfahan by way of the half-ruined town of Yazd-e Khvast which hung spectacularly over the edge of a gorge. Harold's Ford suffered a terminal collapse along the way and had to be abandoned. From Isfahan, Dottie and Marjorie Jebb returned directly to Tehran and to England, but Harold and Vita were now joined by Gladwyn Jebb, Copley Amory from the American Legation, and Lionel Smith, from the Ministry of Education in Baghdad. Jebb brought with him the proofs of *Some People* which had arrived in the diplomatic bag after Harold's departure. This provoked another brief crisis of confidence. 'They read like babbling idiocy,' he wrote in his diary, revealing that he still saw the book as a collection of essays rather than as a whole.[9] James Lees-Milne suggests he was about to destroy the proofs there and then; in *Twelve Days in Persia*, Vita states that he was about to send a telegram cancelling publication; it barely matters. What is clear is that he was still in a state of mind to overreact. Vita talked him down, but he still insisted on transferring the 'responsibility' for publication to her.[10]

Jebb, Smith, and Copley Amory were to accompany Harold and Vita on the second stage of their exit from Persia – which was more adventurous, more romantic, and very much Vita's idea. She wanted to search for wild flowers along the so-called Bakhtiari Road, which meant walking approximately a hundred miles through the Bakhtiari Mountains from the small town of Shalamzar, south-west of Isfahan, to the oilfields near Masjid-i-Suleiman (Masjed Soleyman). On 3 April, the five Europeans plus three Persian servants set off for Shalamzar, by car – a journey which took fully nine hours. The next day they walked. Vita's *Twelve Days in Persia* tells the story in detail. It was a genuinely adventurous journey: the only written record of the area dated back to 1840 and parts of the surrounding country were completely unmapped. The landscape was magnificent: there were snow-capped mountains, savage gorges, worryingly unstable bridges, and grassy open plains. They found all sorts of wild flowers and the bird life was spectacular. They got wet and cross in the rain. They slept in heavy, brown tents. They passed ruined caravanserai and villages built of mud and straw. They ministered to sick villagers. They met holy men and beggars. They received hospitality from local officials and from the nomadic Bakhtiari and Tekhani tribes. Harold, despite his experience of riding and camping around Tehran proved ill-equipped and ill-adapted for this kind of adventure. He wore London suits and thin-soled office shoes, and he had brought no waterproof or overcoat. Worse, he was apt to become irritable or depressed when things became difficult – 'Then it comes on to pour with rain and I have only a flannel suit on. A terrible feeling of despair descends on me. I say that I loathe the Bakhtiari mountains and wish I hadn't come.'[11] He enjoyed the experience in retrospect but was only too happy to return to the 'joys of civilisation.'[12]

Towards the end of the eleventh day, they sighted a distant column of smoke. Smoke, their guide told them, meant 'the Company', as the Anglo-Persian Oil Company was known throughout the region. On the twelfth day they descended to the Plain of Guighir and spent the evening with Sardar Zaffar, the leader of the local tribe, who lived in a tent, but was able to offer them presents of tinned peaches and had Company cars at his disposal: 'Civilisation and the wild were meeting.'[13] The next day, it was all over. They were met by Ronnie Balfour, an artist and illustrator who had stayed at Long Barn in the past and had obtained a job with the Company on the strength of Harold's recommendation. They were driven off, along tarmac roads, through the oil fields, past the huge storage facilities at Ahvaz, to Abadan where the Company operated the world's largest oil refinery. The contrast was extreme. They slept that night in beds in a Company bungalow – luxurious but bookless and soulless and surrounded by a scrape of English garden. Harold was once again the Counsellor from the British Legation. He toured the new gas plant, feigning both comprehension and interest. He met the British Consul and held meetings with Company officials, who, after years of effectively ruling the whole region, were beginning to be worried by a new assertive and interfering attitude on the part of the Shah's government. Harold listened and promised to pass on their views. The one thing he was hoping for, the offer of a job, did not materialise.

At the time, Harold was left with the impression that his letter to Sir John Cadman had either not been taken seriously or not been acted upon. In fact, as James Lees-Milne reveals, Cadman had been interested enough to ask for a confidential approach to be made to Sir William Tyrrell, but Tyrrell had 'absolutely vetoed the idea' on the grounds that Harold was 'too valuable to be spared.' Once back in England, Harold got to hear of the veto but not the reason behind it – a failure of communication which could only have added to his distrust of both the Foreign Office and its Permanent Secretary.

In Abadan, their party broke up. Jebb and Copley Amory returned to Tehran, while Harold and Vita began their long journey back to England, accompanied as far as Baghdad by Lionel Smith. Harold's final departure from Persian soil came when he stepped on board the Company's river steamer which took them slowly up the Shatt al-Arab as far as Basra. From Basra, they took the train to Baghdad. From Baghdad, where they had to wait for a couple of days for seats to become available, they took the Nairn convoy's northern route to Damascus and Beirut. Pausing in Beirut, they took time out to visit two more ancient ruined, cities: Palmyra, on the western edge of the Syrian Desert, and Baalbek in Lebanon's Bekaa Valley. They travelled by train down the coast of Palestine and across to Alexandria, where they took passage with Messageries Maritimes directly to Marseilles. Train to Paris and then to Calais, a channel ferry, a train from Dover and they reached Victoria Station in the late afternoon of 5 May, whereupon – in one of those moments which can only be understood in the context of Harold and Vita's particular relationship – Vita went to stay with Dottie Wellesley and Harold with Raymond Mortimer.

It was a time of reunions and of great emotion. Vita's letters had contained regular news of Ben and Nigel, their doings and their development, and Harold had written to them both during his absence, but it was quite a different matter seeing them for the first time in eighteen months. Ben, now nearly thirteen and at Eton, kept his mouth open all the time. Nigel was ten and grubby. In the manner of fathers reunited with their sons, Harold took them out for dinner at a restaurant and then to a West End cinema. He went round to Cadogan Square to see his parents, but, wisely, kept quiet about his desire to leave the Foreign Office. It was when he returned to Long Barn with Vita and the boys for the weekend that emotion really overcame him. He was overwhelmed by the excitement of being back home and was suddenly and violently sick – though at the same time intensely happy.

Private life was happy, but the shadow of the Foreign Office hung over him. He had failed to get a job – though apart from his letter to Sir John Cadman, it is not clear how hard he tried – and so could not resign, which meant that he had to tell Lancelot Oliphant that he was not prepared to return to Tehran. The news was not well received and was certainly more damaging to Harold's career and his image in the Foreign Office than any fall-out from his mildly controversial, if ultimately accurate, despatch. It was mid-October before his future in the Foreign Office was settled, so for five months during the summer of 1927 Harold was living in a state of uncertainty.

As when he was out of love with the Foreign Office in the summer of 1925, his response was to concentrate on the other strands of his life. Certainly, he picked up the threads of his social life with remarkable speed. Long Barn that summer received a long list of old and new friends – Raymond, Dottie, Eddy Sackville-West, Jean de Gaigneron, Ethyl Smyth, Clive Bell, Leigh Ashton, Gladwyn Jebb. There were visits to Oxford to call on his old friend Gosse, and on Sligger Urquhart, whom he had not seen for some time but with whom he still maintained an intermittent, literary correspondence. Harold and Vita also stayed with Robert Bridges, the Poet Laureate – an experience Harold was disinclined to repeat partly because the food was poor and the drink inadequate, and partly because of Bridges' long dissertations on philosophy, metre and prosody. There were dinners with Clive Bell and Leonard Woolf with whom he discussed everything from homosexuality to imperialism. There was a trip to Richmond in Yorkshire with a party which included the Woolfs and Eddy Sackville-West to see a total eclipse of the sun, an experience which Harold described as 'like some dark wing flashing across the earth.'[14] There was a week spent in Paris with Raymond, who had rented one of the small houses making up the Villa Seurat in Montparnasse – which at the time was home to a remarkable artistic community, including the writer, Frank Townsend, sculptors Arnold Huggler and Chana Orloff, and a number of painters such as Marcel Gromaire, Pierre Bertrand and Jean Lurçat. It was on this trip that Harold met François Mauriac and also employed a young man from Reims to come over to England to teach Ben and Nigel French. This was Maurice Couve de Murville, who became eventually became Prime Minister under de Gaulle. Harold was clearly determined to make up for the intellectual aridity of Tehran – though it is worth noting that he and Raymond also visited the *Folies Bergère*.

Although Harold might not have acknowledged it at the time, the most important event of the summer of 1927 was the publication, on 23 June, of *Some People*. Although he knew that the idea behind the book was original,[16] he never really understood what he had achieved and never really came to terms with its success. He enjoyed the money it brought in – £278 in July 1927 alone, when a three-bedroom house cost only £350.[17] He enjoyed the praise it drew from friends and critics, but while he enjoyed praise, he did not covet popularity. He disliked it when *Some People* – it was usually the 'Arketall' chapter – was the first thing people thought of when he was introduced. Harold wanted to be taken seriously: the classicist, the traditionalist, the Victorian in him, saw recognition as something to be gained for serious books of serious intent, not for something lightweight or trivial, which is how he regarded *Some People*. And his concern was justified insofar as the book did affect his reputation: it did lead people to question whether he could be relied upon, whether his discretion could be trusted.

Initial reviews were mixed, the level of criticism or praise seeming to reflect the relationship of the paper or journal concerned to the British establishment. The *Daily Telegraph* was very unsure and unhappy about Harold's intentions; *The Times* was reserved. The *New Statesmen* understood that Harold was writing a kind of autobiography and compared him to Strachey; the *Nation* (though this was Clive Bell) was full of praise. Whatever the papers said, *Some People* was modern – its structure, its narrative style, its combination of satire and seriousness were all new – and it was accessible; and the public responded, both in Britain and in the United States where the book was published simultaneously. It was an immediate success. It sold. Virginia Woolf, who had been privately critical of Harold's previous books, wrote to say how much she had enjoyed it and that she had laughed out loud. She did not mention the book's commercial success directly, but made it clear that the Hogarth Press would be interested in a sequel: 'You must write another, and for goodness sake, send it to the Wolves.'[18] Her review in the *New York Herald Tribune* was equally positive, suggesting that Harold had broken new ground in the art of biography, though, characteristically, she attributed Harold's informal approach to his subject matter in *Some People* to the example of Lytton Strachey's 'new school'.[19] Cyril Connolly told Harold that *Some People* was 'an important work.'[20] And the book has continued to receive praise. Even Edmund Wilson, in his 1944 attack on Harold's works and character, excepts *Some People* from his strictures.[21] Vladimir Nabokov once claimed that the influence of *Some People* was like a drug which he had to fight against – 'Harold's only comment was that *Lolita* would never have the same influence on him.'[22] John Betjeman praised it; so did Anthony Powell; and today *Some People* remains Harold's most popular book.

At the time, the criticism that *Some People* attracted was not, for the most part, based on literary criteria. The issue was discretion and taste. Absurd though it may seem now, there were many who were ready to consider Harold's character sketches ungentlemanly. Harold's father objected to the book until it became known that King George V had read it and laughed out loud. Naturally enough, Harold's severest critics were in the Foreign Office. He had known from the first that

> There just might be trouble ... [the] sketch of the Lausanne Conference ... is technically a violation of the Foreign Office rule against publishing anything to do with one's official experiences. But I don't care: the book is not in the least malicious or indiscreet.... The only thing that the FO may resent is that I laugh a good deal at people and they may be afraid it will be their turn.[23]

He was right. It was the ridicule and the laughter that caused offence. There can be few precedents for a Secretary of State for India writing to a Foreign Secretary on literary business, but Lord Birkenhead did write to Austen Chamberlain 'expressing the hope [*Some People*] would not prejudice Harold's career in any way.'[24] Tyrrell managed to sow concern and uncertainty by telling Harold publicly that he did not find the book indiscreet – which, of course, suggested that others did. Most outraged of all was Loraine, to whom Harold felt obliged to write a letter apologising for his lack of taste and judgement – and it is true that the picture of 'Lord Bognor' is particularly trenchant. Harold also expressed regret about the 'Titty' chapter, which was written in the belief that Arthur Hope Vere, on whom Titty was based, had died leaving no close relatives, whereas he was survived by a sister who was apparently much upset by the depiction. But in reality, there was little to apologise for and such fuss as the book created quickly died away.

Much attention has been paid to the models for the characters who feature in *Some People*, rather less to what the book says about Harold himself. Nigel Nicolson has observed that

> the book is a record of how the precocious Harold gradually grew up, how he rejected in turn Empire-worship (Miss Plimsoll), the public-school spirit (Marstock), self-conscious aestheticism (Orme), bland affability (Titty), and arrogance (Malone), finding on the way other delights like literature, travel, friendship, work and, what he never specifically mentions, sex.[25]

Some People undoubtedly describes a progress. The question, given the layers of irony woven into the book, is how seriously we should take the portrait of Harold that emerges. The Nicolson of 'Professor Malone' is a successful, slightly self-congratulatory schemer. Yet one is left with the underlying sense that the revenge for which he works so hard is ultimately pointless. The Nicolson of 'Arketall' is a functionary – efficient, correct, subservient, but in the last resort colourless when compared to the eccentric and drunken Arketall. In 'Miriam Codd', he deploys his superior education to crush the hapless Mrs Codd, but in doing so, he not only exposes his selfishness, but is also drawn to acknowledge his 'Kipling feeling' and identify with the bluff, English Colonel.[26] These two characteristics refer back to the first chapter, 'Miss Plimsoll', bringing the book full circle and undermining Nicolson's final triumph as he enters Persia alone. The composite picture is of a young man (the Nicolson of 'Miriam Codd' gives the impression of being younger than the thirty-eight Harold was when he travelled to Persia) who is struggling to maintain his balance in an adult world. At one point, he says 'I have no achievements – and but few recreations.'[27] One cannot take the words at face value – they are said to Miriam Codd by an already ironically-drawn character – but there is a glimpse of the real Harold to be had here. *Some People* is a distorting mirror and proves that Harold was as willing to ridicule himself as he was to ridicule others. Nonetheless, beneath the ridicule, there remains a sense in which 'Nicolson's' insecurity, his lack of balance and the hollowness of all his triumphs, reflect the real Nicolson's view of himself.

33 Berlin

The summer of 1927 was one of the wettest on record and the administrative processes of the Foreign Office ground slowly onward. Harold was active and happy enough down at Long Barn with the boys during their summer holiday, but he lacked purpose and direction. The Woolfs helped by asking him to write something for their recently-established 'Hogarth Lectures on Literature' series and he threw himself into researching what became *The Development of English Biography*. It was not until the middle of August that he received a letter from Walford Selby saying that the Foreign Secretary had agreed to his not returning to Tehran. The bad news was that he would lose his rank of Counsellor and, as there was no suitable role for him in the Foreign Office, he was requested to go to as First Secretary to the Legation in Budapest.[1]

Suddenly, roles were reversed. Harold wanted to resign, but Vita counselled caution. Why? She had been pressing him to leave the Foreign Office. He had shown with *Some People* that he could make money by his writing. Perhaps, having spent the last few months together, she saw how much he still needed the world of politics and diplomacy. Certainly, professional uncertainty made Harold realise how much he needed her. He wrote to her that he felt 'a wrench, a cleavage, a real gulf and gap – just because you go away for one night.'[2] In the end, he chose to argue. He was not, he told Selby, a good choice for Budapest. Because of his work in Paris, he was too closely associated with the Treaty of Trianon and drawing up the current borders of the Hungarian state, both of which the government of Miklós Horthy was seeking to revise. Moreover – and one has to accept that in 1927 this was a serious consideration – in Budapest his inability to dance or to shoot would put him at a social disadvantage.[3]

While the Foreign Office considered, Harold vacillated. He felt he really could resign and not feel bitter about it. It might be difficult financially but 'I have Vita and the boys, and that is more a compensation for anything material.... I have my energy and my talent for writing.'[4] But then again, he decided that all he really wanted was to be in the Foreign Office. He and Vita worked each other up blaming Tyrrell for the way Harold was being treated. Writing to Owen O'Malley, a colleague in Peking who was equally disenchanted with his career, Harold again rehearsed his argument about being in disgrace because of his Persian despatch and the Foreign Office's reaction to it. It was true that Tyrrell did not want Harold in the Foreign Office because he knew that Harold did not like him – Walford Selby made that much clear when he and Harold lunched together in London at the end of September – but the issue of the despatch was in the past. The real problem was that Harold had refused to complete his full tour of duty in Persia. Such a decision was bound to affect the Foreign Office's view of his stability and reliability and, in this respect, Harold was in large measure the author of his own misfortune. Selby, put in the invidious position of go-between, seems to have done his best to plead Harold's case, but to no avail. Would Harold consider Rome? Harold said he would consider it, but Sir Ronald Graham, the Ambassador in Rome, rejected the idea for fear that Harold would laugh at him. Harold had predicted that *Some People* might cause others in the Foreign Office to fear his mockery – although this was the only occasion when the book had a demonstrable impact on his career.

The crunch came in mid-October, more than five months after his return from Persia: 'Get a letter from Walford Selby saying he can't manage to send me to Rome, but will I please go to Berlin at once.' It was a decisive moment. Harold knew that if he turned down Berlin, he would be asked to resign. 'There are few things I would dislike more – and it is bad luck on Vita. But I won't chuck it if I can possibly help. So I accept, gloomily.'[5] Why did he accept? Was it a moment of self-assertion? He had listened to Vita in Tehran, but now – after five months away from it – had he simply come to conclusion that diplomacy was what suited him? Or, now he was back in England, was staying in the Foreign Office simply the line of least resistance? During those five months, he does not seem to have explored any real alternative. He certainly accepted with bad grace: he was, quite exceptionally, rude to his parents when they expressed their approval of his decision. He knew Vita would not understand, however hard he tried to excuse himself or explain: 'Little one, do not be angry with me for being so obstinate and selfish.'[6] Yet the fact remains that Berlin did reinvigorate him. Only a week after arriving (and in total contrast to what he had said before going to Persia), he was writing to Vita, 'I love foreign politics, and I get them here in a really enthralling form.'[7]

When Selby said 'at once', he meant it. Harold embarked on an accelerated round of preparations. There were suits to buy, briefing calls at the Foreign Office to make, farewells to say. He went to visit Edmund Gosse. He had a dinner with Clive Bell and Raymond where he met T. S. Eliot, whose poetry he had learnt to appreciate in Tehran. He delivered the manuscript of *The Development of English Biography*, which he had written at enormous speed, to the Woolfs. He said goodbye to his parents and to the boys. On the morning of 23 October, just nine days after receiving Selby's letter, Vita drove him to Liverpool Street Station where they said another wrenching farewell. As ever, in the strange manner of their relationship, Vita had written a letter, full of love and reassurance, for him to read on the train. Harold replied at once, posting his letter before he boarded the ferry at Harwich. From the Dutch port of Flushing, he took the overnight train, arriving in Berlin's Friedrichstrasse Bahnhof the following morning.

He spent his first few nights in Berlin in the Bristol Hotel on the Kurfürstendamm before moving into his predecessor's apartment at 24 Brücken Allee on the other side of the Tiergarten. The flat was 'so ghastly it is almost funny,'[8] but at least it was comfortable. When Vita made her first visit that December, they spent several days looking for alternatives, but discovered that all Berlin apartments were equally ugly – huge, gaudy, gilt-encrusted public rooms built for show, with tiny bedrooms tucked away and giving onto smelly inner courtyards. In the end, they decided it was best to stay in Brücken Allee and improve the place by importing a shipment of furniture from Ebury Street.

For anyone interested in European politics in 1927, Berlin was the place to be – and Harold, with his immense experience of European politics and security issues, must have felt that here, unlike Tehran, the centre of things was not far away. Germany was in the process of domestic reconstruction and international rehabilitation. The government was led by Wilhelm

Marx, in his second stint as Chancellor, but the key figure was Gustav Stresemann, the Foreign Minister. It was Stresemann's stature as an international statesman that was responsible for the confidence that the Weimar Republic enjoyed among the wartime Allies. In 1923, briefly combining the offices of Chancellor and Foreign Minister, he had seen Germany through the crisis of hyperinflation. In 1924, he had counselled acceptance of the Dawes Plan, which agreed a framework for the payment of reparations. In 1925, he led the negotiations leading to the Locarno Treaties, which appeared to offer an acceptable framework for European security. In 1926, under his guidance, Germany applied for and was admitted to membership of the League of Nations and in 1927 the Control Commission, set up to supervise disarmament, was disbanded. Stresemann believed that recovery and rehabilitation could best be achieved by implementing the terms of the Versailles Treaty and obtaining the cooperation of the Allies. The fact that he received the Nobel Peace Prize in 1926 is evidence that, internationally at least, his efforts were understood and appreciated. Domestically, however, there were many who resented his compliance. In March 1927, the ban on Hitler speaking in public had been lifted and that same month there had been clashes between his supporters and communists on the streets of Berlin, but few people realised the danger that Hitler posed. Communism was generally regarded as a greater threat.

Germany was enjoying an economic miracle, and while the momentum of economic recovery was maintained, Stresemann and the Weimar Republic were safe. Unemployment had fallen; inflation was low; factories were booming; and, in Berlin and the big cities at least, people had money in their pockets. In fact, the miracle was unsustainable: it was being financed by American loans; its proceeds were used to pay Germany's reparations; and there was already a gulf opening up between the prosperous cities and the countryside where an agricultural depression was beginning to hit prices and jobs. Yet at the end of 1927 the fragility of the situation was not immediately obvious.

One person who did foresee trouble was Sir Ronald Lindsay, the British Ambassador. Since the end of the First World War, Lindsay had served in Washington, Paris and Constantinople and was well versed in the political and economic equations on which European security rested. Lindsay was tall, dignified and moustached. Harold found in him a sympathetic intelligence. Neither correct like Loraine nor distant like Robert Clive, Lindsay was excitable and curious, at times academic and at times practical, but always perceptive.

British policy towards Germany, which was to dominate Harold's working life over the next two years, was essentially a balancing act. The First World War had left Britain with an immense burden of debt, and reparations were seen as a way of easing the burden on the British economy. For very practical reasons, therefore – and, in some quarters, for moral ones also – Britain did not wish to see Germany default on its reparation payments. At the same time, the British Government was acutely aware of the dangers of unrest in German society and the risk of a return to economic anarchy and hyperinflation. Lindsay and the British Embassy staff held out a carrot in the form of broad-based support and the prospect of Germany's international rehabilitation; but they also waved a stick, maintaining the pressure required to ensure that reparations continued to be paid. Lindsay's particular concern was to bring forward the date for the final evacuation of Allied troops from the Rhineland, which he believed would remove a major source of irritation between Germany and the Allies, but at the end of 1927 his main worry, and the subject of intense correspondence with the Foreign Office, was his belief that inflationary pressures would return and the economic bubble would burst.

Berlin was at the centre of things in another way as well. Reaction to Germany's militaristic past and to defeat in the First World War had led to an explosion of cultural and intellectual activity. The middle years of the Weimar Republic were a period of extraordinary vitality with Berlin at its heart. At the time Harold arrived, Einstein was teaching at the Kaiser Wilhelm Institute of Physics, and Max Planck held a Professorship at the University of Berlin. Hindemith was teaching at the Berliner Hochschule für Musik, and Schoenberg at the Prussian Academy of Arts. Klemperer was conducting at the Kroll Opera, and Furtwängler at the Berlin Philharmonic. Brecht and Weill were working on *The Threepenny Opera*, which was premiered in August 1928. Max Reinhardt was managing the Deutsches Teater. Fritz Lang was working at Universum Film (1927 was the year of *Metropolis*). Marlene Dietrich had just taken her first major film role in *Café Electrik*. Outside Berlin in Dessau, just an hour by train, Walter Gropius was directing the Bauhaus, where the teaching staff included Paul Klee and Vassily Kandinsky; while down the road in Leipzig, Heisenberg was formulating his uncertainty principle. The list goes on.

Parallel to this explosion in the arts and sciences was a surge of interest in mysticism and the occult and an outburst of decadence, reflected in Berlin's nightlife. Harold's initiation into this aspect of the city's life came less than a week after his arrival when he was taken to the Eldorado, which, although new at the time, was soon to acquire legendary status. The blonde and blowsy women in sequined dresses sitting at the bar turned out to be men, while the men in tweeds and plus fours turned out to be women. In his letter to Vita, Harold claimed he 'was rather shocked and disgusted; these people danced together.'[9]

The Eldorado was just one of many such establishments. They favoured subdued lighting, heavy drapes, gilt mirrors and lush, gaudy decoration. Many would have a particular gimmick – telephones between tables; themed costumes (slaves and gladiators, eighteenth-century French costume, whips and leather); a menu featuring overtly sexual descriptions of the food and drink on offer. All sexual tastes were catered for, but there was a strong emphasis on homosexuality and transvestism. These were the clubs and bars which served as the model for Christopher Isherwood's Kit-Kat Club in *Goodbye to Berlin*, and which attracted both native Berliners and tourists from the rest of Europe and the United States, including many of Harold's visitors.

The British Embassy was (and still is) on the Wilhelmstrasse in the administrative heart of Berlin – the same street as the Chancellery, the Chancellor's official Residence, the Foreign Ministry and the Finance Ministry. It was a solid, neo-classical building, originally built for a German railway magnate in the 1860s, which had become the Embassy in 1874. Arthur Nicolson had been one of the first generation of diplomats to work there. It had closed during the war and reopened in 1919. Sir Neville Henderson, British Ambassador in the years leading up to the Second World War, described the interior as 'musty, cramped and dark.'[10] Certainly, Harold felt no affection for it.

His initial enthusiasm for being back in the swing of foreign politics did not last. He was fascinated by the complexity of the situation and its importance for the future of Europe. He judged, perceptively, that the experience of losing the war had not fundamentally changed the Germans; that they were suffering from 'self-pity' and a lack of confidence, but not 'self-reproach.'[11] But he soon felt underemployed. All he was doing was receiving messages from Whitehall for onward transmission to the German Foreign Ministry and then sending the reply back to the Foreign Office.

One of Harold's first trips out of Berlin was to Kuchelna, just across the Czech border, to visit Prince Lichnowsky, who had been the German Ambassador in London in 1914 and whose bedroom Harold had visited in order to retrieve the incorrect declaration of war. On that occasion, his last words had been, 'Give my best regards to your father.' Harold was touched that thirteen years later his first words were to inquire after Lord Carnock. The estate at Kuchelna was large and the manner of life almost feudal. The villagers doffed their caps when Lichnowsky passed. The house had a number of suites for visitors. There were hothouses and walled gardens. There were liveried footmen, two chefs, and a small army of servants. Yet Lichnowsky recalled that before the war he had been almost immeasurably rich with castles and estates scattered across Germany. The war and its disastrous consequences haunted him. He could talk of little else. Sir Edward Grey had acknowledged how hard he had tried to prevent war, but Lichnowsky believed that had he been in Wilhelmstrasse instead of London he could have succeeded. He was a frail, pathetic figure, living in the past and fed by that very self-pity which Harold had identified as a national characteristic. It was a sad encounter, made worse by Harold's sympathy for his wife, who bore the brunt of his obsession and was 'acutely miserable ... always falling desperately in love with people who are frightened by her passion and run away.'[12] Lichnowsky died less than three months later.

Harold had been in Berlin only a month and was still settling in when Vita made her first visit. He met her on the platform at the Friedrichstrasse Bahnhof and took her to the Brücken Allee apartment. She loathed the city on sight and it is not hard to see why. Harold recognised that, while life in Tehran had appealed to his love of nature and offered him an outdoor lifestyle, Berlin offered no such compensations. Berlin was an urban centre which imposed an urban lifestyle. It was a city for work and for certain forms of play, but nature and the great outdoors were not on offer. There had been periods in Vita's life when she had been out and about in London society, but her social horizons were contracting. These days she preferred the smaller, more intimate gatherings of Bloomsbury and its connections, or just being alone with Virginia or Dottie – and she spent an increasing amount of time in the garden at Long Barn. She had never been a city girl, but now, in her mid-thirties, she was beginning to display the attitudes which would develop into the rural reclusiveness of her later years. Berlin, as a consequence, was hell. She stayed just a week before returning to spend Christmas at Knole with Ben and Nigel. Harold remained in Berlin.

Berlin had been forced upon Harold, but he had hoped that its comparative proximity to England and to Long Barn would make the whole complex issue of his work and Vita's attitude to it easier to cope with. He had even hoped for a mad moment that she might be willing to accompany him, but it was not an idea that ever crossed her mind. She played down her hostility to Berlin because she did not want to make his life more difficult or appear to be criticising him for accepting the posting, but when he showed any signs of ambition or commitment, she was horrified. 'Harold now says he wants to be an Ambassador,' she wrote to Virginia in February 1928, 'but can you see poor Vita as an ambassadress? I can't.'¹³ And then, a few months later, responding to a letter from Harold, 'I was pl ng d into despair this morning by your letter saying that you might have to stay in Berlin till 1930.'¹⁴ There may have been times when she chose not to raise the issue, but the reality is that her hostility to his chosen career never slackened. She saw diplomacy as something that changed or distorted him – 'I *don't* like perfect diplomatists, no I don't. I like Hadji's soft collars – and his laughing eyes – not that white cardboard round his neck and that severe expression.'¹⁵

In the event, Harold found Berlin more difficult to cope with than Tehran. Communications were better, which meant that because he knew more of what was going on at Long Barn or in London, he missed it more and was increasingly homesick. There was now a telephone at Long Barn and from Berlin it was possibly to speak to Vita and the boys five hundred miles away – which he did, but ending the calls upset him so much that they decided to use the telephone only in emergencies. As things turned out, however, the fact that he could return home in less than twenty-four hours was to be a major advantage.

34 Fathers

In his diary, Harold's end-of-year review concluded that 1927 was 'not a bad year.'¹ It had been a year of professional recovery. He had finally recognised that his refusal to return to Tehran was responsible for his disgrace with the Foreign Office, but by that time he also knew Sir Ronald Lindsay had recommended that he be reinstated in the rank of Counsellor. Lindsay was far more influential than Loraine – when he left Berlin in July 1928, he did so in order to take over from Tyrrell as Permanent Under-Secretary – and his recommendation meant that re-promotion was just a matter of time. This effectively closed the Tehran incident and Harold could feel that he had made up any lost ground. Twelve months later, he declared 1928 to be 'one of my worst years. A horrible year.'² The reasons for the verdict were personal rather than professional. Shortly after New Year, while Vita was still at Knole, Lord Sackville was taken ill with influenza. Influenza became pneumonia; pneumonia became pericarditis, and by 19 January he was so ill that Vita sent a telegram asking Harold to come home, but begging him not to fly. (Throughout their lives together, Vita was always opposed to Harold travelling by plane. She equated flying with suicide.) Harold responded immediately. He was fond of his father-in-law, not least because of the support Lord Sackville had given him during the difficult and uncertain period of Vita's affair with Violet. He also understood – perhaps better than anyone else given the similarities between mother and daughter – something of the difficulties Lord Sackville had experienced in his relationship with Lady Sackville; and saw Lord Sackville's apparent indolence and reluctance to take decisions as part of his reaction to those difficulties. Harold arrived at Knole late in the afternoon of 20 January. For the next few days, he sat with his father-in-law by day, sometimes reading out loud from the sick man's favourite books, and by night he slept in the next room in case there should be a crisis. Lord Sackville seemed to rally, but the improvement did not last. On 27 January, Harold, Vita and Olive Rubens were told by Lord Horder – King George V's doctor and the country's leading heart specialist – that there was no chance of a recovery. Lord Sackville died shortly after midnight.

Harold took charge of the situation, dealing with the undertakers, issuing death notices and overseeing all the administrative details. Lord Sackville's funeral service took place on the last day of January in the chapel at Knole. His heavy, lead coffin was then taken to the Sackville vault at the Church of St Michael and All Angels in the small village of Withyham, where the Sackvilles had been interred since the sixteenth century. Harold felt he had lost 'a great friend.'[3] He returned, exhausted, to Berlin, taking with him a brown and white cocker spaniel, which, like his previous dog, he decided to call Henry.

The death of Lord Sackville precipitated a double crisis – in Vita herself and in her relations with her mother. Vita had loved her father, but her relationship with him was bound up with her relationship with Knole. From her earliest days, she had known that she would not inherit the great house; that it was only the accident of her being born a girl that stood in her way. Now that her father was dead, her relations with Knole were severed. Knole would pass to her Uncle Charlie and his American wife, and then in due course to her cousin Eddy. It was no longer her family home. She could no longer wander the courtyards and corridors at will, drawing strength or solace from the house and its history. Her relationship with Knole, as James Lees-Milne points out, was essentially a mystical one: she belonged to it and, spiritually at least, it belonged to her. Uncle Charlie was a straightforward military man who had served in India, Burma, the Boer War and the Somme and risen to the rank of Major-General. He would do his duty, but he did not really want to spend the rest of his life as custodian of Knole.

And Eddy, by his own admission, had no real feeling for the place. Uncle Charlie gave Vita a master key so that she could walk in the gardens, which was kind but did not answer her need. Going back to sort out her father's things was traumatic. Harold saw and understood what was happening, but not even he could enter into the emotional complexities of Vita's relationship with her ancestral home. There was nothing he could do except offer intelligent sympathy. In the end, the person who did most to help Vita manage her reaction to the loss of Knole was probably Virginia Woolf.

Orlando seems to have had its origins in Vita's letters to Virginia describing Moscow in the grip of the icy Russian winter. It grew out of Virginia's intense fascination with Vita's lineage, her aristocratic bearing and confidence. Vita becomes Orlando, a young favourite of Queen Elizabeth I with a vast, ancestral stately home, who lives through the centuries without growing old. He follows a Princess to Russia, goes as Ambassador to Constantinople, metamorphoses into a woman, and returns to the ancestral home where she lives, encountering various key historical personages along the way, right up to the (then) present day, when she achieves literary success with a poem called *The Oak Tree*. Nigel Nicolson has described *Orlando* as 'the longest and most charming love letter in literature.'[4] It is certainly an original work, both satire and biography, blurring the boundaries between fact and fiction. Orlando's change of sex allows for a satirical but serious commentary on the difficulties faced by women in a man's world and also, for those in the know, for an oblique commentary on lesbian and bisexual relationships. If there is a problem with book, it is quite simply that it relies too much on being in the know, on the in-jokes of Bloomsbury and its connections. Yet neither Harold nor Vita saw this. They saw a book which, while a parody, while mocking, and while a fantasy, juxtaposed Vita and Knole across the 400 years that her family had lived there. If Vita could not join the list of those who had earned their place in history by custodianship of Knole, she could achieve immortality through a literary identification with her ancestral home. Harold was quite explicit in encouraging her to see 'a book in which you and Knole are identified for ever ... a unique consolation,' which he and Vita understood but Virginia probably did not.[5]

The book had been conceived and was well under way before Lord Sackville's illness – Vita and Virginia spent part of the autumn of 1927 wandering around Knole picking out details and taking the photographs which were an integral part of the identification between Vita-Orlando and the great house – but it became an important factor in helping Vita cope with the aftermath of her father's death. She saw it as a unique contribution to English literature and felt 'infinitely honoured at having been the peg on which it was hung; and very humble.'⁶ Harold was equally delighted. He did not mind being mocked as Marmaduke Bonthrop Shelmerdine, Esquire, a sea captain bound to do his seafaring duty which took him away from his wife. As ever, the thing he feared most when the book was published in October 1928 was any public revelation of his or Vita's homosexuality, but the book's satirical nature and its esoteric qualities were sufficient to obscure or at least confuse those not already in the circle of knowledge. Moreover, there were other sources which threatened to expose their sexual preferences in a more direct and more damaging way.

The first of these was Roy Campbell, the young South African poet. On one level, this was a classic case of generosity repaid with scorn. Shortly after returning from Persia, Harold and Vita had met Roy and Mary Campbell in their local Post office in the village of Weald. Feeling sorry for the Campbells, who had two young daughters and only £20 a month while Roy sought to establish himself as a writer, the Nicolsons had offered them, rent-free, the use of the cottage in the grounds of Long Barn. The situation became complicated after Harold's departure for Berlin when Vita began an affair with Mary Campbell. Roy found out and, although he was himself sleeping with Dorothy Warren, was furious. There were knife-wielding rows, drinking binges, reconciliations, and threats of divorce, suicide and public exposure. The situation quickly became untenable and in June 1928 the Campbells left Long Barn for the south of France. Whether on sexual grounds or because he disliked receiving their charity, Campbell conceived a deep resentment against the Nicolsons which eventually found expression in wounding attacks and sexual innuendo in his 1931 poem *The Georgiad* and again in his 1934 volume of autobiography, *Broken Record*.

The second potential source of exposure and the second major crisis which faced Harold and Vita in the aftermath of Lord Sackville's death was Lady Sackville, still known in the family as BM or Bonne Mama, though her behaviour did not match the description. Lady Sackville's pride had never fully recovered from the breakdown of her marriage and her decision to leave Knole. Now, she claimed that Vita and Olive Rubens had kept her from Lord Sackville's side during his last illness. She took angry exception to the obituary Harold placed in *The Times*, in particular the statement that Lord Sackville had been happiest during his last years – which she interpreted to mean after their marriage had broken down. While this was quite possibly true and a not unreasonable interpretation of what Harold had written, it was not precisely what he had meant. She began a campaign of vindictiveness and intimidation. She wrote abusive letters to Vita and when Vita tried to mend the breach she threatened to cut Vita's allowance.

She accused Vita of stealing her pearls, making a huge scene in the offices of Pembertons, the family's London solicitors, and screaming that she hoped Vita would be run over and killed. She demanded the return of money, jewellery, carpets and furniture – including the furniture Harold had shipped out to Berlin. She threatened openly to ruin Harold and Vita's lives. She began spreading rumours about them and even telephoned the Foreign Office in an attempt to find out how much Harold earned. Vita was wounded and upset, but she realised that her mother was ill and felt sorry for her. Under other circumstances, Harold, too, might have been sympathetic, but he was fiercely protective of Vita and both angry and apprehensive on his own account. If Lady Sackville made malicious accusations to the Foreign Office, it would not matter that she was ill and deluded: it would be a classic case of no smoke without fire. Back in Berlin, he was sufficiently worried to take pre-emptive action and discuss the matter with Lady Lindsay whom he found very approachable and sympathetic.

Vita spent March in Berlin. She still disliked the city but being there at least meant that she was not at home grieving for her father or worrying what her mother would do next. At the end of the month, in what was their first experience of joint literary recognition, they made a quick trip to Copenhagen: Harold had arranged for Vita to give a lecture on 'Some Tendencies in Modern English Poetry', while he spoke on Byron. Then, as soon as they returned to Berlin, it was time for another agonising farewell: Vita took the overnight train from Friedrichstrasse in order to be back at Long Barn in time for the boys' Easter holidays.

Harold continued to find work unabsorbing and took to spending time in the bar of the Adlon Hotel, literally round the corner from the Embassy on Berlin's famous Unter den Linden. The Adlon, one of Europe's best-known and most luxurious hotels, was a place where journalists gathered and where gossip and rumour – as well as drink – flowed freely. It was a place where Harold met new people, picked up information and enjoyed the convivial atmosphere. Harold was an active social drinker – particularly fond of red wine, but not averse to beer or whisky, or, indeed, to brandy or cognac after a meal. There were undoubtedly many occasions when he drank a bit too much, and not a few occasions when he had a hangover the next morning; but his drinking was never excessive or obsessive, and it never got in the way of his work. It was simply a function of a lively, outgoing, social personality.

Outside work, Harold's life in Berlin became a succession of visitors: some stayed at his flat, some stayed elsewhere; some were interesting, some were irritating; some intellectually stimulating, some attractive. Raymond, of course, was a welcome guest at Brücken Allee, but Eddy Sackville-West irritated Harold by fussing and by dressing in an eccentric and sometimes camp manner. Allen Leeper, who had been Curzon's Private Secretary at the time of Lausanne, came to stay with his wife, Janet. Harold was fond of the Leepers – he and Vita had attended their marriage in 1921 – but their solidly Christian view of the world was at odds with his dislike of organised religion, and their concept of sexual morality was not one he could, or was in a position to, share. The Leepers were followed by Gerald Berners and Gladwyn Jebb, a much more amusing combination. It was through Gladwyn Jebb that Cyril Connolly was introduced in Harold's Berlin orbit. Connolly was only twenty-five, charming, intelligent and entertaining, but already something of a sponger. He flattered Harold, who enjoyed his company and responded with characteristic generosity, either not realising or not caring that Connolly could be extremely two-faced, praising *Some People* in public while condemning it in his diary as 'a most unpleasant book.'[7]

Others passing through the city were Maynard Keynes and his wife, Lydia Lopokova, on their way back from Russia; Sinclair Lewis, the American novelist, author of *Main Street* and *Babbitt*; the increasingly eccentric Ethel Smyth, who wore a tricorne hat which made her look like Frederick the Great and sought to persuade German promoters to put on a concert of her music; Vincent Sheean, last seen in Tehran; Noel Coward, whose energy and talent fascinated, though Harold decided he was essentially a 'bounder'. Unsurprisingly, some of Berlin's floating population provided Harold with just the kind of sexual adventure that had been so lacking in Tehran. Chief among these in his first few months in Berlin was the young Ivor Novello, who was enjoying spectacular success as an actor, singer and composer. Theirs was a short-lived and thoroughly enjoyable fling. Harold, with his life-long inability to manage money, was impressed by Novello's ability to earn and he was also more than a little star-struck.

> I like him so much. He is completely unspoilt by success, and absolutely thrilling about his life. He has contracts which will bring him in £35,000 by November next year. He calculates that if his health lasts he should be able to make about £500,000 before he is forty. He ... says it makes one feel such a fool to be worth so much money simply because of one's profile.[8]
>
> He *fascinates* me. It is an entirely new world.... He *is* so lovely and friendly.[9]

Harold's re-promotion to Counsellor came through in May 1928, just before he returned to England for a month's leave. This time, he chose to come home via Paris and Dieppe, where he took the ferry to Newhaven. Vita was waiting for him and they drove in glorious late spring weather through the Sussex and Kent countryside to Long Barn. Harold was delighted to be home, though his return was a little overshadowed by news of the death of Edmund Gosse and the need to put together an obituary for the *Nation*.

Harold's last communication from Gosse had been a letter of congratulation following the publication of *The Development of English Biography* at the beginning of the year.[10] Although written at speed and although the central distinction between 'pure' and 'impure' biography (that is, between objective biography and biography which is designed to prove a point) strikes one as a little simplistic, *English Biography* is a far from negligible work. It demonstrates Harold's ability to master and synthesise an extraordinary mass of material in a very readable form. It was never going to be a bestseller, but it certainly contributed to the growth of Harold's literary reputation and to this day it remains a key reference on websites and for academic courses dealing with the art and practice of biography, particularly in the United States.

English Biography aroused sufficient interest for Harold to be invited to give a radio talk on the subject. Radio was very much the new medium of the age. The British Broadcasting Company had been formed in October 1922, and experimental broadcasts from station 2LO had begun the following month. Harold had heard his first ever radio broadcast in May 1923 and now entered a studio for the first time. As it happened, Vita had actually beaten him to it, giving her first broadcast a few weeks earlier. It was on the same day as her appalling row with her mother at the solicitors' office and she was still shaking when she sat down in front of the microphone, but she acquitted herself well. Harold was characteristically excited at the prospect of a new experience. His talk also went well and a transcript was published in the *Listener*, but there was no hint of the immense influence that radio would have on his later career. Demand for his magazine articles, however, continued to grow: before leaving Berlin, he had written two articles at £100 each for *Nash's Magazine* and now he wrote another for the same fee. All this pointed to the possibility – which Vita made very sure that he saw – of a life beyond diplomacy.

Another pointer to the future was the presence at Long Barn, during Harold's leave, of Oswald Mosley and his wife Cynthia, or 'Cimmie', the daughter of Lord Curzon. Harold had first met 'Tom' Mosley, as he was known, when he arrived at the Foreign Office in 1918, having been invalided out of the army because of an ankle injury. They had maintained an intermittent acquaintance over the intervening years, but the relationship was to strengthen as Mosley grew politically more influential. Other visitors included Sinclair Lewis, who had just married the influential American broadcaster and journalist, Dorothy Thompson; Vincent Sheean; and, of course, Raymond. Then it was time for another difficult farewell. This time, Harold was left in tears at Liverpool Station, while Vita lost herself driving round the City because she kept thinking about their constant separations.

Sir Ronald Lindsay was due to finish his term as Ambassador and return to London in July, leaving Harold as Chargé d'Affaires for a second time in his career. The prospect of running a major Embassy, if only for a couple of months, revitalised his interest in his work. He had already met Stresemann and dined at the Foreign Minister's official Residence, just a short distance down the Wilhelmstrasse from the Embassy. In one of his *Spectator* articles during the Second World War, he tried to recreate the atmosphere of those dinners and convey the generous character of his host. Stresemann was a family man who liked to have his family around him. He was generous with his wine, his food and his cigars. He never sought to deny or disguise his origins – his father had been a publican and he himself had started life as the Manager of the Saxon Union of Chocolate Manufacturers.

> He would be boisterous, indiscreet, shy and arrogant, gay and gloomy....
> He would speak of art, about which he knew little; of music, about which he knew much; and about politics, which he approached with subtle rage.[11]

The problem was, as Harold knew, that Stresemann was dying of cancer and there was no one of comparable stature to replace him.

The other great figure of the Weimar Republic in those years was the President, Paul von Hindenberg,[12] whom Harold met during the round of farewell meetings, lunches and dinners which preceded the Lindsays' departure. In 1914, at the age of sixty-six, Hindenberg had been called out of retirement and had immediately crushed the Russian armies at the Battle of Tannenberg. After the War, he retired again, but was called out of retirement a second time in 1925 to become President. He was now over eighty and the object of immense respect, even veneration, on the part of the German people. Harold fell for the old man's charm: he 'is an old darling; he has a trick of raising his eyebrows and laughing like a schoolboy.' Characteristically, he responded to Hindenberg as a historical figure, a link between the Weimar Republic and Germany's imperial past. Hindenburg had known Lord Carnock in the years before the First World War; 'he remembered the embassy before it was an embassy ... he had gone up in the first Zeppelin.' Hindenberg was a 'splendid old man,' but whatever else Hindenberg represented, it was not the future.[13]

As in Tehran, Harold was called upon to make a farewell speech on behalf of the whole Embassy to his departing chief. Berlin not being Tehran, and Lindsay not being Loraine, Harold did not feel obliged to take such an imperial line and this time, mercifully, there was no Raymond to criticise. Then, on 1 July, the Lindsays left and Harold found himself in charge.

Lindsay's departure coincided with a change of government: Herman Müller took over as Chancellor on 28 June. This meant an acceleration of the pace of work in the Embassy. Harold's task was to report to Austen Chamberlain and the Foreign Office the composition and policies of the new government. Up to a point, this was not too difficult: Müller's Social Democrats, having increased their share of the vote, remained the dominant party in the governing coalition and major changes of direction were unlikely. The main thing from a British point of view was that Stresemann, ill as he was, remained in control of foreign policy. Stresemann was a strong supporter of what was to become known as the Kellogg-Briand Pact, a somewhat idealistic American initiative which required signatory nations to renounce war as an instrument of national policy. The Pact, which was signed in Paris that August, would have lost all validity if Germany had decided not to participate. Harold's initial assessment was that the new government was the best that Germany could hope for given the available talent, and looked as if it might just have the ability to carry on the task of national reconstruction.[14]

During his period as Chargé, however, and in the months which followed, Harold began to see signs of change. Neither the apparent continuity of government policy nor Stresemann's heroic efforts to rehabilitate Germany internationally could obscure the fact that German society was beginning to fragment. Müller's Social Democrats were by far the largest party in the coalition, but he still needed the support of three coalition partners to command a majority – the German People's Party, the Catholic Centre Party and the German Democratic Party. From the first, the government was riven by internal disagreements as each of the parties sought to pursue their own interests. Moreover, anything the coalition did manage to agree or achieve was violently attacked by the Communists, who had also increased their presence in parliament, on the left, and by the German National People's Party on the right. Stresemann in particular, for all his international prestige, became a hate figure for both right and left, as well as for some inside the coalition, attacked for what was widely seen as his slavish adherence to the demands of the Allies and the terms of the Versailles Treaty.

What the results of the 1928 election did not reveal was the imminence of a seismic shift in German politics, which would see the rise of Hitler and his National Socialist German Workers' Party – soon to become known as the Nazi Party. The overall trend in 1928 showed a move to the left: Hitler's party polled only 2.6% of the votes and lost a couple of seats. Two years later, it would be a very different story. Towards the end of his life, reflecting on the vast difference between the pre-1914 and post-1945 world, Harold claimed that it was the journalists in the Adlon bar who first alerted him to the dangers posed by Hitler and the National Socialists; and he used the story as an example of the need for diplomats to seek out and maintain contacts outside the diplomatic world. At the time, he was sufficiently interested in what they had to say to make a trip to Munich to investigate and judge for himself. On his return he went to see the Papal Nuncio, Eugenio Pacelli (later Pope Pius XII), whose network of Catholic priests in Bavaria were also disturbed by what they had seen and heard of Hitler's growing influence.

From investigating the impact of National Socialism, it was only a short step to investigating the network of paramilitary organisations, veterans' associations and right-wing clubs – some overt, some clandestine – which had sprung up in Germany since the end of the war. Harold saw considerable danger here – not least because the government was doing nothing to curb such organisations, while the military appeared to be actively cultivating them. And the size of these organisations was worrying – by 1930, the League of Frontline Soldiers, or Steel Helmets, had 500,000 members.

Harold reported his concerns to the Foreign Office in a series of despatches, but there was nothing the British Government could do beyond watch and wait. Harold's thoughts on Germany at this period are best summed up in a letter to the Foreign Office dated 7 August 1929. The new Germany, he wrote, was not

> psychologically different from the old. There is, it is true, a strong current against militarism. But this current, which is largely due to the fact that militarism was not successful, is a current which flows in the same old river of German obstinacy and determination. It would take but a slight turn of the tide to set the current swinging in the opposite direction, and carrying with it all the flotsam and jetsam of the very third-rate Social-Democratic politicians.[15]

Fathers

Harold was right in that he saw how Germany might, and did, return to militarism, but he did not identify Hitler and the National Socialists as the catalyst. Few people did. At this stage, they were just one piece of the German jigsaw. By the time he left Berlin at the end of 1929, he thought differently.

Another significant factor in the German equation which Harold did not fully grasp until the end of his Berlin posting was the Jewish issue. This is important in that it raises the question of how far his personal views influenced his political judgement. That Harold held and sometimes expressed anti-Semitic views – views which from a twenty-first-century point of view are completely unacceptable – cannot be doubted. Throughout his life, he would attribute certain characteristics to the Jewish people he knew: that they were liars; that they were oily; that they were pretentious, arrogant and vulgar – and he might extend the characterisation to their art or their writing. It was a habit which became more visceral as he grew older; but neither in youth nor in age would he have dreamed of making his feelings public. To do so would have been unforgiveably rude, and Harold believed in good manners.

Harold's attitude was not uncommon in the years before the Second World War. Writers as diverse as Rudyard Kipling, Thomas Hardy and D. H. Lawrence; politicians including Ernest Bevin, Asquith, Beaverbrook and Winston Churchill: all have been accused of displaying anti-Semitic attitudes and making anti-Semitic remarks. So, too, have most of the Bloomsbury stalwarts: Clive Bell, Duncan Grant, Maynard Keynes and Virginia Woolf. This does not justify or excuse anything, but it does set the context. It may seem surprising that Bloomsbury, so concerned to inspect and analyse their attitudes to all aspects of life, should not have focussed on anti-Semitism, but it seems to have escaped their notice. Barbara Hardy, writing of Virginia Woolf, suggests that she 'participated in the unexamined anti-Semitism of the English middle and upper classes,'[16] and no phrase could better describe Harold's unthinking acceptance of the attitudes of his generation.

Later, after the Second World War, when the fate Europe's Jews was seen in a wholly different context, he might seek to clarify his position in a statement which, however indefensible, is at least honest – 'Although I loathe anti-semitism, I do dislike Jews'[17] – but in Berlin in the 1920s, he simply felt an instinctive dislike for Jewish people. There were exceptions, of course – the most notable being Lali Horstmann, a rich, intelligent Berlin hostess who had had her portrait painted by Augustus John. She was charming. Her husband, Alfred, known familiarly as Freddy, was head of the department in the German Foreign Office dealing with Britain. As such, he was a natural interlocutor and point of reference for Harold, who soon became a regular visitor to their house in Tiergartenstrasse where he met many prominent Berliners and made many useful contacts. The house was full of expensive art which had been bought with Lali's money. She was a von Schwabach, a daughter of one of Germany's most wealthy banking families. By the late 1920s, most of Germany's banks were effectively controlled by Jews. Most of Germany's national newspapers were Jewish-owned. The arts and the entertainment industry were also dominated by Jews. Even the city's sex industry was predominantly a Jewish concern.

The eccentric Ethyl Smyth was one of Harold's visitors. She was intending to stage a concert in Berlin and he somewhat reluctantly hosted a lunch for her, during which she launched into a violent denunciation of what she called the Jewish Republic of Germany. This did not go down well with the guests – the Jewish author Emil Ludwig was present and the musical agency producing her concert was also Jewish – nor was it an original thought. The Weimar Republic was being widely characterised as Jewish. The surprising thing is that Harold does not seem to have seen the danger inherent in this situation, nor the possibility of a major anti-Jewish reaction.

Summer in Berlin was hot and grimy, so Harold rented a flat in Potsdam to be nearer to the lakes and countryside. It took less than an hour to get to the Embassy and it would be a much better place for the boys when they came to visit during their summer holiday. In the meantime, at the beginning of August, the new Ambassador, Sir Horace Rumbold, arrived. He came alone and stayed for just a week in order to present his credentials to President Hindenberg. He would take up his post properly in September. Nonetheless, Harold had to don a top hat, meet him at the station and shepherd him through the presentations and the formalities. Harold was again forced to admit to himself how much he enjoyed running an Embassy – 'I do *not* like Ambassadors arriving when I am in charge,' he told Vita. He knew Rumbold already – they had met at the Lyttons' in 1917 (the weekend when he contracted his venereal infection) and again during the Lausanne Conference – but he did not know him well. Rumbold was an immensely experienced diplomat who had served in Cairo, Tehran, and Tokyo as well as Vienna, Munich and Berlin, and spoke Arabic and Japanese as well as excellent German. Physically, however, he was short and rotund, and it was easy, on first acquaintance, to misjudge him. Harold appears to have done just that, coining the nickname 'Rumby' and describing him as a 'nice old bumble bee.'[18]

Rumbold disappeared until September. Vita and the boys arrived and they all moved into the Potsdam apartment for four weeks, until the boys had to go back to school. The issue of childcare during the summer holidays had already provoked a tense exchange of letters. Vita claimed she liked having them at Long Barn but did not like having to look after them all the time. 'Nor would you,' she added, somewhat provocatively.[19] Harold responded with a lecture on the need to accept one's responsibilities. Vita bridled – 'I should like to see you try it; you would be screaming by the end of the week.'[20] Given that Harold had already agreed to take as much parental responsibility as possible during the summer – hence the Potsdam apartment – it was not an entirely logical exchange, and Harold's contribution was definitely not tactful, but there may have been another explanation. Harold understood that Vita's rebellions against domesticity and what she saw as wifely duties were often associated with periods of new emotional and sexual involvement, and the summer of 1928 was one such period. Mary Campbell had just left for France, although she would reappear briefly in the autumn. Virginia continued to exercise an intensely powerful emotional pull – even more powerful because of *Orlando* – but she was not the sexual partner Vita needed. Vita's excursion into radio talks had brought her into contact with Hilda Matheson, who was in charge of BBC's Talks Department. Hilda was an independent woman, immensely capable and self-reliant, who could hardly have been more different from Vita. She came from a middle-class Scottish background – her father was a Minister – and had fought her way up, attending Oxford University (although women could not be full members of the university in those days), spending the war in British intelligence and then acting as Nancy Astor's Private Secretary following her election to Parliament in 1919. She and Vita did not become lovers until later in the year, but by July Hilda's influence was already in the ascendent. Harold's lecture on responsibility might just have been a reminder of the ground rules.

Harold spent as much time as he could with the boys, doing the things that fathers do with sons in the school holidays. They went to Berlin Zoo (another Jewish-owned concern) which, under the direction of Dr Lutz Heck, had become one of Europe's leading zoos. They also went to the cinema at the zoo: the huge, 2,000-seat Ufa-Palast am Zoo, operated by Universum Film. They swam in the lakes at Potsdam. But Harold was also in demand at work. Britain and France had concluded a Naval Agreement which, although designed to remove inconsistencies in their respective positions on arms limitation, appeared – from a German perspective at least – hostile to Germany. Harold was summoned to the Wilhelmstrassse to explain Britain's position. The Inter-Parliamentary Conference[21] was holding its 1928 meeting in Berlin. Harold had to make himself available for meetings and dinners and brief the British delegation which consisted of a number of important (and some self-important) MPs. Although busy, he was discontented. He was a messenger boy, a host, a besuited diplomatic representative, but his role had no real substance.

On 10 September, Sir Horace Rumbold returned and Harold surrendered control of the Embassy. Two days later, the Nicolson family left Berlin by car, motoring down to Leipzig, across country through the Thüringer Wald to Frankfurt, and then up the Rhine Valley, through to Koblenz and Cologne. The British army of occupation in the Rhineland was based on Cologne so Harold had official calls to pay. It was the first time the boys had seen him acting in his official, diplomatic capacity. They had supper in a restaurant on the quayside within sight of the great cathedral and the Hohenzollern Bridge. Then Harold took the overnight train back to Berlin, leaving Vita and the boys to take the train to Calais and return to England the following morning. The summer was over. Harold returned to the Brücken Allee apartment and to his duties as Counsellor.

The round of visitors, some interesting and some not, continued. In terms of friendship, the most important new contact was John Sparrow, who arrived in Berlin accompanied by Maurice Bowra. Both were young Oxford academics destined for successful academic careers and destined also to remain Harold's lifelong friends. John Sparrow, in particular, became as close to Ben and Nigel as he was to Harold. Eddy Sackville-West visited for a third time in less than a year, full of his new novel, *Mandrake over the Water-Carrier*, which neither Harold nor Vita could understand. Kathleen Drogheda turned up at the Embassy. She had been a young woman, married to the Earl of Drogheda, when Harold and Vita were courting and had attended their wedding. Now, she was married to a Spanish nobleman. With her was her son, Garrett Moore, 'who was our page at our wedding.... You can't imagine the charm and the beauty of that young man.'[22] Vita, whose senses were just as finely attuned to Harold's weaknesses as his to hers, warned him succinctly not to fall in love with Moore.

In terms of Harold's future, the most important visit of the autumn came in October when Ramsay MacDonald, in his capacity as Leader of the Labour Party, made an official visit to meet German leaders and speak to the Reichstag. MacDonald was accompanied by Tom Mosley. This was the first occasion when Harold's association with Mosley took on a professional character and he was impressed with Mosley's energy and determination to do something to revitalise both the Labour Party and British politics as a whole. Since his election as MP for Smethwick in 1926, Mosley's combination of charisma and intellect had made him the Labour Party's rising star; there were suggestions that, should the Party form the next British administration, he might even become Foreign Secretary. And if that did happen, he would be in a position to help Harold return to London and to the Foreign Office. This was Mosley's first visit to Germany in an official capacity and was to prove highly influential. Although his own morals were not beyond criticism – he was an active and unrepentant womaniser – he was shocked by the public sexual activity and the overt homosexuality he saw in Berlin, which he interpreted as evidence of deep, even irredeemable moral degradation. He was equally appalled by the muddled ineffectiveness of the German leadership, which he saw as unable to set social standards or change people's thinking. These were factors which would influence his political thinking and his response to the emergence of fascism.

Two days after MacDonald and Mosley's departure, Harold returned home for a month's leave, mulling over his discontent. One problem was that in the year he had now spent in Berlin, he had not written anything. There are a couple of references to something he calls *Peabody*, apparently a projected novel, but it seems to have been abandoned under the pressure of other events. Whatever plans he may have had for his leave were disrupted by his father's illness. Lord Carnock suffered from a form of progressive arthritis which had begun in the aftermath of his bout of food poisoning in 1894. In later years, he had become extremely frail and bent. He was also somewhat deaf. It was his heart, however, which failed him in the end. He had suffered a series of attacks in 1924, but now, nearly five years later and just past his seventy-ninth birthday, his body was simply worn out. His final days were correct and ordered. 'His mind,' Harold recorded, 'was vigorous and unclouded to the end.'[23] He knew he was dying. He said goodbye to his servants and his family, passed into a coma and died on the morning of 5 November 1928.

On his deathbed, Lord Carnock told Harold how proud he was of Harold's diplomatic achievements and how happy he was that Harold had decided to stay in the Diplomatic Service. Harold was deeply moved and the words added to the distress he felt at his father's death. It had been an understated father-son relationship, but based on genuine affection and mutual respect. While Lord Carnock was never a role model for his son, there is no doubt that Harold admired his father's achievements and saw in him a simplicity and a level of moral certainty which he himself could never hope to attain. At the same time, there is a sense in which Lord Carnock's passing set Harold free. When he had wanted to leave the Foreign Office before, loyalty and the wish not disappoint his father had been among the factors that had held him back. That restraint was no longer there. Lord Carnock also seems to have placed on Harold, rather than his two elder sons, responsibility for ensuring that Lady Carnock should be looked after and should not suffer financial hardship. It was an obligation Harold accepted and fulfilled – but it provoked more bitterness in his relations with Vita than almost any other issue.

Lord Carnock was a private man in a public profession: Harold's sister, Gwen, wrote that 'politics and his family were for him the only reality.'[24] The privacy he liked to maintain around his private life extended to the instructions he left for his funeral, which was principally a family affair. Yet that could not prevent widespread recognition of his professional achievements. Harold arrived back in Berlin on 17 November to find over sixty letters of condolence from current and former members of the Diplomatic Service, from British politicians of all parties, even from members of the German political establishment. Did this contribute to Harold's decision to write his father's life? Certainly, that decision was made immediately on his return to Berlin. The book was to be both a memorial and a personal tribute. By 10 December, Harold had not only written to the Foreign Office requesting permission – such a book would necessarily require access to official papers and would inevitably comment on the conduct of British foreign policy – but also received a reply from Sir Robert Lindsay encouraging him to go ahead. The letter contained an official caveat 'that he must not offend the Germans' but, tellingly, Lindsay also included a note from the Foreign Office Librarian, Stephen Gaslee, whom he had consulted, saying 'go ahead, and don't care a damn.'[25]

Harold now had a book to write, but he remained gloomy. Eddy was staying at Brücken Allee again, and Harold was glad of the company. He liked Eddy, but could not help being irritated by his behaviour at times. In particular, Harold disagreed with Eddy's self-indulgent attitude to the sexual freedoms on offer in Berlin and, at Vita's request, encouraged him to curb his promiscuity – although it has to be said that Harold's own cruising of Berlin's bars was not always as detached and restrained as he might have made it appear. Work remained unchallenging. Rumbold proved a pleasant man to work for, farsighted in his views on Germany, but not an inspiring leader. And Harold himself was no nearer resolving his dilemma over the Foreign Office. On his return, Vita had written almost angrily that

> It's simply sheer misery for me, these perpetual departures of yours; and that's the flat truth. You will never know what it is to me, or how senseless it all seems to one who has neither ambition (of that kind) nor any

sense of public duty.... Oh God, how I hate the Foreign Office, how I hate it with a personal hatred, for all that it makes me suffer.[26]

The problem was, of course, that Harold did have a sense of public duty but, if he were to accommodate Vita's wishes, he would have to deny it. He was cheered by the fact that Vita and the boys were coming out so they could have a German Christmas together, but that did not, in the end, change his verdict on 1928: it was 'not really a wasted year, but a dark one.'[27]

35 Decision

Nineteen twenty-nine was Harold's decisive year: the year in which he finally decided to leave the Foreign Office; the year which, if it did not actually shape, at least set the direction for the rest of his life. It began with thick snow and freezing temperatures, ushering in one of the worst European winters for a long time. Harold's preference at this stage was to return to London and to the Foreign Office. Vita had been pulling strings to this end with Lady Lindsay. Harold had bridled at this in an old-fashioned male manner – 'I won't have my career arranged by women' – but, according to Vita, he was only pretending to be cross.[1]

The first significant event of the year was the great Bloomsbury visit. On 17 January, an excited Vita met Leonard and Virginia Woolf at the Friedrichstrasse Bahnhof and took them to their hotel in the Prinz Albrechtstrasse, just round the corner from the Wilhelmstrasse. Two days later Vanessa Bell and Duncan Grant arrived with Quentin Bell, Vanessa's eighteen-year-old son by Clive Bell. Eddy Sackville-West was making yet another visit to Berlin but, because Vita, Ben and Nigel were all staying in the Brücken Allee apartment, he was obliged to rent a small apartment of his own. As James Lees-Milne suggests, 'the conglomeration of so many precious intellectuals in Berlin, in January, in the snow and slush, was perhaps asking for trouble.'[2] None of the surviving accounts suggest that it was a particularly happy week. Harold, of course, was in his element: he was used to living abroad; he liked having company; he knew his way around; and he spoke excellent German. He seems to have enjoyed meeting up with the rest of the party for lunches and dinners when his Embassy duties allowed. He was happy showing Virginia the sights of Berlin or walking with her in the Tiergarten. He enjoyed the long conversations over dinner with Leonard about the structure of the Diplomatic Service or the future leadership of the Labour Party. He was ready as ever to take the visitors on his now practised tour of Berlin's sleazy nightlife. And he seems to have been unaware of – or perhaps unwilling to acknowledge – the tensions among the rest of the party. Vita was simply happy to be with Virginia – 'you don't know what a difference your week here has made to me.... Formerly, the whole of Berlin was pure loathsomeness to me; now there are just a few places which are invested with romance.'[3]

The rest of the group were less happy. Leonard and Virginia were not natural travellers. They were concerned about spending too much money; Virginia was nervous when not accompanied by Harold or Vita; Leonard did not want to attend the meetings with political figures which Harold had arranged for him. Their English reticence held them back. Duncan Grant and Vanessa Bell were much more at ease outside England, but Vanessa seems to have been particularly unhappy and bitchy throughout the week. Whether or not she understood the relationship between Vita and Virginia, she clearly resented Vita's presence in the group, and was constantly critical of Harold. She saw him only as an establishment figure and could not, or would not, allow him any other qualities. She was perceptive enough to see that Eddy irritated both Harold and Vita, but reached the bizarre conclusion that Eddy was more intelligent than they were. It was an uneasy week.

Ben and Nigel returned to England on 22 January. Bloomsbury returned two days later. Vita stayed on. Harold remained gloomy. Had Vita hoped that Bloomsbury's presence in Berlin would remind Harold what he was missing by not being in London? If so, the tactic did not work. The visit may have relieved Harold's Berlin boredom for a few days, but, if anything, it emphasised his sense of separateness from Bloomsbury. A few weeks later, in March, when Vita suggested buying 37 Gordon Square from Vanessa Bell, Harold was firmly opposed to the idea. They were not part of Bloomsbury and did not want to be. He felt it would be unwise for them to do anything to suggest that they were.

His sense of unease about the future remained and was intensified by an encounter with Frau Stresemann, whom he had previously dismissed as vulgar and stupid. The occasion was a formal Embassy dinner – 'footmen in knee breeches; a sort of Suisse holding a silver topped pole which he banged on the floor every time the door opened; stars and ribbons.' Frau Stresemann was nothing if not direct: 'I know you think I am a fool,' she told Harold, 'but I'm not a fool, and I can tell you that you are wasting yourself *and* your wife on this idiotic profession.'[4]

The weather continued freezing – 'Harold says he shall die if he doesn't escape from Berlin,' Vita told Virginia – so in February they took a week's holiday in Rapallo on the Ligurian coast.⁵ The dining car of their train caught fire and had to be abandoned in Switzerland, but the Alpine scenery was magnificent: the waterfalls were frozen; there was mist in the valleys and sunlight on the peaks. They arrived on a warm evening and strolled by the sea under the orange trees and mimosas, but woke the next morning to snow and cold winds sweeping down from the north. The bad weather did not last. They moved out of their hotel, which they disliked, into a friendly *pensione*, and spent the week walking the rugged coastline and visiting the small fishing ports of the Portofino peninsula. Harold knew he had to make a decision at some point and Vita pressed home her advantage – indeed, she later apologised for nagging him – but the holiday enabled them to escape for a short while into joint fantasy. One day they visited the narrow, brightly-painted fishing village of Camogli and, in an echo of their honeymoon, spent the afternoon playing with the idea of buying a small castle perched on the cliffs above the village. The escape over, they returned to Berlin. Vita left almost at once for Long Barn with a tentative agreement that unless Harold could reach some kind of agreement with the Foreign Office about his future by August, he would resign.

In March, Sir Horace Rumbold asked Harold to undertake a lecture tour which would take him to most of Germany's major cities and last nearly two weeks. This was classic diplomacy and good man management. The fact that the Counsellor from the British Embassy in Berlin was lecturing on cultural issues – Harold's subject would be contemporary English literature – was bound to generate public and press attention. When not lecturing, Harold would have the opportunity to meet local politicians and other figures of influence and try to get some sense of what was happening in the provinces. Rumbold knew Harold was unhappy and uncertain about his future. In sending him off on a lecture tour, he was making the best of Harold's talents, giving him a task he would enjoy and which might just rekindle his enthusiasm for his profession. Harold crossed and recrossed Germany, lecturing twice in the Frankfurt area, then in Cologne, Munich and Hamburg. He concentrated on poetry, taking his audience from the classic poetic diction of Tennyson and Swinburne through to the complexities of T. S. Eliot. He also quoted from *The Land* along the way. He was a good lecturer, capable of entertaining and instructing his audience at the same time. In later life, when he was lecturing more frequently, he could occasionally misread the temper of an audience, but in Germany, where he was less formal in approach than most public speakers, his genuine interest in the subject came across and he was well received – even in Cologne, where he sensed that the audience did not quite follow his argument.

Exposure to Germany outside Berlin deepened Harold's understanding of the country and its culture. In Frankfurt, he was struck by the unutterable respectability of Goethe's early home in Grosser Hirschgraben and then impressed by the city's new, carefully planned and laid-out garden suburbs. In Cologne, he called on the influential Mayor, Konrad Adenauer, who was to become Chancellor of the German Federal Republic after the Second World War. Harold realised immediately that he was in the presence of a remarkable man, but identified 'the manner of a Dictator' in his behaviour.

> It is not a manner which I like, but it is a manner which once seen is never forgotten. I feel I could adopt it at once.... One of the main stunts is to create an atmosphere or rush and flurry around one and to be oneself as calm as the hollow in the centre of a typhoon. Another stunt is to talk to one's subordinates in a very gentle voice but with a sudden flash of a shifty eye.[6]

In Munich, he lunched with the publisher Kurt Wolff, who had effectively discovered Kafka, and he had tea with the great novelist Thomas Mann. Both were optimistic about Germany's future while Stresemann lived. Both were eventually forced to flee to the United States to escape Hitler's Germany.

There was a sad footnote to Harold's visit to Munich. He stayed with his Aunt Clementina, his father's elder sister. Over forty years previously, before Harold's birth and in a world where Kaiser Wilhelm I still reigned and Bismarck was still his Chancellor, she had married the widower and railway functionary, Wilhelm Beemelmans. It was his account of entering Paris with the German army during the Franco-Prussian War which had captivated Harold's five-year-old imagination. Now, poor, elderly and alone – her husband long since dead and her only son killed fighting for the German Empire in 1914 – ostracised by her neighbours because of her English origins, and sustained only by her intense religious faith, Clementina Beemelmans lived on in Germany because she had nowhere else to go. Harold felt desperately sorry for her but was powerless to help. She was a figure left over from a bygone age and would have been even more out of place in her once-native England than she was in her adopted Germany. She died two-and-a-half years later in December 1931.

Despite being struck down by a severe cold in the latter stages of his lecture tour, Harold felt it had been a success, and so did his Ambassador. Once back in Berlin, however, it was quickly forgotten as the endless series of visitors, official and unofficial, once again took control of his life. The Duke and Duchess York – the future King George VI and Queen Elizabeth – passed through Berlin on their return from a royal wedding in Sweden. They stayed at the Embassy and Harold was called upon to help entertain them. He fell heavily for the Duchess' charm – 'a delightful person, incredibly gay and simple' – but was less impressed with the Duke – 'He is just a snipe from the great Windsor marshes.'[7] H. G. Wells, much revered at the time as a social commentator and populariser of scientific ideas, came to deliver a lecture at the Reichstag. It was, Harold concluded, 'rather a disaster' because no one could hear a word that was said.[8] Dinner at the Adlon afterwards, hosted by Albert Einstein, was much more enjoyable. Einstein held a string of important positions – he was Director of the Kaiser Wilhelm Institute for Physics and Professor at University of Berlin – but he immediately endeared himself to Harold by his modesty and his air of total childish innocence and bewilderment. Unofficial visitors included Sybil Colefax, Somerset Maugham and his long-term partner Gerald Haxton, and the fashion designer Edward Molyneux, first met in Paris and now both famous and wealthy.

Meanwhile, Brücken Allee was becoming a mixture of social centre and refuge for a number of Harold's younger friends, to whom he acted as adviser, mentor and – all too often – banker. Raymond, who returned to Berlin in April 1929 and stayed in Brücken Allee, did not altogether approve and it is easy to understand why. No one could object to the presence of Christopher Sykes, who had arrived in Berlin to work as an Attaché at the Embassy. He was the son of Mark Sykes, with whom Harold had worked on the Balfour Declaration, and, although only twenty-one, was already showing signs of a distinctive and original talent – so much so that Harold told him that he was too gifted for diplomacy. Sandy Baird, however, was a different matter. In theory, another prospective diplomat, he arrived with an introduction from Maurice Bowra and immediately fell ill. Harold looked after him, but soon realised that he was dealing with an 'an absolute little bum boy.'[9] Baird was so hopeless and so promiscuous that even Eddy Sackville-West joined in the chorus of disapproval. David Herbert, the Eton-educated son of Lord Pembroke, was equally promiscuous – 'My word, he is hot stuff,' Harold told Vita[10] – but for all his dedication to pleasure, he was more urbane, entertaining and creative than Baird and, consequently, more acceptable company. Then there was Cyril Connolly who returned several times to take advantage of Harold's hospitality. By now,

Harold had realised that 'Cyril is a pleasant guest, easily amused and interesting about things [but] I don't trust him a yard.... He is very thick with Violet Trefusis and I imagine is very disloyal about me when with her.'[11] In the end, Connolly had to be eased out of Brücken Allee because, as James Lees-Milne puts it, 'although Christopher and David were both chronically in debt, they did not sponge.'[12]

It was all very well entertaining visiting dignitaries, meeting and dining with the rich and famous; it was all very well being busy, having young friends and spending extravagantly to keep them happy and amused; but Harold clearly felt he was marking time. True, he was making progress with *Lord Carnock*, but little else seemed to be happening and the pressure from Vita (supported, as ever, by Virginia) did not let up. The crucial moment came in April 1929, when Harold gave a lunch for Robert Bruce Lockhart and Lord Londonderry. Bruce Lockhart was a diplomat-and-intelligence-agent turned journalist. He had been Acting Consul General in Moscow at the time of the October Revolution. He was subsequently imprisoned and sentenced to death for allegedly plotting to assassinate Lenin, and then exchanged for the Russian diplomat, Maxim Litvinov. Harold had first met him in the Foreign Office in 1918.[13] Lord Londonderry, a former soldier and Northern Ireland politician, was a less flamboyant character, but as First Commissioner of Works he was an influential figure in Stanley Baldwin's Cabinet. Their visit was one of many fact-finding trips made by senior British figures to Germany during this period. Conversation over lunch covered the range of foreign policy topics, but at some stage Harold must have said that he was toying with idea of leaving the Diplomatic Service. He went on leave shortly afterwards and apparently thought no more about it, but Bruce Lockhart did not forget.

Harold's hopes at this stage still rested on being recalled to the Foreign Office in London. There was a general election in Britain at the end of May, played out against the background of the Great Depression. The result was a hung parliament and a minority Labour Government. For a few days, Harold lived in hope that Mosley might be appointed to the Foreign Office and recall him, but, in the event, Mosley became Chancellor of the Duchy of Lancaster and the Foreign Office went to Arthur Henderson. Shortly afterwards, Lord Hardinge, now retired, visited Berlin and dined alone with Harold at the Embassy. Harold laid out his problem. Hardinge advised him to wait. The Foreign Office would eventually recall him to a senior position and once that happened, it would be easier to control his career. Hardinge, as a former Permanent Under-Secretary, understood that the Foreign Office moved at its own speed, with its own ends in view, and did not bend

– at least not immediately – to individual requirements. In his heart, Harold understood this, too, but Vita, who railed against the Foreign Office as a juggernaut, never could or would.

Nor was Vita's opinion of the Foreign Office improved that June when, after just a few days of leave at Long Barn, Harold was recalled to Berlin as a matter of urgency. Before he left, however, he and Vita had time to deliver their joint radio broadcast on the nature of marriage. Harold maintained that 'a successful marriage is the greatest of human benefits' and 'must be based on love guided by intelligence.' Vita agreed: 'The caveman plus sweet-little-thing theory is long past. It was a theory insulting to the best qualities of both.'[14] The irony was that the talk was commissioned and produced by Vita's current lover, Hilda Matheson.

Whether because he had recently lost his father, whether because the boys were growing and he was now able to write to them about more adult matters, or whether because of the pressures he felt in the context of his own marriage, the nature of family life and of marriage was a subject which was high on Harold's personal agenda during this period. In addition to the talk with Vita, there had been an earlier radio talk called 'Parents and Children' which centred on the absolute importance of preventing children from being bored and annoying their parents, and, later in the year, there was an article for *Harper's Bazaar* arguing that couples should not be allowed to marry while they were in love. Not everything he said was intended to be taken seriously, but these talks and articles marked a broadening of Harold's range to include social as well as his more normal literary or political subject matter.

Back in Berlin, Harold found himself Chargé once again and plunged into a regime of work. In the mornings and evenings, he wrote *Lord Carnock*. During the day, he struggled to get the German Foreign Office to agree a venue and an agenda for a major reparations conference which was planned for that August. He had given up Brücken Allee in June and was now living in the more impersonal, but still comfortable, Adlon Hotel. The furniture he had imported from Ebury Street to make Brücken Allee habitable had actually belonged to Lady Sackville and he had returned it as a protest at her continuing accusations and rumour-mongering.

Harold was faced with an urgent and complex political situation and he revelled in it. The aim of the proposed conference was to reach agreement on a reduction of German reparations to realistic levels, in line with a plan drawn up by the American industrialist, Owen D. Young, founder of the Radio Corporation of America (RCA). The German Government naturally supported the idea, but also wanted the conference to address the restoration of the Saarland and its coal mines. This did not fit naturally with the rest of the agenda and its inclusion was opposed by the French. In the end, Harold was able to negotiate a compromise which allowed the matter to be raised informally in the margins of the main conference. At the same time, the Germans were insisting on London as the venue, partly because they felt that the British were more sympathetic to their case and partly to annoy the French, who were, indeed, annoyed. Once again, a compromise was reached and all parties were persuaded to agree on the Hague as a suitable location. These various conversations and negotiations revealed an increasing assertiveness on the part of Germany towards the Allies, possibly due to the declining influence of Stresemann, who was now very ill. Harold reported this to London and also drew attention to the way the German Government was evading its treaty obligations and actively misleading domestic public opinion. It was the kind of work he was good at and his reports attracted positive attention in the Foreign Office.

On 22 July, he received a letter from Bruce Lockhart.

> When I was in Berlin in April, you hinted that you might not stay indefinitely in the diplomatic service. I did not take you very seriously but it may be worth while to put the following before you.... Beaverbrook is looking for a man of your ability and your knowledge of men and affairs, and would offer a very considerable inducement for his services. His job would be to write and edit a page like the 'Londoner's Diary' in the *Evening Standard*.... It would bring you into close touch with politics and the politicians again. It would also leave you time for a literary or a political career.[15]

Harold immediately wrote to Vita, who was on a walking and plant-collecting tour in the Val d'Isère with Hilda Matheson and thus not immediately accessible. It is a long, curiously bureaucratic letter, setting out the pros and cons of Beaverbrook's proposal in numbered paragraphs and proposing a plan of action. He intended to ask Bruce Lockhart for more details of the salary and 'what the job entails.' He also intended to ask Leonard Woolf for advice. In the meantime, he asked Vita to send a telegram 'on receipt of this letter' advising acceptance or refusal.[16]

Vita – as if there were any doubt – advised acceptance. So, too, did Leonard Woolf. Virginia also wrote assuring him that it would lead on to better things. Bruce Lockhart telephoned from London to say that Beaverbrook was offering £3,000 a year and a two-year contract to start at the beginning of October. After a flurry of telegrams, Vita left Hilda in

Geneva at the end of their holiday and took a train up to Karlsruhe. Harold drove down from Berlin. They met up on 1 August and for the next four days they wandered slowly north up the Rhine Valley, exploring the towns and villages, discussing their options and what the next step should be. By the time they reached Cologne, where Vita was to take the train back to England, they had drafted a letter which she would deliver on her return. It asked for £4,500 a year and a starting date of 1 January 1930.

Back in Berlin, Harold waited. Hearing nothing, he called Bruce Lockhart who said that Beaverbrook would not pay £4,500 and suggested a meeting when Harold returned to London in September. For Harold, the delay was a relief. From the beginning he had seen the negative aspects of working for Beaverbrook, and now he 'heard from the Ambassador that there are five Legations to be filled ... it is quite likely they will offer me Athens, Belgrade or Bucharest.'[17] Only a few weeks previously, another foreign posting had been the last thing that he wanted. Now, he seized on the idea in order to avoid making a decision. Indeed, despite Vita's attempts to stiffen his resolve, he seemed determined to vacillate.

> You see, Diplomacy really does give me leisure to do literary work of my own and it *does* have advantages such as leave, nice people etc. Moreover (and this is the essential point), if I stay in diplomacy I am certain of being 'successful', or, in other words, getting to the top. You say, with justice, that it is not a very glorious top. I quite agree. Yet I have sufficient knowledge of human nature to realise that it is more satisfactory to succeed on a small scale than fail on a big one. If I end up as an Ambassador I shall always feel (and say) what a wonderful career I could have made for myself in the open market. But if I climb down into the open market and then fail to make good there, I shall regret bitterly not having ... ended as an Ambassador.... Naturally I put against this (1) BM (2) Being separated from you. In the end these factors will probably be determinant. But ... you can't quite expect me to chuck my job at my age in a spirit of light-heartedness.[18]

BM, Lady Sackville, was certainly a factor. She continued to spread malicious gossip to anyone who would listen, accusing the Nicolsons of stealing furniture and jewels in order to pay their debts. She spread gossip about Vita and Virginia. She even tried to influence Ben and Nigel against their parents. Vita tried to explain to the boys that their grandmother was ill, but this was not an explanation Harold would accept. He was uncharacteristically angry. Lady Sackville was 'not mad ... just evil' and he was determined that he and Vita should establish their complete financial independence as soon as possible.[19]

By the end of August, the offer of a Legation seemed to have receded, though there was still the prospect of being made a Minister 'next year.'[20] Before leaving for London, Harold told the Ambassador about Beaverbrook's offer and that he intended to resign. Once in London, he told Sir Ronald Lindsay. Both were sympathetic, and neither sought seriously to dissuade him. It seems odd that Harold should have told them of his intensions before the crucial meeting with Beaverbrook, unless he was still trying, at this eleventh hour, to lever some concession from the Foreign Office.

The interview with Beaverbrook took place in London on 11 September and was followed by dinner a few days later. Harold accepted Beaverbrook's original offer of £3,000 a year. Beaverbrook agreed that, in addition to his work for the *Evening Standard*, Harold could publish one magazine article and give one radio talk a month. Harold also sought and obtained an assurance that he would be allowed to retain his political independence and would not be expected to endorse views or policies that he did not support – which was a sensible, if somewhat academic, way of safeguarding his integrity and also, just possibly, the first indication that he was considering a political career. A contract was drawn up and on 19 September, the *Evening Standard* contained a short paragraph announcing that Mr Harold Nicolson, CMG, had resigned from the Diplomatic Service and would be joining the staff of the paper from 1 January 1930. One is left with the sense that – unsurprisingly – Harold was outmanoeuvred during these negotiations; that Beaverbrook knew exactly what he wanted and what he was prepared to pay for it, whereas Harold, faced with the unfamiliar reality of what we would now call the private sector, was uncertain what he could realistically demand and not at all sure what he really wanted.

He returned for his last three months in Germany to find himself Chargé once again – Sir Horace Rumbold was taking an extended holiday at Taormina in Sicily – and in the middle of another political crisis. The British Government was pressing the German Government to reach a final agreement on a range of outstanding disarmament issues, while, at the same time, refusing to return or offer compensation for German property which had been sequestered during the War. It was an illogical, almost aggressive, stance and Harold, though he dutifully spoke as directed to the German Foreign Ministry, allowed himself more latitude than he might normally have done in letting the Foreign Office know what he thought.

Even though he was in the final weeks of his diplomatic career, Harold did not complain about the responsibility or the amount of work that was thrust upon him. He was not the kind of character to wind down gently. The crisis in relations over disarmament and sequestration subsided. He managed a couple of days in London at the end of October, but had to rush back to Berlin because of the Wall Street Crash. Once again, he found himself working at full stretch, reporting on German reactions to the Crash, on the implications of the sudden financial crisis and on what might happen if the United States reduced the huge loans it was making to Germany (in fact, by 1930, these loans had simply stopped). He also embarked on a new series of lectures – in Weimar, in Hanover, and in Berlin. His subject on this occasion, reflecting the broadening of his interests, was a comparison between English and German psychology. Although it was hardly psychology in a technical sense, rather a broad comparison of how the two nationalities were likely to react to cultural and social phenomena, his views were listened to with interest and respect. At the same time, in the mornings and the evenings, other commitments permitting, he continued to work at *Lord Carnock*. Only Harold's accommodation gave an indication that the end was nigh. The Adlon had proved too expensive and Harold's last few weeks were spent in the grim, crocheted respectability of the family-run Prinz Albrecht Hotel in Niederkirchnerstrasse, five minutes' walk from the Embassy.

Sir Horace Rumbold did not return from Taormina until 12 December, by which time Harold was in the middle of an intensive round of farewell parties and dinners. He had become extremely popular during his two years in Berlin and everyone now seemed to want to feed him or offer him a drink. Some were friends, such as the Horstmanns or Francesco von Mendelssohn, the flamboyant, Jewish art lover, with whom Harold had often cruised Berlin's nightclubs. Some were official contacts, such as Carl von Schubert, State Secretary at the German Foreign Office, or Jacob G. Shurman, the US Ambassador, whose background as a teacher of English Literature (among other things) added a level of understanding to their official relationship. He was even given a special reception at the Chancellery by Chancellor Müller, a signal honour – one cannot imagine Ramsay MacDonald giving a reception at 10 Downing Street for a departing second-in-command at the German Embassy. Harold appears to have been slightly bemused at this sudden popularity, although there is no doubt that he enjoyed it. 'It is extraordinary how nice people are to me here,' he told Vita. 'They really are sorry I am going.'[21] At the same time, he did not hide from himself his real feelings. After lunch with von Schuberts, Harold wrote that he felt 'such a humbug in a way, as these people really do mind my going, and of course I don't care 1½d for them.'²² Consciously or otherwise, these words echo his father's reaction in 1906 when he received the GCMG and a letter of thanks from the King.

Germany's present fascinated Harold, not least because Germany's past had dominated much of his own and his father's life. The imminence of his departure coupled with the imminence of his change of career put him in a mood which mixed reflection and nostalgia. He paid a farewell visit to Weimar, which set him thinking about his time there a quarter of a century before when he was preparing to go up to Oxford. He visited Bismarck's house at Schönhausen in Saxony.

> It was completely untouched and strongly evocative of the past. Harold travelled by train and was met at a wayside station by a large barouche with two horses and a man in a green Jaeger livery. They drove through a wide straggling village with tall trees. An untidy entrance led to a high, rambling house, like an overgrown farmhouse.... The interior was redolent of 1870.... Everything at Schönhausen was simple and dignified.... The impression left on Harold was of the old provincial Germany before the vulgar German Empire came into being.²³

It was an impression and an understanding that informed his attempts during the Second World War to understand what he called 'The German Soul.'²⁴

The British Embassy gave Harold his big farewell dinner at the Buccaneers Club on 15 December 1929: 'there were nearly 40 people – including old Rumbie and the American Ambassador. Speech by Rumbie which gave me a lump in my throat. Speech by me – very restrained but gulpy.... All went off very well.'²⁵ There was a final, less formal dinner with the Rumbolds at the Embassy and two days later, on the afternoon of 19 December, Harold took a cab to the Friedrichstrasse Bahnhof where Lali Horstmann, Francesco von Mendelssohn and a number of other friends waited on the platform to wave him off. Someone gave him a cactus to remind him of how he had once described the way German men cut their hair. It was a low-key end to a diplomatic career that had lasted precisely twenty years and two months.

36   Reasons

So why did Harold do it? Any attempt to understand his life and character must pause at this point to look at what lay behind his decision. Biographers tell an external story in which a character's job and the things that he or she does often appear more important than what happens on their internal landscape. In Harold's life, there were huge continuities – his love for Vita and the boys, his friends, his writing, Long Barn – which spanned the gulf between leaving Germany and the Diplomatic Service in December 1929 and beginning work as a journalist on the *Evening Standard* on 1 January 1930. Yet there is no escaping the fact that the decision changed his life – and not necessarily for the better. As such, it has to be explained.

Some factors are obvious. Vita had resented and disliked diplomacy as a profession even when they were newly-weds in Constantinople – a view perhaps instilled by her mother who referred to it as 'taking trouble over a lot of bedints.'[1] Her pressure on Harold to give up the Foreign Office had only increased with the years, intensified by the views of Virginia Woolf and others in the Bloomsbury set who saw diplomacy not as so much 'bedint' or middle class, but as establishment and unintellectual. On family grounds, it could be argued, Vita had a point. Given that she was not prepared to trail around the world after him, overseas postings meant long separations and frequent partings, which were torture to both of them. Overseas postings also meant that Harold saw very little of his sons during their adolescent years, something of which he was very aware and which almost certainly played a more significant part in his decision than their intermittent presence in the narrative of his life suggests. A return to London and a position in the Foreign Office might have answered much of this. Harold's perceived enemy, Sir William Tyrrell, had departed to be Ambassador in Paris and Sir Ronald Lindsay, whom he had every reason to believe was well disposed, had taken over as Permanent Under-Secretary. A little patience, as Lord Hardinge had suggested, was all that was needed. But Harold would not wait. Again, one has to ask why?

Money is probably the main answer. Harold failed in his attempt to get Beaverbrook to raise his offer of £3,000 a year, but that already represented more than twice his annual salary. While he was overseas his salary was generously supplemented by allowances, but as soon as he returned to London he would receive only his basic salary. Money was important both because Harold always managed to spend whatever he earned and because, for motives of pride and expediency, he wanted to establish his and Vita's financial independence from Lady Sackville, whose behaviour had shocked and alienated him.

Independence from the Foreign Office may have been another, though lesser, factor. James Lees-Milne has suggested that Harold objected to having 'to submit articles and books to official vetos,'[2] but membership of the Diplomatic Service had not so far affected his work, and, with the possible exception of *Peacekeeping*, it is difficult to see that any of his later work would have seriously upset the guardians of the official line. And if independence from the Foreign Office was a factor, it was certainly counterbalanced by the fact that Harold was effectively removing himself from the possibility of a job where he could actively influence the conduct of international affairs – the kind of position he had sought all his life. Unless, of course, he had already decided upon a political career. It is true that around this time Harold seems to have convinced himself he was a socialist, partly because of his experiences in Germany, and partly also on the strength of his friendship with and admiration for Tom Mosley, but in fact his politics were – and were to remain – muddled, and there is nothing to indicate that he held serious political ambitions at this stage. As things turned out, there were occasions later in his career when he could again claim to sit close to the centre of things. As a member of the House of Commons, he could exert an influence on government policy by contributing to the political debate, commenting on events and drawing lessons from them, but this was theoretical rather than practical. He never again exerted the direct influence on the outcome of events that he did at Paris, at Lausanne or while in Berlin.

In any such assessment there must be a 'what if?' What would have happened if Harold had stayed in the Foreign Office? Hugh Trevor Roper, never a friendly critic as far as Harold was concerned, saw him as too frivolous and too much the dilettante to sustain a senior diplomatic position. David Cannadine sees him as lacking the outstanding qualities necessary for his profession, and Derek Drinkwater in his impressive study of Harold's diplomatic legacy suggests that his deliberation and judgement did not equal Sir Arthur Nicolson's. Yet, it is fair to add, these conclusions are in the main based on what Harold decided and did *after* he left diplomacy. For all his frustration with it, the Foreign Office gave Harold security and a sense of belonging. It also gave him confidence. His judgement while he was within the framework provided by the Foreign Office was generally good: even the views he set out in the Tehran despatch which caused so much trouble at the time were seen as justified within twelve months. The contemporary judgement was that Harold would continue his progress upwards. Lord Hardinge suggested that Harold could have his pick of diplomatic postings if he were patient. Rumbold foresaw that he would become 'a young ambassador' and have a 'glittering career'.[3] Robert Bruce Lockhart preferred the adjective 'dazzling'.[4] Arnold Toynbee thought he would have reached the top of his profession.[5] Mosley thought he would have made an excellent ambassador (a backhanded compliment, perhaps, as Mosley saw quite clearly that Harold was not cut out for politics). Harold, fifty-three at the end of 1939 and fifty-nine in 1945, would surely have played a more influential part in the Second World War as a member of the Foreign Office staff or as an ambassador, than he did as a Member of Parliament. Might he, rather than Archie Clark Kerr, have been Ambassador to Russia during the war years? Might he, rather than Duff Cooper, have been the first Ambassador to France after the War? Might he, like his father, have finished his career as Permanent Under-Secretary and Head of the Foreign Office? Or – and this is pure speculation – could there have been a hidden motive here for Harold's decision to resign? Might he have sought to avoid following in his father's footsteps for fear that comparison between them would find him wanting?

The next question is why, given that he had decided to leave the Foreign Office, did he choose to work for the *Evening Standard* and for Beaverbrook? Certainly, the offer came at the right moment, but it was the first one he had received and he does not seem to have gone out of his way to advertise his availability more widely or seek other offers. Nor does he seem to have researched in any detail what was expected of him. It was November – with the contract long since signed and sealed – when he arranged for copies of the *Evening Standard* and its stablemate the *Daily Express* to be sent regularly to Berlin. Only then did the truth sink in.

> They really fill me with alarm. I simply shall be unable to write the sort of sob-stuff they want. They seem to have an unerring eye for just the sort of thing I loathe.... I don't think I am intellectually fastidious but I do loathe slush.[6]

And then there was Beaverbrook himself. By the time he was thirty-five, in 1914, Max Aitken had made a fortune in his native Canada, moved to Britain, become an MP, been knighted by King George V, and begun to build the newspaper empire which was to be his main claim to fame. During the First World War, he received his peerage as the first Baron Beaverbrook, served as Minister of Information, and took over the *Daily Express*. By 1930, he was one of the richest men in Britain, renowned for his brash, capricious,

Harold Nicolson

piratical ways. Harold Macmillan, who worked closely with Beaverbrook during the Second World War, wrote that

> he had a streak of vindictiveness and even cruelty. But he was equally capable of extraordinary kindness, and often his kind actions were towards those from whom he could gain no personal advantage and who could never repay him in any form. His charm could be, if he chose to use it, almost irresistible.[7]

As James Lees-Milne points out, Harold and Beaverbrook were complete opposites. Harold was understandably nervous about how the relationship might work out. In the event, though they disagreed profoundly on many things, on a personal level Beaverbrook treated Harold extremely well.

The decision was made. In terms of Harold's character and interests, it was probably a mistake, but love and money were the factors which swayed him – and he knew that he could not hold out for ever against Vita's pressure and disapproval. Harold, like his father, regarded diplomacy as a noble profession. Accepting Beaverbrook's offer, he knew he was stepping down to write what was, in effect, a political and social gossip column. If he had to leave diplomacy for journalism, a more analytical role on a more up-market paper would have suited him better. Vita, although delighted, understood his feelings and did everything possible to smooth the transition. Virginia, whose support for Vita had so intensified the pressure on Harold, struck a triumphal note which shows how far she failed to understand either Harold or Beaverbrook: 'my word I think you are lucky to have brushed off the bloom of diplomacy and then on to another flower while the sun still shines – What a stallion, what a young blood mare you are, to fling your head, kicking your heels.'[8] That was not at all how Harold felt.

37   Journalist

Harold arrived back in London on the morning of 20 December 1929. Vita met him at Liverpool Street Station and drove straight to the secluded Inner Temple complex, just off Fleet Street. On the first floor of No. 4 King's Bench Walk was a two-bedroom flat, not large, but well proportioned, convenient and quiet. Vita and Hilda Matheson had found it in October and Vita had thrown herself into the task of refitting and redecorating with great enthusiasm. For the first time in her life, she went into Woolworths, where she bought everything from mousetraps and dusters to a tin plate for Harold's dog. She judged it 'the most intoxicating shop.'[1] Harold had seen the flat only briefly before and pretended to be worried that she would put modern pictures on the walls of the bedroom – 'Get a large basin for me to be sick into.'[2]

The Inner Temple is one of the four Inns of Court to which all barristers and judges are required to belong, and has a history stretching back to the Knights Templar in the twelfth century. King's Bench Walk, a terrace of four-storey brick houses sloping down towards the Thames, dates from the seventeenth century, having been rebuilt in 1678 after a fire the previous year, an event recorded in an inscription on the frontage of No. 4. A certain amount of subterfuge had been necessary to obtain the lease. Tenancies were officially reserved for members of the Bar, so it was arranged that the lease should be in the name of Harold's eldest brother, Freddy, now the second Baron Carnock, who was a barrister. Harold was, however, able to apply for membership of the Inner Temple and his status as an Oxford MA allowed him to use the chapel and the library, to eat in Temple Hall or to have food sent across from the kitchen to his flat. It may seem odd for someone who had recently decided that he was a socialist to have accepted the privileges and the Oxford college atmosphere without demur, but Harold's socialism was always emotional rather than practical. The Inner Temple was another club, another family he could join, perhaps to some extent compensating for the loss of the Foreign Office. He revelled in the place and its atmosphere. It remained his London *pied-à-terre* for the next fifteen years.

Christmas was a family affair at Long Barn with Vita and the two boys. In the quiet days that followed, Harold finished the manuscript of *Lord Carnock*, incorporating one or two minor amendments requested by the Foreign Office, and delivered it to his publishers. For New Year, Harold and Vita went to Dottie Wellesley's elegant Georgian house, Penns-in-the-Rocks, just outside Groombridge in Sussex. Together with Desmond MacCarthy, Francis Birrell and the American artist, Ethel Sands, they listened to the chimes of Big Ben on the BBC. Harold felt glad that 1929 was over – 'Not a very happy year for me.'[3] On the morning of 1 January, he travelled up to London from Eridge station to begin his career as a journalist.

First published in 1827, an evening paper since 1859, and locked in protracted rivalry with the *Evening News* since the 1880s, the *Evening Standard* was not quite the Foreign Office, but it was an institution. It was influential, but not profitable. In 1923, with his usual bullish confidence, Beaverbrook had bought a controlling interest from the Mancunian newspaper millionaire, Edward Hulton, determined to make the paper a financial success. The 'Londoner's Diary', which Harold was to write in collaboration with Bruce Lockhart, had been introduced by Hulton as a three column feature 'written daily by gentlemen for gentlemen.'

The offices of the *Evening Standard* were in Shoe Lane, no more than five minutes' walk from King's Bench Walk, but the atmosphere could not have been more different. Despite his concerns and reservations, Harold began work in a generally positive mood. After his second day in Shoe Lane, he wrote:

> I suppose that I shall get into the way of finding these paragraphs [for the 'Londoner's Diary'] leaping ready-armed to mind. At present they are rather a bother to think of, rather a bother to write, and terribly feeble when written. But I shall settle down in time.... Found Bruce Lockhart fussing about in a rush as usual. Rather like all this rush business.[4]

His mood quickly soured. After only a week, he felt he was working 'fruitlessly superficially futilely ... the only news I get is from my friends and that is just the news that I can't publish.'[5] Nor did things really improve. It was not just the work that Harold found unsympathetic. He disliked the people he had to work among – 'On to the *Daily Express* office about books. I see an intolerable man who treats both me and literature as if they were dirt.'[6] Returning from holiday in August, was 'pretty grim.... They didn't seem in the least pleased to see me.... Not hostile exactly, but always on the defensive.' Revealing where his heart still lay, he contrasted this lack of welcome with life in the Foreign Office or an Embassy. He decided his colleagues were 'bedints.'[7] No doubt they had their views about him.

Having decided that he was no good as a columnist, Harold, with characteristic honesty went straight to Beaverbrook and told him that the 'Londoner's Diary' was getting dull. Beaverbrook, of course, denied it and made some 'good suggestions' for improving the column.[8] In fact, as Harold came to recognise over the course of the year, he was a perfectly competent columnist. By October, he could write: 'It is not as if the *Standard* were intolerable: it is perfectly tolerable'[9] and, by the end of the year, 'I have quite found my feet in the *Standard* office – and Beaverbrook likes me.'[10] His dislike of the *Evening Standard* and all that it stood for was based on a combination of intellectual grounds and self-image. It was 'silly work'.[11] It was 'constant hurried triviality which is base for the mind'.[12] And he feared – a fear reinforced in conversation with friends such as Noel Coward – that he would lose not only the reputation that he had built up as a serious writer, but also the ability to write serious books in the future. Working for Beaverbrook put Harold on the periphery: he missed the sense of public service and he did not feel that what he wrote was of any value. This was important because there was a strong moral strain in Harold, the legacy of his upbringing and education, and closely connected to his sense of public duty. As we saw in his reaction to the success of *Some People*, he believed that his work should have a serious purpose, should offer some educational, social, even moral benefit to society. If his work offered no sense of purpose, if he saw it as ephemeral or merely entertaining, he became discontented. The problem was the goose that laid the golden egg – 'I would give my soul to leave the *Standard* but I daren't risk it because of the money;'[13] 'I can't sacrifice Vita and the boys merely for my own convenience.'[14]

While the 'Londoner's Diary' was a weight on Harold's shoulders, he soon found that there were other opportunities in the new world of journalism which were more appealing in themselves and a better indicator of where his future might lie. He had written occasional book reviews in the past, but from April 1930 he became a regular reviewer, taking over the 'Books This Week' column in the *Daily Express* from the playwright St John Ervine and increasing the column's popularity by concentrating on books he liked rather than books which were regarded as important.

He also became a regular broadcaster. At a time when programme-making was surrounded by huge technical constraints, talks were an important part of the BBC's output and, in February 1930, Hilda Matheson arranged for him to give a series of short talks called 'People and Things'. Harold's choice of subject matter was eclectic, ranging from topical events and matters of general interest to more personal, apparently trivial matters. He might discuss the R101 airship disaster; he might dangle a little celebrity interest and talk about his lunch with Charlie Chaplin; or he might describe the character of his dog, Henry. In a world before television, he had the ability to isolate small details and bring to life the scene he was describing – two cooks removing their hats as the Prince of Wales passed by; propping his morning newspaper against his teapot and leaning a fork against it to keep it there; matches and cigarette ends rolling towards him as the Tower Bridge roadway lifted. Harold came across as pleasantly (not threateningly) intelligent, witty, observant and just a little old-fashioned – not in a blimpish or reactionary sense, but just old-fashioned enough to reassure the listener who might find the modern world and the pace of change a little worrying. It is not far-fetched to see in these early radio talks the first, faint precursor of the approach and tone later adopted by Richard Dimbleby and Alistair Cooke.

The listening public responded to Harold's personality and the series was an immediate success. Harold was dismissive of his achievements – 'I have become "famous" as a radio comedian ... a soppy superficial humourist.'[15] He aspired to be a serious writer, and radio, at this stage of its development at least, did not seem to lend itself to profundity or seriousness. Perhaps snobbishly, but at least honestly, he did not seek fame for its own sake and he did not seek a following among the middle-brow, middle-class British public who listened to the radio. In his mind, he distinguished clearly between the renown or reputation which he sought and fame which he did not. It may seem odd that someone who was so soon to embark on a political career should fail to want to develop what we would now call his media profile as a stepping stone towards political success, but these were innocent days and that equation had not yet been written.

Paradoxically, these fears for his future as a serious writer came at a time when his literary reputation had reached new heights. *Lord Carnock* was published on 3 April 1930 to near universal acclaim and not a little sensation. Writing to his mother the previous July, Harold had been quite clear what he was trying to achieve. The book was to be

> a biography and not a history of European diplomacy.... On the other hand, you must admit that father was such a central figure in the foreign politics of his time that it is almost impossible to avoid giving some outline of what was happening beyond.... I want this book to be a monument to a man whom I loved and admired more than I have or shall admire any man.... I wish it to be a book which brings home to ordinary people that unless one thinks war horrible, war will come again. ... It took my generation five years of hell to learn the lesson. But having learnt that lesson one must, one MUST, pass it on to others.[16]

Lord Carnock, then, was intended as a book with a message, and the message is conveyed in a characteristic, low key manner: the facts are selected and marshalled with care; the arguments are balanced and logical. No one reading *Lord Carnock* could accuse Harold of sensationalising his material. He did not need to: the London press did it for him.

On publication day, *Lord Carnock* was the subject of front-page headlines in the *Daily News* and the *Daily Herald*, and it received extensive coverage in most other leading papers and magazines. Harold's account of the events leading up to the outbreak of war in August 1914 was held to shed new light on relations between the main protagonists and on the attitude of the British and French Governments, particularly in relation to their willingness to violate Belgian neutrality. His view, in the Introduction, that Germany was not wholly responsible for the war and his strong condemnation of the war guilt clause in the Versailles Treaty also attracted much attention. The debate continued for several weeks and spread across the Channel to the French and German papers. Only the *Daily Express* and the *Evening Standard* were silent.

> Arnold Bennett, asked by the *Daily Express* to review it, had declined on the grounds that it was not his sort of book. In consequence Beaverbrook derived the impression that the book was not up to much and gave orders that it was not to be boosted in any way. When he woke up on the 3 April to see it splashed across all the other newspapers he was furious.... Panic ensued in Shoe Lane.[17]

We have no record of Harold's reaction to the publicity, but it is clear that the book became – of its kind – a best-seller. We know that he came to consider *Lord Carnock* his best book and it certainly marks a new stage in his development as an author. He writes with a clarity, authority and balance which he had never previously achieved. Gone is the unevenness which characterised *Byron*. The tone is consistent throughout, direct and informative, but capable of irony and allusion, never becoming dry or academic. The twin themes – his father's life and the method and workings of the old-style, pre-war diplomacy which his father represented (the book's subtitle is 'A Study in the Old Diplomacy') – are seamlessly interwoven. And the narrative, which spans seventy years and a huge swathe of European history, is impressively-structured, building gradually as crisis follows crisis to the supreme climax of August 1914 and Sir Edward Grey's fists crashing onto his office table in the knowledge that he had failed to avoid war.

One other development which was to have an immense impact on Harold's reputation took place at the beginning of 1930 – although its importance did not become apparent for another thirty-five years. He had kept a diary in the past: an irregular, scrappy affair in the early years, often little more than a list of names and engagements. Important political events, such as the Paris Peace Conference or the Lausanne Conference, received more detailed treatment; so, too, did his travels in Persia and aspects of his life in Berlin; but from 1 January 1930, he decided he would keep a regular and detailed record of his daily life. The diary was 'typed ... every morning after breakfast on both sides of loose sheets of quarto paper' and by the time Harold was no longer able to keep it in 1964, it had reached some three million words.[18] He told Nigel Nicolson, who edited the diaries in the 1960s, that he wrote it 'because I thought that one day it might amuse you and Ben.'[19] But there was quite obviously more to it than this. Given Harold's historical sense and the use that he made of his Paris and Lausanne diaries in *Peacemaking* and *Curzon*, there can be little doubt that he intended his diaries to be a chronicle of interest and value to future generations.

Harold had been in Berlin for over two years, but on returning to London his social life re-established itself with miraculous ease. He had always been a naturally social animal, never wanting invitations for lunches, dinners and country house weekends. Now, with the additional incentive of a newspaper column to write, having an active social life became a professional duty as well as a pleasure. Even then, the number and range of his friends and acquaintances is astonishing. He achieved, without apparent effort, access to political, literary and social circles which others envied and no doubt fought and intrigued to attain. Beaverbrook understood this from the beginning. It was one of the reasons why he offered Harold a job. Who else, seeing the Prime Minister outside the House of Commons, could say 'Hello, sir. How are you?' and be invited back to Downing Street for a glass of whisky and a chat?[20] Harold and Vita became sufficiently friendly with Ramsay MacDonald to be invited to spend weekends at Chequers – the house near Aylesbury, in Buckinghamshire, which since 1921 had been the Prime Minister's country residence. MacDonald, who came from a very poor background, delighted in his temporary ownership of a sixteenth-century mansion and enjoyed showing it off to friends.

Harold found himself taken up once again by both Sibyl Colefax and Emerald Cunard, London's two leading – and often competing – society hostesses. He and Vita were invited to one of Emerald Cunard's literary dinners at which their fellows guests were the novelist George Moore, Osbert and Edith Sitwell, Evelyn Waugh and Robert Byron. Harold described the evening as 'ghastly'.[21] On the whole, he seems to have preferred Sibyl Colefax's entertainments, recording 'a good party', where the other guests at a lunch were Lady Castlerosse, Diana Cooper, Charlie Chaplin, Lord Lloyd (last seen as High Commissioner in Egypt), H. G. Wells and Tom Mosley.[22] There were 'men only' dinners – such as that hosted by the journalist and Liberal politician, Sir Henry Norman, where Harold found himself sitting next to George Bernard Shaw, while the other guests included Sir John Simon, the Foreign Secretary; Lord Dawson, the King's doctor; Ned Lutyens and A. A. Milne – as well as innumerable smaller lunches and dinners in restaurants and clubs where Harold met and socialised with a huge range of people from all walks of life.

Country-house weekends may not have been as frequent or as splendid as in the Edwardian era, but they still took place. Those to which the Nicolsons were invited generally had a political flavour. Apart from weekends at Chequers, Harold's diary records an invitation in July 1930 to Wilton House, historic home of the Earls of Pembroke. Reginald Herbert, the fifteenth Earl, was the father of David Herbert, who had stayed with Harold in Brücken Allee. The other guests included Winston Churchill and his wife Clemmie; Duff and Diana Cooper; Robert Cecil, the Conservative MP,[23] and his wife; Malcolm Bullock, another Conservative MP; Maurice Baring and Christopher Sykes. This aristocratic party amused itself by dashing into nearby Salisbury for a torchlight procession and community singing as part of the local carnival.[24] A less successful weekend took place that November at the Astors' great house, Cliveden, in Berkshire. Duff and Diana Cooper were again among the guests, as were Tom Mosley and his wife Cimmie; Harold Macmillan and his wife, Lady Dorothy; Oliver Stanley, the Conservative politician, and his wife Maureen; Malcolm Bullock (again); J. L. Garvin, editor of the *Observer*; and the Conservative politician, Bob Boothby. The party did not 'hang together' – the fact that Boothby was having an affair with Dorothy Macmillan and that Harold Macmillan knew it cannot have helped – and although Nancy Astor attempted to enliven things by donning 'a Victorian hat and a pair of false teeth', she did not succeed.[25]

Such guest lists are not, perhaps, interesting reading in themselves, but in examining Harold's life – what he became and what he did not become – it is important to understand how broad was his circle of acquaintance and how few social circles were closed to him.

Although Harold was understandably unsettled after his exit from the Foreign Office, this was not a wasted period. He disliked Shoe Lane, but there is no doubt that it taught him his new trade as a journalist: he developed skills as a reviewer and a broadcaster which he would continue to exploit for the rest of his professional life. But he never learned to love the 'Londoner's Diary', which remained the mainstay of his employment, and his career at the *Evening Standard* lasted less than two years. He left on 22 August 1931, without regret, knowing that he had not been popular and having learnt that 'shallowness is the supreme evil.'[26] By that time, however, he had acquired two new enthusiasms. One was to last the rest of his life and be supremely successful; the other was to be short-lived and more or less disastrous.

38   Sissinghurst

From the moment that Harold and Vita bought Sissinghurst Castle on 6 May 1930, it became the essential background to the rest of their lives. However busy Harold was – however much he was taken up with his life in London, with his life in the House of Commons, with public affairs and social events; despite his deep affection for King's Bench Walk, his constant travelling, and the turmoil of the Second World War – Sissinghurst was his anchor and constantly at the back of his mind. Although sometimes closed up if Vita preferred to spend the winter season in London, Long Barn had been the family home for fifteen years. Harold and Vita had extended it, modernised it and created an extensive formal garden, but Sissinghurst was a project on an altogether grander scale, demanding a far greater level of emotional as well as financial commitment. Harold's love for Sissinghurst was perhaps not as visceral as Vita's, but his commitment and his belief were just as great. Like his love for Vita and the boys, Sissinghurst was a source of stability and continuity in his life. Indeed, it became almost another member of the family.

In the same way that Lord Carnock's death in some sense allowed Harold to break free from the Foreign Office, Vita might well not have chosen to move from Long Barn if Lord Sackville had lived. Long Barn was within walking distance of Knole, but with her father dead and Uncle Charlie in possession, the link was cut. The last lingering impossibility that she might one day return there was gone. She no longer needed its proximity.

The trigger for the move came on 4 March 1930, coincidentally the day on which Vita finished *The Edwardians*, which was to be her biggest-selling book and would help pay for their new home. Long Barn was bordered to the south by Westwood Farm, located on the remarkably named Scabharbour Road. The farm was now to be sold and developed as an intensive chicken farm – which meant chicken houses spreading over the open fields and visible from the terrace at Long Barn. How were they to react? Vita's instinct, characteristically, was to resist. Could they not outbid the poultry farmers? Harold took a longer view.

> Mrs Taylour has offered to sell us the whole of Westwood for £16,000. Vita wishes to offer her £13,000. I have my doubts.... The whole thing [Long Barn and Westwood] together would represent a capital outlay of some £23,000 and for that sum we could get an almost perfect place anywhere else. Long Barn will not improve in amenity as the district gets

built over, and it is neither architecturally or in any other way really ideal.... I do feel that we could find another place which would be more amusing for the boys and in the end more satisfactory to ourselves.[1]

Harold's logic prevailed. Vita began house-hunting and things moved quickly. On Thursday 3 April, while visiting Dottie Wellesley at Penns-in-the-Rocks, she heard about Sissinghurst. On Friday, with Dottie and thirteen-year-old Nigel, she made her first visit and 'fell flat in love with it.'[2] On Saturday, Harold came down from London and made his first visit – 'We get a view of the two towers as we approach. We go round carefully in the mud. I am cold and calm but I like it.'[3] The difference between the two diary entries is eloquent.

On the Sunday, they went back again and made the decision to buy. Then doubts crept in. When the weather was bad, the whole place looked 'big, broken-down and sodden.'[4] Could they afford it? Apparently, Vita could. Just before Christmas she had been to visit her mother at her new home in Streatham in South London. There had been a tentative *rapprochement* (in which Harold had not been included) and now Lady Sackville was prepared to agree that the trustees of the Knole estate should underwrite the necessary funds. Should they afford it? Harold worried about the possibility of socialist legislation penalising landowners (there was a four-hundred-acre farm attached to the property), about not being able to let the fields, and above all about Sissinghurst becoming an enormous black hole into which they would endlessly pour money.

The task they were taking on was immense. 'Sissinghurst Castle,' as Victoria Glendinning succinctly puts it, 'was a ruin, or a complex of ruins, in seven acres of muddy wilderness. There was no electricity or water laid on; there was no single habitable room.'[5] In almost every description of Sissinghurst as the Nicolsons first found it, the word 'mud' features with oppressive regularity. The boys were appalled: 'We haven't got to live here, have we?' asked Nigel.[6] Harold set down his feelings in writing. On the one hand, it would be unwise to buy Sissinghurst because to buy and restore would cost nearly £30,000. And for £30,000, he noted – perhaps a touch wistfully – 'we could buy a beautiful place replete with park, garage, h&c, central heating, historical associations and two lodges.' On the other hand, it was 'most wise' to buy Sissinghurst because 'through its veins pulses the blood of the Sackville dynasty ... [and] we like it.'[7] In truth, as Harold must have known, the decision had already been taken. His more strategic view may have prevailed when it came to leaving Long Barn, but Sissinghurst was Vita's choice. It was her money and it was to be her property: joint ownership was never contemplated – 'The initials VS-W were indelibly branded into the woodwork of the farmcarts and garden tools.'[8]

Sissinghurst touched the powerful romantic seam in Vita's imagination. The name is of Saxon origin and in the early medieval period the land was owned by a family called de Saxingherst. Somewhere towards the end of the thirteenth century, the de Saxinghersts gave way to the de Berhams who owned land throughout Kent and made Sissinghurst their family seat. The de Berhams built a timber-framed manor house on the site, grand enough for Edward I to stay in during his progress through Kent in 1305. In 1533, the estate was bought by one John Baker, a lawyer, a man of politics and power, who had married Catherine Sackville, the daughter of a Sussex knight – allowing Vita to claim that there had been a Sackville at Sissinghurst before Knole. Under John Baker's son, Richard, Sissinghurst reached its apogee. He used the fortune he inherited to create a vast Elizabethan palace with courtyards, a tower, banqueting houses, gardens and a deer park. It was the fame of Baker's creation that led Queen Elizabeth I to pay a three-day visit to Sissinghurst in August 1573. Over the centuries that followed, Sissinghurst's fortunes declined. The house and the park sunk into neglect and ruin. But Vita's romantic, mystical nature responded to the ghost of its Elizabethan glory and to the historical connections with the Sackvilles, as well as to the practical possibilities of creating a garden among the ruins. From the first, she immersed herself in it and identified with it. It was a substitute Knole.

> This husbandry, this castle, and this I
> Moving within the deeps
> Shall be content within our timeless spell
> Assembled fragments of an age gone by ...
> So plods the stallion up my English lane
> And fills me with a mindless deep repose
> Wherein I find in chain
> The castle, and the pasture, and the rose.[9]

Vita knew what she wanted. Once she had seen Sissinghurst, it was unthinkable that she should not possess it, and yet, as with so many of her major decisions – and though she would have loathed the implication – she needed Harold's support and approval before she could go ahead. They made an offer of £12,375: the average house price of the time was £590. On the evening of 6 May, the land agent telephoned to say that it had been accepted. It was a huge challenge, but they felt they were young enough to meet it, and they were immensely excited at the idea of creating something from the ruins. 'Oh my dear dear love,' Harold wrote to her from London the next morning, 'what fun [we] have! Please don't die.'[10]

Harold's life in London, his public life, remained largely unaffected, but when not working in London or travelling, all his efforts – and those of the rest of the family – were focussed on Sissinghurst. Nigel Nicolson remembered that

> We all worked hard, Vita and Harold by inclination, Ben and I because we had nothing else to do.... There was activity all around us, on the farm, on the restorations and in the making of the garden. Ben and I were the labourers, Harold the designer, Vita the plantswoman.[11]

The place was in such a state that for the whole of that first summer it was not even possible to sleep there. On Thursday 16 October, Harold was in London, participating in a broadcast discussion about Germany and knowing, as he did so, that Vita, guarded by her dogs, was spending her first night at Sissinghurst, camping in one of the rooms at the top of the tower. That Saturday, he joined her, but – to no one's surprise – proved ill-adapted to the demands of camping in an isolated brick tower surrounded by a morass of mud. He dramatised the experience in a radio talk called 'The Simple Life' which was broadcast that December. No doubt he exaggerates his inability to light a fire, pump water and cook eggs, for comic effect, but there is equally no doubt that his adaptability in such situations was limited. Harold had always lived, and continued to live, surrounded by servants. He simply had no experience of normal domestic tasks. And yet he did have his practical side. At Long Barn, he had drawn up plans and overseen the work of re-erecting an old timber-frame barn as an additional wing to the main house. Now, at Sissinghurst, he took charge of planning the accommodation and – more important in the eyes of posterity – designing the garden.

Apart from the distinctive brick tower with its twin conical turrets, the main structure at Sissinghurst was the long, Elizabethan gatehouse, once the eastern side of a considerable courtyard. There was also the Priest's House, once an Elizabethan banqueting house, now little more than a ruin, and the South Cottage, which dated from a later era and was merely derelict. Their original plan was to build a connecting wing between the tower and the gatehouse, but this was soon abandoned for a mixture of financial and aesthetic reasons. Instead, Harold developed a scheme which involved restoring the existing structures and distributing the functions of a normal family home between them. The tower was Vita's from the beginning. Only at the top was there any habitable space and this became her study, her private sanctum – so private in fact that Nigel remembered entering it only two or three times in the thirty-two years she occupied it. Harold's study, his bedroom, Vita's bedroom and their shared bathroom were to be in the South Cottage. The boys' bedrooms and bathroom, the kitchen and the family dining room were all to be in the Priest's House. The disadvantage of this scheme was that, apart from the dining room, there was nowhere for the family to gather. Nor was there anywhere for guests to stay. It also meant that the garden became, in effect, part of the house, a space to be crossed and re-crossed in the course of a normal day – delightful perhaps in good weather or on a balmy summer evening, less so in rain or snow. Only in 1935 was part of the gatehouse turned into 'the big room', intended for family use, but for some reason it never worked as a communal space and became the library, while the family continued to live a scattered existence.

This undeniably eccentric arrangement reflected Vita's temperament more than Harold's. Once in possession of Sissinghurst and as time went on, Vita became increasingly taken up with her garden and her writing. Friends might visit; she continued to find lovers and lead a complicated emotional life; but she became gradually more reluctant to entertain or take part in the kind of social life that might have been regarded as normal for someone in her position. There is no doubt that Sissinghurst was inconvenient. It could also be horribly cold – in a bad winter, almost uninhabitable. Pipes froze; lavatories froze; draughts howled under doors; Vita was actually reduced to sitting astride an electric radiator for warmth. Yet she minded the cold and the discomfort far less than Harold, who in his heart of hearts would probably have preferred the kind of house he described in his letter setting out the pros and cons of buying Sissinghurst, a house with central heating and capable of hosting dinners and modest weekend parties. But Harold at least had a choice: he had the beauty and seclusion of Sissinghurst, and he had the more social existence of London and King's Bench Walk.

For Vita, the garden was far more important than the house: the garden and her writing were the two most important things in her life. For Harold, the garden was one interest, although an important one, among many. From the moment the decision to leave Long Barn was made, Vita was looking for somewhere she could create a new and better garden. One of the underlying reasons for leaving Long Barn was that there was little more that they could do with Long Barn's two acres. Sissinghurst was more than three times that size and presented almost unlimited possibilities. They began planning even before they had bought the property.

It was Harold who laid out the shape and structure of the garden at Sissinghurst as it is today. He could see the bigger picture in a way that Vita could not. He employed classical principles, using symmetry and balance to create a series of interlocking, almost private spaces which are linked and flanked by long, open walks giving views onto the Kent countryside. The effect is to make the garden seem bigger than it really is. In this context, Harold could be extremely practical. Nigel Nicolson remembers

> how Harold took me into the field outside the garden wall and planted a stake at the spot which he had carefully calculated on paper, joining it with a string to a second stake with which I walked in a circle using it like a compass, scoring the grass to sketch the position of the yew hedge which we now call the Rondel.[12]

Twenty-three years later, in an article written for the Royal Horticultural Society, Vita paid tribute to Harold's gifts and suggested that in another life he might have been a 'garden-architect'.[13] At the time, however, they did not always see eye to eye.

> Measure the central path in the kitchen garden.... Vita refuses to abide by our decision to remove the miserable little trees which stand in the way of my design. The romantic temperament as usual obstructing the classic.[959]

Given everything else that was happening in his life, it is remarkable how quickly Harold worked. Within two years, most of the main components of the garden as it is today had been laid out, and the hedges and trees which would create the divisions and delineate the structure had been planted. This was Harold's only real involvement with the planting, which was very much Vita's preserve, but here again he took a long view, planting poplar, hornbeam, yew and beech – trees which would take many years to grow and mature.

Vita, too, worked incredibly hard. There were vast amounts of rubbish and debris to be cleared away – bricks and wire, nettles and brambles. There were builders to supervise – H. C. Punnett & Son of Cranbrook. There was a book to be written, for no sooner had she finished *The Edwardians* than she began working on what was to prove another extremely popular novel, *All Passion Spent*. Yet she was soon mapping out the beds and the borders, ordering plants and seeds, and beginning the daunting process of planting huge new areas of garden.

Gradually, as the restoration of the buildings continued, rooms became ready and conditions improved, the centre of gravity shifted from Long Barn to Sissinghurst. There was water; there was electricity; and, at the beginning of 1932, Vita had a telephone installed. Harold seems to have been reluctant to make the final leap, but money was an issue so, in April 1932, Vita arranged to let Long Barn and by May the Nicolson family were fully installed at Sissinghurst. Gradually, too, the garden progressed and matured. Vita experimented with colours, groupings and varieties, and as the plants grew they softened and developed the symmetry of Harold's design. In the summer of 1938, as an experiment, they decided to open the garden to the public for two days. The price of admission was sixpence, to be dropped in a tobacco tin left on an old card table by the entrance. Eight hundred people came.[15]

39 Mosley

Harold Nicolson's involvement with Oswald Mosley and the New Party did not last long – it began early in 1931 and finished abruptly in April 1932 – but it damaged him at the time and has continued to damage his reputation in the eyes of posterity. It shows him at his most naïve and has been principally responsible for the suggestion that, once outside the framework provided by the Foreign Office, he lacked political judgement. If leaving the Foreign Office to work for Beaverbrook and the *Evening Standard* was risky, leaving the *Evening Standard* to work for Mosley and *Action* can only be seen as pure folly. And one has to ask again: what drove Harold to make such a radical change in his life?

Britain had spent most of the 1920s struggling with economic difficulties which stemmed, ultimately, from the need to finance the First World War. Government spending more than halved between 1918 and 1922 and remained at that level throughout the decade. Returning to the gold standard in 1925 caused the pound to rise in value and exports to become more expensive. The whole period was one of sustained recession and deflation. Efforts by employers to cut costs and wages led to the General Strike in 1926. Unemployment remained high, hovering around one-and-a-half million – some 8 to 9% of the work force – and that meant grinding poverty for hundreds of thousands of families. Politicians, however well intentioned, failed to secure the improvements they promised and the 1929 general election ended in a hung parliament and a Labour-led coalition, but, with the coalition partners pulling in different directions, it was powerless to achieve anything at all.

Internationally, as Harold knew better than most, the situation was equally uncertain. The French economy had struggled in the aftermath of the war, although by the end of the decade it seemed to be on the way to recovery. Germany had recovered from hyperinflation but Harold knew how potentially unstable both its economy and its political system were. Italy, under Mussolini, appeared to have achieved a level of political stability, but its economy remained weak – although that was to some extent obscured by propaganda. Eastern Europe and the Balkans were dogged by political and economic instability. It seemed that across the whole of Europe, for the victors and the defeated alike, the First World War and the peace that followed had created more problems than they had solved. Only across the Atlantic in the United States was there significant economic growth – until the Wall Street Crash in October 1929 brought prosperity to an end and shook the world economy to its foundations. This was the background to the emergence of Mosley's New Party and Harold's decision to join it.

Mosley was ten years younger than Harold, born in 1896 to a wealthy, long-established family with estates in Lancashire and Staffordshire. Even as a young man, it was obvious that he was capable of becoming a controversial figure. At Sandhurst, he came top in the cavalry class, but was expelled for a particularly violent retaliation against a fellow student. Attracted by the idea of the new Royal Flying Corps, he became an observer over enemy lines, but broke his leg in a crash landing in 1915. He served in the trenches at the Battle of Loos, but was invalided out of the army in 1917. He went to work in the Ministry of Munitions and ended the war in the Foreign Office, where he first met Harold.

After the war, Mosley embarked upon a political career. In December 1918, he was elected as Conservative MP for Harrow at the age of just twenty-one; eighteen months later he married Cimmie Curzon, the Marquess' second daughter – whom Harold knew well and was extremely fond of. In 1922, he left the Conservative Party as a protest against the Government-sanctioned indiscipline and violence of the infamous Black and Tans in Ireland. In 1924, standing as a Labour candidate, he almost unseated Neville Chamberlain in Birmingham. By 1926, he was back in Parliament as Labour MP for Smethwick. His striking physical appearance, his compelling personality and his undoubted skill as a public and parliamentary speaker made him an obvious candidate for high office; but, by the time MacDonald came to form his government in 1929, Mosley's growing arrogance and egotism had upset a sufficient number of people for him to be excluded from the Cabinet and offered the more junior post of Chancellor of the Duchy of Lancaster.

If Mosley's personality began to tell against him, so too did his personal conduct. London society in the 1920s was not censorious and a degree of sexual licence was tolerated. Mosley's sex life, however, was neither modest nor discreet. He was a serial womaniser. In the ten years following his marriage to Cimmie Curzon, he slept with over thirty women, including his wife's sister and stepmother. This compulsion to seduce any eligible woman who crossed his path – provided she came from the right social background – gradually revealed itself as a part of his rapidly developing and impatient appetite for power.

Mosley was tasked by MacDonald to look at ways of reducing unemployment and in January 1930 he produced the document which became known as the Mosley Memorandum. It attracted criticism not so much for the largely Keynesian measures it proposed but for the radical executive powers it advocated that the Government assume in order to implement them. In May, he used a meeting of the Parliamentary Labour Party to force a Cabinet vote on his proposals. He lost and resigned his ministerial post. Ambitious, impatient and increasingly arrogant, he took his Memorandum to the Labour Party Conference in Llandudno in October, believing he could carry the mass of the Party with him. Again, he forced a vote and, again, he lost, though narrowly. This time, he resigned from the Labour Party and resolved to go it alone, formally launching the New Party on 1 March 1931.

By the second half of 1930, Harold, already disillusioned with journalism, was thinking seriously about a political career, but – and this is immensely revealing about Harold's attitude to politics – he had no clear relationship with any of the parties. He discussed the problem with Beaverbrook who 'talks to me as a father ... urges me not to be a Liberal. Begs me to become a Tory.'[1] Beaverbrook was probably right: Harold would have done best as a reforming Tory in the manner of Harold Macmillan, whom the *Daily Mail* had dubbed a 'semi-Socialist'.[2] Shortly after this, he was approached by Sir John Tudor Walters, the sitting Liberal MP for Penryn and Falmouth, a safe Liberal seat. Sir John would not be contesting the next election: would Harold take it on? Harold was 'much tempted' but in the end turned it down, not because of Beaverbrook's advice, but because he was already drifting closer to Mosley.³ Harold and Vita had been seeing the Mosleys socially – although Vita absented herself when she could on the grounds that she was working at Sissinghurst, but also because she was wholly unreceptive to Tom Mosley's charm and claimed that he gave her the creeps. Harold's diary records several conversations with Mosley about his plans to launch a new political party. In December, in an article for the *Listener*, he attempted a balanced assessment of the Mosley Memorandum and concluded that it was a positive contribution to the national debate. But he was not yet committed: the diary's end-of-year summary says only that he feels he is 'on the verge of politics' and makes no mention of Mosley or his ideas.⁴

Harold was perceptive in attributing a fatherly character to Beaverbrook's attitude towards him. Though there was no meeting of minds, Beaverbrook was genuinely fond of him, and, over the months that followed, as he became ever more committed to the New Party, Harold turned frequently to Beaverbrook, ostensibly to ensure that his political activities did not conflict with editorial policy or his duties at the *Evening Standard*, but also, it seems, on a more personal level looking for approval or even someone against whom to rebel. Beaverbrook, of course, understood the value of opposition and protest: his crusade on behalf of Empire Free Trade – essentially turning the British Empire into a protectionist bloc – was a thorn in the flesh of both the Government and the Conservative Party. He understood the value of what Mosley was doing politically, but clearly, and rightly, saw that Harold needed a more established and establishment career structure.

At the beginning of March, having been asked to serve on the New Party's publicity committee, Harold spoke to Beaverbrook and described his reaction in a letter to Mosley.

> Striding about the room he explained to me how far, far more remunerative it would be for me to attach myself to some more established machine.... And when I, sitting there glum and obstinate, remarked that I did not care for the old parties, he said, 'Go to hell with ye – and God bless ye.'
>
> After which he expressed admiration for yourself and deep sympathy with me in my obstinacy and wrong-headedness.... I might serve on any of your committees if I wished.... I must not boost you unduly in the *Evening Standard*.... But short of that I might do what I liked.⁵

A month later, Harold wrote requesting permission to stand as a New Party candidate in a bye-election. Beaverbrook replied: 'I think you would be mad.... But the decision rests with you, and I have no objection as far as concerns the newspaper work.'[6] In the event, the bye-election did not materialise.

The New Party contested its first bye-election in Newcastle-under-Lyme at the end of April. Harold went up to attend a campaign meeting as part of a panel answering questions. He estimated that there were between 6,000 and 7,000 people present. It was 'at first rather sticky and heavy', but then Mosley got up to speak. Harold had never before seen him in action in front of a big audience – he 'launches on an emotional oration on the lines that England is not yet dead and it is for the New Party to save her.... He is certainly an impassioned revivalist speaker.'[7] Despite the enthusiasm Mosley created when he spoke, the New Party came third in the polls, receiving only 16% of the vote but, crucially, splitting the Labour vote sufficiently to allow the Conservatives to win the seat.

When not pursuing material for the 'Londoner's Diary' or down at Sissinghurst, Harold's life became one of meetings and lobbying. The New Party needed high-level recruits, particularly from the other main parties, but they were slow in coming. In May, Mosley came up with the idea of a weekly paper to act as a mouthpiece for the Party's views. In June, Harold was asked to join the New Party Council. Mosley decided to go ahead with the proposed weekly, which was to be called *Action*, and wanted Harold to edit it. He was being gradually sucked in.

Beaverbrook saw what was happening. He had done all that he possibly could to accommodate Harold's infatuation with the New Party. Now, with impeccable timing, he offered a sensible and suitable alternative. On 18 June, he took Harold out to lunch and made it clear that, if he gave up the New Party, he could become editor of the *Evening Standard*. It was a shrewd offer. Harold might not have been a natural gossip columnist, but, as his radio broadcasts demonstrated, he was a natural communicator able to discuss serious issues in an accessible way. The *Evening Standard* might well have benefitted and Harold would have been able to develop a platform to launch a political career later on. Harold went down to Long Barn and spent the evening with Vita weighing up the options:

> a position of authority on the *Evening Standard* which would mean not merely a very high salary, but also an opportunity of making a decent and influential paper out of it. There is no limit to the possibilities opened by such a prospect.... Alternatively, there is a chance that the New Party within five years would be in such a position as to force a

coalition.... In such a coalition I should certainly be able to ask for the Foreign Office.⁸

He chose the New Party, leaving a second major 'what if?' in his career.

Harold was deluding himself about the New Party and, worse, he knew it – just as he had known before he left Berlin that he was not suited to the 'Londoner's Diary'. As early as May, he found himself urging Mosley against dramatic action. At the beginning of June, Allan Young, the unsuccessful candidate at Newcastle-under-Lyme, told Harold that he was worried about the Party moving to the right and that he was opposed to Mosley's wish for a Youth Movement. By July, Harold was writing, 'I think that Tom at the bottom of his heart really wants a fascist movement.'⁹ A week later, Allan Young and St Loe Strachey, whom Mosley had persuaded to leave the Labour Party, both resigned because they perceived an increasingly fascist tendency in Mosley's policies. And all this came even before Harold left the *Evening Standard* to edit *Action*.

So why did he choose as he did? It was not money. Although initially promised £3,000 a year to edit *Action*, he accepted a lower sum – much of which was, in any case, never paid because the New Party ran out of money. It was not to do with his dislike of popular journalism. The kind of thing with which he was now associated was far worse than anything at the *Evening Standard*: Raymond Mortimer, seeing a poster for *Action* which read 'THE PRIME MINISTER NEEDS KICKING', said it made him want to vomit.¹⁰ It was not, on this occasion, domestic pressure: Vita loathed Mosley, the New Party and everything it stood for. Ambition undoubtedly did play a part, so did dreams. Harold wanted to return to a position at the centre of things and the prospect, however vague, of high political office also lured him on. On the face of it, however, the New Party offered fewer guarantees than staying with Beaverbrook. Did belief play a part? Harold managed to convince Vita – and perhaps himself – that he was joining the New Party 'out of conviction.'¹¹ Such a claim is difficult to gainsay, though it is equally difficult to reconcile with a man who, just a few months previously, had not known which party to join.

Another possible explanation lies in friendship, loyalty and Harold's search for the kind of security that the Foreign Office had provided and which the House of Commons would provide later on. Harold was always loyal to his friends – very often too loyal – and he always kept his word. He had known Tom Mosley a long time. Mosley had been sympathetic when Harold was seeking an escape from Berlin and the Foreign Office. Moreover, it was to Cimmie Mosley, to whom he was devoted (not least out of affection for her father, Lord Curzon), that Harold first pledged his word to join the New Party. Did Harold see the New Party as his new 'family'? Is that why, despite being one of the first to see the fascist direction that the New Party was likely to take, he was the last of Mosley's early recruits to leave? If so, it is shows just how temperamentally unsuited he was to the world of politics.

There is one other possibility which, while speculative, cannot be dismissed out of hand. Was Harold sexually attracted to Mosley? The evidence is limited to a few oddly over-intense phrases (such as 'I am sorry you are ill. For God's sake take care.'[12]), a sense that Harold was in some sense a supplicant in the relationship, and the difficulty of accounting for his actions in any other way. Yet all accounts agree that Mosley had immense personal charisma and a powerful animal, sexual magnetism – qualities he exploited in his career as a seducer, as a public speaker and as a would-be demagogue. He was physically attractive and very fit: a fencing champion in his youth and a skilled boxer (unsurprisingly, he preferred individual sports). He had seen action with the Royal Flying Corps and in the trenches at Loos. Self-assured, combative, an MP at twenty-one, a minister at thirty-three: Mosley was everything Harold was not. While he would never be a hero to Harold in the manner of Dr Pollock or Crowe or Venizelos, an attraction cannot be ruled out, the very unattainability of the prize adding fuel to the fire.

Timing is everything. On 24 August 1931, two days after Harold formally left the *Evening Standard*, Ramsay Macdonald announced the formation of a National Government in order to address the financial and economic crisis facing the nation. In doing so, he split the Labour Party but, by recognising publicly that exceptional times required exceptional measures, he cut the ground from beneath the New Party's feet. Mosley decided that the New Party must forge ahead with its programme and offer an alternative to the established parties. *Action* was part of that programme. The first issue appeared on 8 October and sold 160,000 copies, but momentum stalled immediately and the last issue, published just before Christmas, sold less than 15,000.

Action was a failure from start to finish. As conceived by Mosley, it was to be an uncompromising, hard-hitting journal designed to put across the New Party's views. As edited by Harold from its offices at 5 Gordon Square in the heart of Bloomsbury, it was an amateurish mixture of differing approaches and styles. Mosley's editorials and the political articles written by the Party's inner circle were pure propaganda. Harold's attempts to address political issues were reasoned and logical; his book reviews were witty and thoughtful. Other articles, written by friends such as Osbert

Sitwell and Francis Birrell, or by the philosopher and polymath, Gerald Heard – or, indeed, by the gardening correspondent, Vita Sackville-West – simply did not fit the political intent of the paper.

> I am not a journalist and as such not well suited to be a man who runs a weekly. I see both sides of every question. That is a mistake. [One of the *Action* staff] thinks I am a good editor.... What he really means is that I am a rather nice man.... I should like to make something of this paper. The difficulty is that I am backed and financed by a political party. And even then it is not a party but a rather sly movement.[13]

By the time *Action* hit the streets, Ramsay Macdonald had called an election. The New Party rushed to find candidates. They managed to field twenty-four: 'some were barely literate, and some were frankly disreputable.'[14] Harold was standing for the Combined English Universities – an odd and, even at the time, anachronistic arrangement which allowed members of seven English universities to elect two MPs by proportional representation. There was no physical constituency to visit, which allowed him to continue editing *Action* throughout the campaign. The atmosphere was tense. The New Party had already become a target for communist demonstrators – Mosley had been attacked with a razor in Glasgow and stones had been thrown at meetings – but there was no serious trouble. The result, however, was a complete disaster. Supporters of Ramsay Macdonald's National Government, most of them Conservatives, routed the Labour opposition. Not a single New Party candidate was elected. All but two lost their deposits. They received 0.2% of the vote. The New Party was over before it had begun.

By the end of the year, Harold's main source of income had disappeared – indeed, he had even borrowed money himself to pay off some of *Action's* debts – and he was forced to face up to the stark truth about Mosley: 'I am loyal to Tom since I have an affection for him. But I realise that his views are divergent from my own.... He believes in fascism. I don't. I loathe it.'[15] To make matters worse, he had also fallen out with Sir John Reith at the BBC over his series of talks on 'the New Spirit in Modern Literature'. Forbidden to mention James Joyce's *Ulysses*, which was banned on grounds of obscenity, he refused to continue with the project – a noble, even correct, gesture, but one which did not improve his financial situation.

Even now, after a year in which he acknowledged in his diary that everything had gone wrong and that his connection with Mosley had harmed his reputation, Harold still did not cut loose. He agreed to accompany Mosley on fact-finding visits to Italy and Germany to study 'new political forces born of crisis, conducted by youth and inspired by completely new ideas of economic and political organisation.'[16] They met in Paris. Harold wandered the streets visited by 'incessant memories – the insistence of which show me how much I regret the past' and feeling 'the tug at my heart of diplomacy in all its forms.'[17] In Rome, they met Christopher Hobhouse, a young Oxford graduate, who had been one of the New Party's candidates at the election, and embarked on a series of meetings and visits. Mosley met Mussolini, finding him 'affable but unimpressive.'[18] Harold refused to accompany him and spent his time reading fascist pamphlets which provoked a philosophical passage in his diary.

> I am much impressed by the efficiency of all this on paper. Yet I wonder how it works on individual lives.... It is certainly a socialist experiment in that it destroys individuality. It also destroys liberty.... I admit that under this system you can attain to a degree of energy and efficiency not reached in our own island. And yet, and yet ...[19]

The most enjoyable thing about Rome was spending time with Gladwyn Jebb, a Second Secretary at the Embassy, who was only too pleased to invite Harold to dinner or accompany him on a visit to Mussolini's ambitious scheme to drain the Pontine Marshes.

Mosley was unable to make the trip to Germany, so Harold went without him. He called on his former colleagues, Sir Horace Rumbold and Christopher Sykes. He saw Lady Rumbold. He visited his friend Francesco von Mendelssohn. He was received at the highest levels of government, meeting the Reich Chancellor, Heinrich Brüning. But he was still dissatisfied, thinking about the decisions he had made and their consequences – 'when I last sat at that table I was a person of consequence. And now I have lost all the reputation that I had.'[20] The future of Germany seemed no clearer in 1932 than it had done two years previously when Harold had left. Rumbold's view was that Hitler and his movement – the term 'Nazi' was just beginning to gain currency – had peaked and were beginning to lose ground. Harold, perhaps influenced by the experience of the New Party, tended to agree. But that did not prevent him from noticing that the only topic of conversation in the clubs and bars of Berlin was Hitler.

Mosley continued to move closer and closer to the fascist ideas he had seen in operation in Italy. He came to believe ever more firmly in the importance of the youth movement and the inevitability of violence. These were areas where Harold could not and would not follow him. The emphasis on youth, he told Mosley, would alienate any intellectual support the Party might still hope to muster, and the British would never accept violence as a means of bringing about political or constitutional change. The final meeting took place at Great George Street on 19 April. Mosley revealed that he had been approached, and had rejected, overtures from both the Conservatives and from the Labour Party. He had decided to 'coordinate all the fascist groups with Nupa [the youth wing of the New Party] and thus form a central fascist body under his own leadership.' The New Party was thus dissolved and the way open for the formation of the British Union of Fascists which Mosley launched that October. Harold took the train home from Cannon Street Station with 'battered nerves.' Characteristically, he worried not about the future political complexion of the country but about whether he could be accused of desertion and whether he had 'hurt' Mosley.[21]

40 Recovery

In dealing with Mosley and the New Party, it is important to discount hindsight. No one knew at the time the degree to which Mosley would commit himself to fascist doctrines, nor to what fascism itself would lead. Harold was not alone in finding the New Party and its programme attractive, at least in the early stages. Others who did so included one future Prime Minister, Harold Macmillan; three future Cabinet ministers, Oliver Stanley, David Margesson and St Loe Strachey; and one of the twentieth century's leading economists, Maynard Keynes. Harold's error was to commit himself so publicly and to stay committed for so long. He saw what was happening and should have cut his links with the New Party sooner, but it is not correct to suggest that Harold himself ever had any fascist leanings – indeed, his main contribution to the New Party was to argue against Mosley's move in that direction. Nevertheless, his judgement had been demonstrably poor. He felt his reputation had been damaged. His task now was to restore it.

Writing was his way back. Two years of the *Evening Standard* and *Action* had left Harold no time for his own writing. *Lord Carnock* had been published in 1930, but since then he had written nothing. *People and Things*, published in May 1931, was a collection of extracts from his BBC talks, something he regarded as essentially lightweight. In January 1932, waiting for a train to Berlin and wandering the cold, damp streets of Amsterdam, he thought of writing a second novel, resurrecting the figure of Peabody with whom he had toyed for a while during his Berlin years, but it was not until April that he began writing. By that time he considered he had had 'three good months of quarantine ... and got the poison of journalism out of my system.' Writing a novel was a calculated decision. A historical or a literary study would not make money. *Some People* had been his most successful book financially, but he did not feel he could write an effective sequel: the mood was gone and he did not feel he could recapture the 'good-humoured irony ... [and] youthful irreverence ... at my age.' This may sound slightly exaggerated, given that he had finished *Some People* only five-and-a-half years previously, but it points to a sense, latent in the diaries and letters of the period, that the *Evening Standard* and New Party episodes represented, in his own eyes at least, some kind of loss of innocence.

So it was to be a novel. The initial plan was for 'a dramatic, even a romantic novel,'[1] beginning with 'a heroic figure introduced in the Galerie des Glaces just after the signature of the Treaty of Versailles,'[2] but, pottering about in the woods at Sissinghurst, Harold realised that the heroic was not his natural territory. The novel, which was to become *Public Faces*, developed into a satire with a political and diplomatic theme and a far-from-heroic central character, Arthur Peabody – based loosely on Walford Selby – who is discovered in a verbena-scented bath in his London flat. Once he discovered his tone, Harold wrote, as ever, extremely fast. He went through the usual period of self-doubt – 'Am revising the first eight chapters of my novel. It is foul'[3] – but still finished by 19 July. Three days later, he delivered the manuscript, which ran to nearly 100,000 words, and a photograph for the dust jacket, to Michael Sadleir at Constable.

It was a considerable achievement, but it was not enough for Harold. Within a week, he had begun work on another book. *Peacemaking 1919* could hardly have been more different from *Public Faces*. It was never going to be a best-seller, but, in its own particular way, it is a small masterpiece. It is the second part of Harold's diplomatic trilogy: a history of the Paris Peace Conference, but history with a strong didactic intent, identifying the errors made during the Conference, their causes and consequences. He spent three months researching the book, reading contemporary accounts and drawing on the memories of others who were there.

In the middle of this period, on 6 October 1932, *Public Faces* was published to generally favourable reviews. It is an intriguing book in that it appears to predict the invention of atomic bombs and rocket planes, and also expounds the theory of deterrence through strength. Setting the book in the near future – June 1939 – Harold amused himself by giving a satirical twist to political developments, such as the formation of a Mosley-Churchill coalition with Brendan Bracken as Foreign Secretary. The story is witty and well paced, and reviewers noted that it revealed in full, practical detail the inner processes and workings of the Foreign Office (certain more stuffy members of the Office did not approve). Perhaps the physical world of Whitehall and the Foreign Office is not as fully realised as it might have been. Perhaps, too, the central characters, John Shorland and Jane Campbell, are a touch two-dimensional. With Jane Campbell, in particular, one senses that Harold found it difficult to write from a female point of view, with the result that the portrayal is rather patronising. Nonetheless, *Public Faces* is an entertaining read, and achieved the author's aim of restoring his literary reputation. It also sold well, going through four impressions before the end of the year.

At the end of October, Jack Copper, the Nicolsons' chauffeur, drove Harold over to the village of Churt in Surrey to interview Lloyd George. Harold took with him a list of thirty key questions which the former Prime Minister answered – 'glibly', Harold thought – providing the last pieces of the jigsaw Harold was putting together for *Peacemaking*. He had left Lloyd George to the end, feeling the need to formulate – or reformulate – his own views before approaching the man whose personality had dominated and shaped so much of what had taken place at the Paris Conference. Research and preparation over, he began writing on 8 November, knowing that he would have to finish before the end of the year when he and Vita would be setting off for the United States. In fact, he finished precisely one month later and the manuscript was delivered to Constable well before Christmas. Harold certainly knew the subject as well as, if not better than, anyone else and it is true that the second part of the book consists of Harold's diaries from the Conference, but nonetheless it was an astonishing feat.

Between the demise of *Action* and his departure for the United States, Harold had no paid employment. There were various suggestions and approaches – Beaverbrook suggested he might do the books for the *Sunday Express*; Leonard Woolf proposed him as literary editor of the *New Statesman*; there were approaches from the *Sunday Times* and the *Sunday Dispatch* – but none of them came to anything. There was an indirect and tentative suggestion that he might return to the Foreign Office – apparently originating from his former colleague, Sir Robert Vansittart, now Permanent Under-Secretary – which Harold fended off. He wrote articles and gave the occasional lecture, but for most of the year he concentrated on *Public Faces* and *Peacemaking* and spent as much time as he could at

Sissinghurst. Money was a constant worry – neither Harold nor Vita ever seriously managed to economise. Ben had been unhappy at Eton, but had recovered himself and gained a place at Balliol for the following year. Lady Sackville continued to veer between hostility and wild generosity. And yet despite it all, Harold was happier than he had been for a long time. He was happy with Vita and the diary is full of entries which show him working in the garden and enjoying Sissinghurst: 'Go down to the wood, collect foxgloves in the pram and plant them in the nuttery;'[4] 'Plant water-lilies in the lower lake;'[5] 'Viti and I plant lupins at the end of the moat walk.'[6] At the end of the year, he wrote: 'I do not expect that I shall ever love a year so much as this year.'[7]

This end-of-year assessment, however, was written not at Sissinghurst but on the Norddeutsche Lloyd liner, SS *Bremen*, half way across the Atlantic in the middle of one of the worst storms for many years. Harold's American publisher was Houghton Mifflin. Vita's was Doubleday Doran. The two had combined with the lecture agency, Colston Leigh, to organise a three-month lecture tour for the two of them, criss-crossing the United States. From the perspective of a later age, the idea of a lecture tour seems strange and rather quaint, but in a world before television it was an important opportunity for audiences to see and hear authors, artists, philosophers, architects, celebrities or anyone in the public eye, presenting and discussing their ideas. And it was a lucrative activity for both organisers and lecturers.

Neither Harold nor Vita had been to the United States before. When they did arrive – a day late because of the storm – they found they were famous, or at least that an effective publicity machine had projected certain aspects of each of them to the hungry media. Harold was billed as 'a robust, handsome Britisher, with a keen, witty face' and 'one of the cleverest men in England.' Vita was 'the English noblewoman, novelist and poet.' She was also 'Orlando'.[8] Even before they set foot on shore, they were confronted by reporters and photographers. Once down the gangway, they were greeted by Copley Amory, last seen in Persia, but his was a lone familiar face. They were whisked away to Manhattan, where they were besieged by more journalists and photographers and telephoned by everyone from society hostesses to bootleggers (the US was still in the grip of prohibition). They dined at the Waldorf Astoria; they were given a tour of Manhattan; they visited the Empire State Building. And for the next three months, their lives became a kaleidoscope of media attention, trains, hotels, new cities and new faces, punctuated by lectures.

Harold's first impressions were of scale and energy – 'The lights of the great avenues sparkle like fireflies.... The shadows of huge buildings.... Oh brave new world!'[9] But the United States which Harold and Vita visited in 1933 was no longer the confident and prosperous country which had sought to impose its idealistic beliefs on the peace settlement in Paris in 1919. Nor was it the booming economy of the 1920s which had taken the automobile to its heart, set up the first commercial radio stations and made huge loans to Germany. The Great Depression had brought the economy to its knees: five thousand banks had closed; a quarter of the workforce was unemployed; the hotels where Harold and Vita stayed across the country were luxurious but all too often almost deserted. There were even rumours of a further banking collapse which might lose them the dollars they had come to the Unites States to earn. Yet, in a strange way, all this may have worked to their advantage: part of their attraction for the American public seems to have been that they were – or were presented as being – representatives of an unchanging, aristocratic world, an image of stability in uncertain times. Their lectures, and in particular their prepared but not scripted joint discussions – 'What We Think About Marriage'; 'How To Bring Up Children'; 'Romanticism Versus Classicism' – were massively popular and they frequently found themselves facing audiences of over two thousand.

They began on the East Coast (New York, Boston, Princeton, Yale) and moved by stages westward (Buffalo, Cleveland, Cincinnati, Chicago, Denver, Salt Lake City) to Los Angeles and the West Coast. Sometimes they travelled and spoke together; sometimes their itineraries had them travelling and speaking separately. Vita spoke on 'The Modern Spirit in Literature'; 'Novels and Novelists'; 'D. H. Lawrence and Virginia Woolf' and 'Travels through Persia'. Harold spoke about 'English Biography'; 'The Future of Diplomacy' and 'Literature in the Modern Age'. When they were apart, they wrote to each other at least once a day. In Washington, Harold was received at the White House by President Hoover; and he and Vita stayed with Sir Ronald Lindsay, who was now Ambassador to the United States, at the new British Embassy which had been designed by Ned Lutyens just five years before. Returning to Washington after a rapid trip to a snow-bound Chicago, Harold walked down to the site of the old Embassy and felt sad for Lady Sackville who had once presided there but now seemed such a disappointed and tragic figure.

It was a punishing schedule. They were on public view all the time, having to respond politely and cheerfully to their hosts, to their audiences, to well-wishers, to those in the queue at book-signings and, of course, to the ever-inquisitive journalists. On the whole, Vita managed better than Harold, who sometimes felt the need to bite back, but even when he did, his irony was not always understood: '"Have you and Mrs Nicolson ever collaborated on anything?" "Yes," I answer, "we have two sons." "And what age are they?" she asks.'[10] At the end of March, they gave themselves a holiday. They stayed at Smoke Tree Ranch in California, where the skies reminded them of Persia, and then crossed the desert into Arizona to visit the Grand Canyon, which astonished them both. They returned to New York via Charleston in South Carolina, which had so impressed Harold earlier in the trip that he wanted Vita to see it. At midnight on 15 April, they left New York, once again aboard the SS *Bremen*, and arrived off Cherbourg at dawn five days later. Ben and Nigel, who had been studying French near Tours, came on board for the last leg of the voyage. By eight o'clock that evening, they were back at Sissinghurst. Harold calculated that they had travelled 33,527 miles.

Although she found the constant lionising and attention she received tiring, Vita liked the American people and responded positively to their openness and generosity. As she wrote to Virginia, she felt 'battered but enriched, not only by dollars.'[11] Nevertheless, the influence of the United States upon her was transient. She returned to Sissinghurst, to her writing and to her garden, but she never returned to America. Harold's reaction was more complex and more influenced by his political sense. He could not respond as she did to the people – he appreciated their kindness and their generosity, but the lionising and the well-meaning compliments seemed to him to fail to mask a lack of cultural depth. Too often he found his hosts slow and ponderous in conversation. And the only alternative to those he met was 'the vulgarity of big business or the morons of the farming community.'[12] The whole country seemed to him to live in an eternal present, with no sense of the past and no sense of the future – 'They do not plant avenues for their great-grandchildren.... It gives a ghastly feeling of provisionality.'[13]

If this initial reaction was snobbish and condescending – that of an upper-class Englishman (which Harold was and could never quite escape being) faced with a set of values wholly different from his own – his native intellectual honesty did at least lead him to try and probe deeper. He became fascinated by the contrasts. He saw a country containing such an immense variety of scenery, settlement and architecture that he could only conclude that it had no real unity, that America was 'merely a term for a certain surface of the earth.'[14] He saw an emergent world power with such an 'unenlightened and clumsy' understanding of the rest of the world that Americans necessarily became suspicious of everyone else's motives.[15] These thoughts gave rise to a clutch of articles – 'American and English

Recovery

Humour', 'What Struck Me Most in America', 'Americans and Ourselves', 'In Defence of the American Man' – which appeared in the *Daily Telegraph* and in periodicals such as *The Listener* and *Harper's Magazine*. Like much of Harold's journalism in the 1930s, they are entertaining and perceptive pieces with the anecdotal tone of dinner-party conversation, but they hardly represent a profound response to the United States and its people. In the end, Harold could only define America and its emergence by reference to Britain's loss of influence and greater (as he saw it) cultural depth. It was, as Norman Rose identifies, the 'all too familiar daydream: London would play Athens to Washington's Rome.'[16] And it was an issue which would come to the fore again in 1934 when he was asked to write a biography of a truly American figure.

The Nicolsons had gone to the United States to make money. Between them they earned £3,000. Personal expenses and an enjoyable holiday at the end of the tour meant that they arrived home with some £2,000 in their collective pocket. The problem was that they continued to live beyond their means and that Harold still had no regular income. He agreed to write a regular book review column for the *Daily Telegraph*, but that was nowhere near enough. Another book seemed to be required and, on 1 May, he began researching the third part of his diplomatic trilogy: *Curzon: The Last Phase, 1919–1925*.

Meanwhile, *Peacemaking*, the second part of the same trilogy, was published on 11 June. In Britain, it was received with something approaching rapture and, indeed, it is in some ways Harold's most brilliant and original work. Perhaps because he was writing about what he knew, Harold managed to make the issues, complexities and personalities of a long dead peace conference seem alive and relevant. The first part of the book – 'As It Seems Now' – is an analytical account of the Paris Peace Conference and its proceedings from the perspective of the 1930s. The second part – 'As It Seemed Then' – consists of Harold's diaries from 1919. The whole becomes a remarkable *tour de force* which is detailed, precise, and pointed, dealing not only with the Conference itself but with its political, personal, geographical and social context. American reviewers were more reserved. In part this may have been because of Harold's quite explicit criticisms of President Wilson and the way in which he approached the Conference, but the underlying reason seems to have been a failure to appreciate or understand the detached, even ironic tone, which characterises parts of the book – most notably, of course, the diary extracts. This led some American critics to suggest that Harold was not entirely serious about his subject. The one thing *Peacemaking* did not do, of course, was make money. However brilliant Harold's writing, the book was never going to attract a mass audience. It made just £500.

That Harold would choose to write about Curzon at some stage was probably inevitable. Though his early death and the radical shifts that had taken place in British society and politics since 1925 had diminished his reputation, Curzon remained a major figure on Harold's personal landscape – not just because they had worked closely together. Harold had turned down the opportunity to write the full, official biography of Curzon in 1925 and Ronaldshay's painstaking but dull life had appeared in 1928. Now, at a distance from the Foreign Office and the official view, Harold felt able to concentrate on Curzon's achievements and the way in which his conduct as Foreign Secretary represented a shift in the nature of diplomatic practice. During the summer of 1933, Harold worked with his usual speed and intensity. Despite being denied previously-promised access to personal papers by Lady Curzon (who claimed that she, too, was intending to write a book about her husband), by the end of August he had moved from research to writing and by the end of November he had finished the first draft and the first revisions. The manuscript, together with maps (drawn by Ben) and photographs, was delivered to Constable at the beginning of January 1934.

Intent though Harold was on *Curzon*, it was obvious that another book with a diplomatic theme was not going to solve his financial problems and he continued to cast around for other, more lucrative work. At one point in October, he even considered an invitation from Beaverbrook to return to the 'Londoner's Diary' as the sole editor. Only a letter from Vita's French bank disclosing that she had a balance of £2,600 which she had forgotten about and the strident disapproval of the Woolfs saved him.

Money issues aside, by the end of 1933 Harold's literary and journalistic output had gone a long way towards re-establishing the reputation that (at least in his own eyes) he had lost by his flirtation with Mosley and the New Party. It had not, however, been a year without personal dramas. Ben learnt to drive, then wrecked his car by driving it into a telegraph pole, though without injuring himself. Nigel had appendicitis and was so ill after the operation that the surgeon – the splendidly named Sir Lancelot Barrington-Ward – told Harold and Vita that 'for the next thirty-six hours it must be touch and go.'[17] Both boys were growing up and establishing their personalities, a process which, as in every family, created its own tensions. Harold understood what was happening better than Vita and tried to see it in perspective:

The real difference is that V. and Ben are introverts and Niggs and I are extroverts. Niggs' remorseless logic irritates her as much as Ben's muddle-headedness irritates me. Yet how slight is the irritation really! Our happiness and understanding is so complete that the slightest discordance echoes like a thunderstorm.[18]

One problem which tested even Harold's patience and which could easily have done great damage to the family was Lady Sackville. In May, a couple of weeks before his accident, Ben drove his new two-seater car down to Brighton and made a dutiful visit to his old and increasingly immobile grandmother. The family were accustomed to accusations from Lady Sackville – that Vita or the boys had stolen things from her; that they never wrote to her; that her lawyers would be seeking to repossess various items that she had given them. On this occasion, however, she told Ben about his parents' homosexuality, about Harold's affairs with boys in Persia and Berlin, about Vita's affair with Violet, and about Virginia who she claimed had nearly wrecked their marriage. Ben, by his own account, did not believe her, being more concerned about playing golf the next day, but over dinner that evening he told his parents what had been said.

> It was they who were deeply embarrassed, not I. I took their embarrassment to mean that they were shocked that Lady Sackville should do anything so monstrous. It never occurred to me that they were also distressed that the central drama of their lives was being played back to them by their adolescent son.
>
> I can imagine the conversation that took place as they left the dining-room. The truth was out, but which of them was to confirm it? ... My father with his fastidiousness could never have brought himself to enlighten me; by letter, perhaps, but not face to face. It was my mother who sat on my bed at midnight and into the small hours, and I suppose it was the first intimate talk we ever had.[19]

The truth was out. Ben knew. Nigel was told. Harold and Vita were so appalled at Lady Sackville's behaviour that Harold took medical advice on Lady Sackville's state of mind and legal advice on how any future problems might be dealt with. Ben retold the story later that same month when Leonard and Virginia were lunching at Sissinghurst. Virginia was furious. Perhaps Lady Sackville in the bitterness of old age and loneliness had intended to try and turn Ben and Nigel against their parents. If so, she failed, achieving only a concentration of anger against herself.

In the short term at least, Lady Sackville's revelations had little or no impact on the family – unless it influenced Ben's driving. It was obvious to both boys that their parents were devoted to each other. Life carried on. Ben went off to Florence to study art and Italian. Nigel returned to school where he did extremely well in his School Certificate exams, gaining no less than eight credits. Whether their parents' unusual relationship was to have longer term emotional implications for them is a more open question.

41 Morrow

Mosley was in the past. Harold was no longer involved in either diplomacy or politics. He had worked hard to re-establish the reputation he believed he had lost, but that was not the same as having a clear sense of direction. Writing was immensely important to him – since *Verlaine* in 1921, Harold had published eleven books and *Curzon*, the twelfth, was to appear in May 1934 – but it had always been an additional activity, something to be fitted around the demands made on his time by his profession. Now, he had to accept that writing *was* his profession and to restructure his daily life and his mental attitude accordingly. It was a process he did not find easy and, as was often the case when uncertain about the future, he went travelling, partly as an escape and partly out of a submerged belief that the journey would provide inspiration – which it did. In the event, the inspiration in question proved to have only a limited impact on his future career, but things could have turned out very differently.

At the end of January 1934, Vita and Gwen St Aubyn, Harold's younger sister, drove down to Italy where they rented a hilltop villa called, confusingly, Il Castello, overlooking the Ligurian fishing village of Portofino. Harold was still worrying about money. 'I like being turned out of my dear little suburban home and made to sleep in a ruined tower on a camp bed,' he wrote. 'And I see no reason why, in the present state of our finances, you should not buy the Castello outright.'[1] The reason for the holiday was to provide peace and quiet for Gwen, who had suffered serious head injuries in a car crash the previous year while Harold and Vita were in the United States. Gwen's need for regular treatment at the London Clinic meant that she had spent much of the previous six months at Sissinghurst where Vita had been looking after her. Whether as a consequence of her injuries or Vita's care or for some other reason, Gwen's period of convalescence coincided with a questioning of her role as wife and mother (she had five children) and an upwelling of religious faith, which was to lead her to become a Roman Catholic the following year. She and Vita became inseparable.

Harold decided to join them, but took a circuitous route. It was one of those journeys, increasingly common as he grew older and his reputation increased, studded with well-known names. He travelled to Paris in company with James Lees-Milne, his future biographer, whom he had met during the 1931 election campaign and with whom he was to have a brief affair and a lasting friendship. Lees-Milne was present when Harold called at James Joyce's flat on rue Galilée, just off the avenue Kléber. Unsurprisingly, given their contrasting characters, it was an encounter that never took off. Joyce was wearing his best suit and carpet slippers. Harold, who greatly admired *Ulysses*, was left with the impression of a man of 'brittle and vulnerable strangeness,' who had 'little contact with reality.'[2] From Paris, Harold went via Munich to Vienna, where he was met by Walford Selby, now Minister at the British Legation there. He lectured to the Anglo-Austrian Association. He dined with the Austrian aristocracy – the Prince and Princess Rohan, Prince Schwarzenberg, Countess Palfi – families which remembered all too well life under the Hapsburg monarchy and now sensed revolution in the air again with 'most of the country ... Nazi in feeling.'[3] From Vienna, he travelled down to Portofino, where he called on his old acquaintance Max Beerbohm, whom he found physically much changed, and met the Nobel Prize-winning German dramatist, Gerhardt Hauptmann. He met up with Vita and Gwen and the three of them went to stay with Somerset Maugham at his villa at Cap Ferrat, visiting Cannes, where in the bar of the Carlton Hotel, they met the novelist Michael Arlen.

From Cap Ferrat, the three of them travelled to Morocco where they visited Marrakech, Casablanca, Rabat, Fez and Tangier. It was thirty years since Harold had last visited the country and, although there had been many changes, he still loved the atmosphere and the scenery – 'Walk up in the evening to the cemetery above Bab Guissa ... a story teller with Arabs arrayed around him upon the tombs and rocks. And to the west is the valley of Oued el Fez, the edge of town and the distant snowy mountains, with the dust of returning goats hanging in the evening sun.'[4] The only problem was that, while in Fez, Harold was bitten on the ear by an insect. The bite became infected and by the time he reached England he was so ill that his doctor, Sir Louis Knuthsen, insisted that he be admitted to a nursing home where he spent nearly a week. Harold was delirious and so certain that he was going to die that he rewrote his will, but the crisis passed and he recovered quickly.

Somewhere between Munich and Cap Ferrat, Harold came up with what, in his diaries, he calls 'THE IDEA' or 'my *magnum opus.*' It was to be a six-volume autobiography called *Mutations* (one perhaps not entirely serious diary entry suggests the title 'FA or *Fictional Autobiography*'[5]). He realised from the first that this was not going to be a money-making project and at one point in the diary, he notes (bizarrely): 'I must try and write a play first.'[6] But he was intensely excited: 'It is a great adventure, perhaps the most important thing that I have ever essayed.'[7] He spent a long time debating with himself whether he should write in the first or the third person and the extent to which he should fictionalise his experiences. He wanted to avoid introducing fictional situations because he did not want to end up writing a bad novel. He did not want to write like Proust, whose work he felt contained too many half-truths. He wanted to be sincere and tell the truth, but at the same time – being Harold – he feared that too much truth might wound other people.

The project was never to be realised. Although two later volumes – *Helen's Tower* (1937) and *The Desire to Please* (1943) – have a flyleaf subtitle, *In Search of the Past*, suggesting they are part of a series, the idea had clearly been much diluted by that stage.[8] The main interest, however, is what the concept says about Harold's view of himself and his work at the age of forty-eight and in what was to prove a transitional period of his life. He was clearly trying to come to terms with his new situation.

> I may be wrong, but I feel in the last year I have found myself ... my day-dreams have centred upon the picture of my returning to the Foreign Office as Secretary of State. But now that I am obsessed by THE IDEA all this seems perfectly trivial, and is disclosed as an ... illusion that I am really a man of action.[9]

What brought this on? Re-reading Proust? Consciousness of the essentially transient nature of the many magazine articles and book reviews he was having to write to keep afloat financially? Visiting the Galerie des Glaces in Versailles with James Lees-Milne and knowing that he had been present at a pivotal moment in history? Morocco and the childhood memories it evoked certainly helped develop 'THE IDEA' but they were not its Genesis.

Ambition lay at the heart of it. Harold's ambition was not the obvious kind: he did not long for power or fame for its own sake. But he did want to be recognised as intelligent, as a positive influence on the tide of human events, which is why he wanted so much to be at the centre of political activity. He also wanted to be understood: one reason perhaps why he reacted so strongly when criticised. If he could no longer be a great diplomat or a great politician, he would be a great writer and that, to Harold's traditional mind, meant writing a *magnum opus*. Nor is it beside the point that literary greatness was an ambition Vita would understand and support. To her dying day, however much she loved him, she could never understand Harold's attachment to the political world.

It is a fascinating prospect: Harold's own account and interpretation of his family background and his first fifty years. Why was it never written? Nigel Nicolson recognises that it was 'untypical' of Harold not to have carried the project forward and suggests that this may have been due to the illness which followed the insect-bite in Fez.[10] Norman Rose, more plausibly, suggests that Harold was 'deficient in ruthlessness' and that, consequently, the project 'outran his literary skills.'[11] Harold's stated desire to tell the truth would inevitably have come into conflict with his reluctance to hurt anyone and with his sense of decorum, his gentlemanliness. How, for example, would he have coped with issues surrounding his own and Vita's private lives? Was the world ready for the full story of Vita and Violet or, indeed, of Harold and Raymond Mortimer? To have omitted the private dimension entirely would have been a half-truth of immense proportions. Harold would have been limited not so much by his skill as by his character.

His creativity was not the same as Vita's. He appreciated poetry but could never have written it. The best parts of his novels are drawn from life and from personal experience. For all the charm of *Sweet Waters*, his fiction is competent and entertaining rather than inspired. *Some People*, his most imaginative book, takes reality as its starting point, then extends and exaggerates it. This is not to belittle his achievement, but rather to recognise that his imagination leant more towards the critical and the analytical than the purely or abstractly creative. If the *magnum opus* were to be essentially a history of Harold's life and times, this would be an advantage, but, according to his diary, it was also to be either an autobiography or a biography with 'a serious philosophical shape.'[12] And a philosopher is one thing that Harold was not. He was never truly at home in abstraction. The generalisations he makes about life in his radio talks and magazine articles are not broad, sweeping theories, but lessons drawn from anecdotes or from his observations of people going about their daily lives. The same is true of his reflections on diplomatic and political life. As Derek Drinkwater demonstrates in *Sir Harold Nicolson & International Relations*, there is a case for seeing Harold as a theorist, even a major theorist, in the field of international relations, but that case has to be drawn out of his writings, which are practical in orientation, on diplomacy and international events. Though he published a book entitled simply *Diplomacy* and lectured on 'The Evolution of Diplomatic Method', Harold's stated concern was 'with the actual functioning of modern diplomacy, with the relation between diplomacy and commerce, with the organisation and administration of the Foreign Service.'[13] If he took a historical approach it was because 'I have observed that politicians, unlike diplomatists, have no time to learn the lessons of history.'[14] In attitude at least, Harold fell between the roles of writer and man of action – not irredeemably in terms of his life and career as a whole, but with sufficient force to prevent his all-inclusive design for *Mutations* taking any coherent shape.

This same duality was picked up by the more perceptive reviewers when *Curzon: The Last Phase* was published on 10 May 1934. The *Times Literary Supplement*, taking a positive view, said that 'the philosopher and the biographer struggled for control of his pen.'[15] The American magazine, *Nation*, however, described the book as 'partly a sermon and partly a life' and saw Harold as 'the victim of contrary forces within himself', caught between an awareness of the faults of the past and an unwillingness to trust (or, perhaps better, imagine) a more democratic future.[16] The vast majority of reviews, however, were enthusiastic, even adulatory – and the publication of four extracts in *The Times* in the run-up to publication day boosted sales. Harold was deluged with letters of congratulation both from friends and from public figures. The only really sour note came from Lady Curzon who, having made writing the book more difficult by withholding access to Curzon's papers, now described Harold's portrait of her late husband as a caricature.[17]

Accepted on its own terms and as the third part of Harold's diplomatic trilogy, *Curzon: The Last Phase* is a remarkable book. There are minor inconsistencies, and the 'Terminal Essay' on aspects of diplomatic practice simply does not fit, but one can imagine how, in 1934, the book itself appeared almost radical. Harold pulls together the major strands of what was then the recent political past into a sequential narrative, offering a clear view of the personal and diplomatic mechanisms through which events and crises unfolded and were resolved. Curzon himself comes across as a multifaceted character: imperialist, statesman, negotiator, arrogant aristocrat, sensitive leader. He is a flawed hero, but a hero nonetheless, drawn from life as Harold knew him, and Harold's affection – the genuine affection of one who had experienced the man at his best and at his worst – comes across clearly.

Just two days after the publication of *Curzon*, Harold was driven to Tilbury where he boarded the Swedish Lloyd ship, SS *Suecia*, bound for Gothenburg. From Gothenburg, he took a train to Stockholm where he was greeted by his old friend Archie Clerk Kerr who, since 1931, had rejoiced in the title of Envoy Extraordinary and Minister Plenipotentiary to the King of Sweden. Harold's purpose was to lecture on 'Democratic Diplomacy' to the Swedish-British Society, which he did, receiving an appreciative vote of thanks from the Society's President, but the real significance of the visit was that, while in Stockholm, he first became seriously aware of the way the wind was blowing in Germany. Hitler had become Chancellor in January, and now, according to a German exile who had made his way to Stockholm, many of those who had supported liberal policies were being imprisoned or leaving the country.

On his return to London, Harold, as a member of the Anglo-German Association, lunched with another German exile, Heinrich Brüning, whom he had last met as Reich Chancellor at the beginning of 1932. Brüning, too, was full of dire warnings about what was happening in Germany. His solution, which Harold at this time apparently supported, was to bring back the Hohenzollern monarchy. That was 12 June. Three weeks later came the Night of the Long Knives when Hitler quite literally killed off all political opposition in Germany. It was another indication of what the future would hold and, although it was far too early to contemplate any form of intervention, Harold was one of the first to warn publicly – in a book review in the *Daily Telegraph* on 6 July – that political action would be required to prevent Germany from attacking what he called 'the civilisation' of other countries.

Whether or not *Mutations* would have seen the light of day, or whether it was too big and too complex a project for Harold, it was, initially at least, simply overtaken by events. On 26 June, he was invited to lunch at the London-based investment bank Morgan Grenfell, which was closely linked to the American finance house, J. P. Morgan. Edward Grenfell showed him a letter from Mrs Elizabeth Morrow, widow of the American lawyer, banker and diplomat, Dwight Morrow, who had died suddenly in 1931, asking that Harold should be commissioned to write a biography of her husband. He thought about it for a few days and then accepted.

Sybil Colefax seems to have been responsible for this unexpected invitation. Thomas Lamont, Chairman of J. P. Morgan, was one of her close friends and she had actually introduced him to Harold at one of her fabled society dinners in 1931. It was Lamont who had suggested Harold's name to Elizabeth Morrow, although his recommendation may well have been confirmed via another route. On arrival in New York in January 1933, Harold and Vita had been faced with a huge welcome dinner at the Waldorf Astoria. Among the guests were the pilot, Charles Lindbergh, and his wife, Anne, who was Dwight Morrow's daughter. Harold and Lindbergh met only briefly but apparently they got on well. They were to get to know each other better over the next few years.

A book about Dwight Morrow appeared to offer the prospect of good sales in the United States, and Harold was attracted by the diplomatic theme, albeit in a very different context from his previous work. At the same time, there were some serious issues to be faced. The book was a commission, an official life, and Harold was concerned about his authorial independence – rightly, as things turned out. Some of Morrow's greatest professional successes – in the years before he became a diplomat – had been in the field of corporate and international finance, subjects about which Harold's ignorance was almost total. Moreover, Morrow and his life were deeply American in character, both psychologically and culturally. It would require extensive research and a leap of the imagination for Harold to understand and convey the essential Americanness of his subject. Indeed, he was warned at the outset that he might even face prejudice because he, as an Englishman, had been selected for the task. Between his first investigations into Morrow's life at the beginning of July 1934 and publication in October 1935, Harold made four trips to the United States. The first began in September aboard SS *Berengaria* in a mood of self-pity and self-doubt. One reason for giving up diplomacy was because it separated him from Vita. Now, it seemed that even writing was taking him away from her, and he was still feeling uncertain, even guilty, about choosing a literary career – 'I could have done this biography business when 60, and devoted these thirteen years to real active work.'[18]

In New York, Harold was met by representatives of the Morrow family and of J. P. Morgan. Immigration formalities were reduced to a minimum. A convoy of limousines whisked him the thirty kilometres (twenty miles) to Next Day Hill, a wooded, forty-acre estate on the edge of Englewood, New Jersey, where Morrow himself had died and where Elizabeth Morrow now lived together with Charles and Anne Lindbergh. Harold grew to admire Elizabeth Morrow and to respect the courage she showed in the face of the series of tragedies which confronted her family. The Lindberghs became close friends, for whom he felt 'real affection'.[19] Lindbergh's solo flight across the Atlantic in 1927 had made him a national hero. He had married Anne Morrow in 1929, but their lives were shattered when their first child was kidnapped, ransomed, and then found murdered. J. L. Mencken called it 'the biggest story since the Resurrection' and the Lindberghs found themselves subjected to massive and intrusive press attention. Harold's first visit coincided with the arrest of Bruno Hauptmann, the German carpenter who was eventually convicted and executed for the crime. This redoubled media attention and affected the atmosphere at Englewood. Harold was full of admiration for the Lindberghs' dignity and the way in which, whatever their inner thoughts, they 'made a determined habit of ignoring the Press.'[20]

The Morrows had a summer house at Deacon Brown Point on the island of North Haven, eight miles off the coast of Maine. Harold crossed to the island in the Morrow steam yacht, *St Michael*, piloted by Morrow's personal captain, as porpoises played in the blue waters around him. In an attempt to understand his subject's origins and background, he travelled with Morrow's sister, Alice, to Pittsburgh, where 'factories smoke on every hand and the sluggish waters of the Ohio are fringed with coal dust.'[21] He travelled on to Washington to meet some of Morrow's political associates, staying once again with Sir Ronald Lindsay at the Embassy. From Englewood, he made a number of trips into New York to talk to people at J. P. Morgan who had known and worked with Morrow during his years at the bank. He also lectured on diplomacy to students at Yale. There were moments of personal relaxation – a weekend with Archibald MacLeish in the Massachusetts hills, a weekend with Copley Amory on his family's island off the Massachusetts coast, meetings with the Roosevelt family, not to mention three or four casual sexual encounters in New York about which he boasted to Raymond Mortimer. However, for most of the ten weeks he was in the United States, Harold remained at Englewood, working determinedly – and ably assisted by Miss Schiff, a lady employed by the Morrows – through the vast archive of Dwight Morrow's papers that had been preserved there.

Harold quickly realised that the interesting thing about Dwight Morrow was his character and psychology – 'the mind of a super-criminal and the character of a saint.'[22] The impact he had on other people was more important than his actual achievements. The difficulty was getting an objective description of his subject. Judge Learned Hand said openly that Morrow had an ability to captivate or fascinate people, despite the fact that he lacked charm and was physically revolting. J. P. Morgan himself told Harold that Morrow was ambitious and selfish. To everyone else, he was 'so true, so staunch, so loyal.' Nothing could have brought out more strongly the contrast between Harold, for whom objectivity *was* truth, and the American way of thinking. It aroused within him a quite uncharacteristic degree of anger and frustration, which, being English, he suppressed.

> There is something in the smarminess of Americans which makes me see red.... I feel a sharp, cold knife coming up within me and I want to cut and slash. It is something nastier than any mere intellectual annoy-

ance at the eternal superficiality of the American race. It is something really *unkind*. I longed to say, 'But this is all nonsense and you know it. Dwight Morrow was a shrewd and selfish little *arriviste* who drank himself to death.' ... I could have smashed and bashed their silly heads. I merely sat there glum and silent.[23]

At the beginning of December, Harold took ship for Europe, meeting up with Ben and James Lees-Milne in Paris, before returning to Sissinghurst, where he began the process of turning the huge loose-leaf folder of notes which he had amassed into a coherent narrative.

By the time he returned to New York aboard SS *Berengaria* at the beginning of February 1935, he had a solid first draft of the first fourteen of the book's eighteen chapters. The main purpose of this trip was to visit Mexico, where Morrow had been US Ambassador between 1927 and 1930, but he went first to Englewood, where both Elizabeth Morrow (now 'Betty' in the diaries) and the Lindberghs greeted him almost as a member of the family. Nonetheless, it was a difficult evening. He arrived on the day when the trial of Bruno Hauptmann for the murder of the Lindberghs' child reached its conclusion. The verdict was announced while Harold was talking to Dwight Morrow's nephew. Charles Lindbergh took control of the situation by asking if Harold had been following the case.

> And then quite quietly, while we all sat round in the pantry, he went though the case point by point. It seemed to relieve all of them. He did it very quietly, very simply. He pretended to address his remarks to me only. But I could see that he was really trying to ease the agonised tension through which Betty and Ann had passed.[24]

The original intention had been that Harold should travel to Mexico with Elizabeth Morrow alone, but in the event the Lindberghs came too. They travelled by train, a long and not terribly comfortable journey passing through St Louis and Little Rock, crossing Texas, and reaching the Mexican frontier at Laredo. They eventually arrived in Mexico City which Harold found shabby and dilapidated. Cars awaited them and they were driven eighty kilometres (fifty miles) south to the small town of Cuernavaca. This was the town with which Morrow had fallen in love – 'halfway between the central plateau and the tropical regions of the coast ... huddling its roofs below the Cathedral and around the pink municipal building which was the last palace of Hernando Cortes.' Morrow had bought a small house and extended it to become a place of 'happiness and repose', a weekend retreat where he could 'watch the sunset melt into green behind the mountains while the two volcanoes still glowed pink and violet in the east.'[25] Harold, too, fell in love with the place. He had a cottage and courtyard at the end of the garden. There were blue plumbago flowers, hummingbirds, and the heavy scent of datura. Peasants with huge Mexican hats led donkeys through the streets.

It was in Cuernavaca under these almost idyllic circumstances that Harold finished the main part of the manuscript and here, too, that Elizabeth and Anne Morrow read through the bulk of what he had written. They seemed to understand what he was trying to do and never quibbled at the criticisms he ventured of his subject. Harold, as ever when in the last stages of a book, was smitten with self-doubt – 'it is dull' – but relieved that the family were happy. This was the first time he had written a book without knowing something about the subject before he started and he felt he had learnt a lot in the process. He had also gained 'a real friendship with the Morrow family and this wonderful visit to Mexico.' [26] His departure from Cuernavaca, when the family waved him off from the end of their lane, was an emotional moment.

From Mexico City, he took the train to Guadalajara where he stopped to look at the extraordinary cathedral which was crowded with pilgrims and worshippers. He continued northwards, breaking his journey at Culiacán where he had an interview with Plutarco Calles, the former President and *de facto* dictator of Mexico. Calles had been one of Morrow's principal interlocutors in his struggle to reconstruct the relationship between the United States and Mexico. Harold hoped, rather than expected, that he would gain some insight into Morrow's character but Calles kept on saying, 'Senor Morrow was a man of great judgement and friendliness,'[27] which was no use at all.

Another train journey right across the United States, another transatlantic crossing and Harold was home. But he was off again almost immediately. He had promised to show Nigel, who had inherited his father's love of the classics, the great sites of the ancient world. Harold, Vita, Nigel and Gwen drove to Marseilles, where they picked up a cruise ship destined for Greece and the Greek islands. It was another of Harold's name-studded trips with Hugh Walpole, Sir Henry Lunn and Lady Ravensdale (Lord Curzon's eldest daughter, Mary) among the passengers and Axel Munthe among those he met along the way. The cruise was accompanied by lectures from some of Britain's leading classicists, but when it came to Byron, to Nigel's mingled pride and embarrassment, they turned to Harold. Father and son disembarked at Naples, travelled on to Rome and returned to

England by train. Vita, who was researching her book, *St Joan of Arc*, returned at a slower pace through France with Gwen.

Back again at Sissinghurst on the last day of April, it looked as if the pace of Harold's life might slow down just a little, but it was not to be. On 16 May, Elizabeth Morrow telephoned from Englewood to say that the House of J. P. Morgan was raising objections to some aspects of the book. Harold waited for the dossier to arrive. When it did, it was clear he would have to return to America. By the end of May, Harold was once again in mid-Atlantic, this time on RMS *Aquitania*.

Matters of fact were easily dealt with, but a number of the issues raised by J. P. Morgan's many partners, all of whom had been allowed to have their say, were questions of interpretation which required discussion and mutual understanding. The truth was, Harold decided, that although he had not been critical of the bank, he had not treated it with the 'awed respect' which its partners expected.[28] Moreover, he had not hidden the fact that Dwight Morrow had reservations about it. Criticism from J. P. Morgan was followed by a memorandum from the US State Department's legal adviser, Reuben Clark, complaining about the Mexican chapters. For the first time Elizabeth Morrow's confidence in Harold faltered. Harold, as ever, reacted badly to criticism, and lay awake in 'torments of rage.'[29] In the event, with advice from the journalist, Walter Lippmann, he managed to deal with the J. P. Morgan criticisms, while on close examination the State Department memorandum reduced itself to 'complete nonsense.'[30] Elizabeth Morrow's confidence, which was extremely important to Harold, was restored and he returned home.

There was to be a fourth trip to the United States that summer. Harold took Ben with him and they stayed in idyllic circumstances at the Morrows' summer house on North Haven. The purpose of the trip was to correct proofs and construct an index; when not working Harold enjoyed swimming and waterskiing, cutting down trees and building bonfires. Ben played tennis and went up in Lindbergh's plane. The significance was not so much that *Dwight Morrow* was finished and the proofs despatched to the publishers, but that it cemented the friendship between Harold and the Morrow-Lindbergh family.

Norman Rose sees Harold 'yielding' to the demands from the House of Morgan as an example of the lack of ruthlessness which dogged and damaged Harold's career.[31] While it is true that Harold did lack ruthlessness, he also, throughout his life, allowed personal feelings to influence his judgement and in this case his desire to retain Elizabeth Morrow's good opinion seems the dominant factor.

The influence of American caution and sentimentality has pervaded my style. My fear of hurting Betty's feelings has made me a trifle sloppy. And then the excisions have removed from the book any tang that it might have had. The result is soft and flabby. But in spite of all this Morrow does emerge as a real person, not as a legend. I am not really discontented with the book.³²

Elizabeth Morrow, Charles Lindbergh and George Rublee – Morrow's personal assistant during his later years with whom Harold struck up a friendship – were all warm in praise of *Dwight Morrow*. When it was published in October 1935, the opinion of the reviewers, echoing Harold's own, was one of qualified approval. Harold's skill and hard work could not disguise the fact that, whatever the fascination of his character, Morrow's life was not punctuated by the kind of incidents or achievements which made for a captivating narrative. Moreover, and more important, Harold did not really understand America or the Americans and it showed. It was all very well for Charles Lindbergh to say that he did not see how 'a Britisher' could have written the book,³³ but Lindbergh was no critic. Others recognised that Harold could only interpret the United States in terms of Britain. Perhaps the clearest illustration of this is Harold's assessment of a comment from J. P. Morgan himself.

> I had written, in describing the immense expansion assumed by Morgan's bank at the outbreak of war: 'It ceased to be a private firm and became almost a Department of Government.' I meant that as a compliment. Old J. P. Morgan appears to have regarded it as an insult.... [It] 'will be interpreted as if we were reduced to the status of a department subordinate to the Government.' This is characteristic of both of us. *I feel it the highest compliment to compare Morgan's to the Foreign Office. They* regard it as an insult to suggest that they have any connection with the Government, or any government. But, you see, the whole point of view is different. I regard bankers and banking as rather low class fellows [*sic*]. They regard officials as stupid and corrupt.³⁴

Harold was too steeped in the complexities and sophistries of Europe to appreciate fully the frontier character of certain aspects of American society and politics. And he was too gentlemanly to see the vaulting personal ambition and the defining corporate loyalties of Wall Street as both qualitatively and quantitatively different from those of the City of London. His values and the perspective he cast on his narrative were essentially British.

Despite its failings and the reservations expressed by some reviewers, *Dwight Morrow* sold well, which was a relief to Harold since the project had taken over a year and he had accepted no money for the commission beyond his expenses. He knew that it was not among his best books, but by the time it appeared, in October 1935, he could push that concern into the background because his life had once again changed direction.

42 Election

Even before the Morrows' beach-wagon took the final proofs of *Dwight Morrow* to the post, Harold's certainty of having found himself, his conviction that he was a man of literature not a man of action, had vanished. Sissinghurst, he realised when he returned to it from America, was wonderful but did not satisfy all of him. He still felt he needed a role in the world. In June 1935, shortly before his final Morrow trip to the United States, he had a conversation with Christopher Hobhouse who told him frankly that he did not have a political mind. This was followed the same day by a lunch during which he learnt that Michael Sadleir at Constable thought he would survive as 'one of the leading writers of this age.' Harold was plunged into another round of introspection, leading him once again to the conclusion that he should concentrate on literature.

> My desire to go into politics is motivated by feelings other than real political ambition or aptitude.... I wish to enter public life partly from a sense of curiosity, partly from a feeling of duty, and partly because I have not sufficient confidence in my own literary gifts. Obviously, I should rather be the Proust of England.... If Michael and Christopher are both right, then there is only one alternative. I must devote such years as may remain to me to my *magnum opus* ...[1]

The resolution did not hold. It was an unhappy summer. He loved and needed Vita, as she loved and needed him, but she had her own life and her own interests. Ben was abroad studying in pursuit of his ambition to become an art historian. Nigel was abroad studying German before going up to Oxford. Harold reviewed books for the *Daily Telegraph* and grew frustrated. As the international situation worsened, he felt the pull of old ties.

On 21 August, with Mussolini on the verge of invading Abyssinia, he was invited to one of Emerald Cunard's society lunches where he had the opportunity to exchange a few words with Anthony Eden, who held the unusual position of Minister without Portfolio for League of Nations Affairs at the Foreign Office. 'I felt,' he wrote in his diary, 'that I had touched the fringe of the centre of the problem. But I also felt that in the FO I should have been in the centre of the problem.'[2] This led him to speak to his old friend, Sir Lancelot Oliphant, about the possibility of rejoining the Foreign Office, but he quickly realised he could not go back, and wrote an apologetic letter withdrawing the request. A thoroughly outrageous and drunken weekend in Venice with his old boyfriend Victor Cunard was enjoyable but did not solve the essential problem. The solution came in a phone call on 3 October from Vita's second cousin, who rejoiced in the name and title of Herbrand Edward Dundonald Brassey Sackville, ninth Earl De La Warr, but was generally known as 'Buck'.

Harold had let it be known to friends and acquaintances that he was interested in standing for Parliament, but had not pursued the idea with any great energy. In June 1935, he had put his name forward as a potential Conservative candidate for Sevenoaks, but was not shortlisted (Vita was pointedly not interested – an indication of things to come). Buck De La Warr's phone call was different. He was an influential figure: the first hereditary peer to join the Labour Party and one of the few ministers who had followed Ramsay MacDonald and joined the National Government in 1931. He was now Chairman of the committee which coordinated the allocation of seats between the component parts of the National Government. Would Harold stand as National Labour candidate for West Leicester?

The formation of a National Government in August 1931 had split both the Labour and Liberal Parties. The subsequent general election in October of that year had therefore been fought by the Conservative Party, the National Labour Party and the National Liberal Party, all campaigning together under a National Government banner against Labour and Liberal opposition. The National Government was triumphant and Ramsay MacDonald continued as Prime Minister (in the face of accusations of betrayal and great bitterness on the part of many former Labour colleagues), but it was a strange triumph. His National Labour Party won only 13 seats and the National Liberals only 35, while the Conservatives won 475. MacDonald continued to lead the government until June 1935 when, with his health failing, he stood aside as Prime Minister in favour of the Conservative leader, Stanley Baldwin, but remained as leader of National Labour. The party that Harold was being asked to join and to represent was thus the most junior partner in the National Government and led by an ailing, isolated and unpopular former Prime Minister. He accepted.

Things began to move quickly. A general election was in the offing. The National Labour Party was prepared to accept Harold as a candidate, but it was clear that he would face Labour and Liberal opposition. In this case, he would need the Conservative vote if he were to win. He dutifully went to Leicester to appear before a meeting of the West Leicester Conservative Association. He answered questions on Abyssinia, the topic of the hour, with no difficulty at all, but when it came to 'the mining question' he had to fall back on his charm. 'Well,' said one lady, 'I am sure, Mr Nicolson, if you smile like that, it doesn't matter what you know or don't know.'[3] The West Leicester Conservatives agreed to support him and he was launched.

Then there was the question of election expenses, which would amount to some £1,500. A third would come from National Labour headquarters and a third would come from constituency organisations, but he was expected to pay one third himself. He asked Vita for a loan to be paid for by a mortgage on Long Barn. She raised no objection. She was prepared to make money available, if that was what Harold wanted. What she was not prepared to make available was herself. She would not come up to Leicester. She would not play the candidate's wife. She would not attend meetings, canvass for votes, open bazaars, or do anything of that sort. It was not just that she disliked the workings of democracy, having to ask for the support of ordinary people whom she regarded as 'bedint'; it was not just that her own inclinations were increasingly towards solitude and seclusion; it was a question of her personal independence, which she guarded fiercely. Harold had known this from the beginning. It was, as Vita wrote with some justice, only when 'agents and people started badgering' that he asked her to become involved.[4] In the end, Harold told his supporters that she was 'not very strong and [had] gone to France for a few weeks.'[5]

Harold started on the campaign trail immediately. He made his first big speech, opened Committee Rooms, organised election workers and hired halls for campaign work. He publicly refuted accusations from the Labour candidate, John Morgan, that he had been a fascist. He spoke to communist audiences who sang the *Red Flag* when the meeting was over. He banged on doors and introduced himself. He even attended two football matches. Duff Cooper, who had been the Conservative MP for Westminster since 1931, visited Leicester and made two 'amazing speeches' which, Harold felt, reassured his Tory supporters who were worried about his National Labour tag.[6] Aldous Huxley turned up, in a purely private capacity, offering encouragement and the kind of intellectual conversation Harold had missed during the campaign. In fact, Harold hated campaigning. 'Generally in experiences,' he wrote to Vita, 'there is something, some isolated moment, which one enjoys. I hate and loathe every moment of this Election ... the evening meetings are such absolute HELL that they hang on one's soul all day like a lump of lead.'[7] He might become an MP, but he would never be a man of the people.

Polling was on 14 November. Ben and Nigel were in Leicester with him. So, too, were Gwen's husband, Francis ('Sam') St Aubyn and Copper, the chauffeur from Sissinghurst, both of whom spent the day ferrying voters to and from the polling stations. Vita was at Sissinghurst listening to the radio. It had been raining all day. The De Montfort Hall was laid out with long trestle tables where volunteers counted the votes into bundles of fifty. Morgan was confident and condescending and it seemed that he would win, but the presence of a Liberal candidate had split the opposition vote. Somewhere after midnight, Harold was told he had won with a majority of 150. Morgan demanded a recount. The majority was reduced to 87, but Harold was still the winner. The Returning Officer declared the result. Harold made a short speech. There were cheers, congratulations and champagne. But the congratulations he valued most came from a reporter on the *Leicester Mercury* who had lost money by betting ten to one against him: 'Well, you see,' said the reporter, 'I did not believe that a man as decent as you were could ever be elected in so bitter a contest.'[8]

Of Harold's decency there was never any doubt. He told Vita that, despite the urgings of his supporters, he had put his whole 'philosophy of life' into the election and said nothing of which he need feel ashamed.[9] Though he owed his nomination to aristocratic influence, he had fought a hard and honest campaign and won. Norman Rose's statement that he was 'jobbed into Parliament by an aristocratic relative in time-honoured fashion'[10] is harsh. Harold always saw being elected to Parliament as the greatest triumph of his life.

Nor is there any doubt that he saw Parliament in much the same way as he saw the Foreign Office: it was a club, a family, a privileged coterie. Election gave him the right of membership and placed him once again close to the centre of things. In one sense, the fact that the National Labour Party was now reduced to eight MPs and a handful of supporters in the Lords was probably a good thing. As a member of what was essentially a splinter group attached to a National Conservative Government, it was unlikely that Harold would find himself required to toe a party line that conflicted with his personal beliefs. He made great play of wanting to retain his freedom to speak as he chose in the House – even to the extent, at the beginning of 1936, of refusing an offer to become Ramsay MacDonald's Parliamentary Private Secretary, a decision which caused some offence at the time – but in reality it was something of a fiction. He did accept the position of Foreign Affairs spokesman for National Labour, but as National Labour was anyway part of the National Government it carried no formal responsibilities and he was not in a position to exercise any real influence.

All of which raises a number of questions. What were his personal beliefs? What influence did he wish to exercise? What did Harold Nicolson, MP, stand for? In 1936, he formulated a personal statement of belief in a twenty-eight-page pamphlet called *Politics in the Train*. Harold, ever the classicist, cast his arguments in the form of a Socratic dialogue, imagining a conversation with 'a man whom I had not seen for years' as he travels by train to his Leicester constituency. Even today, it remains a very readable piece – open, honest, and revealing of Harold's general beliefs and sympathies. 'Why on earth,' the man asks, 'do you belong to the National Labour Group?'[11]

Harold accepts that twenty years as a civil servant have left him disinclined to be party-minded. He was once an Asquithian Liberal, but feels that party politics and liberal optimism have become discredited by the First World War and by events in post-war Europe. He believes that politicians should put the country above personal or party interests; he believes in 'imperial responsibility';[12] but not in any form of dogma – 'neither extreme capitalism, nor extreme communism, nor extreme State control, nor extreme competition or *laissez-faire*.'[13] He disclaims any romantic view of the working classes, but sympathises with the poor in an economic system which allows a distribution of wealth so unequal as to be 'uncivilised.'[14] He believes strongly in the role and value of education as a key to the future. He is 'National because I believe in reality. Labour, because I believe in Idealism.'[15]

Politics in the Train is a classic statement of the belief that 'there must be some intelligent and positive middle way.'[16] Harold favours evolution, not revolution. He wants 'to improve everything and destroy nothing.'[17] It is a balanced and well-argued position. He attempts, where he can, to ground his arguments in reality, and if in the end he remains more idealistic and theoretical than practical, that is because he is putting forward a view of the whole political arena rather than writing a detailed manifesto. All the same, it is a work which gives the sense of someone justifying his position rather than seeking to make a political mark.

Christopher Hobhouse was wrong when he said that Harold did not have a political mind. Harold's training and experience left him superbly equipped to analyse the issues and come up with policy solutions. What he did not have was a political personality. In Parliament, he remained a commentator: his best speeches and interventions were the equivalent of the position papers he wrote for the Foreign Office. He could show courage and speak with conviction, but he lacked the capacity to force the issue and take the lead. His sensitiveness to criticism, his concern to be liked and approved of, his very moderation meant that, in a milieu that was much more combative and competitive than the Foreign Office, he was always going to be a follower.

He made his maiden speech in the House of Commons on 19 December 1935, a month after his election. The subject for debate, the League of Nations and Abyssinia, was appropriate and the circumstances mildly dramatic. Mussolini had launched his invasion of Abyssinia that October. France and Britain, while opposed to Italian ambitions, saw Abyssinia as a distraction, creating tensions between themselves and Italy at a time when they hoped to enlist Italian support against an increasingly assertive and aggressive Germany. The French and British Governments sought a way out of the impasse. The Foreign Secretary, Samuel Hoare – tired, in poor health, and on his way to Switzerland for a skating holiday – stopped off in Paris where he met the French Prime Minister, Pierre Laval, and was persuaded to initial an agreement. The so-called Hoare-Laval Pact gave Italy two large zones in the north and south-east of Abyssinia, while offering the Abyssinians the poor compensation of a corridor to the sea at the port of Assab. Details of the pact were leaked to the French press before the British Cabinet had seen them. The British press picked up the story, outraged at the apparent betrayal of Abyssinia. The Prime Minister, Stanley Baldwin, was forced to repudiate the agreement and Hoare resigned as Foreign Secretary.

Harold spoke in the debate that followed. He was nervous but spoke clearly and fluently, with appropriate ironic touches. His central argument, strange though it may sound to our ears, was that there was nothing fundamentally wrong with the terms of the Hoare-Laval Pact. He did 'not think it unwise or unfair that Italy should be granted, in a large area of Abyssinia, such preferential rights as France, to the great benefit of the native population, exercises in Morocco.' Abyssinia had herself conquered the territories concerned and abused them 'in a disgraceful manner.' What was wrong was the way in which the agreement had been reached. Conducting negotiations between Foreign Ministers was a mistake. So, too, was diplomacy by conference. The issue should have been settled under the aegis of the League, not in the 'foetid saloons of the Quai d'Orsay.'[18] Harold's judgement on his performance was that 'the manner was right enough but the matter was too thin.'[19] Nevertheless, maiden speeches are traditionally given a warm welcome in the House of Commons and he received congratulations from an array of political figures, including Baldwin, Ramsay MacDonald, Austen Chamberlain, Eustace Percy and Duff Cooper. He even received a positive notice in *The Times* the next day. His political career, which was to last ten years, was launched.

43 Drama

For Harold, as for Britain and for Europe as a whole, 1936 was a year of drama. Early one morning at the beginning of January, he found himself in Southampton, waiting for the Lindberghs. They had been so persecuted by the American press that they had decided to escape to England. Having crossed from New York on the SS *Bremen*, they were being landed by private launch at an isolated wharf in Southampton docks in order to avoid the attentions of the British press. Privately, Harold considered such precautions extreme, but he wanted to help and travelled with them to Wales, where they were to stay with Anne Lindbergh's brother-in-law; and he continued to look after their interests in a number of ways over the next few months.

A few days later, he was invited by Sibyl Colefax to join her for cocktails, a play – Noel Coward's *Tonight at 8.30* which had just opened at the Phoenix Theatre – and supper afterwards. Only when he arrived did she tell him that the other members of the party were the Prince of Wales and Mrs Simpson. He had met the Prince of Wales previously, but this was his first encounter with Mrs Simpson, whose relationship with the Prince was to shake the foundations of the British monarchy. His first impression was more positive than negative: she was 'bejewelled, eyebrow-plucked, virtuous and wise' and had a positive influence over the Prince, at least insofar as she stopped him smoking during the interval. Nonetheless, the evening left him uneasy: Mrs Simpson was being placed in an 'absurd position' and the Prince of Wales was 'in a mess.'[1]

Another few days and Harold was in the north of Scotland campaigning on behalf of Malcolm MacDonald, Ramsay MacDonald's son and the Colonial Secretary in the National Government. Malcolm MacDonald had lost his seat the previous November and was now standing in a bye-election in Ross and Cromarty. In Dingwall, in a heated bar smelling of beer, whisky and tobacco, they learnt of the death of King George V. They returned to London the next morning and, on 23 January, Harold was in the House of Commons when the Prime Minister proposed a vote of condolence. Both Houses of Parliament then gathered in Westminster Hall as the King's coffin was carried in by six bare-headed guardsmen and placed on a purple catafalque to begin its lying-in-state. The man whom Harold had described only ten days earlier as 'in a mess' was now King.

On Monday 27 January, Gwen had another serious operation. Vita stayed by her bedside until she recovered consciousness and took a room in a hotel so as to be near her. Tuesday was the King's funeral and all London stood still while the gun carriage bearing the coffin passed through the streets from the Houses of Parliament to Paddington, where it was taken by train to Windsor Castle for burial in St George's Chapel. Harold stayed in King's Bench Walk, listening to the minute guns echoing across the city. Then on Thursday, news came that Lady Sackville was dying. Vita left Gwen's bedside and took the first train to Brighton. Harold followed two hours later and arrived at White Lodge just minutes after Lady Sackville had died.

It was the end an era. Harold's relations with Lady Sackville had never really recovered from the crisis which followed the death of Lord Sackville in 1928. He had been polite, even dutiful; there had been times when he had felt sympathy for her; but there had never been any return of the trust and mutual support which had characterised the early years of their relationship. For Vita, it was different. She was, Harold felt, 'shattered, but inwardly ... relieved.'[2]

As Victoria Glendinning has pointed out, there were times, whether in intimacy or estrangement, when the relationship between Vita and her mother resembled that of lovers. They recognised their shared characteristics: the tempestuousness, the irrationality, the passion, the independence, the indifference to the opinion of others. When Vita lost her father, she lost Knole. When she lost her mother, she lost an image of herself: someone whose recognition, if not approval, she sought; someone she believed could and should understand her. Her mother's death accelerated a change in Vita that had been gathering momentum for some time. It was not that her behaviour itself became conventional – it never did – rather that her attitudes moved closer to those traditionally associated with the aristocracy. She hated change and she hated the modern world. She became what, in someone with more political interest and awareness, one might call right wing. It was the end of the romantic and rebellious Vita, who longed to emulate her Spanish grandmother. Henceforth, the English Vita came to dominate. That August, she began to write *Pepita*, the story of her grandmother and her mother, and this, in the judgement of her biographer, 'completed, for good or ill, the exorcism of the Spanish gypsy in herself – an exorcism that her immersion in Sissinghurst, middle age, and, above all, the death of her mother, had begun.'[3]

Harold must have noticed the change. How could he not? A few months before, he had written 'what you like is PASSION and not spent in the least. Real good Triana jealousy and knives. That's what Mar likes. Anything else is just your old armchair.'[4] Now, he was receiving letters from her counselling that 'considered judgement is what really counts in the long run ... this is what wins respect in public life.'[5] But the change in Vita, while it affected her attitudes and to some degree her self-confidence, did not alter her depth of feeling for Harold – nor his for her.

A week after Lady Sackville's death, Harold went down to Brighton and collected her ashes from an oyster shop – where they had been stored overnight in order to avoid the press, who had got hold of the story, and were expected to be waiting outside the undertakers. It was sunny, but bitterly cold with a strong east wind. A fishing boat had been chartered and, accompanied by Lady Sackville's secretary, Cecil Rhind, Harold headed out to sea with spray breaking over the bows. When they were two miles offshore and opposite White Lodge, Harold said a few solemn words wishing Lady Sackville at peace and emptied her ashes into the sea. James Lees-Milne's story that some of the ashes blew back in the wind so that Harold was shaking his mother-in-law's remains out of his overcoat on the train back to London sounds too good to be true.[6]

The immediate impact of Lady Sackville's death was financial. Even after death duties amounting to £46,000, Vita was left with an income of £5,000 a year, while Ben and Nigel would have £1,000 each.[7] This gave the family a much increased level of financial security. It did not, of course, prevent Harold from spending above his income, but it meant that there was no longer any danger of not having the money to maintain Sissinghurst. Nor did they need to sell Long Barn which, that March, was let on a two-year contract to Charles and Anne Lindbergh, who had fallen for its old world charm. Harold told them that it was a happy place and enlisted the help of 'old Mrs Woods' at the local Post Office to make sure that the Lindberghs were not 'bothered' while they were at Long Barn.[8]

Back at Westminster, two issues occupied Harold's attention. The first was the future of National Labour as a party. It had been reduced to only five MPs at the general election. Both Ramsay MacDonald and Malcolm

MacDonald had been re-elected at bye-elections making the total seven, six of whom had ministerial responsibility. (Harold was the only one who did not.) But those re-elections, like Harold's victory in West Leicester, had only been achieved with Conservative support and in the face of implacable hostility from the rest of the Labour Party. In fact, as Harold realised – even when he was writing *Politics in the Train* – National Labour had no future. The fact that the Party, and Harold as one of its representatives, survived in Parliament until 1945 was due only to the coming of the war and the consequent extension of the National Government's term of office.

The second issue, of course, was Hitler. On 7 March 1936, German forces reoccupied the Rhineland. This was an open breach of the Treaty of Versailles, the Locarno Pact and the Covenant of the League of Nations. Under Locarno, the German action should have led to a joint response from Britain and France, but both were paralysed by indecision. The French wanted support in line with Britain's treaty obligations. The British Government under Baldwin was not willing to risk a war which he believed, almost certainly correctly, that the British people would not support. Moreover, there were fears that another European war would open the door for communism to spread westward from Russia into Germany and even France. There were many, inside the Government and out, who saw Hitler and fascism as preferable to communism. Harold, with his understanding of the European situation, had actually guessed that Hitler was about to move into the Rhineland.[9] He did not want war, but believed strongly that a determined reaction from France and Britain – as demanded by the treaties that Britain had signed up to – was not only the honourable course of action, but also the only practical way to demonstrate to Hitler that he had overstepped the mark. On 17 March, he addressed the Foreign Affairs Committee of the House of Commons on the subject of Britain's Locarno obligations. On 18 March, he addressed the Royal Institute of International Affairs (also known as Chatham House after the building which it still occupies) on Britain's moral obligation to support France and suggested the despatch of an international force. On 26 March, in the face of barracking and opposition, he gave a strongly pro-French speech in the House of Commons. It was a sustained campaign which brought Harold into alignment with Winston Churchill, who was now becoming the focal point for those who wanted to stand up to Hitler. He also saw and spoke frequently with Anthony Eden, whose views were broadly the same, but Eden, now Foreign Secretary, was seeking to impose his will from inside the Cabinet and his public freedom of speech and action were more limited.

Outside the House, Harold's reach was truly extraordinary. In the fortnight immediately following Hitler's move into the Rhineland, apart from speaking engagements, he managed meetings with King Leopold III of Belgium; Massigli, the French Foreign Minister; Grandi, the Italian Ambassador; Maisky, the Soviet Ambassador; and the Head of the Political Department of the German Foreign Office. His knowledge and expertise in foreign affairs were recognised when he was appointed Vice-Chairman of the House of Commons Foreign Affairs Committee.

The crisis passed. Hitler's actions had effectively faced down and divided Britain and France. Harold knew that not only had Britain's prestige suffered, but the whole concept of collective security under the League of Nations had been badly, perhaps fatally, damaged. Nonetheless, he did not abandon the idea entirely. Speaking again at Chatham House in July, he suggested that the League of Nations should meet aggression with military force, to which its members should contribute. Later in the year, he was elected to the Executive Committee of the League of Nations Union. He wanted to use the position to push for a reconstitution of the League along stronger and more interventionist lines, but in the event his time was spent combatting left-wing and communist attempts to take over the organisation.

As the Rhineland crisis receded, another began to take shape. On 2 April, Harold was invited to dinner by Mr and Mrs Simpson at their Westminster apartment in the presence of the King. As always, Harold found the King charming. Mrs Simpson he judged 'a perfectly harmless type of American, but the whole setting is slightly second rate.'[10] Two months later he met the King and Mrs Simpson again, this time without Mr Simpson, at one of the last dinners given by Sibyl Colefax in her Chelsea home, Argyll House. This was the occasion when the King made it abundantly clear that he preferred to listen to Noel Coward singing 'Mad Dogs and Englishmen' than to Arthur Rubenstein playing Chopin.

That royal princes should have mistresses was, within their own circle, an undiscussed but accepted fact. That the King should have a mistress was certainly not unknown. The important thing was discretion: the relationship should never come to public attention, nor in any way compromise or conflict with the role or duties of the member of the Royal Family concerned. During his years as Prince of Wales, Edward VIII had had a number of mistresses, some married, some divorced, some both. The problem was that, in his relationship with Wallis Simpson, the new King was unwilling to play by the rules.

From the perspective of an age where royalty is surrounded by intense media interest and speculation, it is difficult to appreciate just how few people knew about the relationship and just how restrained the press and newspapers were until the storm finally broke. Certain sections of London society knew what was going on and talked about it among themselves. The press barons, Beaverbrook and Rothermere, knew but exercised impressive – from a later perspective, scarcely credible – restraint. Whether the King should be allowed to marry the twice-divorced Mrs Simpson and retain the throne, or whether he should abdicate, was eventually to prove a divisive question at all levels of British society. Harold, with his parliamentary and London society connections, knew what was happening and appreciated the gravity of the situation earlier than most. His diaries for 1936 record the incidents which marked the King's increasing commitment to Mrs Simpson and caused growing concern at court and in government: her invitation (with Mr Simpson) to the first official dinner of the new reign; her appearance at Ascot in the royal carriage; the summer cruise (without Mr Simpson) in the Mediterranean on the *Nahlin*; the King's refusal to open a new hospital in Aberdeen, deputing the task to the Duke of York, in order to meet her at the station when (without Mr Simpson) she visited Balmoral. By November, it was clear that serious constitutional issues were at stake. Mrs Simpson's divorce had come through and contradictory rumours were flying around. Sibyl Colefax told Harold that Mrs Simpson had denied that the King had proposed to her, yet the Cabinet and the Privy Council were clearly preparing for a confrontation with the King on the issue. Then came an unexpected and unintentional intervention from the Bishop of Bradford. With the Coronation approaching, and concerned that the new King rarely went to church, the Bishop gave a speech to the Bradford Diocesan Conference which drew attention to the religious significance of the Coronation ceremony and the importance of God's grace in helping the King fulfil his public duties. The Bishop had never heard of Mrs Simpson but his words were widely misinterpreted as an attack on the King's relationship with her. The circle of knowledge could no longer be contained. 'The King and Mrs Simpson' was headline news and the government found itself faced with a quite unprecedented constitutional crisis.

Initially at least, Harold maintained that Mrs Simpson was a decent and well-intentioned woman who was simply out of her depth. Later, as the situation grew more complicated, he came to believe that she must be either 'a fool or a minx,'[11] but he avoided joining the public chorus of disapproval, reserving his criticism for the King, whom he considered should know better – 'What a little ass the man is to plunge us into this disorder!'[12] The King, who all his life had received the cheers and adulation of the British people, expected the 'the country, the great warm heart of the people' to support him, but, in Harold's view, he was wrong: 'The upper classes mind her being American more than they mind her being divorced. The lower classes do not mind her being American but loathe the idea that she has had two husbands already.'[13] Harold understood as well as anyone the gravity of the situation, but, oddly in view of his interest in constitutional matters, his letters and diaries give no indication of how he thought it should be resolved. Like the House of Commons and the British people as a whole, he came to see abdication as the only course, but, as the unprecedented situation unfolded, he remained passive, watching, waiting and recording. What the diaries do give, however, is a remarkable account of events as seen from the House of Commons: the rumours, the hearsay, Churchill's disastrous interventions on behalf of the King, Baldwin's mastery of the House, and the anticlimactic passing of the Abdication Bill on 11 December. 'We are all staggered with shame and distress. I never dreamt it would come to this.'[14]

In the meantime, Harold's own reputation in the House of Commons had suffered a setback. Much of the business of the House during the first half of 1936 had concerned foreign affairs and Harold had made two significant interventions. Neither had repeated the success of his maiden speech, but he had nonetheless become a recognised figure and, when Parliament reassembled for its new session in November, he was asked to second the Address to the Throne which followed the King's Speech. It was an honour to be asked, but Harold was nervous. Edward VIII spoke in the odd, slightly American, slightly Cockney accent that he had assumed – and which all those in the know understood as reflecting the influence of Mrs Simpson. Miss Horsbrugh, the Conservative Member for Dundee, moved the Address in a dignified and uncontroversial manner. Then Harold, dressed in the uniform of the Diplomatic Service (which he had hired from Moss Bros), rose to speak in support. Precedent demanded that he make reference both to his constituency and to previous members who had held the seat. This meant that he had to mention Ramsay MacDonald, still a highly controversial figure with the Labour Party. Harold praised MacDonald as a man who had helped 'create a great party and a great Coalition, a man who, when the acrid dust of controversy has settled, will emerge as a statesman of peculiar vision, as a politician of unsullied integrity'.[15] These sentiments reflected his sense of loyalty and his personal beliefs. They were not intended to be controversial or partisan, but they created uproar in the House. In the right context, Harold could be an entertaining and an instructive speaker, but he lacked the commanding presence necessary to dominate the House of Commons, and in this case, oddly and unusually, he misread both the occasion and his audience. He faltered and nearly broke down, but recovered and managed to finish his speech. It was a disastrous performance. He had hoped to appear 'brave and noble' but in the eyes of the House he looked 'silly and tactless.'[16]

In June, after his interventions on foreign policy, Harold had been mentioned in the press as a likely candidate for ministerial office, but now he feared he had lost his chance. Perhaps he was, as ever, overreacting to criticism, but it was a very public failure and illustrates his broader failure to adapt to the political arena. He loved the House of Commons, its traditions and its club-like atmosphere – and it was in that context that he felt constrained to praise Ramsay MacDonald – but he never adapted to the combative nature of party politics and party prejudices. Chips Channon, now Conservative MP for Southend West, saw 'dear, sentimental, hardworking, gentle Harold ... always a victim of his loyalties.'[17] Harold Macmillan saw a man who cared 'what people thought or said about him ... [and] worried if he was criticised. He wanted to be liked. A fatal propensity.'[18] Harold was, quite simply, not tough enough.

44 Fifty

Tough enough or not, politics was the course he had chosen. On 28 November 1936, he turned fifty – and he hated it, as he hated any landmark indicating that he was growing older. Even had he wished it, it would have been difficult for him to find and embark on an alternative career, but he did not wish it. As an MP, he could combine public service with a position at the political centre and, as the European situation darkened, he concentrated on building – or rebuilding – his reputation in the political and parliamentary arena. However, being a concerned, conscientious, even dedicated MP was not the same as the being the man of action he had envisaged himself only a few years previously. He seems to have realised that he would never achieve any of the great offices of state. In his end-of-year diary entry, he recognises, 'I have dispersed my energies in life, done too many different things, and have no sense of reaching any harbour. I am still very promising and shall continue to be so until the day of my death.'[1]

And he continued to disperse his energies. In August 1936, he crossed the Irish Sea to visit Clandeboye, Lord Dufferin's house. Dufferin was to be the subject of his next book, *Helen's Tower*, and the visit was an attempt to recapture the atmosphere of the place and of that small, privileged part of

Irish society which had been such an important mental anchor for him during his nomadic childhood. That he should embark on such a project shows that he had not entirely given up the image of himself as a Proustian man of letters recapturing the past – especially as this book was eventually to be subtitled *In Search of the Past*. That he should have enjoyed the company of his hosts, Lord Dufferin's grandson and his wife, and revelled in the beauty of the scenery is characteristic. That the experience of revisiting the house should have depressed him and caused him to ask himself what he had done with the intervening forty years is equally characteristic – 'it seems so odd that I should have lived so long and worked so hard ... and have nothing to show for it.'[2] And yet this underlying melancholy – which, had Harold been of a different cast of mind, might have resulted in paralysis of purpose, or even an outburst of philosophical or religious questioning – was not accompanied by any diminution of energy or activity. A couple of weeks after his trip to Ireland, he went to stay with Chips Channon and his wife, who had attended the Olympic Games in Berlin and were now renting Schloss Martin, near Graz in Austria. Apart from Lali Horstmann, the German-Jewish intellectual, whom he had known well during his time in Berlin, Harold found the house party uncomfortably snobbish and rather too well disposed towards Goering, Goebbels and Ribbentrop. From Austria, he went on to stay with Victor Cunard in Venice where he continued writing *Helen's Tower*. From Venice, he travelled to Cap Ferrat to stay with Somerset Maugham. It was the usual name-studded progress. Back in London that autumn, he was extremely active outside Parliament as well as fulfilling his role as an MP. He gave radio talks and lectures, lunchtime speeches and after-dinner speeches, speeches of inauguration and celebration – on one occasion he managed three speeches in a single day. Many of these were political in content, but many also dealt with poetry, biography and the history and theory of diplomacy.

Then, at the beginning of 1937, Harold went to East Africa for ten weeks as a member of a Government commission to report on African education and the status of Makerere College in Uganda. He was persuaded to do so by Buck De La Warr, now Parliamentary Under Secretary for the Colonies, and by Robert ('Rob') Bernays, National Liberal MP for Bristol North, a parliamentary colleague who had become a close friend.[3] Harold was, presumably, pleased to be asked and may have seen the trip as a way of recovering the parliamentary reputation he believed he had lost, but it was a further dispersal of his energies. He had little knowledge of Africa or African affairs and, though he had decided views on the value of traditional, classical education, he could hardly have been accounted an expert.

Nonetheless, he went, seeing in the New Year on a train between Paris and Marseilles, where the members of the commission then boarded the P & O steamer, RMS *Viceroy of India*. In Cairo, he stayed at the Residency with the Ambassador, his old Foreign Office colleague Miles Lampson, peering into the room where he and Vita had stayed during their honeymoon in 1914. The party then flew in an Imperial Airways flying boat to Khartoum – Harold having to beg forgiveness from Vita, who still regarded flying as suicide. From Khartoum, they flew to Entebbe in an RAF bomber which offered very little comfort.

For the next seven weeks, Harold and his colleagues based themselves on Kampala and Makerere College, while travelling extensively in the region – south to Kigoma and Ujiji in Tanganyika, across to Kisumu and Nakuru in Kenya. There was a fair amount of sightseeing: Harold thought the sight of Lake Nakuru in the early morning with its flocks of pelicans and pink flamingos 'probably the loveliest thing I have ever seen.'[4] There were also places and incidents to excite his sense of history. In Khartoum, he was shown the place where General Gordon had been hacked to death and interviewed an old servant, who described the manner of the General's demise. At Ujiji, at the monument marking the spot at which Stanley met Livingstone, he met Livingstone's last surviving servant, who was presented with an ebony and silver cane by the Governor of Tanganyika. The focus of the trip, however, was higher education and Harold worked hard to master the details – and even harder when he returned to England to write the report which took several months to complete. The commission's main recommendation was that Makerere College should become a University College for East Africa and its main success was to extract a £100,000 grant from the Treasury to begin the process.

Harold was always stimulated by new places and new ideas, but despite the interest and excitement, the African trip led nowhere. Seen in the context of Harold's life and intellectual development, its chief relevance is in defining his limitations. Nigel Nicolson summarises its impact concisely.

> His reaction could have been foreseen: it was a mixture of liberal intent and aristocratic disdain. He confessed that he 'loathed the dark races' but felt acutely sorry for them; he had little in common with the junior and middle ranks of the British Colonial civil servants, but was impressed with 'the good they are doing the natives'.... [The] tour left no permanent mark on [his] political outlook, except to confirm his life-long belief that true civilisation existed nowhere outside the inner circles of certain West European capital cities.[5]

His attitude to coloured people, compounded by later stories such as that, again told by Nigel Nicolson, of Harold wiping his plate where a black waiter's thumb had touched it,[6] requires careful assessment. From the vantage point of our age, they are completely inexcusable, but just because Harold appears in many ways wise, liberal and charitable, we should not expect him to be prescient or in advance of his time. Norman Rose, in the index to his biography, groups references to this aspect of Harold's character under 'racism', which is to use a term belonging to a later age.[7] There is no suggestion that Harold behaved rudely or offensively to individuals or that his views caused him to criticise or hold back efforts to improve the life of Britain's colonial subjects. Quite the reverse is true. It is simply that, as with his attitude to Jewish people, he shared the prevailing view of his time – in this case, that black people were intellectually and culturally inferior.

Back in London, the parliamentary session was dominated by foreign affairs and, in particular, by the Spanish Civil War. This, of course, was Harold's strong suit and he intervened in five debates – even when he spoke on the issue of nutrition he drew on his knowledge of middle income families in France, Italy and Germany.[8] There were no disasters, but, while his interventions were perfectly sensible contributions to the debate, they were not particularly memorable: as Harold himself acknowledged, he was not at ease when speaking in the House of Commons. Outside the House, however, his reputation as a speaker was growing and, in April 1937, he was invited to deliver Cambridge University's annual Rede Lecture. His topic was 'The Meaning of Prestige' and he took an unconventional approach: rather than propound a clear thesis, he questioned and challenged, asking what the concept of prestige might mean for an individual or for a nation and then seeking to apply possible answers to the prevailing international situation.

The Royal Family provided another distraction. Harold had known Edward VIII, both as Prince of Wales and as King. He had found him knowledgeable in some areas, but the diaries show him aware of the King's limitations and highly critical of the attitude and the decisions which led up to the Abdication. He had also known the Duke and Duchess of York, being charmed by her, while – at least during their 1929 visit to Berlin – less impressed by the Duke. Yet Harold was never partisan, and avoided being drawn into either of the two camps which divided London society in the months leading up to the Abdication. Soon after the accession of George VI, and only a matter of days after his return from Africa, he found himself invited to dine at Buckingham Palace. Footmen with scarlet and gold epaulettes and powdered hair lined the stairs, and the dining room was a 'mass of gold candelabra and scarlet tulips.' The Prime Minister was there; so were Lord Halifax and Lloyd George and an assemblage of Dukes. The Queen teased Harold 'charmingly' about his 'pink face and [his] pink views' and he was left feeling 'what a mess poor Mrs Simpson would have made of such an occasion ... how wholly impossible that marriage would have been.'[9] Two months later, once again in the full uniform of the Diplomatic Service, he found himself sitting in Poets' Corner in the South Transept of Westminster Abbey watching the rituals attendant on the Coronation of George VI. Harold was a traditionalist and, as such, a natural believer in the value of the monarchy. The monarchy was the public face of Britain and the British Empire and, like millions of other British people, he felt the Abdication as a public humiliation. It caused him to ask what could now be expected of the monarchy and whether it could ever regain the respect of the people. And yet, within months of the accession of George VI, he was discussing with Oliver and Maureen Stanley 'the strange legend of monarchy'[10] and with Ramsay MacDonald the 'real religious sense' with which the new King and Queen had entered on their task.[11]

All of which makes it even stranger that, just another two months later, Harold should have embarked on what James Lees-Milne has called 'a sudden, quixotic and romantic escapade,' the main beneficiary of which was Mrs Simpson, by that time Duchess of Windsor.[12] At the height of the Abdication crisis, Mrs Simpson had left secretly for France, heading for Cannes where she stayed with her old friends Herman and Katherine Rogers. On the way, she stopped on several occasions to telephone the King. At Evreux, she made notes for herself which she accidentally left by the telephone in the Hôtellerie du Grand Cerf and which were found and kept by the proprietor. Harold learned of this from Stephen King-Hall, a fellow National Labour MP, who had recently lunched at the hotel. He contacted the Duchess and offered to retrieve the notes for her. Armed with her letter of authority and an official letter from the French Embassy in London, Harold set off for Evreux and successfully persuaded Monsieur Piaccarella, the proprietor, to hand over the paper, which he then sent to the Duchess in Austria.

It is true that the paper could have been exploited by the press, but did that require Harold to dash off to France in such an uncharacteristically dramatic way, not telling Vita about his mission until he had returned? Was it just a case old-fashioned chivalry? Harold certainly had nothing to gain by his actions and had no wish to ingratiate himself with the Windsors. Was not such gallantry outdated and faintly ridiculous? Roland de Margerie, who wrote the letter from the French Embassy, appeared to think so when he called Harold Don Quixote and likened his exploits to those of Athos, Aramis, Porthos and d'Artagnan.[13] Or could it be that Harold was moved to imitate the combination of drama, romance and kindness which characterised his childhood hero, Lord Dufferin, about whom he was writing in *Helen's Tower*? All we know for certain is that both the Duke and Duchess of Windsor were grateful for Harold's actions and acknowledged the fact in their memoirs.[14] The episode remains something of a mystery, but an entertaining one for all that.

Harold spent the summer at Sissinghurst finishing and revising *Helen's Tower*. He sent it to Constable at the beginning of September and it was published on 15 November. As ever, Harold was unsatisfied and self-critical. The diary reads '*Helen's Tower* is published and there are a few scattered mentions,'[15] when in fact in was widely reviewed and widely praised – the one severely critical reviewer being Evelyn Waugh in *Night and Day* magazine. The problem, of which Harold was aware, is with the narrative technique, which necessarily veers between first person narration of those parts of the story which are within Harold's reach, and third person narration of the more distant parts of Lord Dufferin's career. This is connected to the book's genesis as part of Harold's great Proustian idea. Had Harold continued with the sequence, following the same technique, it might well have come to seem effective rather than awkward, which it can at times in the isolation of a single volume.

Yet a minor issue of narrative technique should not detract from what in other ways is a small masterpiece. *Helen's Tower*, with its memories, questions and speculations, its deliberate descriptions and concentration on the senses, is more than just a biography of Lord Dufferin: it is an evocation of the Victorian era and intended as such. Lord Dufferin's career grew with the Empire, reaching its heights with ambassadorial appointments to Russia, Turkey, Italy, and France in the High Victorian period of the 1880s and 90s, before declining into financial turmoil and illness – his death coming shortly after that of the Queen-Empress he had known and served for fifty years. Harold's writing is equal to his subject, evoking the glory and the pathos, using his childhood self to probe and question, and his adult narrator's voice to allow the play of wit and irony across his subject matter. *Helen's Tower* is a real achievement, founded on Harold's genuine sympathy and admiration for Dufferin himself. And the importance of that foundation was something he understood. Just before *Helen's Tower* was published, he heard of the sudden death of Ramsay MacDonald. The same day, he was approached by his publisher with an invitation to write MacDonald's official biography, but he turned the offer down, on the grounds that he did not admire MacDonald 'morally or intellectually' and could not write a biography of someone for whom he did not have 'real enthusiasm'.[16]

Helen's Tower was not his only publication that autumn. 'The Meaning of Prestige' was published by Cambridge University Press as a small hardback volume, and Constable put out a 250-page volume called *Small Talk*, which brought together a number of essays, articles and radio talks. Ephemeral pieces revisited many years later risk disappointment, but the range of subject matter, coupled with Harold's ability to amuse, reflect and instruct at the same time, make *Small Talk* still worth reading today. Harold himself was, of course, dismissive. His end-of-year diary entry notes that 'my political career has suffered a decline'[17] and that 'I have not fulfilled high hopes,' but at the same time his standing as a literary and a public figure had undoubtedly grown. His books and his many speeches – including one at the end of the year to the Oxford University Conservative Association where he was hosted by the young Edward Heath – had kept him in the eye of a certain, not uninfluential section of the public. Chips Channon had asked Harold to be his literary executor and publish his diaries in the event of his death. Gerald Barry, who was on the board of the *New Statesman* and was Features Editor on the *News Chronicle*, had asked him to write a daily column. Both these requests were refused. Harold even made his first television broadcast – 'I enjoyed it, because it was an experience. But it is certainly an ordeal.'[18] From one perspective this was gratifying, even impressive, but it was not what he wanted. Although conscious that he was not 'sufficiently virile to force myself upon the House, and ... too old to create a gradual impression,'[19] he still craved political success.

45   Munich

The Munich crisis and the period leading up to it was, in many respects, the high point of Harold's political career. It was the one time when he actually did force himself upon the House of Commons as a man of strong convictions who was not afraid to stand up and express them. By doing so, he dramatically raised his political profile and became associated in the public and parliamentary mind with Churchill, Eden, Duff Cooper, Leo Amery, Harold Macmillan, Bob Boothby, 'Bobbetty' Cranborne, Anthony Crossley, Brendan Bracken, Sir Archibald Sinclair and other leading opponents of Neville Chamberlain's policy of appeasing the dictatorial regimes in

Germany and Italy. However, as so often in Harold's life and career, his achievements have an ironic underside. In this case, his political successes, while putting him firmly in the right in the eyes of posterity, signally failed to influence or alter government policy at the time. And those successes came about as a result of a decisiveness normally alien to his character, which, in the end, he could not sustain.

Harold had never lacked strong views on key international issues, but his good manners, his reticence, his fatal ability to see both sides of an argument – all the qualities which made him an English gentleman of the old school – meant that he often lacked fire when putting those views across. He was at his best on paper or in a committee where opposing arguments could be weighed and a balanced conclusion reached. He was, as he admitted in a letter to Vita in February 1938, 'still rather frightened of the House.'[1] It seems to have been Hitler's predatory demands upon Schuschnigg, the Austrian Chancellor, just a few days before that letter, which started him off on a different path.

Up to that point, Harold's year had seemed normal enough. He had taken part in a debate at the Cambridge Union, successfully opposing the motion, proposed by Stephen Spender, that 'Art must be political.'[2] He had dined with Gladwyn Jebb, now Private Secretary to the Permanent Under-Secretary at the Foreign Office, but with classic English decorum and reticence, they had avoided all discussion of foreign affairs and Harold had even refrained from asking why Jebb had to return to the Office after dinner. But once Hitler turned against Austria, Harold's attitude hardened. At the Foreign Affairs Committee on 17 February, he expressed succinctly and forcefully what others had failed to realise: that Hitler had imposed the will of the Nazi Party on the military and that Britain's response should be to 'keep a stiff upper lip, not throw sops or slops about, and, above all, arm.'[3] The speech was well received and Churchill offered his congratulations.

Three days later, on 20 February, Anthony Eden resigned as Foreign Secretary, causing a storm of political speculation across Europe. Ever since Neville Chamberlain had taken over from Baldwin in May 1937, Eden's views on how to deal with Hitler and Mussolini had been diverging from those of the new Prime Minister and the majority of the Cabinet. Moreover, he felt – correctly – that Chamberlain was trying to conduct a personal foreign policy independently of the Foreign Office.

The trigger for Eden's resignation was the issue of talks with Italy about the still-raging Spanish Civil War. Galeazzo Ciano, the Italian Foreign Minister (and also Mussolini's son-in-law), was insistent that if the British wanted talks, they would have to go to Rome. Chamberlain was willing to

Munich

concede. Eden was not. The underlying reason, however, was Chamberlain's blunt rejection of a somewhat naïve though undoubtedly genuine proposal from President Roosevelt that he should launch an American initiative to reduce tensions in Europe. Roosevelt's proposal was made, in strict confidence, to Chamberlain on 12 January. Eden was on holiday at Grasse on the French Riviera, but was summoned home by Alec Cadogan, his Permanent Under-Secretary. Supported by the Foreign Office and Sir Ronald Lindsay – Harold's former chief, who was still Ambassador in Washington – Eden pressed for a positive response. Anything, he argued, which drew the United States out of isolation and into the international arena was worth pursuing. Chamberlain disagreed and sent a discouraging reply. Roosevelt took offence and an important opportunity was lost. Knowledge of this episode, however, was kept within the confines of the Cabinet. To Parliament and to the electorate, Eden's resignation appeared to hang upon a point of diplomatic procedure relating to Italy, and, because he felt obliged to maintain Cabinet secrecy, his resignation speech on 21 February did nothing to clarify matters. It was in the debate that followed that Harold made the speech of his career so far.

By his own account, he was 'not nervous. Only angry.'[4] He was called just before 7.30 p.m. and spoke for a quarter of an hour. His anger stemmed from Hitler's violent speech in the Reichstag the previous day. Harold had been able to listen courtesy of the BBC and had been appalled at Hitler's aggressive demands on Austria and his promises to protect German minorities outside the Reich. In the House, however, Harold concentrated on Italy. Eden's resignation was

> not merely a little point of procedure, but a great question of principle... whether a country which has continuously, consistently, deliberately and without apology, violated every engagement into which she has ever entered can be taken back into the fold with a smile; or whether it is better to make a few concrete conditions before negotiations are resumed.

He did not propose, he said, to attack Signor Mussolini, and then went on to demonstrate how successive Italian Governments had broken every significant international agreement they had signed since 1882. He concluded with a violent attack on the government's foreign policy:

> the rule of law and order, the theory of the League of Nations, the belief in the sanctity of treaties, and the confidence of the world... those great

principles of our policy, those charters of that authority which we have for so many centuries exercised in the world ... now lie tattered at our feet.[5]

The speech was greeted with outrage by Chamberlain's supporters and attacked by several subsequent speakers, but it was greeted with applause by Lloyd George, Churchill and others who opposed the government's weak approach and wanted a firmer line against the dictators. It also marked the end of Harold's chances of getting a ministerial post but, as he wrote to Vita, 'truly, darling, I do not care when such vital principles are involved.'[6]

Having spoken against the government he had been elected to support, Harold, determined as ever to do the right thing, went straight to Leicester to explain his actions to his constituents. Bertie Jarvis, the Chairman of the Conservative Association, warned him that the constituency's mood was resolutely pro-Chamberlain and it would be better to say nothing. The newly self-assertive Harold disagreed, made a wholly unapologetic speech and received a vote of confidence. Jarvis, astonished, admitted that it had been a triumph.

This was a new and tougher Harold. He had found a cause:

The Government may say what they like, but their policy is nothing less than the scrapping of the ideas which have been built up since the war and the reversion to the old pre-war policy of power politics and bargaining.... My own Party has behaved like worms and kissed the Chamberlain boot with a resounding smack.[7]

He was in almost daily contact with Vansittart, who had been replaced as Permanent Under-Secretary at the Foreign Office because of his anti-appeasement views and created Chief Diplomatic Adviser to His Majesty's Government. The title was grand enough but the job had no substance. 'Van' spent much of his time prophesying doom and holding meetings with malcontents such as Harold. Harold was in regular contact with Ivan Maisky, the Soviet Ambassador in London – a useful connection for any MP, but also a suspicious, even defiant one in the eyes of the Government and those who feared 'the Reds' more than Hitler. Indeed, Harold's diary records an incident in May when he stopped at Pratts' Club and met 'three young peers who state that they would rather see Hitler in London than a Socialist administration.'[8] Then there were endless meetings and lunches with individuals and groups, all in one way or another opposed to the Government's foreign policy and seeking to heighten awareness of the

European situation. After a lunch of the Focus Group – 'one of Winston's things' – Harold wrote to Vita that he was not 'going to become one of the Winston brigade'. His leaders, he told her, were Eden and Malcolm MacDonald (at the time Secretary of State for the Dominions and leader of the National Labour Party).[9] Harold, like many others in Whitehall and in the country, recognised Churchill's qualities but did not at this stage see him as a potential war leader. Yet Churchill was soon to become the greatest of Harold's many heroes.

Ten days later, on 12 March, and despite the Austrian Government conceding every demand made upon it, German troops crossed the border. The following day Austria was formally annexed to the German Reich. Diplomatic protests were rejected on the grounds that third parties had no right to interfere in the internal affairs of the German people. Chamberlain refuted this argument in the House on 14 March, but had precious little else to offer.

> I imagine that according to the temperament of the individual the events which are in our minds today will be the cause of regret, of sorrow, perhaps of indignation. They cannot be regarded by His Majesty's Government with indifference or equanimity.... This is not a moment for hasty decisions or for careless words. We must consider the new situation quickly, but with cool judgment.... As regards our defence programmes, we have always made it clear that they were flexible, and that they would have to be reviewed from time to time in the light of any development in the international situation.... Accordingly we have decided to make a fresh review, and in due course we shall announce what further steps we may think it necessary to take.

This time it was Churchill who took the Government to task: 'Why should we assume that time is on our side?' he asked. 'Not only do we need a clear declaration of the Government's policy, but we require to get to work to rally the whole country.'[10]

It was a time of national crisis and Harold as an MP with a recognised expertise in foreign affairs was in a position to make his contribution. Hindsight may suggest that he had again achieved his ambition to be at the centre of things, but the reality was different. Both in the House and in the country, those who opposed Chamberlain's increasingly frantic attempts to maintain peace were a small, though growing, minority. And they were fragmented. To many, Eden appeared the natural leader of such a grouping, but Eden, not wishing to make things worse by challenging Chamberlain directly at a time of national crisis, was not speaking out. Many others looked to Churchill, but an equal number distrusted him. History has shown Harold and those opposed to appeasement to have been right – at least in their assessment of Hitler's and Mussolini's characters and ambitions, and the impossibility of reaching a meaningful agreement with them – but at the time the majority wanted peace and disliked what was widely seen as warmongering. It was this perception that led Harold to be asked to resign his position as Vice-Chairman of the House of Commons Foreign Affairs Committee. 'I knew this to be inevitable,' he wrote, 'but now that it has happened, I am curiously hurt.'[11]

As early as October 1936, Vansittart had had the idea of sending Harold off to the Balkans on a kind of fact-finding, morale-bolstering lecture tour. The project was now revived, though under the auspices of the British Council rather than the Foreign Office, which rather lessened its official prestige. An itinerary was put together which included Romania, Bulgaria and Yugoslavia, but not Czechoslovakia. Nothing could make a greater contrast with Hitler's most recent speech in Königsberg – a messianic rant, received with hysterical approval by his audience, to the effect that his faith in the eternal German God and the German people would make him 'the Leader of the greatest army in the history of the world'[12] – than the middle-aged former diplomat who set off by train from Victoria Station to lecture to invited audiences on 'The British Empire Today', 'The Foundations of British Foreign Policy' and 'Are the British Hypocrites?'

Harold left London on 13 April. Nigel, now in his last months at Oxford, went with him as far as Venice where he was to stay with Ben, who was still studying for his career as an art historian. Harold continued on to Bucharest's Gara de Nord, where he found that his visit was being treated as an event of some significance. Though it was early on a Saturday morning, the Romanian Foreign Office had sent a representative to greet him and the press were out in force. The British Minister in Romania, Sir Reginald Hoare, whisked him off to the Legation with the news that King Carol had invited him to lunch. This proved a double embarrassment: first because he had brought neither tail coat nor top hat with him and had to borrow Sir Reginald's, and second because, during an otherwise delicious lunch and instructive conversation, a bottle of *sal volatile* in Harold's trouser pocket began to leak, its scent wafting across the lunch table and the liquid itself leaving an all-too-visible stain on his seat. Lunch with the King was followed by a concentrated programme of lectures, speeches and other engagements, including meetings with anyone who was anyone in Romanian political life.

After four days in Romania, Harold crossed the Danube by ferry to Ruse (Ruschuk) on the Bulgarian shore, where there were prolonged formal welcomes from the Mayor and other officials. He took the train to Sofia, which he had not visited since he was *en route* to Constantinople at the beginning of 1912. Sofia and the Bulgarians were a great deal less appealing than Bucharest and the Romanians. Nonetheless, he gave his lecture on British foreign policy and worked his way through a meeting with the Prime Minister, a packed press conference and, finally, an audience with King Boris – who used the occasion to let off steam to a foreigner in a way that he could never have done with one of his subjects, and whom Harold found full of good stories. Another train ride and Harold was in Yugoslavia for the third leg of his tour – more lectures, more meetings with political leaders, and an audience with the Oxford-educated Prince Paul, Regent of Yugoslavia. He arrived home at the beginning of May, having spent the train journey writing a very full report which he presented to Vansittart.

Harold had done all that had been asked of him. He had spoken openly and honestly about Britain and the British in a way which he believed had demonstrated Britain's values and strength of purpose in the current, tense international situation. He had avoided controversial statements and promises of British support in the event of war, but he was worried that the countries he had visited and the people he had met would read more into his trip than was actually intended. The whole episode certainly enhanced his reputation in government circles and in Whitehall, and he found himself being used as a sounding board for parliamentary and public opinion by Eden and by David Margesson, the Government's Chief Whip. It was against this background that Vansittart asked him to host an event for Konrad Henlein, leader of the Sudeten Germans.

It had been obvious for some time that Czechoslovakia was Hitler's next target. The country had been in existence less than twenty years and many people – including Vita – saw it as an artificial state, cobbled together from the remains of the Austro-Hungarian Empire. The majority of the population were Czech, but Germans formed the second-largest ethnic group, far outnumbering the Slovaks, Ruthenians, Hungarians, Poles and Croats. They were scattered around the geographical edges of the country, but the highest concentration was in the Sudeten Mountains in the north-west, an industrially valuable region, which bordered Saxony. Tension between ethnic groups was nothing new. There had been protests by the German community as early as 1919 and there is no doubt that the Czech-dominated Government had sought to boost the position of Czechs relative to the other ethnic groups. The Sudeten Germans had naturally looked to

Germany for cultural and economic support, which meant they suffered disproportionate levels of hardship and unemployment when the Great Depression hit and German banks and companies began to fail.

In 1933, when economic conditions were at their worst, a bank clerk named Konrad Henlein emerged as leader of the Sudeten-German Home Front. He made regular visits to London, lobbying the British Government to support the largely legitimate aspirations of the German community within the Czechoslovak state. In the early stages, his public position had been to support the Czech Government in the face of Nazi pressures. From 1937, however, responding to growing pressure within the Sudeten German Party (as the Home Front was now known), he began to move towards the idea of union with Germany. As far as anyone in London was aware, the May 1938 visit was simply the latest in a continuing series. When Harold hosted a tea party at King's Bench Walk, with the idea of introducing him to a cross-section of those who opposed Chamberlain's appeasement policy, no one knew that Henlein had come directly from Berlin where he had received orders to escalate the Sudeten situation to a point where Germany could step in. And no one knew that one of his tasks in London was to assess whether Britain would go to war over Czechoslovakia.

The tea party lasted for two hours and finished with sherry. Harold seems to have been impressed – or taken in – by the balanced nature of the programme Henlein claimed he was putting forward. Henlein's party 'did not claim more than to voice their opinion.... They did not claim to overrule the majority.'[13] He believed Henlein had understood that German occupation of the Sudetenland would mean war. Yet within a week of Henlein's return home, the Czechoslovak Government had been forced into a partial mobilisation of the army to suppress disorder on the streets among Sudeten Germans while the German army was building up large forces on the Czechoslovak border.

The Czech President, Edvard Beneš, was defiant. Chamberlain and the French Prime Minister, Daladier, offered support. So, too, did the Polish and Russian Governments. For once, the diplomatic line held firm and, on 23 May, the German Ambassador in London, Herbert von Dirksen, made an announcement to the effect that Germany had no territorial ambitions in Czechoslovakia. Harold was overjoyed: Hitler had been checked for the first time. Speaking to Clement Attlee, at that time Leader of the Opposition, he suggested that it was 'the turn of the tide.' Attlee, only three years older but a considerably wiser politician, agreed 'so long as the Government do not show cowardice now.'[14]

The crisis passed, but Czechoslovakia's problems remained unresolved.

Harold knew more about the situation and its origins than anyone in the Government. He had, after all, played a leading role in drawing up the country's borders during the Paris Peace Conference and knew why the line had been drawn where it had. Moreover, he had known Edvard Beneš during the Paris Conference and developed a good working relationship with him. Yet, beyond being asked to host a tea party, his expertise was ignored. True, he was a vocal opponent of the Government's foreign policy, but he would have responded positively to any request to help in a time of national crisis and his friends in the Cabinet (Duff Cooper, Oliver Stanley, Malcolm MacDonald, Buck De La Warr) knew that. The fact that he was not asked probably reflects Chamberlain's character – an odd combination of resentment at any public criticism of his actions and a particular arrogance, which expressed itself in the belief that he alone could reach an understanding with the dictators. It was this conviction which led him to act in a way which his interlocutors in Germany and Italy interpreted as weakness.

Harold, for all his initial elation when Germany backed down, was gloomy about the future.

> Ancient traditions and principles were based on the theory that we should protect the weak and defy the strong ... [but] Chamberlain (who has the mind and manner of a clothes-brush) aims only at assuring temporary peace at the price of ultimate defeat. He would like to give Germany all she wants at the moment, and cannot see that if we make this surrender we shall be unable to resist other demands.... If we provoke Germany now (when our defences are in a pitiable state), she will or may destroy us utterly.... And if we do not oppose her she will become so strong that we cannot face [war].[15]

He expressed his frustration in a series of weekly radio talks, unimaginatively entitled 'The Past Week', which began in July and lasted for three months. Although broadcast at 10 p.m., these talks attracted a staggering audience of up to twenty million around the world. For the most part, Harold avoided direct criticism of Chamberlain, contenting himself with a logical demonstration of the flawed basis of British policy, but when September came he found that both his radio talks and a newsreel soundtrack he had recorded had been subjected to Foreign Office censorship – particularly when he documented and criticised Nazi behaviour or suggested that Britain might fight to defend Czechoslovakia. This was only one instance of Chamberlain's increasingly determined attempts to suppress dissent – attempts which later included stimulating constituency revolts and smear campaigns against anti-appeasement MPs and even, in some cases, telephone tapping.

Intense political activity put Harold's social life under pressure, but he still found time to dine with literary figures such as H. G. Wells and George Bernard Shaw, and, as his account of a lunch he attended to meet the author, Karen Blixen, demonstrates, he never lost his sense of humour.

> Ethyl Smyth comes in. She has a telephone box in order to hear but puts it the wrong way round and is absolutely stone deaf. She blows her nose on a muffler. She is rather drunk and doddery. She had come up from Oxford and had spent an hour and a half reading P. G. Wodehouse and drinking sherry. Thus she is wobbly the poor old sweet.[16]

The summer months were calmer, allowing Harold time to reflect on his relationship with his sons[17] and his love for Vita – 'I know that the central thing in myself (the actual main-spring which makes all the little cogs go round) is my love for you ... and, by the way, we shall shortly have a silver wedding.' He took a few days in the south of France, staying once again with Somerset Maugham at Cap Ferrat. While he was there the Duke and Duchess of Windsor came to dine. It was a slightly awkward evening with everyone on their best behaviour. 'I do not think that ex-Kings are very good company,' was Harold's conclusion.[18] From Cap Ferrat, he went with Ben to the Western Isles of Scotland to visit Nigel, who had used the money he had inherited from Lady Sackville to buy the Shiant Islands, three rugged, uninhabited and staggeringly beautiful Hebridean islands half way between Skye and Harris. He also found time to begin writing *Diplomacy*, his attempt to bring some clarity to the theory and practice of the profession he had followed for twenty years. It was a happy and busy period, but well before the end of August he was back in London lunching with Ambassador Maisky and trying to make sense of Russian policy in the Balkans.

By that time, the Germans were once again ratchetting up the tension in central Europe. Negotiations between Henlein's Sudeten German Party and the Czech Government were held to the accompaniment of 750,000 German troops conducting exercises on the other side of the border. At Chamberlain's instigation, Lord Runciman, a Liberal politician recently retired from the post of President of the Board of Trade, was appointed to mediate between the Sudeten Germans and the Czech authorities. When he failed to make progress, Britain began to mobilise the fleet and Chamberlain began to make plans for a personal meeting with Hitler.

Under intense pressure, on 2 September, President Beneš issued the so-called 'Fourth Plan' which conceded virtually all the Sudeten German demands. But it was too late. Acting under orders from Berlin, the Sudeten Germans staged demonstrations which became confrontations with the police. Violence spread and on 13 September, all negotiations ceased. Two days later, in Berlin, Henlein issued a statement demanding that the Sudetenland be united with Germany.

The broader international situation was worsening, too. Italy and Japan had announced that they would support Germany. The Russians had mobilised their fleet. War seemed inevitable; so when the news broke that on 15 September Chamberlain would fly to Germany to intervene personally with Hitler, even Harold felt 'enormous relief.'[19] The meeting took place in the Berghof, Hitler's house in the mountains above the small town of Berchtesgaden, close to what until recently had been the Austrian border. It lasted for three hours. Hitler demanded the immediate annexation of the Sudetenland, but eventually settled for a plebiscite among the Sudeten Germans while giving a guarantee that he had no further territorial ambitions in Czechoslovakia. Over the week that followed, Britain and France again put pressure on the Czech Government to accept, which they eventually did – having been told unequivocally that neither Britain nor France would go to war if the Germans invaded the Sudetenland.

For Harold and those who thought like him, both the terms Chamberlain had agreed and the pressure subsequently put on an independent sovereign state were a source of anger and humiliation. Britain had capitulated. He found Eden 'in the depths of despair' and the young writer James Pope-Hennessy 'almost in tears over England's shame.'[20] Baffy Dugdale, Arthur Balfour's niece and a member of the National Labour Party, claimed she had been physically sick. Harold wrote a letter of protest to Buck De La Warr, Chairman of the National Labour Party, warning him that he was considering both voting against the Government and resigning from the party. He also made his views plain to Robert Barrington-Ward of *The Times* which had taken what Harold saw as a very weak, pro-Government stance – 'Barrington-Ward gets very red, and I fear I do also'.[21]

On 22 September, the same day that Chamberlain set off for his second encounter with Hitler, Churchill called a meeting at his flat in Morpeth Mansions. He was in buoyant mood. He had heard from Downing Street that the Prime Minister was taking with him four clear conditions, agreed by the Cabinet, to put to Hitler. Harold recorded in his diary:

It boils down to this. Either Chamberlain comes back with peace with honour or he breaks it off. In either case, we shall support him. But if he comes back with peace with dishonour, we shall go out against him.... I walk back feeling that we are very near to war. When war comes it will be a terrible shock to the country.... All those of us who said 'we must make a stand' will be branded as murderers.[22]

But it was too late for Czechoslovakia. The vultures were already circling. Hungary was claiming Ruthenia and southern Slovakia. Poland wanted a readjustment of the northern borders – including the area around Teschen which Harold had tried so hard to keep Czech during the Paris Peace Conference. The Czech Government, humiliated by successive concessions, resigned. Chamberlain's meeting with Hitler, this time in the Rheinhotel Dreesen at Bad Godesberg on the Rhine, was little short of disastrous. Hitler raised the stakes, demanding immediate occupation of the Sudetenland. Chamberlain did not press on the conditions he had agreed with the Cabinet. Hitler produced a memorandum which outlined his terms and Chamberlain agreed to circulate it to the French and the Czechs.

War seemed inevitable. Harold saw trenches being dug in London's Green Park. Gas masks were issued. He moved from one meeting to another, and when not talking about the crisis, tried to set down his thoughts on what had gone wrong, who was to blame and what should happen now. On the afternoon of 28 September, Chamberlain rose to address the House of Commons on the European situation. It was a tense occasion. He worked his way methodically and chronologically through the events of the previous month. After an hour, as he was approaching the climax of his narrative, a message was delivered: 'Herr Hitler,' Chamberlain said, 'has just agreed to postpone his mobilisation for twenty-four hours and to meet me in conference with Signor Mussolini and Monsieur Daladier at Munich.' It was, Harold wrote, 'one of the most dramatic moments which I have ever witnessed.'[23] Harold returned to King's Bench Walk and dictated his account of proceedings which he broadcast that evening on the BBC Empire Service. It was a dramatic account of dramatic events, but he left out the fact that when the whole House rose to its feet to cheer Chamberlain, three MPs remained resolutely and defiantly seated – Duff Cooper, Churchill, and Harold himself.

The rest of the story is quickly told. The following morning Chamberlain set off from Heston aerodrome for his third visit to Germany in as many weeks. The talks, held in Paul Troost's newly-completed, neo-classical *Führerbau*, began as soon as he arrived. Hitler announced his intention to invade Czechoslovakia on 1 October. Mussolini produced a proposal based on Hitler's Bad Godesberg demands to which, after prolonged rather than acrimonious discussion, the French and British Prime Ministers agreed. The Munich Agreement was signed at 1.30 a.m. on 30 September. The Czechs were not present and were told what had been agreed afterwards. Before leaving Munich, Chamberlain had a separate and private meeting with Hitler at which a second agreement was signed, expressing, as Chamberlain saw it, 'the desire of our two peoples never to go to war again.' It was this second agreement that he waved on his return to Heston aerodrome.

Chamberlain was given a triumphal welcome home. Crowds mobbed his car. He appeared on the balcony of Buckingham Palace with King George and Queen Elizabeth. Returning to Downing Street, he was prevailed upon to address the crowds from a first floor window with words that would echo down through history – 'this is the second time there has come back from Germany to Downing Street peace with honour. I believe it is peace for our time.'[24]

Duff Cooper, First Lord of the Admiralty, was the only Cabinet Minister to resign, but, though the national mood was one of rejoicing, there was an increasing sense of unease. When Harold made a speech in Manchester attacking Chamberlain and the Munich Agreement – a speech which was heavily criticised in *The Times* – he claimed that members of his audience said to him: 'You have put into words the feeling we woke up with this morning and which we at once suppressed.'[25]

It was when the House of Commons came to debate the Munich Agreement that Harold enjoyed his finest parliamentary hour. He was called towards the end of the third day of a four-day debate. He had kept a low profile in the House since his intervention in the debate following Eden's resignation in February, and, although his views were well known from his radio talks, many MPs wanted to hear what he would say. The chamber filled up when his name was called. He again kept his speech short – just twenty-five minutes – and, again, it was a deceptively simple presentation, encouraging his audience 'to face up to the situation as it really is.' To do otherwise was to seek to escape from reality. He drew on the contributions of other speakers to demonstrate how sophistry could be used to obscure simple truth: the central issue was not Czechoslovakia but the rule of law in Europe. He accused the Government of allowing a big country to crush a small country, thereby reversing the traditional principles of British foreign policy. He demonstrated the chain of causality which meant that 'we have given away not merely Czechoslovakia, not merely the Sudeten

Germans, but we have given away the whole key to Europe.' His peroration quite brilliantly distilled clear principles from the complexities of the situation, but they were not principles invented for the occasion: they were the deeply-held tenets by which Harold had always tried to live his life and, as such, they describe his character as much as his reaction to a particular political crisis.

> I know that in these days of realism those of us who try to keep our election pledges are told that we are disloyal to the party. The actual expression used to me was, 'You must not bat against your own side.' As if it were a game of cricket that was being played in this most revered Assembly. I know that those of us who try to be consistent are accused of having 'one-track' minds, I know that in these days of realism principles are considered as rather eccentric and ideals are identified with hysteria. I know that those of us who believe in the traditions of our policy, who believe in the precepts which we have inherited from our ancestors, who believe that one great function of this country is to maintain moral standards in Europe, to maintain a settled pattern of international relations, not to make friends with people whose conduct is demonstrably evil, not to go out of our way to make friends with them but to set up some sort of standard by which the smaller Powers can test what is good in international conduct and what is not – I know that those who hold such beliefs are accused of possessing the Foreign Office mind. I thank God that I possess the Foreign Office mind.[26]

In the division that ended the fourth day of the debate, Harold and those National Government MPs who opposed appeasement abstained, remaining in their seats while the vote took place and thus causing the maximum embarrassment for the Government. There were only about thirty of them and the Government won the vote comfortably (by 366 votes to 144), but, as Harold recorded, 'it is not our numbers that matter but our reputation.'[27] Among their number were the next three Prime Ministers and eight future cabinet ministers.

46 Outbreak

The first of October 1938, the day after Chamberlain flew back from

Munich, was Harold and Vita's twenty-fifth wedding anniversary. The butler at Knole, Booth, and his wife Emily sent congratulations but otherwise the event went unmarked. Harold had mentioned the anniversary in his letter about their relationship in July ('I know it bores you to realise that we are married'[1]) but presumably Vita did not respond, so on the day itself he did nothing 'since Viti does not like domesticity.'[2]

In fact, Vita was changing. Her mother's death had brought to an end a relationship which was volatile, intense, and of fundamental importance to both of them. *Pepita*, published in 1937, was part tribute and part exorcism of that aspect of Vita's personality which responded so strongly to her mother. One can also speculate that the emotional changes in Vita may owe something to the approach of the menopause. Whatever the reason, there is no doubt that she grew increasingly reclusive. She would take holidays in France or North Africa, usually with Harold's sister, Gwen, but when in England she was ever more reluctant to leave Sissinghurst. She had her friends and her lovers, but she became less and less interested in London and London society. Just a few weeks after Munich, she wrote to Harold that she simply could not attend a dinner at Buckingham Palace for King Carol of Romania. She had taken her jewels out of the bank, but could not 'subscribe any longer to the world which these jewels represent. I *can't* buy a dress costing £30 or wear jewels worth £2,000 when people are starving.'[3] This was a new Vita, socially aware, though not as democratic as this particular quotation might suggest, for her world was always patriarchal, even feudal, in conception. Harold, after some initial irritation, responded to her altered view of the world with enthusiasm (and no little irony) – 'You are quite right, as usual. . . . How can a person of your sensitiveness and imagination doll yourself up in expensive clothes when there are cultured Jewish men and women hiding like foxes in the Grünewald.'[4]

Yet a changed Vita was not necessarily an easier or more contented Vita. Her reclusiveness was matched by a shyness which had never troubled her before. There were periods when she felt lonely and depressed and, to make matters worse, she was not writing. This led to a tendency to drink too much in the evenings. Harold had long grown used to Vita claiming and maintaining her personal and professional independence. He had supported her views and lived his own life accordingly. He had accepted that his political life, which centred on London and was keeping him away from Sissinghurst more than previously, would not involve her. His social life was also London-based, and when he travelled, he travelled alone. Writing to Ben and trying to explain their relationship, Harold acknowledged that Vita was 'a difficult wife' and that 'we have many tastes which are different, many activities we do not share.'⁵ Yet their mutual emotional dependence remained unchanged and they wrote to each other constantly. Thus, although Vita's name may not feature on every page of the narrative of Harold's pre-war and wartime life, she was there, ever present in the background, and the letters and diaries show that all the major (and many of the minor) issues that concerned Harold were communicated to or discussed with her.

Munich left a troubled atmosphere in its wake. Both in Parliament and in the country, the majority still saw Chamberlain as the man who had saved Britain from war, but as day followed day it was a point of view increasingly difficult to maintain. Germany swallowed the Sudetenland and, in doing so, also swallowed the long line of Czech fortifications designed and built to protect the frontier. Poland and Hungary also took large bites of Czech territory. Jewish emigration from Germany increased and with the emigrants came news, still largely anecdotal at this stage, of the persecution and degrading treatment inflicted on those who remained. Germany's anti-British propaganda was becoming ever more strident. It was not a comfortable time.

Both Harold and Vita did things that could be interpreted as self-indulgence but were more probably a form of defiance, a response to the feeling that time was running out. In the summers after the First World War, Harold had enjoyed sailing in Lord Sackville's *Sumerun*, so he borrowed £2,000 from Vita and bought himself a yacht, calling it the *Mar*, perhaps in homage to Lord Sackville who had invented that name for Vita. He also engaged a Captain De'Ath to sail her. Vita went even further. In February 1939, returning from Paris where she had delivered a radio talk in French on *Pepita*, she decided to buy the 200-acre Bettenham Farm, which bordered on Sissinghurst, a television set (still a great and expensive novelty), and a motor mower to replace the horse-drawn one which was used for the lawns and the orchard.

In the aftermath of his Munich speech and abstention, Harold again submitted himself to his constituents and obtained a vote of confidence – though Bertie Jarvis noted that his closely-argued stance did not appeal to the female voters who were solidly pro-Chamberlain. Then he was off again and, for the next seven or eight months, he criss-crossed the country – also venturing abroad to Amsterdam and Brussels – giving lectures and speeches. In London, he participated in debates in the House and attended confidential meetings of the loosely-constituted 'Eden Group.' At Sissinghurst, where he returned when he could, but rarely for more than a day or two, most of his time was taken up writing speeches, radio talks and articles for newspapers and magazines – as well as a lecture on Byron which, despite the pressures of other work, he had agreed to give. It was his work for the BBC that brought his biggest audience. 'The Past Week' had centred on political issues and foreign policy. Now he was given a regular, fifteen-minute slot on Monday evenings when he could speak about anything he chose. Some topics – 'Mass Observation', 'English Public Schools' – had more or less contemporary relevance, while others – 'When I Was Young', 'Life in the Garden' – were more personal. What came across to the millions of radio listeners was Harold's logical but unemphatic defence of reasonable views and reasonable behaviour. It was these talks in 1938 and 1939 which did more than anything else to make him a nationally known figure.

Guy Burgess was working as a producer in the Talks Department and Harold would sometimes go out for a drink or a meal with him after a broadcast. He had met Burgess, later to be exposed as a Russian spy, some years previously, but it was during this period that they got to know each other better. Despite later suggestions, there is no evidence that they ever had an affair. Norman Rose points out that Burgess already had a drink problem, was none too careful about personal hygiene and anything but discreet in his homosexual behaviour, which made him an extremely unlikely sexual partner for Harold.[6] Nonetheless, he found Burgess amusing, as did many people, and though his access to sensitive or secret information was limited he may well have provided Burgess with gossip about individuals and their attitudes which was passed on to Moscow. Burgess certainly played on Harold's reasonableness, feeding him selected pieces of information and leading him to believe that Russian attitudes were more moderate than was in fact the case. However clearly Harold could see through Nazi and, later, Soviet duplicity on a political level, it is clear that with Burgess, as with Henlein, he was not prepared for duplicity when he met it face to face.

Just before Christmas 1938, Harold had lunch at the Reform Club with Henry Wilson Harris, the long-serving and strongly pro-League-of-Nations editor of the *Spectator*. The result was the 'Marginal Comment' column,[7] another vehicle for Harold's views and one which was to last, with occasional interruptions, for the next fourteen years. *The Spectator* allowed even greater latitude in the choice of subject matter than the BBC – topics could and did range from the Italian seizure of Albania to garden design. He assumed an educated and well-read audience, and again presented himself in the persona of the reasonable man: he might sound passionate on a subject where he held strong views, but never beyond the point of balance or reason. And it was this persona, always interesting, always reliable, never extreme, that developed 'Marginal Comment' into something of a national institution. It is difficult to make a meaningful comparison between Harold's journalism and his books. Even when collected, radio talks and magazine articles cannot offer the opportunity for the kind of structured and developed argument that was his strength as a writer and which is fundamental to his longer works. Nonetheless, the journalism remains worth reading. Taken as a whole, it creates a fascinating *pointilliste* picture of the man and his views and demonstrates a remarkable consistency of approach.

A more obvious and more traditional achievement was *Diplomacy*, published in 1939. It is a specialist work, an exploration of why diplomacy is necessary and how it should work. His central thesis is a familiar one: diplomacy is both an art and a profession and the best results are achieved when the professionals are allowed to do their job. He looks at the historical development of diplomacy, the differing diplomatic styles of the main European nations, and the qualities required for a diplomat to be successful. In doing so, he identifies 'the principles and ideals of correct diplomacy' which he sees as 'necessary and immutable.'[8] *Diplomacy* remained recommended reading for new entrants to the Foreign Office for over half a century after its publication; and it is a surprisingly accessible work, full of humourous and ironic touches which elucidate his points and enhance the train of argument – and it is a model of stylistic clarity.

At the time it was published, however, the central theme of *Diplomacy* had a clear application to Chamberlain's conduct of foreign policy and there are some passages which, for all their impersonality, can only be interpreted as fierce criticism of the Prime Minister.

> The dangers of vanity in a negotiator can scarcely be exaggerated. It tempts him to disregard the advice or opinions of those who may have longer experience of a country, or of a problem, than he possesses himself. It renders him vulnerable to the flattery of those with whom he is negotiating. It encourages him to take too personal a view of the nature and purpose of his functions and in extreme cases to prefer a brilliant but undesirable triumph to some unostentatious but more prudent compromise.[9]

Such passages – and there are several – were no doubt read and understood in Downing Street.

That a specialist work of this kind should have received reviews – let alone favourable reviews – in the mainstream press is further evidence of Harold's status as both an acknowledged expert in his field and a popular commentator. In May 1939, he developed his media credentials still further by becoming a television presenter. In tandem with the socialist writer, cartoonist and sometime MP, Frank Horrabin, he made several appearances in front of the BBC's cameras at Alexandra Palace introducing *This Rough Island Story*, a series of vaguely patriotic intent featuring film clips of agricultural and industrial activities.

Meanwhile, Chamberlain's foreign policy was moving, reluctantly and erratically, away from appeasement. In the aftermath of Munich, he appeared to urge rearmament, while at the same time refusing to put the country on a war footing in case Hitler might think he was abandoning the Munich agreement. In early January 1939, Chamberlain and the Foreign Secretary, Lord Halifax, visited Rome and, incredibly, came away 'convinced of the good faith and good intentions of the Italian Government.' Harold was astonished: 'How can he say such a thing at a moment when Italian troops are advancing on Barcelona?'[10] Even protests from senior, old-school Tories such as Lord Lloyd could not puncture Chamberlain's certainty. The visit to Rome was followed by speeches in Birmingham and Blackburn in which he expressed hopes for continued peace and saw trade as the solution to international problems. Yet in between those two speeches, on 6 February, Chamberlain suddenly announced to the House that he felt 'bound to make plain that the solidarity of interest, by which France and this country are united, is such that any threat to the vital interests of France from whatever quarter it came must evoke the immediate co-operation of this country,'[11] a statement which Harold interpreted as 'something like an offensive and defensive alliance.'[12]

Some indication of Harold's status and reputation in the first half of 1939 can be seen in the way the *Manchester Guardian*, a national paper despite its name, suddenly began to champion his cause. On 15 March, after months of raising the political temperature and instigating Slovak agitation for self-rule, Hitler marched into Moravia and Bohemia and Czechoslovakia ceased to exist. The *Manchester Guardian* ran an editorial leader with the headline 'The Gift of Prophecy' and quoted sections of Harold's Munich debate speech which foretold the final destruction of the Czechoslovak state. Harold's speech was accurate, too, in predicting that Germany wanted a lot more than just Czechoslovakia. Before the end of March, Hitler had occupied Memel (Klaipeda) – thus depriving Lithuania of its main port and thirty per cent of its economy – and issued demands for the annexation of Danzig and the Polish Corridor.

At least it was now clear – even to Chamberlain – that appeasement had failed. On 31 March, Chamberlain told the House of Commons that 'in the event of any action which clearly threatened Polish independence ... His Majesty's Government would feel themselves bound at once to lend the Polish Government all support in their power.'[13] On 7 April, which was also Good Friday, Mussolini invaded Albania and Britain and France extended guarantees to Greece and Romania. Harold's intervention in the debate on the Polish guarantee was not a great success. His too gentle nature was on show again. Following the Government's enforced change of direction and rather than say, quite bluntly, 'I told you so', Harold felt sorry for the Prime Minister and sought to bolster him as a man of peace. The speech rather lost its way.

He managed to spend Easter getting the *Mar* ready for the sailing season. Ben was appointed Deputy Surveyor of the King's Pictures. Nigel was working (unpaid) in Newcastle-upon-Tyne with the Tyneside Council of Social Service. Vita opened the garden at Sissinghurst to the public for the first time. But these domestic happenings, however positive, were constantly overshadowed by external events – German renunciation of the Anglo-German Naval Agreement; Hitler signing the Pact of Steel with Mussolini – which marked the accelerating slide towards war.

In June, Sir Ronald Lindsay was due to retire from the Embassy in Washington. He had been there nearly ten years, an unusually long tenure for such an important post and it was not immediately clear who would replace him. The *Manchester Guardian* suggested that Harold was the most appropriate candidate, a view echoed in the *Spectator*. There is no evidence that this idea was ever discussed, or even thought of, within the Foreign Office, but the suggestion boosted Harold's ego. He debated its merits in the privacy of his diary and came to the conclusion that he would have done the job rather well. It was offered to Lord Lothian, who had served in South Africa and the India Office and who, notwithstanding a recent conversion to the Church of Christ Scientist, was felt to be a 'safe' candidate.

The following month, it happened again. With the Chamberlain Government seemingly uncertain how to react to the tide of events, the newspapers began to agitate for changes in the Cabinet. Churchill and Eden were the obvious names for inclusion, but the *Manchester Guardian* called for Harold to be brought in as well. William Crozier, the editor, had from a very early stage been a vocal opponent of Nazi philosophy, but there is no evidence that Harold ever met him, and precisely what provoked this outburst of support he never knew.

The 'Eden Group' had been keeping a low profile in the House of Commons. Despite the guarantees issued in March, the Government was clearly wavering on the Polish issue. Eden felt that attacking Chamberlain would only raise domestic tensions at a time of international crisis, but as the summer approached Harold began to want a stronger line. He intervened angrily when Commander Sir Archibald Southby, a Tory of the old school, attacked Eden and Duff Cooper. He also felt strongly that, in view of the crisis, the House of Commons should not be adjourned for its summer recess. Eden agreed, but again did not wish to oppose Chamberlain, who was adamant that it should. For the first time Harold felt himself pulled in a new direction – Eden 'is now suggesting that we should all toe the line. I would do so were it not for the fact that Winston refuses, and I cannot let the old lion enter the lobby alone.'[14] The Government was always going to win the vote comfortably, but Harold and forty others abstained. The House adjourned and Harold went sailing.

The *Mar* was an old-fashioned, heavy-rigged yawl which required a crew of two in addition to Captain De'Ath to sail her. She made passage from Southampton to Plymouth where Harold and John Sparrow came on board on 4 August. The plan was to head for the west coast of Scotland, perhaps getting as far as the Shiants. It began well, with idyllic days off Falmouth and Mount St Michael, where Gwen St Aubyn's children were living. Then the weather turned against them off Penzance and they were forced back to Weymouth, where Nigel joined them. They crossed to Cherbourg, which they disliked, but they enjoyed St Peter Port. Harold's diary is unusually lyrical: 'The sails tautened, the sea sparkled into foam at our bows, the dim islands slid behind us.'[15] Heading for Brest, they ran into fog and had to turn back again. They arrived in Fowey and went up to the Fowey Hotel to eat. Harold heard the evening news through the open door of the hotel office. France and Germany were mobilising. The next day they sailed up to Plymouth where they received news of the Nazi-Soviet Pact. The holiday was over. Harold put on his suit and took the train from Plymouth's North Road Station to Paddington. Parliament was being recalled.

It is impossible at this distance fully to understand the sense of shock felt in Britain at the news of the Nazi-Soviet non-aggression pact. Germany and the Soviet Union had been hurling ideological insults at each other for years. The British Government had never seen the Soviet Union as a trusted friend, but it was regarded as a potential ally against Hitler. As recently as July, Harold had been discussing with Maisky the prospects for an Anglo-Soviet Agreement (Maisky thought Chamberlain was deliberately dragging his feet). Now Hitler had pulled off an astonishing diplomatic coup and the picture had been turned upside down. British and French guarantees to Poland were worthless without at least tacit Russian support.

Harold's diaries depict the busy, nervous, subdued atmosphere in and around Parliament. As Hitler's rhetoric against Poland grew increasingly shrill, the House of Commons voted through the Emergency Powers (Defence) Bill. British shipping was withdrawn from the Baltic and the Mediterranean. A programme to evacuate three million mothers and children from major cities was announced. Chamberlain came almost daily to a packed, noisy and expectant House to report on the latest developments, but the Government still had no real policy and was being swept along by the tide of events. On 29 August, Neville Henderson, the Ambassador in Berlin, had a final, stormy meeting with Hitler, although Chamberlain continued desperately to seek some agreement which might stave off the inevitable.

On 1 September, Harold was at Sissinghurst sitting in a deck chair in windless heat when he heard that the Luftwaffe had attacked and nearly destroyed the town of Wielun and that armoured Panzer divisions had crossed the Polish border. He was driven up to London, taking his gas-mask with him. He saw barrage balloons hanging over London 'like black spots in the air.'[16] That evening, leaving the Beefsteak Club, he was 'startled to find a perfectly black city' with all lights and electric signs turned off. He made his way to 28 Queen Anne's Gate, the London home of Ronnie Tree, the Conservative MP for Market Harborough, who had been in Berlin during the Night of the Long Knives and was another leading anti-appeasement figure. News came that Churchill was being brought into the War Cabinet and Eden was being given a ministerial job.

On 2 September, the House passed the National Service (Armed Forces) Act which rendered all men aged between eighteen and forty-one liable for conscription, but when Chamberlain appeared there was still no declaration of war. MPs of all parties were dismayed and confused. Bob Boothby famously called upon Arthur Greenwood, the Acting Labour Leader, to 'speak for Britain' and the resulting cheer from the whole House left the Government front bench looking 'as if they had been struck in the face.'[17] The pressure told. At 11.15 on the morning of 3 September, speaking from the Cabinet Rooms in 10 Downing Street, Chamberlain told the nation that 'this morning the British Ambassador in Berlin handed the German Government a final note, stating that, unless we heard from them by 11 o'clock that they were prepared at once to withdraw their troops from Poland, a state of war would exist between us. I have to tell you now that no such undertaking has been received and that consequently this country is at war with Germany.'[18] Harold heard the speech at Ronnie Tree's house on the housemaid's radio. Churchill was not there, but Eden was. So, too, were Duff Cooper, Harold Macmillan, Brendan Bracken, Leo Amery, Sir

Archibald Sinclair, Bob Boothby, and Duncan Sandys: men who were to have a significant influence on the course of events both during the war and in the years afterwards. As they made their way to the House, the sirens sounded and Harold had his first experience of what he called an 'air-raid refuge' with, on this occasion, 'all manner of people from Cabinet Ministers to cooks'.[19] Returning to Sissinghurst that afternoon, he saw that the Sackville standard, which always flew from the flagpole on the top of Vita's tower, had been taken down.

47   Role

Harold's experience of European affairs, and of Germany in particular, had brought him to an early appreciation of the threat posed by Hitler and Mussolini. This drew him into the orbit of Eden, Churchill and the various loose groupings in and around Parliament which constituted the anti-appeasement lobby. Their view, which Harold articulated throughout, rested on a combination of principle – that Britain had a moral duty to stand up for justice and international law – and *realpolitik* – that Hitler's actions were an actual threat to Britain's interests and Britain's security. They did not succeed in changing the Government's foreign policy, but they did clearly state an alternative and keep that alternative before the Government, Parliament and the country. Their aim had been to make the Government recognise the full danger posed by Germany (and, to a lesser extent, Italy) and act accordingly. With the declaration of war, therefore, their purpose was largely achieved.

As a popular broadcaster and commentator as well as an MP, Harold had been a particularly visible critic of the Government. He had acted in accordance with his beliefs, and selflessly insofar as he was now a very unpopular figure in certain key circles within Government and had forfeited any chance of a ministerial post. He did not want war in any active sense, but knew it to be inevitable and right: 'If Anthony had said, "We will consider peace," I should have been wretchedly relieved. As he said "We shall fight to the end," I am stimulated and happy. Yet I dread what I know to be the consequences.'[1] Naturally enough, he wanted to take an active part in the war, but, too old to fight and with parliamentary work effectively limited to the duties of a constituency MP, he needed to find a role.

As for most of the British population, Harold's war was, from the beginning, one of fluctuating emotions. To begin with, he was 'unable to see how the war could be won.'[2] By November 1939, he was writing that 'this war is costing us six million a day and ... I am not certain that we shall win it. We all keep up a brave face and refuse to admit that defeat is possible.'[3] In his more optimistic moments, he believed that 'if we have the will-power, we might win through.'[4] By April 1940, he could identify a 'first stage of acute depression ... [a] second stage, trying to sort my ideas in order. And now there comes a third stage when I feel that we *can* win but that we may fail to do so.'[5]

Much of Harold's early depression and defeatism was caused by uncertainty and lack of knowledge of what was happening. Even though he was an MP – and, later, a junior minister – he had little special access to information and, like everyone else, was largely dependent on the BBC for news. Nor was it helped by the inaction of the Phoney War period and the lack of leadership displayed by the Chamberlain Government. Harold was in no sense a man of action, but most of his heroes were, and even those who were not – Dr Pollock, Sligger Urquhart, Eyre Crowe – can fairly claim to have been leaders of men in a different way. He responded to leaders, to action and change, and to men who made things happen. The war had to be fought – and it was news of action that spurred him towards optimism, even, quite illogically, when the news was bad. Even when the chaotic failure of the Norwegian campaign became apparent, Harold could write: 'We are in a bad way. We shall win!'[6] and, as Nigel Nicolson observes, 'a note of elation permeates the diary after the fall of France.'[7]

Harold responded to leadership in its most traditional sense, too. After meeting the King and Queen at a lunch in July 1940, he wrote to Vita: 'They did me all the good in the world. How I wish you had been there.... [They were] resolute and sensible. *We shall win*. I know that. I have no doubt at all.'[8] Harold was, of course, a traditionalist and a monarchist, but – while it is easy to dismiss or downplay such a reaction from the standpoint of a more cynical age – it is worth remembering that Churchill, Eden, Macmillan, President Roosevelt's emissary, Harry Hopkins, and the President himself all regarded the royal couple's leadership during wartime as inspirational; and that royal tours of the bombed-out parts of London and other major cities had a huge and positive impact on civilian morale.

Eden had joined the Government on the outbreak of war as Secretary of State for the Dominions, but the Eden Group continued to exist and Harold remained a member. Without its titular head the group became somewhat more formal, holding regular Wednesday dinners, chaired by

Leo Amery, at the Carlton Club in St James's Street. Later, it metamorphosed into a 'Watching Committee' under the veteran Conservative politician Lord Salisbury, Bobbety Cranborne's father. The aim was to guard against backsliding and to push an apparently unwilling Chamberlain Government into action. Harold's membership of this coterie is important because, in May 1940, it was their decision to vote against the Government following the debate on the Norwegian campaign which effectively forced Chamberlain to resign. Harold and forty-three others, all technically supporters of the Government, voted with the Opposition. Thirty other Government MPs abstained and Chamberlain's majority was reduced from 213 to 81. He resigned on 10 May. After that, the group began to disintegrate, not least because many of its members achieved ministerial office under Churchill.

Yet Churchill's succession was far from certain. Whitehall gossip suggested that Chamberlain had given him the Admiralty in order to keep him busy and therefore quiet, and Churchill's friends, Harold among them, feared that association with the Government's failures – particularly the Norwegian campaign in which he played a significant part – would tell against him when the moment came. During the course of the Phoney War, Harold, along with many others, had come to see Churchill as the best successor to Chamberlain, but, as his diary makes clear, his decision to vote against the Government and force Chamberlain out was taken with no certainty that Churchill would succeed: 'People are so distressed ... they are talking about Lloyd George as a possible PM. Eden is out of it. Churchill is undermined by the Conservative caucus. Halifax is believed (and with justice) to be a tired man.'[9]

Harold's movement from defeatism to qualified optimism through the early months of the war is roughly paralleled by his success in piecing together of a wartime role for himself. This was not difficult insofar as it was essentially a more focussed and targetted extension of his peacetime work with the media, but it did involve accepting his own strengths and limitations. Harold's need to belong made him a man of institutions and he would have liked a defined institutional role, such as the Foreign Office had provided in 1914, but over the previous ten years he had carved out a public role for himself as a media personality and commentator on events who was trusted by his audience. Society and technology had both moved on since the 1914–18 war and there was an unprecedented need and urgency for the national purpose and national values to be communicated intelligibly to the mass of the people. It was the natural role for Harold. If it lacked the institutional definition he had hoped for, it allowed him (within limits) to maintain an independence of view, it was of national importance, and it was perfectly suited to his talents.

Yet it took an external agency to push Harold in the direction in which his experience and his talents pointed. Three weeks after the outbreak of war, on 25 September 1939, he received a visit at King's Bench Walk from Allen Lane, whose publishing venture, Penguin Books, was just four years old. Lane wanted Harold to write a 'Penguin Special' to explain to the general reader why Britain was at war. He could not have made a better choice. Harold understood the need for such a publication and the need for haste. Less than three weeks later, on 12 October, he delivered the completed typescript and the book was published a month later, in Penguin's familiar deep orange and cream livery, priced sixpence.

The timing of the commission, the speed at which Harold wrote and, above all, the title, have led *Why Britain Is At War* to be seen as a quick, wartime morale-booster. In fact, it has more in common with his diplomatic histories – the first part of *Peacemaking* or the latter part of *Curzon*, or even the later historical work, *The Congress of Vienna* (1948) – than with a pamphlet such as *Politics in the Train*. He begins with the story of brides-in-the-bath serial killer, George Joseph Smith, who murdered each of his three wives in the same way and was only caught because he was 'too stupid or too arrogant to vary his technique.'[10] Harold compares this to the pattern of behaviour repeated by Hitler as he picked off target countries one by one on his way towards European domination. It is a highly effective introduction, wittily ironic and, as such, well calculated to appeal to the English reader, but it also has a thematic relevance, for, in the concise and logical account of events leading up to the outbreak of war which follows – Hitler's early life, *Mein Kampf*, the Rhineland, Austria, Munich, Czechoslovakia, Poland – Harold presents the war as a combination of battle for survival and moral conflict. The battle for survival is, in fact, a battle to punish the murderer of Austria, Czechoslovakia and Poland, and restore a moral dimension to international politics. If that cannot be achieved, Britain herself will be overwhelmed by an immoral and irresistible force.

Harold wrote *Why Britain Is At War* from his own independent point of view. He was not a member of the Government, but he supported the war. He was an acknowledged expert on European affairs, but fiercely critical of the Government's handling of foreign policy. He was patriotic and would do nothing to hinder the war effort, but insisted on honesty and objectivity in recording the events which had led to war. He allows his view of Chamberlain's ineptitude in managing the relationship with Germany and Italy to emerge from the narrative (and he obviously enjoys convenient details such as Hitler and Chamberlain meeting in the very Bad Godesberg hotel where Hitler had planned the murder of Ernst Röhm), but acquits him of deception and dishonesty. Indeed, the objectivity becomes almost painful when Harold attempts to be fair to Hitler.[11] Whatever else it is, *Why Britain Is At War* is not propaganda. But it did nothing to improve Harold's standing in Downing Street. Sir Horace Wilson, who had been Chamberlain's Special Adviser throughout the appeasement period and had recently been promoted to Permanent Secretary at the Treasury and Head of the Home Civil Service, was so furious at Harold's presentation of events that he used his influence to prevent Harold from being considered for an appointment in the Political Intelligence Department of the Foreign Office.[12] Yet the book was an astonishing success. Harold's colleagues in the House were full of praise, among them Eden and, more surprisingly, R. A. Butler, a Chamberlain loyalist, who was to hold a string of cabinet posts in the 1950s and 1960s. And it clearly responded to a public need: by the end of November 1939, it was selling 5,000 copies a day.

Why Britain Is At War contains the occasional contestable judgement and minor contradiction, but considering the speed and circumstances of its composition – with only limited access to official documents – it is a remarkable achievement; and not the least remarkable feature is the concluding section on 'War Aims', in which Harold addresses the need to create and maintain European order after the war. His solution was the creation of a Unites States of Europe in which

> we should continue to manage our local interests in our own manner through our own Parliament ... but ... the extent and nature of our armaments, the general lines of our foreign policy, and the use of our raw materials and credits should conform to general lines laid down by the Central Federal Authority.... Would that in fact be so terrible a sacrifice?[13]

These are sentiments which can still provoke heated debate in the twenty-first century. Churchill reached similar conclusions towards the end of the war and his 1946 Zurich speech is often seen as a pivotal moment in the birth of the European Union. It is interesting that Harold got there first.

In the period between the writing and the publication of *Why Britain Is At War*, Harold made a visit to France with a group of backbench MPs which included Leo Amery and the future Nobel Peace Prize winner, Philip Noel-Baker. They visited the Maginot Line and received a misleading account of its strength and flexibility. They met the former, current and future Prime Ministers (Edouard Daladier, Léon Blum, and Paul Reynaud) and received equally misleading accounts of the country's preparedness and confidence. The visit would be of little significance were it not for the fact that France, as both a political entity and a culture, was to constitute a significant part of Harold's later wartime role. Again, the role was self-elected and resistant to formal definition, but, at a time of huge mutual suspicion, Harold became, in Nigel Nicolson's words, 'the best of interpreters of France to England and England to France.'[14]

Carving out a wartime role for himself and wrestling with huge concepts such as national identity and purpose and the future of Europe led Harold to reflect on his own values and beliefs. Like the audience he was addressing in *Why Britain Is At War*, he, too, needed to be certain what he was fighting for. In his last pre-war diary entry, he records: 'an elderly woman ... shakes her fist at us and shouts that it is all the fault of the rich. The Labour Party will be hard put to it to prevent this war degenerating into class warfare.'[15] He saw 'a great and angry tide ... rising against the governing classes' and realised that the issues it raised would have to be dealt with in the aftermath of the war. This led him to spell out his beliefs in detail:

> I have always been on the side of the underdog, but I have believed in the principle of aristocracy. I have hated the rich but I have loved learning, scholarship, intelligence and the humanities. Suddenly I am faced with the fact that all these lovely things are supposed to be 'class privileges'. The snobbishness of the British people (that factor upon which the aristocratic principle relied and often exploited) has suddenly turned to venom. When I find that my whole class is being assailed, I feel part of them, a feeling that I have never had before.[16]

Both he and Vita understood that, win or lose, the war would be destructive in more than just a physical sense; that it would destroy much in British and European society that they valued. Harold tried to see his own life and attitudes in the context of historical change.

> Thus I, realising dimly that the old Edwardian world of bath salts and ortolans was doomed to disappearance, trained myself from the age of 22 to despise (and thereby not to desire) that shape of civilisation which I foresaw would not last.... I achieved a different and no less self-indulgent form of elegance which seemed to me likely to survive my own lifetime. It consisted of comparatively modest establishments in the

country and in London, and a gay combination of the Café Royal, Bloomsbury, rooms in the Temple, the garden at Sissinghurst, foreign travel, the purchase of books and pictures and the unthinking enjoyment of food and wine.... And now this tide of self-sacrifice is lapping at our feet. We shall have to walk and live a Woolworth life hereafter.[17]

What could be saved from the wreck? What would post-war Britain look like? Harold's answer was 'federalism abroad and Socialism at home.'[18] The promise of socialism, by which Harold meant 'equality of opportunity', was in his view the only way to give the mass of the population something to fight for.[19] He predicted that after the war there would be

some sort of revolution here. We may even have republicanism and a certain amount of persecution of the governing class. But that will die down and we shall find some middle position between the extremes of the pendulum – a modified socialism.[20]

It was a wholly logical answer: his view of society had an evolutionary quality about it – 'The old aristocracy may be derided, as after the Wars of the Roses, but ... some new class will emerge now.'[21] Yet it was a reluctant answer. He did not really believe equality was possible, and although he was 'prepared to see the old world of privilege disappear'[22] in the interests of a fairer society, he did not expect to like it.

This reluctant acceptance that some form of socialist society was inevitable (an opinion, incidentally, shared by Harold Macmillan)[23] stayed with Harold throughout the war. It was a seriously-held view, but one not often aired with his political friends and colleagues – he knew that it would be unpopular, even divisive, and, in any case, winning the war was a far greater priority – yet it influenced his response to many domestic issues. He supported reform of the public schools[24] and of the foreign service,[25] and he was a passionate advocate of the 1942 Beveridge Report which laid the foundations of the modern welfare state. It may also help to explain Harold's post-war decision to join the Labour Party, a decision which otherwise sits oddly with his patrician character and experience.

Harold saw himself as belonging to a transitional stage between the privileged aristocratic past and an egalitarian socialist future. He was never really a socialist. He may at certain times have accepted certain socialist principles and policies, but if labels have to be attached then he was largely an old-fashioned Liberal – a fact which he half-acknowledged on several occasions.[26] Yet if socialism were the inevitable product of the war, he would not oppose it. The old guard (and Vita) might stand against the tide, but, though it might cause him pain and though he might regret the passing of long-established traditions and institutions, Harold preferred to try and play his part in shaping the future. In that sense, he was both generous and tolerant.

48 Minister

At 12.40 p.m. on Friday 17 May 1940, the telephone at Sissinghurst rang.

> Churchill: Harold, I think it would be very nice if you joined the Government and helped Duff at the Ministry of Information.
> Harold: There is nothing that I should like better
> Churchill: Well, fall in tomorrow. The list will be out tonight. That all right?
> Harold: Very much all right.
> Churchill: OK.[1]

It was a short conversation and it came nearly a week after Churchill had become Prime Minister, at the end of his Government-making process. It was also a very junior appointment – Harold was to be a Parliamentary Under-Secretary, the lowest level of salaried ministerial appointment.[2] Yet it was a step: he had his foot on the ministerial ladder and if he performed well, he could quite reasonably look forward to promotion and a bigger, more powerful ministerial job.

Harold's first impressions of life in the Ministry, in a letter to Vita two days later, make odd, almost camp reading. Rather than suggesting a burning desire to make a success of his new job, they hint at the passivity which seems to have characterised his ministerial performance.

> I feel surrounded by friends here which makes it all very pleasant indeed. Our War Room is perfectly thrilling. It is kept going night and day, and there are maps with pins and different coloured bits of wool. The chiefs meet in conference twice a day at 10.30 and 5.30, and the press conference is at 12.30. I have to attend all these, and in addition I shall be given specific branches of work to take over. I have a nice sunny little room.[3]

The Ministry of Information was a war-time expedient. It had existed briefly at the end of the First World War and was revived at the beginning of the Second under Lord Macmillan (no relation to Harold) and then Sir John Reith. Churchill, who disliked Reith, replaced him with Duff Cooper, an old friend and political ally. The Ministry was responsible for publicity, propaganda and censorship and was based, ironically enough, in Bloomsbury – in Charles Holden's art deco Senate House which was requisitioned from London University for the purpose.

Harold's responsibilities were mainly concerned with morale on what was becoming known as the 'Home Front'. In particular, he was responsible for coordinating information and advice to the public concerning the possibility of a German invasion, which, after Dunkirk, was expected almost daily – and was a subject of deep personal concern: Sissinghurst and Vita were only twenty miles from some of the likely invasion beaches. He sat on the Cabinet's Civil Defence Committee which, particularly during the Blitz, was concerned with morale as well as the more practical aspects of civil defence. As Parliamentary Under-Secretary, he was also his minister's deputy in the House of Commons. As Duff Cooper was frequently absent from London on official business or through illness, Harold was often called upon to take his place on the Government Front Bench to answer questions or make statements on the policy and activities of the Ministry. For an aspiring politician, these occasions were – or should have been – crucial opportunities to make a reputation.

Ministerial and parliamentary functions aside, Harold continued to write articles and to broadcast, even though his freedom to express personal opinions was now constrained by Government policy. He broadcast on the BBC's overseas networks in both French and German, extolling British support for the freedom of individuals, families and nations to make their own choices and live as they chose.

Of the friendliness of the Ministry of Information there can be no doubt. Harold and Duff Cooper had been Foreign Office colleagues during the First World War and Cooper genuinely welcomed Harold's appointment. Charles Peake, another former Foreign Office colleague, later to go on to Washington, was among the senior officials with whom Harold worked. The Ministry's Deputy Director General was Walter Monckton, who advised Edward VIII during the Abdication crisis and whom Harold knew from Court circles. Kenneth Clark, Surveyor of the King's Pictures, who had made Ben his deputy the previous year, was also among those present.

Friendliness was one thing, efficiency quite another. In his memoirs, *Old Men Forget*, Duff Cooper describes the Ministry as so large, so voluminous, so amorphous, that no single man could cope with it.... The main defect was that there were too few ordinary Civil Servants in it, and too many brilliant amateurs. Day after day admirable, though temporary, officials would come to me offering their resignation ... because ... [they] had conceived some brilliant idea and put it forward to their official supervisor, who had either turned it down flat or else had altered it.... The presence of so many able, undisciplined men in one Ministry was bound to lead to a great deal of friction, and we were at the same time subjected to a continual bombardment of criticism from without.[4]

Harold recognised that 'the Ministry is ill-organised and mistakes are made', and also saw that its purpose was in a sense incompatible with the British character. It was 'too decent, educated and intellectual'. To succeed, it needed 'crooks'.[5] Cooper simply saw it as unnecessary: 'All foreign propaganda should be under the direct control of the Foreign Office.... Other departments should conduct their own publicity ... [and] meet regularly to ensure the necessary coordination.'[6]

The Ministry was unpopular with the other Whitehall departments, particularly the Foreign Office and the three service ministries – the War Office, the Air Ministry and the Admiralty: there were constant arguments about what information should be made public and who should do it. It was unpopular with the press and the BBC, because the relationship was poorly defined and, where clear, was seen to be both obstructive and intrusive. It was unpopular with MPs who saw it as lumbering, bureaucratic and expensive. And it was unpopular with the British public who conceived it as far more interfering than was actually the case: the phrase 'Cooper's Snoopers' was coined to describe its denizens.

For Harold, this meant that many of his appearances in the House of Commons involved answering hostile questions from MPs – about aspects of censorship (which was either excessive or inadequate depending on the speaker's perspective); about the size, cost and organisation of the Ministry; or about any aspect of the Ministry's activity which might usefully yield a stick to beat it with. Harold was taken to task for a controversial speech given by the historian A. J. P. Taylor who happened to be a member of a local Information Committee.[7] He was called upon to explain why Noel Coward had gone to visit the United States.[8] He had to defend Walter Monckton who, frustrated beyond endurance, had publicly complained that the Ministry had been 'given a pitchfork to deal with a tank.'[9] It was the stuff of parliamentary life, but Harold was too often seen to be excusing or explaining things, and questioners were too often unhappy with his answers. His worst moment came in May 1941 when he was obliged to apologise to the House for inaccurate information released by the Ministry concerning the arrival of Rudolf Hess in Britain – information which had appeared to cast doubt on the conduct of the Duke of Hamilton. It was not his finest hour.[10] Yet even when Harold did have the opportunity to make a larger statement to the House, defending the Ministry and making a perfectly reasonable point, he managed to speak with less than his usual clarity.

> It is not right to compare the activities and actions of the Ministry of Information with the methods of Dr. Goebbels. We are trying to do something quite different.... We are trying in every way ... every day and every night, to gain the confidence not only of our own people, because that we may hope to obtain, but of the whole world, so that we may establish gradually that credit and that repute, that trustworthiness, that credibility which will not only be of great value to us in time of war but will give us the moral authority when peace comes to play our part, which will be a grave and responsible part, in the reconstruction of the world.[11]

Another problem, of course, was the war itself. Within days of Harold taking up office, Belgium surrendered and the Norwegian campaign reached its dismal conclusion. Then came Dunkirk and the fall of France. The Battle of Britain was a victory and might have offered the Ministry an opportunity for some positive propaganda, but its decisive nature was not fully understood at the time and most of the country expected an invasion in its wake.

For Harold, the Battle of Britain brought the war quite literally home. Dogfights were a daily occurrence in the skies above Sissinghurst. Machine gun bullets and pieces of hot shrapnel fell into the garden. Two German pilots were taken prisoner in the village. One Spitfire crashed on Victor Cazalet's estate, about a mile away. Another demolished Staplehurst station five miles away, from which Harold usually took his train up to London. All this seemed to presage invasion. Harold oversaw the drafting and printing of a leaflet: 'If the Invader Comes – What to Do and How to Do it.' Fourteen million copies were printed.[12] It contained six key principles and lots of rather optimistic good advice, but it certainly did not include his own solution. Both he and Vita had cyanide pills which they would take if captured. Harold's name was on the Nazi blacklist.

The disasters continued into 1941. The Blitz affected every major city in Britain. Victories in North Africa were reversed by Rommel, and Wavell was driven back to the borders of Egypt. Yugoslavia and Greece surrendered. The *Bismarck* was sunk, but so was the *Hood*. Operations in Crete were a bloody failure. It was not a good time for those in charge of publicity and propaganda.

All mitigating factors aside, Harold was not a great success at the Ministry of Information. He may not have been a failure, as James Pope-Hennessy, was to assert later,[13] but he does seem to have been swept along by the tide of events rather than seizing the initiative, however difficult that might have been. James Lees-Milne lists a number of colleagues – Professor Mansergh in the Dominions Office, Walter Monckton, Sir Kenneth Clark – who found Harold indecisive, 'not of sufficient calibre', or lacking any gift for politics.[14] Even Gladwyn Jebb, a firm friend and admirer concedes that Harold 'had little organizational capacity ... and was said to spend a great deal of his time coffee-housing.'[15] And again, crucially, he failed to convince the House of Commons.

He got down to Sissinghurst for a night when he could; and he made time, usually over dinner, to see such friends as were still in London or were passing through – James Lees-Milne; James Pope-Hennessy; Somerset Maugham's nephew, Robin; Christopher Hobhouse; John Sparrow; Guy Burgess. But official duties came first: he worked six days out of seven and also did fire-watching duty at the Palace of Westminster one night a week. Yet hard work was clearly not enough.

Dismissal, when it came on 18 July 1941, was ostensibly for political reasons. Churchill wrote that 'changes at the Ministry of Information lead me to ask you to place your office as Parliamentary Secretary at my disposal.'[16] Harold was replaced by a Labour MP, Ernest Thurtle, as Churchill juggled the allocation of ministerial posts among the parties within the coalition, and was offered a governorship at the BBC as a consolation prize. The real reason was the old problem of assertiveness. Rob Bernays had warned him the previous month that he had too much desire to please and too little desire to dominate.[17] Harold knew only too well what was wrong. The previous September, after four months in the job, he had written, 'I lack authority in this place, which is not due to the unwillingness of others, but to my own lack of strength and drive. I am too acquiescent.'[18] But knowing and doing something about it were two different things.

He was devastated by his dismissal, although pleased to receive a note from Duff Cooper saying, 'I think you have received very shabby treatment, and I find that everybody shares this view.'[19] He received numerous expressions of regret at his departure, in person or by letter, from MPs and members of the public. Osbert Lancaster, the cartoonist and another Ministry employee, gave him a drink and then lunch when he needed it most. And yet, as if in confirmation of the verdict, Harold neither made a fuss nor actively sought another ministerial post.

One feels that Harold's intellectual capabilities, his experience, his capacity for hard work and his public profile should have been worth something. According to John Colville, one of Churchill's Assistant Private Secretaries, Duff Cooper could scarcely have made a worse Minister of Information,[20] but he was still promoted to be Chancellor of the Duchy of Lancaster and given an important role in the Far East. But Cooper was a fighter and had asked Churchill directly for another job. Harold still hankered after the Foreign Office, but defeatism had set in – 'If I had more power and drive, I should have been offered Rab Butler's job at the Foreign Office, which I would dearly have loved.'[21]

Another key element was Churchill. Harold had known Churchill since 1908 and they had met on innumerable occasions in the intervening years. They had dined together in London; they had had professional dealings when Harold was in the Foreign Office; and they had met on grand social occasions – at Knole, at Knebworth, and at Blenheim. Harold had even been to stay at Chartwell. When Harold became an MP and, like Churchill, a vocal opponent of the Chamberlain Government's foreign policy, their association became closer and Churchill often congratulated Harold on his speeches and interventions. They were on good terms, but they were never close.

Harold's attitude to Churchill had undergone a gradual change. During the First World War, he had generally approved of Churchill's belligerence but regarded his judgement as erratic, a view he maintained during the Abdication crisis when Churchill's intervention on behalf of King Edward VIII was little short of disastrous. His admiration grew throughout the appeasement period, and by the time Churchill became Prime Minister, he had outstripped all Harold's previous heroes. Churchill could do no wrong and some of the war-time diary entries make almost embarrassing reading.

I love Winston and would not mind if he were unjust to me.[22]

Winston is the embodiment of the nation's will.[23]

My God, my love and admiration of Winston surge round me like a tide![24]

> I cannot bear the thought that this heroic figure should now be sniped at by tiny little men.[25]

Harold Macmillan suggested that Churchill reacted against Harold's slavish admiration.

> The inner group would say, 'Winston, you are talking balls....' Harold was not on these terms. He would look at Winston with adoring eyes like a faithful spaniel. This was not what Winston liked or admired. He did not care for deference.[26]

This rings true, but, as Norman Rose has pointed out, Churchill's reservations about Harold went back further. In 1936, he had been unwilling to allow Harold admission to the Other Club, a select group of diners, membership of which required Churchillian approval.[27] Why should this have been? Rose raises the possibility that Harold's homosexuality might have been the cause, but rightly notes that Churchill was not really bothered about other people's sexual behaviour. Churchill was notoriously loyal to his close friends, but could be unreasonable about those who did not come into that category, such as, for example, General Wavell in whom he could never be persuaded to have confidence. Perhaps Churchill, like Bloomsbury, took Harold at face value, seeing – from his perspective – a charming, intellectual, slightly detached figure; an artist and a theorist, less pragmatic and apparently less whole-heartedly committed to the political struggle than his usual cronies, such as Beaverbrook, Bracken, Macmillan, and Duff Cooper. Harold's sister, Gwen St Aubyn, commented that Harold was 'insensitive in one respect ... he was always laughing at himself, so imagined that others would not mind his laughing at them. Many of them did mind.'[28] Churchill would have minded mockery more than outright disagreement.

To Harold's logical mind, spelling out war aims and offering a vision for the post-war future was an essential part of explaining the reasons for the war and maintaining morale. He conceived the idea of a war aims pamphlet in July 1940 and worked on it in close cooperation with the Foreign Secretary, Lord Halifax. In January 1941, it was ready for submission to the Prime Minister. Churchill, the pragmatist, turned the idea down flat, refusing to make any statement at all on the grounds that 'precise aims would be compromising' by committing the Government to things it might not be able to deliver, and that 'vague principles would disappoint.'[29]

Some months before, however, Harold had spoken on war aims at a private meeting of the Fabian Society. He said nothing controversial and broke no rules, but his speech was printed in the Fabian Society Year Book. The US magazine *Nation*, considering Harold's views newsworthy, turned his text into an article, which was partially reprinted in the *Manchester Guardian*. Churchill exploded, demanding to know 'by what right [Harold] was writing about war aims when he himself had deprecated any mention of them.' Harold was forced to write an apologetic minute detailing how the situation had come about and was pathetically grateful when Churchill replied, 'Please thank Mr Nicolson for his explanation.'[30] It was a small incident and unlikely to have played a part in Harold's dismissal, but it illustrates the difference in temperament and the nature of their relationship. However good a Foreign Office minister or ambassador Harold might have made, he was not going to get the chance while Churchill was in charge.

49 Might-Have-Been

Having lost his ministerial job, Harold's own assessment of his position was bleak.

> I mind more than I thought I should mind. It is mainly, I suppose, a sense of failure.... I come back to the bench below the gangway having had my chance and failed to profit by it. Ever since I have been in the House I have been looked on as a might-be. Now I shall be a might-have-been. Always up to now I have been buoyed up by the hope of writing some good book or achieving a position of influence in politics. I now know that I shall never write a book better than I have written already, and that my political career is at an end. I shall merely get balder and fatter and more deaf as the years go by.... Success should come late in life to compensate for the loss of youth; I had youth and success together, and now I have old age and failure.[1]

And it was true that his political career would never really recover. He was acutely disappointed. When Ben was about to meet him in London, Vita privately warned that the subject was not one to be taken lightly.

In fact, it did not take Harold long to re-establish a role for himself outside Government. It was necessary financially. He always spent whatever he earned and more, so the loss of his ministerial salary was a serious matter. He was naturally delighted when he was invited to resume his 'Marginal Comment' column in the *Spectator* at ten guineas per article. It was also a question of character. He was a patriot, genuinely committed to his country and to the war. It was wrong to be idle at such a time. He threw himself into all sorts of activities, but, although he was soon busy, it took much longer for him to recover confidence in himself and belief in the value of what he could contribute. He was not helped by disobliging articles in *The Times*, hinting that his BBC governorship had been invented simply to find him a job; and in *Truth*, suggesting that his manners were 'lacking in virility' and that he spoke in 'the mincing accents of a Paris salon.'[2] Harold decided to assert himself by publishing his 1939 diary, but realised that it was too recent. It would highlight his political judgement, but it would also recall the bitter divisions of the appeasement years and risk re-opening wounds which, in the middle of a war, were best left to heal. He dropped the idea. Harold's public – his constituents in Leicester, readers of the *Spectator* and listeners to the BBC[3] – would not have noticed any difference in him, but disappointment led to depression, and depression led to pessimism about the war and what might happen afterwards. In the end, his resilience and his inability not to throw himself wholeheartedly into things pulled him through, together with the constant presence of Vita in the background, without whom he felt he would be 'lost and lonely, like a jam-jar floating in the North Sea.'[4] Nonetheless, July 1941 was a watershed in Harold's life and he knew it.

Two years later, in July 1943, when he suffered a sudden loss of confidence, his mind immediately reverted to the same point. He had gone to the House of Commons intending to speak in a debate on education in Africa, but found he could not do it. He wrote to Vita that

> It was ... a great wave of defeatism.... I have never lost confidence in myself to that extent.... I do find it strange that a person of my experience is so much ignored nowadays. I suppose that the fact that I got into the Government (and in a post where I *ought* to have made good) and was thereafter discarded, has created the impression that I am a dud ... what I mind is that it has damaged my self-confidence and that I have not got the guts to assert myself in the face of a reputation for failure. This induces in me moods of depression which themselves increase my diffidence.[5]

Vita's response to this was immensely practical and shows how well she understood him. She had suspected that 'something of the sort was going on in [his] head.' She dismissed his failure to speak as 'mere stage fright.... I don't worry about such temporary lapses, but I do worry about your tendency for dispersal.' There was nothing wrong with his mind, but if he did 'a little stocktaking', he would realise that he was doing too many different things, each of them useful in its own right, but taken together they diluted his energies. She tabulated his activities:

(1) *Marginal Comment*. Altogether admirable, a great success, well worthwhile...
BBC. Financially essential; very useful, if only the position of the Governors can be reformed.
Free French. Yes. Important. You are specially well qualified.
Your own books... One of your strongest suits, which, with curious modesty, you do not esteem nearly highly enough.
House of Commons. Well, obviously you must keep that on.

(2) *Endless Committees and odd speeches and odd articles*, mostly undertaken because you cannot say No.... I was appalled when you said you were going to write a book on the Colonies.

She went on to suggest that he should 'scrap as much of (2) as possible, and ... take up the rebuilding and planning of England ... but I believe you have the idea that it is not sufficiently "public life".'[6]

Even in adversity, then, Harold had tremendous energy. Reading the 'Marginal Comment' articles reprinted in *Friday Mornings 1941–44* and *Comments 1944–48*, the sense of energy comes through in the different *personæ* he adopts to deal with different subjects. Harold is always Harold, thoughtful, literate, sympathetic, trustworthy, but each topic seems to reveal a different aspect of his personality and experience. He can be the politician, arguing a view on the great issues of the war and the world; the well-travelled man explaining the characteristics and complexities of other cultures; the well-connected man, familiar with the political leaders and the crowned heads of Europe; the parliamentarian, conscious of the value of stability, legitimacy and tradition in a disordered world; the horticulturalist, delivering a discourse on weeds; the serious-minded man wrestling with the problems caused by the bombing of works of art in wartime or how to deal with war criminals; the educated man, distracted from the chaos of the world by a poet or a painting or Shakespeare's vocabulary; or the homely philosopher, musing on human nature and human idiosyncrasy. In these various guises, Harold gave his readers short, wonderfully-structured and complete essays, which conducted them through the successive phases of the conflict. Did they help win the war? No. But in a period of total war, they did argue for the maintenance of human decency and intellectual standards, which, Harold and Vita would have said, was what Britain was fighting for in the first place.

Theoretically, Harold's work at the BBC had the same goal. There is no doubt that his appointment as a Governor was a sop for losing his ministerial post – though there is some evidence that Churchill thought the Governors had more power than they actually did – but that did not mean he regarded the job as a sinecure. When asked by Anthony Eden how he liked his new job, he replied that he wished it were more of a job.[7] The BBC had made him a public figure and, naturally enough, he was keen to support and help develop the corporation. The problem was that the size of the organisation, the size of its audience, and the political importance of both, all conspired to create a tangle of interests which made it difficult to identify a corporate policy, let alone develop it. One key issue was the fact that the role of the Governors was not fully defined – and, throughout his career, Harold was always happier stepping into roles which were defined and understood rather than those which he had to carve out for himself. To make matters worse, it was Ernest Thurtle, MP, Harold's ministerial successor, who drew attention to the problem by stating in the House of Commons 'that the Governors were not concerned with the war effort of the BBC and were only concerned with culture and entertainment.'[8] The Chairman of the Governors, Sir (George) Allen Powell, protested to Brendan Bracken, the Minister of Information, but the whole incident only served to demonstrate that neither Government nor the BBC actually knew what it wanted the Governors to do.

Luckily for Harold, an old friend, Asquith's daughter, Lady Violet Bonham Carter, was appointed to the Board at the same time. She had inherited both her father's Liberal principles and his tenacity. Between them, they made it their job to ask awkward questions and clarify their role. There were several minor skirmishes. In August 1943, they both came to the point of resignation when William Haley, Editor of the *Manchester Evening News*, was appointed Deputy Director-General. The issue was one of procedure – Harold and Violet Bonham-Carter considered that the appointment had been made behind their backs – but an apology was offered and the matter petered out. In February 1944, the Director-General, Robert Foot, resigned because he claimed that the Board of Governors was seeking to undermine his authority, but he could not substantiate his claims, withdrew his resignation and, again, the matter petered out. Harold and Violet

Bonham-Carter ceased to be Governors when their five-year term expired in July 1946, but the division of power and function between the Board and the Director-General continued to be intermittently controversial until the BBC became a trust in 2007.

Harold's function – and that of the other Governors – often seems to have been to fend off minor complaints. When the Conservative MP Brigadier Rayner accused the BBC of issuing watered-down bulletins, Harold told him that the BBC simply broadcast the material it received. Harold Strauss, the Conservative MP for Norwich, complained that the BBC was 'almost wholly left-wing';[9] Hore-Belisha, the former Secretary of State for War, claimed he had been ignored and unfairly treated; Churchill created a fuss about the use and pronunciation of European place names; the King objected to the way aspects of his constitutional position were reported. All this was a long way from the role Harold really wanted, which was to play a part in shaping the values, direction and tone of the BBC for the future.

Again, as so often in Harold's public life, there was an inherent contradiction which hinged on differing approaches to a changing world. Harold had fallen out with Sir John Reith in 1931 because he disliked the strict morality which Reith imposed on the BBC's output. He himself was more adventurous and more liberal, but he still saw the BBC as being a moral force and he believed that it was his (and the other Governors') responsibility to direct that force. He wrote to Violet Bonham-Carter: 'Only the BBC can teach the public to think correctly, to feel nobly, to enjoy themselves intelligently, to have some conception of what is meant by the good life.' Sir John Reith would have agreed, but the majority of the current Board apparently did not. Harold was faced with something new.

> Throughout my life ... I have been dealing with people who, if they did not share my opinions, did share, or at least understand, my values.... [Values] formed the 'language' in which we discoursed.... They were the accepted currency with which we interchanged ideas. Suddenly I have found myself faced with a group of people who not only do not understand, but actually do not know, these weights and measures.... I believe they are honestly quite unaware of the standards which to us seem the axioms of life.[10]

Harold believed – it was his 'principle of aristocracy' again – that the BBC should lead, that it should seek to communicate a set of broadly liberal, but still traditional, values: 'learning, scholarship, intelligence and the humanities.'[11] He found himself faced with a modern, democratic principle which held that the BBC should serve – that it should reflect the views of the majority of the people to whom it broadcast and give its listeners what they wanted. This was an opposition which went far beyond the BBC. Harold would continue to fight – as would Vita, who was far more traditional, even reactionary – but it was to be a rearguard action.

Vita might well have put Harold's work on behalf of the Free French in section (2) of her list of his activities: it was unpaid, unofficial (and unwelcome in some official quarters) and the result of personal choice. That she did not was due to their shared and life-long Francophilia. French was, after all, Vita's mother tongue. Harold, while at times not uncritical of the French, had a deep and emotional attachment to French culture and French civilisation. His attitude is best illustrated by the story of his return to France in March 1945 after an absence of more than four years. Disembarking from the boat at Dieppe, he stooped to touch French soil once more. Asked by his porter if he had dropped something, he replied, 'Non.... J'ai retrouvé quelquechose.'[12]

His emotional attachment to the country notwithstanding, it was clear to Harold that whatever political shape post-war Europe might take (and throughout the early 1940s, some kind of federal system seemed to him the most likely outcome), a strong and democratic France would be a prerequisite for stability.[13] In July 1942, he played a leading role in reviving the Anglo-French Parliamentary Committee, which had not met since the fall of France in 1940. Throughout 1943 and the first half of 1944, he participated regularly in a discussion group organised under the auspices of the Royal Institute of International Affairs. He spoke in the House of Commons. The subject came into numerous articles in the *Spectator* and elsewhere. The detail varied according to the context and the progress of the war, but his essential argument was always the same: 'that France should be fully restored to her position of independence and greatness.'[14] The problem was, of course, that any discussion of the future of France had to take into consideration the tall, controversial, and far from universally-beloved figure of General Charles André Joseph Marie de Gaulle.

Harold first met de Gaulle while he was still at the Ministry of Information. It was an official lunch at the Savoy. 'I do not like him', was Harold's initial, uncompromising judgement.[15] During the course of lunch, de Gaulle, with characteristic lack of modesty, loudly claimed: '*La France entière ... c'est la France libre. C'est moi!*' Harold, clearly in no mood to be steamrollered, replied: '*Oh, le Roi Soleil!*' In fact, he stood up to de Gaulle on a number of occasions in a way he certainly never did to Churchill. De

Gaulle did not seem to resent it and they continued to meet after Harold had ceased to be a minister. The relationship took time to develop – a year after they first met, he noted: 'It is the first time I have ever got on with him.'[16] Harold's close connections with France and the French meant that he already knew, or during the course of the war came to know, many of the leading political exiles – René Pleven, Gaston Palewski, Georges Catroux, Emile Muselier. He was appalled at the level of destructive intrigue such a small group could generate. He decided that de Gaulle could be 'treacherous and wrong' but that, in the last resort, he was no worse than the others.[17] He came to understand that de Gaulle's egocentricity and arrogance, while frequently infuriating, were necessary; they were perhaps the only way of bringing together the scattered remnants of the French armed forces and the French body politic in the aftermath of the shattering defeat of 1940. Devoting himself to the cause of France, Harold was effectively devoting himself to the cause of de Gaulle. He worked determinedly for France to be recognised as a political equal in the struggle against Hitler and for de Gaulle to be recognised as her leader.

It was not an easy task. In retrospect, Churchill recognised both de Gaulle's qualities and the reason for his aggressive and ungrateful behaviour: 'He had to be rude to the British to prove to French eyes that he was not a British puppet.... I always admired his massive strength.'[18] But at the time, Churchill was frequently furious at de Gaulle's contrariness and lack of cooperation. Harold found that

> a good deal of my time is spent trying to pour oil on these troubled waters. All might have been well had de Gaulle been an ordinary man. He is not. He is an extraordinary man. He is an eagle with bad habits. Winston, who is a house-trained eagle, does not see claw to claw with him.[19]

With the Americans, things were even worse. Roosevelt, unskilled in French politics and failing to understand the violent emotions aroused by Maréchal Pétain's Vichy regime, continued to deal with Vichy authorities in the hope that they might turn against the Germans and form the basis of a future French Government. On top of this, he simply could not stand de Gaulle. De Gaulle, predictably, reciprocated.

In November 1942, Allied armies landed in French North Africa. In May 1943, de Gaulle moved his headquarters to Algiers. His main rival as leader of the non-Vichy French was General Henri Giraud, an experienced soldier and a hero by virtue of his escape from a high-security prisoner-of-war camp in Königstein Castle near Dresden. Giraud's main strength was that he was backed by the Americans, particularly Roosevelt's Secretary of State, Cordell Hull. In London, Harold continued to act as intermediary, sit on committees and give speeches in support of de Gaulle on the – wholly accurate – grounds that he had far greater recognition and credibility in France than Giraud. For most of 1943, de Gaulle and Giraud were Joint Chairmen of the French Committee of National Liberation. However, de Gaulle's greater political acumen won the day; Giraud was eased out. By the time Harold dined with him in Algiers in April 1944 in the course of a Ministry of Information lecture tour, de Gaulle was sole Chairman of the Committee and the authority of the Committee was recognised by virtually all the French exile and resistance groups, including the Communist Party. De Gaulle greeted Harold 'with what for him is almost warmth' but complained that the Allies were still making life difficult for him – in particular by refusing him the right to send encrypted telegrams to French diplomatic representatives in London.[20] Harold sympathised. The prohibition was made doubly absurd three weeks later when the French Consultative Assembly passed a resolution declaring that de Gaulle's Committee should become the Provisional Government when France was liberated.

This situation led to Harold's strongest and most public criticism of Churchill's wartime government. In a debate on foreign affairs, he spoke directly after the Prime Minister.

> It seems to me and to many Frenchmen that the United States Government, with His Majesty's Government in their train, instead of helping the French and welcoming them, lose no opportunity of administering any snub which ingenuity can devise and ill-manners perpetrate. ... After all, we treat the French as full Allies in Italy; they are fighting for us and with us. In the battle line they have complete equality of status, even a preference, but the moment we get on to the diplomatic field we ignore them and snub them.... I am convinced that this is a grave error of policy.[21]

What Churchill thought is not recorded, but Eden, still Foreign Secretary, publicly congratulated Harold on his stand, suggesting a division of opinion within the Cabinet.

It was not until October 1944 that the British, United States and Soviet Governments simultaneously recognised de Gaulle as leader of the French Provisional Government. It would be too much to claim that this was Harold's doing, that it would not have happened without his efforts: his influence with the Americans was minimal and de Gaulle's combination of genuine ability and egotistic bullying would have won through in the end. At the same time, Harold's role was more than peripheral. Looking back with the knowledge of what happened after the war, it is almost impossible to understand the immense uncertainty of the time. France was defeated and divided. Vichy, the Free French, the Russian-supported Communists, the Resistance, and equivocal figures such as Admiral Darlan and General Giraud based in the French colonies, all claimed to represent France or some aspect of France. There were no agreed official or diplomatic channels between the myriad French bodies and the Allies. There was not even any certainty that there would be a single, unified French state after the war. Against this background, Harold created channels, lobbied, argued, maintained a consistency of view and offered a clear solution to an apparently intractable problem. If it was a solution not always welcomed by those who heard it, it was at least based on years of knowledge and experience of France with a strong dash of *realpolitik*.

And if Harold's efforts were not recognised in Britain, they were in France. Returning to Paris in March 1945 (and staying with Duff Cooper, now British Ambassador to France, at the Residence in rue du Faubourg Saint-Honoré where he had stayed with his Uncle Dufferin more than half a century before), Harold gave two lectures on 'What the British think of the French'. The first was at the Théâtre des Ambassadeurs, in the presence not only of Duff Cooper in his official capacity, but also of both George Bidault, then Foreign Minister in de Gaulle's Provisional Government, and of Marie-Pierre Koenig, the Military Governor of Paris. The second was at the École des Sciences Politiques, attended by diplomatic friends and colleagues and over a thousand students. Both were successful, but the second was followed by a standing ovation, waving, stamping and shouts of 'Bravo!' Harold was, naturally, delighted.

Recognition of a more formal kind came two years later, in July 1947, when René Massigli, now French Ambassador to London, invited Harold to the French Embassy in Knightsbridge to be invested as *Chevalier de la Légion d'Honneur*. Harold, by his own account, was 'overwhelmed by embarrassment' and rather downplayed the award.[22] Was this perhaps because he was honoured alongside Cyril Connolly, about whom he always had reservations? Or because his elder brother Erskine had received the same award in 1916 for his services to France during the First World War? In any event, the citation says everything about official French attitudes towards Harold and his work.

Harold Nicolson

> *Ecrivain, diplomate et homme politique de renommé mondiale, qui n'a pas cessé un instant de croire en la France et en sa destinée. La France possède en lui un magnifique champion de sa cause.*[23]

A contemporary British assessment would have been less enthusiastic.

Throughout the war years, Harold maintained his profile as a commentator on public events, but diplomacy was long past, his political career had slipped backwards and his reputation as a writer was at best on hold. He completed only one full-length work during the period – *The Desire to Please*, which he began in March 1942 and published, after the now traditional period of depression and self-doubt, in May 1943. The book is a life of his great-great-grandfather, Archibald Hamilton Rowan, and the choice of subject is significant. Hamilton Rowan is presented as a man who promised much but achieved little, because of the behaviour of those around him and because of flaws in his own character; a man from an establishment background who threw over the traces of family and tradition by espousing the Irish cause. Was Harold writing himself out of the depression that had set in after losing his ministerial job and, in doing so, identifying with his great-great-grandfather as another might-have-been? The diary for 1942 contains many references to the need for and the inevitability of social reforms. Did the book reflect his alienation from the traditional high Tory principles of his family – or even look forward to his 1947 espousal of the Labour Party which outraged a number of family members and friends?

The Desire to Please is billed as the second part of Harold's *In Search of the Past* project and probably suffers from the fact that Harold did not finish, or at least make further progress, with his *magnum opus*. As part of a larger structure, it might have gained the sense of direction which, standing alone, it lacks. As it is, the personal aspects of the book – family excursions to Killyleagh as a child, his meeting with James Joyce in Paris, an anecdote about a major in the West Kent Yeomanry and a swarm of bees – while not entirely irrelevant to the main theme, seem intrusive and insufficiently integrated into the narrative. Up to this point in his career, Harold's non-literary biographies – *Lord Carnock*, *Curzon*, *Helen's Tower*, even *Dwight Morrow* – had in some sense transcended their subject and connected to broader political or social themes (as would *King George V* when the time came), but *The Desire to Please* does not do this. The subject is too personal and too narrow. Harold seems aware of the problem when, at the beginning of Chapter IV, he writes, 'this book is a study of the interaction of sentiment and reality; it is not a study of Irish politics or history.'[24] Admitting the problem, even in print, did not solve it. Sales were good, partly because

Harold was a recognised name and partly because the war had generated an unexpected and insatiable demand for books about almost anything, but, in the end, Harold's verdict that 'Hamilton Rowan is simply not interesting enough' is probably correct.[25]

For all these different, demanding, complex strands of activity, Harold thought of himself primarily as a Member of Parliament. It was the central strand of his working life and a position of which he was extremely proud. Despite his disappointment at losing his ministerial role, he still attended the House of Commons regularly and the diaries contain a rolling account of the progress of the war, the disasters and the victories, seen through debates in the House and gossip between MPs and other political figures. Like anyone else in such desperately uncertain times, he had his worries and his opinions. Sometimes, he was right – he foresaw the German attack on Russia – but just as often he was wildly wrong – assuming that Australia would be lost to the Japanese, that the Germans would attack Turkey, or that the Allies would achieve 'victory and peace by the spring of 1944 at the latest.'[26] The diaries also show how Parliament held the Government to account during the war, not by taking any active part in the management of the conflict (though many measures were taken to help the war effort by reorganising British society) but by debates and confidence motions which forced upon the Government an awareness of the opinion of the House of Commons and, by extension, of the nation as a whole. They show, too, how Harold maintained his extensive network of connections with diplomats and government representatives of Allied and neutral countries.

He was a good constituency MP. He went regularly to West Leicester to listen to the concerns of the people he represented and worked closely with Bertie Jervis, who had piloted him through the 1935 election and who remained in place throughout Harold's ten years representing the constituency. Awareness of his constituents' morale and knowledge of the issues that mattered to them informed his attitude in debates and discussions in Westminster. Equally, he thought it important that they should understand the real nature of the war and the issues at stake, and he gave speeches on the political realities behind the conflict and speculated on how long it might last.

Harold often learnt of his constituents' concerns from deputations. In November 1943, he received a deputation from members of the Peace Pledge Union, concerned to 'feed the starving men and women of Europe.' They may have had a point, but the issue was more complex than they realised and the fact that they were pacifists did not help their cause. Nonetheless, he did his duty and spoke on their behalf in a debate the following day.

Three weeks later, he received another delegation on an issue which touched him more closely. Oswald Mosley and his second wife – the former Diana Mitford, whom he had married in 1936 – had been released from internment in Holloway prison by the Home Secretary, Herbert Morrison, and were to be kept under house arrest. Morrison's decision caused outrage. Harold found himself faced with a deputation of Leicester factory workers who assumed that any defence of Morrison was 'propaganda' and therefore untrue.

> They will believe anything 'against the Government' and nothing which its defenders can assert.... Hitherto they have been apathetic and have left politics to their own leaders. They are now becoming extremely conscious of politics and very subject to Marxist slogans.[27]

Harold had, in fact, refrained from speaking in support of Morrison in the House the previous week. Loyal to the very last, Harold felt he should speak out in support of a former friend, and in support of a decision he felt was right (Mosley was ill and was, in effect, in prison without having been tried). Raymond Mortimer wisely advised him to 'keep [his] powder for better causes.'[28]

As Vita identified, Harold had a serious problem saying 'No' to people. By 1942, he was a member of more than twenty different committees, all devoted to different causes, and the number of speeches he gave is impossible to estimate. He was constantly being invited to speak by everyone from exclusive London societies and Oxford colleges to small provincial clubs and institutions, and he usually accepted, travelling from the Orkney Islands to Cornwall in the process – at the same time still managing to write his regular column in the *Spectator* and contribute articles or letters to the *Daily Telegraph*, *Nation*, the *Journal of the Anglo-Swedish Society*, *Foreign Affairs*, the *New York Times Magazine*, the *Journal of the Royal Society of St George*, *Cornhill Magazine*, *Current Affairs*, *American Scholar*, *United Empire* and many others. Most of the invitations he received came because of his reputation as an MP knowledgeable about foreign affairs or because of his position as a Governor of the BBC. Being Harold, he usually found himself enjoying both the event and the people he met. Only in retrospect, having pushed himself to the edge, did tiredness lead to a brief bout of disillusion and depression. These activities – the ones that Vita wanted him to give up – were often those that added variety to his wartime life. They kept him on the move and exposed him to a variety of different opinions and perspectives on the war; they also gave him the chance to travel, something denied

Might-Have-Been

to most of the civilian population in wartime; but Vita, who hated the war, disliked being on the move and increasingly disliked meeting people except on her own terms, was unlikely to understand the appeal.

In 1942, he was flown to Dublin to address the Irish Law Society and join in a debate at University College. While there, he took the opportunity to meet President de Valera and discuss Irish attitudes to the war. (He also got himself into trouble when the *Irish Times* misreported some of his remarks and a Conservative MP called for him to be dismissed from the BBC for defeatism.) In November 1943, he was strapped into a dark hole above the bomb-bay of a Mosquito bomber and flown to Sweden. He spent nearly a month in Stockholm, Gothenburg and Helsingborg. He gave lectures on Britain and British policy, met the Crown Prince, visited the Riksdag, and attended banquets, lunches and receptions organised in his honour. His every move was followed by the Swedish press. Harold's reaction was wholly characteristic – 'I could not imagine the fuss that was made of me. I thought they must imagine that I was far more important than I really am. But I think it was merely that they hate the Germans and like welcoming Englishmen.'[29] In April 1944, he flew to Algiers via Gibraltar, continuing on to Tunis before doubling back to Fez and Casablanca. It was another lecture tour, aimed at both the French in North Africa and Allied troops. He was given a huge cheer when he announced that he was following the footsteps of his son, Nigel, who had landed in Tunis a year before. These trips were undertaken at the request of the Ministry of Information who even came up with a proposal that Harold should go to Australia: it foundered on practical difficulties, much to Harold's relief as he feared the Australians would dislike him as a typical old-fashioned Englishman. No wonder Harold asked himself why they did not give him 'a real job instead of these potty little lecture tours.'[30]

Harold wanted to be a Minister: he believed in institutions. He wanted to be at the centre of things and working alongside his hero, Churchill, formulating the policy that would defeat Hitler. But – given that such a role was not open to him; that he was not a man of action, not a natural organiser or administrator, and not a political fighter – it is hard to escape the conclusion that he was probably in the right place and doing the right thing. As a communicator, maintaining morale, explaining complex issues, maintaining belief in the values of western civilisation, working for the creation of a strong and independent France, looking towards the structure of the post-war world, he could make a genuine contribution to the war effort. That it was not quantifiable, that he did not have the support and shelter of one of the great offices or departments of state – which he would greatly have preferred – does not make it valueless. But, for Harold, an official position implied formal recognition and that was what he sought; that was what made the effort worthwhile. As it was, he had to subsist on the applause of an audience, a good review, a crumb of praise from Churchill, Eden or Duff Cooper, or a moment of noisy support from MPs in the House – hoping all the while that formal recognition might follow.

50 Survival

The war affected every aspect of life. Ever since the move to Sissinghurst in 1932, Harold's regular journey to London had involved being driven by Copper, the chauffeur, the five miles to Staplehurst station where he caught the train for Charing Cross. When it arrived, drawn by a steam locomotive in the familiar olive-green livery of the Southern Railway, he would enter a First Class compartment and settle down to read or work for the hour-and-a-quarter it took to transport him to London. From beneath the Italianate façade of Middleton Barry's Charing Cross Hotel he would either walk or take a taxi along Whitehall to the House of Commons.

By July 1941 when Harold ceased to be a minister, a lot had changed. Unlike most people, Harold, as an MP, still had an adequate supply of petrol and could still be driven to the station, though Copper had been called up. All signs had been removed from what was left of the station; the steam locomotives were now in a livery of uniform matt black; the carriages were blacked out; and there were frequent delays because of bomb damage to the line or to the signalling system. The Charing Cross Hotel was still open, but its upper rooms were unusable and many of its windows boarded up because of bomb damage. There were still taxis in London, but they were rarer than previously, many having been converted for fire-fighting or transporting the wounded. So, more often than not, Harold would walk down Whitehall – a potentially hazardous undertaking in the blackout. The House of Commons had been bombed, too, and MPs now conducted their business in the House of Lords.

The worst of the London Blitz lasted from September 1940 to May 1941, coinciding with Harold's time at the Ministry of Information. In November 1940, the Ministry's headquarters, the Senate House, where he was sleeping, received a direct hit. He was thrown out of bed, the corridors were full of thick red dust, the windows on one side of the building had been blown out and the courtyard was full of collapsed masonry, but, amazingly, no one was hurt. In January 1941, King's Bench Walk was badly damaged by a bomb, but Harold was away visiting his constituency in Leicester. He received the news by letter from his secretary, Elvira Niggeman. Bombs and gunfire became the background to London nights. He saw the devastation at first hand – 'To the south, round about Westminster, there is a gale of fire.... To the north there is another fire.... The stump of the spire of Langham Place church is outlined against pink smoke. I walk on under the guns and flares and the droning of the 'planes.'[1] One night at dinner with Gladwyn Jebb in the Travellers Club there was a bomb which set 'the Club swaying slightly as if in an earthquake.'[2] It was a strange time. Harold was conscious that he was living through a crucial moment in history and, perhaps because of that, felt 'strain and unhappiness', but no sense of fear during air raids.[3] The Blitz eased when Hitler turned his attention to Russia in the summer of 1941, but the threat of bombing remained ever present. When Harold did his weekly duty fire-watching at the House of Commons, he slept on a 'truckle bed ... [with] army blankets which are none too clean,'[4] in a Committee Room alongside 'Wright, the waiter, and the man who stokes the boilers.'[5] He did not like roughing it, but he could do it when duty called.

Danger returned to London with the V1s in June 1944 and then the V2s later the same year. In July, Harold was in King's Bench Walk when he was woken by the sound of a flying bomb.

> It cuts out and I know that it is about to descend. I bury my head in my pillow and then comes quite a small crash and no sense of blast through the room. But a second later I hear things falling and splintering in my sitting room and I get up to look. The shutters have been thrown open and the iron bars smashed out. Only one pane is broken.... I put on a greatcoat and go out into the court.... I notice a thick soup-like haze in the air and all today my eyes have been red and smarting.[6]

He was extraordinarily lucky. The worst injury he sustained during the war was when he was knocked down by a taxi in the black-out on his way to Buckingham Palace. He insisted on continuing, although the taxi driver, hearing where he wanted to go, thought he must be concussed or deluded. His face was badly grazed and he cracked a rib, but it could have been worse.

Nonetheless, death was all around. Ronnie Cartland, a young, violently anti-appeasement Conservative and parliamentary colleague (and brother of the novelist, Barbara Cartland) was killed in France in May 1940. Christopher Hobhouse, who had shared King's Bench Walk with Harold for a short period, was blown to pieces during an air raid on Portsmouth in August, just weeks after his marriage. Victor Cazalet was killed while accompanying the Polish General, Władysław Sikorski, when their plane crashed on take off from Gibraltar in 1943. Jack Macnamara, another Conservative MP and a close parliamentary ally, was killed in Italy in 1944. Worst of all, at the beginning of 1945, Rob Bernays disappeared on a flight from Brindisi to Athens which was lost in the Adriatic. Harold was devastated and did what he could to support Bernays' family, including becoming godfather to young Robert Bernays, who was two months old when his father died.

In many ways, however, the war had a deeper effect on Vita than it did on Harold. They had both been born in the Victorian age and grew up as Edwardians, but Vita, with Knole in the background, was much more dependent on the old order than Harold. Her response to the war was twofold. On the one hand, she did not so much ignore it as look beyond it, engaging a new gardener – Jack Vass, who had worked at Cliveden, and, although called up shortly after he arrived, was to return after the war and remain at Sissinghurst until 1957 – and planning the now famous White Garden. Harold realised what was going on: 'Darling,' he wrote, 'how these things take one away from the sorrow of war.'[7] On the other hand, she responded to the national emergency with an old-fashioned, flag-waving, participatory patriotism: volunteering to help organise the Women's Land Army (about which she later wrote a book), stockpiling straw for mattresses, and agreeing to be an ambulance driver in the event of an air raid in the neighbourhood.

Sissinghurst had been on the front line during the Battle of Britain. Now it was under the flight path of German bombers heading to London by night and by day. More than once Vita found herself unable to go to Sissinghurst village because of an unexploded bomb in the road. On another occasion, a blast brought down plaster in her bedroom. The danger was at its worst in the late summer of 1940 when invasion was expected almost daily. There were fears that the Germans would use poison gas and the library was turned into a gas-proof room. Harold gave Vita instructions that in the event of a German landing, she was to load the car with 'food for 24 hours ... your jewels and my diaries.'[8] She was to head west, avoiding main roads, and make for Devonshire where Harold's brother, Freddy, lived. In the back of her diary, Vita made a list of things she would need to take with her – including the worm-eaten statue of Saint Barbara which Harold had brought back from Spain and given her in 1912.

But the strain told. Vita became depressed and her bouts of heavy drinking increased. Harold, disliking confrontation and, conscious that Vita hated being managed, avoided raising the issue directly. The diary and his letters refer tactfully to her muddles and her 'muzziness,' but it is clear that by the spring of 1941, he was becoming worried. He wrote her an unhappy letter in which (prefiguring what was to happen more than a year later) he describes being narrowly missed by a taxi in the street. 'If I really had been taken to hospital in a mess,' he writes, 'then Viti would have been shaken out of her muzzy moods.'[9] In fact, as Victoria Glendinning points out, it was Virginia Woolf's tragic suicide that administered the necessary shock.

Vita had visited Virginia only a few weeks previously and their relationship was showing signs of renewal. The news that she had drowned herself came in a letter from Leonard Woolf and it 'jolted Vita into a realization of her own priorities and responsibilities, into an acceptance of Harold's dependence on her, and of how much she owed him.'[10] Her depression did not disappear overnight, but the shock does seem to have halted a period of decline. Virginia's death was also responsible for another illustration of the curious relationship between Harold and Vita. As soon as he heard the news, Harold hurried down to Sissinghurst to spend the evening with Vita. Not a word was said on the subject between them, though they could write about it afterwards – 'Of course I came down because of Virginia. But I saw no reason to mention the thing. There was nothing that could be said. I just wanted to be with you.'[11]

As the war progressed, Vita became more solitary and out of sympathy with the rest of the world. It was not precisely loneliness, for old friends and lovers – including Violet Trefusis, driven out France – resurfaced, and new friends and admirers appeared; rather that she became increasingly introspective and focussed on her own core concerns. In 1943, she agreed to take part in a poetry reading in support of the Free French attended by the Queen, Princess Elizabeth and Princess Margaret. The list of poets included T. S. Eliot, Edmund Blunden, John Masefield, Edith and Osbert Sitwell, Vita herself, and Dorothy Wellesley (who got too drunk to read and slapped Harold's face when he tried to control her). The following year she and Harold attended a tea party at Buckingham Palace, but such events were rare and Vita was increasingly ill at ease in such surroundings. She preferred to lunch at Castle Farm with Ozzie Beale, the farmer, or make her regular visits to Mrs Drummond at Sissinghurst Place, whom she described to Harold as 'not exciting, but *so* decent.'[12]

Despite a bad back and the first signs of arthritis, she continued to work hard in the garden, but Jack Vass had been called up and she could not do everything. The once-carefully-cut lawns were left to grow hay for the animals, and parts of the garden began to look neglected. When not working in the garden, she tried to write, often staying up by candlelight far into the night. She feared that her creativity was blunted by the war and by her age, but in fact her wartime output was quite respectable. She produced a novel, *Grand Canyon*, which to her dismay was turned down by Leonard Woolf; a work of non-fiction, *The Eagle and the Dove*, about Saint Teresa of Avila and St Thérèse of Lisieux which, because of its emphasis on the comfort that the Roman Catholic faith can offer to certain temperaments, made Harold think she might be thinking of following Gwen and converting (she denied it); and a commissioned work of patriotic intent, *The Women's Land Army*. She also began work on *The Garden*, intended as a companion to *The Land*.

Yet a deep unhappiness remained. She kept the worst of it from Harold – or tried to. He knew she was frequently depressed, although there was little he could do beyond being there when she needed him. She was finding it harder and harder to accept change. The war was an agent of change, so she hated the war and the Germans who caused it. The Allied invasion of North Africa made her understand 'the feelings of St George when he saw the dragon beginning to bleed, the black-blooded worm of evil oozing under his lance.'[13] And when, in 1944, a bomb fell close enough to Knole to blow out some of the windows, her reaction was visceral: 'Those filthy Germans! Let us level every town in Germany to the ground! I shan't care.'[14] And she hated the changes that came, directly or indirectly, as a consequence of the war. By 1942, Gwen St Aubyn (since 1940 Lady St Levan) had been living at Sissinghurst or in a cottage nearby for nearly ten years, but when her husband, Sam St Levan, returned from three years' service abroad, she went to live with him and their children in the family home on St Michael's Mount in Cornwall. And she took Lady Carnock, now well into her eighties, to live there as well – at least while the war continued. Vita was angry, interpreting Gwen's departure as some kind of betrayal. This, compounded by her long-standing resentment at the emotional demands she felt her mother-in-law made on Harold, meant that if Harold managed a visit to Cornwall to see his mother and his sister, it was liable to provoke an outburst of resentment from his wife.

Social change brought about by the war reinforced Vita's innate conservatism. Some of her ideas appear extreme, almost beyond the point of eccentricity. Harold may have supported the Beveridge Report, but Vita saw 'the proletariat being encouraged to breed like rabbits ... as though there weren't too many of them already and not enough work to go round ... and everyone being given everything for nothing ... it all makes me feel very pre-1792.'[15] In 1945, upset by the possibility of a new bus service which would pass along the road near Sissinghurst, an almost feudal Vita with generations of Sackvilles at her shoulder, burst out: 'What a world! It's like drawing up one's own death warrant.... I hate democracy. I hate *la populace*. I wish education had never been introduced.... I don't like tyranny, but I like intelligent oligarchy.'[16] Such outbursts should not be taken too seriously. They were scribbled emotions in letters to Harold, not argued points of view. And no one's emotional state was normal during wartime.

Sissinghurst was underneath the flight path of the V1s. Troops were exercising in Sissinghurst woods and damaging Vita's cherished woodland. A German bomber narrowly missed the tower and crashed in flames into the moat. The winter of 1944–45 was so severe that the pipes and the lavatories froze. In Sissinghurst, Vita had created her own private domain. Every threat, every intrusion from the outer world had to be ruthlessly countered. It was an understandable, if extreme, reaction to the pressures of wartime, but it was one which created particular difficulties for Harold whose inclination and motivation was to engage with and shape that outer world.

Ben and Nigel both joined the army. Harold was proud that they were serving their country, but would not have been human if he had not worried about what might happen to them. When they were sent overseas, he wrote two thousand words to them every week – typed, with the top copy to one and a carbon to the other – letters they both kept and treasured. They make remarkable reading: a blend of news, thoughts, advice, and deep, underlying affection – one side of an imaginary conversation. Ben joined as a private and served with an anti-aircraft battery in Rochester where Victor Cazalet was his commanding officer. Then he became a second Lieutenant in the Intelligence Corps and in 1942 was posted to Italy where he served until knocked down by a lorry at the end of 1944. He spent several months in hospital before being flown home, able to walk but with his whole torso still encased in plaster. Nigel became an officer in the Grenadier Guards, rising to the rank of Captain. He, too, was posted abroad in 1942. He saw action in Tunisia and then fought in the long-drawn-out Allied progress up the Italian peninsula. He returned home from Naples in July 1945.

Harold was lucky: his family survived the war intact. It snowed at Sissinghurst on the night of 30 April 1945. The next morning came the news that Mussolini and his mistress had been murdered by Italian partisans. That evening came the news that Hitler was dead. On the afternoon of 7 May, Vita was gardening in the courtyard, while Harold and Ben, still on medical leave following his injury, were sitting in the sun, when the BBC broadcast the news that Germany had surrendered unconditionally. The three of them climbed Vita's tower and hoisted the Sackville standard that been taken down six years before.

51 Post-War

On 1 January 1944, the *New Yorker* published an extended review of Harold's work by the American critic, Edmund Wilson. 'Through the Embassy Window' is a rather muddled piece which says as much about Wilson as it does about Harold, but it does show how Harold could appear, or be portrayed, in an age of new and radically altered values. Wilson praises Harold's literary gifts and his prose style – 'vivid', 'readable', 'engaging', 'brilliant' – but goes on to claim that Harold's work is fundamentally flawed because Harold himself is trapped in the values and outlook of his aristocratic upbringing and the Foreign Office.[1] He portrays Harold as a *dilettante*, detached from his subject matter and from what Wilson regards as the real world, 'unable to write a good book, with the exception of *Some People*, owing to the fact that between [him] and life there intervened a sheet of glass.'[2] He criticises Harold for failing to understand the 'great social groups and movements' of the age; for failing to understand 'any other kind of life' but his own.[3]

This is ideological criticism. Wilson had come to Marxism during the 1930s. He saw Marxism as a faith, which demanded social engagement and action. From such a perspective, Harold was an easy target, but by caricaturing Harold as an aristocratic Foreign Office official, Wilson was actually demonstrating his failure to understand the subtleties and complexities of both the individual and the society with which he was dealing. Harold thought it absurd that Wilson should see him as 'well-brushed and well-bred.'[4] One could argue that this proves that he was out of touch, yet it was not a black-and-white issue. He was genuinely far less aristocratic in origin and in manner than many of his contemporaries: Gerry Wellesley (who had become Duke of Wellington in 1943), Lord Berners, Tommy Lascelles, or even Vita. And Wilson's charge of superficiality – which Harold was self-deprecatingly inclined to accept – seems to mistake Harold's reluctance to judge, his frequently ironic tone and his evident delight in odd, circumstantial detail, for lack of substance. Vita, perhaps surprisingly objective, recognised immediately where Wilson went wrong. By 'criticising [Harold] for so obviously belonging to a definite class, by birth, education, experience and consequent outlook ... he is falling into a common error of critics which is to demand that a writer shall be something he is not.'[5] And the one thing Harold was not was partisan or ideological.

Wilson's charges worried Harold. In one of his weekly letters to Ben and Nigel, he writes: 'If in truth I have gone through life regarded by the respectable as Bohemian and by the Bohemians as conventional, there must be something very very wrong.'[6] But the central issue was not belonging, however important that was to Harold, but commitment. Wilson was a Marxist and demanded commitment, but Harold was at his most successful as a writer, analyst and commentator when he was uncommitted – when he was able to see both sides of a question; able to judge proportion rather than totality. His emotions always pulled him towards belonging, but his intellect and his intellectual integrity impelled him to take up positions which were balanced (or stranded, depending on one's point of view) between opposing viewpoints. This fundamental duality may have been difficult for Harold to recognise, and even more difficult to accept, but it was at the root of his individuality; and it was to play an important part in his reaction to the post-war world and in the post-war world's reaction to him.

Harold had been at the centre of the Allies' flawed attempt to construct a workable and lasting peace after the First World War. It was natural, once it was clear that the Second World War Allies were going to win, that he should begin to think about the future peace process. It was the methodology rather than the actual treaty terms which concerned him. He returned to *Peacemaking*, which had been written quite deliberately as a how-not-to-do-it guide. Constable agreed to publish a new edition and, in June 1943, Harold wrote a new and detailed introduction consisting of twelve numbered sections explicitly pointing to the contemporary relevance of his analysis.[7]

His next project also centred on the management of the peace, though the approach was more oblique. For well over a year, following the completion of *The Desire to Please*, Harold had no new book on the stocks. The fact that he could anticipate but not actually foresee the end of the war made a third volume of *In Search of the Past* feel somehow inappropriate. It was not until August 1944 that he decided that he would write about the 1814–15 Congress of Vienna, that great gathering of princes, statesmen and diplomats which redrew the map of Europe following the convulsions of the Napoleonic Wars, created a balance of power across the continent, and established the conference system, the Concert of Europe, to maintain it. *The Congress of Vienna* is probably Harold's most underrated book. It was intended from the first to be an exercise in communication – 'So far as I know there does not exist in any simple form a narrative of the events from 1812 onwards. Most of the books are too technical, too detailed or too partial to be of much value to the ordinary reader.'[8] The Introduction, dated 1 September 1945, warns that 'the analogies between the events described in this volume and those which we are now experiencing are so frequent that they may mislead.... Events are not affected by analogies; they are determined by combinations of circumstance.' Nonetheless, Harold's purpose is clear.

> Then as now the common purpose which had united the Nations in the hour of danger, ceased, once victory had been achieved, to compel solidarity.... Then as now there were those who felt that in destroying one menace to the peace and independence of nations they had succeeded only in erecting another and graver menace in its place.[9]

The book is dedicated to Anthony Eden, whose diplomatic skills Harold held in high regard, and carries a beautifully ironic subtitle: *A Study in Allied Unity: 1812–1822*.

Harold began researching the book in the late summer of 1944 and began writing it on 29 December that year. The exigencies of wartime meant that progress was slower than usual and he was still correcting the proofs at the beginning of 1946. *The Congress of Vienna* was thus in his mind as the war in Europe drew to a close, as the truth about Nazi atrocities and Russian deportations emerged, and as the new battle lines for the great post-war confrontation between East and West were drawn up. So it was not accidental that, when he came to speak in the House of Commons in the debate on the Yalta Conference, Harold concentrated on Poland and its new frontiers. It was a good speech and Churchill praised him for it, though it did little beyond putting a brave face on the fact that Britain and the United States were not in a position to resist Soviet pressures in Eastern Europe.

By 1945, Parliament had been sitting for nearly ten years, twice the normal length of a British parliamentary term. It continued to function, to carry on its business and to debate the Government's actions, but it had lost any momentum or initiative that it once possessed. Partly, this was because it badly needed an injection of new blood, but also because the events unrolling across Europe and the Far East were on such a vast scale and the military machine controlling them was so huge that Parliament could do little more than monitor these great developments. Harold was in the House of Commons on VE Day, 8 May 1945, when Churchill made his statement about the German surrender and the whole House trooped across to

St Margaret's, Westminster, which stands in the shadow of Westminster Abbey, 'to give,' in Churchill's words, 'humble and reverend thanks to Almighty God for our deliverance from the threat of German domination.'[10] He was there when the King and Queen came to the Royal Gallery and the King addressed both Lords and the Commons, struggling with his stammer. When the King had finished, Churchill 'waved his top hat aloft and called for three cheers.'[11]

Harold loved the ceremonial of the House of Commons. He loved the club-like atmosphere of its smoking rooms and bars where MPs gathered, where the latest news was discussed and parliamentary deals were brokered. What he disliked was the whole process of being elected, which he and the rest of the House now had to face up to.

The election was a muddle from beginning to end. Even the date was the subject of prolonged wrangling. Churchill had originally wanted an early election, after the end of the war against Germany, but changed his mind and suggested waiting until after the defeat of Japan. Attlee, as Leader of the Labour Party, preferred a date in October by which time there would be a new electoral register. Churchill would not agree and gave Attlee the choice between an immediate election and waiting until Japan was defeated. Attlee would probably have waited, but the Labour Party was demanding change, so Britain's wartime coalition broke up quickly and unceremoniously. Churchill resigned as coalition Prime Minister on 23 May and was reappointed to head a caretaker administration until after the election. As Harold had foreseen in another context, having lost their common purpose, the allies were allies no longer and began to squabble.

Harold's personal position was even more muddled. He wanted to be an MP – that much he knew. But which party should he represent? He had been elected as National Labour, but the National Labour Party had always been something of a fiction and was now defunct. He had been elected to support a National Government, which had now dissolved into its different parties. He had been elected with the support of the West Leicester Conservative Party, but he was not a Conservative. He disliked the old-fashioned Conservative clique in the House of Commons and many of them (with memories of Munich) returned the feeling. He had for a long time foreseen the inevitability of some degree of socialism in Britain after the war, but, like many at the time, he still feared that a Labour Government might institute a confiscatory taxation policy against anyone it considered to be rich; lastly, whatever his feelings about the Labour Party itself, he refused to join any party or alliance of parties which would put him in opposition to Churchill. The previous year, musing on his political identity, he had decided he was 'an Asquithian Liberal',[12] but that was not much use in 1945. So he ended up belonging nowhere.

A fudge was achieved. He stood as a 'National Candidate' and, once again, received the backing of the West Leicester Conservatives, who, in a kind of back-handed compliment, had decided that Harold stood a better chance of opposing Labour than any full-blooded Conservative they might put forward. Yet, once again, Harold's loyalties betrayed him. Churchill remained his hero and his election literature carried the wordy slogan, 'Support Churchill and Vote for Harold Nicolson, the National Candidate', but, as it turned out, Churchill became an electoral liability.

From the very beginning, Harold had understood that the war would result in significant social change and a political move to the left – developments which would work against him. In December 1943, he predicted: 'Nobody in a constituency where the majority are working-class will keep his seat.... I have no chance of remaining the Member for West Leicester.'[13] So when Parliament was formally dissolved on 15 June, he was not optimistic. Nonetheless, he set off for Leicester immediately, installed himself amidst the fading grandeur of the Grand Hotel and launched into a seemingly endless round of visits, public meetings, speeches and house-to-house canvassing. He found the electorate alternately apathetic, bloody-minded and ignorant. He had no right, he was told, to support Churchill when he had been a slavish supporter of Chamberlain.[14] One woman accused him of being 'a bloated landowner who lived in a castle and ground his tenants for rent.'[15] He could have rebutted her on every point, but it showed again how he was perceived by at least some working-class voters – voters who were tired, resentful and longing for change after six years of war. Vita chastised him for getting mixed up in politics when he could have been at home writing books, but, in fact – and though it did not last long – the war had made her more politically engaged than previously. She even agreed, in contrast to 1935, to visit Leicester and speak at a meeting of women voters.

Harold again fought a scrupulously honest campaign. For the most part, he was listened to with respect – 'They are prepared to admit that I am a decent bloke' – but that was all his triumph. He realised only too well that this was no indication of how 'they' would vote.[16] Many Conservatives believed that, whatever the underlying mood of the country, the voters would support Churchill as the man who won the war for Britain. But even Vita, an instinctive Conservative whose admiration for Churchill very nearly matched Harold's, did not think that Churchill had 'the temperament to deal with the immediate difficulties at home.'[17] And Churchill proved her right. In his election broadcast on 4 June, he stated that a

Socialist Government would not be able to allow free speech and 'would have to fall back on some sort of Gestapo.' This was an electoral gaffe of the first magnitude which opened the way for Attlee's celebrated riposte: 'The voice we heard last night was that of Mr Churchill, but the mind was that of Lord Beaverbrook.'[18] Yet Churchill continued to make partisan attacks on the Labour leaders who had worked so closely with him and sustained his government throughout the war years – attacks which were at best ill-judged, at worst offensive, and did not help his cause.

By 1945, Leicester was battered and scruffy. Many other cities had suffered more death and worse destruction, but the bombing had still left over 100 dead, 250 homes and eleven factories destroyed and another 4,500 homes damaged. It was a manufacturing city and its contribution to the war effort had been the production of literally millions of machine parts, gun components, helmets, shoes and items of clothing (one factory alone produced 17.5 million pairs of socks). The workforce had risen to the occasion, but by the end, like most of the British population, they were exhausted. Their clothes were shabby, their food was rationed and their living conditions often basic. It would have been miraculous for Harold to have held his seat. Churchill's clumsy electioneering made the task even harder.

Polling Day was 5 July. Leicester was bathed in sunshine and the turnout was high, but the count was delayed for nearly three weeks because of the need to wait for the votes of the hundreds of thousands of soldiers, sailors and airmen who were serving abroad. On 25 July, Harold, Vita, Ben and Nigel (just returned from Italy) all went up to Leicester. The following morning, at 11.15, Harold learnt his fate. His Labour opponent – Barnett Janner, a local solicitor of Lithuanian Jewish origin – had won by 7,421 votes, a substantial majority. Harold made a short, dignified speech, saying that he had been 'fortunate to have represented West Leicester ... for ten years in the most historic of Parliaments.'[19] Having thanked the West Leicester Conservatives and his campaign workers, the whole family headed for London and Sissinghurst, where they arrived in time for the 9 o'clock news. It was a Labour landslide. Churchill had resigned. Attlee had already been to Buckingham Palace to see the King and was forming a government. That same evening Churchill was preparing to leave 10 Downing Street when someone drew his attention to Harold's defeat. He said: 'The House will be a sadder place without him – and smaller.' Harold, of course, was delighted – it pleased him 'more than anything' – and, as a succinct Churchillian verdict, it is highly quotable, but one wonders how sincerely it was meant. If Churchill did respect Harold, he had done little to show it.[20]

Harold was disappointed but philosophical. At Sissinghurst, he picked up the threads of *The Congress of Vienna* and wrote a remarkably accurate and honest letter to Nigel, who was about to visit West Leicester to talk to the Conservative Association with a view to becoming their next candidate.

> If you examine my political career you will admit that I muddled the logistics of the thing. It is true that I managed to acquire a certain reputation and influence, that I made some good speeches, and that I was almost always right. It is true that I became on terms of intimacy and confidence with most of the leading figures of all parties. But as a career the thing was mucked.... The reason was (apart from personal defects, such as lack of push and daring) that I was not part of a powerful organisation. When I look back I see that I made two fatal errors. The first was when I attached myself to Mosley; the second was when I joined National Labour.
>
> Now why did I make these errors? People would say that it was due to 'lack of political experience and judgement.'... It was due rather to the fact that I allowed myself to be influenced by personal affections and associations without thinking how these would operate at a later date.[21]

Accurate and honest, and very much the same old story. Unfortunately, when he tried to address the problems he had identified, it ended in disappointment and embarrassment.

Harold had clearly decided to be more assertive in searching for a new role for himself. A month before the election and clearly anticipating defeat, he had written to Bill Mabane, Minister of State at the Foreign Office in Churchill's caretaker government, suggesting that he might become Chairman of the British Council. It was a sensible suggestion, but when Labour won the election Harold rightly assumed that the position would be given to someone with a Labour background. Then, after his defeat, he decided that he wanted a seat in the House of Lords, but his attempts to get one were both naïve and gauche.

He was on friendly terms with William Jowitt, a fellow member of the Beefsteak Club. Jowitt had been an MP since 1922, beginning as an Asquithian Liberal before switching his allegiance to Labour. He had also known Attlee, the new Prime Minister, since childhood and, when the new Government was formed, Jowitt became Lord Chancellor. In September 1945, Harold wrote him a letter asking for a peerage, but at the same time setting out conditions: he supported Labour's domestic policy but could not guarantee he would continue to do so; he had always supported

Churchill and Eden and did not now wish to be ranged against them; therefore, if elevated to the Upper House, he would like to maintain his political independence. Later that month, Jowitt told him that the response of his Labour Party colleagues had not been enthusiastic. Harold decided to push the issue and asked for his original letter to be shown to the Prime Minister. Two months later he was told, in passing, by Hugh Seely, the former Liberal MP who had become Lord Sherwood in 1941, that he was an idiot to have turned down a peerage. The next news came from Guy Burgess, who always had the latest Foreign Office gossip: Ernest Bevin, the new Foreign Secretary, had turned Harold down for Chairman of the British Council and the peerage, which was somehow connected with the British Council appointment, had also disappeared. He was understandably confused.

The New Year's Honours List for 1946 appeared without Harold's name in it. Jowitt said that he had expected it to be there, but had subsequently discovered that Lord Addison, Labour leader in the House of Lords, would only allow peerages for Labour Party members. The only exception to the rule would be honours conferred in recognition of war service. Harold then flirted with the idea of returning to Parliament as one of the members for the Combined Universities, but though he put his name forward nothing happened. In April, he told Jowitt that, if offered a peerage, he would, after all, agree to take the Labour whip. But nothing happened.

Why did Harold want a peerage so badly? And why did he not get one? The obvious answer is that he wanted to retain some kind of position close to the centre of political life; a position which offered a platform for his views, and an opportunity to contribute in some way to the task of rebuilding Britain after the war. The advantage of the House of Lords was that it did not require him to go through an election. Was it plain, old-fashioned snobbery? Probably, a little. Certainly, Vita confessed to liking the idea that her sons should become the Honourable Mr Benjamin and the Honourable Nigel Nicolson, and the family played games choosing a title – Lord Cranfield, a defunct Sackville title, was agreed upon. But Harold was much less interested in the social aspects of a peerage and was probably genuine when he claimed to dread its intrusion into domestic life with Mrs Staples, the cook, saying, 'His Lordship is weeding in the nuttery.'[22] What Harold really wanted was recognition. A peerage would be something achieved. It might not cure but would at least lessen the burden of self-doubt that he carried around with him. It would be official, public, institutional – and irrevocable – recognition of his status as a member of the governing classes.

On the face of it, it was a perfectly reasonable idea. Politicians standing down from senior office and retiring ambassadors were regularly elevated to the House of Lords – indeed, one of Harold's oldest friends, Archie Clark Kerr, had just become Lord Inverchapel as reward for four, long and difficult years as ambassador in Moscow. But Harold had not achieved any political office sufficiently senior for his exit from the House of Commons to be marked in that way, and it was sixteen years since he had left the Foreign Office. Thirty years later, talking to James Lees-Milne, Harold Macmillan said that Harold 'ought to have had a peerage.'[23] Which may have been true, but who was to give it to him? Churchill was obviously not going to help and many of those Conservatives who *might* have said a word in his favour – Macmillan, Brendan Bracken, Leo Amery – had lost their seats in the election and had other priorities. Why should Labour help? Harold's approach to Jowitt, beginning in naïvety and ending in desperation, was hardly a recommendation. And he had been National Labour, which, with its associations with Ramsay MacDonald, was seen in some Labour quarters as worse than the Conservatives. Again, although he was known to and liked by members of numerous different groupings, he did not actually belong to any of them. This unedifying saga continued into the spring of 1946. In the meantime, other things were changing.

The day after his defeat in West Leicester, he was told – by Vita who had been holding back the news until after the election – that he would have to leave King's Bench Walk by Christmas 1945. New regulations meant that only practising barristers could live in the Inner Temple. It was another blow and added to Harold's sense that 'chapter after chapter [of his life] was being closed, finished, put away.'[24]

Working together, Harold's secretary Elivra Niggeman and Vita found a new London home for him remarkably quickly and he moved in at the beginning of January 1946. It was a three-storey house in Kensington, 10 Neville Terrace, between the Fulham Road and Old Brompton Road, and just a few minutes' walk from South Kensington tube station. Ben, returned to his position as Deputy Surveyor of the King's Pictures, was to have one floor; Nigel, still in the army and writing a history of the Grenadier Guards, was to have another; and Harold the third. As a serving officer, Nigel had a soldier-servant who, helped by his wife, would look after the three of them. Ben was mainly responsible for the furniture, having inherited many valuable pieces from White Lodge, Lady Sackville's Brighton house. And Harold hated it. He hated it because it was ugly; he hated it because it was cold (and the winter of 1945–46 was one of the worst on record); he hated it because (as he told James Lees-Milne) he associated the name with Neville Henderson and Neville Chamberlain; he hated it because friends (such as James Pope-Hennessey) teased him about

Kensington being dull and respectable; and he hated it because it was not King's Bench Walk. He took to calling it Devil's Terrace, and it remained his London home until 1952.[25]

There were lighter moments. When the atomic bomb was dropped on Hiroshima in August 1945, the press seized on the fact that Harold had apparently predicted such a weapon in *Public Faces*, published in 1932. Was the book based on secret information? In December, Michael Joseph published *Another World Than This*, an anthology of poetry which Vita and Harold had worked on together. The title was taken from 'The Land' and the book was a sudden success, selling 10,000 copies in its first month. Lack of a parliamentary salary meant that Harold's journalism again became more important. He continued his column in the *Spectator*, took up reviewing for the *Daily Telegraph* and accepted whatever commissions came along.

Although no longer an MP, Harold was still in demand for certain official or semi-official jobs, and he no doubt hoped that by agreeing to give a series of lectures in divided, war-torn Greece, or listening to the horrific evidence presented to the International Military Tribunal in Nuremburg, he was bolstering the case for his peerage. The Greek trip, in October 1945 and sponsored by the Foreign Office, took place in the interlude between liberation from the Germans and the outbreak of full-blooded civil war. The atmosphere in Athens was tense: the National Government was weak; right-wing gangs were attacking and killing suspected communists; and the communists were becoming increasingly militant. Harold had long-established credentials as a friend of Greece, but quite how a series of lectures on 'Byron and Democracy' given to educated Athenian audiences was supposed to help the situation is anyone's guess.

He flew, much to Vita's distress. The weather was appalling and it was only on the third morning that the RAF Dakota in which he was travelling could actually take off from Fairoaks near Woking in Surrey. Strapped in and seated on a metal bench along one side of the fuselage, he was horribly uncomfortable. It took eight hours to reach Naples where they spent the night, and another four the next day to reach Athens. He stayed with the Ambassador, Rex Leeper, younger brother of his former colleague, Allen Leeper, who had died in 1935. Leeper welcomed Harold, escorted him during the visit, and took him on outings into the Greek countryside, where his love of the light, the landscape and the culture came back to him like a tidal wave. Leeper also sought Harold's views on the Greek political situation. To Harold – with the benefit of some thirty years' experience of Greek politics and his own intensely pro-Greek bias – the solution was obvious: Britain should intervene actively to support the Greek Government and maintain peace. Harold claimed later that Leeper transmitted this suggestion to London as his own view, but that Bevin was unwilling to make such a commitment. Perhaps surprisingly, this brief reconnection with diplomacy in action did not stimulate Harold to regret that he had never become an Ambassador.

The Nuremburg visit, in April 1946, was again instigated by the Foreign Office: Harold had been suggested as someone who might possibly write an account of the Trials. He travelled with George Clerk, who had been his Head of Department during the First World War and Ambassador in Paris in the 1930s. Harold was much moved by the atmosphere and the profound seriousness of the court proceedings. The idea of a book came to nothing, but the visit did result in one of his most remarkable *Spectator* articles. Published shortly after his return, it is only 1,500 words, but it addresses the fundamental issues raised by the International Military Tribunal and conveys some of Harold's most deeply-held beliefs in a manner which can only be described as statesmanlike. The characteristic irony is gone. Faced with men who have committed inhuman crimes, he displays his humanity, not by proposing leniency or understanding, but by an insisting that clear and agreed values must underpin any such process of judgement – and his arguments remain relevant to the treatment of war criminals to this day. Harold did not deny the difficulty posed by the victors putting the vanquished on trial, but he saw that to give the vanquished a serious and fair trial was itself an 'affirmation of profound human values.'[26] The process that gave Goering, Hess, Ribbentrop, Keitel and so many others the right to make a full and detailed statement of their case was nothing less than civilisation asserting itself in the face of barbarism.

Three weeks after the *Spectator* article came the publication of *The Congress of Vienna* with its direct bearing on the management of the peace. Whether Harold had taken some of Edmund Wilson's criticisms to heart or whether he was simply matching his manner to his subject matter and seeking the best way to get his message across, *The Congress of Vienna* marks something of a departure from Harold's previous work. It is certainly not dull: the narrative is well paced; the characters are clearly drawn; and there is plenty of sharp, circumstantial description. Yet the tone is more consistently serious throughout, at times approaching the academic, and the authorial 'I' is missing, something which is not common in his work. The timing – just a month ahead of the new Paris Peace Conference where the Allies were to negotiate treaties with Italy, Bulgaria, Hungary, Romania, and Finland – was deliberate. It increased the possibility of the book being noticed, which was good from the point of view of sales, and it also increased the chances of the book being understood as its author intended.

However, an even better opportunity to communicate his views on the peace and on the future of Europe to a mass audience was about to materialise. His five-year term as a Governor of the BBC expired in May, but the Director General, William Haley, approached him with a proposition which was as simple as it was brilliant. It was the manner of Haley's appointment in 1943 which had very nearly caused Harold and Violet Bonham-Carter to resign from the Board, but Harold had since come to appreciate Haley's understanding of the relationship between the BBC and its audience – an understanding clearly evident in the suggestion that Harold should cover the Paris Peace Conference for the BBC. He left for Paris on 23 July 1946.

Haley's offer was generous. Harold would be paid sixty guineas a week for two fifteen-minute talks on the Home Service, one on the Overseas Service and a fourth on the French Service – although, with his characteristic ability to mismanage money, he booked himself into the Ritz on place Vendôme until he realised that the cost of his room alone would eat up his BBC pay, whereupon he decamped to the cheaper (but still very comfortable) Hotel Grand, just around the corner. The Peace Conference was held in the Palais du Luxembourg and Harold was given a studio in the main part of the palace where the delegates gathered and held their formal sessions. From there, or from an alternative studio in the Hotel Scribe, again close to place Vendôme, his talks went out to an audience which the BBC estimated at up to twenty million. His Home Service talks were broadcast at peak listening time, on Sundays and Wednesdays immediately after the six o'clock news. He was supported throughout by Gibson Parker, the Head of the BBC's Paris team, and by Donald Hall, a former Foreign Office official, who was now heading the BBC's European Service. He was also supported, though unofficially, by his old friend, Pierre de Lacretelle, who checked his French scripts for errors but declared that Harold's French was so good that there was no need to do so.

Given the level of recognition that Harold was accorded as both broadcaster and expert on foreign affairs, it was hardly surprising that he himself, and particularly his connection with the 1919 Peace Conference, should become the subject of media attention. Apart from 'a dotard in the Brazilian delegation' with an unreliable memory, he was apparently 'the only survivor of the former peacemaking.' Interviewed by the *New York Times* about the differences, Harold disabused his questioner of the notion that 'they were giants in those days.' He thought James F. Byrnes, the US Secretary of State 'more effective than President Wilson; Bevin ... a stronger and finer character than Lloyd George ... Bidault [the French Prime Minister and Foreign Minister] ... a far more suitable person than Clemenceau.'[27] These remarks, somewhat forcefully expressed for the benefit of his American interviewer, certainly represented what he thought and they clearly indicate that he approached the conference in a positive frame of mind, even if his hopes were soon to be scaled back.

Harold's access must have been the envy of every journalist in Paris at the time. Outside the conference sessions, he was, in effect, an honorary member of the British delegation, which was led by Bevin, whose strength of character and straightforward, common-sense grasp of major issues Harold greatly respected – 'Believe me, 'arold, our trouble is that the Russians are frightened and the Yanks bomb-minded.'[28] Also in the delegation were A.V. Alexander, the Minister of Defence; Hector McNeil, a junior Foreign Office Minister; Oliver Harvey, a senior Foreign Office official soon to succeed Duff Cooper as Ambassador to Paris; and Harold's old friend Gladwyn Jebb. He met Bidault on a number of occasions and was introduced to Jacques Duclos, the French communist leader ('an unbelievably repulsive man ... slimy with cleverness'[29]). He met Molotov and Vyshinsky, who led the Soviet delegation. He met Mackenzie King, the Canadian Prime Minister. He was on particularly good terms with the Romanians. He knew Karl Gruber, the Austrian Foreign Minister, and some of the Italian delegation. He seems, however, to have had only minimal contact with the Americans. Paris was full, too, of other old friends who had views on events – Duff Cooper, the British Ambassador; Jan Smuts, still in his second term as Prime Minister of South Africa; Léon Blum, the former and future French Prime Minister; Osbert Lancaster; Emerald Cunard.

The Conference began on 29 July 1946. Harold sat in the gallery of the auditorium of the French Senate, reflecting on the fact that he was a pundit not a participant. He wrote to Vita that 'looking down upon Gladwyn sitting as a delegate in a plush armchair did give me a slight twinge; but not of envy; merely the "elderly failure" twinge.'[30] From the first, he was conscious of the theatrical nature of the Conference and, despite his own not insignificant profile, the intrusive nature of the media – 'It is like a first night at Her Majesty's or Covent Garden.... American photographers creep about, now on the stage, now off the stage, flashing their cameras. It might be Hollywood itself.'[31] Yet, for all that he was old-fashioned, he was not closed-minded.

I cannot adapt myself to this sort of Conference. It is a public performance, not a serious discussion. Yet the new method may achieve something in a different way. It becomes more and more interesting the more I consider it.[32]

Harold had always favoured diplomatic negotiations being conducted in private, slowly and deliberately, by professionals who were – or should be – self-effacing insofar as, while they might be constrained by a national policy, they did not have to play to a political constituency. In one of his last broadcasts from the Conference, he suggested that 'best outcome of 1946 would have been a realization that conferences must begin with confidential negotiation before moving on to the public consideration of the results of that negotiation.'[33] There was, however, an additional factor in play at Paris in 1946 which rendered the Conference very different from that of 1919 or any others that had preceded it. In 1919, vast territories had been carved up and reallocated. The issue had been who ruled them, not how they were ruled or how new or existing states might interact with each other. It was the 1946 Paris Conference more than any other occasion which marked the emergence of two opposing blocs, each guided by fundamentally different economic and social principles, or, in Harold's phrase 'two conceptions of the proper use of power.'[34] Indeed, it is possible to argue that, while the intensity of media interest in the Paris Conference may have been bad for diplomacy, it did serve to reinforce Churchill's famous 'Iron Curtain' speech, delivered at Fulton, Missouri, that March, and bring home to millions the depth and seriousness of the East–West political divide. The Conference itself, with both sides playing to the gallery, was disorderly: 'Instead of Open Covenants openly arrived at, we have open insults openly hurled.'[35]

Another complication was the voting system – an innovation necessitated by the need for smaller states to be able to register their views without slowing the Conference to a snail's pace. It was, in Harold's view, flawed from the start. To his mind, it was nonsensical for Abyssinia's vote to carry equal weight with that of the United States. Moreover, with voting anything but secret, the smaller states felt obliged to line up behind either the Americans and the British or the Russians, with the result that the East–West divide was emphasised and any inclination to express an independent view was smothered by the requirement to be partisan. It was a first taste of the Cold War to come.

Harold's treatment of the East–West divide was characteristically fair-minded and, not for the first time, his ability to see both sides of a question got him into trouble. He not only insisted that the Russian point of view was worthy of consideration, but also sought to understand why they behaved as they did; why they chose to make negotiation all but impossible. The Russians, he concluded, were

> not trained in the courtesies of international intercourse.... They do not for one moment realise the impression which they are creating. We take as deliberate insults remarks which are merely stock-in-trade remarks and part of the current terms of Russian propaganda.[36]

In one of his radio talks, the text of which was subsequently published by the *Daily Worker*, Harold suggested that Russia 'was not wholly in the wrong.'[37] This caused distress among the members of the British delegation, including Gladwyn Jebb, who seemed to feel that he should toe the party line – though this attitude was not shared by Bevin; despite his total exasperation with Molotov, he had reached much the same conclusion as Harold about the origins of Russian intransigence.[38] Harold put up a robust defence. Did they wish to check his scripts before they were broadcast? If they did not, then they must allow him to develop his own theme in his own way. The Conference was not the House of Commons. Negotiations were not about scoring debating points. Russia might become the enemy, but she was not the enemy yet – 'It is our job to be patient and wise and sensible.'[39]

Harold was researching, writing and broadcasting four talks a week, as well as writing his *Spectator* column, a piece for the French paper, *Le Figaro*, and his book reviews for the *Daily Telegraph*. Vita made a twenty-four-hour visit at the end of August on her way to the south of France, accompanied by Raymond Mortimer; and Harold returned home for a week's holiday at the end of September. Otherwise he continued his punishing schedule from 29 July until 17 October. Being in Paris, he did not fully realise the impact that his talks and his views were having: his public profile had never been higher and his public influence never greater – hence, perhaps, the concern of the British delegation when his views diverged from the official line. At first, the size and impersonality of his worldwide audience bothered him – 'since the whole secret of broadcasting is to address oneself to a *personal* audience.' He solved the problem by inventing an 'imaginary person, sympathetic yet ignorant, interested but uninformed ... a woman of 35 who has experienced great unhappiness in life.'[40] The talks were immensely successful. Plaudits came from all directions. Alan Moorehead, one of the great war correspondents, sought Harold out in Paris to tell him that the British public interpreted the conference only through his talks and that he could have no conception how influential they were.[41] The *Irish*

Times called them 'outstanding'.⁴² The BBC was deluged with fan mail. Perhaps the greatest compliment came from R. A. Butler – who, having held a junior ministerial post at the Foreign Office during the Munich crisis, had not always seen eye-to-eye with Harold – when he said that the talks had 'induced the ordinary public to take an interest in foreign affairs' for the first time.⁴³

It was characteristic of Harold that, despite great personal success, his interest remained focussed on the wider world. At the beginning of October, his mood was darkened when the BBC arranged for a recording of the verdicts of the Nuremburg Tribunal to be sent to Paris. He listened with his colleagues in the Scribe Hotel and was sickened. He had supported the process, but, not for the first time, disliked the reality of the consequences which flowed from it – 'I cannot bear it ... I see the glistening surface of the disk revolving piteously, ticking off the lives of other men.'⁴⁴

By that time, the Conference was approaching its end. Eleven years previously, in 1935, he had written that 'more misery has been caused to mankind by the hurried drafting of imprecise or meaningless documents than by all the alleged machinations of the cunning diplomatist.'⁴⁵ Yet that is exactly what happened in Paris: 'During the first six weeks the Conference dragged itself along painfully ... during the last four weeks there was a breathless scramble to conclude.' A straw poll taken among the correspondents covering the Conference found that fifty-six thought it had been a failure, thirty-one thought it had been a success and thirty-three thought it had been a farce.⁴⁶ Gladwyn Jebb, seeing things from an insider's perspective, thought that 'within ... limits, good and constructive work was done ... in spite of the national passions, which were often unrestrained.'⁴⁷ On the whole, Harold agreed, though he was conscious that much of it had been 'so farcical in so many ways.'⁴⁸ Looking to the future, however, his concern was that 'much bitterness and much distrust has been created.'⁴⁹

52 Labour

Back at home, Harold was in demand. He spoke at Chatham House on 'Peacemaking 1919 and 1946' and was quickly signed up for a weekly international-affairs broadcast on the BBC's Overseas Service. Over the weekend of 7–8 December, he wrote no fewer than eight talks or articles. Yet, as so often, the aftermath of a period of intense activity – in this case combined with a landmark birthday, his sixtieth – led to a bout of introspection and self-doubt. He noticed no intellectual decline in himself, but was conscious of the beginnings of physical decline, in particular the first indications of deafness. He no longer, so he told himself, had any desire 'for office or power in any sense', but regretted what he saw as 'literary ill-success', attributing it to the fact that he was 'not intelligent enough' to write any better. He did acknowledge that 'to have three people in my life such as Viti and Ben and Nigel is something greater than all material success', but the overall effect was of a man seeing the glass half-empty.[1]

Neither his own nor the general assessment of his literary reputation was well served by the appearance, at the beginning of December, of a slim volume entitled *The English Sense of Humour*. It was published as a deluxe edition by Dropmore – rather than Constable, his usual publisher[2] – and Ben commented, unkindly but not necessarily inaccurately, that 'the exterior [was] superior to the interior.'[3] The book – Harold called it an essay – attempts to define and analyse different types of humour and laughter in a manner which is partly systematic, partly psychological, and definitely dull. The tone is often that of an undergraduate essay and there is a distinct sense that what might have been an interesting, ephemeral, 'Marginal Comment' has been unnecessarily stretched to over fifty pages. Raymond Mortimer described it as 'very bad and sham philosophy.'[4] He was right.

A couple of months later, at the end of February, Harold wrote from 10 Neville Terrace to the Secretary of the Kensington Branch of the Labour Party asking what he needed to do to enrol as a party member. There was no particular political mystery to his decision, though it had been some time coming. He admitted in his diary that there was 'some truth in [the] accusation' that he was doing it to get a peerage and that he hated being out of Parliament. He 'could never have become a Tory' and it would have been 'madness to become a Liberal. Therefore becoming Labour [was] the only alternative to dropping out.' There was nothing new in this beyond the decision to act. Harold saw his integrity as his 'most valued possession' and in his own mind he believed he was doing the right thing. He worried that other people might doubt him, but what he dreaded most of all were the rows his decision might cause and the hurt it might cause to others, particularly Vita and his mother.[5]

The mystery was why he should still feel the need for a political position. His career as an MP had been disappointing, and his earlier, clumsy pursuit of a peerage had resulted only in disappointment, yet as a broadcaster and journalist he had achieved international recognition and huge popularity, giving him a public platform that most politicians would have envied. He had seen the importance of the media in Paris, but had not read the message. 'I never feel that being able to broadcast is a respectable gift,' he wrote while still in Paris.[6] And again, reflecting on life on the occasion of his sixtieth birthday: 'I [do not] relish the idea that my reputation rests not so much on my political or literary work, as upon my journalistic and broadcasting work.'[7] Harold recognised but he was not willing to accept the values of the new, democratic age. He still wanted his place at the centre of things conferred by the political establishment. It was a failure to change and to adapt.

Reaction to Harold's decision to join the Labour Party was mixed, even within his own family. Vita's reaction, the one he feared beyond all others, was one of slightly amused calm. She wrote that she was glad about the National Trust – of which he had just been appointed Vice-Chairman – but 'not sure about the Labour Party.'[8] Ben had little interest in politics and, according to James Lees-Milne, who knew him well, 'doubtless ... did not mind in the least.'[9] Nigel was in a very different position. He had been adopted as Conservative candidate for Harold's old constituency in West Leicester. It put him in an awkward position: 'the father joins the young revolutionary party, the son the staid and solid party.'[10] There was no doubt that the Conservatives of West Leicester, who had supported Harold in the 1945 election, were shocked, but Nigel did not seek to duck the issue. He publicly defended his father's decision and used it to define his own position.

> I respect him for his decision. Naturally I cannot agree with it, for if I did I would be a Socialist myself. I will be no less staunch a Conservative because of his attitude, and he, needless to say, will not be affected by mine.[11]

It was a generous attitude – and not one which was shared by Lady Carnock, who accused Harold of betraying his country, or by Harold's brother, Freddy, who assumed he would now resign from his clubs. Harold was devoted to his mother and was family-minded enough to help Freddy as he gradually collapsed into chronic alcoholism, but he was unmoved by their political disapproval.

Friends and political colleagues were also mixed in their reaction. Within the Labour Party itself, his decision attracted surprisingly little attention. A number of Labour intellectuals, such as Noel (later Lord) Annan, took Harold under their wing, although the diarist and (later) Cabinet minister Richard Crossman made some characteristically acerbic remarks. The most sensible reaction came from Anthony Eden, a staunch though not a hardcore or right-wing Tory. Rebuking Emerald Cunard for her criticism of Harold's decision, he said that Harold was 'a person apart' who had 'every right to make his own decisions', though his subsequent statement that 'he will do a world of good in the Labour Party' was to prove less than accurate.[12]

In April, Harold went to a Labour Party gathering, a meeting of the Haldane Society, and hated it. He was, he wrote afterwards, 'a theoretical socialist. I do feel profoundly that we can only avoid totalitarianism or tyranny by a planned socialist economy. I believe we can achieve it in this country without destroying the freedom of the individual.' But vegetable soup, liver-and-bacon and beer with the *Red Flag* to follow were too much for him.[13] The truth was that the majority of his friends and contemporaries, those with whom he felt socially at ease, were Conservatives. Yet his beliefs – and his conviction that beliefs had to be acted upon – led him to join the Labour Party. He had again stranded himself between two groups.

In practice, once the mild media interest had died down, Harold's life continued unchanged. Nineteen forty-seven was, by his standards, a quiet summer. He visited Lady Colefax and met the Duke and Duchess of Windsor, for whose rather purposeless existence he felt sympathy. He attended a French Embassy lunch in honour of André Gide who was about to receive an honorary Doctorate of Law from Oxford University. Gide was worried that there might be undergraduate demonstrations in protest at his homosexuality: Harold assured him that there might be mockery but not disapproval. He discussed war and proverbs with the Chinese Ambassador. He received his *Légion d'Honneur* from the French Ambassador. He lunched and dined with political friends, including Gladwyn Jebb, keeping abreast of developments in the increasingly tense relationship with what was now being seen as the Soviet bloc. He went to a Buckingham Palace garden party on the day when the engagement was announced of Princess Elizabeth and Lieutenant Philip Mountbatten. He was invited to dine at No. 11 Downing Street by Hugh Dalton, the Chancellor of the Exchequer. And in September, he made an extended visit to Switzerland, visiting Geneva, Neuchâtel, Colombier and Lausanne, exploring the background to his next book which was to be a biography of the Swiss-born writer, politician and liberal political thinker, Benjamin Constant. During the trip, he was taken by the former British Consul in Geneva to lunch with the exiled Queen of Italy. Harold, who, with age, showed a tendency to judge the company by the menu, did not enjoy himself – 'We were given a few mushrooms on toast with custard over them, and then the bits of chicken. The latter must have been very old when it died and must have enjoyed ill health for years. But it was served on magnificent plates.'[14] It was hardly a dull life, but by November, Harold was feeling depressed at the bittiness of his professional existence and unwanted by the wider world. He discussed with Vita how to allocate his time now that he had 'dropped out of public life' and did 'nothing of any real importance.'[15]

That neither Harold nor Vita were forgotten in senior political circles was demonstrated that December. The Council of Foreign Ministers, meaning the foreign ministers of the Allied Powers, were meeting in London and Harold and Vita were both invited to the official reception at Buckingham Palace. Attlee asked to be introduced to Vita – he was a deep admirer of *The Land* and could quote several passages by heart. Harold went off to talk to Bidault, the French Prime Minister. He was taken to one side by Bevin and given a blow-by-blow account of his attempts to find out what Molotov really wanted out of the Council meeting. Two days later, Vita received a letter informing her that she was to become a Companion of Honour – her name, it later emerged, having been put forward personally to the King by Attlee. That was Friday. The following Tuesday, Harold received a phone call which was a direct consequence of his decision to join the Labour Party, and which would disrupt his life for the next three months, put *Benjamin Constant* on hold, and finally put an end to his political career and ambitions.

The phone call was from Transport House, the Labour Party's London headquarters and it came from the party's Assistant National Agent, Len Williams. The sitting Conservative MP for Croydon North, Henry Willink, who had been Minister for Health during the latter part of the war, was resigning from Parliament. Would Harold fight the seat on behalf of the Labour Party? In the Labour landslide of 1945, Willink had held the seat for the Conservatives by 607 votes. Half way through the parliamentary term, the tide was swinging back again and in the November municipal elections the Conservatives had made significant gains at Labour's expense. Harold was not expected to win the seat, but it was important that the Labour vote did not drop drastically below the 1945 level. This was not what Harold wanted. If he could not have a seat in the House of Lords, then he wanted a safe Labour seat in a constituency where he would not have to fight a serious election – though in reality there was no earthly reason why the Labour Party should have given him either. But he had joined the Labour Party out of conviction and was now being asked as 'a great favour' to take on Croydon North.[16] If he wished his membership of the Party to be taken seriously he had little choice.

On 17 December, Len Williams and the organiser of the Labour Party's Southern Regional Council, Frank Shepherd, accompanied him to a meeting of the constituency party in suburban South Norwood. From the beginning, it felt wrong – 'I feel like a cow being led garlanded to the altar, and they probably regard me as a very doubtful old horse.'[17] The atmosphere of the meeting was not good. Only ten people turned up. Harold was the only candidate and one lady claimed he was being forced upon them by Transport House. He made a statement outlining what he saw as his disadvantages: his association with Mosley and National Labour; his support for Churchill, his 'inability to be violent or denunciatory', his upper class background. Harold sensed his small audience were unhappy, but only one man spoke up and said that he was too right wing. When it came to the vote, he was adopted by a majority of eight to two.

If the atmosphere was wrong, so, too, was Harold's attitude. Even before the date of the bye-election was fixed he was referring to his 'Croydon crucifixion'[18] – a period of suffering he had to undergo in order to achieve his peerage. Christmas was quiet, with the family together at Sissinghurst. In the New Year, he called on Herbert Morrison, the Deputy Prime Minister, who was pleasant and helpful and made it clear that victory was not really expected – 'if you win this seat, you will be given the VC.'[19] Because Willink had still not actually resigned and the election date could not be fixed, Harold stole a few days in Paris. He spent the time hunting down some of Benjamin Constant's haunts and houses, guided by Pierre de Lacretelle, who had lost all his money and become a morphia addict. He was still charming, but in some way out of reach. On 30 January, Harold accidentally gatecrashed a cocktail party at the British Embassy, hoping to speak to Sir Oliver Harvey, who had just taken over as Ambassador from Duff Cooper. It was then he discovered that polling day would be 11 March and that his Conservative opponent would be a local businessman called Fred Bennett.

The Croydon North bye-election of 1948 seems to be have been something of a period piece, fought against a background of bad weather – 1947–48 was another appalling winter – inadequate heating and poor food. The country was still recovering from the war. Bomb damage and wartime neglect were still visible. Fuel was still rationed and shop windows, many of them displaying nothing more than piles of tinned food, could not be lit up at night. Double-decker trams ran down the High Street and North End. Trolley buses ran along Tamworth Road and Station Road. There were queues each evening outside the Empire, the Odeon, the Scala and the Savoy to see *Miracle on 34th Street, Brighton Rock, The Ghost and Mrs Muir* or *The Treasure of the Sierra Madre*. The candidates toured the streets in black pre-war cars with loudspeakers on the roof. Campaign posters were printed in stark black capitals – 'VOTE NICOLSON LABOUR'.

It was a solo performance from Harold. Ben, struggling to combine his role as Deputy Surveyor of the King's Pictures with the editorship of the art-historical *Burlington Magazine*, which he had taken on the previous April, was indifferent to anything to do with politics. Nigel could not risk coming anywhere near Croydon without creating a storm in West Leicester, although he wrote, privately, that he wanted Harold 'unreservedly, unashamedly, to bring off this triumph.'[20] And Vita was on a long-planned British Council lecture tour of North Africa, so the issue of explaining why she would not support her Labour candidate husband did not arise. Harold's campaign headquarters were cold and draughty with holes in the windows and doors that would not shut. The only place to eat was a tiny restaurant where he could get 'fish and chips and coffee' – not, he reflected, a diet to which he was accustomed.[21] His hotel, described in ironic but affectionate detail in one of his 'Marginal Comment' columns, had clearly seen better days. His room, under the snow-covered eaves, was freezing. He had a gas fire, and a gas ring on which he could boil a kettle. Hot water in the shared bathroom was limited. For him, as indeed for the other people staying there, many of them permanent or long-term residents, it was a grim existence. Yet Harold, who so often found it difficult to relate to strangers or people from different walks of life, was genuinely sympathetic. The residents, faced with a menu of 'vegetable soup ... haricot mutton, and ... steamed fruit sponge and custard, or raspberry mould' were 'an example of quiet dignity in times that are sparse and tough.' And he realised that managing 'such a hotel in modern conditions,' he wrote, 'must be a dispiriting task.'[22]

Harold conducted his usual scrupulously honest campaign. He appreciated the efforts of his campaign workers and did his best to live up to their expectations. He went to call on and be photographed with an eighty-nine-year-old trade unionist. He was photographed talking to a housewife in a grocery shop. He climbed ladders and spoke to builders working on the roof of an unfinished house. Sometimes, he actually believed he was doing good and began to feel 'more comfortable as a Labour man than [he] ever did as a hybrid.'[23] At other times, however, friends such as James Pope-Hennessy and James Lees-Milne were amazed at his awkwardness with people he regarded as uneducated. And it is true that his mood does appear to have swung back and forth between appreciation of the human warmth he encountered and fury at the ignorance and stupidity of some of the electorate.

As the campaign continued, his spirits generally lifted. Partly this was simply the excitement of battle and partly the result of another meeting with Herbert Morrison. Throughout his life, Harold would always be buoyed up by encouragement or compliments from someone he saw as an important or senior figure – it was an aspect of his hero worship. In the middle of the campaign, he again lunched with Morrison who told him: 'Men of your class who join the movement make fools of themselves by trying to put on proletarian airs.... What I like about you is that you never pretend to be anything but yourself.'[24] This produced a new elated feeling of belonging: he felt at ease in the Labour movement and enjoyed the decency of the people around him.

Senior Labour figures such as Richard Crossman and Hector McNeil came down to speak on Harold's behalf, but the Conservatives, too, wheeled out their big guns. Even Churchill came down to support Harold's opponent, and the fact that his daughter, Mary Soames, was having a baby in the local maternity hospital was held to boost the Tory cause. Harold's greatest coup came when he was door-to-door canvassing in the presence of a BBC radio team. He actually managed to persuade a Mrs Briggs to vote Labour rather than Conservative and to encourage her builder husband to do the same. It was not a put-up job, although Harold was convinced that it would sound like one. Unfortunately, the programme was to be broadcast on the Overseas Service and could have no impact on the election.

Thursday 11 March was sunny and clear, if cold. Vita had sent a telegram from Tunis saying that she was thinking of him. Harold spent the day being driven around the constituency, encouraging campaign staff and voters alike. The turnout was huge – up 17.5% on 1945. Harold escaped to London for dinner with Ben and Nigel, returning to Croydon for the count. A win was never expected: the question was by how much he would lose and whether the Labour vote would hold up. In the end, he lost by 11,664, but the Labour vote actually increased by over 1700. It had been a huge effort of will, and he was not actually disappointed by the result. As he wrote to Vita: 'I did well on the whole.... I should not like to represent Croydon, which is a bloody place. Nor should I like to be in the present House. All has turned out for the best, and what is more, it is OVER, and without disgrace.'[25]

The next morning, Harold returned gratefully to Sissinghurst. He was tired, but he could not rest completely. There were book reviews and the following week's 'Marginal Comment' column to be written. He decided to write about the Croydon North bye-election. It was a serious mistake. 'Losing a Bye-Election' was published on 19 March. Harold reflects that 'all elections have about them an atmosphere of unreality.' The candidate is forced to take part in what is essentially a theatrical performance to which Harold felt himself unsuited. His theme is the artificiality of the whole process – 'I much dislike trying to produce within nineteen days a synthetic version of myself which, in effect if not in intention, must inevitably be a distorted version.' The same sense of artificiality applies to the constituency which is 'a line drawn around an arbitrary number of streets and houses' and, as such, has no core of identity with which the inhabitants can identify or to which they can feel loyalty. He describes the unreality of the candidate's situation, using the extended analogy of a racehorse being groomed and put through his paces ahead of a race by its trainer and his staff. He concludes by lamenting his inability to be single-minded even in the pursuit of sincerely held convictions and regretting that he 'may have been a disappointment to [his] trainer and the stable hands.'[26]

Norman Rose has called the piece a 'splenetic tirade' which it is not. James Lees-Milne has called it 'tactless ... mocking and flippant', which it is, although the mockery is largely self-mockery. The real problem is that it is misleadingly detached and one-sided. This is not the Harold Nicolson who in his private diary could write that his Labour colleagues were 'decent people' and that 'it is a joy for me to be on their side.'[27] He was making some serious points. Much of what he said about the artificiality of the process and the nature of the constituency was true. What made it objectionable was the tone. Had he voiced his criticisms directly, in the logical, argued manner of his Nuremburg article, with suggestions for change or improvement, the reaction would almost certainly have been different. But the detachment, the irony and the lack of positive suggestions for change made it appear that he did not really care, and caused real offence.

Why did he do it? Was he just letting off steam? Who was he writing for? Did he not understand that to the people he worked with on the ground, the Labour Party and its policies were matters of continuing commitment and belief, not to be dismissed when the bye-election was over? His dining companions at the Travellers or the Beefsteak might have been amused, but it is hard to imagine who else would have been. Or did he imagine that the voters of Croydon North and the *apparatchiks* of Transport House simply did not read the Conservative-oriented *Spectator*? Just a couple of days later, Nigel criticised his father for having 'no powers of calculation' which meant that he could never foresee where his actions would land him.[28] The remark cannot be described as prophetic for the article had already been published, but Harold certainly never anticipated the effect his words would have. His campaign staff were upset. They felt that he had not taken them or the election seriously. The constituents of Croydon were insulted. Whatever they felt about their locality, they resented the criticisms of a man, who, by his own admission, had been parachuted in for a mere nineteen days. Transport House were furious. Harold had been their choice; they had been made to look foolish; and they had an effective veto on whose names would be put forward for a peerage. As Morrison said later, when the question was raised: 'The boys wouldn't like it.'[29]

The strange thing is that Harold does not seem to have realised the stir of disapproval his article created. He watched New Year and Birthday Honours Lists come and go, at first with disappointment and then with resignation. It was not until two years later, in February 1950, that Philip Jordan, Attlee's Public Relations Adviser, told him why his name had never appeared.

53 Proposition

Harold's defeat in the Croydon North bye-election marked a watershed. It was not immediately apparent, because both he and Vita continued to hope that Cranfield (the name chosen for his putative title) would come, but in fact his political career was dead, if not – in his own mind, at least – quite yet buried. By the time he returned to Sissinghurst on 12 March 1948, he had been out of Parliament for more than two-and-a-half years. In that time, only his BBC role in Paris had brought him close to the political centre of things, but Harold continued to regard broadcasting as a lesser activity. As time went by, he slipped gradually further from the political mainstream.

Harold's hopes of a peerage were kept alive by an encounter with Attlee that April at an American Embassy reception in honour of Mrs Roosevelt. 'Now mind, Harold,' the Prime Minister told him, 'don't say you will abandon politics and return to your writing. We have other things we want of you.'[1] This could have been misleading, but it is more likely that Attlee was simply not aware of the state of feeling in Transport House. As he waited and as he thought about it, Harold – with characteristically honest self-analysis – noticed 'a fat grub of snobbishness' growing in his consciousness. Again, this seems to have been a reflection of his increasing distance from the corridors of power. In 1945, his desire to remain within the governing classes was based on continuing the kind of role he had played in the Commons. He had views on Greece, on managing the peace process, and on the future of Europe which he wanted heard in Government, and the

House of Lords offered the platform he needed. By 1948, he was placing more emphasis on recognition and reward for what he had achieved in the past. For some reason, he suddenly decided that he had 'always hated the name 'Nicolson' as being a common and plebeian name.' Hereditary peers could change their name; life peers could not; so he wanted to be a hereditary peer. He believed that 'at my age I ought not to mind such things', whereas in fact increasing age brought to Harold – as it does to many if not to most people – an increasing social and intellectual conservatism.

He did not go into a sudden decline. He remained passionately interested in foreign affairs. For all his personal prejudices against Jewish people, he supported the establishment of the state of Israel – though keenly aware of the violence which had characterised the last years of the British Mandate. Perhaps thinking back over thirty years to the basement offices in the Foreign Offices where he and Mark Sykes drafted the Balfour Declaration, he wrote: 'All the pleasure I might have felt at this realisation of the hopes of Zionism is clouded by the fear of war and the humiliation we have suffered.'[2] And, four months later, when the Stern Gang murdered the United Nations' Mediator, Count Bernadotte of Sweden, he was deeply and genuinely shocked, not just at the murder but at what it would mean for Chaim Weizmann – 'his life's work sullied by these ghetto thugs.'[3] He rejoiced in the unexpected victory of President Truman over New York's Republican Governor, Thomas Dewey. And, like most of Britain, he was deeply concerned about what was happening in Europe as the Cold War escalated with the Soviet blockade of Berlin, the Berlin Airlift, and then the advent of the Russian atomic bomb. Yet he was no longer in close contact with the policymakers and decision-takers of Whitehall and there is an understandable sense of distance. His comments on events are sometimes accompanied by statements which verge on the bitter or the apocalyptic. Of the Stern Gang atrocity, he wrote: 'It is not fair on our generation, who possess all the susceptibilities created by the old order, to have to face the atrocities of the new.'[4] Of the UN: 'The whole organisation has been turned into nonsense.'[5] Of Berlin: 'The Barbarians are at the gate.'[6] He had made such comments before, but now they come to seem less argued and more embedded in his reactions.

With the ending of his political career, Harold did not retire to the country – he continued to travel right up until his last years, and he maintained a London home until he was approaching seventy-nine – but Sissinghurst, and particularly the garden, gradually assumed a greater centrality in his life. Waking up in Neville Terrace in London, he would 'think of the view over the lilacs which I get from my bedroom window' and he believed that he gained 'more from Sissinghurst than anyone else.'[7] It had always been the one part of life he shared wholly with Vita – although there were occasions when it brought out the differences of temperament between them.

> In the afternoon, I moon about with Vita trying to convince her that planning is an element in gardening. I want to show her that the top of the moat-bank walk must be planted with forethought and design. She just wishes to jab in the things which she has left over ... which 'will give a lovely red colour in the autumn.' I wish to put in stuff which will furnish shape to the perspective. In the end we part, not as friends.[8]

And it remained a fundamental element in both their lives. 'How fortunate we are,' Vita wrote at the beginning of 1950, 'to have both indoor and outdoor occupations. If we can't garden, we can write.'[9]

The garden fulfilled different functions at different times. It was a reference point in a disturbed world: Harold contrasted its beauty by moonlight with the horror of the Stern Gang's violence as if that might bring him understanding. It was an escape, a succession of private spaces that allowed the individual to withdraw or escape from the rest of the world. It was a technical interest: they corresponded over plant names, when particular plants bloomed, whether they needed sunshine or shade. It was an achievement: it possessed 'a quality of mellowness, of retirement, of unflaunting dignity, which is just what we wanted to achieve'[10] and Harold referred to the pleached Lime Walk between the Rose Garden and the Nuttery on the south side of the garden as 'My Life's Work'. It was an ambition: Harold wanted to make it one of the loveliest gardens 'in all England.'[11] And it was beauty in its own right, to be enjoyed and appreciated without reference to anything else, yet at the same time linked to the deep feeling they both had for England and for the Weald of Kent.

In a sense, Vita had been prescient in February 1947 when she wrote that she was glad about the National Trust but not sure about the Labour Party: gardens, ancient buildings, libraries – the landmarks of traditional British culture – and their preservation were to play a major part in Harold's life, and to a lesser extent in her own, until they approached old age. Harold had first become involved with the National Trust at the very end of 1944 when he joined its Historic Buildings Committee which had Lord Esher, a former soldier and senior official in the India Office, as its chairman; James Lees-Milne as its Secretary; and Gerry Wellesley, an architect himself with some very decided opinions about ancient buildings, as one of its members. He was soon co-opted onto both the General Purposes Committee and the

Executive Committee and, in 1947, became the Executive Committee's Vice-Chairman, a post he retained until 1961.

Harold enjoyed the work of the Trust, as did Vita. Her weekly gardening columns in the *Observer*, which began in 1946, rapidly established her as a national gardening icon and she was asked to serve on the Trust's Gardens Committee. Shortly after Harold had become the Trust's Vice-Chairman, he and Vita, accompanied by James Lees-Milne, took a hectic ten-day tour round the west of England during which they visited some forty historic houses, as well as cathedrals and other monuments. Many of the houses and their contents were remarkable but in a desperately poor state of repair. In the years immediately after the war, the cult of the English country house, which was to become a huge cultural phenomenon and launch Britain's heritage industry in the 1960s and 70s, had yet to take off. The Trust's dilemma at the time, which Harold understood, was that while they might just have enough money to save a beautiful house from destruction, they did not have enough to maintain it properly.

In addition to the National Trust, at the beginning of 1949, Harold became a Trustee of the National Portrait Gallery. The appointment seems to have stemmed from an occasion, two years previously, when he had lectured at Burlington House in the presence of Queen Mary on the portraits painted by Sir Thomas Lawrence during the Congress of Vienna. Ben had organised the exhibition shortly before taking over as editor of the *Burlington Magazine*, which he gradually turned into Britain's most prestigious art-historical magazine. In 1951, Harold was elected Chairman of the London Library. T. S. Eliot was elected President at the same time. The Library, located in St James's Square, founded in 1841 by Thomas Carlyle and counting Thackeray, Dickens, George Eliot and Gladstone among its former members, was one of Harold's favourite institutions and he retained the chairmanship until 1957. Also in 1951, he served a term as President of the Classical Association, another honour which meant much to him. He gave a lecture on 'Nature in Greek Poetry', which was later broadcast on the BBC Third Programme.

Harold was rapidly becoming one of the great and the good: that select upper stratum of British society – very much the preserve of the establishment – which makes up the committees and supplies the chairmen of charities, trusts, commissions, enquiries and other public bodies. He was Harold Nicolson, CMG, the distinguished author, commentator and broadcaster, lecturer and public speaker, former diplomat, former Minister and MP. Although no longer a member of the governing classes, his name was now joined with those who enjoyed a certain pre-eminence among the governed.

As if to confirm that this was the direction in which life was moving, on 3 June 1948, he received a letter from his old friend Tommy Lascelles, who since 1943 had been Private Secretary to King George VI, asking him to call at Buckingham Palace. Harold knew that a State Visit to Australia and New Zealand was planned for 1949 (although it never took place owing to the King's illness) and feared that he might be asked to go and give a series of lectures to coincide with the trip. The only other possibility was the official biography of King George V, about which there had been rustlings in the literary undergrowth.

It was the biography. When Harold was ushered into Lascelles' office the following week, he was told that the King wanted a biography of his father, and he wanted it written while certain key people, such as Tommy himself, Sir Owen Morshead, the Royal Librarian, and presumably – though her name was not mentioned – Queen Mary, who had just passed her eightieth birthday, were still alive. Certain, unnamed people had been asked (Harold discovered later that one of them was the historian George Trevelyan) and his had been the name most often suggested. The King and the Queen had agreed. Only Queen Mary remained to be consulted.

Harold did not commit himself immediately. He wrote a letter to Vita setting out the advantages and disadvantages. Lascelles had assured him that he would not be expected to tell untruths, to praise or exaggerate, but had made it clear that he might be required to 'omit things and incidents which were discreditable.' It would take three or four years. He would have unfettered access to the Royal Archive, but there would be no financial assistance, even with secretarial help. He could, however, make whatever contractual arrangements he wished with a publisher. The real question was whether it would be 'possible to write the life in a way that [would] be really interesting, really true, while keeping to the convention of royal portraits.' Vita was more suspicious. She feared that 'Tommy's employer probably has a Divine Right attitude' and might interfere. Elvira Niggeman, who was also consulted, took the solidly practical view that it would give him the anchor he needed and stop him 'doing silly things like Croydon'.

Harold accepted. There was never really any doubt that he would. It was an honour to be asked and the project suited him completely. He would be able to write 'the history of my own times.'[12] It was an indication also – whatever he or anybody else thought of his life's achievements – of his incredible reach: in March he had been grass roots canvassing for the Labour Party and now, in June, he was being asked to write a sensitive royal biography. It would be sensitive not just because King George V was the current King's father, but also because the old King was known to have been reticent, unexciting, and lacking in charm – characteristics which would not lend themselves to easy portrayal in print. By accepting Lascelles' proposition, Harold was also acknowledging the end of his political career – Vita, he understood, would 'not be at all depressed by such a realisation'[13] – but it was a decision he knew he would not regret. And, on this occasion, he was right.

Harold set about organising himself for the task. He immediately decided he could no longer write his regular articles for *Le Figaro*, much to the editor's distress, and, in January 1949, he swapped three book reviews a week in the *Daily Telegraph* for a single review in the *Observer*, a column he was to continue writing until 1963. But the main thing was to complete *Benjamin Constant*. Nearly all the research had been done and he was able to start writing on 20 June 1948. Things went slowly at first, but, after another trip to Paris where he was helped again by Pierre de Lacretelle and also by his French diplomat friend, Roland de Margerie, he recovered his normal fluency and wrote furiously throughout the summer.

The choice of Benjamin Constant as a subject was very much conditioned by Harold's love of all things French, for, although born in Lausanne to a family which had been living in Switzerland for two hundred years, Constant was French in both culture and outlook. He was an intellectual; a writer; a publisher; a political thinker and theorist with a strongly liberal point of view; a politician; a serial turncoat; a lover; a conversationalist. V. S. Pritchett, quoted on the inside cover of the American edition of Harold's biography, described him as 'an inexhaustibly interesting neurotic'. Moreover, Constant was twenty-two in 1789, so his adult life spanned the Revolution, the Napoleonic adventure, the Restoration of the Bourbons, and the July Revolution of 1830 which established the constitutional monarchy of Louis-Philippe – forty years which are crucial to any understanding of France and French consciousness.

Harold's account of Constant's life does not, as one might have expected, emphasise the British connection – Constant was, after all, partly educated at Edinburgh University, spent a few wild but influential weeks travelling around England at the age of twenty, and, partly as a result, regarded Britain as the country to which the rest of the Europe should look in order to safeguard civil liberties and political freedoms. Instead, he stands back from political analysis and from a psychological approach, presenting the narrative of Constant's life as objectively as possible, as – in his own words – 'a simple cautionary tale'.[14]

In his Author's Note, Harold lists twenty-one categories of people to whom this cautionary tale is addressed. Three seem to encompass

Constant's father, while the remaining eighteen apply to Constant himself, thus giving the impression at the outset that Harold either disapproves of Constant or regards his life as an example of how not to manage things. There is also the sense, as with *The Desire to Please*, that he might be writing about someone with whom he half-identifies. The cautionary tale is addressed, among others,

> to politicians who experiment in short cuts; to intellectuals who, on entering the political arena, imagine that they manifest superiority by calling themselves independents; to those who seek in the applause of the ignorant compensation for their inability to acquire the esteem of them that know; to elderly gentlemen who lack the dignity to surrender in time to middle age ... to those who keep diaries.'[15]

These are some of Harold's favourite themes, and relevant to his own mistakes in life. Yet somehow this does not seem sufficient foundation for a biography. The narrative is, as usual, well paced and structured, but like *The Desire to Please*, *Benjamin Constant* suffers from the lack of a central thesis. It somehow fails to suggest why Constant is an important figure. Also – unusually for the mature Harold – there are times when the book lacks stylistic fluency. Having weaned himself off the authorial 'I' with *The Congress of Vienna*, Harold now becomes sometimes a little too impersonal – what Vita referred to as his 'police court style'.[16]

The book was finished and sent to Constable on 9 September, although it was not published until the summer of 1949. It received respectful but not enthusiastic notices – although, for once, Raymond Mortimer was full of praise, and the reviewer in the *Times Literary Supplement* was perceptive enough to notice parallels between the author and his subject. Two weeks after despatching his manuscript, Harold flew to Berlin.

The Russian blockade had begun. The western half of the city was now an island which had to be supplied with food, water and fuel by a thundering, twenty-four-hour delivery service of British, American and French planes. The Foreign Office was concerned about morale in the isolated city, especially among the British forces stationed there, faced, as they were, with a daily bombardment of Soviet propaganda. Harold was called upon to deliver a series of lectures designed to bolster social and cultural values on the western side of the ideological divide. It was a nightmarish trip. Of course, he had to fly, much to Vita's terror. He gave his lectures. The British Commander in-Chief and Military Governor General, Sir Brian Robertson, gave it as his opinion that the Russians would not provoke war. Harold was not so sure. The ruin of Berlin appalled him and saddened him to the point of tears. In the Press Club in Grünewald, there was a single light bulb and he had the 'sense of living in a dugout'.[17] He also had a bad cold.

Journalism and broadcasts continued, some of them reflecting on his experiences in Berlin. Then, in October, he went to Dublin to address the Trinity College Philosophical Society, and tacked onto the trip a visit to his maternal grandmother's house, Shanganagh Castle. It had been turned into a girls' school, and a beautiful avenue of trees leading down to the sea had been felled: the whole experience was chilling. In November, he fulfilled an obligation to the National Trust by going to Buckland Abbey, near Plymouth, to consider plans for creating a modern, residential flat for the caretaker to be fitted within the existing building. And he honoured his commitment to Rob Bernays' widow by visiting preparatory schools in Bath where she was considering sending her two sons. In the meantime, he took what opportunities he could to seek out and talk to people who had known George V. But it was not until the end of November that he began thinking seriously how to approach such an enormous task, and it was not until the beginning of January 1949 that he made his first visit to Windsor Castle.

54 Biographer

On both sides of his family, Harold's background was aristocratic. Few people can have done less to exploit their aristocratic status than Sir Arthur and Lady Nicolson, as they were during Harold's youth. Indeed, they were so unassuming and so unsmart that Lady Sackville considered them 'bedint'. Nonetheless, Harold was brought up among aristocratic and titled people. Throughout his life, he met kings and queens and princes and was neither overawed nor embarrassed in such company. His historical studies gave him an understanding of the importance of titles and he had an excellent grasp of the interconnecting family trees of the royal families of Europe.

But he was not a courtier, and, by agreeing to write the life of King George V, he was, in that sense, entering a new world – a world where the monarchy, its reputation and its continuity must always come first. During their meeting in Buckingham Palace, Lascelles had told him that he would not be writing 'an ordinary biography' but 'a book about a very ancient national institution'.[1] Sir Owen Morshead told him explicitly that 'your first duty will always be to the Monarchy.' This provoked a diary entry claiming that he had 'no mystic feeling about the Monarchy' and regarded it 'merely as a useful institution'.[2] In fact, Harold's attitude to the British monarchy was, somewhat like the position of the monarchy itself, curiously undefined. His response to the Abdication in 1936 and to the role played by King George VI and Queen Elizabeth during the War was much more than a response to an institution, however useful. At the same time, he was not an uncritical monarchist. He had seen the collapse of monarchies across much of Europe without great regret and certainly did not believe that kingship endowed its possessors with particular or special qualities. One of the fascinating aspects of *King George V* is that it is a working out of Harold's own understanding of the position of a constitutional monarch. It is no accident that the chapters dealing with the constitutional crisis of 1931 and that dealing with the royal prerogative and the exceptional circumstances faced by George V on his accession were the first to be written and the first to be shown to Lascelles for official approval.[3]

The world of the courtier is all-encompassing – everything focuses on the person and the role of the monarch – and, although not required to become a courtier himself, Harold soon found that the world of the royal biographer made similar demands. By anyone else's standards he continued to lead a busy and varied life, but for the next three years *King George V* was the mainstay of his working life, overshadowing everything else. As Elvira Niggeman had foreseen, it was a blessing. Those three years saw not only the production of a major literary work, but also the transition from his political – or post-political – period, to a later stage of life when, however much he might carp, he came to accept his role as writer, commentator and member of the cultural chapter of the great and good.

He presented himself at Windsor Castle on 6 January 1949. It was a cold, wet, Thursday morning. He went to Sir Owen Morshead's room where he had his first sight of George V's copious but largely uninformative diaries. Morshead took him across to the great Round Tower which overshadows the rest of the castle and which housed the Royal Archive. Here, he was introduced to Mary Mackenzie, the Registrar of the King's Archive, whose help and whose knowledge, as Harold put it, 'sustained me through many a dark day when the north-east wind howled along the Thames Valley and my light was low.'[4] The archive seemed to promise much fascinating material, but it was enormous. He was also shown a small office which was his for the duration. It was cold, especially when the north-east wind howled, but the view over lower parts of the castle and the River Thames towards Marlow, Henley and the Chiltern Hills beyond was spectacular.

His first task was to establish a routine which would help him cope with the huge number of documents he needed to consult. He had a standing invitation to stay with the Lascelles at their apartment in the castle. The problem was that the Round Tower shut at four-thirty every afternoon which left him homeless and unoccupied until the evening. Moreover, he quickly found that there was a limit to the number of manuscript documents he could read in a single day without straining his eyes. So, in the end, he preferred to make the daily commute to Windsor from Neville Terrace. The scale of the task also caused Harold to change his long-established method of research and composition. Normally, he would work his way carefully through his source materials, noting and summarising in loose-leaf notebooks. When he had finished, he would write the book rapidly and sequentially using the notes he had accumulated. The sheer volume of documentary material and the complexity of the issues involved meant he had to change this. *King George V* was researched and then written piece by piece, and not in chronological sequence.

Thematically, too, Harold had decisions to make. When the prospect of writing the book had been discussed at Neville Terrace, Ben, characteristically, had been opposed to the whole idea, but Nigel, while warning against any suppression of the truth, had added that people would be interested to know 'exactly how far the King exercised his authority.'[5] The idea clearly took root. In the 'Author's Note', Harold makes it plain that rather than attempt a comprehensive examination of the King's attitude to all the events of his reign, he was extracting what he saw as the main theme of the reign and seeking to answer two questions: 'How does a Monarchy function in a modern state?' and 'To what extent were the powers and influence of the Monarchy diminished or increased during the twenty-five years of King George's reign?'[6] These questions hold the key to the book and to its enduring interest. They give it the kind of connection to broader social and political themes beyond its subject which was present in *Lord Carnock*, *Curzon* and *The Congress of Vienna* (among others), but lacking in *The Desire to Please* and *Benjamin Constant*.

The other side of Harold's research was interviewing members of the Royal Family, political figures and others who had known or had dealings with the late King. The biography which he had been asked to write was not a personal biography, nor a portrait of George V as an individual – that had already been done by John Gore, who had published *King George V: A Personal Memoir* in 1941 – but rather a public life which would centre on the King's attitude to and involvement in the great political issues of his reign. Hence the full title: *King George the Fifth: His Life and Reign*. Nonetheless, it was essential for Harold to build up a full picture of the man. He was interested in the idea of monarchy and naturally curious, so he enjoyed his glimpses of what went on behind the public façade, but his real need was to understand the character of the man during whose reign unprecedented changes overtook both Britain and its Empire. In Chapter VIII, 'Monarchy', Harold writes that 'although ... the executive *powers* of the King are strictly limited ... the *influence* he retains, although indefinable, is very great.'[7] That influence depended on the man's character, so the formative influences and consequent characteristics of the King were thus very much a legitimate and relevant aspect of Harold's investigations.

Some of his informants were clear and helpful. The Earl of Cromer, a former diplomat who had served as Lord Chamberlain – the senior official of the Royal Household – from 1922 to 1937, was precise in his assessment of the King: a man with a sense of humour, very conscientious, expecting his views to be listened to by ministers and others, and dominant in his own household. Others were less so. Herbert Morrison said simply: 'Your old boy was a good King, and so is this one. We may consider ourselves damned lucky.'[8] Some offered a small insight: Sir Kenneth Clark described how slowly the King wrote, forming his letters like a schoolboy. Others gave clues: the Duke of Windsor told Harold that he would never understand George V until he saw York Cottage, the villa on the Sandringham Estate in Norfolk which was the King's favourite home.

The key interview, with Queen Mary, took place on 21 March 1949 in Marlborough House. Queen Mary – christened Victoria Mary Augusta Louise Olga Pauline Claudine Agnes – was herself a great-granddaughter of King George III and an immensely regal figure. She had originally been engaged to King George V's elder brother, Prince Albert Victor, but he died of pneumonia only six weeks after their engagement. A year later, in May 1893, she became engaged to the then Prince George. The marriage took place that July and was, by all accounts, genuinely successful. She was as devoted to the King as he was to her, but she was also dedicated to the cause of the British monarchy, and when Edward VIII abdicated her support for George VI was total. In 1949, she was eighty-two and the focus of great patriotic devotion, not only as the mother of King George VI, but also the Queen who, together with her husband, had acted as a figurehead for the country and the Empire through the dark and difficult years of the First World War. Harold's comment was: 'She made me feel the meaning of the phrase *grande dame*.'

The interview was extremely important for Harold, less for its content, though she did speak openly about the King's character – his loyalty, his truthfulness, his attachment to familiar people, places and things – than because her distrust or disapproval could easily have made for difficulties when he presented his text for approval. As it was, when the time came, Queen Mary made only a few minor corrections and excisions. The fact that she had known Harold's parents no doubt helped establish good relations. When asked after Vita, Harold said, quite truthfully, that she had been taken ill in Granada on a recent trip to Spain and that he 'had had a sort of feeling about it.' Queen Mary told him that she and the King had always known what was happening to each other during their rare separations.[9]

Harold soon discovered that writing a royal biography could create situations which had about them an air of unreality. In March 1950, he attended a reception at the French Embassy as part of a State Visit by the French President, Vincent Auriol. Having had a few words with the President he found himself buttonholed by King George VI – 'just the man I want to see' – who talked to him about the book for twenty minutes and invited him to stay at Windsor (an event which never transpired because of the King's illness). He then spoke to the Queen and Princess Elizabeth before being 'seized by the arm' and invited to lunch by Churchill, who also wanted to talk about the book. He and Churchill were then joined by Attlee, the Prime Minister. As Harold wrote to Vita, it sounded like 'something one has made up in one's bath.'[10]

Harold never cared for George V. He felt from the beginning that the late King lacked charm and closer acquaintance neither improved nor altered that assessment: 'He is all right as a gay young midshipman. He may be all right as a wise old King. But the intervening period when he was Duke of York ... is hard to manage or swallow. For seventeen years he did nothing but kill animals and stick in stamps.'[11] In this sense, David Cannadine is right, in his 1983 review of Kenneth Rose's *King George V*, when he describes Harold's work as 'more a triumph of will than of empathy, of tact rather than tolerance.'[12] It was also a triumph of wit and command of English that allowed the transformation of the much-quoted passage above into the tactful description of a man who 'lived the life of a private country gentleman, unostentatious, comparatively retired, almost obscure.... When not out shooting, he would play with his children, read aloud to his wife, visit the farms, dairies and pheasantries, go round the kennels and stables.'[13]

At their first meeting, Morshead told Harold that 'the House of Hanover, like ducks, produce bad parents. They trample on their young.'[14] The Earl of Cromer had previously told Harold that the King brought up his children on the basis that 'I was always frightened of my father; they must be frightened of me.'[15] Then Lord Hardinge, a former Assistant Private Secretary to Edward VIII and Private Secretary to George VI, the son of the Lord Hardinge who had filled so many different roles in the Foreign Office, told him that George V was a brute to his children. He would shout at his sons and humiliate them in front of the staff and servants, but the staff and servants themselves never received an unkind word.[16] Here was an issue which could not be ignored and would require careful handling in print – and it certainly did not make the King any more attractive as a personality. It could not be ignored because, although not mentioned in the book, the behaviour of one of those sons had caused the Abdication which, at the time Harold was writing, was thirteen years distant but not forgotten either within the Royal Family or by the public. The published text confronts the issue head on, but, again, with masterly tact.

> Even in this political biography it is necessary – if only to assure the reader that no single issue has been shirked – to make some allusion to the fact that the King failed to establish with his children, at least until they married, those relations of equable and equal companionship that are the solace of old age. How came it that a man, who was by temperament so intensely domestic ... should have inspired his sons with feelings of awe amounting at times to nervous trepidation?[17]

It was not until October 1949 that Harold followed the Duke of Windsor's advice and visited York Cottage. The Duke, he decided, was right. The house did explain the King. Harold did not hide his dismay.

> It was, and remains, a glum little villa, encompassed by thickets of laurel and rhododendron ... enlivened by very imitation Tudor beams.... [The] Doulton tiles and stained glass fanlights are indistinguishable from those of any Surbiton or Upper Norwood home.... This most undesirable residence became [King George V's] favourite home for thirty-three years.[18]

David Cannadine suggests that the lack of sympathy would have been mutual; that Harold's 'intellectual pretensions, Labour Party loyalties and homosexual proclivities would hardly have endeared him to the late King.'[19] While quite possibly true, Harold's task was not to sympathise but to explain. He needed to convey, without belittling or giving offence, the ordinariness of George V's personality. Here was a man whose formal education was lacking; who kept a regular diary for more than fifty years without conveying anything of his inner life; whose greatest secret was apparently that as a young man, 'he used to sleep with a girl in Southsea and another in St John's Wood, whom he shared with his elder brother;'[20] who could be moved to tears by a novel called *Wrong on Both Sides*, 'composed in the revolting manner of *Little Lord Fauntleroy*';[21] who had no musical tastes whatsoever; and who could feel at home in the ugliest surroundings simply because they were familiar. Yet the same man became the acknowledged figurehead and leader of the British Empire at its greatest extent and during the most devastating war in its history; presided over constitutional changes affecting some 48 million people in Britain and some 480 million throughout the Empire as a whole – changes which continue to resonate into the twenty-first century; and ensured the continuation of the British monarchy at a time when most other European kingdoms and empires were disintegrating and making way for republics.

Harold began his research in earnest in January 1949 and wrote the first words that April. Thereafter the book grew steadily, section by section, each part being submitted to Tommy Lascelles, King George VI and Queen Mary as it progressed. At the end of 1949, he noted in his diary: 'I find it a fascinating pursuit and enjoy my work,' but could not resist adding: 'I am conscious that it furnishes me with an excuse for doing nothing else.'[22] Both the structure and style evolved as he wrote. In a letter dated 25 July 1950, he told Vita

> you are right in thinking that I should make my book less documentary and more alive. I shall certainly try at later stages to introduce more vivid pictures of people and places.... But I am sure that in a book of this length it would be a mistake to try and be 'bright'. One has just got to be intelligent. I am enjoying the book, with a purely personal enjoyment. I like the treasure-hunt element in delving into papers.[23]

He finished delving on 8 August 1951 and went up to the top of the Round Tower to celebrate. By 19 September, he had finished the main text. 'I have enjoyed it immensely,' he noted. 'It was hard, hard work, but I think the result is pretty solid. I have a Gibbon feel.'[24] But there was still work to be done – genealogical trees, the index, the illustrations and the checking and correcting of the proofs. It was not until 11 January 1952 that he received a letter from Lascelles saying that King George VI had read the last part and had no revisions to suggest. The manuscript was sent to Constable the same day. It had taken three years.

55 Meanwhile

Before beginning work on the *King George V*, Harold had negotiated an agreement with Constable which would give him a royalty of 2s 6d in the pound, or 12.5%, on each book sold. By the standards of the time, this was a good – though not wildly generous – arrangement, but, of course, he would earn nothing until the book was written and published. In the meantime, he needed to keep himself afloat financially.

Professional life soon settled into a familiar routine. He wrote two weekly articles for the *Observer*: his 'Marginal Comment' and his new book review column – which rapidly grew in popularity, though it never approached the popularity of Vita's gardening column in the same paper.[1] He was so practised by now that his book reviews almost wrote themselves. They read rather formally by today's standards, but, except on rare occasions, they are carefully thought through and, while not uncritical, always manage to say something entertaining and positive. For example, reviewing George Orwell's *1984* (Orwell, as it happened, was another of the *Observer's* lead reviewers), he wrote that the novel had neither 'the high imaginative force of Aldous Huxley's *Brave New World*, or the self-contained logic of Mr. Orwell's own *Animal Farm*.... Inconsistencies of detail prevent our surrendering ourselves wholly to Mr. Orwell's thesis: but it is an excellent thesis none the less.'[2] If he could not find anything positive to say about a book, he simply chose not to review it.

He continued to be a familiar and popular figure on the BBC. He gave his talks on foreign affairs for the Overseas Service and was in demand on both the Home Service and on television for discussion programmes, such as *The Brains Trust*, a precursor to the later *Any Questions*, where a panel of eminent people drawn from politics, academia, the arts and the media gave their views on questions posed by the audience – 'Is knowledge better than wisdom?', 'Ought girls to do national service as well as boys?', 'Is the English sense of humour cyclical?', 'What existing legislation should be repealed?'[3] Among his fellow panellists – giving some indication of how the BBC saw Harold's public status – were Violet Bonham Carter; Noel Annan; Kenneth Clark; the Liberal peer, Lord Samuel; and the philosophers, C. E. M. Joad and Bertrand Russell.

During the writing of *King George V*, Harold tried to cut down his lecturing commitments, mainly on the grounds that they tended to take him away from London and thus took up too much time. The principles – or feelings – that had led him to join the Labour Party were still in evidence insofar as he preferred to lecture to audiences that were predominantly working class: a preference which led him to the East End of London and to audiences with a large number of West Indian immigrants whom he doubted understood his views on tolerance and the democratic state. An exception to this self-imposed rule was a trip to Switzerland in May 1949 when he lectured at Lausanne, Geneva and Zurich. In the audience at Lausanne, he found the Scottish-born former Queen of Spain, Victoria Eugénie (or Ena), who had been living in exile since 1931. She had known Harold's father when he was Ambassador in Madrid at the time of her marriage to King Alfonso XIII in 1906, and she remembered Harold himself who had been formally presented to her as a very junior diplomat in 1911.

Harold also continued with his many committees, particularly the National Trust, which he greatly enjoyed and which provoked at least one bizarre experience. Following the death of George Bernard Shaw, Harold and James Lees-Milne, who was at the time Secretary of the National Trust's Country House Committee, visited Shaw's house at Ayot St Lawrence in Hertfordshire, which he had bequeathed to the Trust. Shaw had been cremated only two weeks previously and his ashes, mixed with those of his wife, had been deposited in spoonfuls on the flowerbeds and paths of the garden. Harold considered bringing some of Shaw back to the garden at Sissinghurst in an envelope, but decided that the idea might be in bad taste.

One feature of the three years he spent writing *King George V* was Harold's gradual loss of interest in politics. Foreign affairs continued to fascinate him. Like everyone else, he followed the events of the Korean War and worried about its potential to escalate into another global conflict; he was concerned when the Iranian Prime Minister, Mosaddegh, nationalised the Anglo-Iranian Oil Company; but, though he continued to give his BBC talks on foreign affairs and though they were no less incisive, it is clear that such matters occupied less of his time and less of his mind than in the past. As for domestic and party politics – which had never been his strongest suit – he ceased to take any active part whatsoever. He veered between deciding that joining the Labour Party was the worst mistake of his life and voting Labour in the elections because 'I am really unhappy deep inside about the condition of my beloved country.'[4] He was concerned that Herbert Morrison, who took over from Bevin as Foreign Secretary in March 1951, was not sufficiently experienced in foreign affairs for the job. He recorded the hopes and expectations of the Labour Government in the run-up to the 1950 election. He noted Harold Wilson's resignation from the Cabinet in April 1951. But it was little more than a passing interest.

His real domestic political interest was Nigel, who between February 1950 and February 1952 fought as a Conservative candidate in three elections, in three different constituencies. Harold followed his son's political fortunes keenly, any remaining Labour principles overridden by family loyalty. The 1950 general election was held early in the year. It is measure of how far Harold was already removed from the political consciousness of the nation that he received only a handful of requests to comment on the issues and the inter-party arguments of the campaign – and these he declined because, with Nigel now standing as Conservative candidate in West Leicester, he felt that anything he said was likely to be picked up and inflated or misrepresented by the press in order to create a story. Vita's letters to Nigel provide an interesting sidelight on the campaign: they positively cluck with solicitude. She sent him honey, a cake, ginger biscuits and a tin of turkey, and she promised to come up to Leicester 'at any moment' if he wanted – an attitude very far removed from the one she displayed when Harold was fighting the same seat.[5] Polling day was 23 February and there was a massive turnout of over 83%, which has never been equalled since. Despite a significant swing to the Conservatives which reduced the Labour majority to just five seats, Nigel was heavily defeated. It was hardly a surprise. Harold, listening to the results at the Dorchester Hotel in London, at a glittering party hosted by Lord Rothermere, felt 'sick for a moment, but not really shattered' and then returned to his champagne.[6]

The second Labour Government lasted only eighteen months. Nigel, having shown himself a credible candidate in Leicester, was offered the chance to contest Falmouth. A new constituency in 1950, it had a Labour majority of just under 2,000, so there was a realistic chance of winning. Polling day was 25 October 1951. Harold spent the night at the BBC giving a series of commentaries for the Overseas Service on the progress of the election results. He left at 4 a.m. but was back at Broadcasting House by 10.30. Soon after midday, it was evident that the Tories would have a majority and that the Liberal Party was crumbling. His hopes rose, but, when it came, Nigel's result left him 'sick at heart.'[7] Nigel had cut the Labour majority by half, but still failed to take the seat. Harold continued broadcasting updates on the Overseas Service until late that afternoon when the final shape of the new Parliament was clear. Less than a month short of his sixty-fifth birthday, his stamina was undiminished.

Before the end of the year, Harold's disappointment turned to joy when Nigel was adopted as the candidate for Bournemouth East and Christchurch. A bye-election had become necessary because, with the return of Churchill as Prime Minister, the sitting MP, Brendan Bracken, had been offered a seat in the House of Lords. Bournemouth was an entirely different kind of constituency: the safest of safe Conservative seats. In 1950, Bracken's majority had been nearly 15,000. In 1951, it had risen to 17,500. Polling day, 6 February 1952, was complicated by the announcement of the sudden death of King George VI. Harold, who had gone down to Bournemouth to support Nigel, seems to have been less worried about the King than the possibility that Conservative voters might stay at home out of shock. In the event, Nigel was elected with a majority just short of 14,000 and in his victory speech was able to claim that he was the first MP to be elected in the reign of Queen Elizabeth II. Harold was 'wild with relief'[8] and two weeks later watched proudly from the Strangers' Gallery as Nigel took his seat in the House of Commons.

Ben's progress through life was, as ever, less dramatic. In 1949, he had resigned as Deputy Surveyor of the King's Pictures and decided to devote himself full time to the *Burlington Magazine*. The following year, he moved out of Neville Terrace into a flat in St George's Square, Pimlico. This was not so much a bid for independence – he was thirty-five at the time[9] – as the next stage in his slow, deliberate and single-minded pursuit of his career as art historian and editor of the *Burlington*, which was to last until his death in 1968. Time spent at I Tatti in the 1930s had been an inspiration to Ben, but now, set on his course, not even the disapproval of Bernard Berenson, who told Harold and Vita that Ben was 'wasting his energies on the *Burlington*' could deflect him.[10] Neither Harold nor Vita ever really understood what motivated Ben; nor do they seem to have taken in the immense respect in which he was held by the London and, as time went on, by the European art world. On the whole, Harold was more accepting of Ben's self-absorbed approach to life and was rewarded with a deep and enduring affection. With Vita, however, the relationship was one of alternating highs and lows: with Ben feeling that she was trying to invade his world and she that he was locking her out.

Vita herself was a cause for concern. In March 1950, after a cardiograph, her doctor warned her not to overtax herself. She took sufficient notice of the warning to take a short break at Violet Trefusis' house in Saint-Loup-de-Naud in northern France, but immediately on her return chased off to Durham to receive an Honorary Doctorate. Shortly afterwards, there was a reception to celebrate fifty years of the Wallace Collection, which had been established in Hertford House in Marylebone by Sir John Murray Scott, Lady Sackville's admirer. For once, Vita agreed to attend a London event – though she had to borrow an evening dress – but, accordingly to James Pope-Hennessey, she looked 'very blue and ill'. The following weekend,

Pope-Hennessey was at Sissinghurst – as was Violet, with whom all fences were now mended – but, again, Vita looked 'amazingly, frighteningly ill'.[11] How much of this did Harold realise or understand? Certainly, Vita tried to keep it from him – and he could be immensely unobservant at times – but it was also part of the privacy they allowed each other within their relationship that such things were never discussed if one of them did not want to. Only in August, when Vita told him that she was writing another novel, did Harold put on paper the fact that he was aware of her poor state of health and his concern that writing another novel would add to the strain and anxiety she was already suffering. Violet certainly realised Vita was unwell and persuaded them both to visit her in Italy later that summer.

Violet had a car, a Fiat, in France, which she wanted to sell in Italy. The plan was for Harold and Vita to cross to St Loup and drive south in Violet's car, meeting up with her in Florence and then staying at L'Ombrellino, a beautiful villa overlooking Florence, which was owned by her parents – and which appealed to Harold because Galileo had once lived there. Given the past, the idea of Harold sharing a holiday with Violet or Violet sharing a holiday with him might seem strange, but they had both mellowed and Harold had a great ability to forgive. Normally, Vita, who loved driving, would have driven all the way unassisted – Harold disliked driving and was not very good at it on the occasions he tried – but she was under orders not to tire herself and so asked Copper, the Sissinghurst chauffeur, to accompany them. They drove through Paris and headed south-east towards Dijon. From Dijon, they drove to the Val d'Isère, crossing into Italy via the Col du Mont Cenis and Susa, west of Turin. They stayed a night in Alessandria and then moved on to Rapallo, where Harold realised that he had left a document case with his passport and the longhand manuscript of three chapters of *King George V* in Alessandria. The papers were never recovered. For another writer, this might have proved disastrous, but Harold's comprehensive notes, his clarity of mind and the speed at which he wrote meant that it was little more than a setback. He seems to have been more worried about the public demonstration of his incompetence than the loss itself.

Their week in Florence was relaxed, but still sociable. Bernard Berenson, now eighty-five, invited them to spend a day at Casa al Dono near Vallombrosa, a summer retreat which was in fact owned by his private secretary, Nicky Mariano. It was at Casa al Dono that they heard that Sibyl Colefax had died. The age when she and Emerald Cunard, the two great hostesses, had dominated London society was long past: Sibyl had been in a wheelchair and very frail when Harold and Vita had last seen her.

Nonetheless, Harold had been fond of her and her death was a genuine shock. Looking forward rather than backwards, the same day also saw Nicky Mariano introduce the Nicolsons to another Berenson protégé, a girl called Luisa Vertova, whom Ben was later to marry. Another engagement was lunch with the writer and historian, Harold Acton, who lived in the remarkable fifteenth-century Villa La Pietra, just outside Florence and whom, perhaps surprisingly, Harold had never previously met. The warmth of Italy, the relaxed atmosphere, and the easy circumstances of their friends were a relief after the stresses, strains and rationing of post-war Britain, so when they returned to England, by train, at the end of September, they both felt refreshed. Vita's health had recovered and she began to write *The Easter Party* while Harold returned to *King George V* with a renewed sense of purpose – but there were further difficulties ahead.

Christmas at Sissinghurst was always a family affair. Both Harold and Vita preferred it that way – and it was, in any case, difficult to ask guests to stay when the accommodation was spread throughout the garden in such an unconventional and, to most people, inconvenient way. Christmas 1950, however, was different: they had a guest, the novelist, Rose Macaulay, and, not content with having a guest, they even gave a cocktail party for her to meet local friends. The initiative, surprisingly, seems to have been Vita's, but although successful – she was sorry when Rose Macaulay left – it was not repeated.

At the beginning of the new year, Harold's mother became seriously ill. After the war, she had returned to London from Cornwall and taken a small house in Tedworth Square, Chelsea, where she lived with Harold's eldest brother, Freddy, who, for some years, had been sinking into alcoholism. Now, in her nineties, she was diabetic and both her sight and her memory were failing. It was obvious that she would not last much longer. Her illness and the subsequent family upheavals laid bare a never-quite-resolved area of difference between Harold and Vita.

Vita never responded to the concept of duty or responsibility, whether to family or to larger entities such as society or nation: her motivation was always emotional. Her relationship with her mother had been hugely, even violently, emotional. Her attitude and actions during the Second World War were determined by love of England and hatred of Germany, not by any moral sense that she *should* work to defend the country. Harold was almost the opposite. He was not an unemotional man – far from it – but, whether from heredity, upbringing or education, he did not believe in displaying or indulging his emotions. Loyalty, honour and duty, however, were concepts which evoked a powerful response in him, motivated his diplomatic and political careers and also guided his relationship with his parents. This was something Vita could never understand.

Vita had had a kind of respect for Harold's father. Small, elderly, and charming, he made no demands on her; and, as she says in her contribution to the Epilogue of *Lord Carnock*, 'He was impressive, not insignificant.'[12] Lady Carnock, by contrast, was not impressive. In Vita's eyes, she was old-fashioned, lacked assertiveness, and her attitudes were 'bedint.' Vita's views on her parents-in-law were identical to those Lady Sackville had expressed on meeting the Nicolsons for the first time in 1912 – and they only changed insofar as her resentment of Lady Carnock deepened as the old lady aged and the demands she made on Harold increased.

'My mother is too pathetic for words,' Harold wrote on 17 January 1951. 'She just sits and cries.' Tedworth Square was only a short walk from Neville Terrace and he visited every day to sit by his mother's beside. Gwen was also there every day and she engaged a nurse so Lady Carnock need never be left alone. Both Harold and Gwen found that worse than waiting for their mother to die was watching their brother disintegrate. Freddy was already an alcoholic, but with the decline of his mother he lost any self-control he had ever possessed. Every evening he would go to the Anglesea Arms in Selwood Terrace or the Cooper's Arms in Flood Street and drink until he had to be carried home. It was a horrible time. Harold told Vita and the boys to keep away. He felt it would be worse if they saw 'the ugliness of it all'. He was 'not unhappy. Only ashamed and hurt and disgusted.' And he wanted to hide his shame.[13] Vita did make one visit to Tedworth Square before the end. It was 'all pretty grim – Freddy drunk downstairs, and his mother dying upstairs.' She took Harold off to the Victoria and Albert Museum and to Kew Gardens to try and cheer him up, but the weather was cold and rainy.[14] Nevertheless, he was grateful for her visit.

Lady Carnock died on Good Friday, 23 March, and was cremated on 28 March. Harold wrote a letter to Vita in which attempted facetiousness fails to mask his emotions – 'My dear old Mummy is no more than a handful of dust. I dislike having ceased suddenly to be anybody's son.'[15] Lady Carnock's ashes were buried in the St Levan family chapel on St Michael's Mount. Harold, Vita, Ben and Nigel all travelled down to Cornwall for the ceremony. It was the only time Vita ever visited St Michael's Mount. Under other circumstances, one would have expected the romance of the Mount, with its tidal causeway, its castle and its long history to have appealed to her, but relations with Gwen remained strained – another family tension of which Harold, who was closer to his sister than to his two brothers, was very conscious – and she never returned.

Lady Carnock's death was not the end of family problems. Freddy could no longer look after himself and was temporarily removed to a nursing home. To Harold, the obvious solution was for Freddy to move into that part of Neville Terrace vacated by Ben a few months earlier, but Vita 'was hotly against it; she said it was too much for [Harold], not fair on Nigel, and that the Parrotts – the couple who looked after the household – would leave.'[16] Yet, at the same time, she wrote to Harold that she had offered the novelist, Ivy Compton-Burnett, a refuge at Sissinghurst if she needed it. Compton-Burnett had recently lost her long-time companion, Margaret Jourdain, and Vita said she could not bear to think of her grief and loneliness. This provoked an extraordinary outburst from Harold, not simply contrasting the care and generosity she displayed towards her friends with her indifference to his relatives, but also contrasting himself and Vita in class terms, associating her with aristocratic indifference and himself with middle class humanity. It is a dispute that seems as if it should belong to a younger relationship, not to a couple approaching their thirty-eighth wedding anniversary. And it suggests also some kind of unhealed wound or unresolved inferiority complex on Harold's part.

> Mar has no sense of family obligation. I suppose it is a bedint rather than an aristocratic feeling. You toffs think so much about Norman blood that you forget about the wretched Freddies and Aunt Amys of this world. Anyhow I do not think Freddy will live for long. I want to feel if he dies that I have done something at least to render the last stage of his life less horribly miserable than it threatens to be. But why does Mar get into such a state about Ivy Compton-Burnett; why is she such an angel to the Trouts, Mrs Carey, Mrs Lamon, and old Mrs Drummond; why does she fuss about sending flowers to Elvira's Mum: – when she has no feeling at all about Aunt Cecilie and never thought for one moment of sending flowers to my Mum.

He was undoubtedly very angry, and his attempt to conclude on a more affectionate note – 'But I love you for it none the less' – is thoroughly unconvincing.[17] Freddy was eventually moved into the ground floor of Neville Terrace in July. Between them, Harold, Nigel, the Parrotts and a male nurse coped with his continuing decline.

Domestic harmony appears to have been re-established. In May 1951, they visited the newly-opened South Bank Exhibition, part of the Festival of Britain and designed to celebrate Britain's recovery from the war, as well as commemorating the centenary of Prince Albert's Great Exhibition of 1851.

Dominated by the ultra-modern Skylon Tower, the aluminium and concrete Dome of Discovery and the uncompromisingly modernist Royal Festival Hall, and with contemporary murals and a public funfair thrown in, it was not – at least on the face of it – the kind of event calculated to appeal to the Nicolsons. Nevertheless, they were both 'entranced from the first moment' and, although, as Harold recorded, 'it is rather a nuisance that we keep on running into the King and Queen', they enjoyed themselves 'uproariously'.[18] Harold's 'Marginal Comment' column following the visit is possibly the most upbeat of his career.

There was still an undercurrent of uncertainty in their relationship. The following month, Harold was deeply shocked by the defection of Guy Burgess and Donald Maclean '(1) because it shames my dear old profession; (2) because it will make everyone suspicious of quite innocent people; (3) because it will enrage the Americans; (4) because I fear poor Guy will be rendered very unhappy in the end.'[19] The incident depressed him so much that Vita became worried and he had to reassure her. 'No, my darling,' he wrote on 12 June, 'I am not hiding anything from you. I have not become involved in a spy ring nor have I become connected in any way with Guy's disreputable habits.'[20] Nonetheless, the fact that Vita could think it possible tells its own story.

Life continued. That autumn, before he finished the main text of *King George V*, they took a ten-day holiday in the West Country, touring National Trust properties and their gardens. In January 1952, just days after *King George V* had been sent to the printers, Harold set off to lecture in Copenhagen, which he had visited only once before, in 1928. He found it 'a graceful city' and particularly enjoyed a visit to Elsinore.[21] His host, a Danish brewer called Jerichow, was convinced that Shakespeare had visited the Danish Court with a company of English players. Returning home just long enough to see Nigel elected, he was off again – this time on a British Council-sponsored lecture tour of Italy and Greece. In Italy, he was concerned that his lecture – 'The Old Diplomacy and the New', the same one he had given in Copenhagen – did not go well because his audience could not decide whether he was being flippant or serious. In Greece, he lectured on 'Constitutional Monarchy' in Athens, met the Prime Minister, paid a visit to Delphi and went on to Salonika to lecture at the university there on 'Nature in Greek Poetry'. This was the lecture he had previously given in Liverpool as President of the Classical Association and it had also featured as a radio talk the previous year. The Ambassador in Rome was Sir Victor Mallet who had been in the Embassy in Stockholm when Harold had made his wartime visit to Sweden in 1943. The Ambassador in Athens was

Meanwhile

Sir Charles Peake who had been a close colleague at the Ministry of Information. Did Harold ever wonder what might have been? Back in London, he took part in a series of radio discussions. One involved the French writer and inventor of Maigret, Georges Simenon; another was with the novelist, Sir Compton Mackenzie, with whom Harold discussed getting old. Then he was off again, this time to Paris, to lecture at the Sorbonne.

As Harold had predicted, Freddy did not have long to live. He died at the end of May. He was only four years older than Harold. His military career had begun promisingly enough: he had been ADC to the Viceroy of India, Lord Hardinge, between 1911 and 1912 and had been decorated for bravery during the First World War. Leaving the army in 1919, he had studied law and been called to the bar, but his legal career had never taken off and his later years had been a study in failure and disappointment. Caring for his mother had been his only real purpose in life and when she died, Freddy fell apart. Harold was thrown into a reflective mood.

> I walk with Viti in the garden after dinner when all the half-light plays upon the flowers. It is peace unutterable, but in my heart there is great sorrow for Freddy. There ought to be relief, I suppose, that he is eased of all his loneliness and self-contempt, and that he died without suffering. ... I feel an aching pity for him.... Why should I live in such beauty and surrounded by so many affections and interests, when poor old Freddy (who never thought an unkind thought about anyone) was condemned to a life so ineffective and miserable?[22]

He hated the whole idea of growing old and losing his physical and mental agility. In his radio discussion with Sir Compton Mackenzie, he had called it the greatest of human tragedies. And his mood was not lightened when, just a few days later, he heard of the death of his old friend Desmond MacCarthy.

If anything positive could be salvaged from Freddy's death, it was that Harold and Nigel could now leave the hated house in Neville Terrace. The leasehold of flat C1, Albany, Piccadilly, had become vacant. Harold and Nigel were to share it with John Sparrow, who was practising law at that time but was shortly to become Warden of All Souls' College, Oxford. The move took place in July. The Albany was everything that Neville Terrace was not. An eighteenth-century mansion, built round a courtyard and divided into flats, it had long been the preserve of a particular social elite: past inhabitants included Lord Byron, Lord Macaulay, Lord Curzon and Herbert Beerbohm Tree.[23] It was, in effect, a particularly high-class club and

Harold loved it. It remained his London base until 1965 when a combination of age, infirmity and lack of money caused him to give it up and retire to Sissinghurst.

At the end of July 1952, Harold received three copies of *King George V* from the printers. It was a substantial and well-produced volume of 570 pages, with dark blue covers and a gold 'GR V' monogram on the front. Harold sent copies to Queen Elizabeth II, who had come to the throne that February, and to the Queen Mother, then went to Marlborough House in person to present the third copy to Queen Mary. King George V's widow was now eighty-five. Queen for twenty-five years and Queen Mother (though she never used the title) for a further sixteen, she had devoted her life to upholding the dignity of the Royal Family and its position in British society. She used the word 'dignified' to describe Harold's book and signed the copy he had brought with him, adding the inscription: 'This is a noble work about my dear husband.'[24]

Two weeks later, on 14 August, *King George V* was published to almost universal acclaim. A *Times* leader; two pages in the *Manchester Guardian*; paeans of praise from the left-leaning Kingsley Martin in the *New Statesman* and the right-leaning Duff Cooper in the *Daily Telegraph*; a huge article in the *News Chronicle*. A letter of praise from the new Queen; praise from Lord Samuel, who had twice been Home Secretary under George V; from the old-school historian G. M. Trevelyan; from the novelist, Nancy Mitford; from his good friends, the often pedantic Raymond Mortimer and the frequently contrary James Pope-Hennessey. It was a concentrated outburst of recognition and praise such as few writers ever experience. Only the Glasgow MP, Walter Elliott, expressed reservations in the *Observer*, but even then he sounded irritable rather than critical; and Hugh Trevor-Roper, a persistent critic of Harold's, grumpily asserted that the book was 'Royal hagiography', though he admitted that he had not read it.[25] The public responded and despite a price of two guineas – at a time when an office worker's wage was approximately £11 6s[26] – 10,000 copies were sold in the two weeks after publication and over 25,000 in the first year.

It was the kind of recognition Harold had always claimed he wanted – based on solid intellectual and literary effort, but he was rapidly developing a contrary strain of his own. 'I suppose I ought to feel elated,' he wrote. 'But somehow I am rather indifferent and do not feel any inner feelings of satisfaction. Christabel [Maclaren] says it is due to my "loss of vitality". Yes, I am becoming an old man.'[27]

David Cannadine has written that

Nicolson's book in particular did as much to confirm George's reputation as a good king as it did to confirm his own reputation as a good writer, and established a model for royal biography successfully followed by Lady Longford on Queen Victoria, Sir Philip Magnus on Edward VII, Lady Donaldson on Edward VIII, James Pope-Hennessy on Queen Mary and Sir John Wheeler-Bennett on George VI.[28]

Which is praise indeed. Yet there is a sense in which time has not been kind to *King George V*. Harold's careful reticence and his studied tact in the face of difficult issues satisfied the Royal Family at the time. It also satisfied critical opinion and the general public, but does it satisfy readers of a later generation?

Attitudes to the Royal Family have changed since 1952 and one cannot ask writers to anticipate such changes. Harold was a gentleman who would never have wished to give offence; and at the time he was writing George V's widow was still alive and his son still on the throne. For all that, he did at least acknowledge (even if he did not pursue) areas of difficulty in George V's character, tastes, and behaviour towards his children in a way that would not have been acceptable a generation previously. In that sense, *King George V* marked a step forward in royal biography, though the fact that the Royal Family objected to very little that Harold wrote suggests that he was hardly pushing at the boundaries. As a constitutional and political history of the reign, its main focus, *King George V* remains a remarkable (and remarkably readable) achievement, but later generations will undoubtedly find a stiffness in Harold's handling of the character of the monarch and aspects of his personal relations; and, for all Harold's professed lack of sympathy for his subject, they will detect the scent of hagiography. That is probably inevitable. Harold was a man of his time: he was born into the Empire of Queen Victoria and grew to manhood in the reign of the King Emperor. As a diplomat and then a politician, he worked within the structures of the Empire. His attitude to the monarchy was in some ways analogous to his attitude to the Foreign Office. He saw its faults and disliked some of its attitudes, but it was an accepted part of the national framework he had always known and he could not imagine life without it. Compared with Kenneth Rose's book of the same name, Harold's *King George V* certainly seems a little too respectful, a little lacking in the investigative impulse, but Rose was born nearly forty years after Harold and he was writing in the 1980s. Times had changed.

56 Reward

The publication of *King George V* did not mark the end of Harold's career, but with hindsight it did mark the beginning of the end. At the time, at the age of sixty-five, he seemed to stand on the pinnacle of success. The chorus of praise was so loud and so widespread that he gloomily expected a critical reaction to set in, but it never did. That May, before publication, Harold had asserted that his 'life's work was finished.'[1] This seems to have been no more than one of his regular bouts of pessimism and he was, in any case, plainly wrong. He had at least eight years of active working life left: he would continue to publish books, give his radio talks, write articles and reviews, and travel. All the same, there was a change – or rather, a failure to change.

Harold had already achieved membership of the great and the good. The next few months and years saw his transition to the status of national treasure – but that, in Britain, is a two-edged sword. The recognition is genuine enough, but there is an implication that those who attain such national recognition must have passed the peak of their achievement. It is not a status accorded to those who promise great things in the future. Harold was no longer striving to be other than he was. He remained both active and energetic, but – while he continued to work hard at the things that interested him – he showed less interest in new ideas: he had lost his sense of ambition. That is not necessarily a criticism. By anybody's standards, he had led an active and interesting life and, by most standards other than his own, he had been highly successful. He claimed not to be elated by his success, but he certainly enjoyed public and institutional recognition, and now, in his mid-sixties, it was natural that he should pursue familiar paths and seek to enjoy them. It would be harsh to suggest that someone so busy, someone who, between 1955 and 1962, would publish five books of widely differing kinds, was resting on his laurels, but it became progressively true – at least by comparison with his previous life.

Immediately after publication day, while letters of congratulation were still arriving and fulsome reviews still appearing, Harold and Vita set off on another National Trust tour. They visited Wales and Northern Ireland, returning via Yorkshire and Norfolk. In Northern Ireland, they stayed at Clandeboye. It was Vita's first and indeed only visit. For Harold, it was a special place, redolent of childhood holidays, of his mother and her family – the kind of memories recalled in the early pages of *The Desire to Please*. Vita, however, took against it on sight, finding the house ugly and the furniture and paintings disappointing. Of course, it did not compare with Knole, but one senses again that unresolved area: Vita's unwillingness to allow Harold's family background any status or validity equal to her own. Harold, no doubt, sensed it, too, but this time there was no explosion – but perhaps he was making a point when, as they were on the point of leaving, he disappeared and was found rolling down a big grassy bank in the garden, just as he had done as a child, getting grass stains on his suit in the process.

While on tour, Harold received a letter from Tommy Lascelles telling him that the Queen wished to offer him a KCVO.[2] This provoked another unedifying outburst of *angst* over titles and status. Harold did not want a knighthood and had, at some stage, intimated as much to Lascelles. Lascelles wanted to know if he would change his mind. Harold and Vita thought a knighthood was 'bedint' and middle class and considered turning it down, but – of course – he eventually found a formula which allowed him to accept . 'I quite see,' he wrote to Lascelles, 'that after the reception the book has had, [a lesser award] might suggest to people that my biography had not been accorded full royal approval. To maintain my objections might be considered churlish and embarrassing.'[3]

He was appointed KCVO in the New Year's Honours for 1953. In his diary he noted that Eustace Percy, with whom he had joined the Diplomatic Service forty-two years previously, was now Lord Percy, and grumbled that

> a knighthood is a pitiful business, putting me in the third eleven. I know that the KCVO is not supposed to be an assessment of my contribution to life, but rather a present from the Queen for a service to the Monarchy. But other people do not realise that.... So one is really much more snobbish and vain than one imagines.[4]

Yes, would seem the only possible answer.

Was the Queen told of Harold's reservations? In February, he went to Buckingham Palace for his investiture. After she had placed the sword first on his left shoulder and then on his right, she told him, 'This is a personal present.'[5]

King George V established Harold in the royal orbit. Even before publication, in August 1952, the Queen Mother had paid a visit to Sissinghurst and spent an afternoon walking in the garden. Then in March 1953, the Duke of Windsor invited Harold to lunch and asked him for help in writing an article on constitutional monarchy. Harold was amazed that the Duke, of all people, should have been commissioned to write on the subject, but he took the manuscript away and made a number of suggestions and corrections. The article, expanded to a short book, was published the following year as *The Crown and the People 1902–1953*. Just a few days after his lunch with the Duke, Harold and Vita travelled down to Windsor where they attended the funeral of Queen Mary in St George's Chapel. In June, however, for the Coronation of Queen Elizabeth II, they went to the Traveller's Club and watched the service in Westminster Abbey on television. Harold was 'much moved.'[6] It all suggests a remarkable degree of involvement for a man who claimed to regard the monarchy as no more than a useful institution.

In the wake of the knighthood, other honours came thick and fast. He was asked to speak at the annual dinner of the Royal Academy, an event which did not go particularly well. Surprisingly, given his immense experience of public speaking, Harold was nervous – though the fact that he had to follow not only Field Marshal Alexander, Supreme Commander in the Mediterranean during the war and now Governor General of Canada, but also Winston Churchill, cannot have helped. He was awarded Honorary Doctorates from King's College Durham, University College Dublin and the University of Glasgow – actually receiving these necessitated criss-crossing the country and much ceremonial – and he was elected an Honorary Fellow of his old college, Balliol. Harold had neither distinguished himself nor greatly enjoyed his years there as an undergraduate, but his Fellowship was now 'of all honours this earth ... the one I most desire.'[7] Oxford, and Balliol in particular, provoked an emotional, even sentimental, response.

In his writing, in his public life and even in his personal life, Harold was shy of expressing his emotions directly – even with Vita, he often found it easier to express his feelings in letters than face to face – but that does not mean he was unemotional. On the contrary, his emotions ran deep, but he felt more comfortable expressing them through the indirect codes of language and behaviour that his character, upbringing and education dictated. In this respect, it may be that the diaries, on which we rely for so much of our understanding of his life, give a misleading impression of how much of his feelings he actually gave away in day-to-day contact. Yet, as Harold aged, his emotional side began to express itself more directly, often in the form of sentimentality, until, in the last years of his life when senility had taken hold, he had almost no control over his emotions at all and would burst into tears at the slightest provocation – even watching football on television, despite his lack of interest in or knowledge of the sport. Balliol was almost guaranteed to provoke an emotional response; so, too, were children and anything connected with his mother.

Reward

On 30 March 1953, quite unexpectedly, Nigel rang up to say that he was engaged to Philippa Tennyson-d'Eyncourt. Harold and Vita were delighted. Philippa's first visit to Sissinghurst a few days later was carefully choreographed by Nigel. He conducted her round the garden and then introduced her first to Harold and then to Vita. Everyone appears to have been nervous. Harold's good nature and enthusiasm carried him through, but Vita had been drinking to calm her nerves and became flustered and muddled. In the event, the initial awkwardness passed off quickly and Philippa became a much-loved member of the family and a great support to Harold in his old age. For all that, Harold's assessment of his future daughter-in-law, contained in a letter to Ben, shows him in a peculiarly old-fashioned light. Philippa was 'very pretty in a rather chocolate box way ... not in the least bedint.... Obviously straight and reliable and competent and decent. Not clever in the intellectual sense ... [but] enormously presentable.'[8] There is nothing wrong with any parent wanting a suitable partner for their offspring, but Harold's reaction is both patronising and snobbish. As James Lees-Milne (no wild social progressive himself) says, what reason was there to suppose that she should be 'bedint'?[9] And if his initial reaction to his daughter-in-law showed him as old-fashioned, his subsequent conversation with her father made him seem completely out-of-date. Walking in the garden at Sissinghurst with Sir Eustace Gervais Tennyson-d'Eyncourt, he raised the question of a dowry, to be told firmly – and correctly – that dowries went out with the First World War.[10]

Nigel and Philippa were married in the sixteenth-century elegance of St Margaret's, Westminster, on 30 July 1953. The reception was held in Fishmongers' Hall, the Livery Hall belonging to the Worshipful Company of Fishmongers, of which Philippa's father was a member and, later, Prime Warden. Nigel gave a speech which reduced both Harold and Vita to tears.

It was not all unsullied happiness: Harold managed to work himself into an emotional state over the issue of Lady Carnock's emeralds. Many years previously, his mother had been presented with a gift of emeralds by the Shah Nasr-ed-Din. She had had them made into a choker which she gave to Vita, but Vita never liked it, quite possibly because it came from Harold's mother, and had only ever worn it once – when she attended the coronation of Reza Shah during Harold's time in Persia. The idea was that the emeralds should now be passed on to Philippa, but Harold suddenly took it into his head to resent the fact that the gift should come from Vita, who had never cared for his mother or for the emeralds. After much agonising, he decided that, although the emeralds were Vita's, he should be the one to give them to Philippa and he wrote a letter saying that he wanted her 'to look at them as a present from my mother.' He confessed that he was 'rather sensitive about my dear mother and like to think that you will remember at least *about* her when you put this jewel round your lovely neck.'[11] It would hardly have mattered if Harold had not made such heavy weather of it and if it did not, again, point to the unresolved tension between himself and Vita about his family.

That October, when Nigel announced that Philippa was expecting a child, Harold's reaction was – predictably and naturally – one of great delight, yet there is something in the tone of his letter to her which is not natural.

> Now, horrible, sordid and ignorant as this remark may seem, the same experience has revealed itself to 240,000,003 women, even during this present year. I know this is not the same. Other babies are just population statistics, but this one is endowed with beauty, power, a lovely singing voice, profound domestic affections and a good eye for a horse.
> ... I may perhaps be allowed to murmur that the same thing *has* occurred before in the history of mankind.[12]

Harold's characteristic irony has become facetiousness and his wit has become a forced jocularity. The same tone permeates another letter to Philippa written that Christmas: 'By this morning's post I received your Christmas present – six handkerchiefs of white samite, mystic, wonderful, which will be preserved for those great occasions when I dine with Emperors and Princes or Queen Mothers or Mrs Henry Channon.'[13] There can be no doubt of the genuineness of Harold's feelings for Philippa, but it is as if, having fought shy of expressing emotion for so long, he is not quite sure how to manage it without embarrassing himself and so hides behind ponderous linguistic bravado.

Nigel's marriage meant that he moved out of the Albany flat, his place being taken by a young man called Colin Fenton, whom Harold had met while dining at All Soul's with John Sparrow. Between them, Sparrow and Fenton played an important role in looking after Harold in his London life as he grew older. Harold struggled at first with Nigel's absence, but consoled himself in the conventional manner that Nigel had his own life to live and that he himself had gained a daughter-in-law and that there would be grandchildren. Nonetheless, it took a few months for him to adjust to the new situation.

Part of the problem was that, after *King George V*, Harold needed another project. He continued to be busy and to write: one June day in 1953, he wrote a review of Samuel Butler, an obituary notice for the *Observer* in case Winston Churchill should die, and a radio talk – 5,000 words in all. But this was all rather routine. He gave up his 'Marginal Comment' column in the *Spectator* at the end of 1952, explaining to the horrified editor that the strain of finding new subjects – he had written 670 columns in all – was greater than writing his book reviews for the *Observer*, which he proposed to continue. In 1953, he was invited to deliver Oxford University's Chichele Lectures, named after a fifteenth-century archbishop and given under the auspices of All Soul's College, where John Sparrow was Warden. The four lectures on 'The Evolution of Diplomatic Method' took up some of his time that autumn. Delivered in November 1953, and published in book form the following year, they form a closely-argued account of the evolution of diplomacy from Ancient Greece to the first half of the twentieth century and they show Harold's total grasp of his subject and his material, but, again, this was familiar ground.

The project which eventually emerged was *Good Behaviour*, a survey of the origins and development of manners. It was published in September 1955 and dedicated 'To Juliet, aged one', Harold and Vita's first grandchild, whose appearance, in June 1954, had been greeted with great joy and made Harold feel, for a short while at least, 'thirty years younger.'[14] By Harold's standards, *Good Behaviour* had a long gestation. He had had the idea for the book and started making notes as early as October 1952, but the idea refused to take shape until December 1953 when he woke to find that 'the plan of my book on Manners has suddenly become quite clear during the night.'[15] Even then, it took him a full year to write – including the obligatory period of disillusion and depression half-way through – and the final draft was not completed until the very end of 1954.

After the formality of *King George V*, *Good Behaviour* marks a return to a more relaxed and personal style. The authorial 'I' returns and the narrative is full of odd digressions and personal reminiscences – memories of the families with whom he stayed while studying German in the years before the First World War; a description of the coronation of Reza Shah in Persia in 1926; memories of his grandmother describing the life of a young girl in the Victorian era. The narrative obviously rests on a vast amount of research and scholarship, but there is no sense of strain or indigestion. It is a quirky, entertaining read – written, Harold observes, in a 'mood of inquisitive and benevolent optimism'[16] – and reviewers remarked on the ease of Harold's style, which rather annoyed him since he had always, and with some justification, prided himself on his prose style.

The problem with *Good Behaviour* is that in many ways it is too personal.

Harold Nicolson

Its subtitle, *A Study in Certain Types of Civility*, suggests selection, and indeed Harold selects just those types of civility he understands and which interest him. He does not disguise this – quite the reverse. The opening sentence states that the book 'is neither a social history nor a manual on etiquette.'[17] He makes it clear that he has chosen to ignore 'the mass manners of the United States'[18] because 'there are certain elements in American civilisation which, as a European, I find it impossible to understand,'[19] and, in the chapter on the manners of the Far East, he states unambiguously that 'my ignorance of the subject is unredeemed by any glow of sympathy, any impulse of attraction.'[20] One of Harold's central assumptions is that manners originate with the upper classes and gradually spread downwards through society – an argument far from universally true in his own lifetime (if one thinks, for example, of the Bright Young Things of the 1920s or the communists and fellow travellers of the 1930s) and wholly undermined by his own prediction that American manners will 'in the end set the tone for the whole of the free world.'[21] And there are numerous, less sweeping assertions which are less than fully argued. Perhaps this was just a reaction against the formality, precision and necessary balance of *King George V*. In the end, the combination of an idiosyncratic choice of material and an informed, somewhat dogmatic, approach gives Harold a platform to air his preferences and prejudices in an amiable manner. The book is nearly three hundred pages long, but for all its length and detail, it still manages to suggest Harold at a dinner party, after a few glasses of wine, laying down the law about manners and the way people used to behave.

Harold's reputation and his personality ensured that he remained a popular guest at both official dinners and private dinner parties in the capital. In addition, during the period when he was writing *Good Behaviour*, his friends developed the habit of dropping into the Albany flat for early evening drinks. These gatherings began accidentally but soon developed into something of an institution – so much so that Harold, with characteristic self-mockery, called them as his *Grandes Levées*. Apart from John Sparrow and Colin Fenton, there was a shifting population which mixed old friends, such as Raymond Mortimer, Sir Alan Lascelles, Bob Boothby, Violet Bonham Carter and Sir William Haley, now editor of *The Times*; young friends, such as James Pope-Hennessy, Robin Maugham and James Lees-Milne; and newer friends, such as Hugh Thomas, the historian, and Kenneth Rose.

He continued to be active in his many societies – the Keats-Shelley Memorial Association, the Classical Association, the National Trust, the London Library, the National Portrait Gallery; he continued to open and speak at literary events and literary festivals; and he continued to travel. In August 1954, he and Vita made a trip to the Dordogne. She was writing *Daughter of France*, a life of Anne Marie Louise d'Orléans, Duchess of Montpensier, also known as La Grande Mademoiselle, and they visited places associated with her life. They also visited the home village of Alain-Fournier – *Le Grand Meaulnes* having long been a favourite of Harold's – and the house where George Sand was brought up. Returning to England, Harold shot off to open a Book Festival in Nottingham. Passing through Leicester, he was struck by the contrast between urban Britain and the beautiful French landscapes he had just visited. In January 1955, he visited Germany, lecturing in Munich, Bonn and Berlin. The German authorities treated him as a VIP and there were banquets, official dinners and press conferences all along the way. Back in London again, Harold and Vita attended a lunch at Buckingham Palace for the Shah of Persia (Mohammed Reza Shah, the son of the Shah whose coronation they had attended thirty years previously) and Queen Soraya. A few days later, Harold travelled to Portugal, having been asked to assess the effectiveness of the British Council Institute in Lisbon. On the way, he broke his journey in Paris to stay with Gladwyn Jebb, the new British Ambassador to France, and then travelled on to Lisbon non-stop, to avoid spending a night on the soil of Franco's Spain. In Portugal, there were more receptions, dinners and visits laid on for him.

It was a full and busy life, and there is no doubt that Harold enjoyed it. Despite his occasional protestations, he enjoyed the luxury, the privilege and the attention. In the world's eyes, he was a success and these were its trappings.

57 Health

At the beginning of 1955, Harold was sixty-eight. He had his regrets about life and, from time to time, he suffered moments of depression and self-doubt, but he was, by and large, a happy, lucky and contented man. True, he was wholly incapable of managing his financial affairs and he was constantly battling to find the money to pay his income tax – a situation which had worsened following the massive success of *King George V*. And true, he was becoming deaf, but despite various alarms and excursions over the years – for he was also something of a hypochondriac – his health had stood up very well, especially as he smoked too much and, despite numerous good resolutions, was always ready to enjoy a glass of sherry, champagne, wine, whisky or brandy. That was about to change.

A medical check-up in November 1954 had disclosed an irregular heartbeat. It was, he was told, nothing to worry about, although he did decide to rewrite his will as a result. During his trip to Lisbon, he suffered from repeated nosebleeds and was given a series of injections in the buttock by an elderly Portuguese nurse. By the time he returned home, it was apparent that the injections had affected the sciatic nerve and he was in agonising pain for several weeks, scarcely able to hobble between rooms. To make matters worse, he had to have several teeth extracted. Feeling sorry for himself, he travelled down to Sissinghurst and went to bed. On 11 March 1955, having spent most of the day correcting the proofs of *Good Behaviour*, he decided to have a bath. In the bathroom, he blacked out. It lasted only a moment, but the left side of his mouth was twisted and Vita could barely understand what he was saying. The doctor was called and confirmed that he had had a stroke. Mercifully, it was a mild one and his brain was unaffected. That evening, he was even able to continue correcting his proofs, and, although ordered to rest for two weeks, he still managed to write his *Observer* reviews and prepare his radio talks as if nothing had happened. Ten days later, Vita, worried about Harold and not in the best of health herself, tumbled down the stairs of her tower, bruising herself badly and cracking her sacrum. It was not the happiest time at Sissinghurst.

Harold returned to London in the first week of April. Vita wrote to him, urging him to spend more time at Sissinghurst writing books and less time in London giving radio talks and serving on committees. She recognised that, despite or because of their ailments, the three weeks they had spent together had removed tensions and 'something valuable has come out of it.'[1] But their problems were not yet over. Harold received another warning about his heart: he was prescribed digitalis and forbidden any heavy work, including – much to his dismay – gardening. Then, in the middle of May, having gone down to Sissinghurst for the weekend, he had another stroke. Again, it was a mild one. Dr Parish, their local GP, said it was no more than an arterial spasm, but warned Harold that such spasms could lead to 'real apoplectic strokes.'[2] He would have to be careful in future.

This procession of health-related problems was interrupted by the welcome, even startling, news that Ben, who had shown little interest in relationships up to that point, was engaged to Luisa Vertova, the art historian whom Harold and Vita had met when visiting Bernard Berenson at Casa al Dona some five years before. And there was more good news when

Nigel was re-elected in the May general election with a substantially increased majority. But to prevent too much celebration, Harold received a savage demand for surtax from the Inland Revenue: at a time when the average weekly wage was £9 for men and £5 for women, he was required to pay £2,279, on top of the substantial sum which he had already paid. Despite the warnings of friends and helpful suggestions from his publishers about how his income and the tax upon it could be managed, he had made only the vaguest provisions for his tax liabilities. In the short term, he would have to borrow – again – from Vita. And he decided to write another book.

Harold had always worried about his health, and he was of an age now when his friends and contemporaries – those who had not died during the war – were beginning to thin out. Sybil Colefax had died in 1950; so had Lord Berners; Archie Clark Kerr in 1951; and Duff Cooper in 1954. Harold found the death of Duff Cooper, four years his junior, particularly affecting, and writing his entry for the *Dictionary of National Biography* an emotional experience. Having had his own intimation of mortality, it would have been easy for Harold to withdraw from London life and spend more time at Sissinghurst. In his diary account of his second stroke, he anticipates becoming 'a semi-invalid', but that – to his credit – is just what he refused to do.[3] And the decision to write another book, *Sainte-Beuve*, was probably less a response to the taxman than an act of defiance in the face of ill health.

But before he could begin *Sainte-Beuve* – and only a couple of weeks after his second stroke – Harold and Vita set off for Florence to attend Ben's wedding. They travelled by train to reduce the strains on their health, but the whole expedition was fraught with worry. In the event, everything went well. They stayed with Bernard Berenson, now aged ninety, at I Tatti; the ceremony took place in Palazzo Vecchio in the centre of Florence (which appealed to Harold because of its historical importance and to Vita because it embodied Italian culture) in front of an Assessore who acknowledged the English party to the marriage by displaying his knowledge of Shakespeare; and they were both delighted with their new daughter-in-law. Nonetheless, they were pleased to return home without further disasters.

As the summer progressed, Harold gradually resumed his normal life, though he did make an effort to accept fewer engagements, particularly public dinners, and he settled down to work on *Sainte-Beuve*. Even then, it was an odd choice of subject, and it is certainly one which requires explanation today. The back cover of the first edition of *Sainte-Beuve* states that

> Harold Nicolson contends that this book is the payment of a debt of gratitude.... As a young man he derived so much information and pleas-

ure from reading Sainte-Beuve that he has always regarded him as a friendly guide who first introduced him to French life and literature. He has again and again referred to Sainte-Beuve's writings not only as a storehouse of curious information and wise criticism, but also as a library for occasional delightful readings.[4]

That Harold, whose mastery of the French language was acknowledged even by the French themselves, should have understood and appreciated that Sainte-Beuve was a master stylist is not surprising. That he should have found items to arouse his curiosity was perhaps inevitable, given that Sainte-Beuve's collected newspaper articles, *Causeries du Lundi* and *Nouveaux Lundis*, run to eighteen volumes. That he found in Sainte-Beuve a library of delightful readings is quite another matter.

Born in Boulogne in 1804, Sainte-Beuve longed to achieve success as a poet or a novelist, but it was as a biographer and critic that he achieved lasting recognition. He longed for a stable and fulfilling personal life, but neither his temperament nor his physique would allow it: he was naturally timid and apprehensive, while at the same time given to unpredictable outbursts of bad temper; he was also physically unattractive, short, portly and prematurely bald. Moreover, he suffered from a physical disability which prevented him enjoying a normal sex life. Professionally, Sainte-Beuve was not unsuccessful, but his private life trailed broken and disrupted friendships. Only his love for Adèle, the wife of his close friend, Victor Hugo, stands out, but even this was a tortured and ultimately unsatisfactory affair. His great work, published in seven volumes, is a comprehensive history of Port Royal, a Cistercian Abbey not far from Versailles, which was caught up in many movements of great cultural and spiritual significance between its foundation in 1204 and its destruction five centuries later. *Port-Royal* took over twenty years to write. It is immensely detailed, beautifully written and very dull.

It is tempting, though unfair, to say that the same is true of Harold's work. Certainly, *Sainte-Beuve* is a beautifully-constructed book and written with immense clarity. It would be impossible – and Harold does not try – to pretend that Sainte-Beuve was an attractive figure. He clearly respects Sainte-Beuve's intellectual honesty, but does not seek to disguise his 'personal vanity, his liability to be impressed by the last person he had spoken to, his inveterate disloyalty' and 'unpleasant habit of promiscuity.'[5] This gives his approach a sense of balance: he avoids both the hint of hagiography that characterised *King George V*, and the moral disapproval which some critics saw in *Verlaine* and *Swinburne*.

Harold began work on *Sainte-Beuve* in the summer of 1955. In the spring of 1956, he went to Paris to visit and absorb the atmosphere of certain key places in Sainte-Beuve's life. There was a strong nostalgic element to the visit in that, staying at the Embassy where Gladwyn Jebb was now Ambassador, he slept in the very same room where he had slept as a small boy, during the visit which provides the basis for the opening pages of *Helen's Tower*. The Jebbs provided Harold with the mixture of care and assistance that he was beginning to need when he travelled: Gladwyn provided what Harold claimed was the best bottle of claret he had ever drunk (Mouton Rothschild 1948), and Cynthia Jebb accompanied him on his Sainte-Beuve explorations, enlisting the help and knowledge of Nancy Mitford and Antonia Pakenham (who, as Antonia Fraser, was herself later to become a well-known historical writer). Harold finished the book that October and it was published in 1957. Friends and reviewers were complimentary and Harold's style was, justly, praised. Yet the fact remains – and despite Harold's largely successful attempts to place Sainte-Beuve's life within the literary and cultural context of the time – for most readers, both then and now, neither Sainte-Beuve himself nor his works are an interesting enough subject for a full-length book.

At the beginning of 1956, Harold was asked, out of the blue, to stand for election as Oxford Professor of Poetry. It is not a traditional Professorship. Anyone with an Oxford degree is entitled to vote and the person elected serves a five-year term during which his or her main duty is to give three lectures a year. Yet the Professor of Poetry also acts as a figurehead for the University's attitude to and belief in the value of poetry and it was a genuine honour to be asked, although the honour, as Harold would discover, had revealing implications in terms of cultural politics. His first reaction, or so he claimed, was to refuse, but he immediately succumbed, admitting that he was 'always carried away by the mention of Oxford even on a pot of marmalade,' and was duly nominated.[6] The other candidates were W. H. Auden and the Shakespeare specialist and academic, Professor G. Wilson Knight. Harold reasoned that the Professorship was an academic honour and that Auden, though a fine poet, had done nothing to deserve that kind of award. He also made it very clear, in a letter to Vita, that he thought it 'pretty cool for Auden to claim all the rewards and honours this country can give him while deserting her in her hour of danger.'[7] Auden's departure for the United States in 1939 and his decision to stay there during the Second World War had not been forgotten, particularly at Oxford, and this led a number of members of the University to see Harold, a distinguished writer on poetry who had lectured on the subject and fought to maintain cultural values during the difficult years of the war, as the right man to oppose him. It was natural that those supporting Harold should, in general, be older people with more traditional attitudes to poetry; people for whom the memory of wartime behaviour was still a matter of importance. Both the *Sunday Times* and the *Manchester Guardian* seized on this and Harold's supporters were characterised as old school, reactionary, conservative, even right wing, while Auden's were seen as go-ahead and progressive. Harold had never been a radical, but there had been incidents – the publication of *Some People*, joining the New Party, opposing Munich, joining the Labour Party – which marked him out as something more than a creature of the *status quo*. But now, in the eyes of the media at least, Sir Harold Nicolson, KCVO, CMG, author of *King George V*, was, justly or unjustly, firmly associated with the forces of conservatism. It was a transition he did not welcome.

In the event, Auden received 216 votes to Harold's 192 and Wilson Knight's 91. It was, as Harold recognised, the correct decision, and he felt that he had avoided humiliation.

Nineteen fifty-six was a climactic year for British politics and one which marked a temporary revival in Harold's interest in politics. Colonel Gamal Abdel Nasser had been among the leaders of the coup which overthrew King Farouk of Egypt in 1952. He took an increasingly nationalist stance and began to look to Russia and the Warsaw Pact for military and financial assistance. Tension had been mounting for some time, but on 26 July 1956, shortly after becoming Egypt's President, Nasser felt able to challenge British supremacy in the Middle East. He sent Egyptian forces to seize control of the Suez Canal and announced its nationalisation, at the same time as closing it to all Israeli shipping. Britain and France, who had been the main shareholders in the Suez Canal Company, were outraged. Nasser's actions were, at best, controversial in terms of international law and existing treaties, but they also publicly exposed the weakened international position of Britain and France. Anthony Eden, Prime Minister for just over a year in the wake of Churchill, and still haunted by the cost of refusing to stand up to Hitler at Munich, was determined that Nasser should not get away with it. So, too, was the French Prime Minister, Guy Mollet. But they were slow to act. International opinion demanded the exploration of peaceful options to resolve the crisis and the Unites States would not back the use of force.

It was a pivotal moment in British history and Harold was among those who appreciated its significance from the beginning. He had been strongly of the opinion that Britain should seek to prevent the nationalisation of the canal, but once it happened he recognised that Nasser had 'won all along the line.' As early as 31 July, he was correctly predicting that, particularly in a presidential election year, the Americans would 'not stand for anything that might lead to war in order to defend British oil-interests and our lifeline with the Empire.' As a result, he foresaw 'increased tension in Anglo-American relations.'[8] He understood also that, however distasteful it might seem and however dangerous it might be, Britain was no longer in a position to dictate terms in international disputes of this kind. As he wrote to Vita, 'we *have* ceased to be a Great Power and must cut our coat according to our very cheap cloth.'[9] Harold's terminology may have smacked of the early decades of the century, but his analysis was accurate.

The summer of 1956 was cool and wet. There were initiatives, debates and resolutions, but no progress. Questions were asked about Eden's leadership and whether his Foreign Secretary, Selwyn Lloyd, was a strong enough character for the job. In the meantime, Harold and Vita became grandparents for the second time when Ben's wife, Luisa, gave birth to a girl, Vanessa. Harold privately regretted it was not a boy, but was otherwise happy. Vita spent a night in hospital after a dangerous allergic reaction to a wasp sting. At the beginning of October, they went on holiday, accompanied by Philippa, to northern Spain, Harold having been pressured into giving up his objection to setting foot on Spanish soil while Franco ruled.

While overt diplomacy continued to get nowhere, Eden and Mollet had been holding secret talks with the Israelis and had concocted a plan which they believed would allow them to break the deadlock. On 29 October, Israeli forces attacked Egypt. Twenty-four hours later, Britain and France intervened, claiming that their purpose was to separate the combatants and prevent the war escalating. Harold was appalled. International security and the way in which countries conducted their foreign policies had been his lifelong study. Now, Britain, his own country, was taking advantage of an illegal Israeli invasion. Not only that, it was defying the political will of the United Nations which had voted almost unanimously for a ceasefire (only Britain, France, Israel, Australia and New Zealand opposed the idea); it was risking lasting hostility if not open war with the Arab world; and it was courting economic disaster, for the United States was threatening financial sanctions and Saudi Arabia was threatening to impose oil sanctions. And all this for a dubious point of principle, because Nasser had not actually shut the canal – except to the Israelis – and shipping was passing through unhindered.

Harold could also see that the crisis would have an impact on Nigel's parliamentary career. Bournemouth Conservatives were a very traditional band and Nigel had already alienated some of them by voting in support of the abolition of the death penalty. If he followed his instincts and spoke out against military intervention in Suez, he risked alienating a great many more. From the beginning, it was a divisive issue. The Labour Party, the Liberal Party, and the trades unions were strident in their opposition. Most Conservatives supported the government, but a minority, which included Nigel, stood up for what they saw as the principles of international law and were victimised by their own supporters as a result. When Nigel explained to his Bournemouth Conservatives why, when it came to a vote in the House, he intended to abstain rather than support the government, he was rewarded with 'murmurs of "Traitor!" and "Renegade!"'[10]

Militarily, intervention was successful, but politically it was a disaster. Britain's economy had been a constant source of worry since the war and, faced with sanctions, would simply have collapsed. Eden was forced to agree to a ceasefire and a withdrawal of troops before the end of the year. In later years, President Eisenhower regarded his refusal to support Britain and France as his greatest foreign policy mistake, but at the time the attitude of the Unites States meant that the international weakness of Britain and France was not only exposed but put on public display. It was a complete humiliation. Eden subsequently resigned on health grounds. Macmillan took over as Prime Minister; Britain, so recently ruler of the world's greatest empire, rapidly increased the pace of decolonisation and withdrawal from a world role.

Harold, of course, held no official position and had no access to Government information, but Nigel kept him informed of events in Parliament and he picked up information from his fellow diners at the Beefsteak and the Travellers. Nor had he any platform to air his views, but he made sure that everyone knew what he thought, even to the extent – according to James Lees-Milne – of picking arguments with Tory members of the Beefsteak.[11] As early as 2 November, Harold and Nigel had begun to suspect 'some collusion between the French and the Israelis to which we were a consenting party.'[12] Eden denied it, but Harold still saw Suez was 'an act of insane recklessness and an example of lack of all principle.'[13] It was 'truly one of the most disgraceful transactions in the whole of our history.'[14] And, with his understanding of the concept of balance in international affairs, Harold was among the first to realise that when the Russians invaded Hungary and had seven divisions closing in on Budapest, Britain had 'no right to speak a word of criticism.'[15] It was Eden whom Harold blamed most for the shambles of Suez. During the Munich period and in the early days of the war, he had seen Eden as his natural leader, but it now seemed that Eden had learnt the wrong lesson from Munich. The lesson was not simply that dictators must be opposed with force; rather that foreign policy must be conducted in accordance with moral principles and international law. In politics, unlike literature, Harold's traditional stance did not align him with the forces of conservatism.

On 21 November, just as the first United Nations troops were landing at Port Said to police the ceasefire, Harold celebrated his seventieth birthday. It was a Wednesday and, as usual during the week, he was in London. Vita, although not present herself, and Elvira Niggeman had choreographed the day. The first thing was the delivery of an envelope containing a cheque and a letter. The letter was signed by eleven of Harold's friends who described themselves as the originators of a scheme to find him a suitable birthday present.[16] They realised that raising a subscription suggested that he was being treated like an ancient monument, but they thought money more suitable than silver or a picture (unstated was the fact that they also knew he was constantly in financial trouble) and had opened the list up to all Harold's friends. The cheque was for £1,370 (the average price of a house was about £2,000). Harold was amazed, embarrassed, and somewhat perturbed that some of the names on the list were people he barely knew and others he did not recognise at all. His second present was a surprise visit from Philippa and his grand-daughter Juliet, now aged two. Elvira Niggeman wrote to Vita that 'it was a moving moment when [Harold] had on his overcoat and was looking down at Juliet in her overcoat, both staring at each other unblinkingly and bridging that gulf between ... the old and the very young.'[17] That evening, Harold was given a birthday dinner by seven of his closest friends at a private room in the Garrick Club.[18] He could never claim to be neglected or unloved.

The fall-out from Suez continued to rumble round the political firmament for many months, but at the beginning of December it became personal when the Bournemouth East and Christchurch Conservatives passed a resolution of no confidence in Nigel. Harold was sad, but he fully supported what Nigel had said and done. Looking back on the Suez crisis as the end of the year approached, he emphasised the moral dimension of events. Throughout a lifetime of diplomacy and commentary on foreign affairs, he had consistently called for international relations to be guided by moral values rather than extremes of realism or idealism. That was what he saw and supported in Nigel's opposition to the government. More important, that was what he expected to see in his country's foreign policy and in the actions and utterances of his country's leaders.

It seems strange to me that at the age of seventy I should have been so passionately moved by the whole business. Of course there was a personal interest in the effect on Nigel. But apart from that, the moral issue affected me as much as anything since Munich. My admiration for the Hungarians and my realisation of the immense importance of Russia suppressing by force a movement which was patently a working class movement, were nothing like the intense shame and sorrow of the Suez episode. It meant much to me that a Prime Minister who had made his reputation by his moral courage should out of exasperation have violated his principles and told his country a series of shameful lies.[19]

58   Cruising

Harold understood economics in the abstract. He understood that Britain could no longer sustain the cost of the Empire and its vast web of international commitments, but he could never have formulated an economic policy to address the situation. With his personal finances, it was much the same. He knew he had to live within his means; he did not, in theory at least, object to paying tax; but he was incapable of anticipating his liabilities and controlling his spending in order to meet them. By 1956, the era of post-war austerity was drawing to an end, but the British tax regime remained both complicated and aggressive. The basic rate was 47.5%. Marginal tax rates on unearned income, which included certain types of royalty payments, could reach 97.5% or 19s 6d in the pound. Harold was still battling with the huge tax demands generated by the success of *King George V* when he received his unexpected birthday present. So, not unreasonably, he decided to spend it.

Less than two months after his birthday, on 15 January 1957, he and Vita embarked at Southampton on the Royal Rotterdam Lloyd liner *Willem Ruys*, destination Java.[1] The journey there and back would take two months. This first cruise was a luxury that the generosity of Harold's friends enabled them to afford, but an annual winter cruise soon became a necessity: it was the first of six they took together. They called at Cape Town, Colombo and Singapore before arriving in Jakarta. Then, after a week in Java, they returned by the same route, making an additional call at Las Palmas. Along the way, they were met and looked after by friends or friends of friends, by the Commissioner General in Singapore, by the Ambassador and his staff in Indonesia. Even on board ship, they appeared to enjoy a degree of privilege, being entertained personally by the Captain throughout the voyage and allowed access to the bridge.

Privilege clearly meant different things to the two of them. For Harold, it was kindness and courtesy based on his reputation and recognition of what he had achieved during his life. He enjoyed the attention; he enjoyed being taken on trips and being asked to stay by Ambassadors; but privilege was not, ultimately, important to him. He was not given to pulling rank or demanding special treatment. Because Vita had so rarely travelled with Harold in his official roles, she had less experience of this kind of privileged treatment, but – perhaps for that reason, or perhaps because she was Vita with all the heredity of the Sackvilles behind her – it meant more to her. There were undoubtedly times when she expected special treatment and created a fuss if she did not get it. Yet what they both enjoyed most about the cruise was not so much the sight-seeing and the experience of new places, but the quiet routine of shipboard life.

They spent most of their time reading and writing in their separate cabins, joining to go down to meals together or to participate in the ship's social life – which ranged from cocktail parties to bingo. For Harold, shipboard routine was more relaxed than his London life. He could enjoy a moderately social existence and meet a few interesting people, without the demands that were normally made on him to make speeches or appear at formal dinners and ceremonies. He watched himself becoming less impatient. For Vita, however, it was probably the most socially active period of her life for some years. At home in Kent, she rarely met new people and usually objected to attending receptions and dinners. The difference here was that she felt in control: she was happy to socialise in the evening because it was part of the routine and did not prevent her from working all day at *Daughter of France*.

They arrived back in Southampton on 17 March. It was not the happiest of homecomings. Nigel's parliamentary future was in doubt because of his opposition to Suez. The Bournemouth East Conservatives had passed another motion, this time describing him as a traitor to his country and seeking to adopt a new candidate for the next election, but Nigel was refusing to resign. There was trouble, too, at Sissinghurst where one of the gardeners had become a communist and walked out. Harold was soon back in the swim. He attended a dinner at Buckingham Palace and discussed nuclear weapons with the Labour leader, Hugh Gaitskell. He called on the new Prime Minister, Harold Macmillan, as part of a delegation petitioning that no executions be carried out in the wake of the most recent troubles in Cyprus. He also started the process of turning the diary he had kept during the cruise into a travel book, *Journey to Java*. 60,000 words of diary were turned into a 100,000 word book between 31 March and 14 June – an impressive achievement for a man who had had two strokes. He finished correcting the proofs on 4 September and the book was published on 21 November. (The technology may have been less advanced, but the process of seeing a book into print was much faster in those days.)

Journey to Java was not well received by reviewers and, ominously, Raymond Mortimer was reticent on the subject, but it sold well and generated much interest among Harold's reading public. He claimed to have received more letters about *Journey to Java* than any of his other books – a fact which, with characteristic contrariness, he resented because the book had been easy to write. In stylistic terms, it is certainly not vintage Nicolson. There is an uncharacteristic scrappiness and clumsiness at times, although the diary format of the book means that such things matter less than they might have done in a more formal context. What lets the book down, and what the reviewers noted, is a rather forced humour, not dissimilar to that found in his letters to Philippa. In Harold's best writing – *Lord Carnock*, *Curzon: The Last Phase*, *Helen's Tower* – his observations are expressed in an unforced manner and carry with them his trademark irony. In *Journey to Java*, he is working too hard for his effects. It is possible that he was to some extent drawing on the example of Lord Dufferin, whose *Letters from High Latitudes*, employed – indeed, originated – the irreverent, humorous style of travel writing which was to be adopted later by many other British travel writers, perhaps the most notable being Peter Fleming and Robert Byron. But in *Journey to Java* it does not work.

It does not work because it strikes a discordant contrast with the other central strand of the book. The originality of *Journey to Java* lies in Harold's use of a travel narrative to support what appears to be – and to some extent is – a philosophical investigation. In the opening chapter, he says

> I propose to examine a problem that has long interested me, namely the problem of contentment. I always have the feeling that, considering that we live in a world of chaos and transition, I ought to be more unhappy than I am.... I want to examine whether the disillusion bequeathed by the French Revolution to the nineteenth century is in any way different from that which has been left us by our social revolution and two horrible wars. Is it a fact that the *maladie du siècle* of the nineteenth century produced languorous melancholy, whereas that of the twentieth

century is distinguished by fear and anger? ... Are energy and apathy, courage and anxiety, no more than personal accidents or are they symptomatic of an age?[2]

Harold explores these and other related questions through an account of his reading during the cruise. It is an extensive list, including Galen, Robert Burton, Kierkegaard, Rousseau, Goethe, Epicurus, Colin Wilson, Diogenes, Lucretius, Mill, Hume and others. This philosophical investigation counterpoints the daily events of the cruise and Harold's reflections are often illustrated by or contrasted with his fellow passengers and the people he and Vita encounter during their stopovers in port. Yet what emerges is not so much a philosophical conclusion – for, in the last resort, Harold did not have a philosophical mind: he was a critic and a historian and less confident in the realm of abstracts – but a self-portrait in ideas and attitudes. In this sense, *Journey to Java* is a companion piece to *Some People*.

In order to get a clearer perspective on himself, Harold invents Sydney Culpepper, the one fictional character in the book. Culpepper is Harold's *alter ego*. He is intelligent, educated and rich enough not to need to work. He is also homosexual and served a prison sentence for soliciting when he was eighteen. This experience, it is implied, has left him both isolated and fearful of exposure, an observer rather than a participant, shy but at the same time defiant, even cynical. He is also a way of dramatising some of Harold's thoughts about contentment and their 'conversations' become a kind of Socratic dialogue in which Culpepper, who frequently manages to deflate Harold's self-importance, gets most of the best lines. A younger or a braver man might have avoided the need for Culpepper altogether and spoken from personal experience, but Harold was neither. For him, homosexuality was not a matter for personal guilt, but it was a matter for public shame. An inner circle knew the truth, and a larger group may well have guessed, but as far as the public were concerned he was the husband of Vita Sackville-West, the writer and gardener. At the age of seventy-one, he was not about to change his attitude. But Culpepper's homosexuality does show how Harold felt his own sexual orientation to be an important factor in determining his attitude towards society and towards life in general.

In the end, *Journey to Java* probably belongs to the category of interesting failures – but it is genuinely interesting, much more so than *Sainte-Beuve*. Harold may not have achieved all he set out to, but the book is a genuine attempt to take travel literature in a new direction.

The cruise had undoubtedly done Harold good and, all things considered, he was in good health. Indeed, for a period he risked becoming something of a bore, recounting the experience of his two strokes, and telling anyone who would listen that he felt no decline in his mental powers. He became fascinated by the (possibly apocryphal) story that Catherine the Great had had a stroke while sitting on the lavatory. He continued to spend the week in London at C1, Albany, pursuing his public life, while John Sparrow and Colin Fenton kept an eye on his well-being. There were the usual dinners and lectures and committees – his National Trust duties, in particular, continued to give him great pleasure. There were reviews, articles and broadcasts – one of the most revealing being his contribution to a BBC Overseas Service programme which sought to justify the identity and values of 'the West'. Of course, this was the height of the Cold War and the borderline between genuine cultural analysis and propaganda was necessarily blurred. It was an age when the West felt challenged not only by Soviet power and ideology, but also by nationalism among the Arab and African nations which were either taking or being granted their independence. These new values evidently meant nothing to Harold: his views remained those of an old-fashioned, back-to-the-wall English classicist. On the radio, he expressed himself in more measured tones, but his diary summary captures the essence of what he believed: 'The whole of modern civilisation, including the hydrogen bomb, derives from the Mediterranean basin, and the east is no good at all except at poetry and art. I despise everything east of Suez ... with the exception of the Chinese, for whom I have a deep respect.'[3]

Old-fashioned attitudes, this time shared by Vita, were in evidence again that September when Philippa gave birth to a boy. Although delighted with their first two grandchildren, the fact that the succession of the Nicolson male line was now secured – and, moreover, that the new arrival, Adam, was in line to succeed to the Barony of Carnock or, in Harold's exaggerated phrase, 'heir to the lairds of Skye'[4] – was a source of unregenerate dynastic pride to them both. Sissinghurst, by contrast, divided them. It was 'passing through a period of nervous strain': the old barn was falling down and Harold contacted Tommy Lascelles, who had retired from his royal duties and was now Chairman of the Historic Buildings Council, about obtaining financial assistance for its repair. Tommy could not help with the barn but did offer to organise and pay for repairs to the tower and the front porch. To Harold, this was how things were done. The repairs needed doing. Tommy was an old friend and could help. It was a sensible and practical solution. Vita, however, was ruled by her emotions. The clattering and the shouting of workmen erecting scaffolding around her sanctuary – and, worse, the fact that they came from the Ministry of Works – outraged some ancient sense of ownership. She took herself off to Suffolk with her artist friend, Edie Lamont.

Vita's health was becoming a matter for concern. Her arthritis pained her much of the time. In November, she had three wisdom teeth extracted and then almost immediately succumbed to a bout of flu, from which she had barely recovered when she and Harold embarked at Liverpool for a second cruise in December 1957. Their ship, the *Reina del Mar*, was the latest (and, as things turned out, the last) addition to the Pacific Steam Navigation Company fleet and their destination was Valparaiso in Chile. Things did not begin well. Within twenty-four hours of leaving Liverpool, Vita went down with a fever which lasted intermittently for nearly two weeks and was not helped by a severe Atlantic storm which also made her violently sick. The ship's doctor did not think it anything serious, but Harold was consumed with worry. Feeling lonely and isolated without Vita, he was befriended and consoled by Jewell Allcroft, the wife of Philip Magnus-Allcroft, the biographer of Gladstone, Kitchener and Edward VII. The Magnus-Allcrofts[5] were to be fellow passengers on this and on several future cruises.

Once Vita recovered, their shipboard routine became a repeat of the previous year. She would breakfast in her cabin and work until the evening. Harold would swim, breakfast in the restaurant and then retire to his cabin to work. She was still working on *Daughter of France*, while he was reading and making notes for what was to become *The Age of Reason*. Shortly after finishing *Journey to Java*, Harold received a proposal from the editor of the *Observer*, David Astor, that he should go on a world tour, writing articles on the countries he visited and interviewing world leaders such as Mao, Khrushchev, Nehru and, Eisenhower. The idea of having one last opportunity to be at the centre of things was tempting, but he feared that his health would not stand the strain and so declined. He then toyed with the idea of a book about minor Victorian poets, such as James Bailey, George Mogridge and Edward Slow. Perhaps luckily, this was supplanted by a suggestion from Doubleday, his American publishers, that he should write a history of the eighteenth century. It was a slightly daunting prospect for Doubleday wanted a substantial volume – when published the book ran to 400 pages – but it was a period that interested him and, perhaps more to the point, for he was again a matter of interest to the tax authorities, he would be paid £3000.

Harold refused to go on shore at Bermuda because Vita was still ill, but, as the cruise progressed and she recovered, they began to enjoy themselves. The itinerary was a leisurely one and the *Reina del Mar* called at Nassau,

Havana, Kingston, La Guaira, Curaçao and Cartagena before passing down through the Panama Canal and making her way slowly down the South American coast to Valparaiso. As before, they were entertained and taken on trips to tourist sites and places of interest by friends of friends or by Ambassadors and their wives; and, as before, during the turnaround week, they were able to stay at the British Embassy, this time in Santiago. The only untoward incident was at La Guaira in Venezuela on the return leg of the voyage. They had been intending to experience a drive up the motorway (such things did not yet exist in Britain) to Caracas, but were prevented from going ashore by the revolution which overthrew President Jimenez.

They arrived home to a cold Sissinghurst on 9 February 1958 and picked up the threads of life in England. Harold's attitudes were hardening daily. He responded to two articles in Books and Art by Humphrey Clinker which accused him of being 'cultured, snobbish and urbane.' He was unapologetic: 'I am writing for an educated public ... it would be absurd for me to put on a proletarian tone.'[6] Dining with C. P. Snow, he was impressed by the Snows' account of 'sterilised, dehydrated, pasteurised and fridgidaired' food. 'That is what we shall come to,' he wrote, 'a tasteless, common-man age.'[7] It was an old man's view of the world: 'The sense of authority has decayed and the young revolt against the old and the irresponsible against the responsible.'[8] On a more positive note, he was full of praise for James Pope-Hennessey's life of Queen Mary; he enjoyed a visit to Horace Walpole's villa, Strawberry Hill, near Twickenham; the American Ambassador awarded him a diploma from the New York Academy of Literature; and the German Ambassador presented him with *Das Grosse Verdienstkreuz mit Stern*, an award for 'distinguished men who have rendered services to Germany.'[9] In December, at David Astor's invitation, he lunched with Igor Stravinsky, who praised *Some People* and *Journey to Java*, but greatly pleased Harold by saying that his best book was *Lord Carnock*.

Nigel's relationship with the Conservative Association in Bournemouth East had not improved and two separate issues seemed likely to make it worse. The first was the Wolfenden Report, which had been published in September 1957 but was only debated in Parliament in November 1958. The Report recommended that homosexual behaviour between consenting adults in private should no longer be a criminal offence. The matter was undoubtedly controversial and Nigel, for obvious reasons and also because he was naturally liberal in his approach to social issues, wanted to speak out in favour of a change in the law. Such an attitude would undoubtedly do further damage to his image and his position in ultra-conservative Bournemouth East, but his attitude to opposition had hardened and made him more determined to speak out. Harold himself could hardly have opposed Wolfenden's recommendations, but he neither spoke out nor wrote anything in support. Fear of exposure had been a guiding principle for over fifty years and it was too late to change now – especially as that fear was shared and reinforced by Vita. His one diary comment suggests that he thought public attitudes were not ready for a change in the law.

The second issue concerned Weidenfeld & Nicolson, the publishing company Nigel had formed with George Weidenfeld in 1946 and which had gradually increased its business and reputation over the intervening years. Weidenfeld & Nicolson was proposing to publish Vladimir Nabokov's *Lolita*, the (now) classic novel of middle-aged Humbert Humbert pursuing and ultimately seducing a twelve-year-old girl. Many of those who had read the book (and many who had not) regarded it as obscene and Nigel was aware that for his firm to publish it would further damage his standing with the Bournemouth Conservatives – indeed, he had been told so quite explicitly by senior party officials. Harold and Vita urged him strongly not to publish and Harold worked himself up into a frenzy worrying about his son's future. He approached Weidenfeld asking him to drop the idea of publication and even roped in J. B. Priestley to support his case – this from the man who in 1931 had broken with the BBC when forbidden to mention James Joyce's *Ulysses* on air.

Nigel comes out of the story well, acting in accordance with his own liberal convictions and a showing a sense of integrity to match his father's. Faced with pressure from the Attorney General and the Chief Whip to drop the idea of publication, he proposed that a single copy should be published to test the reaction of the Director of Public Prosecutions who was responsible for pursuing prosecutions for obscenity. There was much toing and froing in Westminster but eventually – assisted, perhaps, by the fact that the Prime Minister himself was a liberal-minded publisher, and on the evening when a reception for Nabokov and his wife was in progress at the Ritz – George Weidenfeld was told that there would be no prosecution. *Lolita* sold 100,000 copies in its first month. For all that, there can be little doubt that the controversy was the final nail in Nigel's Bournemouth coffin. When the final vote was taken in February 1959, he lost by 91 votes and was officially deselected. An alternative candidate stood in the 1959 election and Nigel never returned to Parliament.

Harold and Vita received this news in the middle of the Indian Ocean, approaching Bombay on their return from the Far East. They had set off from Sissinghurst on 5 January, crossed to Boulogne and travelled by train to Marseilles where they joined a Messageries Maritimes ship, SS *Cambodge*, which was to take them to Yokohama and back. Philip and Jewell Magnus-Allcroft were again among the passengers. Also on board was Michael Pitt-Rivers, whose prosecution for buggery in 1954 had brought both a prison sentence and the kind of exposure that Harold so greatly feared, but had also been instrumental in leading to the formation of the Wolfenden Committee. With him was his new wife, Sonia, who had previously been married to George Orwell. On the second day at sea, Harold began writing *The Age of Reason*.

From Marseilles, they crossed the Mediterranean to Port Said, which Harold had last seen in 1937. Both the place and the people had been much westernised in the intervening years and he disliked the change. They passed through the Suez Canal, which provoked thoughts of Britain's recent humiliation and Nigel's troubles, and down the Red Sea. At Aden, they were given a tour of the Crater and the old city by the Governor's ADC. They called at Djibouti, where Vita received the news that her beloved Alsatian, Rollo, had died. They sailed across the Indian Ocean to Bombay and Colombo and then on to Singapore, Saigon, Hong Kong, and Manila, reaching Kobe a month after leaving home. Their impressions of the places were necessarily fleeting – Hong Kong was beautiful, Macao (to which they crossed from Hong Kong) fascinating, and Manila enchanting. The place where they stayed longest, Japan, was the place they liked least. They disembarked at Kobe and travelled by train to Osaka, through a landscape of industrial desolation. At Kyoto, the temples and gardens failed to move them, and when they reached Tokyo, where they were delighted to be able to escape the city and stay in the British Embassy with the Ambassador, Dan Lascelles, who had been a junior diplomat in Berlin when Harold had been Chargé d'Affaires in 1928. For both Harold and Vita, the mysteries of the East were a closed book and would remain so.

Arriving in Colombo on 25 February on the return leg of their voyage, Harold found himself in the news. A local newspaper reporter was waiting to interview him about Guy Burgess, who had held a press conference in Moscow to announce that he was seeking safe conduct to return to England to visit his mother, who was dying. Among other things, Burgess had said that Harold Nicolson was the one friend from his past with whom he kept in regular touch. It was typical of Harold that, although disgusted by Burgess's treachery and defection and thoroughly disliking his alcoholic excesses, he continued to write to him because he felt sorry for his foolishness and because he remembered the young, sharp and promising Guy who had joined the BBC in the 1930s. As Harold told the reporter, there was nothing in his letters to Guy that he was ashamed of – James Lees-Milne suggests that he had taken care when writing that this should be the case.[10] Harold may have had nothing to be ashamed of, but he was still suddenly seized with fear that public exposure of his friendship with Guy Burgess would further damage Nigel's political chances. So often these days, and usually unnecessarily, his thoughts seemed to turn to public reaction and the whole issue of what people might think. The interview with the reporter in Colombo made him so tense that he was physically sick.

Back home by the middle of March, Vita's first act was to adopt an abandoned collie, which she named Ben, to take the place of her much-lamented Rollo. Her second was to take four silver urns, which in the distant past had belonged to Seery, and sell them so that she and Harold could afford a cruise the next winter. Then at the beginning of April, she was taken ill with what was diagnosed as viral pneumonia. Harold, as usual, was both consumed with worry and hopeless at doing anything practical to help. Vita was looked after by a succession of friends and helpers, who disagreed with each other and gave Harold contradictory advice. While she was ill, their daughter-in-law, Luisa, visited and told them that her marriage to Ben was not going well; the head gardener resigned; and Harold was invited to lunch at 10 Downing Street to meet the French Prime Minister, Couve de Murville, who in 1927 had been the boys' French tutor. Vita was ill for eight weeks, fuming at being forced to miss the arrival of spring in the garden at Sissinghurst. It was not until June that her health improved. June also saw the arrival of Ursula Codrington. Officially, she was meant to be Vita's secretary, but in practice she became a live-in companion who helped look after both Vita and Harold.

The summer of 1959 was hot and sunny and the fame of the garden was growing. The weather, concern for Vita, and the fact that he was writing *The Age of Reason*, meant that Harold spent more time than usual at Sissinghurst that year. Sometimes, in the afternoons when the garden was open to the public, he and Vita would stand together in the shade of the archway of the tower watching the steady stream of visitors – or 'shillings' – and answering their questions. For all their differences, their relationship remained absolutely solid. That September, returning to London on a Tuesday morning, Harold wrote: 'Why should I experience such a spurt of pleasure at seeing the tower of Staplehurst church catch the sun through the fog? And why should that pleasure be doubled if you are there to share it? Oh bless you, my saint, for giving me such a happy life.'[11] Two months later, Vita returned the compliment:

You've gone away again, into the different life you lead in London. It's an odd sort of life we have evolved for ourselves – me here, and you in London, and then both of us in our real home over the ends of the week, so happy and quiet and busy. Few people would understand it, in fact people often think that we are on the verge of divorce. How wrong they are.[12]

Christmas was a quiet one at Sissinghurst, but interrupted on Boxing Day by the arrival of an outside broadcast unit from CBS. The American journalist Ed Murrow, who was in Switzerland, hosted a discussion on the function of diplomacy between Harold in Kent, Charles Bohen, the US Ambassador to the USSR, in New York, and Clare Luce Booth, former US Ambassador to Italy, who was in Los Angeles. Harold was fascinated by the technology. Vita was outraged by the intrusion.

Two days later, they set off for their fourth cruise, crossing to Calais and taking the train to Venice, where they spent New Year 1960, and boarded the Lloyd-Triestino steamer, *Europa*, which would take them to Cape Town and back. The *Europa* was the most luxurious and comfortable ship so far and they slipped immediately into their established shipboard routine. Vita was writing *No Signposts in the Sea*, which was to be her last novel, while Harold was continuing *The Age of Reason*. They passed through the Suez Canal and called at Aden before turning south and following the East African coast. Zanzibar left a positive impression, but Harold's main feeling about the countries they visited – Somalia, Tanganyika, Mozambique – was that self-government would only embed 'corruption, impoverishment and cruelty.'[13] The real shock was South Africa, where they called at several ports and gained a fuller picture of the country than during their brief visit on their first cruise in 1957. Apartheid had become official policy in 1948 and had been strengthened since H. F. Verwoerd became Prime Minister in 1958; both Harold and Vita were shocked and outraged at the treatment of the black population. Harold's reaction, in a letter to Nigel and Philippa, is an honest one. If it mixes a patriotic sentimentality, to which with age he was increasingly prey, with racial attitudes which are wholly unacceptable by today's standards and unenlightened even in 1960, it must also be seen against the fact that racial discrimination was both common and legal in Britain at the time.

> You know how I hate Negroes and how Tory Vita is. But I do hate injustice more than I hate Negroes, and Vita screams with injustice.... You have no idea how shocking it all is. The complete police state. How happy we are with our freedom and Parliamentary Questions! I could

not live in this Nazi country in constant fear of the Gestapo.... God bless our little island. God bless her as a jewel of justice.[14]

Although still a supporter of the Labour Party – he had recorded a brief broadcast in support of Labour policies the previous June – Harold was also, perhaps for historical reasons, an admirer of Harold Macmillan and he was delighted when, on 3 February, just a few days after he and Vita had left South Africa, Macmillan delivered his famous 'Winds of Change' speech, making it clear that Britain was completely opposed to apartheid.

When the *Europa* docked in Venice, they went to stay for a few days with the traveller and travel writer, Freya Stark, at her home in Asolo, returning to Sissinghurst on 19 February. Once again, they picked up the threads of life in England.

Harold wrote fewer reviews and articles now and he gave fewer radio talks, but his status as a national treasure and arbiter of culture remained unchallenged. American television came to interview him in the Albany. Harold played up to his old-fashioned image saying that he was glad the porters wore top-hats because it prevented him being mistaken for one, and that he liked the idea of the Albany being a privileged sanctuary because 'highly developed civilisations specialise in variety, whereas lower civilisations impose uniformity.'[15] He was invited to the most exclusive dinners, such as that given by the American Ambassador, John Hay Whitney, for the Queen Mother, when the other guests included the Prime Minister and his wife, and the Chancellor of the Exchequer. In May, the French Government decided to promote him to Commander of the Legion of Honour.

Domestic life was happy; he was respected and sought after; he still contrived to be active and enjoy life in the day-to-day. Yet there were deep-seated worries. He was beginning to suspect that Vita's bouts of fever and weakness – she had had another one soon after their return in February – were more than just a viral illness. His physical health was holding up, but he worried that his mental powers were failing. He finished *The Age of Reason* in May 1960, but it had proved harder than he had expected and he was far from happy with the result – and, on this occasion, with more reason than usual. Then, of course, there was the constant problem of money: the Inland Revenue had presented him with another massive tax bill – this time for £1,500.

59 Endings

When *The Age of Reason* was delivered to the publishers in May 1960, Harold received the third and final instalment of the £3,000 due under his contract with Doubleday. Most of it went directly to pay the Inland Revenue. The problem of his finances was now acute. Although he was earning less than he had done, he was not exactly poor: the problem was his refusal to economise. As James Lees-Milne, who was close to him at this time, points out, both the London flat and his secretary, Elvira Niggeman, were expensive and both were luxuries for a man who had no position in public life, yet Harold refused to consider giving up either. To do so would be an admission of defeat and a surrender to his advancing years, which he was not prepared to make: there was always an element of vanity in Harold's maintenance of his self-image. And then there was his habit of treating his friends to lunches and dinners. This was something he had always done and something he enjoyed – and, in any case, many of the younger ones simply could not afford to pay for themselves. But Harold was not a man to choose the cheaper restaurant or the cheaper bottle of wine; as a habit, it was ruinously expensive.

Harold's social life remained extremely full. Any attempt to name all those with whom he dined, lunched or had a drink during the final years of his London life would reduce these pages to a guest list. Some were figures from public life; some were from the world of the arts; some were well known; some seemed likely to achieve fame; some never achieved anything. Broadly, they fell into two categories. There were the old friends: those had had some connection with his past life as diplomat, politician and writer – people as diverse as Clive Bell, Raymond Mortimer, Tommy Lascelles, Diana Cooper, Gladwyn Jebb, Kenneth Clark, Bruce Lockhart, Noel Annan and Maurice Bowra, to take an almost random selection. The second group were those he had originally met socially rather than professionally. John Sparrow, James Lees-Milne and James Pope-Hennessey were the seniors of this group, which also included younger friends, such as Kenneth Rose, Robin Maugham, Colin Fenton, Howard Ricketts (one of Weidenfeld & Nicolson's authors), and Christopher Gibbs, the antique dealer and style icon. If some of these younger men were more than willing for Harold to take them to expensive restaurants, they repaid him with genuine affection and looked after him while he was in London. James Lees-Milne tells the story of Harold being taken in a bubble car to Christopher

Endings

Gibbs' garret-like flat overlooking St Pauls for a riotous evening out.[1] He was never for a moment lonely or neglected.

But that did not solve the money problem. In the end, that was left to Nigel. Having refused to borrow money from Vita, Harold had come up with the somewhat unlikely idea that he would be able to persuade one of the City of London's Livery Companies to pay him £5,000 to write a book, thus securing the Albany flat, Elvira Niggeman and his London lifestyle for another three years. Nigel persuaded George Weidenfeld to offer the sum of £5,000 over two years for Harold to write a book on the subject of monarchy. It was a generous gesture, and not only financially. Monarchy was a subject which Harold understood. He would have to research the book, but not to the extent that almost any other subject would have involved. Yet he was conscious of the effort which starting a new subject from scratch would demand and it worried him.

Vita was ill again that summer and did not recover until September. Even though the money issue was solved for the moment, Harold remained in low spirits, depressed by Vita's continuing poor health, by the death of Nye Bevan, and by growing tensions in Cuba and the Congo. He had no strong feelings over the epoch-making American election in November 1960 when Kennedy defeated Richard Nixon, though he noted that he disliked 'candlesticks in high positions.'[2] There were times when ageing did not bring out the best in Harold, and such off-hand, dismissive language ('candlesticks' meant Roman Catholics) revealing deep, underlying prejudices became increasingly common.

In December 1960, *The Age of Reason* was published. It did not get a good reception. Harold had tried to tell the story of the eighteenth century through a series of chapter-length portraits of individuals – such figures as Saint-Simon, Pierre Bayle, Louis XIV, Peter the Great, John Addison, Cagliostro and John Wesley. It was a good, even ambitious, idea, but unfortunately poorly executed. The style is recognisably Harold Nicolson, despite numerous repetitions and misprints – which on this occasion cannot be blamed on the speed of composition – but it offers no real analysis of the period with which it deals. Indeed, it often reads like an impressive summary of its sources, which, in the end, is what it is. The individual stories are interesting in themselves and packed with incident; and, as ever, there are numerous instances where Harold seeks to inject life into the narrative with sharp descriptions of the characters, their habits or their surroundings, but on this occasion they are not as effective as usual. Too many of these characteristic passages – Vita's 'Hadji bits' – fall flat: the details deployed seem almost perfunctory and the irony misses fire so that the overall effect is one of self-parody. From another writer, *The Age of Reason* might not be judged a bad book, but coming from someone with Harold's stylistic and analytical gifts, it marks a distinct falling off. The reviewers recognised it and Harold knew it.

Vita was ill again that December and spent a few days in a nursing home, but with the New Year they were off again, departing from Genoa on 8 January 1961 on board SS *Augustus* and heading for Buenos Aires. The annual cruise had become much more than a luxury for them both by this stage. It had become an end in itself. Harold liked 'the great emptiness' of the Atlantic; Vita preferred passing islands and watching the coastline; but they both preferred days at sea to days spent in harbour. Harold relished the comfort and the luxury; the opportunity to read, work and rest without the distractions of daily life around him. Vita needed an escape from her always complex net of lovers, ex-lovers and friends; and from Sissinghurst, the garden she loved but which also made great physical demands upon her. Vita would be sixty-nine in March and, although she was well during this cruise – and during most of 1961 – her health was obviously fragile. Her thoughts began to turn to the past and to mortality. The previous November she had written to Harold that 'in our advancing age, we love each other more deeply than ever, and also more agonisingly since we see the inevitable end.'[3] This had been followed by a second letter reflecting on her affair with Violet and how much she had hurt him. The cruise seems to have allowed her to push such worries into the background.

The routine was unchanged. Harold was working on *Monarchy*; Vita was writing a book about dogs, to be called *Faces*. Ambassadors met them at the quayside, gave them lunches and took them sightseeing. On the whole, they disliked Brazil, but thought Rio de Janeiro spectacular and particularly enjoyed their visit to the Botanical Gardens. Montevideo was spoilt for Vita by the sight of a herd of cows waiting outside a slaughterhouse, though Harold was interested to be shown the spot where the *Graf Spee* had been scuttled in 1939. Neither of them liked Buenos Aires or the Argentinians, whom they found rude. Shipboard social life, including games of bingo, was relaxed and undemanding. The Magnus-Allcrofts were again fellow passengers and they all got on well, except when Harold's irritability broke through. Philip Magnus-Allcroft was twenty years younger than Harold and took the conventions more lightly. His appearance in the dining room wearing Bermuda shorts outraged Harold who told him to go and dress properly. The incident would mean little had it not provoked, as Norman Rose points out, an angry anti-Semitic outburst in Harold's diary about 'the insensitiveness of the Jews [being] one of their many abominable traits.'[4]

On the outward leg of the voyage, as they approached Lisbon, they received a telegram telling them that the current Lady Sackville, the American wife of Vita's Uncle Charlie, had died. Vita had never liked her; nor had Harold; and Vita's personal dislike was intensified by the fact that for the last thirty-three years Anne Sackville had been chatelaine of Knole. It was sad for Uncle Charlie, but for Vita it was a liberating death. Back in England, she felt free to return to Knole for the first time in thirty years, lunching with her now ninety-year-old uncle and casting a highly critical eye over the refurbishment and alterations carried out by the National Trust, which had acquired Knole after the end of the Second World War when Uncle Charlie realised that it was no longer possible for him to maintain the vast house. Vita saw her visit as the end of a long exile. Something else she did on returning to England was to give up her gardening articles for the *Observer* which she had been writing since 1946. With the benefit of hindsight, many of her actions at this time have a sense of completion about them, a settling of accounts.

A death which upset Harold a great deal more than that of Anne Sackville was that of Richard Rumbold, one of his younger friends, whom he had met during the war. Richard was loveable, gifted and damaged by his family (both his mother and his sister committed suicide), by his religious sensibilities (he was a devout Roman Catholic who managed to get himself excommunicated) and by the war (during which, despite acts of great bravery, he managed to get himself court-martialled). Harold had done everything he could to help him through a succession of troubles and Richard in return had looked upon Harold as an almost omnipotent father figure. When, in March 1961, following his return from South America, Harold heard that Richard had taken his own life, it depressed him greatly and fuelled his dislike of the Roman Catholic Church which he felt had made Richard's life more difficult.

London life became increasingly ceremonial. He enjoyed the slightly bizarre affair when the remains of Coleridge were dug up and then reburied. There was a dinner to meet the King and Queen of Greece; a Royal Academy dinner attended by Field Marshal Montgomery, Tommy Lascelles, T. S. Eliot and a very old and frail Winston Churchill; a Garrick Club dinner with Siegfried Sassoon; and the unveiling of a plaque to Walter de la Mare. In March, the journalist Kenneth Harris visited the Albany on four occasions to interview Harold about his life. The interviews were to serve as the basis for a series of articles which would be published in the *Observer* later that year to mark Harold's seventy-fifth birthday. He enjoyed the experience, partly because old men enjoy talking about their lives, but also because Harris was a gifted interviewer – 'an excellent interrogator'.[5] On his death in 2005, the *Guardian* obituary noted that 'Harris's strength as an interviewer lay in his ability to talk to his subjects on equal terms without sounding either aggressive or patronising.'[6] Certainly his articles about Harold are sympathetic without being sycophantic: they give a remarkable picture of both Harold himself and his understanding of social, political, cultural, even religious issues; and, in doing so, they show how highly he was regarded among the reading and thinking classes of the time.

There were other positives, too, particularly in his relationship with his grandchildren, Juliet and Adam. In one letter to Vita, he recounts a visit to Nigel and Philippa's house in Limerston Street in Chelsea and gives a verbatim record of his conversation with them on the subject of his age. In another, he recalls what was obviously a moving moment at Sissinghurst with 'Juliet running down the path between the big yews and flinging her arms round me.'[7]

Yet there was another and sadder side to the picture. Getting old is not an easy process, and Harold found it particularly difficult to accept. He disliked the feeling that the interest he aroused in people was based on what he had been not what he was. He knew that he no longer sparkled at dinner parties and that he was becoming increasingly deaf – unable, for example, to hear the speeches at the Royal Academy dinner and reduced to judging Macmillan's performance on his physical delivery alone. Always diffident about displays of emotion, he now shied away completely from awkward issues or situations. Vita's letter the previous year, in which she had discussed her relationship with Violet and their homosexuality, ended 'Oh, what a very unexpected letter.... You won't like it, because you never like to face facts.'[8] James Lees-Milne recounts a sad yet revealing episode when Vita's dog, Dan, had a heart attack in her tower room. Vita was distressed and in tears. Harold could only go outside and wait in case she called for him. He did not lack sympathy, but simply could not express it – 'I was NOT being indifferent, only muddled ... now that I am senile I have got worse than ever.'[9] And yet there were times when the Loyal Toast, the mere thought of Sissinghurst or some wholly commonplace event would provoke a sudden rush of sentimentality. Equally, a minor lapse in dress, language or behaviour could provoke an uncontrollable outburst of irritation.

He was not senile – though, sadly, that was to come – but his intellectual abilities were faltering. He knew it in himself, but it was brought home forcibly that September. Nigel had received the finished manuscript of *Monarchy* from his father's hands on 23 August. A month later he wrote a letter saying that it was not acceptable for publication. The problem was simple: Harold's sense of structure had deserted him.

> The original intention ... was that each chapter would deal with a different aspect of kingship: thus, the King as a Magician, the Warrior-King, the feudal King, the Constitutional King, and so on.... This was an excellent idea. But after the first two chapters he abandons it for a strictly narrative history.... But that is not all. For a book on this subject, surely we should have more than a passing reference to Napoleon, something about the Tsars, about the Court of Spain, about the French Revolution, about the Holy Roman Empire after Charlemagne, even about the great kings of Poland and Scandinavia? But there is nothing about any of these.[10]

Nigel's generosity as a son had rebounded on him as a publisher. He knew that his father had struggled in writing the book, but he also knew that, if published as it stood, Weidenfeld & Nicolson's French, German, Italian and American partners would cancel their contracts. He chose not to explain all this to Harold face-to-face, but to write a letter, and he wrote the letter not to Harold, but to Vita, asking her to intervene with Harold on his behalf. This curious, roundabout procedure was apparently designed to soften the blow to Harold's pride, but it also suggests that Harold may not have been the only Nicolson who disliked facing up to potentially emotional situations.

In fact, though it was a great blow to his pride, Harold accepted Nigel's criticisms with a combination of resignation and sadness – 'What is really meant is that I am getting gaga, and cannot really do such sort of books at my age'[11] – and he sympathised with his son for having to write such a letter. The task of restructuring the book and adding significant amounts of new material proved almost too much of a challenge. It took him until the end of the year, and even then he did not so much finish as reach a point where he recognised that no more could be done without scrapping the whole thing and starting again. Nigel, Vita and Harold himself all realised that this was a significant moment.

Even before Nigel's letter and the problems over *Monarchy*, Harold's money problems had resurfaced. He had again massively underestimated his tax bill and had no reserves to meet the additional £1,400 he was required to pay. It was probably this which led him to sign a conditional contract for *The Age of Romance*, which was conceived as a companion piece to *The Age of Reason*. The subject was certainly one which interested him and in the brief period between, as he thought, finishing Monarchy and being faced with Nigel's reaction, he began reading and researching the new book, but after the enforced revision of Monarchy the idea simply dropped out of sight.

On 21 November 1961, Harold turned seventy-five. On the weekends leading up to the birthday, the *Observer* published Kenneth Harris's interviews. These stimulated a response from readers not because they were in any sense revelatory, but because they gave such a complete picture of the man. Harold emerges as a man of privileged birth and upbringing, an educated man, a snob perhaps but a nice one: a man recognisably of his particular class and generation. And yet, at the same time, it is evident that he does not quite fit the stereotype. Here is someone who upholds the value of Latin and Greek and the discipline of a classical education, but calls himself a Liberal Socialist and claims to hate Tories; who takes his philosophy of life from Aristotle but regrets that a lack of scientific knowledge has held him back in life; who identifies Asquith (not Churchill) as the greatest man he has ever known; who regrets the democratisation of culture but strongly supports the National Health Service. Whatever one says of Harold's mix of attitudes, it was not stereotypical.

The day itself was Tuesday and, as usual on a weekday, he was in London. Private celebrations seem to have been muted, but public interest was sufficient for him to be interviewed on the *Today* programme on the BBC Home Service. He described his performance as a 'shattered old bronchial voice discoursing on youth and happiness.'[12]

After a cold and frosty Christmas at Sissinghurst, Harold and Vita set off on their sixth annual cruise, only this time they did not go alone. They were accompanied by Edie Lamont, who was now living at Chart Sutton, some ten miles north of Sissinghurst. Vita had known Edie since 1947 but had only become emotionally attached to her over the past two or three years, and the relationship had deepened still further since the death of Edie's husband in 1961. Harold did not particularly care for her, but, as it turned out, her presence was a godsend. On 19 January 1962, the three of them took the 8.05 train from Waterloo to Southampton Docks. Ben and his daughter, Vanessa, surprised them by turning up at the station to say goodbye. Luisa was not there. Ben – another Nicolson who disliked facing up to situations – had asked Vita to tell Luisa that he wanted a divorce; their marriage was effectively over. On the train, Vita suffered a sudden gynaecological haemorrhage. She told Edie but not Harold and tried to behave normally. As soon as they boarded the ship, she went to her cabin to rest.

The cruise aboard SS *Antilles* was little short of a disaster. Vita was ill for more or less the whole trip. The ship's doctor patched her up sufficiently for her to go ashore in Barbados, where they lunched with Harold's former House of Commons colleague, Ronnie Tree, in his palatial villa, but that was as much as she could manage. For the most part, she stayed in her cabin and longed to get back to England. Harold went ashore by himself in Trinidad to visit the Governor-General, Lord Hailes, formerly Patrick Buchan-Hepburn, with whom he had shared a tent on a fishing trip in Persia in 1926. Vita could not hide the fact that she was ill, though she sought to conceal, from Harold at least, how ill. The Magnus-Allcrofts were once again on board, as were Evelyn Waugh and his daughter, Margaret, but the sociability of previous cruises could not be recaptured. Harold was worried, uncertain, unsettled and irritable. He resented the sympathy he was offered; he resented the small kindnesses that people showed him as indications of age and infirmity; and, at the root of his dissatisfaction, he resented Vita's dependence on Edie, which kept him at a distance from her.

This cruise was shorter than its predecessors. They were back at Sissinghurst by 15 February and Vita began a round of visits to doctors, being referred ever upward. Harold and Vita's relationship was based on mutual love, trust and honesty, but at this crucial time their inability to communicate directly with each other seems to have caused them both misery. Vita felt 'really ill' but could not bear to tell Harold and so tried to hide it. Harold, deceived, thought she might be getting better 'but she never lets me know.'[13] On 23 February, Vita went to the Royal Free Hospital in London for more tests. Edie accompanied her. When she returned, she told Harold about the haemorrhage she had suffered on the train. He was deeply shocked. As a result of the tests, it was decided that she should have a hysterectomy as soon as possible. She returned to the Royal Free on 27 February. Again, Edie went with her. Harold was in a dreadful state and the letter he wrote that day swings wildly between a child-like confession that 'I am not as brave as you and I miss my Mummy who would comfort me' and an almost formal statement that, if asked, he will 'merely say that you are "in hospital for observation".'[14]

The operation took place on 1 March 1962. The surgeon telephoned Harold at the Albany and told him that Vita had cancer. Harold's reaction – 'I feel like fainting, but drink some sherry'[15] – speaks volumes. He was devastated but he would not and could not show it. Those closest to him – Ben and Nigel, Elvira Niggeman, James Pope-Hennessey, James Lees-Milne – understood and supported him as best they could, but there were others, many of them friends of Vita, who mistook his apparent external calm for a failure to understand how ill Vita was. They were wrong: he did understand, but he continued to hope.

In fact, there was little hope. It was over a month before Vita's condition was stable enough for her to leave hospital. She returned to Sissinghurst on 6 April, but she was barely able to do more than get up to eat before she was exhausted and had to return to her bed. Nigel, Philippa, Juliet and Adam came to see her on Easter Sunday. She rallied a little towards the end of April and was able to appreciate the garden – Copper wheeled her around in a chair – but the rally did not last. It was an agonising period. She was ill and weak but suffered acutely from 'the boredom of being ill.... The days seem endless.'[16] Harold's diaries chart a course of uncertainty, worry and desperate, self-deceiving hope. At the end of May, Vita began a course of X-ray treatment at Pembury Hospital, just outside Tunbridge Wells, but she was not strong enough to continue. On 1 June, their local GP told Harold firmly that he must face the fact that she was unlikely to recover. Nigel came down that evening to be with him. Vita died, the following day, 2 June 1962, at 1.15 p.m. Harold picked some of her favourite flowers and placed them on her bed.

In public at least, he remained in control. Vita's funeral took place on 5 June in Sissinghurst parish church. Leaving the church, he shook hands with the Bishop of Dover, who officiated, and managed to thank one or two old friends who had come down from London to attend the service. He returned to London the following week and tried to continue something approaching his normal life, but he was 'like a man in a trance' and it could not last long.[17] Inwardly, he was completely devastated and, as he confessed to Philippa, when alone would frequently collapse and cry. He never recovered from Vita's death and the process of his own mental and physical decline accelerated rapidly.

Under the terms of Vita's will, Nigel inherited Sissinghurst and perhaps the most positive thing to happen in the aftermath of Vita's death was that he, Philippa and the two children moved in. This gave Harold a sense of security – someone to come home to – which he badly needed, as well as someone to look after him. Philippa became a substitute correspondent and a line from one of the letters he wrote to her, quoted by James Lees-Milne, shows what he was going through: 'What hurts me most is when I forget that Vita is dead and think, "I must tell her in my letter tomorrow; it will amuse her," and then the lance of memory swoops and pierces me with a cry.'[18]

That summer, John Sparrow and James Pope-Hennessey took him to Bergamo in Lombardy for a few weeks. He enjoyed the flight over the Alps and sitting in the sun reading and making notes; and he enjoyed it when Nigel joined them and they visited the printers where 500,000 copies of *Monarchy* were being printed in four languages. But the interest was passing: nothing now aroused the level of interest and response that he would previously have shown. And when *Monarchy* was published at the end of the year, he showed none of his usual concern for its reception. In fact, *Monarchy* sold reasonably well, although, assessed critically, it remains a thoroughly disappointing book. Harold's text, which itself can only be described as patchy, seeks to explore the concept of kingship; Weidenfeld & Nicolson's production aims at the glossy, coffee-table market; and resulting book falls between the two stools.

In January 1963, he visited the United States and insisted that he should go by himself. Nigel and Elvira Niggeman organised things so that he would be looked after without appearing to be managed. Nigel and Howard Ricketts saw him off at the station; Noel Coward and Sir John Wheeler-Bennett watched over him during the crossing on the *Queen Mary*; contacts from the *New Yorker* and the *New York Times* shepherded him around New York; and Minna Curtiss, whom he had known since he and Vita spent a few restful days at her farm in Massachusetts during their tour of the United States thirty years previously, accompanied him through a round of lunches and receptions in Washington. He saw old friends, such as Copley Amory, Anne Lindbergh and W. H. Auden. He saw famous men, such as the political commentator and philosopher, Walter Lippman; the former Presidential candidate and now US Ambassador to the UN, Adlai Stevenson; and the journalist Alistair Cooke, whose 'Letter from America' was already well established on the BBC. His stock in America was just as high as in Britain and he was given a remarkably warm welcome wherever he went.

He was buoyed up by the attention he received and the generosity of his hosts, but, in the end, it was all too much. He returned home emotionally exhausted and also, one suspects, deeply frustrated that he was no longer capable of analysing and putting down on paper all that he had seen and heard on his travels in the way that would have been natural to him just a few years previously. The birth of Nigel and Philippa's third child, Rebecca, in April revived him, but only a little. In May, he had another stroke. Again, it was a mild one, but for a while the right side of his face dropped and he had difficulty speaking.

By the summer of 1963, he could no longer write his book reviews for the *Observer*. His standards of dress, table manners and personal cleanliness all began to slip. The latter, in particular, meant that it was necessary for him to have a male nurse. A young man called Tony King was engaged and quickly became a favourite. King accompanied Harold to Bergamo that September, where they met John Sparrow and stayed for two weeks, and when in London would guide him from the Albany to the Beefsteak or the Travellers Club and back again. In March 1964, they went on a trip to Greece and then, that June, to Paris. Harold's greatest enjoyment was seeing the pleasure his much younger companion gained from the sights and the new places; otherwise he just simply sat in the sun and remembered. Tony King stayed with Harold for a year. It was a brief, late friendship and could not be repeated. Harold's subsequent male nurses were mere figures with whom, in his decline, he was unable to establish any sort of relationship.

And, as ever, there was money. Nigel took effective charge of his father's finances which, once the *Observer* book reviews had ceased, consisted solely of a cash legacy of £10,000 from Vita – and this was being rapidly consumed by the need to pay for a male nurse and by Harold's continued insistence on maintaining the Albany flat. Nigel wanted to edit and publish his father's diaries. Harold did not see that they would interest anyone, but Nigel was a publisher and understood the attraction that the material would have. In his autobiography, *Long Life*, Nigel writes:

> I obtained an advance of £3,000 from Collins, and £6,000 from the *Observer* for the serialisation rights.... I edited a volume a year for three years, 1965–7, taking time off from my own books.... The three volumes were published at yearly intervals. They were best-sellers, and I suddenly found myself enriched by £30,000, of which I kept one third and devoted the balance to sustaining poor Harold for the rest of his life. He was pleased by his success, but said to me with a flash of his old humour, 'It's rather sad to think that of all my forty books, the only ones that will be remembered are the three I didn't realize I'd written.'[19]

It is sad also that when Harold's financial problems were finally solved, he should have been unable fully to appreciate the fact.

The rest of the story can be quickly told. Harold finally left the Albany in 1965 and lived permanently in the South Cottage at Sissinghurst. His steady mental decay meant that he was soon unable to read or write. When friends came to see him, he would not recognise them or he might try and hide behind a newspaper. To friends or to strangers he encountered in the garden, he could be unpredictably rude and, as a consequence, was sometimes assumed to be drunk. He would cry often, sometimes when reminded of Vita, sometimes at the sight of a small child, sometimes at a meaningless event on television. He was well looked after but the strain on Nigel and Philippa was immense. In November 1966, they gave a dinner at Sissinghurst for his eightieth birthday at which Kenneth Rose thought him to be in better form than at any time in the previous two years. He ate pheasant and drank champagne, answered questions about his life and his regrets, chanted some verses of Omar Khayyam in Farsi, and appears generally to have enjoyed once again being the centre of attention. But it was a last, brief glimpse of the Harold Nicolson who had sparkled at London dinner tables. The last eighteen months of his life were mere existence. On Wednesday, 1 May 1968, just a few minutes after midnight, as he was undressing for bed, he suffered a heart attack and died.

60 Epilogue

In accordance with the instructions he left, Harold was buried not with Vita among the Sackvilles in Withyam Church, but by himself in Sissinghurst churchyard. To James Lees-Milne, this was 'a final gesture of good breeding, a determination not to intrude where he did not belong.'[1] It could equally be seen as a final failure to assert himself.

Harold led what most people would regard as a charmed life. He came from a loving and stable background. He had an excellent education. As a diplomat, his work in Paris and Lausanne helped shape the history of the twentieth century. As a writer, he gained an international reputation for his thoughtful and readable interpretations of history. As a journalist and broadcaster, he informed and entertained audiences of millions in Britain and throughout the world. As a diarist, he left a record of events and people during the central decades of the twentieth century, and in particular during the Second World war, which is second to none. As a garden designer, he planned and laid out one of the most beautiful gardens in England. As a committee man, he used his influence to further the cause of knowledge and culture at a time when much of England's heritage seemed under threat. Even as a politician, he made a significant contribution to the policy debate in the period leading up to the Second World War and, albeit briefly, achieved ministerial status. He was awarded a CMG at thirty-five and was given a knighthood as a personal gift of the Queen. He was honoured by the French and Federal German Governments. He was welcomed as a guest by royalty across Europe and by Ambassadors and politicians around the world. And he was half of a wholly remarkable, if not untroubled, marriage which lasted forty-nine years. He was not exactly lacking in achievements, in worldly success, or in recognition.

Yet there hovers round him a sense, if not of actual failure, at least of disappointment or failed hopes. He was a successful diplomat who never quite broke into the inner circle. His political career promised well, but in the end never took off, damaged by his poor political judgement and an embarrassing tendency towards hero worship. He never gained the seat in the House of Lords that he wanted, but received a knighthood which he considered very much a consolation prize. The books which made his name at the time are now mostly out of print, and the diaries, for which he is best known, are fascinating but not the kind of intellectual memorial he would have wanted.

When I first started thinking about this book, I thought of borrowing the title of one of Harold Nicolson's own books and calling it *The Desire To Please*, because it seemed to me that the trait he identified in his great-great-grandfather was a driving force, or indeed a driving weakness, in his own character. His desire to please, to charm, to be liked and appreciated, was symptomatic of a deep-seated need to belong. Throughout his life, he was constantly searching for a group, an institution, some recognised or defined social body that would accept him. Acceptance gave him the reassurance he needed and bolstered the sense of identity that he felt he lacked.

Self-doubt is a human universal and Harold worried to varying degrees and at various times about failing intellectual powers, about his figure, his health, his receding hairline, his strength of character, his ability to earn money, and whether he was bringing his children up properly. Such worries are normal enough, even in someone with his background, but they never left him. Perhaps one of the reasons for his hero worship was that he saw in his heroes evidence of the self-assurance, certainty and success he felt he lacked. I think Harold would have liked to have been a hero to others; that he really wanted to be seen as a leader – of thought if not of men. It was a status he would never attain. He was loved, respected and admired, but never quite a hero. He was not that sort of person.

Then there is the question of happiness. Harold was almost always cheerful, but that is not quite the same thing. Vita was not, as he recognised, an easy wife, but they undoubtedly loved each other deeply. There may have been areas of the relationship where he conceded more than he gained, but he, too, enjoyed considerable freedom, which no traditional marriage would have offered. He loved his sons and enjoyed spending time with them. For all that, Harold was not a natural family man. Although there are numerous references in the letters and diaries to his happiness at being with his family, there is also an underlying sense that the happiness he feels on such occasions arises from a recognition that, given all his advantages, he *ought to be* happy, but that a part of him remains unfulfilled. The problem is that, while he appreciated his family and Sissinghurst, he did not judge his own success or failure in terms of family life. It was in the public sphere that he judged himself and expected others to judge him.

Harold always had half-an-eye on history and it cannot go unmentioned that in his lifetime he saw some of the most radical changes that human society is ever likely to see. He was born into a world where the horse was the dominant form of transport, where the telephone was just coming into public use and where manned flight was still widely held to be impossible. In Turkey and in Persia, he had lived in societies which were, to a significant degree, still medieval in character. When he died, the internal combustion engine had taken over, television pictures were beamed across the Atlantic by satellite, and scheduled flights linked all the world's major cities. He had lived through the two most destructive wars in the history of mankind. And despite the wars, he had seen the population of the planet more than double to over 3.5 billion, ushering in the age of mass consumption and mass culture.

If the values he absorbed during a privileged, traditional Victorian and Edwardian upbringing failed to cope with the political, social and cultural changes which began with the First World War and rolled forward with gathering momentum during the rest of his life, he cannot altogether be blamed. He liked to think of himself as a rebel, but that was the last thing he was. He seems to have mistaken the natural difference between generations, differences of style or of manner, for something much more fundamental. He was never a radical, never a creature or supporter of the avant-garde. Bloomsbury saw him as establishment. The judgement stuck and was reinforced in the 1960s and 70s when the lines between the establishment and the rest of the world were, albeit crudely, re-emphasised, putting Harold Nicolson, CMG, KCVO, biographer of King George V, very much on the wrong side. But Harold's views were frequently not those of the establishment. He did adapt to change, much more than is often suggested. He saw and acknowledged that the future would belong to a more equal society which exalted the common man. He did not necessarily like it, but he tried in his own way to respond. In the end, he was a traditionalist – which is not the same as a conformist and not the same as a conservative.

Harold lived a nomadic childhood and became a nomadic adult. The amount of time he spent travelling was phenomenal. He travelled to see places; he travelled for work; he travelled to see friends; he travelled to learn or research. He spent days in cars, on trains and on ships, staying in hotels, in Embassies, with friends or friends of friends. Long Barn and, later, Sissinghurst were supposedly his roots, his anchors, but in fact he spent far less time there than he did in London – in King's Bench Walk, Neville Terrace, the Albany – or off on his travels. Perhaps that is revealing. He may, towards the end of his life, have accepted that he had reached a certain point and could go no further, but he never felt he had reached his destination. His life was a permanent state of becoming, not of being.

When a memorial service was held for both Harold and Vita in St James's Church in Piccadilly on 16 May 1968, John Sparrow characterised Harold as 'a nineteenth-century Whig leading an eighteenth-century existence in the twentieth century.'[2] That is a rather complicated definition. It acknowledges Harold's historical perspective but misses an essential ordinariness about him. Rob Bernay's wartime description of Harold was 'a national figure ... of the second degree.'[3] Bernays, as much as anyone, saw that Harold was ambitious, but was held back by his own basic decency; that it was his inability to be formidable, to be assertive, to put his own interests first, which prevented him rising above the second degree. Again, that may be true, but it is not the whole story.

Above all, Harold Nicolson was a decent man. He had great gifts as well as perfectly normal doubts, failures and insecurities. Because of the times in which he lived, because of the people he knew, and because of the vast amount of documentation he and Vita left behind, his life seems to us now to have been acted out on a kind of magnified stage. His prejudices, too, are magnified: his Europe-centred views on culture, his unreasoned and unacceptable attitudes to Jews and to black people. But despite his prejudices, despite his difficulties in expressing emotion and his sometimes muddled response to changes in society, Harold lived a life which emphasised human decency. His values were not exceptional: he stood for balance, reason, fairness and the common good. They were the values he derived from history and from experience – and they were the values he employed to interpret history and the events of his own lifetime for the benefit of later generations. They were also the values he maintained, with great personal integrity, throughout his life, whatever the rest of the world was doing and whatever other people said. Perhaps that sort of approach was never going to propel Harold Nicolson into the front rank of public life, but it is why he is worth remembering.

Notes

Abbreviations used in the notes:

HN   Harold Nicolson
JLM   James Lees-Milne
JLM, Vol. 1 James Lees-Milne, *Harold Nicolson*, Volume 1
JLM, Vol. 2 James Lees-Milne, *Harold Nicolson*, Volume 2
VSW   Vita Sackville-West
VW   Virginia Woolf

Source books are indentified by the name of the author. Their titles and full publishing information will be found in the Bibliography (page 573).

Nicolsons, pages 1–11
1. HN diary, 9 August 1938.
2. Sellar, 'Clan History of the Nicolsons of Skye'. Consulted 24.06.2012.
3. *Lord Carnock*, p.5n.
4. JLM, Vol. 2, p.108.
5. Not John Nicolson in 1629 as claimed in Rose, p.2. There were, in fact, four Nicolson baronetcies created within the Baronetage of Nova Scotia.
6. *Lord Carnock*, p.5n.
7. *Lord Carnock*, p.5.
8. JLM, Vol. 1, p.2.
9. *The Desire to Please*, p.3.
10. *Lord Carnock*, p.7.
11. *Lord Carnock*, p.6.
12. *Lord Carnock*, p.7.
13. *Lord Carnock*, p.7.
14. *Lord Carnock*, p.9.
15. *The Desire to Please*, p.3.
16. *Lord Carnock*, p.5.
17. *Lord Carnock*, p.7.
18. *Lord Carnock*, p.7.
19. *Lord Carnock*, p.7.
20. *Lord Carnock*, p.9.
21. *Lord Carnock*, p.10.
22. *Helen's Tower*, pp.5–6.
23. JLM, Vol. 1, p.384.
24. *Lord Carnock*, p.246.
25. *Lord Carnock*, p.271.
26. *Lord Carnock*, p.335.
27. *Lord Carnock*, p.7.
28. HN Diary, 30 March 1932.
29. JLM, Vol. 1, p.5.

Hamiltons, pages 11–17
1. *Helen's Tower*, p.39.
2. *Helen's Tower*, p.36.
3. JLM, Vol. 2, p.353.
4. *Lord Carnock*, p.31.
5. *Desire to Please*, p.8.
6. *Desire to Please*, p.1.
7. *Desire to Please*, p.5.
8. *Desire to Please*, p.6.
9. *Desire to Please*, p.13.
10. *Desire to Please*, p.14.
11. *Desire to Please*, p.183.
12. *Desire to Please*, p.28.

Harold Nicolson

Childhood, pages 17–28

1. *Lord Carnock*, pp.29–30.
2. *Lord Carnock*, pp.43–44.
3. Peter King (ed.), p.94.
4. JLM, Vol. 1, p.251.
5. *Lord Carnock*, p.76.
6. Companion of the Most Distinguished Order of St Michael and St George; Knight Commander of the Indian Empire.
7. JLM, Vol. 1, p.240.
8. JLM, Vol. 1, p.2.
9. *New York Herald Tribune*, 30 October 1927, quoted in JLM, Vol. 1. p.312.
10. *Some People*, p.vii.
11. Rose, p.5n.
12. *Some People*, p.2.
13. *Helen's Tower*, pp.29–30.
14. *Lord Carnock*, p.80.
15. Tuchman, *The Proud Tower*, 'The Patricians', pp.3–59.
16. Tuchman, *The Proud Tower*, p.22.
17. *Helen's Tower*, facing p.236.
18. *Helen's Tower*, p.1.
19. *Helen's Tower*, p.23–24.
20. There has been some controversy over the origin of the phrase, 'the sick man of Europe' (Christopher La Bellaigue, *New York Review of Books*, 8 March 2001 & 5 July 2001), but it is usually attributed to Tsar Nicholas I.
21. Mansel, pp.320–21.
22. *Lord Carnock*, p.88.
23. *Lord Carnock*, p.102.
24. *Lord Carnock*, p.102.
25. *Lord Carnock*, p.106.
26. *Some People*, pp.10–11. In JLM, Vol. 1, p.5, Harold's victim is his mother's maid rather than Miss Plimsoll, which perhaps reinforces the argument for Miss Plimsoll being a composite figure.
27. Not 1891 as stated in *Lord Carnock*, p.108.
28. *Lord Carnock*, pp.9–10.
29. *Lord Carnock*, p.73. In *Some People*, HN suggests they travelled in HMS *Arethusa*, but *Arethusa* appears to have been serving in the Far East at the time.
30. *Some People*, p.14.
31. Battleships-Cruisers.co.uk, HMS *Bellona*. Consulted 28.06.2012.
32. Not 1899, as suggested in *Some People*, pp.15–16.
33. *Lord Carnock*, p.113.
34. *Lord Carnock*, p.113.
35. *Lord Carnock*, p.109.
36. HN, 'On Becoming Sixty', *Comments 1944–1948*, pp.211–15.
37. *Helen's Tower*, pp.12–13.
38. *Some People*, p.14.
39. *Helen's Tower*, p.9.
40. *Some People*, p.13.
41. *Some People*, p.15.
42. *Some People*, p.15.
43. JLM, Vol. 1, p.5.
44. JLM, Vol. 1, p.5.
45. Rose, p.8.
46. *Helen's Tower*, pp.31–32.
47. *Helen's Tower*, p.23.
48. JLM, Vol. 1, p.4.

School, pages 28–38

1. HN letter to Jocelyn Brooke, 17 October 1950, quoted in Rose, p.12.
2. HN, 'Thucydides'. *Comments 1944–1948*, p.290.
3. JLM, Vol. 1, p.6.
4. Quoted in JLM, Vol. 1, pp.6–7.
5. HN, 'Corporal Punishment', *Comments 1944–1948*, p.227.
6. HN Diary, 27 July 1933.
7. *People and Things*, p.86.
8. HN Diary, 27 July 1933.

9   *Some People*, p.21.
10 HN Diary, 27 July 1933; *Some People*, p.22.
11 HN Diary, 27 July 1933.
12 HN, 'How to Read Books', *Small Talk*, p.163.
13 HN, 'How to Read Books', *Small Talk*, p.164.
14 HN, 'How to Read Books', *Small Talk*, pp.163–4.
15 Rose, p.12.
16 *Helen's Tower*, pp.263–4.
17 JLM, Vol. 1, p.11.
18 *Some People*, pp.28–31.
19 HN letter to parents, 19 March 1901, quoted in JLM, Vol. 1, p.10.
20 *Some People*, p.23.
21 HN letter to parents, 13 December 1903.
22 *The Listener*, 24 December 1943.
23 HN Diary, 30 March 1932.
24 HN Diary, 10 November 1942.
25 HN Diary, 21 November 1946.
26 *Some People*, p.23.
27 HN Diary, 30 March 1932.
28 Rose, p.12.
29 JLM, Vol. 1, p.11.
30 HN, 'Corporal Punishment', *Comments 1944–1948*, p.229.
31 *Some People*, pp.31–32.
32 Quoted in Rose, p.13.
33 *Some People*, p.33.
34 HN letter to parents, 21 November 1903.
35 *Some People*, p.23.
36 *Some People*, p.33.
37 HN letters to parents, 25 October 1903, 21 November 1903, 13 December 1903.
38 Rose, p.17.
39 JLM, Vol. 1, p.12.
40 *Some People*, p.23.
41 HN letter to parents, 13 December 1903.
42 HN letter to parents, 15 October 1903.
43 HN letter to parents, 13 December 1903.

Weimar, pages 38–42
1   HN Diary, 16 October 1958.
2   HN letters to parents, 18 April 1904, 24 July 1904, 14 August 1904.
3   HN to Lady Nicolson, 4 April 1904.
4   HN to parents, 24 February 1910.
5   JLM, Vol. 1, p.14.
6   Rose, p.18.
7   HN to parents, 24 July 1904.
8   HN to parents, 14 August 1904.
9   HN to parents, 21 August 1904.

Oxford, pages 42–58
1   HN to parents, 14 October 1904; JLM, Vol. 1, pp.18–19.
2   Speech to St Catherine's dinner, Balliol College, 25 November 1930.
3   HN Diary, 25 November 1930.
4   HN, 'On Learning Foreign Languages', *Small Talk*, p.210.
5   Figures taken from Hobsbawm, *Industry and Empire: The Birth of the Industrial Revolution*.
6   HN, 'The Boat Race', *Comments 1944–1948*, p.162.
7   The Rhodes Scholarship programme was started by the British businessman and imperialist Cecil Rhodes to bring students from the countries of the British Empire, Germany and the United States to Oxford.
8   HN to parents, 23 October 1904.
9   JLM, Vol. 1, p.20.
10 HN to parents, 23 October 1904.
11 Jones, *Balliol College: A History*, p.233, note 17.

Harold Nicolson

12 Balliol College Archives & Manuscripts, Francis Fortescue Urquhart Photographs. Consulted 30.06.2012.
13 Nigel Nicolson, *Long Life*, p.61.
14 HN review of Cyril Bailey, *Francis Urquhart*, *Daily Telegraph*, 6 November 1936, quoted in JLM, Vol. 1, p.22.
15 *Some People*, pp.47–48.
16 JLM, Vol. 1, p.23.
17 JLM, Vo. 1, p.24.
18 HN to Lady Nicolson, 12 February 1905.
19 HN to Sir Arthur Nicolson, 26 February 1905.
20 JLM, Vol. 1, p.21.
21 Sir Arthur Nicolson, 'Diplomatic Narrative', quoted in *Lord Carnock*, p.162.
22 HN, 'The King of Spain', *People and Things*, pp.164–71.
23 *Some People*, pp.42–44.
24 *Some People*, p.45.
25 JLM, Vol. 1, p.22.
26 *Some People*, p.46.
27 Balliol College Archives & Manuscripts, Francis Fortescue Urquhart Photographs. Consulted 30.06.2012.
28 JLM, Vol. 1, p.26.
29 Knight Grand Cross of the Most Distinguished Order of St Michael and St George.
30 *Lord Carnock*, p.196.
31 *Lord Carnock*, p.197.
32 *Lord Carnock*, pp.204–05.
33 *Lord Carnock*, p.205.
34 *Lord Carnock*, p.205.
35 HN, 'Tzarist Russia', *Friday Mornings 1941–1944*, p.16.
36 *Lord Carnock*, p.205.
37 HN, 'Tzarist Russia', *Friday Mornings 1941–1944*, pp.13–14.
38 HN, 'Tzarist Russia', *Friday Mornings 1941–1944*, p.15.
39 HN, 'Tzarist Russia', *Friday Mornings 1941–1944*, p.13.
40 JLM, Vol. 1, pp.28.
41 Balliol College Archives & Manuscripts, Patrick Houston Shaw-Stewart (1888-1917), War Poet. Consulted 30.06.2012.
42 HN, 'The Edwardian Week-End', *Small Talk*, p.77.
43 HN to VSW, 1 August 1926.
44 Nigel Nicolson, *Long Life*, p.3.
45 HN letter to parents, 30 April 2007, quoted in JLM, Vol. 1, p.30.
46 HN, 'Our Youngers and Betters', *Small Talk*, p.87.
47 HN, 'Post-War Undergraduate', *Comments 1944–1948*, p.280.
48 HN, 'Tzarist Russia', *Friday Mornings 1941–1944*, p.13.
49 *Some People*, p.46.
50 HN Diary, 29 November 1930.
51 HN Diary, 3 June 1942.
52 HN Diary, 6 May 1953.

Preparation, pages 58–66

1 JLM, Vol. 1, p.32.
2 HN Diary, 16 August 1907, quoted in *Lord Carnock*, pp.248–9.
3 *Lord Carnock*, pp.245–6.
4 *Lord Carnock*, pp.249–50.
5 Henderson, *Water Under The Bridges*, pp.32–33.
6 Robert K. Massie, *Dreadnought*, p.599.
7 Ponsonby (ed.), *Letters of the Empress Frederick*, p.209.
8 *Lord Carnock*, p.239.
9 'Jeanne de Hénaut' was written before most of the *Some People* chapters and was published separately by Leonard Woolf's

Hogarth Press in 1924. Harold told his parents that the picture of Jeanne was 'drawn straight from life'. HN to parents, 14 January 1927.
10 Some People, p.93.
11 HN to parents, 9 January 1907.
12 Some People, p.85.
13 Some People, p.94.
14 Some People, p.95.
15 JLM, Vol. 1, p.34.
16 HN to Lady Nicolson, 20 April 1908.
17 Good Behaviour, p.224.
18 Good Behaviour, p.221.
19 Good Behaviour, p.223.
20 JLM, Vol. 1, p.34.
21 HN, 'A Portrait of Winston Churchill', Life, 16 April 1948, quoted in Rose, p.22. Rose places this incident during Harold's undergraduate years, but Churchill did not join the Cabinet until May 1908 and was not thirty-four until the end of November that year.
22 HN to parents, 6 December 1908.
23 Good Behaviour, p.221.
24 HN to F.F. Urquhart, 9 April 1909, quoted in JLM, Vol. 1, pp.36–37.
25 JLM, Vol. 1, p.37.
26 Good Behaviour, p.146.
27 Rose, p.311, note 19.
28 HN to F.F.Urquhart, 22 September 1909, quoted in JLM, Vol. 1, p.38.
29 Rose, p.29 (179 cm; 67 kg).
30 HN to parents, 19 October 1909.

Office, pages 66–72
1 HN to parents, 19 October 1909.
2 HN to parents, 5 January 1910, quoted in Rose, p.31.
3 HN, 'The Reform of the Foreign Service', Friday Mornings 1941–1944, pp.119–23
4 HN to parents, 19 October 1909.
5 Tuchman, The Proud Tower, p.20.
6 HN to parents, 6 December 1908.
7 HN, 'The Edwardian Week-End', Small Talk, pp.73–81.
8 HN, 'The Edwardian Week-End', Small Talk, pp.78–79.
9 HN, 'The Edwardian Week-End', Small Talk, p.81.
10 JLM, Vol. 1, p.41.
11 Tuchman, August 1914, p.13.
12 HN to parents, 21 May 1910.
13 Lord Carnock, p.319.
14 Lord Carnock, p.335.
15 HN Diary, 19 July 1941.
16 HN to parents, 19 October 1909.
17 HN to parents, 22 November 1909.
18 HN to parents, 13 May 1910.
19 Rose, p.36.
20 HN to VSW, 31 July 1913.
21 Rose, p.37.
22 HN to parents, 22 November 1909.

Courtship, pages 73–78
1 JLM, Vol. 1, p.43.
2 Portrait of a Marriage, pp.31–32.
3 VSW to HN, 5 November 1910.
4 JLM, Vol. 1, p.43.
5 Portrait of a Marriage, p.32.
6 Good Behaviour, pp.23–24.
7 HN to parents, 5 July 1911. JLM, Vol. 1, p.45 states that Harold returned to England in June, but this is clearly incorrect.
8 HN to JLM, 8 January 1935.
9 Portrait of a Marriage, p.34.
10 Glendinning, p.42.
11 Portrait of a Marriage, p.34.
12 Portrait of a Marriage, p.36.

13 JLM, Vol. 1, p.48.
14 *Portrait of a Marriage*, p.36.
15 JLM, Vol. 1, p.48; Glendinning, pp.4–45.
16 *Portrait of a Marriage*, p.36.
17 Glendinning, p.46.
18 VSW to HN, 23 January 1912.
19 *Vita and Harold*, p.19, note 1.

Vita, pages 78–85
1 Tuchman, *The Proud Tower*, pp.4–5.
2 Glendinning, pp.9–11.
3 Glendinning, p.11.
4 Glendinning, p.11.
5 VSW, *Knole and the Sackvilles*, p.35.
6 VSW, *Knole and the Sackvilles*, p.209.
7 VSW to HN, 15 February 1913.
8 VSW to HM, 21 October 1958.
9 Glendinning, p.2.
10 Glendinning, p.3.
11 Glendinning, p.3.
12 American-Presidents.org, Chester Arthur and Victoria Sackville. Consulted 02.07.2012.
13 Glendinning, p.5.
14 Glendinning, p.1.
15 Glendinning, p.24.
16 Glendinning, p.28.
17 *Portrait of a Marriage*, p.28 & p.32.
18 *Portrait of a Marriage*, pp.33–34.
19 JLM, Vol. 1, p.44.
20 *Portrait of a Marriage*, p.42 & p.37.
21 Glendinning, p.42.

Constantinople, pages 85–97
1 The war was also notable for the first ever instance of aerial bombardment when bombs were dropped from Italian airships onto Libyan troops.
2 JLM, Vol. 1, p.51.
3 JLM, Vol. 1, p.51, note 18.
4 *Some People*, p.49.
5 *Some People*, pp.49–50.
6 Waugh, p.32.
7 HN diary, 7 May 1912, quoted in Rose, p.51.
8 JLM, Vol. 1, p.54 and note 21.
9 JLM, Vol. 1, p.54.
10 VSW to HN, March 1912.
11 VSW to HN, 23 July 1912.
12 VSW to HN, 23 July 1912.
13 VSW to HN, 21 June 1912.
14 Later sixth Earl of Harewood, not to be confused with Sir Alan 'Tommy' Lascelles, Harold's friend and later Private Secretary to King George VI and Queen Elizabeth II.
15 Lady Sackville's diary, quoted in Glendinning, p.45.
16 VSW to HN, August 1912.
17 Glendinning, p.50.
18 HN diary, 1 September 1912, quoted in JLM, Vol. 1, p.56.
19 VSW diary, 29 September 1912.
20 VSW to HN, 18 March 1912.
21 HN diary, 11 October 1912.
22 *Portrait of a Marriage*, p.38.
23 Glendinning, pp.50–51.
24 Also known as the Treaty of Lausanne; Ouchy is the lakeside suburb (or *quartier*) of Lausanne.
25 For some reason, Montenegro declared war on 8 October, the day Harold left London for Bologna, but as it had no common border with Turkey, nothing happened.
26 JLM, Vol. 1, pp.56–57.
27 Mansel, p.364.
28 JLM, Vol. 1, p.57.
29 *Sweet Waters*, p.141.
30 *Sweet Waters*, pp.128–9.
31 HN diary, 4 December 1912.

32 VSW diary, 18 November 1912.
33 HN to VSW, 14 January 1913.
34 VSW to HN, 30 January 1913.
35 VSW to HN, 4 March 1913.
36 VSW to HN, 17 April 1913.
37 HN to VSW, 24 January 1913.
38 HN to VSW, 3 March 1913.
39 HN to parents, 30 March 1913.
40 VSW to HN, 4 March 1913.
41 *Portrait of a Marriage*, p.3 7.
42 Glendinning, p.52.
43 *Portrait of a Marriage*, p.94n.
44 HN to VSW, 19 May 1913.
45 *Portrait of a Marriage*, p.39.
46 *Portrait of a Marriage*, p.95.

Marriage, pages 97–103
1 *Portrait of a Marriage*, p.97.
2 VSW to HN, 31 August 1913.
3 HN to VSW, 19 September 1913.
4 *Portrait of a Marriage*, p.194.
5 *Portrait of a Marriage*, p.42.
6 *Portrait of a Marriage*, p.41.
7 JLM, Vol. 1, p.66.
8 HN diary, 4 October 1913.
9 VSW, *Passenger to Tehran*, pp.20-21.
10 HN diary, 2 November 1913.
11 Glendinning, p.69.
12 JLM, Vol. 1, p.68.
13 VSW to Lady Sackville, quoted in Glendinning, p.70.
14 HN to VSW, September 1914, quoted in Glendinning, p.73.
15 *Portrait of a Marriage*, p.42.
16 HN to parents, 20 December 1913.
17 Glendinning, p.71.
18 *Portrait of a Marriage*, p.43.
19 Glendinning, p.71.
20 Lady Sackville's diary, quoted in Glendinning, p.72.
21 *Portraits of a Marriage*, p.43.
22 VSW to HN, 9 July 1914.

War, pages 103–116
1 *Lord Carnock*, p.403.
2 Sir Arthur Nicolson to Sir George Buchanan, Ambassador to Russia, 30 June 1914, quoted in *Lord Carnock*, p.410.
3 *Lord Carnock*, pp.xiv–xv.
4 Massie, p.881.
5 Massie, p.879.
6 *Lord Carnock*, p.422.
7 *Lord Carnock*, p.423.
8 JLM, Vol. 1, p.75.
9 *Lord Carnock*, p.426.
10 HN to VSW, 4 August 1914.
11 JLM, Vol. 1, p.79.
12 HN to VSW, 22 August 1917.
13 VSW Diary, 30 May 1915.
14 VSW to HN, November 1915.
15 HN to VSW, 22 May 1916.
16 HN to VSW, 22 April 1916.
17 HN to VSW, 22 August 1917.
18 HN, 'The Balfour Declaration', *Comments 1944–1948*, p.222.
19 HN, 'The Balfour Declaration', *Comments 1944–1948*, p.222–3.
20 HN, 'The Balfour Declaration', *Comments 1944–1948*, p.223.
21 HN, 'The Balfour Declaration', *Comments 1944–1948*, p.224.
22 *Peacemaking*, p.35.
23 JLM, Vol. 1, p.87.
24 HN to VSW, 18 October 1917.

Revelation, pages 117–124
1 Violet Keppel became Violet Trefusis when she married Major Denys Robert Trefusis on 16 June 1919, in the middle of her affair with Vita.
2 *Portrait of a Marriage*, pp.33–34.
3 Glendinning, p.67.
4 VSW to HN, February 1917.
5 Glendinning, p.86; Rose, p.76.
6 Ozzie Dickinson, Harold's friend,

was also an intimate of Lady Sackville.
7   HN to VSW, 25 October 1919.
8   Rose, p.76.
9   Glendinning, p.80.
10 Glendinning, p.81.
11 JLM, Vol. 1, p.367.
12 Glendinning, p.86–87.
13 Sackville slang for 'frightened'.
14 HN to VSW, 7 November 1917.
15 HN to VSW, 7 November 1917.
16 Quoted in Rose, p.70.
17 HN diary, 13 March 1918.
18 *Portrait of a Marriage*, pp.105–06.
19 VSW to HN, 23 November 1960.
20 HN to VSW, 23 April 1918.
21 HN to Hugh Walpole, 25 April 1918.

Violet, pages 124–134
1   HN to VSW, 28 April 1918.
2   HN to VSW, 28 April 1918.
3   HN to VSW, 28 April 1918.
4   HN to VSW, 28 April 1918.
5   HN to VSW, 9 May 1918.
6   VSW to HN, 11 May 1918.
7   JLM, Vol. 1, p.88.
8   VSW to HN, 11 May 1918.
9   HN to VSW, 3 June 1918.
10 HN to VSW, 4 September 1918, quoting Lord Denman's decision.
11 HN to VSW, 9 September 1918.
12 HN to VSW, 9 September 1918.
13 HN to VSW, 9 September 1918.
14 HN to VSW, 2 September 1918.
15 VSW to HN, 1 October 1918.
16 Violet Keppel to VSW, 29 October 1918, quoted in JLM, Vol. 1, p.103.
17 *Peacemaking*, p.9.
18 HN to VSW, 11 November 1918.
19 HN to VSW, 5 December 1918.
20 HN to VSW, 6 December 1918.
21 HN to VSW, 7 December 1918.
22 Glendinning, p.99.
23 *Peacemaking*, p.221.

Peace, pages 134–153
1   *Peacemaking*, p.76.
2   *Peacemaking*, p.41.
3   *Peacemaking*, p.143.
4   *Peacemaking*, pp.143–4.
5   *Peacemaking*, p.160.
6   *Peacemaking*, p.161.
7   *Peacemaking*, p.164.
8   *Peacemaking*, p.170.
9   *Peacemaking*, p.184.
10 *Peacemaking*, p.vii.
11 *Peacemaking*, pp.31–32.
12 *Peacemaking*, p.44.
13 *Peacemaking*, p.46.
14 HN diary, 9 January 1919, *Peacemaking*, p.228.
15 *Peacemaking*, p.219.
16 HN diary, 10 January 1919, *Peacemaking*, p.230.
17 HN diary, 10 January 1919, *Peacemaking*, p.230.
18 HN to VSW, 10 January 1919.
19 HN to VSW, 17 January 1919.
20 HN diary, 14 January 1919, *Peacemaking*, p.236.
21 HN diary, 16 January 1919, *Peacemaking*, p.240.
22 HN diary, 18 January 1919, *Peacemaking*, p.242.
23 VSW to HN, 27 January 1919.
24 HN to VSW, 2 February 1919.
25 HN to VSW, 8 February 1919.
26 HN to VSW, 9 February 1919.
27 HN diary, 5 February 1919, *Peacemaking*, p.258.
28 HN diary, 27 February 1919, *Peacemaking*, p.272.
29 HN diary, 5 March 1919, *Peacemaking*, p.277.
30 HN diary, 21 February 1919, *Peacemaking*, p.266.

31 HN diary, 8 February 1919, *Peacemaking*, p.259.
32 HN diary, 10 February 1919, *Peacemaking*, p.260.
33 HN diary, 28 February 1919, *Peacemaking*, p.273.
34 HN diary, 13 February 1919, *Peacemaking*, p.262.
35 HN diary, 25 February 1919, *Peacemaking*, p.269.
36 HN, 'Cure for Overwork', *Small Talk*, pp.224–32.
37 HN diary, 17 February 1919, *Peacemaking*, p.263.
38 HN diary, 27 February 1919, *Peacemaking*, p.273.
39 HN diary, 2 March 1919, *Peacemaking*, pp.275–6.
40 HN diary, 30 April 1919, *Peacemaking*, pp.318–9.
41 HN diary, 15 March 1919, *Peacemaking*, p.284.
42 HN to VSW, 18 March 1919.
43 VSW to HN, 20 March 1919.
44 *Portrait of a Marriage*, p.113.
45 *Portrait of a Marriage*, p.112.
46 Violet Keppel to VSW, 14 April 1919.
47 HN to VSW, 26 & 29 March 1919.
48 HN to VSW, 10 June 1919.
49 HN diary, 2 April 1919, *Peacemaking*, p.293.
50 HN diary, 3 April 1919, *Peacemaking*, pp.293–4.
51 HN diary, 4 April 1919, *Peacemaking*, p.299.
52 HN diary, 5 April 1919, *Peacemaking*, p.303.
53 HN diary, 4 April 1919, *Peacemaking*, p.301.
54 HN diary, 5 April 1919, *Peacemaking*, p.304.
55 HN diary, 10 April 1919, *Peacemaking*, p.309.
56 HN diary, 2, 4 & 5 April 1919, *Peacemaking*, pp.293, 294, 301, 304.
57 HN diary, 28 April 1919, *Peacemaking*, p.317.
58 HN to VSW, 4 July 1919.
59 HN diary, 24 June 1919, *Peacemaking*, p.364.
60 VSW to HN, 1 June 1919.
61 *Portrait of a Marriage*, p.114.
62 HN to VSW, 28 June 1919.
63 HN diary, 28 June 1919, *Peacemaking*, p.370.
64 HN diary, 28 June 1919, *Peacemaking*, p.371.

Crisis, pages 154–166

1 HN diary, 28 June 1919, *Peacemaking*, p.368.
2 HN to VSW, 14 July 1919.
3 HN to VSW, 19 July 1919.
4 JLM, Vol. 1, p.137.
5 HN to Lord Carnock, 25 February 1919.
6 HN to VSW, 8 August 1919.
7 HN to VSW, 29 November 1920.
8 HN to VSW, 15 September 1919.
9 VSW to HN, 19 October 1919.
10 HN to VSW, 25 October 1919.
11 HN to VSW, 29 October 1919.
12 HN to VSW, 3 December 1919.
13 VSW to HN, 5 December 1919.
14 HN to VSW, 9 December 1919.
15 Commander of the Order of St Michael and St George.
16 VSW to HN, 8 January 1920.
17 HN to VSW, 8 February 1921.
18 VSW to HN, 1 February 1920.
19 HN to VSW, 3 February 1920.
20 VSW to HN, 7 February 1920.
21 Lady Sackville quoted in JLM, Vol. 1, p.148; Rose, p.80.
22 *Portrait of a Marriage*, p.125.
23 *Portrait of a Marriage*, p.126.
24 *Portrait of a Marriage*, p.127.

25 *Portrait of a Marriage*, p.128.
26 Glendinning, p.108.
27 BBC talk, 17 June 1929.
28 Rose, p.84.

Author, pages 167–181
1 VSW to HN, undated January 1920.
2 JLM, Vol. 1, p.150.
3 HN to VSW, 5 January 1915.
4 I often have this strange and penetrating dream / Of an unknown woman, whom I love and who loves me, / And who each time is neither wholly the same / Nor wholly someone else, and who loves me and understands — Paul Verlaine, *Mon Rêve Familier*.
5 *Curzon*, p.249.
6 *Curzon*, p.249.
7 HN to VSW, 20 May 1920.
8 Glendinning, p.111.
9 Glendinning, p.113.
10 HN to Michael Sadleir, 26 October 1920, quoted in Rose, p.113.
11 Gilmour, p.261.
12 It has not proved possible to trace the article. It may not have been published.
13 Not *L'Echo de Paris* as stated in JLM.
14 HN to VSW, 8 February 1921.
15 JLM, Vol. 1, p.161.
16 *Sweet Waters*, p.190.
17 HN diary, 28 February 1921.
18 JLM, Vol. 1, p.161.
19 JLM, Vol. 1, p.161.
20 *Times Literary Supplement*, 17 March 1921.
21 *The Observer*, 20 March 1921.
22 HN diary, 20 March 1921.
23 Wilson, pp.53–58.
24 *Verlaine*, pp.73–75.

25 *Verlaine*, pp.203–04.
26 *Verlaine*, p.225.

Balance, pages 182–188
1 *Portrait of a Marriage*, pp.132–3.
2 JLM, Vol. 1, p.169.
3 HN diary, 6 October 1921.
4 JLM, Vol. 1, p.172.
5 HN to Michael Sadleir, 6 August 1921.
6 HN to VSW, 27 August 1921.
7 HN to VSW, 20 September 1921.

Tennyson, pages 188–193
1 HN, 'Writing Books', *Spectator*, 7 September 1945.
2 HN, 'Writing Books', *Comments 1944–1948*, pp.124–5.
3 JLM, Vol. 1, p.174.
4 HN diary, 23 February 1922.
5 *Tennyson*, p.174.
6 *Tennyson*, p.34.
7 HN, 'Writing Books', *Comments 1944–1948*, p.125.
8 *Tennyson*, p.170.
9 *Tennyson*, pp.170–1.
10 HN diary, 5 September 1922.

Curzon, pages 193–200
1 *Curzon*, p.273.
2 JLM, Vol. 1, p.178.
3 *Curzon*, p.274.
4 Gilmour, p.27.
5 JLM, Vol. 1, p.156.
6 HN diary, 2 February 1922.
7 HN diary, 2 February 1922.
8 JLM, Vol. 1, pp.155–6.
9 HN diary, 2 March 1922.
10 *Some People*, p.143.
11 *Some People*, p.143.
12 *Some People*, p.154.
13 HN to VSW, 1 February 1923.
14 HN diary, 28 December 1922.

Lausanne, pages 200–211

1. Gilmour, p.555. There is some confusion about the valet's real name. I have followed Gilmour, but JLM calls him Tippendale, whereas Nigel Nicolson in *Letters* calls him Chippendale.
2. *Some People*, p.142, makes an anachronistic reference to the Southern Railway which did not, in fact, come into being until 1923. Rose makes the equally anachronistic claim that the train was the Golden Arrow which did not run from London to Dover until 1929.
3. *Curzon*, pp.288–9.
4. *Some People*, p.153.
5. *Curzon*, p.289.
6. *Some People*, p.156.
7. *Curzon*, p.289.
8. *Curzon*, p.290.
9. HN, 'The Fall of Mussolini', *Friday Mornings*, p.182.
10. *Curzon* p.290.
11. Still officially known at this stage by the unwieldy name of the Kingdom of Serbs, Croats and Slovenes.
12. HN to VSW, 24 January 1923.
13. *Curzon*, p.290.
14. HN diary, 22 December 1922.
15. HN diary, 3 February 1923, quoted in *Curzon*, p.345.
16. HN diary, 22 December 1922.
17. HN diary, 3 February 1923, quoted in *Curzon*, p.345.
18. HN to VSW, 28 November 1922.
19. JLM, Vol. 1, p.188.
20. Lord Curzon to Lady Curzon, 22 December 1992, quoted in Rose, p.121.
21. Rose, p.323, note 12.
22. Rose, p.323, note 12.
23. VSW to HN, 12 December 1922.
24. Sheridan, p.315.
25. HN diary, 30 December 1922.
26. JLM, Vol. 1, p.195.
27. HN to VSW, 23 November 1922.
28. HN to VSW, 2 January 1923.
29. HN to VSW, 9 January 1923.
30. JLM, Vol. 1, p.197.
31. HN diary, 3 February 1923.
32. *Curzon*, p.348. The 'diary kept by a member of Lord Curzon's staff' quoted in *Curzon* is a slightly amplified and dramatised version of Harold's original diary.
33. *Curzon*, p.349.

Bloomsbury, pages 211–216

1. *Curzon*, p.318.
2. Bell, *Art*, p.27.
3. HN to VSW, 18 December 1922.
4. VSW to HN, 19 December 1922.
5. VSW to HN, 10 January 1923.
6. VSW to HN, 12 January 1923.
7. Bell (ed.), *The Diary of Virginia Woolf, Vol. II, 1920–1924*, 15 December 1922, p.212.
8. *The Diary of Virginia Woolf, Vol. II*, 19 February 1923, p.241.
9. *The Diary of Virginia Woolf, Vol. II*, 17 March 1923, 256.
10. JLM, Vol. 1, p.202.
11. JLM, Vol. 1, p.202.
12. VW to Pernel Strachey, 3 August 1923, quoted in JLM, Vol. 1, p.202.
13. Glendinning, p.142.
14. VW to Jacques Raverat, 1 June 1933, quoted in De Salvo and Leaska (eds), *The Letters of Vita Sackville-West to Virginia Woolf*, p.10.
15. VSW to HN, 3 August 1938.
16. VW to VSW, 1 September 1929.
17. VW to Lytton Strachey, 23 March 1924, quoted in JLM, Vol.

Harold Nicolson

1, p.216.
18 Bell (ed.), *The Diary of Virginia Woolf, Vol. II*, 5 July 1924.
19 VW to VSW, 23 February 1929.
20 VSW to HN, 26 December 1925.
21 HN to VSW, 8 January 1926.
22 HN to VSW, 17 December 1926.
23 HN *Diary*, 14 July 1925.

Byron, pages 216–223
1 VW to Pernel Strachey, 3 August 1923, quoted in JLM, Vol. 1, p.202.
2 JLM, Vol. 1, p.203.
3 JLM, Vol. 1, p.205.
4 *Byron*, p.vii.
5 *Byron*, p.61.
6 *Byron*, p.viii.
7 HN to VSW, 4 April 1923.
8 HN to VSW, 15 June 1923.
9 HN to VSW, 2 September 1923.
10 HN diary, 4–19 September 1923.
11 HN diary, 4–19 September 1923.
12 HN to VSW, 2 September 1923.
13 *Swinburne*, p.106.
14 HN diary, 20 September 1923. Accounts of the supper party vary. JLM claims that it was organised by Jack Squire, editor of the *London Mercury*, and took place at 'Goldoni's, a modest restaurant in Rupert Street' (JLM, Vol. 1, p.208). Edward Marsh's biographer claims that Marsh gave the supper at the Carlton and that the guests were more distinguished than Harold suggests, including John Singer Sargent and Somerset Maugham (Hassall, p.511).

Affair, pages 223–236
1 HN to VSW, 12 February 1924.
2 HN to VSW, 5 October 1923.
3 *Byron*, p.170.

4 HN to VSW, 5 October 1923.
5 HN diary, 18 October 1923.
6 *Portrait of a Marriage*, p.195.
7 Tuchman, *The Proud Tower*, p.28.
8 HN to VSW, 20 September 1921.
9 *Portrait of a Marriage*, p.195.
10 HN diary, 28 October 1923.
11 Quoted in *Portrait of a Marriage*, p.195.
12 Lady Sackville's diary, 3 November 1923, quoted *Portrait of a Marriage*, p.195.
13 JLM, Vol. 1, p.211.
14 HN diary, 31 December 1923
15 HN diary, 1 January 1924
16 HN diary, 31 December 1923
17 HN diary, 15 January 1924
18 Norwich (ed.), *The Duff Cooper Diaries*, p.173
19 King George V diary, 22 January 1924, quoted in *King George V*, p.384
20 HN diary, 26 January 1924.
21 HN diary, 24 January 1924
22 Norwich (ed.), p. 190
23 HN diary, 29 January 1924
24 JLM, Vol. 1, p.215
25 Lady Sackville's diary, 24 January 1924, quoted in *Portrait of a Marriage*, p.197
26 Lady Sackville's diary, 1 February 1924, quoted in Glendinning, p.135
27 Glendinning, p.135
28 Glendinning, p.136
29 VW to Lytton Strachey, 23 March 1924, quoted in JLM, Vol. 1, p.216
30 *Byron*, pp.1–2; p.10; pp.81–82; pp.97–98
31 *Byron*, pp.41–61
32 *Byron*, p.21
33 *Byron*, p.41
34 JLM, Vol. 1, p.218

35 HN diary, 4 April 1924
36 Geoffrey Scott to VN, quoted in Glendinning, p.137
37 HN to VSW, 23 July 1925
38 Glendinning, pp.136–7

Policy, pages 237–244
1 Quoted in Glendinning, p138.
2 Drinkwater, p.123.
3 JLM, Vol. 1, p.222.
4 HN diary, 28 September 1924.
5 JLM, Vol. 1, p.222.
6 HN diary, 7 March 1924.
7 JLM, Vol. 1, p.223.
8 VSW to HN, quoted in Glendinning, p.142.
9 HN to VSW, 4 December 1924.
10 HN diary, 6 January 1925.
11 HN diary, 6 January 1925.
12 HN diary, 22 January 1925.
13 HN, 'British Foreign Policy Considered in Relation to the European Situation,' pp.311–8.

Change, pages 244–253
1 *Spectator*, 4 April 1925.
2 Gilmour, p.xii.
3 Gilmour, p.417.
4 Gilmour, pp.379–81.
5 *Lord Carnock*, p.3 28.
6 HN diary, 24 May 1925.
7 HN diary, 24 May 1925.
8 HN to VSW, November 1924, quoted in Glendinning, p.141.
9 Glendinning, p.142 & p.144; JLM, Vol. 1, p.228.
10 HN diary, 7 June 1925.
11 HN to VSW, 2 July 1925.
12 HN to Raymond Mortimer, 27 July 1925.
13 HN to Raymond Mortimer, 24 July 1925.
14 HN to Raymond Mortimer, 27 July 1925.

15 Raymond Mortimer to HN, 16 August 1955.
16 HN diary, 23 September 1925.
17 JLM, Vol. 1, p.240.
18 HN diary, 24 September 1925.
19 JLM, Vol. 1, p.241.
20 HN to Raymond Mortimer, quoted in Rose, p.137.
21 Ben Nicolson to HN, [October 1925] quoted in JLM, Vol. 1, p.241.
22 Nigel Nicolson to HN, [October 1925] quoted in Glendinning, pp.146–7.
23 Bell, *Bloomsbury Recalled*, p.136.
24 HN to Raymond Mortimer, 3 November 1925.
25 HN diary, 4 November 1925.

Journey, pages 253–260
1 HN to VSW, 4 November 1925.
2 HN to VSW, 6 November 1925.
3 HN to VSW, 9 November 1925.
4 JLM, Vol. 1, p.244.
5 Jasper Brinton, unpublished memoirs, quoted in Haag, *Alexandria: City of Memory*, p.129.
6 JLM, Vol. 1, pp.244–5.
7 Haag, p.156.
8 Burg El Arab did revive in the 1930s, but as a desert retreat for Alexandria's privileged Europeans rather than as a settlement for the Bedouin.
9 *People and Things*, p.62.
10 HN to VSW, 24 November 1925.
11 Dodge, p.26.
12 HN to VSW, 24 November 1925.
13 VSW, *Passenger to Tehran*, pp.55–56.
14 HN diary, 26 November 1925.

Legation, pages 260–268
1 HN to VSW, 28 November 1925.
2 Gladwyn, p.21.

3   King (ed.), p.91.
4   Gladwyn, p.21.
5   King (ed.), p.91.
6   HN to VSW, 10 December.
7   HN to VSW, 1 December 1925.
8   HN to VSW, 3 December 1925.
9   HN to VSW, 10 December 1925.
10 HN to parents, 13 December 1925.
11 HN to VSW, 12 December 1925.
12 HN to VSW, 24 December 1925.
13 HN to parents, May 26 1926.
14 HN to Clive Bell, 26 December 1925.
15 Gladwyn, p.25.
16 HN to VSW, 24 December 1925.
17 HN to VSW, 26 June 1926.
18 HN to VSW, 12 May 1926.
19 HN to Clive Bell, 26 December 1925.
20 HN to VSW, 4 September 1926.

Visit, pages 269–277
1   VSW to VW, 21 January 1926.
2   VSW to HN, 17 December 1925.
3   VW to VSW, 15 January 1926.
4   VSW, *Passenger to Tehran*, p.40.
5   VSW, *Passenger to Tehran*, p.52.
6   VSW, *Passenger to Tehran*, p.53.
7   VSW to VW, 9 March 1926.
8   HN to parents, 11 March 1926.
9   VSW to VW, 9 March 1926.
10 VSW, *Passenger to Tehran*, pp.67–70.
11 VSW to Lord Sackville, quoted in Glendinning, p.157.
12 HN to Clive Bell, 19 March 1926.
13 Mohammed Hossein Mirza Firouz Khan.
14 Dowson, p.55.
15 VSW to VW, 8 April 1926.
16 JLM, Vol. 1, p.269; HN to VSW, 15 November 1925.
17 VSW to VW, 8 April 1926.
18 VSW, *Passenger to Tehran*, p.97.
19 VSW to VW, 15 March 1926.
20 VSW to VW, 8 April 1926.
21 VSW to VW, 17 April 1926.
22 HN to parents, 29 April 1926. Nasr-ed-Din Shah gave Arthur Nicolson a diamond-encrusted snuff box and Catherine Nicolson a string of emeralds when they left Persia in 1888.
23 HN to parents, 29 April 1926.
24 HN to VSW, 6 May 1926.
25 HN to VSW, 7 May 1926.
26 VSW to HN, 6 May 1926.
27 Raymond Mortimer to VSW, 7 May 1926, quoted in JLM, Vol. 1, p.273.
28 *Portrait of a Marriage*, pp.208–09.
29 VSW, *The Land*, p.96.

Chargé, pages 277–289
1   Quoted in JLM, Vol. 1, p.274.
2   Harold's portrayal of John Nichols as Swinburne's personal Mephistopheles has been challenged as 'nefarious (and false),' Meyers, pp.392–424.
3   HN to VSW, 28 October 1942.
4   HN to Clive Bell, 17 May 1926.
5   HN to VSW, 1 July 1926.
6   HN to VSW, 17 June 1926.
7   HN to parents, 22 January 1926.
8   HN, 'The Revision of the Treaty of Sèvres', pp.12–15.
9   Cronin, p.724.
10 HN to VSW, 1 August 1926 and 5 August 1926.
11 HN to VSW, 10 July 1926.
12 JLM, Vol. 1, p.285.
13 Gladwyn, pp.26–27.
14 HN to parents, 26 August 1926.
15 HN to Sir Percy Loraine, 16 July 1926.
16 HN to Austen Chamberlain, 30 July 1926, quoted in Rezun, p.87.

17 Zirinsky, pp.639–63.
18 HN, 'Anglo-Persian Relations', pp.812–20. It is noteworthy that when published in 1968, with Reza Shah's son still on the throne of Iran, the British Government chose not to publish Harold's more damning criticisms of the Shah.
19 Lancelot Oliphant's notes on 'Anglo-Persian Relations', quoted in Rose, pp.146–7.
20 Austen Chamberlain's notes on 'Anglo-Persian Relations', quoted in JLM, Vol. 1, pp.291–3.
21 HN to Raymond Mortimer, 29 December 1926.
22 *Hansard*, 5 October 1938, Vol. 339, c434. Consulted 12 July 2012.
23 HN to VSW, 10 November 1926.
24 Zirinsky, pp.639–63.
25 HN to VSW, 1 October 1926.
26 HN to VSW, 7 November 1926.
27 VW to VSW, 24 June 1927.
28 HN to VSW, 12 December 1926.
29 HN to VSW, 7 January 1926.
30 HN to VSW 14 November 1926.
31 HN to Michael Sadleir, 31 December 1926.
32 HN to Clive Bell, 11 August 1926.
33 HN to parents, 14 January 1927.
34 HN to VSW, 19 November 1926.
35 HN diary, 21 November 1926.
36 HN to parents, 21 November 1926.
37 HN diary, 1 January 1927.

Return, pages 289–298
1 VSW to VW, 2 February 1927.
2 VSW to VW, 9 February 1927.
3 VSW diary, quoted in Glendinning, p.173.
4 VSW to Raymond Mortimer, 10 February 1927.
5 VSW to VW, 23 February 1927.
6 Glendinning, p.173.
7 HN diary, 12 March 1927.
8 VSW to VW, 23 February.
9 VSW, *Twelve Days in Persia*, p.31.
10 HN diary, 2 April 1927.
11 JLM, Vol. 1, p.304; VSW, *Twelve Days in Persia*, p.17.
12 HN diary, 8 April 1927.
13 *Portrait of a Marriage*, pp.210–11.
14 VSW, *Twelve Days in Persia*, p.117.
15 HN diary, 29 June 1927.
16 HN to parents, 14 January 1927.
17 Constable's account for July 1927, quoted in Rose, p.327, note 45.
18 VW to HN, 15 June 1927.
19 VW, *New York Herald Tribune*, 30 October 1927.
20 HN to VSW, 16 May 1928. It should be noted that Connolly, always inclined to be jealous of those who sold well, described the book privately as 'most unpleasant.' See Rose, p.150.
21 Wilson, pp.53–58.
22 JLM, Vol. 1, p.313.
23 HN to parents, 14 January 1927.
24 JLM, Vol. 1, p.310.
25 *Some People*, p.xiii.
26 *Some People*, p.182.
27 *Some People*, p.169.

Berlin, pages 298–305
1 Walford Selby to HN, 19 August 1927.
2 HN to VSW, 12 September 1927.
3 HN to Walford Selby, 21 August 1927.
4 HN diary, 28 August 1927.
5 HN diary, 14 October 1927.
6 HN to VSW, 24 October 1927.
7 HN to VSW, 3 November 1927.
8 HN to VSW, 25 October 1927.
9 HN to VSW, 3 November 1927.
10 UK in Germany, Embassy

Harold Nicolson

History. Consulted 2 August 2014.
11 HN to parents, 28 May 1928.
12 HN to VSW, 9 December 1927.
13 VSW to VW, 29 February 1928.
14 VSW to HN, 12 July 1928.
15 VSW to HN, 4 November 1927.

Fathers, pages 305–321
1 HN diary, 31 December 1927.
2 HN diary, 31 December 1928.
3 HN diary, 31 December 1928.
4 *Portrait of a Marriage*, p.201.
5 HN to VSW, 13 October 1928.
6 VSW to HN, 11 October 1928.
7 Quoted in Rose, p.150.
8 HN to VSW, 14 April 1928.
9 HN to VSW, 16 April 1928.
10 Though originally intended for publication in 1927, which is the commonly quoted publication date, it appears that delays at the Hogarth Press meant that *The Development of English Biography* did not actually appear until 1928, the date given in later editions.
11 HN, 'Herr von Ribbentrop', *Spectator*, 14 January 1944.
12 In full, Paul Ludwig Hans Anton von Beneckendorff und von Hindenberg.
13 HN to VSW, 2 July 1928.
14 HN, 'Herr Müller's Policy Declaration', pp.159–61.
15 HN, 'Germany and the Rhineland', pp.488–90.
16 Barbara Hardy, untitled review, *Boston Review*, October–November 1997. Consulted 24 January 2011.
17 HN diary, 13 June 1945.
18 HN to VSW, 3 August 1928.
19 VSW to HN, 7 August 1928.
20 VSW to HN, 10 August 1928.
21 Later styled the Inter-Parliamentary Union.
22 HN to VSW, 6 October 1928.
23 *Lord Carnock*, p.436.
24 *Lord Carnock*, p.434.
25 JLM, Vol. 1, p.383.
26 VSW to HN, 16 November 1928.
27 HN diary, 31 December 1928.

Decision, pages 321–332
1 VSW to VW, 12 January 1929.
2 JLM, Vol. 1, p.360.
3 VSW to VW, 25 January 1929.
4 VSW to VW, 31 Janury 1929.
5 VSW to VW, 29 January 1929.
6 HN to VSW, 15 March 1929.
7 HN to VSW, 25 May 1929.
8 HN to VSW, 16 April 1929.
9 HN to VSW, 12 April 1929.
10 HN to VSW, 16 May 1929.
11 HN to VSW, 18 May 1929.
12 JLM, Vol. 1, p.370.
13 He was also a member of the team that won the Russian football league championship in 1912.
14 BBC radio talk, 17 June 1929, quoted in *Portrait of a Marriage*, pp.189–90.
15 Robert Bruce Lockhart to HN, 17 July 1929.
16 HN to VSW, 22 July 1929.
17 HN to VSW, 8 August 1929.
18 HN to VSW, 26 August 1929.
19 HN to VSW, 29 August 1929.
20 HN to VSW, 26 August 1929.
21 HN to VSW, 16 December 1929.
22 HN to VSW, 17 December 1929.
23 JLM, Vol. 1, pp.386–7.
24 HN, 'The German Soul', *Spectator*, 29 August 1941.
25 HN to VSW, 16 December 1929.

Reasons, pages 333–336
1 JLM, Vol. 1, p.56.

2 JLM, Vol. 1, p.388.
3 Sir Horace Rumbold to HN, 16 September 1929, quoted in Rose, p.163.
4 Bruce Lockhart, p.17.
5 Drinkwater, p.25.
6 HN to VSW, 14 November 1929.
7 Macmillan, *The Blast of War*, p.85.
8 VW to VSW, 17 September 1928, quoted in Rose, p.163.

Journalist, pages 336–343
1 Quoted in Glendinning, p.221.
2 HN to VSW, 16 December 1929.
3 HN diary, 1 January 1930.
4 HN diary, 2 January 1930.
5 HN diary, 8 January 1930.
6 HN diary, 26 March 1930.
7 HN diary, 24 August 1930.
8 HN diary, 5 June 1930.
9 HN diary, 28 October 1930.
10 HN diary, 31 December 1930.
11 HN diary, 18 October 1930.
12 HN diary, 31 December 1930.
13 HN diary, 18 October 1930.
14 HN diary, 28 October 1930.
15 HN diary, 18 October 1930.
16 HN to Lady Carnock, 7 July 1929.
17 JLM, Vol. 2, p.5.
18 Nigel Nicolson (ed.), *Diaries and Letters 1930–1939*, p.13.
19 Nigel Nicolson (ed.), *Diaries and Letters 1930–1939*, p.14.
20 HN diary, 28 January 1931.
21 HN diary, 21 July 1930.
22 HN diary, 31 October 1931.
23 Robert Cecil was the grandson of Lord Salisbury, who later became the fifth Marquess. Although an MP, Cecil was sometimes referred to by the junior title, Lord Cranborne.
24 HN diary, 5 July 1930.
25 HN diary, 29 November 1930.
26 HN diary, 22 August 1931.

Sissinghurst, pages 344–350
1 HN diary, 20 March 1930.
2 VSW diary, 4 April 1930, quoted in Glendinning, p.223.
3 HN diary, 5 April 1930.
4 HN diary, 13 April 1930.
5 Glendinning, pp.223–4.
6 Nigel Nicolson, *Long Life*, p.199.
7 HN to VSW, 24 April 1930.
8 Nigel Nicolson, *Long Life*, p.199.
9 VSW, 'Sissinghurst', 1930.
10 HN to VSW, 7 May 1930.
11 Nigel Nicolson, *Long Life*, pp.201–02.
12 Nigel Nicolson, *Long Life*, p.202.
13 VSW, 'The Garden at Sissinghurst Castle', November 1953.
14 HN diary, 27 September 1933.
15 Adam Nicolson, *Sissinghurst: An Unfinished History*, p.282.

Mosley, pages 350–359
1 HN diary, 5 November 1930 and 30 November 1930.
2 Macmillan, *Winds of Change*, p.248.
3 HN diary, 25 November 1930.
4 HN diary, 31 December 1930.
5 HN to Sir Oswald Mosley, 4 March 1931.
6 Lord Beaverbrook to HN, 24 April 1931.
7 HN diary, 29 April 1931.
8 HN diary, 18 June 1931.
9 HN diary, 17 July 1931.
10 Raymond Mortimer to Edward Sackville-West, 26 November 1931, quoted in JLM, Vol. 2, p.24.
11 VSW to Raymond Mortimer, 5 January 1931, quoted in Rose, p.168.

12 HN to Sir Oswald Mosley, 4 March 1931.
13 HN diary, 2 November 1931.
14 JLM, Vol. 2, p.22.
15 HN diary, 2 November 1931.
16 *Action*, 17 December 1931.
17 HN diary, 1 January 1932.
18 HN diary, 7 January 1932.
19 HN diary, 6 January 1932.
20 HN to VSW, 25 January 1932.
21 HN diary, 19 April 1932.

Recovery, pages 359–368
1 HN diary, 11 April 1932.
2 HN diary, 12 April 1932.
3 HN diary, 22 June 1932.
4 HN diary, 12 April 1932.
5 HN diary, 6 May 1932.
6 HN diary, 6 October 1932.
7 HN diary, 31 December 1932.
8 Nigel Nicolson (ed.), *Diaries and Letters 1930–1939*, p.129.
9 HN diary, 5 January 1933.
10 HN diary, 2 March 1933.
11 VSW to VW, 28 March 1933.
12 HN to VSW, 23 February 1933.
13 HN diary, 24 February 1933.
14 HN to Raymond Mortimer, 15 March 1933, quoted in Rose, p.177.
15 HN to Raymond Mortimer, 6 April 1933, quoted in Rose, p.178.
16 Rose, p.178.
17 HN diary, 13 July 1933.
18 HN diary, 24 December 1933.
19 *Portrait of a Marriage*, p.182.

Morrow, pages 368–380
1 HN to VSW, 1 February 1934.
2 HN diary, 4 February 1934.
3 HN diary, 5 February 1934.
4 HN diary, 6 March 1934.
5 HN diary, 11 February 1934; 18 February.
6 HN diary, 9 February 1934.
7 HN diary, 19 February 1934.
8 The series title appears in such an unobtrusive way that most readers are likely to miss it.
9 HN diary, 11 February 1934.
10 Nigel Nicolson (ed.), *Diaries and Letters 1930–1939*, p.167.
11 Rose, p.181.
12 HN diary, 11 February 1934.
13 *Diplomacy*, p.15.
14 *The Evolution of Diplomatic Method*, p.71.
15 JLM, Vol. 2, p.47.
16 *Nation*, 8 August 1934, pp.165–6, quoted in Drinkwater, p.27.
17 Gilmour, p.xii.
18 HN diary, 22 August 1934.
19 HN to VSW, 14 October 1934.
20 HN diary, 1 October 1934.
21 HN to VSW, 17 November 1934.
22 HN to VSW, 26 October 1934.
23 HN to VSW, 17 November 1934.
24 HN to VSW, 14 February 1935.
25 *Dwight Morrow*, p.338.
26 HN to VSW, 9 March 1935.
27 HN to VSW, 11 March 1935.
28 HN to VSW, 2 June 1935.
29 HN diary, 4 June 1935.
30 HH diary, 5 June 1935.
31 Rose, p.184.
32 HN diary, 7 June 1935.
33 HN diary, 10 July 1935.
34 HN to VSW, 1 June 1935.

Election, pages 380–386
1 HN diary, 19 June 1935.
2 HN diary, 21 August 1935.
3 HN to VSW, 18 October 1935.
4 VSW to HN, 28 October 1935.
5 HN to VSW, 23 October 1935.
6 HN to VSW, 2 November 1935.
7 HN to VSW, 7 November 1935.
8 JLM, Vol. 2, p.69.
9 HN to VSW, 15 November 1935.

10 Rose, p.192.
11 *Politics in the Train*, p.5.
12 *Politics in the Train*, p.10.
13 *Politics in the Train*, p.19.
14 *Politics in the Train*, p.14.
15 *Politics in the Train*, p.27.
16 *Politics in the Train*, p.13.
17 *Politics in the Train*, p.27.
18 *Hansard*, League of Nations and Abyssinia, 19 December 1935, Vol. 307, c2079 & c2081. Consulted 12 July 2012.
19 HN diary, 19 December 1935.

Drama, pages 386–393
1 HN diary, 13 January 1936.
2 HN diary, 30 January 1936.
3 Glendinning, p.285.
4 HN to VSW, 16 December 1935.
5 VSW to HN, 2 July 1936.
6 JLM, Vol. 2, p.74.
7 At 2010 values, these sums equated to approximately £2.3 million, £250,000 and £50,000.
8 HN diary 5 March 1936.
9 HN diary, 24 February 1936.
10 HN diary, 2 April 1936.
11 HN diary, 30 November 1936.
12 HN to VSW, 10 December 1936.
13 HN diary, 30 November 1936.
14 HN diary, 3 December 1936.
15 *Hansard*, Debate on the Address, 3 November 1936, Vol. 317 cc17-21. Consulted 14 July 2012.
16 HN diary, 7 November 1936.
17 Channon, *'Chips': The Diaries of Sir Henry Channon*, 20 September 1936, p.147.
18 Lees-Milne, *Through Wood and Dale*, p.236.

Fifty, pages 393–399
1 HN diary, 31 December 1936.
2 HN diary, 1 September 1936.

3 There has been speculation, based on comments in Bernays' letters and diaries, that he and Harold were lovers for at least part of Harold's ten years in parliament (http://en.wikipedia.org/wiki/Robert_Bernays). This may or may not be true. What is more important is that Bernays, who had a better understanding of the House of Commons and its moods than Harold, looked after Harold during his early years in Parliament and that they shared a common attitude towards many social and political issues.
4 HN diary, 8 February 1937.
5 Nigel Nicolson (ed.), *Diaries and Letters 1930–1939*, p.291.
6 Nigel Nicolson, *Long Life*, p.4.
7 The *OED* (1989) records that the word first appeared in the United States in 1936, but was probably coined by Magnus Hirschfeld whose book, *Racism*, was translated into English in 1938. The term did not enter common usage until after 1945.
8 *Hansard*, 18 June 1937, Vol. 325 cc778-779. Consulted 14 July 2012.
9 HN diary, 17 March 1937.
10 HN diary, 17 March 1937.
11 HN diary, 27 May 1937.
12 JLM, Vol. 2, p.91.
13 Nigel Nicolson (ed.), *Diaries and Letters 1930–1939*, p.305, note 2.
14 Duke of Windsor, *A King's Story*, 1951; Duchess of Windsor, *The Heart Has Its Reasons*, 1956.
15 HN diary, 15 November 1937.
16 HN diary, 10 November 1937.
17 HN diary, 31 December 1937.
18 HN to VSW, 28 October 1937.

19 HN diary, 31 December 1937.

Munich, pages 399–412
1 HN to VSW, 17 February 1938.
2 HN diary, 26 January 1938.
3 HN diary, 17 February 1938.
4 HN to VSW, 22 February 1938.
5 *Hansard*, 21 February 1938, Vol. 332 c99 and c104. Consulted 14 July 2012.
6 HN to VSW, 22 February 1938.
7 HN to VSW, 25 February 1938.
8 HN diary, 18 May 1938.
9 HN to VSW, 2 March 1938.
10 *Hansard*, 14 March 1938, Vol. 333, cc.52, 94–95. Consulted 15 July 2012.
11 HN diary, 29 March 1938.
12 Comicism.tripod.com, Koenigsberg. The speech was given on 25 March but not broadcast until 11 April when Harold heard it. Consulted 15 July 2012.
13 HN diary, 13 May 1938.
14 HN diary, 23 May 1938.
15 HN diary, 6 June 1938.
16 HN diary, 2 May 1938.
17 HN diary, 7 June 1938.
18 HN diary, 5 August 1938.
19 HN diary, 14 September 1938.
20 HN diary, 19 September 1938.
21 HN diary, 20 September 1938.
22 HN diary, 22 September 1938.
23 HN diary, 28 September 1938.
24 Faber, *Munich: The 1938 Appeasement Crisis*, pp.5–7.
25 HN diary, 1 October 1938.
26 *Hansard*, 14 March 1938, Vol. 333 cc45-169. Consulted 15 July 2012.
27 HN diary, 6 October 1938.

Outbreak, pages 412–421
1 HN to VSW, 11 July 1938.
2 HN diary, 1 October 1938.
3 VSW to HN, 14 November 1938.
4 HN to VSW, 15 November 1938.
5 HN to Ben Nicolson, 27 January 1938, quoted in JLM, Vol. 2, p.97.
6 Rose, p.223.
7 The column in fact began life as 'People and Things', changing its name in 1940.
8 *Diplomacy*, p.7.
9 *Diplomacy*, p.119.
10 HN diary, January 15 1939.
11 *Hansard*, 6 February 1939, Vol. 343 c623. Consulted 16 July 2012.
12 HN diary, 7 February 1938.
13 *Hansard*, 31 March 1939, Vol. 345 c2415. Consulted 16 July 2012.
14 HN diary, 2 August 1939.
15 HN diary, 19 August 1939.
16 HN diary, 1 September 1939.
17 HN diary, 2 September 1939.
18 BBC.co.uk, The Transcript of Neville Chamberlain's Declaration of War. Consulted 16 July 2012.
19 HN diary, 3 September 1939.

Role, pages 421–428
1 HN diary, 11 September 1939.
2 HN diary, 5 September 1939.
3 HN diary, 25 November 1939.
4 HN diary, 17 September 1939.
5 HN diary, 5 April 1940.
6 HN diary, 3 May 1940.
7 Nigel Nicolson (ed.), *Diaries and Letters, 1939–1945*, p.97.
8 HN to VSW, 10 July 1940.
9 HN diary 4 May 1940.
10 *Why Britain is at War*, p.10.
11 *Why Britain is at War*, p.31.
12 JLM, Vol. 2, p.125.
13 *Why Britain is at War*, p.159.
14 Nigel Nicolson (ed.), *Diaries and Letters, 1939–1945*, p.19.
15 HN diary, 3 September 1939.

16 HN diary, 13 January 1940.
17 HN diary, 4 June 1941.
18 HN diary, 16 July 1940.
19 HN diary, 12 July 1940.
20 HN diary, 21 June 1942.
21 HN diary, 29 September 1940.
22 HN diary, 3 August 1940.
23 HN diary, 23 October 1942.
24 HN, 'The Future of the Public Schools', *Friday Mornings 1941–1944*, pp.115–18.
25 HN, 'The Reform of the Foreign Service', *Friday Mornings 1941–1944*, pp.119–23.
26 HN diary, 1 November 1942 and 28 June 1944.

Minister, pages 428–435

1 HN diary, 17 May 1940.
2 Also called Parliamentary Secretary, but not to be confused with Private Secretary (a civil service post) or Parliamentary Private Secretary (an unpaid ministerial aide). The most senior ministerial rank is Secretary of State or Minister, followed by Minister of State and then Parliamentary Under-Secretary.
3 HN to VSW, 19 May 1940.
4 Cooper, *Old Men Forget*, pp.285–6.
5 HN diary, 3 August 1940.
6 Cooper, p.288.
7 *Hansard*, 24 October 1940, Vol. 365 c1144. Consulted 02.01.2012.
8 *Hansard*, 6 August 1940, Vol. 364 cc33-34. Consulted 02.01.2012.
9 *Hansard*, 10 July 1941, Vol. 373 cc306-7. Consulted 02.01.2012.
10 *Hansard*, 27 May 1941, Vol. 371 cc1701-3. Consulted 02.01.2012.
11 *Hansard*, HC Deb 27 May 1941, Vol. 371 c1826. Consulted 31.12.2011.
12 The Spitfire Site, Stories of the Battle of Britain 1940 – Preparing for Armaggedon. Consulted 29.01.12.
13 HN diary, 2 January 1942.
14 JLM, Vol. 2, pp.144–5.
15 Gladwyn, p.97.
16 Nigel Nicolson (ed.), *Diaries and Letters, 1939–1945*, p.178, note 2.
17 HN diary, 25 June 1941.
18 HN diary, 29 September 1940.
19 Nigel Nicolson (ed.), *Diaries and Letters, 1939–1945*, p.179, note 2.
20 Colville, p.781.
21 HN diary, 19 July 1941.
22 Quoted in JLM, Vol. 2, p.142.
23 HN diary, 14 January 1942.
24 HN diary, 27 January 1942.
25 HN diary, 27 February 1942.
26 Lees-Milne, *Through Wood and Dale*, p.235.
27 Rose, p.224.
28 Lees-Milne, *Through Wood and Dale*, p.152.
29 Rose, p.245.
30 HN diary, 11 February 1941; Nigel Nicolson (ed.), *Diaries and Letters, 1939–1945*, p.144, note 1.

Might-Have-Been, pages 435–448

1 HN diary, 19 July 1941.
2 JLM, Vol. 2, p144; 'Bracken in Bloomsbury', *Truth*, 25 July 1941.
3 BBC governors were not allowed to broadcast, but Harold was occasionally made an exception.
4 HN to VSW, 22 July 1941.
5 HN to VSW, 14 July 1943.
6 VSW to HN, 15 July 1943.
7 HN diary, 4 December 1941.
8 HN diary, 9 October 1941.
9 HN diary, 16 December 1941.
10 HN to Lady Violet Bonham-Carter, 28 August 1943, Nigel

Nicolson (ed.), *Diaries and Letters 1939–1945*, pp.313–14.
11   HN diary, 13 January 1940.
12   HN to Ben & Nigel Nicolson, 11 March 1945.
13   HN, 'Allied War Aims', *New Republic*, 26 February 1940, pp.272–5.
14   *Hansard*, December 1943, Vol. 395 c1600. Consulted 20.01.2012.
15   HN diary, 20 January 1941.
16   HN diary, 21 January 1942.
17   HN diary, 9 June 1942.
18   Churchill, p.451.
19   HN diary, 13 April 1943.
20   HN diary, 21 April 1943.
21   *Hansard*, 24 May 1944, Vol. 400 c790. Consulted 20.01.2012.
22   HN diary, 8 July 1947.
23   Nigel Nicolson (ed.), *Diaries and Letters, 1945–1962*, p.101, note 1.
24   *The Desire to Please*, p.61.
25   HN diary, 22 June 1942.
26   HN diary, 21 June 1942.
27   HN diary, 3 December 1943.
28   HN diary, 19 November 1943.
29   HN to Ben & Nigel Nicolson, 7 November 1943.
30   HN diary, 23 November 1943.

Survival, pages 448–454
1   HN diary, 16 April 1941.
2   HN diary, 20 September 1940.
3   HN diary, 19 September 1940.
4   HN diary, 8 October 1942.
5   HN diary, 20 November 1941.
6   HN diary, 24 July 1944.
7   HN to VSW, 14 December 1940.
8   HN to VSW, quoted in Glendinning, p.304.
9   HN to VSW, 31 March 1941.
10   Glendinning, p.316.
11   HN to VSW, 2 April 1941.
12   Glendinning, p.319.
13   VSW to HN, 10 November 1942.
14   VSW to HN, 16 February 1944.
15   VSW to HN, 2 December 1942.
16   VSW to HN, 7 February 1945.

Post-War, pages 454–469
1   Wilson, pp.53–58.
2   HN to Ben & Nigel Nicolson, 21 February 1944.
3   Wilson, pp.53–58.
4   HN to Ben & Nigel Nicolson, 21 February 1944.
5   VSW to HN, 23 February 1944.
6   HN to Ben & Nigel Nicolson, 21 February 1944.
7   It is called 'Introduction to the Edition of 1943', but because of wartime difficulties the edition was not published until 1944.
8   HN diary, 6 January 1945.
9   *The Congress of Vienna*, pp.vi–vii.
10   HN diary, 8 May 1945.
11   HN to Nigel Nicolson, 17 May 1945.
12   HN diary, 28 June 1944.
13   HN to Ben & Nigel Nicolson, 3 December 1943.
14   HN to VSW, 19 June 1945.
15   HN to VSW, 22 June 1945.
16   HN to VSW 3 July 1945.
17   VSW to HN, 30 June 1945.
18   Quoted in Jenkins, p.792 & p.793.
19   HN diary, 26 July 1945.
20   HN diary, 1 August 1945.
21   HN to Nigel Nicolson, 30 August 1945.
22   HN to VSW, 28 September 1945.
23   Lees-Milne, *Through Wood and Dale*, p.236.
24   HN diary, 29 July 1945.
25   JLM, Vol. 2, pp.195–6.
26   HN, 'The Nuremburg Trials', *Spectator*, 10 May 1946.
27   HN diary, 4 August 1946.

28 HN diary, 6 September 1946.
29 HN diary, 10 September 1946.
30 HN to VSW, 29 July 1946.
31 HN diary, 29 August 1946.
32 HN diary, 5 August 1946.
33 Drinkwater, p.107.
34 HN, 'Peacemaking in Paris: Success, Failure or Farce', p.190.
35 HN, 'The Need for Leadership at Paris', p.269.
36 HN diary, 17 August 1946.
37 HN diary, 9 August 1946.
38 HN diary, 6 September 1946.
39 HN diary, 9 August 1946.
40 HN diary, 27 July 1946.
41 HN diary, 2 October 1946.
42 Quoted in Rose, p.272.
43 HN diary, 22 October 1946.
44 HN diary, 2 October 1946.
45 HN, 'Modern Diplomacy and British Public Opinion', pp.599–618.
46 HN, 'Peacemaking at Paris: Success, Failure of Farce?', p.190.
47 Gladwyn, p.192.
48 HN diary, 8 October 1946.
49 HN diary, 16 October 1946.

Labour, pages 469–478
1 HN diary, 21 November 1946.
2 An enlarged volume called *The English Sense of Humour*, containing the title essay and six others dating from between 1930 and 1951, was was published by Constable in 1956.
3 HN diary, 6 December 1946.
4 HN diary, 5 January 1947.
5 HN diary, 28 February 1947.
6 HN diary, 2 October 1947.
7 HN diary, 21 November 1946.
8 VSW to HN, 7 March 1947.
9 JLM, Vol. 2, p.205.
10 Nigel Nicolson's diary, quoted in Nigel Nicolson (ed.), *Diaries and Letters, 1945–1962*, p.92.
11 Nigel Nicolson (ed.), *Diaries and Letters, 1945–1962*, p.93, note 4.
12 HN diary, 2 April 1947.
13 HN diary 25 April 1947.
14 HN to VSW, 8 September 1947.
15 HN diary, 10 November 1947.
16 HN diary, 11 December 1947.
17 HN diary, 17 December 1947.
18 HN diary, 7 January 1948.
19 HN diary, 15 January 1948.
20 Nigel Nicolson to HN, 28 February 1948.
21 HN to VSW, 24 February 1948.
22 HN, 'A Surburban Hotel', *Comments 1944–1948*, pp.296–300.
23 HN diary, 29 February 1948.
24 HN diary, 4 March 1948.
25 HN to VSW, 12 March 1948.
26 HN, 'Losing a Bye-election', *Comments 1944–1948*, p.301–05.
27 HN diary, 4 March 1948.
28 HN diary, 21 March 1948.
29 HN diary, 13 February 1950.

Proposition, pages 478–485
1 HN diary, 5 April 1948.
2 HN diary, 15 May 1948.
3 HN diary, 17 September 1948.
4 HN diary, 17 September 1948.
5 HN diary, 14 October 1948.
6 HN diary, 16 July 1948.
7 HN to VSW, 7 May 1948.
8 HN diary, 29 December 1946.
9 VSW to HN, 3 January 1950.
10 HN diary, 26 October 1948.
11 HN to VSW, 3 July 1951.
12 HN to VSW, 8 June 1948.
13 HN to VSW, 9 June 1948.
14 *Benjamin Constant*, p.ix.
15 *Benjamin Constant*, p.x.
16 JLM, Vol. 2, p.236.
17 HN to VSW, 26 September 1948.

Harold Nicolson

Biographer, pages 485–491
1. HN to VSW, 8 June 1948.
2. HN diary, 17 January 1950.
3. Chapter XXVI, 'Financial Crisis 1929–1931'; Chapter XXVII, 'National Government 1931'; Chapter VII, 'The Monarchy'.
4. *King George V*, p.vii.
5. HN diary, 12 June 1948.
6. *King George V*, p.v.
7. *King George V*, pp.119–20.
8. HN to VSW, 4 March 1949.
9. HN diary, 21 March 1949.
10. HN to VSW, 9 March 1950.
11. HN diary, 17 August 1949.
12. Cannadine, p.56.
14. HN diary, 7 January 1949.
15. HN diary, 21 July 1948.
16. JLM, Vol. 2, pp.234–5.
17. *King George V*, p.365.
18. *King George V*, p.51.
19. Cannadine, p.3.
20. JLM, Vol. 2, p.234.
21. *King George V*, p.39, note 1.
22. HN diary, 31 December 1949.
23. HN to VSW, 25 July 1950.
24. HN diary, 19 September 1951.

Meanwhile, pages 492–503
1. Four book collections of Vita's gardening articles were published: *In Your Garden* (1951); *In Your Garden Again* (1953); *More for Your Garden* (1955) and *Even More for Your Garden* (1958).
2. *Observer*, 12 June 1949.
3. HN diary, 24 May 1949.
4. HN to VSW, 18 October 1951.
5. VSW to Nigel Nicolson, 6 February 1950.
6. HN diary, 24 February 1950.
7. HN diary, October 1951.
8. HN diary, 7 February 1952.
9. JLM, Vol. 2, p.239.
10. JN diary, 23 September 1950.
11. Quoted in Glendinning, p.365.
12. *Lord Carnock*, p.435.
13. HN to VSW, 16 March 1951.
14. Quoted in Glendinning, p.368.
15. HN to VSW, 28 March 1951.
16. Glendinning, p.369.
17. HN to VSW, 17 April 1951.
18. HN diary, 4 May 1951.
19. HN diary, 8 June 1951.
20. HN to VSW, 12 June 1951.
21. HN diary, 22 January 1952.
22. HN diary, 31 May 1952.
23. There is an ongoing dispute over whether it is 'Albany' or 'The Albany'. Harold preferred 'Albany' but was by no means consistent in his usage. Lord Curzon, no mean pedant in such matters, used the definite article.
24. JLM, Vol. 2, p.251.
25. Rose, p.281.
26. £2.20 and £11.30.
27. HN diary, 17 August 1952. Christabel was Christabel Aberconway, the wife of Henry McLaren, second Baron Aberconway. They lived at Bodnant in Denbighshire, where Harold and Vita were staying.
28. Cannadine, p.3.

Reward, pages 504–511
1. HN diary, 18 May 1952.
2. Knight Commander of the Royal Victorian Order. Admission to the Order comes as a personal gift from the reigning monarch as a recognition of personal service to the monarchy.
3. HN to Sir Alan Lascelles, 31 August 1952.
4. HN diary, 3 January 1953.
5. HN diary, 26 February, 1953.

6   HN diary, 2 June 1953.
7   HN diary, 6 May 1953.
8   HN to Ben Nicolson, 5 April 1953.
9   JLM, Vol. 2, p.269.
10 Rose, p.285.
11 HN to Philippa Nicolson, 30 July 1953.
12 HN to Philippa Nicolson, 13 October 1953.
13 HN to Philippa Nicolson, 28 December 1953.
14 HN diary, 9 June 1954.
15 HN diary, 8 December 1954.
16 *Good Behaviour*, p.3.
17 *Good Behaviour*, p.1.
18 *Good Behaviour*, p.15.
19 *Good Behaviour*, p.17.
20 *Good Behaviour*, p.39.
21 *Good Behaviour*, p.15.

Health, pages 511–520
1   VSW to HN, 5 April 1955.
2   HN diary, 15 May 1955.
3   HN diary, 15 May 1955.
4   *Sainte-Beuve*, back of dust jacket of first edition.
5   *Sainte-Beuve*, p.169 & p.226.
6   HN diary, 25 January 1956.
7   HN to VSW, 1 February 1956.
8   HN diary, 31 July 1956.
9   HN to VSW, 1 August 1956.
10 HN to VSW, 8 November 1956.
11 JLM, Vol. 2, p.297.
12 HN to VSW, 15 November 1956.
13 HN diary, 31 October 1956.
14 HN diary, 2 November 1956.
15 HN diary, 4 November 1956.
16 Diana Cooper, Rupert Hart-Davis, A. P. Herbert, Gladwyn Jebb, Enid Bagnold Jones, L. E. Jones, Rose Macaulay, Raymond Mortimer, Alan Pryce-Jones, John Sparrow, Gerry Wellesley.
17 Elvira Niggeman to VSW, 21 November 1956.
18 Lawrence Jones, Alan Pryce-Jones, Rupert Hart-Davis, Raymond Mortimer, John Sparrow, Colin Fenton, James Lees-Milne.
19 HN diary, 15 December 1956.

Cruising, pages 520–531
1   The *Willem Ruys* achieved notoriety in 1985 when, under a new name, *Achille Lauro*, she was hijacked by the Palestinian Liberation Front off Egypt and one of the passengers, a disabled American of Jewish origin, Leon Klinghoffer, was killed and his body thrown overboard.
2   *Journey to Java*, pp.7–8.
3   HN diary, 13 June 1957.
4   HN diary, 12 September 1957.
5   Philip Magnus wrote under his original name, but when he married Jewell Allcroft he added her surname to his.
6   HN diary, 18 March 1958.
7   HN diary, 1 May 1958.
8   HN diary, 14 May 1958.
9   HN diary, 16 October 1958.
10 JLM, Vol. 2, p.311.
11 HN diary, 8 September 1959.
12 VSW to HN, 24 November 1959.
13 HN diary, 4 February 1960.
14 HN to Nigel & Phillipa Nicolson, 24 January 1960.
15 HN to VSW, 17 March 1960.

Endings, pp.532–543
1   JLM, Vol. 2, p.324.
2   HN to VSW, 9 November 1960.
3   VSW to HN, 8 November 1960.
4   HN diary, 2 February 1961; Rose, p.295.

5   HN to VSW, 9 March 1961.
6   Hattersley, *Guardian*, 2 July 2005.
7   HN to VSW, 30 May 1961.
8   VSW to HN, 23 November 1960.
9   HN to VSW, 10 October 1961.
10 Nigel Nicolson to VSW, 20 September 1961.
11 HN diary 21 September 1961.
12 HN diary, 21 November 1961.
13 VSW diary, 15 February 1962; HN diary, 18 February 1962.
14 HN to VSW, 27 February 1962.
15 HN diary, 1 March 1962.
16 VSW to HN, 16 May 1962.
17 JLM, Vol. 2, p.346.
18 HN to Philippa Nicolson, 31 July 1962, quoted in JLM, Vol. 2, p.347.
19 Nigel Nicolson, *Long Life*, pp.15–16.

Epilogue, pages 543–546

1   JLM, Vol. 2, p.354.
2   JLM, Vol. 2, p.354.
3   HN diary, 27 September 1944

Bibliography

Unless otherwise indicated, the place of publication is London.

Works by Harold Nicolson
  Paul Verlaine. Constable, 1921.
  Sweet Waters. Constable, 1921.
  'The Revision of the Treaty of Sèvres', *Documents in British Foreign Policy 1919–1939*, Series 1, Vol. 17, 18 January 1921. HMSO, 1970.
  Tennyson: Aspects of His Life, Character and Poetry. Constable, 1923.
  Byron: The Last Journey. Constable, 1924.
  Swinburne. Constable, 1926.
  Some People. Constable, 1926. Quotations in the text are taken from the new edition published by Oxford University Press in 1983.
  'British Foreign Policy Considered in Relation to the European Situation'. *Documents in British Foreign Policy 1919–1939*, Series 1, Vol. 27, 20 February 1925. HMSO, 1968.
  'Anglo-Persian Relations'. *Documents in British Foreign Policy 1919–1939*, Series 1A, Vol. 2, 30 September 1926. HMSO, 1968.
  'Herr Müller's Policy Declaration'. *Documents in British Foreign Policy 1919–1939*, Series 1A, Vol. 5, 4 July 1928. HMSO, 1973.
  'Germany and the Rhineland'. *Documents in British Foreign Policy 1919–1939*, Series 1A, Vol. 6, 7 August 1929. HMSO, 1975.
  Lord Carnock. Constable, 1930.
  People and Things. Constable, 1931.
  Public Faces. Constable, 1932.
  Peacemaking 1919. Constable, 1933. Quotations in the text are taken from the 1944 edition.
  Curzon: The Last Phase 1919–1925. Constable, 1934.
  Dwight Morrow. Constable, 1935.
  Politics in the Train. Constable, 1936.
  Diplomacy. Constable, 1939. Quotations in the text are taken from the 3rd edition, Oxford University Press, 1963.
  Why Britain is at War. Penguin, 1939.
  Friday Mornings 1941–1944. Constable, 1944.
  Another World Than This (edited with Vita Sackville-West). Michael Joseph, 1945.
  'The Need for Leadership in Paris'. *Listener*, 29 August 1946.
  The Congress of Vienna: A Study in Allied Unity: 1812–1822. Constable, 1946.

Harold Nicolson

'Peacemaking in Paris: Success, Failure or Farce'. *Foreign Affairs*, Vol. 25, No. 2, January 1947.
Tennyson's Two Brothers. (Text of 1947 Leslie Stephen Lecture). Cambridge: CUP, 2014.
Comments 1944–1948. Constable, 1948.
King George V: His Life and Reign. Constable, 1952.
The Evolution of Diplomatic Method. Constable, 1954.
The English Sense of Humour and other Essays. Constable, 1946.
Good Behaviour. Constable, 1955.
Journey to Java. Constable, 1957.
The Age of Reason 1700–1789. Constable, 1960.
Monarchy. Weidenfeld & Nicolson, 1962.

Works by Vita Sackville-West

Poems of East and West. John Lane, 1917.
Heritage. Collins, 1919.
The Dragon in Shallow Waters. Collins, 1921.
Orchard and Vineyard. John Lane/Bodley Head, 1921.
The Heir: A Love Story. Heinemann, 1922.
Challenge. New York: George.H.Doran, 1923. 1st UK edition, Collins, 1974.
Grey Wethers. Heinemann, 1923.
Seducers in Ecuador. Hogarth Press, 1924.
The Edwardians. Hogarth Press, 1930.
All Passion Spent. Hogarth Press, 1931.
Sissinghurst. Hogarth Press, 1931.
The Land. Heinemann, 1933.
Passenger to Tehran. Hogarth Press, 1926. Quotations in the text are from the new edition published by Arrow Books in 1991.
Twelve Days: Account of a Journey Across the Bakhtiari Mountains of Southwestern Persia (also published as *12 Days in Persia*). Hogarth Press, 1928.
Knole and the Sackvilles. Ernest Benn, 1922. Quotations in the text are from the new edition published by the National Trust in 1991.
The Women's Land Army. Michael Joseph, 1946.
The Garden. Michael Joseph, 1946.
'The Garden at Sissinghurst Castle'. *Journal of the Royal Horticultural Society*, November 1953.
No Signposts in the Sea. Michael Joseph, 1961.

Other printed sources

Bell, Clive, *Art.* Chatto & Windus, 1913.
Bell, Oliver, ed. *The Diary of Virginia Woolf, Vol. II, 1920–1924.* Hogarth Press, 1984.
Bell, Quentin, *Bloomsbury Recalled.* New York: Columbia University Press, 1996.

De Salvo, Louise and Mitchell Leaska, eds. *The Letters of Vita Sackville-West to Virginia Woolf.* Hutchinson, 1984.
Bruce Lockhart, Robert, *Retreat From Glory.* Putnam, 1935.
Cannadine, David, 'Rose's Rex'. *London Review of Books,* Vol. 5, No. 17, 15 September 1983.
Channon, Sir Henry, *'Chips': The Diaries of Sir Henry Channon.* Phoenix, 1996.
Churchill, Winston, *The Second World War: II, Their Finest Hour.* Cassell, 1949.
Coates, Willson Havelock, Anne Steele Young & Vernon F. Snow, eds. *The Private Journals of the Long Parliament.* New Haven, Connecticut: Yale, 1982.
Colville, John, *The Fringes of Power: Downing Street Diaries, 1939–1955.* Hodder and Stoughton, 1989.
Cooper, Duff, *Old Men Forget.* Rupert Hart Davis, 1953.
Cronin, Stephanie, 'Opposition to Reza Khan within the Iranian Army 1921–1926'. *Middle East Studies,* Vol. 30, No. 4, 4 October 1994.
Dodge, Toby, *Inventing Iraq.* New York: Columbia University Press, 2003.
Dowson, Jane, *Women's Poetry of the 1930s: A Critical Anthology.* Routledge, 1996.
Drinkwater, Derek, *Sir Harold Nicolson & International Relations.* Oxford: OUP, 2005.
Dufferin, Lord, *Letters from High Latitudes.* John Murray, 1857.
Faber, David, *Munich: The 1938 Appeasement Crisis.* New York: Simon & Schuster, 2008.
Fleming, Peter, *Bayonets to Lhasa.* Rupert Hart-Davis, 1961.
Gilmour, David, *Curzon.* Papermac, 1995.
Gladwyn, Lord, *The Memoirs of Lord Gladwyn.* Weidenfeld & Nicolson, 1972.
Glendinning, Victoria, *Vita: The Life of V. Sackville-West.* Weidenfeld & Nicolson, 1983.
Haag, Michael, *Alexandria: City of Memory.* New Haven, Connecticut: Yale University Press, 2004.
Hassall, Christopher, *Edward Marsh.* Longmans, 1959.
Hattersley, Roy, 'Kenneth Harris'. *Guardian,* 2 July 2005.
Henderson, Sir Neville, *Water Under The Bridges.* Hodder & Stoughton, 1945.
Hobsbawm, Eric, *Industry and Empire: The Birth of the Industrial Revolution.* New York: New Press, 1999.
Jones, John, *Balliol College: A History.* Oxford: OUP, 1988.
King, Peter, ed. *Curzon's Persia.* Sidgwick & Jackson, 1986.
Lees-Milne, James, *Through Wood and Dale, Diaries 1975–1978.* John Murray, 1998.
Lees-Milne, James, *Harold Nicolson,* 2 Volumes. Chatto and Windus, 1980–1981.
Macmillan, Harold, *Winds of Change.* Macmillan, 1966.
Macmillan, Harold, *The Blast of War.* Macmillan, 1967.
Mansel, Philip, *Constantinople.* Penguin, 1995.

Massie, Robert K., *Dreadnought*. Pimlico, 1993.
Meyers, T. L., 'On Drink and Faith: Swinburne and John Nichol at Oxford'. *Review of English Studies* 55, Oxford University Press, 2004.
Nicolson, Adam, *Sissinghurst: An Unfinished History*. Harper Collins, 2008.
Nicolson, Juliet, *The Great Silence: 1918–1920 Living in the Shadow of the Great War*. John Murray, 2010.
Nicolson, Nigel, *Long Life*. Putnam, 1998.
Nicolson, Nigel, *Portrait of a Marriage*. Weidenfeld & Nicolson, 1973.
Nicolson, Nigel, ed. *Harold Nicolson: Diaries and Letters 1930–1939*. Collins, 1966.
Nicolson, Nigel, ed. *Harold Nicolson: Diaries and Letters 1939–1945*. Collins, 1967.
Nicolson, Nigel, ed. *Harold Nicolson: Diaries and Letters 1945–1962*. Collins, 1968.
Nicolson, Nigel, ed. *Vita and Harold. The Letters of Vita Sackville-West and Harold Nicolson 1910–1962*. Weidenfeld & Nicolson, 1992.
Nicolson, Nigel, ed. *The Harold Nicolson Diaries 1907–1963*. Weidenfeld & Nicolson, 2004.
Norwich, John Julius, ed. *The Duff Cooper Diaries*. Phoenix, 2006.
Ponsonby, Sir Frederick, ed. *Letters of the Empress Frederick*. Macmillian, 1929.
Powell, Anthony, *To Keep the Ball Rolling*. Penguin, 1983.
Rezun, Miron, *The Soviet Union and Iran*. Institut Universitaire de Hautes Études, Geneva, 1981.
Rose, Norman, *Harold Nicolson*. Jonathan Cape, 2005.
Self, Robert, *Neville Chamberlain: A Biography*. Ashgate, 2006.
Sheridan, Clare, *Nuda Veritas*. Thornton Butterworth, 1927.
Tuchman, Barbara, *The Proud Tower*. Papermac, 1980.
Tuchman, Barbara, *August 1914*. Papermac, 1980.
Waugh, Evelyn, *Brideshead Revisited*. Chapman & Hall, 1945.
Wilson, Edmund, 'Through the Embassy Window'. *New Yorker*, 1 January 1944, pp.53–58
Windsor, Duchess of, *The Heart Has Its Reasons*. Michael Joseph, 1956.
Windsor, Duke of, *A King's Story*. Cassel, 1951.
Zirinsky, Michael P., 'Imperial Power and Dictatorship: Britain and the Rise of Reza Shah'. *International Journal of Middle East Studies*, Vol. 24, No. 4 (November 1992), Cambridge University Press.

Internet sources

American-Presidents.org, Chester Arthur and Victoria Sackville. http://www.american-presidents.org/2007/05/chester-arthur-and-victoria-sackville.html
Balliol College Archives & Manuscripts, Francis Fortescue Urquhart Photographs. http://archives.balliol.ox.ac.uk/Exhibitions/exhib09.asp

Balliol College Archives & Manuscripts, Patrick Houston Shaw-Stewart (1888-1917), War Poet. http://archives.balliol.ox.ac.uk/Past%20members/PHStewart.asp

Battleships-Cruisers.co.uk, HMS Bellona. http://www.battleships-cruisers.co.uk/hms_bellona.htm

BBC.co.uk, The Transcript of Neville Chamberlain's Declaration of War. http://www.bbc.co.uk/archive/ww2outbreak/7957.shtml

Comicism.tripod.com, Koenigsberg. http://comicism.tripod.com/380325.html

Hansard, League of Nations and Abyssinia, HC Deb, 19 December 1935, Vol. 307 cc2017-127. http://hansard.millbanksystems.com/commons/1935/dec/19/league-of-nations-and-abyssinia#S5CV0307P0_19351219_HOC_365

Hansard, Debate on the Address, HC Deb, 03 November 1936, Vol 317 cc14-74. http://hansard.millbanksystems.com/commons/1936/nov/03/debate-on-the-address#S5CV0317P0_19361103_HOC_55

Hansard, Ministry of Health, HC Deb, 18 June 1937, Vol. 325 cc729-810. http://hansard.millbanksystems.com/commons/1937/jun/18/ministry-of-health#S5CV0325P0_19370618_HOC_44

Hansard, Foreign Policy, HC Deb, 21 February 1938, Vol. 332 cc52-156. http://hansard.millbanksystems.com/commons/1938/feb/21/foreign-policy#S5CV0332P0_19380221_HOC_283

Hansard, Foreign Policy (Austria), HC Deb, 14 March 1938, Vol. 333 cc45-169. http://hansard.millbanksystems.com/commons/1938/mar/14/foreign-affairs-austria

Hansard, Policy of His Majesty's Government, HC Deb, 05 October 1938, Vol. 339 cc337-454. http://hansard.millbanksystems.com/commons/1938/oct/05/policy-of-his-majestys-government#S5CV0339P0_19381005_HOC_222

Hansard, Great Britain and France, HC Deb, 06 February 1939, Vol. 343 c623. http://hansard.millbanksystems.com/commons/1939/feb/06/great-britain-and-france#S5CV0343P0_19390206_HOC_109

Hansard, European Situation, HC Deb, 31 March 1939, Vol. 345 cc2415-20. http://hansard.millbanksystems.com/commons/1939/mar/31/european-situation-1#S5CV0345P0_19390331_HOC_226

Hansard: Local Information Officer (Speech, Oxford), HC Deb, 24 October 1940, Vol. 365 cc1143-5. http://hansard.millbanksystems.com/commons/1940/oct/24/local-information-committee-officer#S5CV0365 P0_19401024_HOC_204

Hansard, Mr Noel Coward (Visit, United States), HC Deb, 06 August 1940, Vol. 364 cc33-34. http://hansard.millbanksystems.com/commons/1940/aug/06/mr-noel-coward-visit-united-states#S5CV0364 P0_19400806_HOC_257

Hansard, Personnel (Civil Service Rules), HC Deb, 10 July 1941, Vol. 373 cc306-7. http://hansard.millbanksystems.com/commons/1941/jul/10/ personnel-civil-service-rules#S5CV0373P0_19410710_HOC_165

Hansard, Rudolf Hess, HC Deb, 27 May 1941, Vol. 371 cc1701-3. http://hansard.

millbanksystems.com/commons/1941/may/27/rudolf-hess#S5CV0371P0_19410527_HOC_161

Hansard, Ministry of Information, HC Deb, 27 May 1941, Vol. 371 cc1815-26. http://hansard.millbanksystems.com/commons/1941/may/27/ministry-of-information#S5CV0371P0_19410527_HOC_498

Hansard, War Situation and Foreign Affairs. HC Deb, 15 December 1943, Vol. 395 cc1575-647. http://hansard.millbanksystems.com/commons/1943/dec/15/war-situation-and-foreign-affairs#S5CV0395P0_19431215_HOC_330

Hansard, Foreign Affairs. HC Deb, 24 May 1944, Vol. 400 cc762-829. http://hansard.millbanksystems.com/commons/1944/may/24/foreign-affairs#S5CV0400P0_19440524_HOC_307

Hardy, Barbara, untitled review. *Boston Review*, October-November 1997. http://bostonreview.net/BR22.5/hardy.html

Sellar, David, Clan History of the Nicolsons of Skye. http://www.clanmacnicol.org/BriefHistory.htm.

The Spitfire Site, Stories of the Battle of Britain 1940 – Preparing for Armaggedon. http://spitfiresite.com/2010/06/battle-of-britain-1940-fear-of-invasion.html

UK in Germany, Embassy History. http://archive.today/qOu4

Index

Adam, Paul, 142
Adb El Aziz, Sultan, 25
Addison, Lord, 461
Adenauer, Konrad, 324
Alexander of Battenburg (King of Bulgaria), 23
Alexander of Battenburg (son of Princess Beatrice), 32
Alexander, A.V., 466
Alexander, Field Marshal, 506
Alexander, King of Greece, 172–3
Alfonso XIII, King of Spain, 50, 75, 493
Allcroft, Jewell, 525, 528
Amery, Leo, 399, 420, 423, 425, 462
Amory, Copley, 292, 294, 362, 375, 541
Andrew, Prince of Greece, 205–6
Annan, Noel, 471, 492, 532
Arlen, Michael, 251, 369
'Arketall', see Tivendale
Arnold, Thomas, 7
Arthur, President Chester, 82
Ashton, Dorothy, see Wellesley, Dorothy
Ashton, Leigh, 289–90, 295
Asquith, Elizabeth, see Bibesco, Elizabeth
Asquith, H.H., 29, 73, 79, 242, 245, 252, 315, 538
Asquith, Margot, 242
Astor, David, 525–6
Astor, Nancy, 317, 343
Astor, William Waldorf, 97, 107
Attlee, Clement, 406, 457, 459–60, 473, 478, 489
Auden, W.H., 515–16, 541
Auriol, President Vincent, 489

Bailey, Cyril, 46–47
Baird, Sandy, 325
Baldwin, Stanley, 229, 234, 241–2, 245, 326, 381, 385–6, 389, 392, 400
Balfour, A.J. (later Earl Balfour), 69, 112, 114, 116, 127–8, 139, 144–5, 154–7, 160, 248
Balfour, Ronald, 183, 263, 293
Baring, Maurice, 121, 208, 343
Barrington-Ward, Robert, 409
Barry, Gerald, 399
Beaverbrook, Lord, 240, 315, 328–30, 333, 335–9, 341–2, 352–5, 361, 361, 366, 391, 434, 459
Beemelmans, Clementina, 4, 8–9, 324
Beemelmans, Wilhelm, 9–10, 324
Beerbohm Tree, Sir Herbert, 68, 190, 501
Beerbohm, Max, 31, 369
Bell, Clive, 183, 211–16, 248, 268–9, 272, 278, 289, 295–6, 300, 315, 321, 532
Bell, Gertrude, 255, 259, 270
Bell, Quentin, 253, 321
Bell, Vanessa, 248, 321–2
Benedict XV, Pope, 112–13
Beneš, Edvard, 139, 144, 406–7, 409
Bentinck, Charles, 224
Berenson, Bernard, 225–6, 495–7, 512–13
Berenson, Mary, 225
Bernays, Robert, 394, 432, 450, 485, 546
Berners, Lord, 68, 130, 134, 186, 225, 310, 454, 513
Berry, Walter, 241

Bertie, Arthur ('Tata'), 48–49, 63, 66, 68, 77, 79
Betjeman, Sir John, 29, 120, 296
Bevan, Aneurin, 533
Bevin, Ernest, 315, 461, 464–6, 468, 473, 493
Bibesco, Elizabeth, 143, 248
Bibesco, Prince Antoine, 143
Bidault, Georges, 443, 466, 473
Bildt, Baron, 107
Birrell, Francis, 248, 337, 357
Blixen, Karen, 408
Bloomsbury Group, xiii, 180, 211–16, 226, 228, 237, 239, 242, 248–9, 253, 279–80, 307, 315, 321–2, 333, 545
Blum, Léon, 426, 466
Blunden, Edward, 451
Bohen, Charles, 530
Bonar Law, Andrew, 196, 229
Bonham Carter, Lady Violet, 438–9, 465, 492, 510
Booth, Clare Luce, 530
Boothby, Robert, 343, 399, 420–1, 510
Borden, Sir Robert, 144
Boris, King of Bulgaria, 405
Bowra, Maurice, 318, 325, 532
Bracken, Brendan, 249, 361, 399, 420, 434, 438, 462, 494–5
Bramly, Wilfred ('Bramly Bey'), 257
Bratianu, Ion, 144
Briand, Aristide, 175
Bridges, Robert, 295
Brooke, Jocelyn, 29
Brooke, Rupert, 120, 208
Browning, Oscar, 64
Bruce Lockhart, Robert, 326, 328–9, 335, 338, 532
Brüning, Heinrich, 358, 373
Buchan-Hepburn, Patrick (Lord Hailes), 268, 535
Bullock, Malcolm, 343
Burgess, Guy, 415, 432, 461, 500, 528–9
Butler, R.A. ('Rab'), 425, 433, 469
Byron, Clara Allegra, 226

Byron, Lord, 1, 126–7, 179, 208–9, 216, 218–20, 223–6, 228, 233–5, 237, 309, 377, 415
Byron, Robert, 342, 522

Cadman, Sir John, 290–1, 293–4
Cadogan, Alec, 401
Caird, Edward, 46
Calles, President Plutarco, 377
Cambon, Jules, 141–2
Campbell, Kenneth Hallyburton, 84, 107
Campbell, Mary, 308, 317
Campbell, Roy, 308
Campbell-Bannerman, Sir Henry, 53
Campbell-Gray, Ian, 248
Carnock, Lord Arthur; upbringing and education: 4–7; joins Foreign Office: 8–9; character: 10–11; early career: 17–24, 86–87, 253–4, 260–1; Minister to Morocco: 25–26, 28; 29, 32, 37–8, 42–3, 48; Ambassador to Spain: 49–50; Ambassador to Russia: 53–4, 58–60, 197, 208; Permanent Under-Secretary at Foreign Office: 70–71, 76, 78, 105, 108, 136, 139; 90, 100, 101, 110–12, 205, 246, 303, 313; death: 319–20; 334, 340, 485, 498
Carnock, Lady Catherine, 11–21, 26, 28–29, 36, 39, 40, 42, 49, 66, 90, 160, 320, 452, 470–1, 497–9, 506–8
Carol, King of Romania, 404, 413
Cartland, Ronald, 449
Catroux, Georges, 441
Cazalet, Sir Victor, 176, 431, 450, 453
Cecil, Lord Robert, 112–13, 123, 129
Cecil, Robert, 343
Chamberlain, Austen, 242–4, 247, 250, 252, 285, 297, 313, 386
Chamberlain, Neville, 351, 399–403, 406–12, 414, 416–20, 422–5, 433, 458, 462, 488

Index

Channon, Sir Henry ('Chips'), 176, 393–4, 399
Chaplin, Charlie, 339, 342
Charles I, Emperor, 122
Charles I, King, 4, 12
Churchill, Clementine ('Clemmie'), 111
Churchill, Sir Winston, 28, 63, 111, 119, 178, 194, 214, 242, 244, 248–9, 315, 343, 361, 389, 392, 399–400, 402–4, 408–10, 425, 428–9, 432–5, 438–42, 447–8, 456–62, 467, 474, 476, 489, 494, 506, 535, 538
Clark Kerr, Archibald ('Archie'; later Baron Inverchapel), 68, 72, 74, 77, 79, 112, 335, 373, 462, 513
Clark, Reuben, 378
Clark, Sir Kenneth, 429, 432, 488, 492, 532
Clay, Sir Charles, 51
Clemenceau, Georges, 133, 139, 141, 151, 153–4, 466
Clerk, Sir George, 108, 111–12, 116, 131, 464
Clive, Magdalen, 286–7
Clive, Sir Robert, 286–7, 289, 291, 301
Cocteau, Jean, 91, 142–3, 155, 272
Codrington, Ursula, 529
Colefax, Lady Sibyl, 121, 180, 182, 189, 214, 252, 325, 342, 373, 386, 390–1, 472, 496
Compton-Burnett, Ivy, 499
Connolly, Cyril, 29, 296, 310, 325–6, 443
Constant, Benjamin, 472, 474, 483–4
Constantine, King of Greece, 172, 174, 195
Cook, Sir Joseph, 144
Cooke, Alistair, 339, 541
Cooper, Lady Diana, 189, 230, 342–3, 532
Cooper, Duff, 189, 230, 335, 343, 382, 386, 399, 407, 410–1, 419–20, 428–30, 432–4, 443, 466, 502, 513

Cooper, Reginald, 33, 48, 68, 77, 88, 108, 112
Copper, Jack, 361, 383, 448, 496, 540
Coward, Noel, 310, 338, 386, 390, 430, 541
Cradock-Hartopp, Charles, 183, 224, 255–6
Cranborne, Lord ('Bobbetty'), 399
Crichton Stuart, Lord Colum Edmond, 61
Cromer, Earl of, 488–9
Crossley, Anthony, 319
Crossman, Richard, 471, 474
Crowe, Sir Eyre, 70–1, 108, 113, 129, 139, 154, 172–5, 179, 185, 200, 206, 230, 238, 241, 244, 246–7
Cunard, Sir Bache, 133
Cunard, Lady Emerald, 121, 133, 180, 342, 381, 466, 472
Cunard, Victor, 133, 166, 183, 381, 394
Curzon, Lady, 206, 214, 230, 245, 252, 366, 372
Curzon, Lord, 18, 43, 64, 100, 160, 172–5, 177, 179, 184–5, 194–212, 217, 219, 221–2, 229–30, 232, 239, 242, 244–7, 252, 261, 263, 366, 372, 501
Cutting, Iris, 226
Cutting, Lady Sibyl, 225, 227, 236

Daladier, Edouard, 406, 410, 426
Dalton, Hugh, 472
d'Annunzio, Gabriele, 156
Darlan, Admiral François, 443
Daryush, Elizabeth, 272
Dawson, Lord, 342
de Bunsen, Sir Maurice, 75
de Gaigneron, Comte Jean, 140, 166, 295
de Gaulle, General Charles, 440–3
de Hénaut, Jean, 56, 61–62, 66
De La Warr, Buck, 381, 394, 407, 409
de Lacretelle, Pierre, 88–89, 91, 140, 207, 210, 465, 474, 483
de Margerie, Roland, 397, 483

581

de Murville, Maurice Couve, 295, 529
de Valera, Eamon, 447
Dickinson, Oswald ('Ozzie'), 118, 121
Dimbleby, Richard, 339
Dobbs, Sir Henry, 259
Drinkwater, John, 183
Drogheda, Kathleen, 318
Drummond, Sir Eric, 150, 168–9
Duca, Ion, 206
Dufferin, Lady, 13, 17, 21, 28, 252
Dufferin, Lord, 13–15, 17–19, 21, 24, 33, 43, 47, 99, 393, 398, 443, 522
Dugdale, Baffy, 409

Eden, Sir Anthony, 381, 389, 399–401, 403, 405, 409, 411, 418–23, 425, 438, 442, 456, 472, 516–19
Edward VII, King, 10, 50, 53, 60, 69, 242
Edward VIII, King, 78, 229, 386, 390, 392, 396, 488, 505
Einstein, Albert, 302, 325
Elgin, 9th Earl (Viceroy of India), 43
Elgin, Lord (8th Earl), 5, 7
Eliot, T.S., 272, 288, 300, 323, 451, 481, 535
Elizabeth, Princess, *see* Elizabeth II, Queen
Elizabeth, Queen (consort of King George VI), 325, 397, 411, 486, 489, 502
Elizabeth II, Queen, 451, 472, 489, 502, 506
Elliott, Walter, 502
Ervine, St John, 339

Fenton, Colin, 508, 510, 524, 532
Firbank, Ronald, 47, 51, 88
Flecker, Helle, 223
Flecker, James Elroy, 223
Fleming, Eve, 183
Foch, Maréchal, 128, 175
Foot, Robert, 438
Forster, E.M., xiii

Franz Ferdinand, Archduke, 103, 105, 153
Freese, Reverend, F.E., 38–41
Fry, Roger, 214, 248

Gaitskell, Hugh, 521
Gaslee, Stephen, 320
George V, King, 78, 105, 224, 229–30, 242, 252, 296, 335, 387, 482, 485–90, 503
George VI, King, 78, 325, 396–7, 411, 482, 489, 491
Georges-Picot, François, 129
Gibbs, Christopher, 532–3
Gide, André, 142, 472
Giraud, General Henri, 441–3
Goossens, Sir Eugene, 223
Goschen, George, 17
Gosse, Edmund, 180, 190, 192, 208, 217, 234, 242, 247, 252, 277, 295, 300, 311
Graham, Sir Ronald, 299
Grandi, Dino, 390
Grant, Duncan, 213, 248, 315, 321–2
Granville, Lord, 8
Grenfell, Edward, 373
Grenfell, Julian, 55
Grey, Sir Edward, 60, 70–71, 101, 105–6, 111, 136, 304, 341
Grosvenor, Rosamund, 74, 84–85, 90–92, 94, 96, 99, 102, 107
Gruber, Karl, 466

Haig, Field Marshal Douglas, 154
Haley, Sir William, 438, 465, 510
Halifax, Lord, 397, 417, 423, 434
Hall, Donald, 465
Hamilton, Archibald Rowan, *see* Rowan, Hamilton
Hamilton, Hans, 11
Hamilton, Hariot Rowan, *see* Dufferin, Lady
Hamilton, James, 11–12

Index

Hamilton, Mary Catherine Rowan, see Carnock, Lady
Hankey, Sir Maurice, 138
Hardinge, Sir Charles (later Lord), 66, 82, 111–13, 116, 123, 139–40, 150, 172, 174, 326, 333
Harington, General Sir Charles, 194–5
Harris, Henry Wilson, 415
Harris, Kenneth, 535–6, 538
Harvey, Oliver, 466, 474
Hauptmann, Gerhardt, 369
Heard, Gerald, 357
Heath, Edward, 399
Henderson, Arthur, 326
Henderson, Sir Neville, 59, 303, 420
Henlein, Konrad, 405–6, 408–9
Herbert, David, 325
Herbert, Reginald (15th Earl of Pembroke), 343
Hitler, Adolf, 301, 314–5, 358, 373, 389–90, 400–1, 404, 406, 408–11, 417–21, 424–5, 453
Hoare, Sir Reginald, 404
Hoare, Sir Samuel, 385
Hobhouse, Christopher, 358, 380, 384, 432, 449
Hoover, President Herbert, 363
Hopkins, Harry, 422
Hore-Belisha, Leslie, 439
Horner, Edward, 55
Horrabin, Frank, 417
Horsbrugh, Florence, 392
Horstmann, Alfred, 315
Horstmann, Lali, 315, 332, 394
Horthy, Miklós, 299
Hull, Cordell, 442
Hulton, Edward, 338
Hussey, Rev. Arthur, 29
Huxley, Aldous, xiii, 189, 382, 492, 459

James I and VI, King, 3, 12, 56, 80
James, Henry, 69, 241

Janner, Barnett, 459
Jarvis, Bertie, 402, 414
Jebb, Gladwyn (later Lord Gladwyn), 261, 263, 266–9, 271–3, 292, 294–5, 310, 358, 400, 432, 449, 466, 468–9, 472, 511, 515, 532
Jebb, Marjorie, 289, 291–2
Joad, C.E.M., 492
John, Augustus, 143, 183, 315
Jonescu, Take, 138
Jordan, Philip, 478
Jowett, Benjamin, 43–44
Jowitt, William, 460–2
Joyce, James, 357, 369

Kemal, Mustapha (Atatürk), 168, 172, 191, 193–6, 204
Keppel, Alice, 163, 167
Keppel, Colonel George, 163
Keppel, Violet, see Trefusis, Violet
Keyes, Sir Roger, 200, 204, 207
Keynes, John Maynard, 180, 213, 216, 226, 237, 310, 315, 359
King, Tony, 542
King-Hall, Stephen, 397
Kitchener, Lord, 100, 114, 197
Knatchbull-Hugessen, Hughe, 48
Knoblock, Edward, 132, 140
Knox, Ronald, 56
Koenig, Marie-Pierre, 443
Kun, Béla, 148–50, 167

Lamont, Edie, 525, 538
Lamont, Thomas, 373
Lampson, Sir Miles, 238, 395
Lancaster, Osbert, 433, 466
Lane, Allen, 424
Lascelles, Sir Alan ('Tommy'), 68, 79, 454, 482–3, 485–6, 491, 505, 510, 524, 532, 535
Lascelles, Sir Daniel, 528
Lascelles, Viscount, 90–92, 190
Laval, Pierre, 385
Lavery, John, 119

583

Lawrence, D.H., xiii, 187, 315, 363
Lawrence, T.E., 256
Layard, Sir Henry, 17
Learned Hand, Judge, 375
Leeper, Allen, 138, 145, 148–9, 182, 200, 202, 209–10
Leeper, Rex, 138, 463–4
Lees-Milne, James, 76, 88–89, 369–70, 376, 462, 471, 475, 480–1, 493, 510, 539
Leopold III, King of Belgium, 390
Lewis, Sinclair, 310, 312
Lichnowsky, Prince, 106–7, 303–4
Lindbergh, Anne, 373–4, 378, 386, 388, 541
Lindbergh, Charles, 373–4, 376, 378–9, 386, 388
Lindemann, Frederick, 248
Lindsay, Lady, 309, 321
Lindsay, Sir Ronald, 301–2, 305, 312–13, 320, 330, 333, 363, 375, 401, 418
Lippman, Walter, 378, 541
Lister, Charles Alfred, 55
Lloyd George, Sir David, 114, 131–2, 136, 141, 144, 151, 154–5, 174–5, 177–9, 192, 194, 196, 361, 397, 403, 423
Lloyd, Sir George (later Lord Lloyd of Dolobran), 255–7, 342, 417
Loch, Henry Brougham, 7
Loch, James of Drylaw, 4
Loch, Mary Clementina, 4
Londonderry, Lord, 326
Lopokova, Lydia, 360
Loraine, Sir Percy, 252, 260, 263–7, 272–5, 278–81, 283–7, 297, 301, 395
Lowther, Sir Gerald, 87, 93, 101
Lloyd, Selwyn, 517
Lubbock, Sir Percy, 236
Lunn, Sir Henry, 377
Lutyens, Sir Edwin, 83, 110, 112, 119, 121, 130, 143, 228, 270
Lytton, Victor, 2nd Earl of, 119

Macaulay, Rose, 497

MacDonald, Malcolm, 386, 389, 403, 407
MacDonald, Ramsay, 230, 232–3, 238, 240–1, 318, 342, 352, 356–7, 381, 384, 386, 388, 392, 397, 398–9
Mackenzie King, William Lyon, 466
Mackenzie, Sir Compton, 501
Mackenzie, Mary, 486
MacLaren, Christabel, 253, 502
MacLean, Donald, 500
MacLeish, Archibald, 248, 272, 375
MacMahon, Sir Henry, 129
Macmillan, Lady Dorothy, 343
Macmillan, Sir Harold, 56, 336, 343, 352, 359, 393, 399, 420, 422, 427, 434, 521, 531, 536
Macnamara, Jack, 450
Magnus-Allcroft, Philip, 502, 525, 528, 534, 539
Maisky, Ivan, 390, 402, 408, 419
Mallet, Sir Louis, 101, 119
Mallet, Sir Victor, 101, 119, 500
Mann, Thomas, 324
Mansergh, Professor Nicholas, 432
Margaret, Princess, 451
Mariano, Nicky, 496–7
Marlborough, Duchess of, 239, 248
Marlborough, Duke of, 248
Marsh, Sir Edward, 119, 176, 183, 208, 223
'Marstock, J.D.', 33, 36, 297
Marx, Wilhelm, 301
Mary, Queen (consort of King George V), 78, 228, 242, 481–2, 488–9, 491, 502, 506
Masefield, John, 451
Massigli, René, 390, 443
Matheson, Hilda, 317, 327
Maugham, Robin, 432, 510, 532
Maugham, Somerset, 325, 369, 394, 408
McCarthy, Desmond, 215–6
McNeil, Hector, 466, 476
Melville, John (Earl of Leven; Earl of Melville), 48, 69

Milne, A.A., 342
Mirza Firouz, Prince, 272
Mitford, Diana (Lady Mosley), 446
Mitford, Nancy, 502, 515
Mohammed Reza, Shah of Persia, 511
Mohammed VI, Sultan of Turkey, 196
Mollet, Guy, 516–17
Molotov, Vyacheslav, 466, 468, 473
Molyneux, Edward, 158, 325
Monckton, Walter, 429–30, 432
Moore, Garrett, 318
Moore, George, 342
Moorehead, Alan, 468
Morgan, J.P., 373, 375, 378–9
Morgan, John, 382–3
Morrell, Lady Ottoline, 248
Morrison, Herbert, 466, 474, 476, 478, 488, 493
Morrow, Dwight, 373–9
Morrow, Elizabeth, 373–4, 376–9
Morshead, Sir Owen, 482, 485–6, 489
Mortimer, Raymond, 216, 249–54, 268, 270, 273, 275–6, 278–81, 286, 290, 294–5, 300, 309, 312, 325, 355, 446, 468, 470, 484, 502, 510, 522, 532
Mosley, Cynthia ('Cimmie'), 311, 343, 355
Mosley, Oswald ('Tom') 311–12, 318–19, 326, 335, 342–3, 350–9, 446
Mountbatten, Philip, Duke of Edinburgh, 206, 472
Müller, Herman, 313, 331
Munthe, Axel, 377
Murrow, Ed, 530
Muselier, Emile, 441
Mussolini, Benito, 196, 199, 201–2, 207, 221, 229, 358, 400–401, 404, 410–11, 418, 453

Nabokov, Vladimir, 296, 527
Nairn Brothers, 257–8
Nansen, Fridtjof, 205

Nasr-ed-Din, Shah, 18, 260–1, 271, 275, 507
Nicolson, Adam, 524, 536, 540
Nicolson, Sir Arthur, *see* Carnock, Lord
Nicolson, Benedict ('Ben'), 107, 126, 130, 134, 143, 146–7, 179, 223, 228; career as art historian: 246, 380, 404, 418, 429, 462, 475, 481, 495; 251–2, 270–1, 276, 294–5, 304, 318, 321–2, 329, 347, 362, 364, 366–8, 376, 378, 383, 388, 435, 453, 459, 470–1, 475–6, 487, 498; marriage to Luisa Vertova: 512, 529, 538–9
Nicolson, Lady Catherine, *see* Carnock, Lady
Nicolson, Clementina, *see* Beemelmans, Clementina
Nicolson, Erskine, 18, 443
Nicolson, Sir Frederick William Erskine, 4–8, 24, 58
Nicolson, Frederick ('Freddy', 2nd Baron Carnock), 17, 29, 30, 98, 337, 450, 471, 497–9, 501
Nicolson, Gwendolen, *see* St Aubyn, Gwendolen
Nicolson, Sir Harold George; family background: 1–17; birth and early years: 18–28; classical education: 27, 33, 44, 65, 218–19, 225, 384, 524; school: 28–37; Morocco: 25–27, 369–71; Oxford (and Balliol College): 33, 37, 42–49, 51–52, 55–58, 146, 176, 506; visits St Petersburg: 53–55, 58–59; joins Foreign Office: 66–71; homosexuality: 36–37, 51, 72, 85, 117–18, 120, 133, 128, 166, 230, 268, 367, 523, 526–7; meets Vita: 73–75; posting to Madrid: 75–76; posting to Constantinople: 85–89, 92–95, 101–2; marriage: 97–100; Long Barn: 109–10, 183; Balfour Declaration: 114–16; response to Vita–Violet relationship: 124–8,

585

Harold Nicolson

Nicolson, Sir Harold George, (*cont.*)
response to Vita–Violet relationship (*cont.*) 130, 133, 140, 143, 147–8, 152, 158–66; Paris Peace Conference (1919): 134–60; Lausanne Conference: 200–11; relations with Bloomsbury Group: 211–216, 248, 280, 322; affair with Raymond Mortimer: 249–50, 253; posting to Tehran: 251–2, 260–75, 278–83, 288–9; despatch from Persia: 284–7; posting to Berlin: 299–305, 309–10, 312–15, 317–18, 321–32; success as broadcaster: 311, 330, 339–40, 343, 354, 399, 407, 415, 465; anti-semitism: 315–16, 534, 546; leaves Foreign Office: 328–30, 333–6; works for Beaverbrook: 335–6, 338–9, 343, 353–4; Sissinghurst: 344–50, 362, 380, 479–80, 524, 534, 546 ; involvement with New Party: 350, 354–9; lecture tour of the US: 362–5; idea for *magnum opus*: 370–1, 444; visits US for *Dwight Morrow*: 374–8; MP for West Leicester: 381–6, 457–9; visits Africa: 394–6; attitude to black people: 396, 530–1; opposition to appeasement: 399–412, 414, 417–21; at Ministry of Information: 428–35; governor of BBC: 432, 436–40, 447, 465; advocate of France: 440–4; broadcasts on Paris Peace Conference (1946): 465–9; involvement with National Trust: 471, 480–1, 485, 493, 500, 504, 524; joins Labour Party: 471–2; stands in Croydon North bye-election: 473–8; royal biographer: 482–3, 485–92; candidate for Oxford Professor of Poetry: 515–16
Another World Than This, 463
Benjamin Constant, 483–4
Byron: the Last Journey, 218–20, 233–4
Comments 1944–1948, 437
Curzon: the Last Phase 1919–1925, 245–6, 366, 372
Diplomacy, 371–2
Dwight Murrow, 379–80
Friday Mornings 1941–1944, 437
Good Behaviour, 509–10
Harold Nicolson: Diaries and Letters (3 volumes), 542
Helen's Tower, 12–14, 21–22, 32, 393, 398–9
Journey to Java, 522–3
King George V: His Life and Reign, 502–3
Lord Carnock, 320, 340–41
Monarchy, 533, 536–8
Paul Verlaine, 170–1, 179–81, 185
Peacemaking 1919, 360–1, 365–6
People and Things, 359
Politics in the Train, 384
Public Faces, 360–1
Sainte-Beuve, 513–14
Small Talk, 399
Some People, 19–29, 25, 30, 32–33, 35–37, 47, 51, 88–89, 198, 208, 255, 295–8
Sweet Waters, 173, 187–8
Swinburne, 237, 277–8
Tennyson: Aspects of His Life, Character and Poetry, 190–3, 216–17
The Age of Reason, 533–4
The Age of Romance (unwritten), 537
The Congress of Vienna: A Study in Allied Unity 1812–1822, 455–6
The Desire to Please, 444–5
The Development of English Biography, 298, 311
The English Sense of Humour, 470
The Evolution of Diplomacy, 509
Why Britain is at War, 424–5
Nicolson, Juliet, 509, 519, 536, 540

Index

Nicolson, Mary Clementina, 4
Nicolson, Nigel, 2, 98, 112, 117, 126, 130, 134, 179, 259–60, 269–72, 276, 294–5, 304, 318, 321–2, 329, 345, 347–9, 364, 366–8, 377, 380, 383, 388, 404, 408, 418–9; army career: 447, 453, 462; political career: 460, 471, 475, 494–5, 513, 517–21, 526–7; publishing career: 527, 533, 536–7, 541–2; 477, 487, 498, 501, 539; marriage to Philippa: 507–8, 524, 536, 541, 543
Nicolson, Norman (clan chief), 2
Nicolson, Philippa, 507–8, 517, 519, 524, 536, 540–1, 543
Nicolson, Rebecca, 541
Nicolson, Thomas, 3–4
Nicolson, Vanessa, 517, 538
Nicolson, Major General Sir William, 4
Niggeman, Elvira, 449, 482, 519, 532, 541
Noel-Baker, Philip, 425
Norman, Sir Henry, 342
Novello, Ivor, 176, 310

Oliphant, Lancelot, 123, 196, 251–2, 283, 285, 287, 294, 381
O'Malley, Owen, 299
Origo, Iris, see Cutting, Iris
'Orme, Lambert', see Firbank, Ronald
Orpen, William, 143
Orwell, George, 492
Osborne, D'Arcy, 177

Pacelli, Eugenio, 314
Painlevé, Paul, 142
Pakenham, Antonia, 515
Palewski, Gaston, 441
Peake, Sir Charles, 429, 501
Pemberton, Richard Oliver ('Crooked'), 55, 63
'Pepita' (Victoria Josefa Durán y Ortega), 81, 83, 95, 388

Percy, Lord Eustace, 61, 66, 79, 134, 138, 386, 505
Philipp, Prince of Hesse, 186
Pius XII, Pope, see Pacelli, Eugenio
Pleven, René, 441
'Plimsoll, Miss', 20, 24–25, 27, 297
Plumer, Field Marshal Lord, 257
Poincaré, Henri, 141, 194–5, 201–2, 210, 221–2, 232
Pollock, Dr Bertram, 33–37, 48, 66, 219
Ponsonby, Arthur, 230
Pope-Hennessey, James, 409, 432, 462, 475, 495–6, 502, 510, 526, 532, 539–40
Powell, Anthony, xii, 296
Powell, Sir George Allen, 438
Priestley, J.B., 527
Proust, Marcel, 146

Ravensdale, Lady Mary, 377
Rawnsley, Willingham, 216
Rayner, Brigadier Sir Ralph, 439
Reith, Sir John, 357, 429, 439
Reynaud, Paul, 426
Reza Khan, Shah of Persia, 264–6, 274–5, 279–85, 287, 509
Ricketts, Howard, 532, 541
Rimbaud, Arthur, 181
Robertson, General Sir Brian, 484
Rodd, Sir Rennell, 130
Ronaldshay, Lord, 245, 366
Roosevelt, President Franklin D., 401, 441
Rose, Kenneth, 489, 503, 510, 532, 543
Ross, Janet, 226
Rothermere, Lord, 240, 391, 494
Rowan, Archibald Hamilton, 16, 444–5
Rubens, Olive, 99, 102, 107, 151, 228, 306, 308
Rubens, Walter, 77, 102
Rumbold, Sir Horace, 119, 200, 217, 316, 318, 320, 323–331, 335, 358

587

Harold Nicolson

Rumbold, Richard, 535
Russell, Bertrand, 248, 492
Rylands, George, 248

Sackville, Lady Anne (wife of Lord Charles Sackville), 306, 535
Sackville, Lord Charles ('Uncle Charlie'), 306–7, 344, 535
Sackville-West, Eddy, 89, 295, 306–7, 310, 318, 321, 325
Sackville, Lord Lionel (Vita's father), 73, 77, 82–83, 91, 96, 98, 102–3, 107, 109–10, 133–4, 143, 151, 168, 182, 191, 227–8, 252, 305–6, 308
Sackville-West, Lord Lionel (Vita's grandfather), 81–3
Sackville, Lady Victoria ('BM'; Vita's mother), 73–74, 77–78, 81–83, 89–91, 96–100, 103, 107–10, 130, 132–4, 143, 151, 158–9, 163, 168, 187–8, 211, 227–9, 231, 233, 237, 252, 308–9, 329, 334, 345, 362–3, 367, 387–8
Sackville-West, Victoria Mary ('Vita'); reputation as writer: xiii, 119, 188, 287–8, 290, 473; attitude to public service and diplomacy: 9, 101, 108, 111, 272–3, 290–1, 304–5, 320–1, 327, 333, 382, 458, 497; relationship with HN: 73–75, 77–78, 89–91, 94, 98–100, 109–10, 167–9, 129, 147, 152, 155, 158, 160–2, 165, 182–3, 235–6, 241, 250, 253, 268, 271, 273, 317, 414, 451, 500, 529–30; Englishness: 80–81, 273, 277; family background: 79, 81–83, 95, 388; relationship with Knole: 79–80, 306–7, 346, 535; childhood: 81–83; relationship with Rosamund Grosvenor: 84–85, 91–92; relationship with Violet Trefusis: 84, 95–96, 117, 123–4, 126–7, 129–34, 142, 147, 152, 158–60, 162–4, 171–2, 174; relationship with mother: 97–98, 103, 107–8, 143, 159, 308–9, 329, 387–8; gardens and gardening: 101, 109, 344, 347–50, 480–1, 492; relationship with Dorothy Wellesley: 176, 186, 189–90, 235, 294; relationship with Virginia Woolf: 211–14, 269, 271, 307, 322; affair with Geoffrey Scott: 226–9, 231–2, 236; relationship with Hilda Matheson: 317, 327, 328; attitude to Sissinghurst: 344–46, 348, 388, 450, 453, 524, 534; changing attitudes: 413, 440, 450–3; health: 495–6, 512, 517, 529, 531, 533–4, 538–40
Sadleir, Michael, 169–70, 173, 183, 289, 360, 380
Sainte-Beuve, Charles Augustin, 514–15
Salisbury, Lord (3rd Marquis), 78, 248
Salisbury, Lord (4th Marquis), 245, 423
Sands, Ethel, 337
Sandys, Sir Duncan, 421
Sargent, John Singer, 69
Sassoon, Siegfried, 186, 208, 535
Scott, Geoffrey, 225–8, 231–2, 235–6, 246, 252, 269
Scott, Sir John Murray ('Seery'), 83, 90, 97
Seely, Hugh (Lord Sherwood), 461
Selby, Walford, 230–2, 250–1, 298–300, 360, 369
Senhouse, Roger, 248
Shaw, George Bernard, 342, 408, 493
Shaw-Stewart, Patrick, 55, 90
Sheean, Vincent, 279, 281, 310, 312
Shepherd, Frank, 474
Sheridan, Clare, 207
Shurman, Jacob G., 331
Simenon, Georges, 501
Simon, Sir John, 342
Simpson, Mrs Wallis, *see* Windsor, Duchess of

Sitwell, Edith, 189, 342, 451
Sitwell, Osbert, 112, 119, 225, 288, 342, 356, 451
Sitwell, Sacheverell, 112, 225
Smith, Lionel, 292, 294
Smuts, Field Marshal Jan, 148–51, 183, 466
Smyth, Dame Ethel, 248, 295, 310, 316, 408
Snow, C.P., 526
Soames, Mary, 476
Sonnino, Sydney, 133
Southby, Commander Sir Archibald 149
Soutzo, Princess Hélène, 146
Sparrow, John, 318, 419, 432, 501, 508–10, 524, 532, 540, 542, 546
Spender, Stephen, 400
Squire, Jack, 183, 235, 237, 278
St Aubyn, Francis ('Sam'), 383, 452
St Aubyn, Gwendolen ('Gwen'), 26, 41–42, 99, 320, 368–9, 377–8, 387, 413, 434, 452, 498
St Levan, Lord, *see* St Aubyn, Francis
St Levan, Lady, *see* St Aubyn, Gwendolen
St Petersburg, 10, 52–60, 63, 66, 71–72
Stambolov, Stefan, 23–4
Stamboulski, Alexander, 206, 220
Stancioff, Dmitri, 177
Stanley, Annie, 73
Stanley, Maureen, 343, 397
Stanley, Oliver, 343, 359, 397, 407
Stanley, Captain Sir Victor, 73
Stark, Freya, 531
Stern Gang, 479–80
Stevenson, Adlai, 541
Stolypin, Pyotr, 53–54, 58
Storrs, Ronald, 257–8
Strachey, Lytton, 179–80, 213, 214–17, 233, 237, 248, 296
Strachey, St John Loe, 233, 245, 355, 359

Strauss, Harold, 439
Stravinsky, Igor, 526
Stresemann, Frau Kate, 322
Stresemann, Gustav, 301, 312–13, 324, 328
Swinburne, Algernon Charles, 179–80, 223, 237, 241, 247, 277–8, 323
Sykes, Christopher, 325, 343, 358
Sykes, Sir Mark, 113–16, 128–9, 145

Talbot, Sir Gerald, 205–6
Tennyson, Alfred Lord, 179–80, 188–92, 200, 213, 216–17, 220, 323
Tennyson-d'Eyncourt, Sir Eustace Gervais, 507
Tennyson-d'Eyncourt, Philippa, *see* Nicolson, Philippa
Terry, Ellen, 68, 73, 190
Thomas, Hugh, 510
Thompson, Dorothy, 312
Thurtle, Ernest, 432, 438
Tilea, Virgil, 138
Tittoni, Tommaso, 154
Tivendale, 200, 202, 208
Toynbee, Arnold, 151, 335
Trefusis, Denys, 132, 147, 158, 166, 176
Trefusis, Violet, 84, 94–96, 99, 102–3, 107, 117, 123–4, 126–7, 129–34, 140, 143, 146–7, 152, 157–60, 162–7, 170–2, 174, 176, 182, 212, 236, 241, 326, 241, 326, 451, 495–6
Trevelyan, George, 482, 502
Trevor Roper, Hugh, 334, 502
Truman, President Harry S., 479
Tyrrell, Sir William, 70–71, 90, 144, 200, 205–7, 221–2, 230, 246–7, 252, 285, 287, 293, 297, 299, 305, 333
Tyrwhitt, Gerald, *see* Berners, Lord

Urquhart, F.F. ('Sligger'), 46–8, 51–2, 66, 76, 176, 217, 295

Vansittart, Sir Robert, 61, 178, 198, 230, 361, 402, 404–5

Venizelos, Eleftherios, 112, 130, 132, 139, 144, 156–8, 168, 171, 173, 175–6, 195–6, 204–5, 219, 235, 356
Vere, Arthur Hope, 297
Verlaine, Paul, 170, 179–81
Vertova, Louisa, 497, 512
Victoria Eugénie, Princess (later Queen of Spain), 50, 75, 493
Victoria, Queen, 6–7, 19, 23, 32, 50, 60, 69, 186, 200, 230
von Hindenburg, President Paul, 312–13, 316
von Mendelssohn, Francesco, 331–2, 358
von Schubert, Carl, 331
Vyshinsky, Andrey, 466

Wales, Prince of, *see* Edward VIII, King
Walpole, Hugh, 121, 124, 183, 377
Walton, William, 189
Warner, Christopher, 263, 266, 269
Warren, Dorothy, 269, 308
Warren, Sir Herbert, 216
Wauchope, General, 243
Waugh, Evelyn, xiii, 28, 56, 342, 398, 539
Weidenfeld, George, 527, 533
Weizmann, Dr Chaim, 114, 459
Wellesley, Dorothy ('Dottie'), 102, 130, 176, 183, 186, 189–91, 212, 228, 233, 235, 248, 251–2, 269–70, 289–92, 294–5, 337, 345
Wellesley, Gerald, ('Gerry'; later Duke of Wellington), 68, 72, 79, 100, 102, 108, 116, 130, 176, 183, 186, 190, 193, 214, 221, 221, 226, 252, 454, 480
Wellington, Duke of, *see* Wellesley, Gerald
Wells, H.G., 345, 342, 408
Weygand, General Maxime, 185, 204
Wheeler-Bennett, Sir John, 503, 541
Whitney, John Hay, 531

Willink, Henry, 473–4
Wilson Knight, Professor, 515–16
Wilson, Edmund, 180, 296, 454–5
Wilson, President Woodrow, 113, 129, 134–7, 141, 145, 151, 154, 365
Wilson, Sir Henry, 129
Wilson, Sir Horace, 425
Windsor, Duchess of, 386, 390–2, 397–8, 408, 472
Windsor, Duke of, *see* Edward VIII, King
Wodehouse, Jack, 183
Wolff, Kurt, 324
Woolf, Leonard, 212, 215, 237, 268, 288, 295, 321–2, 328, 361, 367, 451–2
Woolf, Virginia, 20, 179–80, 211–14, 215–17, 233, 235, 237, 248, 269–74, 276, 288, 290, 296, 304, 307, 315, 317, 321–3, 326, 328, 333, 336, 363–4, 367, 451

York, Duchess of, *see* Elizabeth, Queen
York, Duke of, *see* George VI, King
Young, Allan, 355
Young, Owen D., 327
Yussopuv, Prince Félix, 55

www.ingramcontent.com/pod-product-compliance
Lightning Source LLC
Chambersburg PA
CBHW030243010526
44107CB00030B/1324/J